D0580644

Interactive Teaming

Enhancing Programs for Students with Special Needs

THIRD EDITION

CAROL CHASE THOMAS
University of North Carolina – Wilmington

VIVIAN IVONNE CORREA
University of Florida

CATHERINE VOELKER MORSINK
Slippery Rock University of Pennsylvania, Dean Emerita

Merrill
Prentice Hall

Upper Saddle River, New Jersey
Columbus, Ohio

Library of Congress Cataloging in Publication Data

Thomas, Carol Chase.
    Interactive teaming : enhancing programs for students with special needs / Carol C. Thomas, Vivian I. Correa, Catherine V. Morsink.
       p.   cm.
    Includes bibliographical references and indexes.
    ISBN 0-13-019236-8 (casebound)
       1. Handicapped children—Education—United States. 2. Team learning approach in education—United States. 3. Communication in education—United States. 4. Group guidance in education—United States.   Correa, Vivian, Ivonne. II. Morsink, Catherine Voelker. III. Title.
    LC4031.T46   2001
    371.9—dc21   00-027037

Vice President and Publisher: Jeffery W. Johnston
Executive Editor: Ann Castel Davis
Editorial Assistant: Pat Grogg
Production Editor: Sheryl Glicker Langner
Design Coordinator: Diane C. Lorenzo
Photo Coordinator: Anthony Magnacca
Cover Designer: Linda Fares
Cover art: Steven Schildbach
Production Manager: Laura Messerly
Electronic Text Management: Marilyn Wilson Phelps, Karen L. Bretz, Melanie N. Ortega
Director of Marketing: Kevin Flanagan
Marketing Manager: Amy June
Marketing Services Manager: Krista Groshong

This book was set in Zapf Calligraphic by Prentice Hall. It was printed and bound by R. R. Donnelley & Sons Company. The cover was printed by Phoenix Color Corp.

Photo Credits: pp. 2, 36, 116, 230 by Anthony Magnacca/Merrill; pp. 78, 156, 194, 342, 368 by Ann Vega/
Merrill; p. 270 by Scott Cunningham/Merrill; pp 308, 434 by Barbara Schwartz/Merrill; p. 400 by Tom Watson/Merrill.

Copyright © 2001, 1995, 1991 by Prentice-Hall, Inc., Upper Saddle River, New Jersey 07458.
All rights reserved. Printed in the United States of America. This publication is protected by Copyright and permission should be obtained from the publisher prior to any prohibited reproduction, storage in a retrieval system, or transmission in any form or by any means, electronic, mechanical, photocopying, recording, or likewise. For information regarding permission(s), write to: Rights and Permissions Department.

Merrill
Prentice Hall

10   9   8   7   6   5   4   3   2   1
ISBN 0-13-019236-8

Dedication

To my parents, John B. E. and Geraldine M. Chase; sister, Janene E. Chase; godmother, Ann R. Corley; and mentor, Alma Lee Allen, for their love and support.

CAROL CHASE THOMAS

To my husband, John C. Ziegert, for his support and assistance with editing, and to my family for their continued love and support throughout the years.

VIVIAN IVONNE CORREA

To my husband, John Knight, for his patience, love, and support, and to Carol Chase Thomas, Vivian Ivonne Correa, and Linda Lenk, to whom the torch is passed.

CATHERINE VOELKER MORSINK

Preface

Interactive teaming in special programs is a new concept of service delivery for school-age students who are currently placed in special education programs or are at risk for referral to such programs. The model proposed in this book is based on several assumptions:

◆ An increasing number of students are failing in the traditional public school program, both in general and in special education.

◆ The needs of individual students are too complex to be handled by a single professional working in isolation, and the needs of all of these groups of students are too diverse to be addressed by the knowledge base of a single profession.

◆ Increased diversity in cultural differences, both between professionals and families and among professionals from different cultures, further exacerbates the difficulty both of providing effective instructional programs and of developing effective communication systems.

◆ The time of trained professionals and the scarce resources of public education systems are too valuable to be wasted on uncoordinated or duplicated efforts that produce marginal results for students with special needs.

The opening paragraph and items listed above were the beginning ideas of the preface to the first edition of *Interactive Teaming*, published in 1991. As the third edition goes to press 9 years later, the same assumptions are still present and the need for effective teaming models is even greater. The number of students served in special education programs continues to grow, and the cultural diversity of the population continues to increase. The time professionals have for collaboration and the resources of school systems seem to diminish instead of increase.

During this same time span, much attention has been given to organizational models or school restructuring/reform efforts that call for skills in collaboration and teaming. Total quality management, school-based and site-based management, macro-system reform efforts, inclusion and transition models, and early childhood intervention programs all require collaboration and team decision making to be successful.

The interactive teaming model described in this text is based on transdisciplinary teaming and collaborative consultation models. The model focuses on two concepts:

1. *Consultation:* The sharing of knowledge by one professional with another.
2. *Collaboration:* Mutual efforts between professionals and parents to meet the special needs of children and young people.

The model includes key elements of total quality efforts, adult learning theories, and recognition of the importance of sensitivity to cultural differences.

This text is divided into three parts, each with several supporting chapters. Part I provides a foundation and overview of the contextual framework within which current and future programs for serving students who have disabilities and are at risk will need to be provided. The emergence of a new population of school-age students and the need for a new, coordinated model of implementing special services are highlighted. In Part I an outline of this model and comparisons with existing models are provided. The historical development of the new model includes a brief discussion of the models that preceded it: the medical model, the triadic model of consultation, the refinement of the triadic model to collaborative consultation, and the further extension to variations of the school-based and teacher assistance teams. Each represents a step closer to the interactive teaming model proposed in this text; the strengths and documented factors in the effectiveness of previous models have been incorporated into the new proposal.

In Part II the facilitating factors that make the teaming model work are outlined, and the barriers to effective team functioning are addressed. The facilitating factors include understanding the roles and perspectives of team members, enhancing communication skills, developing service coordination skills, empowering team members through professional development, and supporting family involvement. Each factor is presented through a review of the relevant literature with descriptions and examples of applications.

Part III features implementation of interactive teaming in four contexts: programs for (1) students from culturally and linguistically diverse backgrounds, (2) infants and preschoolers with disabilities, (2) students with mild disabilities, and (4) students with severe disabilities. The necessary knowledge and skills of team members are described in their roles as direct service providers and as consultants/collaborators who provide indirect services.

Although the intervention strategies, team members, and their specific interactive processes differ by settings, all teams operate within the framework of problem identification, intervention, and evaluation of effectiveness. A concluding chapter features an extended case study showing how the model is applied, and provides guidelines for implications of interactive teaming for the future.

The guidelines by which the interactive team operates are modifications of those used in school-based management teams. The culture of the school—its values and rules—provides the contextual framework for establishing its goals. Teachers, parents, and other team members—rather than administrators and specialists—are empowered to analyze problems, make decisions, and evaluate programs designed to attain common goals. These goals are related to the provision of effective educational service programs for the students on whom the team focuses its efforts.

This book was developed by an interactive team, each member serving as consultant and collaborator to the two other members. In reality, each chapter has three coauthors. To avoid redundancy, however, the authorship of each chapter indicates only the person who was the primary developer. Carol Chase Thomas authored Chapters 2, 3, 5, and 11; Vivian Correa authored Chapters 8, 9, 10, and 12; and Catherine Morsink authored Chapters 1, 4, 6, 7, and 13.

ACKNOWLEDGMENTS

Revising a textbook invariably turns out to be much more of a challenge than anticipated, especially when the authors are located in different states and have many other roles and responsibilities. We are fortunate in that we shared a common commitment to the goal of advancing the interactive teaming model, and that we had excellent supporters in this endeavor. We appreciate the constructive suggestions provided by the reviewers of the revision plan: Judith J. Ivarie, Eastern Illinois University; Donna Kearns, University of Central Oklahoma; Rosanne Pirtle, Marian College (IN); and Diane T. Woodrum, West Virginia University.

Our students in undergraduate and graduate courses provided invaluable insights on how the text could be improved. We also wish to thank Lee Brinkley, Laura Nelson, and Holly Greenoe for their assistance. Special thanks to Linda Lenk for providing school-based examples and review of content, and to Kristin Young for her summary and application of content in a medical setting. Ann Castel Davis and Pat Grogg at Merrill are always helpful and encouraging persons with whom to work.

A number of other individuals were supportive of this endeavor and deserve our thanks: Linda Baker, Grace Burton, Bailey and Whitney, Linda Taylor, Cricket, Dolores Daugherty, Phyllis Kendziorski, Jay Hertzog, and Mary Kay Dykes.

CAROL CHASE THOMAS
VIVIAN IVONNE CORREA
CATHERINE VOELKER MORSINK

Discover the Companion Website Accompanying This Book

The Prentice Hall Companion Website: A Virtual Learning Environment

Technology is a constantly growing and changing aspect of our field that is creating a need for content and resources. To address this emerging need, Prentice Hall has developed an online learning environment for students and professors alike—Companion Websites—to support our textbooks.

In creating a Companion Website, our goal is to build on and enhance what the textbook already offers. For this reason, the content for each user-friendly website is organized by topic and provides the professor and student with a variety of meaningful resources. Common features of a Companion Website include:

For the Professor—

Every Companion Website integrates **Syllabus Manager**™, an online syllabus creation and management utility.

- **Syllabus Manager**™ provides you, the instructor, with an easy, step-by-step process to create and revise syllabi, with direct links into Companion Website and other online content without having to learn HTML.
- Students may logon to your syllabus during any study session. All they need to know is the web address for the Companion Website and the password you've assigned to your syllabus.
- After you have created a syllabus using **Syllabus Manager**™, students may enter the syllabus for their course section from any point in the Companion Website.
- Clicking on a date, the student is shown the list of activities for the assignment. The activities for each assignment are linked directly to actual content, saving time for students.
- Adding assignments consists of clicking on the desired due date, then filling in the details of the assignment—name of the assignment, instructions, and whether or not it is a one-time or repeating assignment.

◆ In addition, links to other activities can be created easily. If the activity is online, a URL can be entered in the space provided, and it will be linked automatically in the final syllabus.

◆ Your completed syllabus is hosted on our servers, allowing convenient updates from any computer on the Internet. Changes you make to your syllabus are immediately available to your students at their next logon.

For the Student—

◆ **Topic Overviews**—outline key concepts in topic areas

◆ **Electronic Bluebook**—send homework or essays directly to your instructor's email with this paperless form

◆ **Message Board**—serves as a virtual bulletin board to post—or respond to—questions or comments to/from a national audience

◆ **Chat**—real-time chat with anyone who is using the text anywhere in the country—ideal for discussion and study groups, class projects, etc.

◆ **Web Destinations**—links to www sites that relate to each topic area

◆ **Professional Organizations**—links to organizations that relate to topic areas

◆ **Additional Resources**—access to topic-specific content that enhances material found in the text

To take advantage of these and other resources, please visit the *Interactive Teaming: Enhancing Programs for Students with Special Needs* Companion Website at

www.prenhall.com/thomas

Contents

III IMPLEMENTATION OF INTERACTIVE TEAMING

Context and Foundations

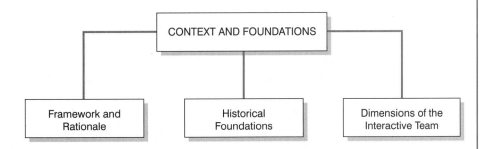

OVERVIEW

The first part of this text provides perspectives on historical, current, and future service delivery systems for students who have special needs. In Chapter 1, the population for whom people on an interactive team will need to be concerned is described. The chapter also includes a review of past and current service delivery approaches and some of the problems inherent in the implementation of those systems. The chapter concludes with a summary of the research on effective schools, a description of models that emphasize collegial problem solving among professionals, and an application showing the factors that set the tone for effective interactive teaming.

Chapter 2 begins with a summary of the historical and legal foundations that have contributed to the development of consultation, collaboration, and teaming models. Selected consultation and teaming models are described, along with their impediments and positive features. In Chapter 3, the dimensions of the interactive team are identified and explained. The interactive teaming model is presented, and an application illustrating implementation of the model is provided.

1

Framework and Rationale for Interactive Teaming

Topics in this chapter include:

- Definition of interactive teaming.
- Why interactive teaming is needed now.
- Legal basis for special services.
- Limitations of traditional approaches.
- Promising new practices from which the components of inter-active teaming are derived.
- An application that sets the tone for success of an interactive team.

Janice, a classroom teacher in a middle school, became a teacher because she wanted to make a difference in the world—to excite students about social issues and creative writing—to help young people learn, and discover, and grow. She is the kind of person who should be a teacher. She is bright, knowledgeable, enthusiastic, empathic, and optimistic about the future.

Yet, two years ago, Janice was on the verge of dropping out of the profession. She had been given more students than she thought she could handle, and when she tried to refer those with learning and behavior problems to the school's special programs, she was told these students would be placed on the "waiting list." The principal explained that the special programs were overloaded because there were too many students with special needs in her suburban school: students whose parents had divorced, students addicted to drugs and stealing to support their habits, and students—barely more than children themselves—who were pregnant.

Janice felt discouraged and isolated. She and the other teachers in her building went into their classrooms and closed their doors, trying to cope single-handedly with their students' bored expressions, lack of ambition, and belligerence. Worst of all, Janice thought nobody else cared. Parents didn't come to PTA meetings; they didn't seem to care. The other teachers gathered in the faculty lounge only to gossip and collapse between classes; they didn't seem to care. But that was two years ago.

Today we see a new Janice. She is a member of an interactive team, consulting and collaborating with other professionals and with parents to design and carry out plans that make her programs for students with special needs more effective. Sometimes the team is just two people—Janice and the special education teacher, for example. Sometimes, if a student has severe or multiple disabilities, a larger group is gathered to work as a team. Sometimes Janice is the consultant, the expert who knows more than the others about the specific subject area with which a student is having difficulty. At other times, Janice is a collaborator, working with others to carry out the decisions made on the student's behalf by those who make up the team. She now considers her job more challenging and more rewarding because she thinks the team makes better decisions than each person could make alone. She also feels that she is part of a dynamic learning community.

Janice, the teacher described in the vignette, has developed a new enthusiasm for teaching as a result of being part of a professional group—an interactive team—that shares responsibility for students with special needs. In this chapter, *interactive teaming* is defined, and a rationale is presented for why interactive teaming is needed in today's schools and in the schools of the future. The times when interactive teaming is most appropriately used—when decisions need to be made about the program for students with special needs—are described. The limitations of current approaches are discussed, and the components of promising new practices from which the new interactive teaming model is derived are described.

DEFINITION OF INTERACTIVE TEAMING

The word *teaming* is used here to mean professional and parental sharing of information and expertise, in which two or more persons work together to meet a common goal. In this case, the goal is to provide the best possible educational program for a given student with special needs. The *interactive team* is one on which there is mutual or reciprocal effort among and between members of the team to meet this goal.

Note that interactive teams do not operate in isolation to serve students with special needs. Instead, they operate within the context of other macro-level teams. These include strategic planning teams, which guide decisions in partnerships across the boundaries of schools, businesses, and community agencies. Macro-level teams also encompass district-wide teams focused on extended school service or quality improvement, and the university/school district teams that monitor professional development schools with student teachers. The interactive teams described in this text are micro-level versions of these larger teams, illustrative of school and business trends in collaboration.

Each team member may engage in *consultation*, any activity in which he or she is the expert who possesses more knowledge or skill than other team members about the issue being discussed. When the team member consults, she does this by sharing knowledge or skills, or by explaining or carrying out actions that demonstrate this knowledge. As a member of the interactive team, however, she shares knowledge in a reciprocal rather than an authoritarian manner. On an interactive team, the consultant is not always the same person; the person who consults possesses the necessary knowledge and expertise on a given topic at a particular time. The team member, such as Janice, may be a consultant on the academic subject of teaching creative writing; at the same time, Janice may also be the recipient of consultation from the school psychologist, who has more knowledge about behavior management. Similarly, the parent might be the consultant on the home behavior and history of the student, while being the recipient of the speech-language therapist's recommendations on language development.

The team member also engages in *collaboration*, a mutual effort to plan, implement, and evaluate the educational program for a given student. Collaboration is cooperative rather than competitive. It consists of joint or coordinated actions by team members to reach their common goal. For example, if Janice is a member of a team working with a gifted student who has cerebral palsy and requires an adapted computer for creative writing, she would collaborate with the special education teacher, the occupational therapist, the adaptive technology specialist, and the student's parents to plan, implement, and evaluate the student's special program. Although most team discussions are held face to face, it is also possible for a team to communicate through e-mail or interactive video technology as a way to save time and reduce distance.

The application of the designing of a camel by a committee (Figure 1.1) illustrates the spirit and process that an interactive team displays as members shift between consultative and collaborative roles. Just as these specialists with diverse backgrounds and disparate vocabularies have functioned together to design a product for the desert that is superior to that which any one of them could have designed alone, so too can members of the interactive team respond to the demanding environment facing educators in the coming years. As we shall see, tomorrow's education and health-related professionals will not be facing stable, happy, eager students from the "grassy meadows" of affluent suburban schools. They will be largely placed in desolate rural areas or in urban blackboard deserts, where the majority of their students live in poverty, come from single-parent homes, speak another language or represent another culture, and have largely abandoned their hope that education is the key to a better future.

WHY INTERACTIVE TEAMING IS NEEDED NOW

This model of consistent consultation, collaboration, and team-based decision making is especially vital now because of the increase in the number of school-age students who are disabled or at risk for school failure. Because there are so many students who experience difficulties, and because their difficulties are so complex, education, social services, and medical professionals working in isolation are unable to provide these students with appropriate educational programs.

Target Population

The target population served through interactive teaming practices is the group of school-age students who are currently identified as having special needs and who have been placed in special education programs or included in the regular classroom with related special services. It also includes students who are at risk for being placed in such programs and students experiencing school failure without placement.

Students in Special Education Programs.   Those students classified as disabled are defined by Public Law 94-142, the Education of All Handicapped Children Act, passed by the U.S. Congress in 1975, amended in 1990 (P.L. 101-476) and

The Camel: A Horse Designed by a Committee

No doubt you have heard that a camel is a horse designed by a committee. Well, it's true. I know, because I was there. I'll tell you what took place. It was mid-morning on the 30th; the entire committee assembled and seated themselves.

"Acme Caravans Incorporated is opening a new market. They have the exclusive franchise for a trans-Sahara trade route and have invited our company to submit a proposal on an order for twenty horses to carry the trade goods, and forty more to carry the caravan's supplies and the pack horses' food and water. This committee is to develop our company's response."

"So they want sixty horses. Model 701B I suppose?"

"Maybe we should think about that. Remember, we used the 701B horse for that high-mountain job last winter, and it floundered when the snow was loose packed and powdery. The sand may be just as bad."

"You have a point there. The 701's small feet sank too deep. Maybe we need a model with a larger foot size."

"Yeah, make it about twice the diameter—maybe padded somewhat on the bottom so it will really spread out."

"Hey, that sounds good. Just like snow shoes—I mean, sand shoes."
"Anything else?"

"Well, yes. Two front toes would give a better grip than just one."

"OK. Let's make it two front toes on each foot. Got that?"

"I've read in the North Africa tour book about the extreme temperatures—135 degrees in the daytime and 40 degrees at night."

"What are you saying? Do you think we should increase the R rating of the exterior covering of the 701B?"

"Insulation pays off in the long run. And besides, don't you still get a tax break on weatherproofing?"

"How about an extra six inches of thick hair and fur on the back and head, and a couple of inches all around?"

"Not a bad idea. As for colors, mauve and taupe are really in this year."

"I don't know. I'm more inclined to the earth tones."

"Why don't we give some choices? Perhaps from a light sand beige to dark chocolate?"

"Is something bothering you?"

"Well, yes. The insulation is OK, but it may cause a real buildup of internal heat at maximum RPMs."

"I don't know. I thought we might gear it down to about two-and-a-half MPH as the cruising speed. At that rate we can keep the heat-loss/heat-gain pretty well balanced."

"We can still have a passing gear that can get its speed up to Mach point-oh-five when necessary."

Figure 1.1
Decision making by the interactive process.

Source: From "The Camel: A Horse Designed by a Committee" by Noojin Walker (March 1988). *The Clearing House, 61*(7), pp. 329–330, 1988. Reprinted with permission of the Helen Dwight Reid Educational Foundation. Published by Heldref Publications, 4000 Albemarle St., N.W., Washington, DC 20016. Copyright © 1988.

"Sounds good. This fur will also protect the skin from the abrasion of the hard-blowing sand."

"Speaking of sand, do you remember the attempted helicopter rescue in Iran? That sand and dust really clogged up the choppers' air intake."

"Played heck with their vision, too."

"What we need is a way to keep the sand out of the system. Can we change the nostril of the 701B from an open hole to perhaps a slit that can open and close on demand?"

"Sure."

"And while we're at it, we can modify the eyelids and brow so that they are somewhat over- hanging."

"And increase the number and length of the eyelashes?"

"Definitely! You can't overestimate the value of keeping the vision protected."

"Neat! And these sand and wind protection features can also double as glare reducers. Man! That sun is bright!"

"Excuse me, but I have recalculated the heat-loss/heat-gain and the two-point-five MPH."

"So?"

"Well, we're going to have to lengthen the stride and cut down on the leg action if we are going to keep the heat from building up."

"OK, so what do you figure?"

"It needs a stride that will require legs that are eight meters tall."

"Wow! That would be one tall 701B! How would you ever get it loaded—with a crane?"

"Can't you adjust its thermostat? What's its operating temperature range any-how?"

"Well, it's the usual plus-or-minus one degree tolerance."

"Let me figure—yeah, that's much better. If the internal temperature could vary 10 or 12 degrees with no burnout, it would let us shorten the stride some, and shorten the legs without increasing the leg action and RPMs."

"It would still be taller than the 701B, but we can program it so that it kneels down to be loaded or mounted."

"If it's going to kneel, do you think we should extend the insulation to the knees—maybe some fur pads there? That sand gets fiercely hot."

"Good idea."

"I don't know whether to mention this or not, but if we increase the operating temperature range to 12 degrees, this modified 701B won't need to sweat as much."

"What does this mean?"

"Sweating and its evaporation is a cooling mechanism. It's not going to need it."

"Well, what does that mean?"

"It's not going to lose as much water—not nearly as much."

Figure 1.1, *continued*

8

"You know, if it doesn't lose much water by sweating, and if we were able to add the right kind of reserve water tank, it might be able to go a week or more without having to be refilled."

"These legs are long enough to let us hang a belly tank underneath just like the jet fighters."

"No good! No good! It would not leave enough height underneath to give good clearance over those rough bushes."

"And besides, when it knelt down to be loaded, it would be awfully uncomfortable—mashing all of that water."

"OK, then, let's put it on top."

"Hey, what's that going to look like—a big hump sitting up there?"

"Sure, but that's not all bad. It will be a good base to secure the loads to."

"Right. And the rider will have a much better field of vision."

"Should it have one hump or two?"

"Good question. Why don't we configure two models and let the buyer decide which one he wants?"

"Hmmm. A one-hump and a two-hump model. Marketing will like that."

"I don't know. How are we going to keep all of that water from sloshing around inside that hump as it gets empty? Do you plan to use tubes and baffles?"

"My suggestion is to make it somewhat collapsible. Fill the hump with fibrous connective tissues, sort of like your tubes and baffles. And pack the whole thing with fat. You know fat allows for a lot of water absorption. I figure it can carry 10 percent of the total body weight right there in that hump—or humps."

"I get it. As the fat and water are used the hump gets smaller. Sort of a built-in gauge to tell you how much is still left."

"Super plan! We could also modify the metabolic processes so that the water metabolized from the fat stays right inside the system."

"Sure. Any water that can be saved or recycled is just that much less that it will have to drink en route."

"Will that be a problem—I mean modifying the metabolism?"

"Not really. Our subcommittee has planned a truly rugged digestive system. So far, we can fuel this baby with any kind of desert vegetation—cactus, brush, and even those bitter thorny- bushes. And if necessary, it can digest dried fish, bones, leather, even a blanket."

"That's enough; we get your drift. So actually it can carry enough food and water in that hump to last for a week or more, and also eat almost anything along the way."

"Where are we with the payload?"

"Our calculations show that it will be able to carry about a half-ton, for a week or more, at a steady pace of $2\frac{1}{2}$ miles an hour."

"Is there any danger of overloading it?"

"Not much. We can build in a warning mechanism—groaning, followed by bellowing, and that sort of thing."

"Right on! And as the critical weight is approached, it can be programmed to spit at the loader to get his attention."

"Excellent proposals! With all of these warnings I figure we can load it to within one straw of breaking its back."

"Gee! This modification is really an improvement over the original 701B, at least in this terrain."

"But what is the cost?"

"Well, our cost subcommittee projects that if we use all natural materials and no plastics, the unit cost will be just a little more than the cost of the standard 701B horse. But because it doesn't require the exotic fuel, the extra water, and the support units to carry it all, we calculate that the total job will be about a 50 percent saving to Acme Caravan."

"Great!"

"OK, what about a name?"

"What do you think of CARAVAN MODEL ECONOMY LANDCRUISER?"

"Not bad. It's a little long, but. . . . "

"Group?"

"Sure. That's good. We can market it as CAMEL. It's easier to say. The ad group will love it."

"Good work. I guess that takes care of this business. Unless there is anything else, the committee is adjourned."

Figure 1.1, *continued*

again in 1997 (P.L. 105-17) as the Individuals with Disabilities Education Act. These are students with the following: specific learning disabilities, mental retardation, hearing impairments, visual impairments, speech or language impairments, emotional disturbance, orthopedic impairments, autism, traumatic brain injury, and other health impairments. Because of these conditions, the law permits these students to receive special education and related services. A total of 4,817,503 children and youth at risk or with disabilities, ages 0–21, were served in special programs during the 1990–1991 school year. The number of children and youth with disabilities rose from 4.8% in 1976–1977 to 7.1% in 1990–1991 and to 10.6% in 1994–1995 (U.S. Department of Education, 1997). Students ages 6–21 were initially classified most often as learning disabled, speech impaired, mentally retarded, and seriously emotionally disturbed. These four categories represented almost 94% of the total number of children classified in 1990–1991 as disabled (U.S. Department of Education, 1992). In 1995–1996, approximately 5 million students ages 6–21 were identified as disabled, with 51% of these classified as "learning disabled" and 20% as having speech and language impairments (Lipsky & Gartner, 1998). Only those students who have been formally identified, placed in special programs, and labeled according to the procedures specified in P.L. 94-142, amended as the Individuals with Disabilities Education Act (IDEA), are classified as "disabled." These are not, however, the only students in need of the services of the interactive team.

Students at Risk for School Failure.   The term *at risk* was originally defined by Reynolds (1989) as follows: "The term *at risk* . . . refers to children who fall into various categories for which the base rate (or group frequency) for experiencing educational difficulties is relatively high" (p. 129).

Reynolds (1989) further specified that children who are either disabled or at risk are classified together as students with special needs:

> Special needs children show one or more of the following characteristics which have significance for educational planning: (a) they are not responding positively to the instruction offered to them in basic academic skills (usually reading); (b) their social behavior in school is unacceptable; (c) they are falling badly behind classmates in learning in academic subjects; (d) they have significant physical limitations or major health problems; (e) English is not their primary language (often associated with important cultural differences as well); or (f) they are extremely limited in experiences which provide background for formal education. (p. 130)

The new amendments to the IDEA allow the states the option to provide special services for students who are at risk but have not yet been classified. This is essentially an option to extend the "developmental disabilities" classification to students through the age of 9; it has been adopted by some states but not by others. According to Turnbull and Cilley (1999), this is an attempt to prevent students from needing placement. Some special educators believe, however, that service to students at risk constitutes a diversion of funds from those within the protected class specified by law.

There has been an increase in the number of children who meet the criteria for services specified in the Individuals with Disabilities Education Act, and who are being identified, classified, and served according to the requirements of the law. There has also been an increase in the number of these students who are currently being educated, at least part time, in the regular classroom. McLesky, Henry, and Hodges (1998) indicate that there was an increase of 12.8% in the number of students identified as disabled in the 6 years between 1988–1989 and 1994–1995.

Basing their findings on data from the annual reports to Congress, McLesky et al. (1998) have used the measure "cumulative placement rate," which is the total number of students ages 6–17 classified as disabled and placed in a given setting, divided by the total number of students in the U.S. population ages 6–17, times 1,000. These authors further point out that the total number of students with disabilities placed in resource rooms and separate school settings declined (by 16% and 20%, respectively), and those placed in separate classes increased slightly (by 5%), while those placed in general education classrooms increased significantly (by 60%) within the 6-year period. Data from the 17th Annual Report to Congress (U.S. Department of Education, 1995) show that nearly 40% of all children with disabilities were being served in the regular classroom at least 80% of the time in the school year 1993–1994. Lipsky and Gartner (1998) view the data from the 19th Annual Report (school year 1995–1996) from a different perspective, stating that 55% of children with disabilities are not fully included in regular classes after more than two decades since the passage of P.L. 94-142.

The category of exceptionality that is growing most rapidly and is most controversial is that of learning disabilities. McLesky, Henry, and Hodges (1998) point out that the number of students identified in the learning disabilities category grew by 70% between 1988–1989 and 1994–1995. Spear-Swerling and Sternberg (1998) refer to the increase in learning disabilities as an "epidemic." They suggest changing the way children are tested and classified for learning disabilities, as well as recommending that special educators serve as learning specialists who work with low-achieving students in addition to those who are classified as disabled.

Sack (1998) shows that there are still large discrepancies across the nation in the diagnosis of children with special needs, particularly in the category of learning disabilities. Hocutt, Cox, and Pelosi (1984) conducted the original national study of special education placement issues, which pointed out that the number of students labeled as disabled in a given school district was determined by the norms of the school district. As early as 1984, this study revealed that it was difficult to separate students who were labeled as disabled from those with characteristics that place them at risk for school failure, and that minority students were more often placed in special programs if they were from families with low socioeconomic status. The original national companion study by Pyecha, Kullgowski, and Wiegerink (1984) indicated further that special education placement issues were related to funding patterns, and that when the number of students identified as having one categorical label decreases, the number classified into another category is likely to increase. Although issues of classification and placement remain controversial, one thing is clear: With 53.2 million children entering school in the fall of 1999 (an increase of 0.5 million over fall 1998), ever-increasing numbers of them will need special assistance.

Increase in Students at Risk

Recently, the number of school-age students considered to be at risk has increased; the students include those with low academic achievement, poor task completion, and social maladjustment (Morsink & Lenk, 1992; Stevens & Price, 1992). Those who have studied this phenomenon have found a correlation between poor achievement and intense poverty. In schools with the highest poverty levels, 47.5% of the students have low achievement levels (Reeves, 1988). In addition, it has been shown that the newest groups of immigrant children and those with racial, cultural, and linguistic differences are at risk for school failure (First & Carrera, 1988; National Coalition of Advocates for Students, 1985). Other demographic changes and related social problems have combined to create a large number of students who are identified as disabled or at risk in the school population. Jacobson (1998) has shown that there are half a million children now in foster care, a 74% increase, linked primarily to their parents' crack cocaine addiction. These children often exhibit anger and difficulty in concentration and are more likely to have learning disabilities or emotional problems with which their teachers are unable to cope. Similarly, Rafferty (1997–1998), reporting on the increased number of homeless children, stresses that this group is among those at greatest risk for school failure.

It is estimated that 1 in 500 to 600 newborns suffer from fetal alcohol syndrome and 1 in 300 to 350 have some fetal alcohol effects (Burgess & Streissguth, 1992). Between 15,000 and 30,000 children are affected with HIV (Stevens & Price, 1992). Each year 37,000 babies, born weighing less than 3.5 pounds, live to experience significant learning difficulties (Bartel & Thurman, 1992). In addition, 7.5 million students have emotional problems severe enough for counseling; and 2.2 million are abused or neglected, according to Mernit (1990). The effect of lead poisoning, largely from ingestion of paint, is also a factor in the increase of children at risk for failure (Needleman, 1992). The implications of these conditions for increases in special programs are clear.

Demographic Changes.   Demographic changes that have taken place during the past 40 years have implications for the education system that will impact the learning of school-age children. Many of these changes were projected by Hodgkinson (1988) and summarized by Reeves (1988).

According to Reeves (1988), the median income for parents under the age of 25 dropped by 45% in the 16 years ending in 1986, while the overall U.S. family income rose by 20%; for the richest two fifths of families, the income level rose 27%. One in every five children was classified as living in poverty. Ninety-five million women were raising children alone; many of them are represented in the lowest levels for family income. These increases in poverty levels also intensified risk factors: poor nutrition and health care, neglect, abuse, and violence (Fleischner & Van Acker, 1990).

Other demographic changes, as they relate to the education of students with special needs, were summarized by Thomas, Correa, and Morsink (1995) and by Corrigan (1996) from a variety of databases. Among the most significant generic changes are the aging of the population and the increased proportion of young persons who are at risk for school failure. Changes in family structure have also caused fewer children to have the emotional advantages of two-parent families and after-school care.

Related Social Problems in Secondary Students.   In addition to the dramatic changes in demography, school-age students face a number of social problems that increase the likelihood they will have school-related difficulties. These social problems have led to an increase in the number of secondary-level students with special needs, which place them at risk for school failure. These data have been summarized in a national report by the Education Commission of the States (ECS; Brown, 1985), in a study sponsored by the Carnegie Corporation (Hechinger, 1992), and more recently in the daily news. They include dramatic increases in teenage pregnancy, crimes, and drug abuse, with an alarming increase in the incidence of violence. Homicides are now the third leading cause of death for people between 10 and 19 years of age in the United States.

Adolescents in this country are at much higher risk of death than in other industrialized countries (Hechinger, 1992). Thirty-nine percent of youth aged 12–24 state that violence has increased in their schools and that they are afraid (Carey & Parker, 1999). Fifteen percent of the public stated that violence/gangs was the biggest problem facing local schools, according to a 1998 Gallup poll (Rose & Gallup, 1998).

Ten million people in the United States are addicted to alcohol; 7 million children of these alcoholics are in the public schools, children with special needs and potential future problems (Leerhsen & Namuth, 1988); the incidence of problem drinking in high school seniors is up 300%; and it is estimated that 10% to 20% of our adolescents abuse alcohol (Brown, 1985).

The ECS also reported 700,000 high school dropouts and another 300,000 truants in 1984. The issue of high school dropouts remains a major concern to the superintendents of our urban school districts (Superintendents, 1988). In addition, at least 3.4 million children in schools have a limited ability to use English, and even among those who graduate, the functional illiteracy rate is greater than 30% (Will, 1986).

In a policy report by the U.S. Department of Labor, it was found that these conditions will seriously affect the future of the workforce. The Secretary's Commission on Achieving Necessary Skills (SCANS) estimates that more than half of our youth leave school without the knowledge and skills to acquire and retain a good job. This commission recommended that all students master the essential "workplace know-how": basic skills, thinking skills, and personal qualities, plus five competencies, which enable them to use resources, interpersonal skills, information, technology, and systems in a productive manner (Secretary's Commission on Achieving Necessary Skills, 1991).

There is a high rate of discouragement and hopelessness among our youth. The report of the ECS (Brown, 1985) indicated that 10% to 15% of youth aged 16–19 were alienated, disadvantaged, or both. In-depth interviews with 100 school-leavers over an 8-year period indicate that, although some step out and drop back in, those who leave do so because they find little support at school (Altenbaugh, Engle, & Martin, 1995). These students, unless provided with assistance, are in danger of becoming a new "underclass." Eitzen (1992) suggests that "... some young people act in antisocial ways because they have lost their dreams" (p. 590). The real-life students behind these data are at risk for school failure; if they become parents, they are in danger of perpetuating the same conditions that will place their own children at risk.

LEGAL BASIS FOR SPECIAL SERVICES

The interactive team operates in response to a 1975 federal law, the Education of All Handicapped Children Act (P.L. 94-142), amended in 1990 and again in 1997 as the Individuals with Disabilities Education Act. A detailed explanation of the 1997 amendments is provided by Turnbull and Cilley (1999), using the six principles that form a framework for the law: (1) zero reject, (2) nondiscriminatory evaluation, (3) appropriate education, (4) least restrictive educational placement, (5) procedural due process, and (5) parent and student participation. The implications most relevant for the interactive team are summarized here.

The intent of the law is to provide persons with disabilities an equal opportunity to participate in and contribute to society. Money flows from the federal level through the states to the local education agencies to assist them in implementing the law, providing special education and related services for students classified as disabled or at risk for school failure, and in need of services. New provisions of the law also allow some of the costs of special services to be shared by other public agencies in addition to schools. New emphasis is placed on the removal of architectural barriers and on comprehensive planning to provide a sufficient supply of appropriately trained teachers and other personnel. Restrictions are placed on suspension of services for students whose behavior results from their disability, a team decision is required for any change in placement, and an appeal process is specified. New regulations make an effort to balance the rights of the IDEA student with those of others to ensure school safety. New regulations also specify that the same persons serve on the student's evaluation/placement team and on the team that develops the individual educational plan. Nondiscriminatory evaluation procedures and parental participation/consent are strengthened, while requirements for participation in the regular curriculum and in the postschool transition services and development of the preschool individualized family services plan are clarified. Bilingual education and behavioral interventions are encouraged when deemed necessary by the team, and mediation of differences is encouraged prior to requests for due process hearings.

Most important for operation of the interactive team is the amended law's clarification of requirements for serving students in the "least restrictive appropriate educational placement." The placement is focused on the academic curriculum, but can also include other components of the school day, such as lunch and recess and, in some cases, even extracurricular activities. According to Turnbull and Cilley (1999), it is presumed that the general education program is appropriate unless shown to be inappropriate. Case law requires collection of evidence on attempted modifications (supplemental aids and services) prior to the team's decision for placement in a more restrictive environment. Turnbull and Cilley (1999) summarize the rules for decision making on placement in the appropriate educational environment, now included in the law:

1) educational benefit to student
2) nonacademic benefit to student
3) possible negative effects of general class placement
4) costs involved in accommodating placement. (p. 44)

Yell (1998) further specifies that, in assuring placement in the least restrictive environment, school districts are required to have access to the entire range of placements, from which they may choose the best match for the individual student's needs. This range extends from the regular classroom through special schools, such as the Pioneer Center in Pittsburgh, for example (Vail, 1997). Neither "inclusion" nor (the older term) "mainstreaming" are required in this effort to balance both the educational and social benefits to the child with a disability and the effect of placement on others, including classmates and the teacher. Yell (1998) concludes:

1. Mainstreaming is not required if a student with disabilities will not receive educational benefits from a regular classroom;
2. Mainstreaming is not required if any marginal benefit would be significantly outweighed by benefits obtained only in a separate instructional setting;
3. Mainstreaming is not required if the child is a disruptive force in the general education classroom. (p. 72)

LIMITATIONS OF TRADITIONAL APPROACHES

Interactive teaming represents a proposed alternative to the traditional programs serving students who are disabled and at risk, because it has been shown that these programs have limited effectiveness. Frequently, services are delivered primarily through the individual efforts of regular and special education teachers who staff "lower tracks" or special pull-out programs, and through social services personnel who provide a variety of related services that may be uncoordinated. "Top-down" bureaucratic fixes show limited value; voucher programs are relatively untested and frequently exclude students with disabilities. All of these programs are limited in their effectiveness, and none has typically incorporated interactive teaming. The inability of special education teachers to provide consistently high-quality instruction, the presence of marginal professional and parent interactions and follow-up, and a narrow understanding of the change process are among the major limitations in these current approaches.

Poor Quality of Instruction in Tracking and Pull-Out Programs

In an effort to provide for the educational needs of students with disabilities or those at risk, many schools in the 1980s and 1990s divided students into groups, or tracks, in which the more able learners were separated from those with learning difficulties. Oakes (1986) summarizes the history and effects of tracking, pointing out that it contributes to a mediocre education for more than 60% of our students, in addition to perpetuating social and economic inequality. Tracking offers advantages for only the top 40% of students. The curriculum for that top 40% is based on high-level content, while that of the lower track students consists of workbooks and ditto sheets; also, top-track students receive more of the teacher's instructional time and work in a more positive classroom climate. This structure, according to Oakes, appears to buy increased achievement for the few at the expense of apathy and mediocrity for the many students. In later research, it is acknowledged, however, that it is not easy to overcome the barriers in the power structure and entrenched procedures that would allow schools to eliminate these tracking systems (Oakes, Wells, Yonezawa, & Ray, 1997).

It also appears that it is extremely difficult for teachers in pull-out programs to provide special students with adequate direct instruction or feedback. Although designed to provide additional individualized instruction for students with special needs, many programs in which remedial students are isolated and pulled out of the regular classroom are providing less actual instruction than that available in the mainstream classroom. Haynes and Jenkins (1986) found that disabled students in Washington State, placed in resource rooms for reading instruction, spent 52% of their time doing private seatwork without the teacher's assistance, and only 25% of their time actually reading. At the same time, their classroom teachers, assuming that these students were being provided with reading instruction in the resource room, provided them with no additional instruction in the classroom.

Allington (1987), who has studied a large number of remedial programs in New York, has also shown that students in these programs receive a low quality of instruction, and that they spend the majority of their time just sitting—staring at mounds of seatwork—and waiting for the teacher to come and help them. This unfortunate reality also has been observed in special education programs in Florida, where observations were made in nearly 100 classrooms during a 2-year period (Algozzine, Morsink, & Algozzine, 1987; Fardig & Morsink, 1985). In Minnesota, it was found that remedial students received an average of only 45 minutes a day of active academic responding (Graden, Thurlow, & Ysseldyke, 1982). These difficulties have caused reform advocates to continue their call for more inclusive instruction (Lipsky & Gartner, 1998).

It is equally unfortunate that these same students are often receiving inadequate instruction in the regular classroom. Anderson, Hiebert, Scott, and Wilkinson (1985) have suggested that students in the primary grades spend 50% to 70% of their time working independently. Rupley and Blair (1987), in observation of 12 primary teachers' monitoring of seatwork tasks in reading, have indicated that 50% of these teachers assigned seatwork before conducting reading instruction, that they assigned the same seatwork to the entire group, and that only 10% of these teachers modeled the task before asking students to complete it.

One of the major difficulties with the programs offered for students at risk is that they present repetitive content, using remedial drills that are not challenging. Knapp, Turnbull, and Shields (1990) have summarized the difficulties of remedial programs, concluding that the traditional remedial curriculum may intensify student failure through delay of more interesting work or because it does not provide a meaningful context for learning activities. Levin (1986) has developed "accelerated learning" for students at risk, a curriculum similar to the high-level, creative problem solving traditionally offered only to gifted students. This approach has been found to increase both the learning rate and the enthusiasm of students at risk.

"Top-Down" Bureaucratic Solutions

One of the most common responses to poor performance on the part of students is to "raise the standards." Barth (1998) has discussed the relative merits of the most widely recognized state standards for student achievement. The Virginia standards, for example, are praised because they state clearly what students should learn in academic subjects at each grade level. At the same time, they are flawed because they are rigid in specifying grade-level mastery without regard for individual learning time requirements. Cross (1998) also points out that competition exists among states to see which can set the highest standards, an action that can result in standards that are unreasonably high.

Existing state standards have much in common, and Cross (1998) believes they may constitute a bottom-up set of national standards by 2003. If this happens, concurrently with new IDEA language that requires participation in testing by students with disabilities, the results will likely be mixed. Accountability ensures that the achievement of students with disabilities is of concern to school districts. It also presents a dilemma for students who do not meet standards; neither retention in grade nor social promotion are particularly good options. Retention has, in fact, risen nationally to an average as high as 32%; it is a practice shown to have negative long-term effects on student achievement and to contribute to students' disengagement from school (Owings & Magliaro, 1998). Social promotion has also been widely criticized.

French (1998) has provided an in-depth review of the experiences of state-mandated educational reform in one state that replaced earlier consensus-based learning frameworks. These top-down reforms excluded practitioners' input and resulted in narrow, prescriptive academic standards with high-stakes facts-based tests. He expresses concern that such reforms are limited in effectiveness, and encourages greater collaboration. When schools continue to perform poorly, some states impose "takeovers" with state-appointed superintendents and strict accountability for boards, a procedure that has demonstrated mixed results (Bushweller, 1998).

Some reformers have the opinion that public schools have been unable to respond effectively to the needs of students who are increasingly diverse; they have proposed alternative private or charter schools (Nathan, 1998), often with vouchers for students. According to the Phi Delta Kappa national policy summary (Center on National Education Policy, 1996), even if private school enrollment doubled as a result of vouchers, the majority (78%) of students would still attend public schools. Scarce resources would have been diverted from programs that serve the vast majority of students and given to a small number of private programs. When for-profit management companies have invested in the business of charter schools, they have frequently chosen to restrict their clientele, rationalizing that their limited resources make it difficult to serve students with disabilities (Zollers & Ramanathan, 1998). In other cases, students with disabilities have been mismanaged in charter programs (Farber, 1998). Although business and industry leaders profess an interest in improving education, they frequently express caution about investing in education for the most difficult students, those at risk for school failure (Walsh, 1998). Although top-down standards and new models for schooling may offer improvement for students with disabilities or risk factors, this remains to be shown. French (1998), in his case study of state-mandated reform, issues this alert:

> In the end, while this narrow, authoritarian approach to standards and assessment may result in overall increases in student achievement and pockets of significant achievement in some districts, the achievement gap between low-income students, students of color, and more affluent white students will most likely continue to remain large and may possibly even widen. (p. 190)

Marginal Professional and Parent Interactions

One of the major limitations of previous special programs is that they have not led to an increase in either professional or parent/professional interactions. Although intended to provide coordinated programs for students with special needs, many efforts have resulted in further fragmentation of special services. Johnston, Allington, and Afflerbach (1985) found that students who are taught in separate settings (regular and special class) often receive entirely different, conflicting approaches to reading instruction. They found the majority of specialists did not know what kind of instruction the child was receiving in the regular classroom, and only 8% of the classroom teachers could identify the materials used in the special class.

It has been found also that social services for high school students with mild to severe special needs are isolated and fragmented (Boone, 1990; Farrar & Hampel, 1987). In their on-site study of 15 urban high schools, Farrar and Hampel found that the relationships among a variety of social services professionals were ambiguous and informal, though appearing to be bureaucratic. These programs lacked department heads, had no systematic operating procedures, were flawed by little information about related community agencies, and were plagued by endless paperwork. Students with similar problems in these schools were provided with a variety of disparate services, while departments failed to share responsibilities.

These authors acknowledge that it is difficult to establish coordinated programs for students' problems in which the diagnosis is ambiguous (e.g., depression) or for which the prescription is controversial (e.g., teen pregnancy). They also point out that some of the social programs have changed in scope and responsibility, that the larger schools often have a totally differentiated staff of specialists, and that new programs come and go in response to fads and available funding. The result is that many existing social services lack continuity and coordination.

Traditional programs are also limited by a lack of meaningful parental participation in decision making. Pfeiffer (1980) has found that minimal parental involvement in the team decision-making process, particularly as it relates to the Individual Educational Program (IEP) conference, is one of the major problems in traditional special education programs. Boone (1990) has found that parental participation is also minimal in the Individual Transition Planning (ITP) conference that enables the adolescent to make the transition from school to the adult world. A low rate of participation is characteristic of parents who represent cultural and linguistic minorities (Boone, 1990; Lynch & Stein, 1987).

New regulations in IDEA will strengthen the role of parents, require participation by general education personnel, and improve decision making by keeping the team membership constant across placement and program planning functions (Turnbull & Cilley, 1999). All of these changes support the rationale for teaching teamwork. The importance of parents' contributions to the education of their children has been increasingly recognized as essential for school reform (Fullan & Watson, 1997; Toch, 1999; White, 1997). Similarly, it is widely recognized that successful schools, both for the majority of students (McLaughlin & Schwartz, 1998) and for students with special needs (Hobbs & Westling, 1998) are those that have a common focus on student learning, with goals that are collaboratively determined. There is a need to provide this type of preparation to beginning teachers (Hobbs & Westling, 1998). Wadsworth (1997) and Switzer (1996) have shown further that deep divisions exist in the views of teacher educators, front-line K–12 educators, and the general public regarding definitions of quality in education and teacher preparation. Pipho (1997) issues an urgent plea for needed collaboration in her request that we just try to get along.

Limited Understanding of the Change Process

New proposals offered without regard for the major factors that facilitate change are not likely to be implemented effectively (Cuban, 1988; Fullan, 1993; Fullan & Watson, 1997; Skrtic, 1987). Some proposals have been offered without an understanding of the structure of schools and in the absence of significant input from the people most affected by the changes—the classroom teachers.

The structure of schools is a major barrier to any proposed change. Most teachers are still very isolated in their classrooms (Wadsworth, 1997). Classrooms in schools all over the nation are very much alike. In a major study of 525 high school classrooms, researchers found that although classrooms had different "personalities"—climate, community, administration, relationships among staff—they were alike in their "deep structure" (Tye, 1987). Their curriculum, policies, and reliance on test scores as measures of success were similar. These classrooms had an average size, with students seated noninteractively in rows while teachers engaged in frontal teaching and demonstrated "safe" control over learning. These commonalities were found in urban, rural, and suburban schools, regardless of socioeconomic status.

Fullan (1993) has emphasized that school change is extremely slow, requiring a minimum of 3 to 6 years. Skrtic (1987) points out that "it has always been so" because schools are locked into patterns that dictate grades and commonality and separate rooms. He suggests that schools faced with new problems can add new programs or create new classes, but they cannot incorporate new structures. When forced to change, teachers may simply pretend to do so, while continuing to operate as usual behind closed doors. Cuban (1988) expresses the same concern about the structure of schools and their resistance to change, pointing out that we need to study previous effective changes to determine those that have succeeded, and to ask—before changing—about the effect of this change on the system and on society.

Emphasis on excellence in the late 1990s, like the similar movement in the late 1980s, was characterized by the establishment of new standards, which appeared exclusionary; that movement created high levels of polarization between professionals (Wadsworth, 1997; Shaw, Biklin, Conlon, Dunn, Kramer, & DeRoma-Wagner, 1990).

Current trends are more consistent with the recommendations of Hobbs and Westling (1998) and of Shaw et al. (1990) for an inclusionary model that provides appropriate education for students with disabilities within the context of the total system. For example, recent trends in educational measurement encourage students to monitor the quality of their own work (Strickland & Strickland, 1998; Wiggins, 1991). Other proposals for reform in vocational education also have potential to benefit students at risk and those with disabilities. These include work in units with relevance beyond the classroom, which feature collaborative learning, use of resources outside the school, flexible use of time, and allowing students to express learning in their own language or in other creative ways (Newmann, 1991).

Because of marginal budgets and the high cost of education, there is also a growing interest in cost effectiveness. In a study of special education costs, Pyecha, Kullgowski, and Wiegerink (1984) studied the budgets of eight school districts in five states from 1980 through 1983. They found that personnel represented the greatest costs for special programs (64% to 92%) and that transportation costs had also increased. As a result, most school districts were forced to decrease their expenditures for professional development and materials, increase class size, place students in "least restrictive programs," and place students into categories with the maximum advantages in funding.

It appears, then, that a society in which the value system equates individual worth with economic productivity, and which classifies people according to a medical model of disability, is unlikely to respond to the need for change unless it can be shown that this change will have a positive economic effect.

PROMISING NEW PRACTICES

Some new practices, based on the concepts that underlie the model of interactive teaming, offer promise for program improvement. These practices are derived from the summary of research on effective schools which focuses on teams that have been able to facilitate academic achievement and social adjustment in students who are at risk for school failure. These practices also appear to enhance the effectiveness and morale of the professionals who implement them.

Effective Schools Research

From a summary of the research on effective schools, it can be determined that schools in which there is a central mission, on which the school works as a team, are more effective than those in which there are individual teacher goals. In schools with a central mission, productivity, morale, and effectiveness increase (DeBevoise, 1984; McLaughlin & Schwartz, 1998), and the teacher's sense of isolation (Wadsworth, 1997) is lessened (Ashton & Webb, 1986). According to Stedman (1985), these schools have several things in common: personal attention to students; skillful use of teachers; parental involvement; emphasis on ethnic studies; student responsibility for school affairs; and preventive teaching as opposed to remediation. Summaries by Guthrie (1998) and by Wang, Haertel, and Walberg (1997) also stress the importance of school leadership, collaboration, and ability to respond to individual students' needs.

Ashton and Webb (1986), in an extensive study of a teacher's sense of efficacy, have shown that feeling a lack of efficacy is often related to the teacher's belief that he or she is isolated in the futile attempt to solve complex problems. This is particularly true in schools with a high concentration of students at risk (Liedel-Rice, 1998; Olson & Rodman, 1988; Rosenholtz & Kyle, 1984). In an ethnographic study on the socialization of teachers, Blase (1985) has shown that beginning teachers become less creative and less involved with students over time, and that they need support systems from within to prevent them from becoming traditionalists or authoritarians who focus on low-order skills. The most effective schools are those in which the members of the staff are able to collaborate in the effort to improve the quality of their services to students. Thousand and Villa (1990) add that teachers who operate within collaborative teams report high levels of morale and a sense of empowerment.

Representative Samples of Promising Practices

The demographic and social changes in today's classrooms represent a new population of students and a new set of circumstances that cannot be addressed by old mandates. Successful reform needs to include provisions for collaborative activity at a collegial level. Samples of promising practices include the following:

◆ There are new models for assessment of student progress, including the use of student projects and portfolios, through which students with a range of abilities and learning preferences can show what they know (Strickland & Strickland, 1998). This type of assessment is translated more readily into the improvement of instruction when it is continuous and based on multiple sources of evidence (Darling-Hammond and Falk, 1997).

◆ Increasing numbers of teacher preparation programs are beginning to incorporate instruction on collaboration into their curriculum, both through modeling by university faculty (e.g., Hohenbrind, Johnston, & Westhoven, 1997; Welch,

1998) and through design of field-based experiences (Hobbs & Westling, 1998; Morsink, 1999).

◆ Technology applications provide expanded opportunities for collaboration. Higher education and K–12 faculty are able to collaborate across time and space, "visit" each other, participate in conferences with distant experts, and create shared simulations and products (Baston & Bass, 1996). Similarly, students previously labeled "at risk" have been able to work together productively in projects such as creation of a web site (Brodsky, 1998).

Community-wide teams, implementing the model of extended-service schools (National Center for Schools and Communities, 1998; O'Neil, 1997) and those listening/communicating effectively to public concerns about schools (Kernan-Scholss & Plattner, 1998) have been able to provide services and obtain substantive support from their constituents.

Total Quality Management

Total quality management (TQM), a special form of teaming, was initially implemented and is used largely in business and industry settings (Lawler, 1993). It is viewed as a vehicle for the improvement of processes within the system. Most TQM programs focus on ways to reduce errors in processes, making them more effective in providing services. TQM is a variation on other collegial problem-solving models, such as quality circles, self-management teams, shared decision making and school-based management (Thomas, Correa, & Morsink, 1995).

TQM, an innovation by Deming (1986) and also based on the concepts of Csikszentmihalyi (Schmoker & Wilson, 1993), was the catalyst for postwar economic recovery in Japan. It combines principles from psychology, leadership, and statistics into a systematic plan for continuous improvement of services.

TQM, which is beginning to be used in school restructuring, incorporates the principles of interactive teaming, and is most often referred to as total quality education (TQE) in the school context. Schmoker and Wilson (1993), indicating that site-based management alone has not produced higher achievement in schools, have summarized the use of total quality principles and analyzed the factors that account for their success. Schmoker and Wilson note that, in business and industry, as in school applications, the appearance of TQM principles fails without willingness to empower workers and to trust them. Successful schools use these simple principles, without becoming rigid Deming disciples. They also caution that real improvement takes time—probably 5 years, although morale may improve sooner. Specific problems may be identified and solved, building on success. Continuous improvement through use of data and team analysis is a common element in all of the successful programs.

Schmoker and Wilson (1993) indicate that the TQM principles have been applied successfully in a variety of schools. They also note that it is important for implementers to ask questions, such as these:

◆ Are employees working together on the most important problems?

◆ What data are used to determine priorities?

◆ Are we making progress? What works and doesn't work?

◆ How can we improve?

THE COMMON ELEMENTS CONTRIBUTING TO INTERACTIVE TEAMING

The most promising proposals for improving schools' responsiveness to the increased number of students with special needs are those that include the features of teacher empowerment, shared "ownership" of problems, and the common goal of providing each student with the best possible program. These same features are incorporated into interactive teaming. Friend and Cook (1996) have emphasized the importance of voluntary participation among equals to establish mutual goals through shared responsibility as essential in successful collaboration. Goodlad (1984) has stressed that the common patterns of teacher isolation, with top-down mandates for change and improvement, lead only to superficial compliance. Stedman (1987) has pointed out that several factors involving collaboration account for the successes in the effective schools research, such as the emphasis on community participation and ownership, shared governance by teachers, and the emphasis on student responsibility. Wilson and Firestone (1987) have given examples of ways in which innovative leaders can work around the bureaucratic structures in schools to facilitate collaboration (e.g., help teachers network their skills, encourage a buddy system for parents, enhance communication among constituents).

Among the successful attempts to encourage teaming in new teachers are those that provide mentors (Bunting, 1988) or involve coaching (Leggett & Hoyle, 1987). The practices that facilitate teacher collaboration include opportunities to develop lesson plans and units, to talk together about new ideas, and to observe each other in classrooms (Little, 1981). All of these approaches involve some form of interactive teaming, although the implementers have not used that label.

History of Success

The most encouraging thing about the use of interactive teaming is that it has been successful even in schools with the most difficult students. These are schools that have a large number of students who are disabled or at risk, particularly minority students who do not believe that school achievement is related to economic gain (Olson & Rodman, 1988). They are schools with the worst combination of poverty, low parental achievement, and racial and cultural isolation. The staff members are the newest and least prepared teachers—those trained to work with an average and ideal student population that no longer exists.

Olson and Rodman (1988) point out that the old excuses for school failure—the poor home environments of a few students—are no longer valid when these limitations are representative of the majority of the student population. One of the successful team responses to school failure has been implemented in New Haven, Connecticut, by a team of Yale University, public school, mental health, and community personnel (Comer, 1989; O'Neil, 1997), and extended throughout the nation to several other school districts (Schmoker & Wilson, 1993). In this program, success has been attributed to the collaborative contributions of people with diverse areas of expertise. Comer has also been able to document improvement in the educational achievement of parents as well as their children.

Three school districts in Hammond, Indiana, have initiated a collaborative program to train new professionals to work in urban schools by designating one school in each district as an urban education center (Olson & Rodman, 1988). Task forces representing the teaching staff, administration, and community will reach consensus on the curriculum, entrance criteria, and implementation plan for the new program.

Maeroff (1993) describes some effective teams used to facilitate school change. First offered through leadership academies, such as those sponsored by the Rockefeller Foundation at the University of New Mexico and Michigan State University, these teams grew in strength as they developed the support of colleagues, learned new process skills, facilitated an academic excellence atmosphere, and forged new links with business and the community. According to Maeroff, some of the factors that increased the team's ability to succeed in making changes are as follows:

◆ Set important priorities for school.
◆ Model appropriate skills and interactions.
◆ Anticipate resistance, provide responses.
◆ Interact with peers in school and help community become involved.
◆ Keep sense of humor, positiveness.
◆ Find time to work together.
◆ Maintain communication.

Maeroff (1993) indicates that teams may initially believe that their school's problems (lack of budget, time, clear mission, knowledge; temporary staff, unions) are so severe, the team cannot be of much help. It is important for the team to focus on the major problems of students, rather than seeming to deal with superficial issues.

Smith (1992) describes the common strengths of teams in which university and school partners have come together to agree on common goals for professional practice. In a survey of the 38 programs that won the Association of Teacher Educators (ATE) Distinguished Program in Teacher Education awards, 1977–1989, it was found that award-winning programs had common factors. These factors included practical or clinical collaboration, which featured both learning how to teach and acquisition of interpersonal relationship skills for the participants. Most had a governance team with representatives from both partners, and a structure that allowed for the relationship of theory to practice. Characteristics that seemed to enable partnerships to survive over time included equality between partners, emphasis on significant school-based programs with collaboration in the settings where education occurs, and the assignment of responsibility based on participants' skills.

These successful teams—both micro teams that function within a school, and macro teams that extend to include school partnerships—have a common element: They are planned and implemented by representative, interactive participants, as opposed to being mandated by legislatures or district administrators. They follow the recommendations of the Carnegie report for new governance structures, and they respond to the concerns of the chief state school officers that schools cannot help the most difficult students without providing a whole range of special services (Olson & Rodman, 1988). Teacher and related professional competence, combined with the belief that even the most difficult students can learn, are viewed as essential elements in the success of these teams.

Decision Points in Teaming

Figure 1.2 illustrates the differences between a traditional system of serving students with special needs and the proposed system called *interactive teaming*. It follows the five decision points modified from the work of Salvia and Ysseldyke (1988), initially identified as referral, screening, classification, instructional planning, and evaluation of pupil progress.

At decision point 1 in a traditional system, referral is costly and time consuming; there is often a backlog of referrals, and students may have to wait a long time before services can begin. In the interactive teaming model, a prereferral team meets to discuss the educational needs of a student even before a referral is made. At this stage, the team members might be able to resolve the problem and eliminate the need for costly referral.

Decision point 2 involves screening. In a traditional system, this means the student is tested by several isolated specialists and that the data from testing may not be well integrated. Screening is most often followed by classification—the identification of the student as having a disability. Interactive teaming proposes joint problem solving by members of the team to ensure that multiple inputs are received before making the decision about classification.

Decision point 3, services, is most often characterized in a current system by the delivery of expert advice by consultants who tell the practitioner what to do with the student, and by the individual efforts of teachers to provide remedial instruction. In interactive teaming, "services" are characterized by coordinated consultation and collaboration among the members of the team.

Decision point 4 involves the development of an instructional plan. In a traditional system, the IEP is often written before the meeting and presented to par-

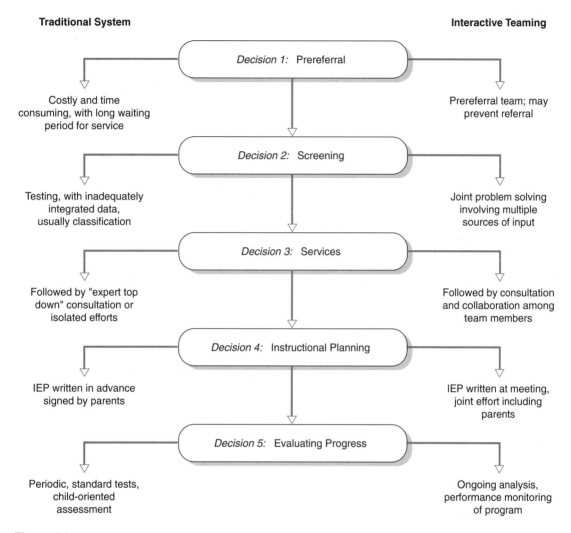

Figure 1.2
Contrasts between the traditional system and the proposed model for interactive teaming.

ents for their signature. In interactive teaming, the IEP is written during the meeting, and represents the joint efforts of team members, including parents.

At decision point 5, evaluation, the child is traditionally given periodic tests focused on standardized measures of achievement to determine whether he or she has mastered the prescribed program content. In interactive teaming, the focus of evaluation is on the program; measurement is ongoing and the analysis is focused on ways in which the team can change the program to increase its effectiveness.

APPLICATION OF INTERACTIVE TEAMING

Working as an effective team member is much more challenging than working alone. The team members have differing perspectives, speak varying "languages," and demonstrate a range of behaviors that results in both effective and ineffective resolution of problems. Figure 1.3 gives an example of effective interactive teaming in action.

This application takes place in a university-related urban professional development school. The team includes a third grade classroom teacher, a student teacher, a university faculty member, and a school principal. The application shows how careful observation, direct but respectful communication, and the willingness of participants to learn by listening can set the tone for successful interactive teaming.

Monica, a student teacher seeking certification in elementary and special education, observed an incident that troubled her. It was during a group activity, in which the children were sitting on the floor or at their desks, listening attentively while the teacher read them a story. Gary, a boy whose desk was next to the teacher's, stood up in the middle of the story and made sweeping motions in the air as he talked seemingly to himself. The teacher kept reading and the other children kept listening to the story, though a few of them seemed momentarily distracted by Gary's behavior. At the end of the day, Monica asked for a team meeting that involved the classroom teacher, the university supervisor, and the school principal.

Student Teacher (ST): Ms. Michaels, I don't want you to think I am criticizing you, but I'm really confused about something I saw today. I guess when you just start out in student teaching, it is hard to put everything together that you've learned in your methods classes and make sense out of what you see in the classroom.

Classroom Teacher (CT): I'm pleased that you feel comfortable about questioning what you see me doing.

University Supervisor (US): I agree. That's why we choose people like Ms. Michaels as cooperating teachers. And I'm glad that you are making astute observations and thinking about what you see, Monica.

School Principal (PR): Absolutely! Our philosophy includes the acceptance of the behaviors children bring with them to school, and the understanding that they all have different learning styles. We view children's behaviors as opportunities for problem-solving. What is it you would like to talk about?

ST: (explains her observation, then continues...) Well, it's just that Gary's behavior could have been disruptive, and it could spread to the other kids. If it was my class, I'd be afraid things would get out of control. Shouldn't you have done something to let the others know this wasn't the behavior you expected? I mean, like said you liked the way Gail was sitting and listening so quietly? Not a big deal, but just a gentle reminder of the rules?

Figure 1.3   Setting the tone for effective interactive teaming.

US: You were relating your observation to what you had learned about positive reinforcement, then? What was the effect of Ms. Michaels' response on Gary's behavior?

ST: Well, he kept on making these motions and talking to himself for a minute or so, and then he sat back down. It looked like he was drawing a picture or something, and he was still off-task.

CT: It must have seemed to you that I was doing selective ignoring? And you were afraid the other kids would take advantage of that and get off-task too?

PR: Actually, when we developed Gary's IEP, we talked about how best to adapt and accomodate his special learning needs. Gary can't sit still very long, and he learns best through physical activity. When we assess what our students have learned, we let them show what they know in a variety of ways—through art, music, construction of models—in addition to writing. This applies to all of the students, of course, but it does make the classroom a more supportive environment for students with special needs.

US: I see Ms. Michaels has the picture Gary drew. Is that the one...

CT: Yes, see he has a picture of a boy, and he is winding up to throw a pitch in the ball game, just as was happening in the story I was reading.

ST: Wow! So he was not only listening, but he was understanding what you read and reacting to it. Talk about "on task!" What would have happened, Ms. Michaels, if you had tried to stop Gary from standing up and moving around?

CT: Based on data I've kept on him in the past, he would have tuned out—stopped listening altogether. Or, he might have flipped out and had a tantrum.

US: Yes, in frustration because you were actually stopping him from learning. I'll have to incorporate this example into my methods class. But how did the other students know that Gary's behavior wasn't a problem or that they shouldn't do that too?

CT: Well, we talk a lot about individual differences in our room, and the children just accept each other's learning styles.

PR: It's just the way the whole staff thinks about teaching and learning. We're a team.

ST: And you just did the same thing for me! I learn best by asking questions about what I see and trying to figure out how that fits in to what I think I know. Thanks for making me feel like I was part of the team, and not just some outside critic with unrealistic expectations.

Figure 1.3, *continued*

SUMMARY

Educators and related professionals now experience intensified pressures to collaborate in the solution of increasing education-related problems for these reasons:

◆ The majority of our students have complex special needs.

◆ Traditional programs are ineffective in serving the increasing numbers of students with complex special needs.

◆ Proposed solutions that do not take into account the body of knowledge about the process of change will not be any more effective.

Those who have summarized the research on effective schools suggest the following:

◆ Teachers in these schools are committed to a central mission.

◆ This mission is focused on maximizing the educational opportunities for students.

◆ Teachers in effective schools work together as a team to achieve this goal.

The model proposed in this book—interactive teaming—is a response to the nation's increasingly complex problems in special needs programs because it incorporates the features of teacher empowerment, community responsiveness, and professional collaboration, all of which characterize effective schools for students who have disabilities or are at risk.

The interactive team is a group that functions at the highest level of professionalism because it involves both consultation and collaboration. The interactive teaming model includes components that have been used previously to provide services to students with mild disabilities and in programs that provide educational, medical, and social services to students with severe disabilities. The historical foundations and specific dimensions of interactive teaming will be described in detail in the following two chapters.

ACTIVITIES

1. Observe interactive teaming in your own classroom or clinical program, or interview a person who teaches in such a program. How do the students in this program differ from those in your classes when you attended school? In what ways are the professionals in this program collaborating (or failing to collaborate) to provide effective educational and medical services for students with complex needs?

2. Describe your attitudes about or past experiences with activities in which you were asked to interact with other professionals to develop an educational product or program. In what ways did your experiences lead you to be optimistic about the benefits of interactive teaming? Pessimistic? What, in your opinion, has to happen if collaboration is to succeed?

3. Imagine that you have an unlimited budget and the power to implement any type of programs you choose that would serve the growing number of students with special needs. Describe the program(s) you would implement.

REFERENCES

Algozzine, K., Morsink, C., & Algozzine, B. (1987). In search of differentiated instruction: An analysis of teaching behaviors in self-contained special education classrooms. *Florida Journal of Teacher Education, 4*, 62–70.

Allington, R. (1987, October). Current practice and future directions: Implementation of categorical programs: Reading instruction. In *The education of students with special needs: Gearing up to meet the challenges of the 1990s*. Symposium conducted at The Wingspread Conference, Racine, WI.

Altenbaugh, R., Engel, D., & Martin, D. (1995). *Caring for kids: A critical study of urban school leavers*. London: Falmer Press.

Anderson, R., Hiebert, E., Scott, H., & Wilkinson, I. (1985). *Becoming a nation of readers: The report of the commission on reading*. Washington, DC: National Institute of Education.

Ashton, P., & Webb, R. (1986). *Making a difference: Teachers' sense of efficacy and student achievement*. New York: Longman.

Bartel, N., & Thurman, K. (1992). Medical treatment and educational problems in children. *Phi Delta Kappan, 74*(1), 57–61.

Barth, P. (1998, March). Virginia's version of excellence. *The American School Board Journal*, pp. 41–43.

Baston, T., & Bass, R. (1996). Teaching and learning in a computer age. *Change, 28*(2), 42–47.

Blase, J. (1985). The socialization of teachers. *Urban Education, 20*, 235–256.

Boone, R. (1990). The development, implementation, and evaluation of a preconference training strategy for enhancing parental participation in and satisfaction with the individual transition conference (Doctoral dissertation, University of Florida, 1989). *Dissertation Abstracts International, 51*(3), 618A.

Brodsky, N. (1998). Think quest content motivates youngsters to collaborate on web-based projects. *T.H.E. Journal, 25*(6), 55–56.

Brown, R. (1985). *Reconnecting youth: The next stage of reform*. Denver, CO: Business Advisory Commission, Education Commission of the States.

Bunting, C. (1988). University-public school collaboration in the preparation of teachers: The North Carolina model. *The Clearing House, 61*, 315–316.

Burgess, D., & Streissguth, A. (1992). Fetal alcohol syndrome and fetal alcohol effects: Principles for educators. *Phi Delta Kappan, 74*(1), 24–30.

Bushweller, K. (1998). Do takeovers work? *The American School Board Journal, 185*(8), 16–18.

Carey, A., & Parker, S. (1999, April 22). Fear of classmates. *USA Today*, p. 1.

Center on National Education Policy. (1996). *Do we still need public schools?* Bloomington, IN: Phi Delta Kappa.

Comer, J. (1989). Children can: An address on school improvement. In R. Webb & F. Parkay (Eds.), *Children can: An address on school improvement by Dr. James Comer with responses from Florida's Educational Community* (pp. 4–17). Gainesville, FL: University of Florida, College of Education Research & Development Center in collaboration with the Alachua County Mental Health Association.

Corrigan, D. (1996). Teacher education and interprofessional collaboration: Creation of family-centered, community-based integrated service systems. In L. Kaplan & R. Edelfelt (Eds.), *Teachers for the new millenium* (pp. 142–171). Thousand Oaks, CA: Corwin Press.

Cross, C. (1998, October 21). The standards wars: Some lessons learned. *Education Week, XVIII*, pp. 32, 35.

Cuban, L. (1988). A fundamental puzzle of school reform. *Phi Delta Kappan, 69*, 341–344.

Darling-Hammond, L., & Falk, B. (1997). Using standards and assessments to support student learning. *Phi Delta Kappan, 78*, 190–198.

DeBevoise, W. (1984). Synthesis of research on the principal as instructional leader. *Educational Leadership, 41*(5), 14–20.

Deming, W. E. (1986). *Out of the crisis.* Boston: MIT Center for Advanced Engineering Studies.

Eitzen, S. (1992). Problem students: The sociocultural roots. *Phi Delta Kappan, 73,* 84–590.

Farber, P. (1998). The Edison project scores—and stumbles—in Boston. *Phi Delta Kappan, 79,* 506–511.

Fardig, D., & Morsink, C. (1985). *Classroom observations of SLD, EH, and EMH teachers using the Florida Performance Measurement System.* Gainesville, FL: University of Florida, Department of Special Education.

Farrar, E., & Hampel, R. (1987). Social services in American high schools. *Phi Delta Kappan, 69,* 297–303.

First, J., & Carrera, J. (1988). *New voices: Immigrant students in U.S. public schools.* Boston: National Coalition of Advocates for Students.

Fleischner, J., & Van Acker, R. (1990). Changes in the urban school population: Challenges in meeting the need for special education leadership and teacher preparation personnel. In L. M. Bullock and R. I. Simpson (Eds.), *Critical issues in special education: Implications for personnel preparation* (pp. 73–91). Denton: University of North Texas.

French, D. (1998). The state's role in shaping a progressive vision of public education. *Phi Delta Kappan, 80,* 185–194.

Friend, M., & Cook, L. (1996). *Interactions: Collaborative skills for school professionals* (2nd ed.). New York: Longman.

Fullan, M. (1993). *Change forces.* London: Falmer Press.

Fullan, M., & Watson, N. (1997). *Building infrastructures for professional development: An assessment of early progress.* New York: Rockefeller Foundation.

Goodlad, J. (1984). *A place called school: Prospects for the future.* New York: McGraw-Hill.

Graden, J., Thurlow, M., & Ysseldyke, J. (1982). *Instructional ecology and academic responding time for students at three levels of teacher-perceived behavioral competence* (Research Report No. 73). Minneapolis: University of Minnesota, Institute for Research on Learning Disabilities.

Guthrie, J. (1998, November 21). 20/20 vision: A strategy for doubling academic achievement in America by the year 2020. *Education Week, XVIII,* 24–25.

Haynes, M., & Jenkins, J. (1986). Reading instruction in special education resource rooms. *American Educational Research Journal, 23,* 161–190.

Hechinger, F. (1992). *Fateful choices: Healthy youth for the 21st century.* New York: Carnegie Corporation.

Hobbs, T., & Westling, D. (1998). Promoting successful inclusion through collaborative problem-solving. *TEACHING Exceptional Children, 31*(1), 12–19.

Hocutt, A., Cox, J., & Pelosi, J. (1984). *A policy-oriented study of special education's service delivery system. Vol. I. An exploration of issues regarding the identification and placement of LD, MR, and ED students* (RTI Report No. RTI/2706-06/OIFR). Research Triangle Park, NC: Research Triangle Institute, Center for Educational Studies.

Hodgkinson, H. (1988). The right schools for the right kids. *Educational Leadership, 45,* 10–15.

Hohenbrind, J., Johnston, M., & Westhoven, L. (1997). Collaborative teaching of a social studies methods course: Intimidation and change. *Journal of Teacher Education, 48,* 293–300.

Jacobson, L. (1998, September 7). One-on-one. *Education Week, XVIII,* 42–47.

Johnston, P., Allington, R., & Afflerbach, P. (1985). The congruence of classroom and remedial reading instruction. *Elementary School Journal, 85,* 465–477.

Kernan-Scholss, A., & Plattner, A. (1998). Talking to the public about public schools. *Educational Leadership, 56*(2), 18–21.

Knapp, M., Turnbull, B., & Shields, P. (1990). New directions for educating the children of poverty. *Educational Leadership, 48*(2), 4–8.

Lawler, J. (1993, April 2). Quality is a matter of teamwork. *USA Today,* pp. 4–5B.

Leerhsen, C., & Namuth, T. (1988, January 18). Alcohol and the family. *Newsweek,* pp. 62–68.

Leggett, D., & Hoyle, S. (1987). Preparing teachers for collaboration. *Educational Leadership, 44,* 58–63.

Levin, H. (1986). *Educational reform for disadvantaged students: An emerging crisis.* West Haven, CT: National Education Association Professional Library.

Liedel-Rice, A. (1998). *Program follow-up study of former urban student teachers in their second through sixth year of teaching.* Slippery Rock, PA: SRU College of Education, unpublished manuscript.

Lipsky, D., & Gartner, A. (1998). Taking inclusion into the future. *Educational Leadership, 56*(2), 78–81.

Little, J. (1981). School success and staff development. In *The role of staff development in urban desegregated schools, executive summary.* Washington, DC: National Institute of Education.

Lynch, E., & Stein, R. (1987). Parent participation by ethnicity: A comparison of Hispanic, black, and Anglo families. *Exceptional Children, 54,* 105–111.

McLesky, J., Henry, D., & Hodges, D. (1998). Inclusion: Where is it happening? *TEACHING Exceptional Children, 31*(1), 4–10.

Maeroff, G. (1993). Building teams to rebuild schools. *Phi Delta Kappan, 74,* 512–519.

McLaughlin, M., & Schwartz, R. (1998) *Strategies for fixing public schools.* Cambridge, MA: Pew Forum, Harvard Graduate School of Education.

Mernit, S. (1990). Kids today. *Instructor,* 35–43.

Morsink, C. (1999). *21st century teachers for a better future* (Final Report to Howard Heinz Endowment). Slippery Rock, PA: SRU College of Education, unpublished manuscript.

Morsink, C., & Lenk, L. (1992). The delivery of special education programs. *Remedial and Special Education, 13*(6), 33–43.

Nathan, J. (1998). Heat and light in the charter school movement. *Phi Delta Kappan, 79,* 499–505.

National Center for Schools and Communities. (1998). *Community schools in the making: Conversations supporting children and families in the public schools.* New York: Fordham University Center.

National Coalition of Advocates for Students. (1985). *Barriers to excellence: Our children at risk.* Boston: Author.

Needleman, H. (1992). Childhood exposure to lead: A common cause of school failure. *Phi Delta Kappan, 74*(1), 35–37.

Newmann, F. (1991). Linking restructuring to authentic student achievement. *Phi Delta Kappan, 72,* 458–463.

Oakes, J. (1986). Keeping track, part 1: The policy and practice of curriculum inequality. *Phi Delta Kappan, 68,* 12–17.

Oakes, J., Wells, A., Yonezawa, S., & Ray, K. (1997). Equity lessons from detracking schools. In A. Hargreaves (Ed.), *Rethinking educational change with heart and mind* (pp. 43–72). Alexandria. VA: ASCD.

Olson, L., & Rodman, B. (1988, June 22). The unfinished agenda, part II. *Education Week,* pp. 17–33.

O'Neil, J. (1997). Building schools as communities: A conversation with James Comer. *Educational Leadership, 54*(8), 6–10.

Owings, W., & Magliaro, S. (1998). Grade retention: A history of failure. *Educational Leadership, 56*(1), 86–88.

Pfeiffer, S. (1980). The school-based interprofessional team: Recurring problems and some possible solutions. *Journal of School Psychology, 18,* 389–394.

Pipho, C. (1997). The possibilities and problems of collaboration. *Phi Delta Kappan, 78,* 261–262.

Pyecha, J., Kullgowski, B., & Wiegerink, R. (1984). *Special education costs and funding trends and their relation to the provision of special education and related services.* Research Triangle Park, NC: Research Triangle Institute, Center for Educational Studies.

Rafferty, Y. (1997–1998). Meeting the educational needs of homeless children. *Educational Leadership, 55*(4), 48–52.

Reeves, M. S. (1988, April 27). Reform at 5: The unfinished agenda, part 1. *Education Week,* pp. 14–23.

Reynolds, M. (1989). Students with special needs. In M. C. Reynolds (Ed.), *Knowledge base for the beginning teacher* (pp. 129–142). Oxford, England: Pergamon Press.

Rose, L., & Gallup, A. (1998). The 30th annual Phi Delta Kappa/Gallup poll of the public's attitudes toward the public schools. *Phi Delta Kappan, 80*, 41–56.

Rosenholtz, S., & Kyle, S. (1984). Teacher isolation: Barrier to professionalism. *American Educator, 8*, 10–15.

Rupley, W., & Blair, T. (1987). Assignment and supervision of reading seatwork: Looking in on 12 primary teachers. *The Reading Teacher, 40*, 391–393.

Sack, J. (1998, June 8). Special ed designation varies widely across country. *Education Week, XVII*(1), 20–21.

Salvia, J., & Ysseldyke, J. (1988). *Assessment in special and remedial education* (4th ed.). Boston: Houghton Mifflin.

Schmoker, M., & Wilson, R. (1993). Transforming schools through total quality education. *Phi Delta Kappan, 74*, 389–395.

Secretary's Commission on Achieving Necessary Skills. (1991). *What work requires of schools: A SCANS report for America 2000*. Washington, DC: U.S. Department of Labor. (ERIC Document Reproduction Service No. ED 332 054)

Shaw, S., Biklin, D., Conlon, Dunn, J., Kramer, J., & DeRoma-Wagner, V. (1990). Special education and school reform. In L. M. Bullock and R. L. Simpson (Eds.), *Critical issues in special education: Implications for personnel preparation*. Denton, TX: North Texas University.

Skrtic, T. (1987). *An organizational analysis of special education reform*. Washington, DC: The National Inquiry into the Future of Education for Students with Special Needs.

Smith, S. (1992). Professional partnerships and educational change: Effective collaboration over time. *Journal of Teacher Education, 43*(4), 243–256.

Spear-Swerling, L., & Sternberg, R. (1998). Curing our "epidemic" of learning disabilities. *Phi Delta Kappa, 79*, 397–401.

Stedman, L. (1985). A new look at the effective schools literature. *Urban Education, 20*, 295–326.

Stedman, L. (1987). It's time we changed the effective schools formula. *Phi Delta Kappan, 69*, 215–224.

Stevens, L., & Price, M. (1992). Meeting the challenge of educating children at risk. *Phi Delta Kappan, 74*, 18–23.

Strickland, K., & Strickland, J. (1998). *Reflections on assessment: Its purposes, methods, and effects on learning*. Portsmouth, NH: Boynton/Cook.

Superintendents. (1988). *Dealing with dropouts: The urban superintendents' call to action*. Washington, DC: U.S. Government Printing Office.

Switzer, T. (1996, October 3). Disconnect: Education deans and faculty, teacher education and schools. Presidential address at annual meeting of the Teacher Education Council of State Colleges and Universities, Baltimore, MD.

Thomas, C., Correa, V., & Morsink, C. (1995). *Interactive teaming: Consultation and collaboration in special programs* (2nd ed.). Upper Saddle River, NJ: Merrill/Prentice Hall.

Thousand, J., & Villa, R. (1990). Sharing expertise and responsibilities through teaching teams. In W. Stainback and S. Stainback (Eds.), *Support networks for inclusive schooling: Integrated interdependent education*. Baltimore: Paul H. Brookes, 151–166.

Toch, T. (1999, January 18). Outstanding schools. *US News and World Report*, pp. 48–51.

Turnbull, R., & Cilley, M. (1999). *Explanations and implications of the 1997 amendments to IDEA*. Upper Saddle River, NJ: Merrill/Prentice Hall.

Tye, B. B. (1987). The deep structure of schooling. *Phi Delta Kappan, 69*, 281–283.

U.S. Department of Education (1992). *To assure the free appropriate public education of all children with disabilities* (Fourteenth Annual Report to Congress on the Implementation of the Individuals with Disabilities Education Act). Washington, DC: National Association of State Directors of Special Education.

U.S. Department of Education (1995). *Seventeenth annual report to Congress on the implementation of the Individuals with Disabilities Act*. Washington, DC: Author.

U.S. Department of Education (1997). *Nineteenth annual report to Congress on the implementation of the Individuals with Disabilities Act.* Washington, DC: Author.

Vail, K. (1997). Special pioneers. *The American School Board Journal, 184*(12), 16–21.

Wadsworth, D. (1997). *Different drummers: How teachers of teachers view public education. A report from Public Agenda.* New York: Public Agenda.

Walsh, M. (1998, September 23). High-risk investors eye education opportunities. *Education Week, XVIII*(1), 12.

Wang, M., Haertel, G., & Walberg, H. (1997). *What do we know: Widely implemented school improvement programs.* Philadelphia, PA: Mid-Atlantic Educational Lab, Temple University.

Welch, M. (1998). Collaboration: Staying on the bandwagon. *Journal of Teacher Education, 49,* 26–34.

White, S. (1997, November). Family friendly schools. *The American School Board Journal, 184,* 31–33.

Wiggins, G. (1991). Standards, not standardization: Evoking quality student work. *Educational Leadership, 48*(5), 18–25.

Will, M. (1986). *Educating students with learning problems: A shared responsibility.* Washington, DC: Office of Special Education and Rehabilitation Services.

Wilson, B., & Firestone, W. (1987). The principal and instruction: Combining bureaucratic and cultural linkages. *Educational Leadership, 45,* 18–23.

Yell, M. (1998). The legal basis of inclusion. *Educational Leadership, 56*(2), 70–73.

Zollers, N., & Ramanathan, A. (1998). For-profit charter schools and students with disabilities. *Phi Delta Kappan, 80,* 297–304.

2 Historical Foundations of Consultation, Collaboration, and Teaming

Topics in this chapter include:

- Description of the historical and legal foundations of consultation, collaboration, and teaming.
- Definitions of consultation, collaboration, and teaming.
- Models of consultation, collaboration, and teaming.
- Dimensions and goals of consultation, collaboration, and teaming.
- Competencies and processes in consultation and teaming.
- Impediments and positive features of consultation and teaming.
- An application illustrating these approaches.

Dan Hayes, a school psychologist, is responsible for the assessment of students in three schools in the district. The district also expects its psychologists to serve as consultants and team members in their assigned schools. Dan has commented often on the variance in how well he believes he is able to meet that expectation in his three assigned schools.

At the meetings at Maxway Elementary, Dan feels primarily like a reporter. The assistant principal, Mrs. Payton, is in charge of all meetings to discuss students, and she prides herself on running brief and efficient meetings. The usual format is to have Dan and his colleagues present their assessment data and recommendations in round-robin fashion. However, questions and discussion are not encouraged because of the extra time involved, and Mrs. Payton says such talk among professionals usually only confuses the parents. After the professionals make their reports, Mrs. Payton provides a summary and a list of options to the parents. The parents usually are silent listeners until this point, and Dan thinks they often are intimidated by the number of professionals present and Mrs. Payton's business-like approach. He has commented to his colleagues that more often than not, the parents select the first option presented and rarely ask questions. He has tried to talk to Mrs. Payton about various ways to enhance the input of the professionals, but the response always has been "Why make things more complicated than they are? We've always done it this way, and I don't want to change now. Our meetings go quickly, so let's not do anything that might prolong them."

At Zion Primary School, Dan believes his role is more like that of a consultant, but he is uncomfortable with being introduced to the parents as the "expert" and viewed as the one whose recommendations should carry the most weight. Because the principal at Zion does not like to ask his staff to attend meetings regularly, Dan finds that he frequently has to attend several meetings to discuss the same issues on a single child because not all the personnel are willing or able to meet at the same time. In addition to the strains this places on his schedule, Dan is aware that trying to attend several meetings is a hardship for some parents.

In contrast to these two schools, when Dan attends meetings at Anderson Middle School, he feels like more of a team member. The principal, Mr. Gutierrez, has identified one day per week as a meeting day, and he encourages his staff to be available for meetings on students or curriculum matters. Mr. Gutierrez posts the schedule for the meetings on students and lists which teachers and professionals need to attend. Although he attends the meetings, he contributes as a team member rather than as team leader. The leadership role *is rotated among Dan, a special educator, a regular classroom teacher, and the counselor, based on a schedule they designed at the beginning of the year.*

Input from the parents is encouraged, and all the professionals value the exchanges and ideas among the team members. Team members frequently consult and collaborate with others outside of the group meetings, and any additional information or strategies obtained in those sessions are shared at the beginning of each team meeting. Dan thinks the situation at Anderson is advantageous to all of the people involved, and that the quality of the decisions made is much higher than at his other two schools.

This vignette illustrates various processes professionals and parents can engage in to share information on students. It also describes the effects the setting and attitudes can have on what actually occurs and how well people are able to fulfill their roles. In this example, Dan was able to complete the assessment tasks expected of him in a similar way at all three schools. However, implementation of the aspects of his role that involved consulting and serving as a team member varied markedly among the three schools. This variance was due to the attitudes of the team members on what should be done by whom, who is considered the "expert," the leadership style implemented, the value placed on input from others, and a lack of willingness to change. However, at Anderson Middle, Dan was able to be a consultant, collaborator, and team member—and his colleagues also were able to serve in those roles.

The interactive teaming model proposed in this text has been developed as an attempt to take into account the myriad factors affecting the provision of educational and other types of program services for students with special learning and behavioral needs. In addition, appropriate implementation of the model should reduce the discrepancies in how services are delivered and how professionals and parents interact.

The model is built on components of various approaches and service delivery alternatives that have been presented and researched primarily in the fields of special education and school psychology. However, it is important to note at the outset that interactive teaming includes not only psychologists and special educators, but also parents and other professionals who are concerned with the welfare and education of children. These professionals include regular classroom teachers, physicians, social workers, counselors, physical and occupational therapists, adapted physical educators, assistive technology specialists, speech-language clinicians, and other related services personnel.

This chapter includes a selected review of the literature on consultation, collaboration, and teaming models advanced during the past two decades. The models are defined and their characteristics delineated. Dimensions or characteristics of these models, programmatic goals, and competencies of personnel involved in implementation are described. Finally, impediments or barriers and effective features of the models are summarized.

HISTORICAL AND LEGAL FOUNDATIONS

Professional Viewpoints: Early 1970s

In the early 1970s, professionals in special education and school psychology began to comment on the changes needed in their fields to improve services to students with special needs and the professionals who were working with or teaching those students. Deno (1970) presented a model of service delivery for special education students that included consultation services as the first level above total regular classroom integration. Lilly (1971) stated that professionals needed to change how they viewed children with mild learning and behavioral problems, and how they behaved toward those students. He suggested that rather than labeling the *students* as exceptional, the *situation* should be considered exceptional.

Instead of functioning in a direct service role with students with mild disabilities, Lilly (1971) proposed that special educators serve in a support and training role for the regular classroom teachers who would have primary responsibility for educating the children. Fine and Tyler (1971) also commented on the idea of support for teachers from school psychologists. They called for psychologists to move away from the limited test-and-report approach to one that focused more on teacher consultation and the development of interpersonal functioning and helping relationships.

Legal Influences: 1970s, 1980s, and 1990s

A legal impetus for teachers, psychologists, and others to work together on concerns about students with special needs appeared in 1975 in Public Law 94-142, the Education for All Handicapped Children Act. Although child study teams existed in some systems before this (Pryzwansky & Rzepski, 1983), certainly the law and its accompanying regulations served as a catalyst for professionals working together. Section 121a.532(e) of P.L. 94-142 states: "The evaluation is made by a multidisciplinary team or group of persons, including at least one teacher, or other specialist, with knowledge in the area of suspected disability." The law also specified cooperation to "insure that the placement decision is made by a group of persons, including persons knowledgeable about the child, the meaning of the evaluation data, and the placement options." Kaiser and Woodman (1985) noted that this law removed the primary decision-making role on special education placement from the school psychologist and placed it with a team of people including parents, speech pathologists, teachers, school administrators, nurses, physicians, social workers, and counselors.

The passage of Public Law 99-457, Education of the Handicapped Act Amendments of 1986, further strengthened the idea of professional collaboration or teaming, in this case to meet the needs of young children. Part H of this law requires states to "develop and implement a statewide comprehensive, coordinated, multidisciplinary, interagency program" for early intervention services. This legislation includes children from birth through age 2 who have been diagnosed as having a mental or physical condition that is likely to result in a disability. At the discretion of a state agency, it can also include children who are considered at risk for developmental problems (Siders, Riall, Bennett, & Judd, 1987).

Public Law 94-142 was amended again in 1990 by Public Law 101-476, the Individuals with Disabilities Education Act (IDEA). In this legislation the exceptionalities of autism and traumatic brain injury were added, and references to "handicapped children" were changed to "children with disabilities." The law stipulated increased collaboration among special educators, classroom teachers, and related services personnel, and placed more emphasis on transition services for students age 16 or older. The latest amendments to the Individuals with Disabilities Education Act were passed in 1997, and the regulatory provisions were issued in March 1999. In general, the three themes in the 1997 IDEA amendments are (1) increased emphasis on parental participation in decision making, (2) participation of children with disabilities in the general curriculum, and (3) development of behavioral intervention/management plans. (For additional information, see Turnbull & Cilley, 1999, the most recent IDEA regulations, or refer to the U.S. Department of Education-funded web site at http://www.ideapractices.org.) As Coben, Thomas, Sattler, and Morsink (1997) noted, each version of the law addressed issues that called for increased collaboration and involvement of families and a range of professionals in program design and implementation for students with disabilities.

Section 504 of the Rehabilitation Act of 1973 is a civil rights law that prohibits discrimination on the basis of disability. As Fishbaugh (1997) commented, Section 504 complements the special education mandates of IDEA with procedural requirements that often parallel IDEA. The Americans with Disabilities Act of 1990 also provides strong legal and civil rights support for equality of opportunity and the value of individuality. Discrimination on the basis of disability is forbidden, and the barriers that prohibit people with disabilities from participating in activities in public locations must be removed. As businesses, public service agencies, and educational institutions have begun the process of implementing these laws, consultation and teaming approaches among employees and employers have been used.

Expanding Applications: Late 1970s, 1980s, and 1990s

Starting in the late 1970s, consultation and teaming approaches began to receive attention beyond the original proposals for support and helping relationships and the legal requirements for identification and placement. Special issues on consultation and collaboration appeared in such professional journals as *Behavioral Disorders* (Nelson, Neel, & Lilly, 1981), *Teacher Education and Special Education* (1985), *Remedial and Special Education* (1988), *Preventing School Failure* (1991), *Journal of Teacher Education* (1992), *Remedial and Special Education* (1996), and *Journal of Learning Disabilities* (1997).

Consultation and collaboration received much support as:

◆ An effective way to reduce regular educators' referrals for special education services (Adelman & Taylor, 1998; Cantrell & Cantrell, 1976; Ritter, 1978; Sindelar, Griffin, Smith, & Watanabe, 1992).

◆ A way to diminish the need for labeling or providing differentiated services for mildly disabled students whose academic and behavioral needs are similar (Bruskewitz, 1998; Morsink & Lenk, 1992; Newcomer, 1977).

◆ A skill all teachers need to respond to changing school practices (e.g., Denemark, Morsink, & Thomas, 1980; President's Commission on Teacher Education, 1992).

◆ A viable service delivery alternative for students with mild disabilities (cf. Friend, 1988; Reynolds & Birch, 1982).

◆ A requirement for the success of students in mainstreamed classrooms (Friend, 1984; Nelson & Stevens, 1981; Safran & Barcikowski, 1984; Salend, 1994; Simpson & Myles, 1990; Wood, 1992).

◆ An approach to dealing with the unique needs of secondary-level pupils (Huefner, 1988; Patriarca & Lamb, 1990; Tindal, Shinn, Walz, & Germann, 1987).

◆ An important element in infant and preschool programs (Hanline & Knowlton, 1988; Lowenthal, 1992).

◆ An area needing more research in response to the Regular Education Initiative (Lloyd, Crowley, Kohler, & Strain, 1988).

◆ A model for transition planning (Sileo, Rude, & Luckner, 1988).

◆ A strategy to reduce teacher burnout (Cooley & Yovanoff, 1996).

In addition to the special issues of journals previously cited, a new journal focusing on consultation was initiated in 1990, the *Journal of Educational and Psychological Consultation*. A number of textbooks targeted for special educators, psychologists, and other related professions were published on the topics of consultation, collaboration, and teaming in the late 1980s and early 1990s. These texts include *Psychological Consultation* (Brown, Pryzwansky, & Schulte, 1991); *Consultation, Collaboration, and Teamwork for Students with Special Needs* (Dettmer, Thurston, & Dyck, 1993); *Interactions: Collaboration Skills for School Professionals* (Friend & Cook, 1992); *Consultation Concepts and Practices* (Hansen, Himes, & Meier, 1990); *Collaborative Consultation* (Idol, Nevin, & Paolucci-Whitcomb, 1994); *Effective School Consultation* (Sugai & Tindal, 1993), and *Collaboration in the Schools* (West, Idol, & Cannon, 1989). In the late 1990s the number of texts available on collaboration and teaming increased dramatically including revised texts by Friend and Cook (1996) and Brown, Pryzwansky, and Schulte (1998), and new books such as *Collaborative Practitioners, Collaborative Schools* (Pugach & Johnson, 1995); *Teamwork Models and Experience in Education* (Garner, 1995); *Models of Collaboration* (Fishbaugh,

1997); *Collaboration: A Success Strategy for Special Educators* (Cramer, 1998); *Interprofessional Collaboration in Schools* (Mostert, 1998); and *Collaborative Decision Making: The Pathway to Inclusion* (Tiegerman-Farber & Radziewicz, 1998).

Consultation also has been recognized and supported by professionals inside and outside special education settings, as well as in various other types of service delivery programs. In an article for school counselors, Umansky and Holloway (1984) commented on the changes in education that created the need for counselors to serve as consultants. Physical therapists are finding an increasing amount of their role descriptions to be consulting with teachers (cf. Lindsey, 1985). Physicians have supported the concept of consultation and collaboration, and they believe their input is necessary in treating all aspects of a child's functioning (cf. Brown, 1987; Marshall & Wuori, 1985). Alternative programs for young children, such as day-care and home-based programs, are utilizing consultation as a way to meet professional development needs (Jones & Meisels, 1987; Klein & Sheehan, 1987; Trohanis, 1981). Community-based programs for people with developmental delays have implemented consultative services (e.g., Como & Hagner, 1986; Powers, 1986). In addition, consultation has been used to address the needs of people with physical disabilities who live in rural settings (e.g., Moore & Allen, 1986).

Examples of teaming approaches in a variety of settings also have been documented in the literature. Major journals have run topical issues on teaming, including *Teacher Education and Special Education* (Egan & Bluhm, 1981) and *School Psychology Review* (1983). Kaiser and Woodman (1985) noted that rehabilitation centers and mental health clinics have provided ongoing integrated team services for their clients. Vocational and industrial educators have begun advocating a team approach for meeting the needs of students who are at risk or have special needs (Feichtner & Sarkees, 1987; Spencer-Dobson & Schultz, 1987). Transitional programs for preschoolers (Brown, 1987) and adults with special needs (Edgar, 1988; Hasazi, Furney, & DeStefano, 1999) cite teaming as a key aspect. Ancillary personnel, such as physical and occupational therapists, support teaming as a way to fit into the total school system or program functioning (e.g., Lindsey, O'Neal, Haas, & Tewey, 1983; McAfee, 1987). Stahlman (1995) advocated a teaming approach in the education of the deaf and children with hearing impairments. Collaboration and teaming models received extensive support in three educational arenas in the late 1990s. These three arenas were middle schools, inclusion settings, and school reform initiatives.

Teachers and administrators in middle schools have implemented collaboration and teaming models in their efforts to reconfigure their schools from a junior high approach. As Gable, Hendrickson, and Rogan (1996) noted, "Collaboration holds special promise at middle school where the organizational structure is well suited to interdisciplinary teamwork" (p. 235). They described collaborative teams comprised of teachers from various content areas along with one or more specialists that engaged in structured problem-solving processes to examine curricular goals and needs of individual students. Ryan and Paterna (1997) described how teachers in Alaska used collaborative teaming to correlate general and special education services with the student's educational objectives and cooperative lesson planning. Clark and Clark (1997) suggested that interdisciplinary teaming allows better use of faculty members' skills and improved strategies for dealing with diverse populations. Erb (1997) found that implementation of teaming approaches in middle schools resulted in higher student achievement in math, reading, and language arts.

Stanovich (1996) called collaboration "the key to successful instruction" (p. 39) in schools where inclusion is being implemented. O'Shea, O'Shea, and Algozzine (1998) noted that changes in demographics, school standards and student performance expectations, instructional practices, and service delivery models necessitated the use of collaborative and teaming approaches. Hobbs and Westling (1998) observed that the "degree of success of inclusion can be related to several factors, perhaps the most important being teachers' preparation, attitudes, and opportunity for collaboration" (p. 13). Idol (1997) commented that the best configuration for providing inclusive programs is the use of teams of professionals and parents.

The school reform movement is the third arena where collaboration and teaming models have received much attention and endorsement by researchers (cf. Pugach & Warger, 1996). Neubert and Stover (1994) suggested that schools for the 21st century will encourage teaming among teachers, and ideal schools will be characterized as collegial and collaborative. The National Commission on Teaching and America's Future (1996) noted that teachers currently do not have enough time with their colleagues, and that one of the turning points that will indicate progress is when all teachers have access to high-quality professional development and regular time for collegial work and planning. Darling-Hammond (1997) and Danielson (1996) described the importance of teaming models as ways to support curriculum alignment and professional development. O'Shea, Williams, and Sattler (1999) observed that educational reformers studying teacher effectiveness found that teaming was an essential component. Pugach and Johnson (1995) commented:

> Many developments in the reform-minded educational scene over the past 15 years have converged to encourage educators to rethink the role of adult–adult relationships in schools and to realize the value of professional collaboration and the need to establish it soundly as an expectation for teachers. (p. 6)

The Council for Exceptional Children supported the importance of consultation, collaboration, and teaming by inclusion of these areas in the *CEC Common Core of Knowledge and Skills Essential for All Beginning Special Education Teachers* (Swan & Sirvis, 1992). The *Common Core* is composed of 107 knowledge and skill statements in eight categories. Examples of statements and categories related to consultation and collaboration are listed below:

Skill #25. Collaboration with parents and other professionals involved in the assessment of students with individual learning needs.

Category VII.   Communication and Collaborative Partnerships

Knowledge #85.   Importance and benefits of communication and collaboration, which promotes interaction with students, parents, and school and community personnel.

Knowledge #87.   Developing individual student programs working in collaboration with team members.

Skill #90.   Use collaborative strategies in working with students, parents, and school and community personnel in various learning environments.

Skill #93.   Encourage and assist families to become active participants in the educational team.

Skill #95.   Collaborate with regular classroom teachers and other school and community personnel in integrating students into various learning environments.

In the most recent revision of the standards, the Council for Exceptional Children (1998) continued to stress the importance of collaboration and teaming and also emphasized cultural and family issues. An excerpt from the Common Core is included below:

Category 7.   Communication and Collaborative Partnerships Knowledge:

K1   Factors that promote effective communication and collaboration with individuals, parents, and school and community personnel in a culturally responsive program.

K2   Typical concerns of individuals with exceptional learning needs and appropriate strategies to help parents deal with these concerns.

K3   Development of individual student programs working in collaboration with team members.

K4   Roles of individuals with exceptionalities, parents, teachers, and other school and community personnel in planning an individualized program.

K5   Ethical practices for confidential communication to others about individuals with exceptional learning needs.

K6   Roles and responsibilities of the paraeducator related to instruction, intervention, and direct services.

K7   Family systems and the role of families in supporting child development and educational progress.

The extensive support for consultation, collaboration, and teaming from a variety of viewpoints and service delivery options, along with legal mandates and support from key professional organizations, make further exploration of these approaches vital. The next sections will define consultation, collaboration, and teaming, discuss characteristics and processes, and delineate how aspects of these approaches are part of the foundation for interactive teaming.

CONSULTATION AND COLLABORATION

Definitions

The variety of definitions of consultation frequently is due to the differences in the philosophical views and professional roles of the authors. Based on their extensive review of the literature, West and Idol (1987) concluded that consultation has at least three general meanings: *medical,* in which a doctor calls on the expertise of another physician for counsel; *organizational,* which involves change in a system; and *mental health,* in which a consultant provides assistance to another professional on problems the latter may be experiencing with a client.

Tharp (1975) described consultation as a triadic process in which the consultant attempts to bring about changes in a target person through a consultee or mediator. Bergan's (1977) definition included two forms of consultation, depending on whether the goals were considered to be long range (*developmental* consultation) or designed to remediate an immediate problem (*problem-centered* consultation). Brown, Wyne, Blackburn, and Powell (1979) noted that consultation is a process involving the establishment of trust and communication and "joint approaches to problem identification, the pooling of personal resources, to identify and select strategies that will have some probability of solving the problem that has been identified, and shared responsibility in the implementation and evaluation of the program or strategy that has been initiated" (p. 8). Idol-Maestas (1983) focused on the support regular classroom teachers can gain from consultants that will help them cope with students' academic and social behavior problems. Conoley and Conoley (1982) emphasized the voluntary and nonsupervisory design of a consultative relationship.

Medway's (1979) definition included the phrase *collaborative problem-solving* to describe the interaction that occurs among professionals. The collaborative nature of consultation has received much attention in the literature for school psychologists (cf. Gutkin & Curtis, 1982; Piersel, 1985). Hawryluk and Smallwood (1986) noted: "Regardless of theoretical orientation, school consultation is based on the premise that positive change in student behavior can be produced indirectly when a consultant engages with teachers or other school personnel in collaborative problem solving" (p. 519).

Special educators also have advocated this collaborative approach. Idol, Paolucci-Whitcomb, and Nevin (1986) defined *collaborative consultation* as follows:

> An interactive process that enables people with diverse expertise to generate creative solutions to mutually defined problems. The outcome is enhanced, altered, and produces solutions that are different from those that the individual team members would produce independently. The major outcome of collaborative consultation is to provide comprehensive and effective programs for students with special needs within the most appropriate context, thereby enabling them to achieve maximum constructive interaction with their nonhandicapped peers. (p. 1)

In the second edition of their textbook, Idol and her colleagues (1994) noted: "The process creates synergy, with different outcomes that are better than the original solutions that any team member would produce independently" (p. xi).

Heron and Harris (1987) included the concept of professionals working together in consultation by stating: "It is a collaborative, voluntary, mutual problem-solving process that may or may not involve the achievement of several subordinate objectives and that leads to the prevention or resolution of identified problems" (p. 3).

Friend and Cook (1992) also noted the importance of collaboration and defined it as "A style for direct interaction between at least two co-equal parties voluntarily engaged in shared decision-making as they work toward a common goal" (p. 6).

Aldinger, Warger, and Eavy (1991) defined teacher consultation as follows:

A problem-solving process which takes place over a period of time and has a number of stages. Consultation focuses on a current work problem of the consultee. The consultant and consultee pool expertise or work together for purposes of analyzing and solving classroom problems. (p. 2)

Dettmer et al. (1993) defined school consultation and the role of consultant as follows:

School consultation is activity in which professional educators and parents collaborate within the school context by communicating, cooperating and coordinating their efforts as a team to serve the learning and behavioral needs of students.

A school consultant is a facilitator of communication, cooperation, and coordination who consults, collaborates, and engages in teamwork with other educators to identify learning and behavioral needs, and plan, implement, and evaluate educational programs to meet those needs. (p. 14)

Brown et al. (1998) approached consultation from a human services perspective:

Human service consultation is defined as a voluntary problem-solving process that can be initiated and terminated by either the consultant or consultee. It is engaged primarily for the purpose of assisting consultees to develop attitudes and skills that will enable them to function more effectively with a client, which can be an individual, group, or organization for which they have responsibility. Thus, the goals of the process are two-fold: enhancing services to third parties and improving the ability of consultees to function in areas of concern to them. (p. 6)

Fishbaugh (1997) noted the linkage between educators and human services in her definition of collaboration: "Collaboration means working together for a common end. As educators and human services professionals collaborate, they should do so with a knowledge of different models for collaborating, and recognition of the different purposes for their collaborative practice" (p. 4).

Mostert (1998) described the potential for student involvement in his definition:

> Collaboration is a style of professional interaction between and among professionals, parents and families, and, where appropriate, students themselves to share information, to engage in collaborative decision making, and to develop effective interventions for a commonly agreed upon goal that is in the best interests of the student. (p. 16)

Sugai and Tindal (1993) emphasized a behavior-analytic approach to consultation and collaboration. In the preface of their book, they state:

> Consultation is defined as a structured series of problem-solving steps or interactions that occur between two or more individuals. We emphasize the development and modification of solutions from information that is systematically obtained and analyzed within the context of the immediate problem. (p. viii)

Welch and Sheridan (1995) observed that other factors may influence the implementation of collaboration: "Collaboration is a dynamic framework for efforts which endorses interdependence and parity during interactive exchange of resources between at least two partners who work together in a decision making process that is influenced by cultural and systemic factors to achieve common goals" (p. 11).

Cramer (1998) commented on the importance of focus on goals and situational assessment:

> Effective collaboration consists of designing and using a sequence of goal-oriented activities that result in improved working relationships between professional colleagues. Collaboration rests on the ability to accurately assess the demands of the situation, develop appropriate expectations, and initiate actions that will enable collaboration to occur. (p. 3)

A final point in defining consultation is clarifying what it should *not* be. Pryzwansky (1974) stated that consultation should not be an "expert" providing some type of prescription. Gutkin and Curtis (1982) distinguished between the traditional medical model approach that focused on psychological problems as mental illnesses, and the current approach to consultation that is based primarily on behavioral psychology. West and Idol (1987) also pointed out the difference between consultation and counseling by stating that the former should be focused on issues, whereas the latter tends to be focused on individuals.

Distinguishing consultation from collaboration also is important. Hansen et al. (1990) noted that consultation differs from collaboration, because collaborators carry joint responsibility for situations and in consultation the consultee retains ownership of the case or program. Aldinger et al. (1991) stated, "In essence, collaboration is an alternative to the expert approach in consultation" (p. 4). Schulte and Osborne (1993) commented that collaboration and consultation are two distinct processes. Collaboration is an interactive, planning, decision-making process involving two or more team members. Whereas consultation also is a problem-solving process involving two or more people, consultation is "an *indirect* helping process that empowers the consultee. The collaborative process involves two or more individuals in a *direct* helping process" (Brown et al., 1998, p. 7).

Models

West and Idol (1987) identified 10 models of consultation from their examination of the literature in special education and school psychology. Three of the models they described are discussed here because they are essential to an understanding of interactive teaming. Those models are *triadic* (and its relationship to collabora-tive), *organizational,* and *behavioral* consultation.

As previously indicated, *triadic consultation* (Tharp, 1975; Tharp & Wetzel, 1969) involves three people: consultant, mediator, and target. Tharp (1975) describes the roles of each person as follows:

1. The *target* is the person with the problematic behavior, the change of which is the primary goal of the directed influence.
2. The *mediator* is the person with the available means of social influence for effect-ing that goal.
3. The *consultant* is the person with the knowledge to mobilize the mediator's influence. (p. 138)

In the triadic model, the target may be a student or an adult in whom others believe a behavior change is desirable. The mediator is a parent, teacher, or other professional who will be attempting to bring about a behavior change in the tar-get. The consultant can be a parent, teacher, administrator, or other professional who has expertise to share regarding strategies to change the behavior.

In the illustration of the triadic model in Figure 2.1, the existence of two dyads within the model is also shown in the bottom part of the box. The dyads are con-sultant–mediator and mediator–target. Each influences the other, and there is an indirect influence of the consultant on the target, as shown by the dotted line in the top diagram.

Collaborative consultation (Idol et al., 1986) is essentially an extension of the tri-adic model. Idol et al. specified that the target typically is a student with some type of problem, the mediator usually is a regular classroom teacher, and the con-sultant can be a special educator, speech therapist, principal, or the like. Although the authors commented that this model can result in collaboration and sharing among professionals with various types of expertise, implementation has primar-ily focused on a triadic relationship among regular and special educators attempt-ing to meet the needs of students with special characteristics.

Organizational consultation (e.g., Brown, Kiraly, & McKinnon, 1979; Gallessich, 1982) focuses on the process of change in the systems of an organization or group of people. The interactions among group members, interrelationships among subsystems, shared decision making, and communication skills are highlighted in

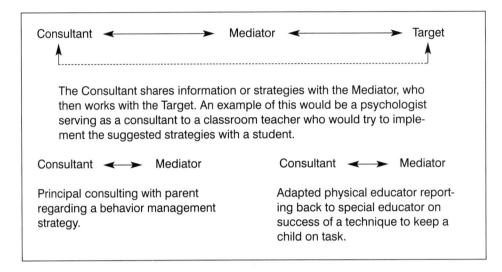

Figure 2.1
The triadic model.
Source: From "The Triadic Model of Consultation: Current Considerations," by R. G. Tharp, 1975. In C. Parker (Ed.), *Psychological Consultation: Helping Teachers Meet Special Needs.* Reston, VA: The Council for Exceptional Children, p. 137. Adapted by permission.

this model. The consultant can be anyone within the system and is viewed primarily as a facilitator of the group process.

Behavioral consultation (Bergan, 1977) is based on social learning theory and the application of the principles of applied behavior analysis. The primary emphasis is on student behavior change, so it can be considered a client-centered and problem-solving approach (Piersel, 1985). Proponents of behavioral consultation, especially in recent years, also have indicated the importance of considering a child's interactions within a total environmental system to understand influences on behavior (Cipani, 1985; Friend, 1988; Hawryluk & Smallwood, 1986), and they have noted that some degree of change will occur in the consultee's behavior as a result of involvement in the consultative process (Gutkin, 1986).

The defining features of this consultation model are the use of direct observation methods resulting in problem definitions in observable and measurable terms, identification of target behaviors for change, and the use of data-based intervention and assessment methods (Hawryluk & Smallwood, 1986). Sugai and Tindal (1993) focus their behavior-analytic and best practices approach to consultation on the learned nature and lawfulness of behavior and the potential for change by manipulating aspects of the environment.

Dimensions

The dimensions or characteristics of consultation can be affected by the emphasis or focus of the consultant. However, Gutkin and Curtis (1982) identified a set of core characteristics they believe are present in almost all the models they reviewed:

1. *Indirect service delivery:* Working on a child's behavior through another professional rather than directly with the child.

2. *Consultant–consultee relationship:* Establishment of an open and trusting relationship.

3. *Coordinate status:* Viewing the consultee as an equal, rather than operating in a hierarchical power structure.

4. *Involvement of the consultee in the consultation process:* Active participation of the consultee throughout the process.

5. *Consultee's right to reject consultant suggestions:* The freedom to select among the options presented instead of being pressured to follow along with every recommendation.

6. *Voluntary nature of consultation:* Participants are involved because they recognize a need and want some assistance, not because they are being forced to attend.

7. *Confidentiality:* The information provided is not shared with others who are not involved in the consultation process.

The dimensions or elements of collaboration are similar to those of consultation listed above. Cook and Friend (1991) noted that collaboration is a voluntary endeavor. In addition, they commented that individuals who collaborate *share a common goal, share responsibility for decisions and accountability for outcomes,* and *must believe in parity;* that is, each participant has something valuable to contribute and the *contributions are valued by others.* Mostert (1998) cited the same dimensions as those listed above and added *communal trust, collective involvement, action for problem solving, collaborative resources, confidentiality,* and *focus on the student as priority.*

The critical elements of collaborative consultation were identified by Villa, Thousand, Paolucci-Whitcomb, and Nevin (1990). They stated that participants *value one another as possessors of unique expertise, distribute task and relationship functions* among members of the group, *hold one another accountable,* and *monitor and adjust emphasis on task and relationship behaviors.*

Goals

Some authors stress the *helping relationship* goal of consultation and collaboration (e.g., Fine & Tyler, 1971), whereas others focus more on the *training* or *teaching* of another professional such skills as assessment, programming, management, and monitoring (e.g., Idol-Maestas, 1983; Parker, 1975). West and Idol (1987) summarized aspects of the latter goal by noting that consultation can provide remedial services for presenting problems, as well as attempt to increase consultee skills to prevent—or more effectively respond to—future problems. In their review of six consultation service delivery models, Idol and West (1987) noted that they focused on three types of outcomes: changes in students, changes in teachers, and changes in systems. Pugach and Johnson (1990) commented that consultants can provide the stimulus for general classroom teachers to change their instructional practices to "increase the likelihood that students with learning and behavior problems will be successful" (p. 240).

Brown et al. (1979) presented a comprehensive list of goals for consultation that included (1) placing high priority on the psychological development of the student, (2) using parent and community resources to assist the student, (3) enhancing the skills of consultees, (4) facilitating communication among professionals, (5) improving human relations in the school, and (6) increasing educational achievement of students. Idol et al. (1994) described other possible positive outcomes of collaborative consultation: changes in the collaborators and changes in the organization. They stated that as a result of engaging in the collaborative process, the collaborators are expected to:

1. Increase their individual knowledge bases by learning from each other.
2. Improve their interpersonal skills (communication, group interaction, and problem solving).
3. Make cognitive and emotional shifts in their own intrapersonal attitudes toward how to be more effective team members and toward what the learning possibilities might be for learners who have special needs or who are currently experiencing school failure. (p. xii)

Fishbaugh (1997) described the goals of collaboration as follows:

The overriding goal is student achievement; but in order to reach that goal collaboration may be used to provide technical assistance to teachers as they work with students to practice new techniques. Collaboration may be employed to provide support among teachers as they work with especially difficult students or as they strive for personal professional development. Collaboration among educators may be necessary for solving immediate or long-range individual student or school-wide challenges. (p. 5)

Competencies

Studies in the area of competencies considered necessary for effective consultation have focused on those needed by consultants as well as by consultees. The interactive and confidential nature of consultation makes empirical measures difficult to obtain, so the research has tended to take the form of recommendations, consensus ratings among professionals, or self-reports. As Brown et al. (1998) noted, skills needed by consultants are frequently described by authors, but characteristics of effective consultants have received little attention by researchers.

Special educators who serve as consultants typically are in the role of resource teacher (Voltz, Elliott, & Harris, 1995). The consultant aspect of this role has been the topic of considerable debate since the mid-1980s in terms of whether (1) this is an appropriate expectation (Brown et al., 1979); (2) it is an important element for the success of mainstreaming (Speece & Mandell, 1980); (3) principals and regular classroom teachers see it as a vital part of the resource role (Evans, 1981); (4) special educators feel confident in the role (Aloia, 1983); and (5) it is an expectation or policy by the state departments of education (West & Brown, 1987).

Recommendations regarding competencies generally are similar to those presented by Haight (1984). She stated that the consultant role requires specific knowledge in a variety of areas; skills in analysis, problem solving, and synthesis; and the ability to promote human relations, communication, and skill development in others. Friend (1984) surveyed resource teachers, regular classroom teachers, and principals regarding their views on the skills needed for consultation. All three groups of educators indicated that the skills usually considered integral to a consultative role should be possessed by resource teachers. West and Cannon (1988) conducted a study to identify the competencies needed by both regular and special educators in working in a collaborative consultation model. These authors used a Delphi method to survey 100 interdisciplinary experts in 47 states. The competencies that received the highest ratings were in the areas of personal characteristics, collaborative problem solving, and interactive communication. In their review of the literature, Brown et al. (1998) identified five primary characteristics needed by consultants. The characteristics are (1) a high level of awareness of his/her values—especially important in cross-cultural consultation; (2) ability to solve problems; (3) high levels of ego development including increased self-awareness and reliance on self-generated standards; (4) ability to establish working alliances including empathy, genuineness, and positive regard; and (5) willingness to take interpersonal risks.

The training to develop consultation competencies typically is included in programs for health and medical practitioners (Courtnage & Healy, 1984) and school psychologists and counselors, but such training is less often a part of the course of study for special educators (Salend & Salend, 1984) and even more limited—if present at all—for regular educators. Training programs have been described that use a variety of approaches, such as single-subject measurement designs (Idol-Maestas, 1983), interactive video (Evans, 1985), collaboration between university faculty and field-based teachers (Paolucci-Whitcomb & Nevin, 1985), and collaboration among postdoctoral-level personnel from various departments (McClellan & Wheatley, 1985). However, as Gable, Young, and Hendrickson (1987) noted, training in consultation competencies is still limited in most programs, and if it is available, it is usually at the graduate instead of the undergraduate level. A summary of programs designed to teach special educator skills in consultation can be found in Idol and West (1987). An inservice and preservice curriculum for teachers, support staff, and administrators has been developed by West et al. (1989).

As collaboration-based service delivery models in educational settings have increased, the roles and activities of educators have been impacted accordingly (Foley & Mundschenk, 1997). In a survey of elementary and special educators serving students with behavior disorders, respondents were asked to identify collaboration competencies (Foley, 1994). The competencies identified were similar to those previously described for consultants but also included recognition of the importance of the roles of fellow collaborators, e.g., (1) knowledge and skill in communication skills; (2) knowledge of professional roles and responsibilities of colleagues; (3) knowledge and skill in the use of a variety of assessment and instructional approaches; (4) knowledge of general education curricula; and (5) knowledge and skill in modifying and adapting methods, materials, and evaluation systems to meet students' needs. Pugach and Johnson (1995) described the following dimensions of collaborative professionals: recognition of the complexity of collaboration, acknowledgment of the creativity of working with others, enjoyment of the social nature of joint problem solving, and reflection on professional practice. Blanton, Griffin, Winn, and Pugach (1997) described collaborative teacher education programs that are designed to prepare both general and special educators. Hudson and Glomb (1997) also outlined programs at several universities that focus on collaboration instruction for all educators.

Process

The process implemented in consultation is based on the focus, type of problem, and the people involved. Although described in a variety of terms by different authors, the process generally includes the steps listed in Figure 2.2 (compiled from Aldinger et al., 1991; Brown et al., 1998; Cipani, 1985; Dettmer et al., 1993; Gutkin, 1993; Heron & Harris, 1987; Idol et al., 1986; Kampwirth, 1987; Kurpius, 1978; Sugai & Tindal, 1993).

1. *Establishing the relationship*—meeting and establishing trust with the consultee.
2. *Gathering information*—checking a variety of sources to get background on the problem.
3. *Identifying the problem*—determining the history and frequency of the problem, defining it in measurable terms.
4. *Stating the target behavior*—considering whether the behavior needs to be increased or decreased, and by what criteria the behavior is to be judged.
5. *Generating interventions*—discussing options to consider, selecting ones to try.
6. *Implementing the interventions*—putting the interventions into effect and collecting data on their success or failure.
7. *Evaluating the interventions*—determining whether the desired outcomes have been reached and modifying as necessary.
8. *Withdrawing from the consultative relationship*—ending the process when the goal has been reached or an agreement is made not to continue.

Figure 2.2
The process of consultation.

TEAMING

Definitions

The definitions delineated in the literature on teaming frequently are very similar, although emphases may vary slightly depending on the model being defined. Pfeiffer (1980) noted that a team is an organized group of professionals from different disciplines who have unique skills and a common goal of *cooperative problem solving*. Abelson and Woodman (1983) commented on *interdependence* among team members, and the relationships and norms that help control team and individual behavior. Bailey (1984) observed that teams learn, grow, and change as they attempt to collaborate. Dettmer et al. (1993) stated that consultation, collaboration, and teaming share two characteristics: "engaging in interactive processes and using specialized content to achieve shared goals" (p. 16). They also noted that collaboration and teamwork allow participants the opportunity to build on the strengths of their colleagues. Katzenbach and Smith (1999) distinguished a team from a group of people who have been given a common assignment in the following definition:

> A team is a small number of people with complementary skills who are committed to a common purpose, performance goals, and approach for which they hold themselves mutually accountable. (p. 45)

Models

Three models of teams, as well as three types of committee approaches, have been identified. The teaming models are described first: multidisciplinary, interdisciplinary, and transdisciplinary. These three models are illustrated in Figure 2.3.

The *multidisciplinary team* developed from the medical model as people with expertise in various fields shared their observations about a patient, and frequently those findings were reported to one person (Hart, 1977). Pfeiffer (1981) stated that the "key elements of a multidisciplinary team are a common purpose, cooperative problem solving by different professionals who possess skills and orientations, and a coordination of activities" (p. 330).

An *interdisciplinary team* may include the same members as the multidisciplinary team, but in this model the team members evaluate a child and then meet as a group to discuss their observations. Bailey, Helsel-DeWert, Thiele, and Ware (1983) described the interdisciplinary process by saying it "is at one level, the complex interaction of individual skills, professional and personal priorities, client needs, group dynamics, and institutional regulations. At its heart, however, is the individual participant and his or her ability to contribute in a way that facilitates meeting group goals" (p. 248).

The *transdisciplinary team* was developed to attempt to reduce the fragmentation of services that often occurred in the other two models (Hart, 1977). In this

Figure 2.3
Model of teams.

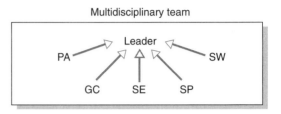

Multidisciplinary team

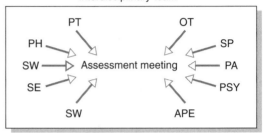

Interdisciplinary team

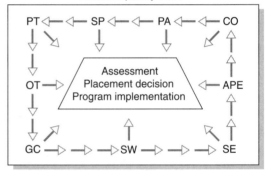

Transdisciplinary team

Key:
PA = Parent
GC = General education classroom teacher
SE = Special educator
SP = Speech/language clinician
SW = Social worker
PH = Physician
PT = Physical therapist
OT = Occupational therapist
APE = Adapted physical educator
PSY = Psychologist
CO = Counselor

approach, interdisciplinary services may be used to make the initial assessment and develop an implementation plan. Golightly (1987) said the major factor that distinguishes transdisciplinary teams from the other models is the extension through the program implementation phase. Sailor and Guess (1983) stated, "The transdisciplinary approach is an education/treatment model that effectively integrates program goals and objectives from various disciplines and professions. The integration begins in the assessment process and extends through direct programming effort" (p. 207). Lyon and Lyon (1980) advocated the transdisciplinary approach over the other two because it promotes more efficient use of the expertise from various professionals. Gast and Wolery (1985) also supported the transdisciplinary approach because it would allow for multiple interventions to occur concurrently for a child. The model has been used most frequently with students with severe disabilities, but it also could be used with children who have other types of exceptionalities (Golightly, 1987). (See Orelove & Sobsey, 1991 for additional comparisons of the three models and implementation for children with multiple disabilities.)

Dimensions

The characteristics of the transdisciplinary approach apply most directly to the interactive teaming model so they will be summarized here and examined in more detail in Chapter 3. Lyon and Lyon (1980) cited the following characteristics:

1. *Joint team focus*: The various professionals involved in serving a child need to work together.
2. *Professional development approach*: Each professional will need to share information and skills with other group members.
3. *Role release implementation*: Roles and responsibilities must be accepted and shared among group members.

Orelove and Sobsey (1991) identified other characteristics of a transdisciplinary model, including the following:

1. *Indirect therapy approach:* Team members serve as consultants to others rather than providing only direct service to students or clients.
2. *Multiple lines of communication:* Regular team meetings are conducted to share information, knowledge, and skills among participants.
3. *Integration of services:* Planning is based on a common set of goals, and therapies and services are integrated instead of delivered in isolation.

Trimble and Miller (1996) described ways administrators could maximize team functioning in secondary schools by sharing authority, cultivating teacher leadership, training all team members, using situational leadership, modeling effective team leader behaviors, providing incentives, supporting the teams, and moving teams beyond managerial functions.

Goals

The two obvious goals for teaming approaches are similar to the ones described for consultation: *improvement in treatment or education for a child with special needs,* and the *training of professionals in skills beyond their own areas of expertise.* Other benefits espoused for teaming approaches include improved accuracy for assessment and placement decisions, reduction in referrals to special education (Korinek & McLaughlin, 1996), a forum for sharing a variety of perspectives, the development and evaluation of programs, providing consultative services to parents and community members, and an extension of psychoeducational services into schools (cf. Kaiser & Woodman, 1985; Orelove & Sobsey, 1991; Pfeiffer, 1980, 1981; Reynolds, Gutkin, Elliott, & Witt, 1984). Pryzwansky and Rzepski (1983) cited the technical assistance, role enhancement, and professional development opportunities available through a school-based team approach. Siders et al. (1987) noted that a transdisciplinary team model facilitated viewing the child and family as part of an ecological system. Stanwood (1988) also noted the importance of viewing the child as part of a "school–family systems orientation," and commented on how that perspective could contribute to improvements in the functioning of a school system administrative placement committee. Thomas (1986) suggested implementation of a team approach as a strategy to reduce the high school dropout rate.

Mahcr and Hawryluk (1983) recommended consideration of individual, group, and organizational needs, and they provided a set of questions to consider when attempting to identify the tasks or goals that might be appropriate for a team to address in school situations:

1. What educational services and programs are to be provided to individual, group, and organizational clients?
2. To provide appropriate programs to these clients, what educational service delivery tasks need to be accomplished?
3. Within what period of time must task accomplishment occur?
4. Given the tasks that have been identified, which ones might be effectively and efficiently carried out by means of one or more versions of a team approach?
5. What specific kinds of teams might be used? (pp. 181–182)

In their work with business organizations implementing teams, Katzenbach and Smith (1999) cited four "key lessons" they learned. These lessons also apply to educational and human services settings:

1. Significant performance challenges energize teams regardless of where they are in an organization. Performance is the primary objective, and a team remains the means, not the end.
2. Organizational leaders can foster team performance best by building a strong performance ethic rather than by establishing a team-promoting environment alone.
3. Biases toward individualism exist but need not get in the way of team performance.
4. Discipline—both within the team and across the organization—creates the conditions for team performance. Groups become teams through *disciplined*

action. They *shape* a common purpose, *agree* on performance goals, *define* a common working approach, *develop* high levels of complementary skills, and *hold* themselves mutually accountable for results (excerpted from pp. 12–15).

Competencies

Although special educators and psychologists, as well as those from other disciplines, have been expected through role descriptions and legal mandates such as P.L. 94-142 to participate as team members, the number of training programs designed to improve competencies in this area remains limited. In their national survey of preservice teacher training programs, Courtnage and Smith-Davis (1987) found that of the 360 responses received from a possible 513 programs, only 52% of the respondents indicated that they had some degree of training on teaming. Moreover, only 34 of those institutions said the training was required in a separate course or practicum setting; the remainder indicated that the training was included in other courses or experiences.

The competencies that have been identified as important for teaming are typically included in articles about programs or course work at various institutions. Additional information may be found in the 1981 special issue of *Teacher Education and Special Education* (Egan & Bluhm, 1981), in the text by Blanton et al. (1997), or in the article by Quigney (1998).

Foley and Mundschenk (1997) noted that the current emphasis on teaming results in at least three implications for preservice and inservice teacher preparation: (1) need for reciprocal cross-disciplinary training, (2) knowledge of the professional perspectives of others, and (3) inclusion of joint instructional and behavior management methods courses, collaboration seminars, and practicum experiences. Katzenbach and Smith (1999) stated that team members need to have technical or functional expertise, problem-solving and decision-making skills, and interpersonal skills such as risk-taking, active listening, and objectivity.

In the past 15 years a number of universities have developed programs designed to improve various teaming skills. Courtnage and Healy (1984) described a preservice program at the University of Northern Iowa that was designed to assist prospective educators in developing skills in the referral, evaluation, and staffing processes in schools. The program is competency and procedure based, and includes course work as well as a practicum experience. Siders et al. (1987) outlined a model transdisciplinary graduate program at the University of Southern Mississippi at Hattiesburg. Their program is focused on developing leadership skills in professionals from various disciplines who will be working with children with disabilities. This program also is competency based and offers several options for field placement sites.

A third program description was provided by Hudson, Correa, Morsink, and Dykes (1987) of the University of Florida. This preservice program includes a course on transdisciplinary teaming that is taken concurrently with a field-based internship. The six competency areas developed in the program are interpersonal communication, collaborative consultation, case management, power and politics in schools, parent conferences, and awareness of cultural diversity. These competency areas are similar to the collaboration training curriculum for preservice and inservice educators developed by West et al. (1989), which includes the following components: consultation theory/models; research on consultation theory, training, and practice; personal characteristics; interactive communication; collaborative problem solving; systems change; equity issues and values/belief systems; and evaluation of consultation effectiveness.

Rosenberg and Rock (1994) described a field-based program developed in a collaborative arrangement among Johns Hopkins University, two urban local education agencies, and the Maryland State Department of Education. This program was based on an interdisciplinary orientation and included course work in collaborative programming. Hudson and Glomb (1997) included the following areas in their programs at Southern Utah University, Utah State University, and Arizona State University West: perspectives and attitudes, nonverbal communication skills, verbal and listening skills, and strategies for problem solving, cooperative planning, and managing conflict. Lesar, Benner, Habel, and Coleman (1997) described a program at the University of Tennessee for preparing elementary education teachers for inclusive settings, and noted the importance of integrating additional skills and knowledge into courses and practica. O'Shea et al. (1999) described how collaboration skills were essential in the teaming process between general education and special education preservice teachers in the program at Slippery Rock University of Pennsylvania.

Another example of collaboration between general education and special education faculty to design a comprehensive teaming program was described by Duchardt, Marlow, Inman, Christensen, and Reeves (1999). The program at Northwestern State University of Louisiana resulted in a number of positive outcomes including the development of collegial and collaborative skills and formation of teaching and learning partnerships.

Process

The process or sequence of steps in teaming is determined by the type of need presented and the purpose (e.g., identification, IEP development, change in placement) of the meeting(s). Thus, if the purpose of a meeting is to develop an IEP, the sequence of steps might include the sharing of progress data and the establishment of annual goals by the parents and professionals. If the purpose is a change in placement, team members will need to present their data and justification for the change. One example of a detailed sequence of the major steps for a referral process was outlined by Courtnage and Healy (1984). The steps are displayed in Figure 2.4.

Fishbaugh (1997) noted that the "use of teaming requires shared leadership, goal setting, and decision making" (p. 114). She listed four steps in the implementation of the teaming process:

Major flow steps of the referral and interdisciplinary meeting process

1. Gather initial student information.
2. Complete initial checklist for identifying behaviors of concern.
3. Designate concerned behaviors and determine the need for data collection.
4. Determine procedures to collect additional data.
5. Collect additional data, analyze data, and formulate a referral decision.
6. Complete referral form.
7. Prepare the pupil for referral.
8. Describe the need for an evaluation meeting and give roles of participants.
9. Determine relevant student information needed for presentation at evaluation meeting.
10. Prepare for evaluation meeting.
11. Evaluate the evaluation meeting—procedures and affective domain.
12. Describe the need for an IEP meeting and give roles of participants.
13. Determine relevant student information needed for presentation at IEP meeting.
14. Prepare for IEP meeting.
15. Evaluate the IEP meeting—procedures and affective domain.
16. Describe the need for the re-evaluation meeting and give roles of participants.
17. Determine relevant student information needed for presentation at re-evaluation meeting.
18. Prepare for re-evaluation meeting.
19. Evaluate the re-evaluation meeting—procedures and affective domain.
20. Describe the need for referring special education students after placement.
21. Activate referral and staffing follow-up activities for those special education students who indicate: (a) unusual progress, (b) significant academic behavior problems, (c) a need for outside resources.

Figure 2.4
The process of teaming.
Source: From "Interdisciplinary Team Training: A Competency- and Procedure-Based Approach" by L. Courtnage & H. Healy, 1984, *Teacher Education and Special Education, 7,* 3–11. Copyright © 1984 by Special Press. Reprinted with permission of Special Press and the Teacher Education Division of the Council for Exceptional Children.

1. Team focus—team members should identify a team vision, goal, or purpose.
2. Role sharing—team roles include a team leader or facilitator, team recorder, team reporter, and team observer.
3. Individual accountability—each team member has to share responsibility for achieving team goals.
4. Team processing—group processing serves as the team critique in order to monitor team effectiveness. (p. 114)

Mostert (1998) emphasized that the reasons for forming teams and possible ramifications must be considered. He stated that the reasons why a team is being formed should be clear, considerations for how other work responsibilities might be affected must be examined, the team plan should be discussed with administrators, the types and amount of resources needed should be identified, and the procedures under which the team will operate must be clarified.

Committee Approaches

Four additional examples of groups of professionals collaborating to provide services to children and adolescents are *teacher assistance teams* (Chalfant, Pysh, & Moultrie, 1979), *school consultation committees* (McGlothlin, 1981), *prereferral intervention models* (Graden, Casey, & Christenson, 1985), and *collaborative inclusion teams* (Gibb, Ingram, Duches, Allred, Egan, & Young, 1998). All four approaches use many of the consultation strategies previously described, and they often are referred to as collaborative consultation models because the educators involved provide indirect services to students. Another similarity is that they all are designed to assist teachers in making appropriate referrals, as well as to support teachers who are providing services in inclusive settings or working with students who do not qualify for special services. The committees could be considered interdisciplinary in composition, although they often are composed primarily of regular and special educators with occasional involvement from administrators and parents. As typically implemented, they would not be viewed as transdisciplinary because they are not involved in all of the procedures for a child from assessment to implementation; rather, they are designed to address day-to-day problems that may arise in a particular school or to serve as prereferral screening committees to determine if a student needs to be continued in the referral process and considered for placement in a special program.

Of the three approaches, the prereferral intervention model has been implemented most often by state and local school systems and has received increased attention from researchers. Graden (1989) stated a preference for the term *intervention assistance*, because she thought this more accurately reflected the component of collaboration, and noted that the use of a team in and of itself did not create problems; rather, the functioning of the team as collaborative or expert advice giving made the difference. Pugach and Johnson (1989a) described prereferral intervention as a progressive concept because it promotes interactions between general or regular educators and special educators, and results in sharing of problem-solving strategies for students who do not qualify for special services.

Several reviews of research have delineated the positive outcomes of prereferral intervention, including increases in abilities of teachers to meet a variety of needs, improvements in teachers' attitudes toward students with learning and behavior problems, decreases in overidentification of students as having disabilities, and positive changes in student achievement and behavior (cf. Bahr, Whitten, Dieker, Kocarek, & Manson, 1999; Morsink & Lenk, 1992; Nelson, Smith, Taylor, Dodd, & Reavis, 1991; Sindelar, Griffin, Smith & Watanabe, 1992). However, several authors also have pointed out the problems with quality and validity of research on prereferral (Safran & Safran, 1996; Sindelar et al., 1992), the need for additional training on interventions and formative and summative evaluation procedures (Nelson et al., 1991), the importance of striving to achieve parity between classroom teachers and specialists (Pugach & Johnson, 1989b), and the significance of administrator support on consumers' satisfaction (Kruger, Struzziero, Watts, & Vacca, 1995).

IMPEDIMENTS AND BARRIERS

Consultation

The factors that can hinder the implementation of consultation result from a number of causes. The fact that professionals have existed as separate entities for such a long time—and frequently have established their own "language" and "turf"—often makes communication difficult (cf. Reppucci & Saunders, 1974). Differences in levels of skill and expertise, as well as the number and type of responsibilities, flexibility in working environment, and differing views of the status of one's position can present problems (Parker, 1975). The contrast between real and ideal time to do consultation often presents a challenge for the educators involved (Evans, 1980; Gerber, 1991). Consultants may find that even when the time is available, the consultees are resistant to their suggestions (Hughes & Falk, 1981; Idol-Maestas & Ritter, 1985), or the tendency to train specific interventions rather than a problem-solving approach weakens credibility for the process (Goodwin & Powell, 1981).

Other impediments include lack of the following: role definition (Haight, 1984), standardization of consultation (Kratochwill & Van Someren, 1985), training for consultants and consultees and inservice programs (Idol & West, 1987; Johnston, 1990), and policies and leadership at the state level (West & Brown, 1987). Kampwirth (1987) cited two more barriers: the consultant attempting to be all things to all people, and those involved in the process becoming discouraged when change is not immediately evident. Underfunding and faulty assumptions about program effectiveness were mentioned by Huefner (1988). Fuchs and Fuchs (1996) noted that consultation tends to compete with special education placement.

Lack of consistent implementation of consultation also has been problematic. As Lilly (1987) noted in an article 16 years after his original description of the concept, "consultation has been written about more than it has been practiced in special education" (p. 494). Friend (1988) called for conceptual clarity, professional preparation, and mature discussions of the aspects of various models. Johnson, Pugach, and Hammitte (1988) described pragmatic barriers (e.g., insufficient time, overwhelming caseloads) and conceptual barriers (e.g., differences in the thinking of special educators and classroom teachers, problems with hierarchies among education professionals). Welch (1998) echoed many of these same barriers to collaboration a decade later: conceptual barriers, pragmatic barriers such as time and logistics, attitudinal barriers, especially the belief that change should be immediate, and professional barriers due to lack of training or differences in training.

As the 1980s ended, Greer (1989) commented that collaboration had "come to mean almost solely linkages structured for the sake of such institutional goals as cost-effectiveness, logistical expedience, and managerial convenience. It has come to be a sort of administrative axle grease used to reduce bureaucratic wear and tear" (p. 191). Hansen et al. (1990) pointed out the effect of cultural differences on the implementation of consultation and collaboration. Witt (1990) questioned whether a collaborative relationship could be established given the typical hierarchical nature of consultation being provided by "experts" in school settings. Phillips and McCullough (1990) called for the institutionalization of a collaborative ethic, use of ecologically sensitive standards for selection of program formats to be used, and delineation of specific implementation guidelines. Ten years after Greer's article, Morsink (1999) described the barriers encountered in implementation of a collaboration project designed to prepare elementary teachers to work in urban settings. She noted barriers such as confusion about responsibilities, lack of time for collaboration, and the challenges of creating a common mission among different educational entities.

Teaming

A number of barriers to teaming have been cited in the literature. The lack of participation in team meetings, particularly that of regular educators, is a problem frequently identified by authors (e.g., Ysseldyke, Algozzine, & Allen, 1982). Quality of decisions made and ensuring shared decision making were two concerns cited by Pfeiffer (1980). Organizational barriers to focusing on school–family relationships were mentioned by Pfeiffer and Tittler (1983). Inadequate resources, including personnel, and lack of procedures to evaluate team functioning were mentioned by Maher and Hawryluk (1983).

Yoshida (1983) stated that teams frequently do not operate as participatory groups, but rather as forums for powerful people to develop support for their opinions. Fleming and Fleming (1983) noted that team members often do not make positive changes in team functioning when the process is not going well; instead, they blame problems on the perceived weaknesses of other members rather than taking responsibility for the team's effective operation. These authors also mentioned four challenges facing teams: reduction of stress, efficient use of time, developing the skills and knowledge base of all members, and assigning available resources appropriately. Problems cited by Abelson and Woodman (1983) were increased role ambiguity, duplication of effort, and confusion regarding the responsibility for decisions. Bailey (1984) attributed team dysfunctions to a lack of consideration of teams as developing and changing units composed of subsystems that need to function in a cohesive manner. Lack of training for team members was a frequently cited source of difficulty (e.g., Kaiser & Woodman, 1985; Nevin, Thousand, Paolucci-Whitcomb, & Villa, 1990).

Tindal, Shinn, and Rodden-Nord (1990) also commented on limitations of time as a barrier to developing joint relationships. They also cited impasses in consen-

sus decision making, differences in anticipated working relationships, and difficulties with program evaluation. In their discussion of transdisciplinary teams,
Orelove and Sobsey (1991) grouped factors that hinder teams into three categories: (1) philosophical and professional challenges (differences in philosophy
and orientation of team members, diminishment of professional status, and isolation of parents); (2) interpersonal challenges (threat of training others and threat
of being trained, role conflict or ambiguity); and (3) administrative challenges
(failure to understand the approach, resistance to change, concern about professional ethics and liability). Mostert (1998) identified similar barriers and included
lack of collaborative skills and varying levels of experience of team members.

Walther-Thomas, Bryant, and Land (1996) noted that as inclusive models continue to be introduced, "it is important for building level teams to resist temptation and allow themselves adequate planning and preparation time before new
services are implemented" (p. 257). These authors described both classroom-level
and building-level issues that should be addressed in order for teaming services
to be effective.

POSITIVE FEATURES

Although the barriers described in the preceding section have resulted in some
implementation problems for consultation, collaboration, and teaming models,
the approaches have several positive features that remain important for consideration. These features are highlighted here and then explored further in the next
chapter in terms of their relationships to the interactive teaming model.

The first positive feature is the opportunity for the development of professional skills. Although consultation approaches often are viewed as one "expert"
providing information to another, in the collaborative consultation models it is
recognized that *all* parties have knowledge to share with others. In teaming
approaches the range of possible interactions and knowledge exchange becomes
even greater because of the number of people from various fields who are
involved. In the transdisciplinary teaming model in particular, the opportunities
are enhanced because the team operates on a basis of professional sharing from
the time of the initial assessment through the implementation phase. An additional benefit that should result from such professional interactions is an increase
of collegiality among the people involved, rather than a feeling of individuals
operating in isolated situations.

The second feature is the one of primary importance: the potential for
improved services for students with special needs and at-risk children. Professionals meeting to share perspectives and knowledge and striving to provide a
cohesive and comprehensive array of services will be much better able to address
the variety of needs presented by such children than educators, health professionals, or social services operating independently. The results of several studies
on consultation and teaming show positive gains for students, as well as
improvements in skills and attitudes of teachers (cf. Adamson, Cox, & Schuller,

1989; Givens-Ogle, Christ, Colman, King-Streit, & Wilson, 1989; Idol-Maestas, 1983; Nelson & Stevens, 1981; Polsgrove & McNeil, 1989).

A third positive feature of consultation and teaming involves the legal support and mandates that exist for these two approaches. Most states have a continuum of service delivery alternatives that include some form of consultation or collaboration. Also, as mentioned earlier in the chapter, The Education for All Handicapped Children Act and subsequent amendments mandate team decision making for assessment, placement, and transition planning processes.

What follows is an example of how consultation and teaming might be implemented in response to the referral of Peter, a child suspected of having a mild hearing loss. The case study illustrates the interaction and information that can be obtained from an individual who has certain areas of expertise (e.g., consulting), and shows how knowledge and strategies can be shared among a group of professionals (i.e., teaming).

◇ ◇

Application

Observation. Peter is a fourth grader whose teacher, Mr. Fort, has noted that he appears to be having difficulty hearing. In the past two weeks, Mr. Fort has observed that as he walks around the room dictating words for a spelling test, Peter turns in his seat so he is always facing the teacher. Mr. Fort also has noticed several times that if Peter was looking away when the directions for an assignment were given, as the other students began to work he would raise his hand and ask for an explanation of the task. Today Mr. Fort watched Peter on the playground. Whenever Peter's best friend Andrew would call to him, Peter would not respond unless he was looking at Andrew at the time. Several times Andrew had to run after his friend to get him to join in the activities.

Consultation. Mr. Fort mentions his concerns about Peter to the school nurse, Ms. Schlichting. She asks Mr. Fort questions about Peter's background, such as any previous concerns being listed on the cumulative folder, any recent illnesses, any changes in his articulation of words, and so on. Because Mr. Fort is not aware of any previous concerns, illnesses, or speech changes, Ms. Schlichting suggests that a form be sent home to Peter's parents securing permission for her to do some basic auditory screening. After those results are obtained, she will decide whether to recommend that the parents consider taking Peter to a physician for an examination to determine a medical cause of the problem or to an audiologist for additional testing. She also describes the two major types of hearing loss, conductive and sensorineural, and the effects of each.

Teaming. At the weekly team meeting, Mr. Fort describes his concerns about Peter to his colleagues. Ms. Greenoe, the speech-language clinician, asks questions about Peter's attentiveness and verbal responses to questions in class. Ms. Nelson, the counselor, inquires about Peter's interactions with his friends and whether he appears to be withdrawn or aggressive. She also asks if Peter acts frustrated about being left out of activities because of his lack of response to conversations or invitations to play. Ms. Brinkley describes the behaviors of a student with a hearing impairment in her fifth-grade class and offers some suggestions to Mr. Fort on how to key in on Peter's facial expressions and actions to determine if he is following the discussions and explanations in class.

The special educator, Mr. Cox, also offers some suggestions on how to emphasize key words and use the blackboard effectively so Peter can focus in on those cues. He recommends that Mr. Fort contact Peter's mother to inquire if she has noticed similar behaviors, and to suggest that Peter's hearing be tested either at school or by a physician.

At the conclusion of the discussion, Mr. Fort agrees to call the mother, and he also has a list of other possible indicators of a hearing loss to consider as he observes Peter while waiting for the test results. In addition, he has strategies to help ensure that Peter is able to follow classroom activities.

◊ ◊

SUMMARY

An examination of consultation, collaboration, and teaming reveals that:

◆ These approaches have been advocated by professionals from various disciplines for at least the past 25 years.

◆ A legal basis for the approaches exists in federal laws such as P.L. 94-142 and amendments to it, as well as in state and local education agency service delivery alternatives.

◆ A variety of models have been reviewed in the literature.

◆ Dimensions, goals, competencies, and processes are similar in many instances.

◆ The approaches have barriers that can interfere with successful implementation.

◆ Among the positive features for consultation, collaboration, and teaming are the documented gains for students and professionals.

◆ Several components of consultation and teaming approaches that have been described in this chapter are incorporated into the interactive teaming model proposed in this text. The specific dimensions of interactive teaming will be presented in the next chapter.

ACTIVITIES

1. Construct a table listing the benefits and disadvantages of consultation and teaming. Compare your list with those of your classmates or colleagues. What

similarities or differences were noted? Were any of the differences due to professional training or role (e.g., special educator, psychologist, social worker)?

2. Interview an administrator and a parent about their preferences for consultation, collaboration, or teaming. List reasons they prefer one over the other or a combination of the two approaches. How were their preferences affected by previous experiences?

3. Explain how you think consultation, collaboration, and/or teaming could be incorporated into your role. Address such areas as how you would include time for these activities in your daily and weekly schedules, what groups of professionals you are likely to interact with, and what barriers you might encounter.

4. Describe the professional growth opportunities you believe you would gain from being involved in consultation, collaboration, and/or teaming approaches. How would your job change? Would you need additional training to feel that you could be an effective consultant, collaborator, or team member?

REFERENCES

Abelson, M. A., & Woodman, R. W. (1983). Review of research on team effectiveness: Implications for teams in schools. *School Psychology Review, 12,* 125–136.

Adamson, D. R., Cox, J., & Schuller, J. (1989). Collaboration/consultation: Bridging the gap from resource room to regular classroom. *Teacher Education and Special Education, 12,* 46–51.

Adelman, H. S., & Taylor, L. (1998). Involving teachers in collaborative efforts to better address the barriers to student learning. *Preventing School Failure, 42*(2), 55–60.

Aldinger, L. E., Warger, C. L., & Eavy, P. W. (1991). *Strategies for teacher collaboration.* Ann Arbor, MI: Exceptional Innovations, Inc.

Aloia, G. F. (1983). Special educators' perceptions of their roles as consultants. *Teacher Education and Special Education, 6,* 83–87.

Bahr, M. W., Whitten, E., Dieker, L., Kocarek, C. E., & Manson, D. (1999). A comparison of school-based intervention teams: Implications for educational and legal reform. *Exceptional Children, 66*(1), 67–83.

Bailey, D. B. (1984). A triaxial model of the interdisciplinary team and group process. *Exceptional Children, 51,* 17–25.

Bailey, D. B., Helsel-DeWert, M. J., Thiele, J., & Ware, W. B. (1983). Measuring individual participation on the interdisciplinary team. *American Journal of Mental Deficiency, 88,* 247–254.

Bergan, J. R. (1977). *Behavioral consultation.* Columbus, OH: Merrill.

Blanton, L. P., Griffin, C. C., Winn, J. A., & Pugach, M. C. (Eds.). (1997). *Teacher education in transition: Collaborative programs to prepare general and special educators.* Denver, CO: Love Publishing Co.

Brown, B., Pryzwansky, W. B., & Schulte, A. C. (1991). *Psychological consultation.* Boston: Allyn & Bacon.

Brown, B., Pryzwansky, W. B., & Schulte, A. C. (1998). *Psychological consultation: Introduction to theory and practice.* Needham Heights, MA: Allyn & Bacon.

Brown, D., Wyne, M. D., Blackburn, J. E., & Powell, W. C. (1979). *Consultation: Strategy for improving education.* Boston: Allyn & Bacon.

Brown, L. F., Kiraly, J., & McKinnon, A. (1979). Resource rooms: Some aspects for special educators to ponder. *Journal of Learning Disabilities, 12,* 56–58.

Brown, W. (1987). Rainbow connection instructional guide. *Techniques, 3,* 257–259.

Bruskewitz, R. (1998). Collaborative intervention: A system of support for teachers attempting to meet the needs of students with challenging behaviors. *Preventing School Failure, 42(3),* 129–134.

Cantrell, R. P., & Cantrell, M. L. (1976). Preventive mainstreaming: Impact of a supportive service program on pupils. *Exceptional Children, 42,* 381–386.

Chalfant, J. C., Pysh, M. V., & Moultrie, R. (1979). Teacher assistance teams: A model for within-building problem solving. *Learning Disability Quarterly, 2,* 85–96.

Cipani, E. (1985). The three phases of behavioral consultation: Objectives, intervention, and quality assurance. *Teacher Education and Special Education, 8,* 144–152.

Clark, S. N., & Clark, D. C. (1997). Exploring the possibilities of interdisciplinary teaming. *Childhood Education, 73(5),* 267–271.

Coben, S. S., Thomas, C. C., Sattler, R. O., & Morsink, C. V. (1997). Meeting the challenge of consultation and collaboration: Developing interactive teams. *Journal of Learning Disabilities, 30 (4),* 427–432.

Como, P., & Hagner, D. (1986). *Community work development: A marketing model.* Stout, WI: Stout Vocational Rehabilitation Institute. (ERIC Document Reproduction Service No. ED 274 775)

Conoley, J. C., & Conoley, C. W. (1982). *School consultation: A guide to practice and training.* New York: Pergamon Press.

Cook, L., & Friend, M. (1991). Principles for the practice of collaboration in schools. *Preventing School Failure, 35(4),* 6–9.

Cooley, E., & Yovanoff, P. (1996). Supporting professionals at-risk: Evaluating interventions to reduce burnout and improve retention of special educators. *Exceptional Children, 62(4),* 336–355.

Council for Exceptional Children (1998). *What every special educator must know: The international standards for the preparation and licensure of special educators* (3rd ed.). Reston, VA: Council for Exceptional Children.

Courtnage, L., & Healy, H. (1984). Interdisciplinary team training: A competency- and procedure-based approach. *Teacher Education and Special Education, 7,* 3–11.

Courtnage, L., & Smith-Davis, J. (1987). Interdisciplinary team training: A national survey of special education teacher training programs. *Exceptional Children, 53,* 451–458.

Cramer, S. F. (1998). *Collaboration: A success strategy for special educators.* Needham Heights, MA: Allyn & Bacon.

Danielson, C. (1996). *Enhancing professional practice: A framework for teaching.* Alexandria, VA: Association for Supervision and Curriculum Development.

Darling-Hammond, L. (1997). *The right to learn: A blueprint for creating schools that work.* San Francisco: Jossey-Bass.

Denemark, G., Morsink, C. V., & Thomas, C. C. (1980). Accepting the challenge for change in teacher education. In M. C. Reynolds (Ed.), *A common body of practice for teachers: The challenge of Public Law 94-142 to teacher education.* Washington, DC: The American Association of Colleges of Teacher Education.

Deno, E. (1970). Special education as developmental capital. *Exceptional Children, 37,* 229–237.

Dettmer, P., Thurston, L. P., & Dyck, N. (1993). *Consultation, collaboration, and teamwork for students with special needs.* Boston: Allyn & Bacon.

Duchardt, B., Marlow, L., Inman, D., Christensen, P., & Reeves, M. (1999). Collaboration and co-teaching: General and special education faculty. *The Clearing House, 72(3),* 186–193.

Edgar, E. (1988). Transition from school to community: Promising programs. *Teaching Exceptional Children, 20,* 73–75.

Egan, M. W., & Bluhm, H. P. (1981). *Teacher Education and Special Education, 4*(1).

Erb, T. O. (1997). Meeting the needs of young adolescents on interdisciplinary teams. Reviews of research. *Childhood Education, 73*(5), 309–311.

Evans, R. J. (1985). *Special education consultation: Interactive video simulation: Adults, teachers, and consultants.* (ERIC Document Reproduction Service No. ED 258 423)

Evans, S. (1980). The consultant role of the resource teacher. *Exceptional Children, 46,* 402–404.

Evans, S. (1981). Perceptions of classroom teachers, principals, and resource room teachers of actual and desired roles of the resource teacher. *Journal of Learning Disabilities, 14,* 600–603.

Feichtner, S., & Sarkees, M. (1987). Working together: The special needs team. *Vocational Education Journal, 62,* 22–24.

Fine, M. J., & Tyler, M. M. (1971). Concerns and directions in teacher consultation. *Journal of School Psychology, 9,* 436–444.

Fishbaugh, M. S. E. (1997). *Models of collaboration.* Needham Heights, MA: Allyn & Bacon.

Fleming, D. C., & Fleming, E. R. (1983). Problems in implementation of the team approach: A practitioner's perspective. *School Psychology Review, 12,* 144–149.

Foley, R. M. (1994). Collaboration activities and competencies of special educators serving students with behavior disorders. *Special Services in the Schools, 8*(2), 69–90.

Foley, R. M., & Mundschenk, N. A. (1997). Collaboration activities and competencies of secondary school special educators: A national survey. *Teacher Education and Special Education, 20*(1), 47–60.

Friend, M. (1984). Consultation skills for resource teachers. *Learning Disability Quarterly, 7,* 246–250.

Friend, M. (1988). Putting consultation into context: Historical and contemporary perspectives. *Remedial and Special Education, 9*(6), 7–13.

Friend, M., & Cook, L. (1992). *Interactions: Collaboration skills for school professionals.* New York: Longman Publishers.

Friend, M., & Cook, L. (1996). *Interactions: Collaboration skills for school professionals* (2nd ed.). White Plains, NY: Longman Publishers.

Fuchs, D., & Fuchs, L. S. (1996). Consultation as a technology and the politics of school reform. *Remedial and Special Education, 17*(6), 386–392.

Gable, R. A., Hendrickson, J. M., & Rogan, J. P. (1996). TEAMS supporting students at risk in the regular classroom. *The Clearing House, 69*(4), 235–238.

Gable, R. A., Young, C. C., & Hendrickson, J. M. (1987). Content of special education teacher preparation. Are we headed in the right direction? *Teacher Education and Special Education, 10,* 135–139.

Gallessich, J. (1982). *The profession and practice of consultation.* San Francisco: Jossey-Bass.

Garner, H. G. (1995). *Teamwork models and experience in education.* Boston: Allyn & Bacon.

Gast, D. L., & Wolery, M. (1985). Severe developmental disabilities. In W. H. Berdine & A. E. Blackhurst (Eds.), *An introduction to special education* (2nd ed.). Boston: Little, Brown and Company.

Gerber, S. (1991). Supporting the collaborative process. *Preventing School Failure, 35,* 48–52.

Gibb, G. S., Ingram, C. F., Duches, T. T., Allred, K. W., Egan, M. W., & Young, J. R. (1998). Developing and evaluating an inclusion program for junior high students with disabilities: A collaborative team approach. *B.C. Journal of Special Education, 21*(3), 33–44.

Givens-Ogle, L., Christ, B. A., Colman, M., King-Streit, S., & Wilson, L. (1989). Data-based consultation case study: Adaptations of researched best practices. *Teacher Education and Special Education, 12,* 46–51.

Golightly, C. J. (1987). Transdisciplinary training: A step forward in special education teacher preparation. *Teacher Education and Special Education, 10,* 126–130.

Goodwin, J., & Powell, T. H. (1981). Toward a more effective consulting teacher: Some strategies. *Education Unlimited, 3,* 14–16.

Graden, J. (1989). Redefining "prereferral" intervention as intervention assistance: Collaboration between general and special education. *Exceptional Children, 56,* 227–231.

Graden, J. L., Casey, A., & Christenson, S. L. (1985). Implementing a prereferral intervention system: Part I. The model. *Exceptional Children, 51,* 377–384.

Greer, J. (1989). The prime factor in education. *Exceptional Children, 56,* 191–193.

Gutkin, T. B. (1986). Consultees' perceptions of variables relating to the outcomes of school-based consultation interactions. *School Psychology Review, 15,* 375–382.

Gutkin, T. B. (1993). Cognitive modeling: A means for achieving prevention in school-based consultation. *Journal of Educational and Psychological Consultation, 4,* 179–183.

Gutkin, T. B., & Curtis, M. J. (1982). School-based consultation. In C. R. Reynolds & T. B. Gutkin (Eds.), *The handbook of school psychology.* New York: Wiley.

Haight, S. L. (1984). Special education teacher consultant: Idealism versus realism. *Exceptional Children, 50,* 507–515.

Hanline, M. F., & Knowlton, A. (1988). A collaborative model for providing support to parents during their child's transition from infant intervention to preschool special education public school programs. *Journal of the Division for Early Childhood, 12,* 116–125.

Hansen, J. C., Himes, B. S., & Meier, S. (1990). *Consultation concepts and practices.* Upper Saddle River, NJ: Prentice Hall.

Hart, V. (1977). The use of many disciplines with the severely and profoundly handicapped. In E. Sontag, J. Smith, & N. Certo (Eds.), *Educational programming for the severely and profoundly handicapped.* Reston, VA: The Council for Exceptional Children, Division on Mental Retardation.

Hasazi, S. B., Furney, K. S., & DeStefano, L. (1999). Implementing the IDEA transition mandates. *Exceptional Children, 65*(4), 555–566.

Hawryluk, M. K., & Smallwood, D. L. (1986). Assessing and addressing consultee variables in school-based behavioral consultation. *School Psychology Review, 15,* 519–528.

Heron, T. E., & Harris, K. C. (1987). *The educational consultant: Helping professionals, parents, and mainstreamed students* (2nd ed.). Austin, TX: Pro-Ed.

Hobbs, T., & Westling, D.L. (1998). Promoting successful inclusion through collaborative problem-solving. *Teaching Exceptional Children, 31*(1), 12–19.

Hudson, P. J., Correa, V. I., Morsink, C. V., & Dykes, M. K. (1987). A new model for preservice training: Teacher as collaborator. *Teacher Education and Special Education, 10,* 191–193.

Hudson, P., & Glomb, N. (1997). If it takes two to tango, then why not teach both partners to dance? Collaboration instruction for all educators. *Journal of Learning Disabilities, 30*(4), 442–448.

Huefner, D. S. (1988). The consulting teacher model: Risks and opportunities. *Exceptional Children, 54,* 403–414.

Hughes, J. N., & Falk, R. S. (1981). Resistance, reactance, and consultation. *Journal of School Psychology, 19,* 134–142.

Idol, L. (1997). Key questions related to building collaborative and inclusive schools. *Journal of Learning Disabilities, 30*(4), 384–394.

Idol, L., Nevin, A., & Paolucci-Whitcomb, P. (1994). *Collaborative consultation* (2nd ed.). Austin, TX: Pro-Ed.

Idol, L., Paolucci-Whitcomb, P., & Nevin, A. (1986). *Collaborative consultation.* Rockville, MD: Aspen Systems Corporation.

Idol, L., & West, J. F. (1987). Consultation in special education (Part II): Training and practice. *Journal of Learning Disabilities, 20,* 474–494.

Idol-Maestas, L. (1983). *Special educator's consultation handbook.* Rockville, MD: Aspen Systems Corporation.

Idol-Maestas, L., & Ritter, S. (1985). A follow-up study of resource/consulting teachers: Factors that facilitate and inhibit teacher consultation. *Teacher Education and Special Education, 8,* 121–131.

Johnson, L. J., Pugach, M. C., & Hammitte, D. J. (1988). Barriers to effective special education consultation. *Remedial and Special Education, 9*(6), 41–47.

Johnston, N. S. (1990). School consultation: The training needs of teachers and school psychologists. *Psychology in the Schools, 27,* 51–56.

Jones, S. N., & Meisels, S. J. (1987). Training family day care providers to work with special needs children. *Topics in Early Childhood Special Education, 7,* 1–12.

Kaiser, S. M., & Woodman, R. W. (1985). Multidisciplinary teams and group decision-making techniques: Possible solutions to decision-making problems. *School Psychology Review, 14,* 457–470.

Kampwirth, T. J. (1987). Consultation: Strategy for dealing with children's behavior problems. *Techniques: A Journal for Remedial Education and Counseling, 3,* 117–120.

Katzenbach, J. R., & Smith, D. K. (1999). *The wisdom of teams: Creating the high-performance organization.* New York: HarperCollins Publishers.

Klein, N., & Sheehan, R. (1987). Staff development: A key issue in meeting the needs of young handicapped children in day care settings. *Topics in Early Childhood Special Education, 7,* 13–27.

Korinek, L., & McLaughlin, V. (1996). Preservice preparation for interdisciplinary collaboration: The intervention assistance teaming project. *Contemporary Education, 68*(1), 41–44.

Kratochwill, T. R., & Van Someren, K. R. (1985). Barriers to treatment success in behavioral consultation: Current limitations and future directions. *Journal of School Psychology, 23,* 225–239.

Kruger, L. J., Struzziero, J., Watts, R., & Vacca, D. (1995). The relationship between organizational support and satisfaction with teacher assistance teams. *Remedial and Special Education, 16*(4), 203–211.

Kurpius, D. J. (1978). Consultation theory and process: An integrated model. *Personnel and Guidance Journal, 56,* 335–339.

Lesar, S., Benner, S. M., Habel, J. & Coleman, L. (1997). Preparing general education teachers for inclusive settings: A constructivist teacher education program. *Teacher Education and Special Education, 20*(3), 204–220.

Lilly, M. S. (1971). A training based model for special education. *Exceptional Children, 37,* 745–749.

Lilly, M. S. (1987). Response to "Consultation in special education" by Idol and West. *Journal of Learning Disabilities, 20,* 494–495.

Lindsey, D. (1985). A model performance appraisal instrument for school physical therapists. *Clinical Management, 6*(5), 20–26.

Lindsey, D., O'Neal, J., Haas, K., & Tewey, S. (1983). *A cooperative adventure: Physical therapy services in North Carolina's schools.* Raleigh, NC: State Department of Public Instruction.

Lloyd, J. W., Crowley, E. P., Kohler, F. W., & Strain, P. S. (1988). Redefining the applied research agenda: Cooperative learning, prereferral, teacher consultation, and peer-mediated interventions. *Journal of Learning Disabilities, 21,* 43–52.

Lowenthal, B. (1992). Collaborative training in the education of early childhood educators. *Teaching Exceptional Children, 24*(4), 25–29.

Lyon, S., & Lyon, G. (1980). Team functioning and staff development: A role release approach to providing integrated educational services for severely handicapped students. *Journal of the Association for the Severely Handicapped, 5,* 250–263.

Maher, C. A., & Hawryluk, M. K. (1983). Framework and guidelines for utilization of teams in schools. *School Psychology Review, 12,* 180–185.

Marshall, R. M., & Wuori, D. F. (1985). Medical and education literature on physician/teacher collaboration. *Journal of School Health, 55,* 62–65.

McAfee, J. K. (1987). Integrating therapy services in the school: A model for training educators, administrators, and therapists. *Topics in Early Childhood Special Education, 7,* 116–126.

McClellan, E., & Wheatley, W. (1985). Project RETOOL: Collaborative consultation training for post-doctoral leadership personnel. *Teacher Education and Special Education, 8,* 159–163.

McGlothlin, J. E. (1981). The school consultation committee: An approach to implementing a teacher consultation model. *Behavioral Disorders, 6*, 101–107.

Medway, F. J. (1979). How effective is school consultation? A review of recent research. *Journal of School Psychology, 17*, 275–282.

Moore, E., & Allen, D. (1986). *An outreach program: Addressing the needs of the physically impaired in rural communities.* (ERIC Document Reproduction Service No. ED 285 370)

Morsink, C. (1999). *21st century teachers for a better future* (Final Report to Howard Heinz Endowment). Slippery Rock, PA: Slippery Rock University College of Education.

Morsink, C. V., & Lenk, L. L. (1992). The delivery of special education programs and services. *Remedial and Special Education, 13*(6), 33–43.

Mostert, M. P. (1998). *Interprofessional collaboration in schools.* Needham Heights, MA: Allyn & Bacon.

National Commission on Teaching and America's Future (1996). *What matters most: Teaching for America's future.* New York: National Commission on Teaching and America's Future.

Nelson, C. M., Neel, R. S., & Lilly, M. S. (1981). Consultation as a support system for behaviorally disordered pupils and their teachers. *Behavioral Disorders, 6*, 75–81.

Nelson, C. M., & Stevens, K. B. (1981). An accountable model for mainstreaming behaviorally disordered children. *Behavioral Disorders, 6*, 82–91.

Nelson, J. R., Smith, D. J., Taylor, L., Dodd, J. M., & Reavis, K. (1991). Prereferral intervention: A review of the research. *Education and Treatment of Children, 14*, 243–253.

Neubert, G. A., & Stover, L. T. (1994). *Peer coaching in teacher education* (Fastback 371). Bloomington, IN: Phi Delta Kappa Educational Foundation.

Nevin, A., Thousand, J., Paolucci-Whitcomb, P., & Villa, R. (1990). Collaborative consultation: Empowering public school personnel to provide heterogeneous schooling for all—or, who rang that bell? *Journal of Educational and Psychological Consultation, 1*(1), 41–67.

Newcomer, P. (1977). Special education for the mildly handicapped: Beyond a diagnostic and remedial model. *Journal of Special Education, 11*, 153–165.

Orelove, F. P., & Sobsey, D. (1991). *Educating children with multiple disabilities: A transdisciplinary approach* (2nd ed.). Baltimore: Paul H. Brookes Publishing Co.

O'Shea, D. J., Williams, A. L., & Sattler, R. O. (1999). Collaboration across special education and general education: Preservice teachers' views. *Journal of Teacher Education, 50*(2), 147–157.

O'Shea, L. J., O'Shea, D. J., & Algozzine, R. (1998). *Learning disabilities: From theory toward practice.* Upper Saddle River, NJ: Merrill/Prentice Hall.

Paolucci-Whitcomb, P., & Nevin, A. (1985). Preparing consulting teachers through a collaborative approach between university faculty and field-based consulting teachers. *Teacher Education and Special Education, 8*, 132–143.

Parker, C. A. (1975). *Psychological consultation: Helping teachers meet special needs.* Reston, VA: The Council for Exceptional Children.

Patriarca, L. A., & Lamb, M. A. (1990). Preparing secondary special education teachers to be collaborative decision makers and reflective practitioners: A promising practicum model. *Teacher Education and Special Education, 13*, 228–232.

Pfeiffer, S. I. (1980). The school-based interprofessional team: Recurring problems and some possible solutions. *Journal of School Psychology, 18*, 388–394.

Pfeiffer, S. I. (1981). The problems facing multidisciplinary teams: As perceived by team members. *Psychology in the Schools, 18*, 330–333.

Pfeiffer, S. I., & Tittler, B. I. (1983). Utilizing the multidisciplinary team to facilitate a school-family systems orientation. *School Psychology Review, 12*, 168–173.

Phillips, V., & McCullough, L. (1990). Consultation-based programming: Instituting the collaborative ethic in schools. *Exceptional Children, 56*, 291–304.

Piersel, W. C. (1985). Behavioral consultation: An approach to problem solving in educational settings. In J. R. Bergan (Ed.), *School psychology in contemporary society: An introduction.* New York: Merrill/Macmillan.

Polsgrove, L., & McNeil, M. (1989). The consultation process: Research and practice. *Remedial and Special Education, 10*(1), 6–13, 20.

Powers, M. D. (1986). Promoting community-based services: Implications for program design, implementation, and public policy. *Journal of the Association for Persons with Severe Handicaps, 11*, 309–315.

President's Commission on Teacher Education. (1992). American Association of State Colleges and Universities.

Preventing School Failure. (1991). Vol. 35(4).

Pryzwansky, W. B. (1974). A reconsideration of the consultation model for delivery of school-based psychological services. *Journal of Orthopsychiatry, 44*, 579–583.

Pryzwansky, W. B., & Rzepski, B. (1983). School-based teams: An untapped resource for consultation and technical assistance. *School Psychology Review, 12*, 174–179.

Pugach, M. C., & Johnson, L. J. (1989a). Prereferral intervention: Progress, problems, and challenges. *Exceptional Children, 56*, 217–226.

Pugach, M. C., & Johnson, L. J. (1989b). The challenge of implementing collaboration between general and special education. *Exceptional Children, 56*, 232–235.

Pugach, M. C., & Johnson, L. J. (1990). Fostering the continued democratization of consultation through action research. *Teacher Education and Special Education, 13*, 240–245.

Pugach, M. C., & Johnson, L. J. (1995). *Collaborative practitioners, collaborative schools.* Denver, CO: Love Publishing Co.

Pugach, M. C., & Warger, C. L. (Eds.). (1996). *Curriculum trends, special education, and reform: Refocusing the conversation.* New York: Teachers College Press.

Quigney, T. (1998). Collaborative teacher training for special and general educators: Rationale and recurring themes. *B.C. Journal of Special Education, 21*(3), 20–32.

Remedial and Special Education. (1988). Vol. 9(6).

Reppucci, N. D., & Saunders, J. T. (1974). Social psychology of behavior modification: Problems of implementation in natural settings. *American Psychologist, 29*, 649–660.

Reynolds, C. R., Gutkin, T. B., Elliott, S. N., & Witt, J. C. (1984). *School psychology: Essentials of theory and practice.* New York: Wiley.

Reynolds, M. C., & Birch, J. W. (1982). *Teaching exceptional children in all America's schools* (rev. ed.). Reston, VA: The Council for Exceptional Children.

Ritter, D. R. (1978). Effects of a school consultation program upon referral patterns of teachers. *Psychology in the Schools, 15*, 239–243.

Rosenberg, M. S., & Rock, E. E. (1994). Alternative certification in special education: Efficacy of a collaborative, field-based teacher preparation program. *Teacher Education and Special Education, 17*(3), 141–153.

Ryan, S., & Paterna, L. (1997). Junior high can be inclusive: Using natural supports and cooperative learning. *Teaching Exceptional Children, 30*(2), 36–41.

Safran, S. P., & Barcikowski, R. S. (1984). LD consultant information in mainstreaming: Help or hindrance? *Learning Disability Quarterly, 7*, 102–107.

Safran, S. P., & Safran, J. S. (1996). Intervention assistance programs and prereferral teams: Directions for the twenty-first century. *Remedial and Special Education, 17*(6), 363–369.

Sailor, W., & Guess, D. (1983). *Severely handicapped students: An instructional design.* Boston: Houghton Mifflin.

Salend, S. J. (1994). *Effective mainstreaming: Creating inclusive classrooms* (2nd ed.). Upper Saddle River, NJ: Merrill/Prentice Hall.

Salend, S. J., & Salend, S. (1984). Consulting with the regular teacher: Guidelines for special educators. *The Pointer, 28*, 25–28.

School Psychology Review. (1983). Vol. 12(2).

Schulte, A. C., & Osborne, S. S. (April, 1993). What is collaborative consultation? The eye of the beholder. In D. Fuchs (chair), *Questioning popular beliefs about collaborative consultation.* Symposium presented at the annual meeting of the Council for Exceptional Children, San Antonio, TX.

Siders, J. Z., Riall, A., Bennett, T. C., & Judd, D. (1987). Training of leadership personnel in early intervention: A transdisciplinary approach. *Teacher Education and Special Education, 10*, 161–170.

Sileo, T. W., Rude, H. A., & Luckner, J. L. (1988). Collaborative consultation: A model for transition planning for handicapped youth. *Education and Training in Mental Retardation, 23,* 333–339.

Simpson, R. L., & Myles, B. S. (1990). The general education collaboration model: A model for successful mainstreaming. *Focus on Exceptional Children, 23*(4), 1–10.

Sindelar, P. T., Griffin, C. C., Smith, S. W., & Watanabe, A. K. (1992). Prereferral intervention: Encouraging notes on preliminary findings. *The Elementary School Journal, 92,* 245–259.

Speece, D. L., & Mandell, C. J. (1980). Resource room support services for regular teachers. *Learning Disability Quarterly, 3,* 49–53.

Spencer-Dobson, C. A., & Schultz, J. B. (1987). Utilization of multidisciplinary teams in educating special needs students. *Journal of Industrial Teacher Education, 25,* 68–78.

Stahlman, B. L. (1995). When teaming goes right. *Perspectives in Education and Deafness, 14*(2), 9–11.

Stanovich, P. J. (1996). Collaboration—The key to successful instruction in today's inclusive schools. *Intervention in School and Clinic, 32*(1), 39–42.

Stanwood, B. (1988). *Effective utilization of multidisciplinary teams.* Unpublished manuscript. Wilmington: University of North Carolina–Wilmington, School of Education.

Sugai, G. M., & Tindal, G. A. (1993). *Effective school consultation: An interactive approach.* Pacific Grove, CA: Brooks/Cole.

Swan, W. W., & Sirvis, B. (1992). The CEC common core of knowledge and skills essential for all beginning special education teachers. *Teaching Exceptional Children, 15*(1), 16–20.

Teacher Education and Special Education. (1985). Vol. 8(3).

Tharp, R. G. (1975). The triadic model of consultation: Current considerations. In C. A. Parker (Ed.), *Psychological consultation: Helping teachers meet special needs.* Reston, VA: The Council for Exceptional Children.

Tharp, R. G., & Wetzel, R. J. (1969). *Behavior modification in the natural environment.* New York: Academic Press.

Thomas, C. C. (1986, March). *Problem-solving strategies for school assistance teams.* Paper presented at the Region II Exceptional Children Administrators Staff Development Conference, Atlantic Beach, NC.

Tiegerman-Farber, E., & Radziewicz, C. (1998). *Collaborative decision making: The pathway to inclusion.* Upper Saddle River, NJ: Merrill/Prentice Hall.

Tindal, G., Shinn, M. R., & Rodden-Nord, K. (1990). Contextually based school consultation: Influential variables. *Exceptional Children, 56,* 324–336.

Tindal, G., Shinn, M., Walz, L., & Germann, G. (1987). Mainstream consultation in secondary settings: The Pine County model. *Journal of Special Education, 21,* 94–106.

Trimble, S., & Miller, J. W. (1996). Creating, invigorating, and sustaining effective teams. *NASSP Bulletin, 80*(584), 35–40.

Trohanis, P. L. (1981). *Consultation and the TADS experience* (Occasional Paper Number 1). Chapel Hill: The University of North Carolina. (ERIC Document Reproduction Service No. ED 224 227)

Turnbull, R., & Cilley, M. (1999). *Explanations and implications of the 1997 amendments to IDEA.* Upper Saddle River, NJ: Merrill/Prentice Hall.

Umansky, D. L., & Holloway, E. L. (1984). The counselor as consultant: From model to practice. *School Counselor, 31,* 329–338.

Villa, R., Thousand, J., Paolucci-Whitcomb, P., & Nevin, A. (1990). In search of new paradigms for collaborative consultation. *Journal of Educational and Psychological Consultation, 1,* 279–292.

Voltz, D. L., Elliott Jr., R. N., & Harris, W. B. (1995). Promising practices in facilitating collaboration between resource room teachers and general education teachers. *Learning Disabilities Research and Practice, 10*(2), 129–136.

Walther-Thomas, C., Bryant, M., & Land, S. (1996). Planning for effective co-teaching: The key to successful inclusion. *Remedial and Special Education, 17* (4), 255–264, Cover 3.

Welch, M. (1998). Collaboration: Staying on the bandwagon. *Journal of Teacher Education, 49*(1), 26–37.

Welch, M., & Sheridan, S. M. (1995). *Educational partnerships: Serving students at risk.* Ft. Worth, TX: Harcourt Brace.

West, J. F., & Brown, P. A. (1987). State departments of education policies on consultation in special education: The state of the states. *Remedial and Special Education, 8*(3), 45–51.

West, J. F., & Cannon, G. S. (1988). Essential collaborative consultation competencies for regular and special educators. *Journal of Learning Disabilities, 21, 28,* 56–63.

West, J. F., & Idol, L. (1987). School consultation (Part I): An interdisciplinary perspective on theory, models, and research. *Journal of Learning Disabilities, 20,* 388–408.

West, J. F., Idol, L., & Cannon, G. (1989). *Collaboration in the schools: An inservice and preservice curriculum for teachers, support staff, and administrators.* Austin, TX: Pro-Ed.

Witt, J. (1990). Collaboration in school-based consultation: Myth in need of data. *Journal of Educational and Psychological Consultation, 11,* 367–370.

Wood, J. W. (1992). *Adapting instruction for mainstreamed and at-risk students* (2nd ed.). Upper Saddle River, NJ: Merrill/Prentice Hall.

Yoshida, R. K. (1983). Are multidisciplinary teams worth the investment? *School Psychology Review, 12,* 137–143.

Ysseldyke, J., Algozzine, B., & Allen, D. (1982). Participation of regular education teachers in special education team decision making. *Exceptional Children, 48,* 365–366.

3 Dimensions of the Interactive Team

Topics in this chapter include:

- Discussion of the bases for the team's work.
- A model of an interactive team.
- Descriptions of the aspects of team membership and leadership.
- Procedures for implementing the interactive teaming process.
- An application illustrating the contrast between a successful and unsuccessful team meeting.

◇ ◇

When the Jordans' son, Dontaye, was 4 years old, he became seriously ill in the middle of the night. Hearing her son crying, Mrs. Jordan checked on Dontaye and found him to have a very high fever. She awakened her husband, and they took the boy to the emergency room. On the way to the hospital, Dontaye had a seizure.

The pediatrician at the hospital diagnosed the problem as a respiratory infection and said the seizure was caused by the high fever. He prescribed a baby-aspirin substitute and an antibiotic and assured them that Dontaye would be much improved in 48 hours when the medication began to take effect. The Jordans took Dontaye home feeling optimistic that their son would soon be back to his energetic, talkative, happy-go-lucky self.

Two days later, however, Dontaye was still listless and unresponsive. His mother called their family pediatrician, who said to give the medication one more day, and if he still was not improved to bring him in for an appointment. The next day Dontaye did not talk at all when his mother awakened him. She immediately dressed him and took him to the pediatrician. Dr. Corley examined Dontaye and noted that the infection had caused respiratory distress and an asthma-like condition. She prescribed another medication and suggested that he not return to his preschool program for at least another week.

After a week, Dontaye seemed better, so his parents sent him back to his preschool program. At the end of the first day, his teacher called. She said Dontaye was withdrawn and that during playtime the recreation specialist had commented that he displayed autistic-like behaviors, such as twirling and flapping his hands. The next day the director of the preschool called. He said that Dontaye seemed to have lost some of his language skills and that he was striking out at peers when they approached him. He inquired whether Dontaye could have suffered brain damage or emotional trauma from the infection and suggested that his parents might want to consider moving him to a preschool for children with disabilities.

Now extremely concerned and confused, Mrs. Jordan called Dr. Corley again and suggested that she talk with the people at the preschool about how the respiratory infection could be affecting Dontaye's behavior. Mrs. Jordan said she was feeling like a "go-between," trying to relay all the messages from one person to the next, and she stated that she would like everyone involved to meet to share their observations, discuss possible causes, and suggest what needed to be done. Dr. Corley agreed to come to a meeting the following week.

The Jordans contacted the preschool personnel, who also agreed to attend a meeting. At the meeting, all the professionals shared their observations about Dontaye, and his parents commented on his behavior at home. Although at first they were quite defensive, eventually the educators agreed they might have been hasty in labeling some of Dontaye's behaviors as autistic or brain damaged. The educators and parents discussed some strategies for interacting with Dontaye. Everyone agreed to meet again in three weeks to discuss any changes or improvements that might occur after all of the medication had been taken.

The effects of professionals and parents operating in "separate worlds" are illustrated at the beginning of this vignette. When no one is in charge, everyone functions as a separate entity, even though each individual is concerned with the same child. Consequently, communication does not occur and the results often are fragmented services for a child and confusion for adults. After the Jordans were able to get the professionals to communicate, the situation improved, but much time and energy could have been saved if the people involved had been able to operate within a team framework from the beginning.

In Chapter 1, *interactive teaming* was defined as a mutual or reciprocal effort among and between members of a team to provide the best possible educational program for a student. The strength of this approach is the potential for effective, comprehensive, and cohesive services when all the people involved work together instead of functioning as separate individuals or disciplines. As stated in Chapter 2, interactive teaming includes features from the collaborative consultation and transdisciplinary teaming models used primarily in special education and school psychology. In addition, interactive teaming incorporates components identified in recent research on effective schools and school-based management (e.g., David, 1989; Goodlad, 1997; Lezotte, 1989; National Commission on Teaching and America's Future, 1996), decision-making processes, adult learning, and total quality management (Berry, 1991; Deming, 1986; Walton, 1990), recognizing that all the components and factors must be implemented within the context of a school or institutional program for at-risk students or those with identified special needs. In addition, barriers that have interfered with the implementation of other models described in the previous chapter must be addressed.

This chapter provides an examination of the dimensions of interactive teaming. Incorporated in the dimensions are the purposes and objectives of the model, description of the competencies of team members, and processes and procedures for implementation. Some of the barriers and limitations of other approaches that were cited in Chapters 1 and 2, including the absence of decision-making processes and dissimilar goals, are discussed as part of the explanation of the dimensions. Part II of the text, Facilitating Factors, provides additional information on how to address potential barriers to interactive teaming, such as a lack of understanding of roles, the process of change, miscommunication, ineffective leadership, insensitivity to cultural diversity, and limited family involvement.

Recent literature on collaboration, effective schools, total quality management, leadership, and teaming models contains several factors, parameters, or dimensions identified as necessary for the success of the students and the satisfaction of the professionals involved. Wangemann (cited in Wangemann, Ingram, & Muse, 1989) reviewed the literature on successful collaborations and noted that the following "ingredients" are essential:

1. Clarity of purpose.
2. Complementary dissimilarity between the partners.
3. Overlapping self-interests.
4. Sufficient time to build bridges of communication and trust.
5. Clarification and coordination of roles and responsibilities within the partnership.
6. Shared ownership.
7. Emphasis on action rather than structure building.
8. Adequate resources.
9. Leadership from key administrators.
10. Institutional commitment to the satisfying of mutual self-interests.
11. An ongoing system for research and evaluation.
12. An understanding of each institution's culture.

Harrison, Killion, and Mitchell (1989) reported on their attempts to implement site-based management in a school district in Colorado. They said the lessons learned from their mistakes included recognition of the following needs: (1) clarification of concepts and terms at the beginning, (2) definition of roles and then support and modeling of the new role expectations, (3) provision of training for school personnel and on-site support for administrators, and (4) preparation for the process of change and implications resulting from change.

Phillips and McCullough (1990) identified five key requirements for developing and implementing school-based collaborative approaches. The first is that administrative support must progress from a primarily managerial and facilitative focus to action-oriented participation. The second requirement is that systematic program development, multilevel planning, and decision making must occur. Third, membership on the team must be composed primarily of people from the consumer group (i.e., general education teachers) rather than specialists. This factor will help people develop ownership and commitment to the goals. Fourth, feasibility must be considered when choosing interventions and formats to be used. Finally, they pointed out that resistance to collaboration and teaming can be reduced through practical and specific professional development.

Laycock, Gable, and Korinek (1991) noted the following considerations for selecting collaborative structures: (1) process of program planning should be collaborative, (2) underlying philosophical assumptions should guide choices made,

(3) structures should be compatible with existing collaborative structures, (4) alternatives can be combined to enhance the delivery of services, (5) planning teams should adapt models to fit current needs, and (6) program adjustments should be based on evaluation data.

Characteristics that maximize effectiveness of teams were described by Elliott and Sheridan (1992). They noted the importance of shared leadership and ensuring that the group used problem-solving guidelines. They also stated the necessity of planning activities, agenda setting, clarifying communication, participation of group members, use of conflict management strategies, and review of group processes.

The literature on leadership and total quality management also stresses certain aspects designed to enhance team functioning. Covey (1991) emphasized the significance of shared values or governing principles, and said strategies, structures, systems, skills, and styles will flow from these values. Blankstein (1992) endorsed the philosophy of Deming (1986) as a framework within which to integrate developments such as teacher participation and site-based management. This philosophy endorses the idea that the role of management or leadership is to improve the system or organization so that individuals can work together. Several of Deming's (1986) principles are especially relevant to teaming models: (1) Create constancy of purpose for improvement of products and services, (2) adopt and institute leadership, (3) break down barriers between staff areas, (4) institute a vigorous program of education and self-improvement for everyone, and (5) put everybody in the organization to work to accomplish the transformation.

O'Shea, O'Shea, and Algozzine (1998), drawing on the work of Larson and LaFasto (1989) and others, identified eight characteristics of effective teams. They stated that effective teams share common goals, are results driven, have competent members, have a unified commitment to their work together, work together in a collaborative climate, hold high standards of excellence, have principled leadership, and receive external support and recognition.

Hanson and Widerstrom (1992) described elements necessary for successful preschool special education programs. These elements included interagency collaboration, commitment from decision makers, shared ownership and decision making among participants, adequate resources to support planning and coordination, ongoing training and technical assistance, evaluation, and family involvement. Hasazi, Furney, and DeStefano (1999) identified similar factors in their examination of model sites for implementation of the IDEA transition mandates: (1) incorporation of system-wide, student and family-centered strategies; (2) fostering of effective and substantive interagency collaboration; (3) facilitation of systemic professional development; (4) a visionary, supportive, and inclusive form of leadership; (5) coordination of an integrated set of reform efforts; and (6) emergence of connections among a variety of local and federal transition initiatives.

Fishbaugh (1997) described several hallmarks of effective teams: face-to-face interactions, positive interdependence, trust, assessment of team functioning, and individual accountability. She summarized the components of successful change efforts as illustrated in Figure 3.1.

Involvement *of All Pertinent Stakeholders*
Administration
Faculty
Support Personnel
Special Services Personnel
Parents
Community Agencies
Local Businesses
Government Entities

Team Building *Among Stakeholders*
Shared Visioning
Shared Planning
Delegated Responsibilities
System for Problem Management
Evaluation Plan

Commitment *of All Involved*
Follow-Through
Revisions as Needed

Resources *to Support Change*
Technical Expertise
Materials and Funding

Leadership *to Maintain Focus*

Figure 3.1
Components of successful change efforts.
Source: From *Models of Collaboration* by M. S. E. Fishbaugh, 1997, Needham Heights, MA: Allyn & Bacon. Reprinted by permission.

Katzenbach and Smith (1999) focused on what they considered team basics: skills, accountability, and commitment. They illustrated the various components of each area as shown in Figure 3.2.

Based on the research of these authors and others who have been involved in the study or implementation of models that contain components similar to interactive teaming, 10 dimensions have been identified that are considered essential:

1. Legitimacy and autonomy.
2. Purpose and objectives.
3. Competencies of team members and clarity of their roles.
4. Role release and role transitions.
5. Awareness of the individuality of team members.
6. Process of team building.
7. Attention to factors that affect team functioning.
8. Leadership styles.
9. Implementation procedures.
10. Commitment to common goals.

Each of these dimensions is examined in more detail in the remainder of this chapter.

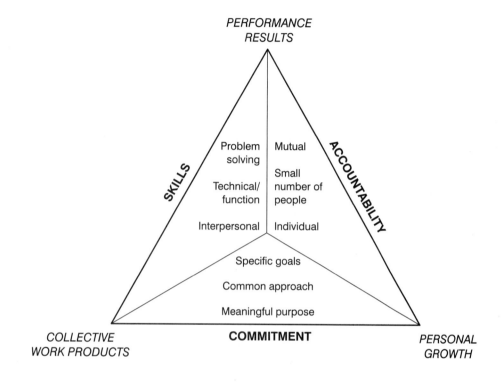

Figure 3.2
Team basics.
Source: Reprinted by permission of Harvard Business School Press. From *The Wisdom of Teams: Creating the High-Performance Organization* by J. R. Katzenbach and D. K. Smith. Boston, MA, 1999. Copyright © 1999 by McKinsey & Co., all rights reserved.

BASES FOR INTERACTIVE TEAMING

Legitimacy and Autonomy

To be successful, any group must have a reason to exist and the freedom to operate. Team decision making and consultation with families are stipulated by Public Laws 94-142, 99-457, 101-476, and amendments to the Individuals with Disabilities Education Act (IDEA); therefore, the legitimacy of a framework such as interactive teaming is supported by law, as well as by a recognition of the need to collaborate by professionals in various fields (cf. Turnbull & Cilley, 1999, or the IDEA web site at http://www.ideapractices.org). However, even if a legal basis exists and teaming is endorsed by individuals, the team and its decisions must be valued by organizations, administrators, and staff to be effective (Maher & Hawryluk, 1983; Phillips & McCullough, 1990).

A second consideration is the necessity of autonomy and the support for this concept. Time and support personnel must be provided for team members so they are able to plan and reflect together, and to be responsive to the accountability measures that often accompany increased autonomy (Pugach, 1988). Johnson, Pugach, and Devlin (1990) identified six steps for developing a more collaborative environment that included the following: (1) sanctioning of collaborative efforts by the administration, (2) providing assistance for teachers with clerical work and other noninstructional tasks, (3) organizing meeting times for teachers to engage in mutual problem solving, and (4) reserving faculty or in-service meeting times for collaboration.

Team members and others in organizations should recognize that the composition of a team may differ at various times due to the specific needs of a child (Golightly, 1987; Orelove & Sobsey, 1991) and the culture and priorities of a district or school (cf. Orlich, 1989). Given these considerations, part of team autonomy is realizing that the "constellation" of people involved may change over time, depending on the purpose of the information sharing (e.g., assessment results) or decision making (e.g., placement, intervention design) about a student or client. As a result, all members of a team may not be involved in every interaction. Consultation and collaboration between individuals or among subgroups should be viewed as enhancing the overall effectiveness of a team and contributing to team consistency and cohesiveness. The interactive teaming model and illustrations of how consultation and collaboration can occur among members are shown in Figure 3.3.

Purpose and Objectives

A team needs an identified purpose, objectives, and performance goals to guide its actions (Katzenbach & Smith, 1999). The major purpose of interactive teaming is to share information and expertise to ensure that the best possible decisions are made and effective programs are implemented. The types of decisions an interactive team can be involved in include those identified by Salvia and Ysseldyke (1988): referral, screening, classification, instructional planning, and evaluation of pupil progress. (See Chapter 1 for definitions of these terms.) Specific objectives will be derived from the decisions made and the roles people will play in implementing those decisions (cf. Gutkin, 1996). For example, a social worker may participate in an interactive team meeting at which the decision is made to place a child in a special education program. She is aware of a community program that offers free tutoring for economically disadvantaged students, and she thinks this child would qualify. Her objectives are to determine eligibility, make the necessary contacts if the child is eligible, and then assist with communication with the child's grandmother, who is acting as guardian.

Figure 3.3
The interactive teaming model.

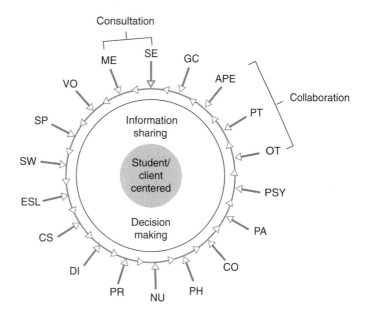

Note: Not all of these persons will need to be present at every meeting.

Key:

PA = Parent	PSY = Psychologist
GC = General education classroom teacher	NU = Nurse
SE = Special educator	CO = Counselor
SP = Speech/language clinician	PR = Principal
SW = Social worker	DI = Dietician
PH = Physician	CS = Computer specialist
PT = Physical therapist	ESL = English as a second language
OT = Occupational therapist	VO = Vocational specialist
APE = Adapted physical educator	ME = Migrant educator

ASPECTS OF TEAM FUNCTIONING

Competencies of Team Members and Clarity of Their Roles

Team members should first be able to demonstrate competencies in their own disciplines before they are expected to acquire knowledge in other areas (Siders, Riall, Bennett, & Judd, 1987). In addition to the discipline-specific competencies, they will need to be competent in the areas previously described as essential for consultants and team members: collaborative problem solving, interactive communication, leadership, awareness of cultural diversity, referral, and evaluation (cf. Blanton, Griffin, Winn, & Pugach, 1997; Courtnage & Healy, 1984; Hudson, Correa, Morsink, & Dykes, 1987; Quigney, 1998; West & Cannon, 1988). Maher and Hawryluk (1983) cited several other considerations for selection of team members: (1) a willingness to receive training in other areas, (2) the ability to participate in a problem-solving situation, (3) possession of enough time to contribute to team processes, and (4) the potential for implementing their own tasks as identified by the team.

Along with attainment of individual competencies, team members must be accurate in their perceptions of the competencies and roles of others (Orelove & Sobsey, 1991). At times members may be unclear about the expertise of people from different disciplines or the roles those people should play in a team situation. Clarity of roles and expertise is essential and will be explored further in Chapter 4.

Role Release and Role Transitions

In addition to understanding the roles and recognizing the competencies of others, team members must be able to "release" their own knowledge and share it with others. *Role release* has been defined by Lyon and Lyon (1980) as referring "to three levels of sharing between two or more members of an educational team: general information, informational skills, and performance competencies" (pp. 253–254). They described the first level as sharing knowledge about basic procedures or practices; for example, a special educator explaining to the principal the behavior management system he is using in his classroom. Informational skills include teaching others to make judgments; for example, an adaptive physical educator teaching a regular classroom teacher how to determine if a child is using a correct skipping motion in a game. The third level, performance competencies, includes training another person to perform specified skills, such as an occupational therapist teaching a parent how to use an adaptive feeding device with a child who has a severe disability.

A similar conception of sharing roles and expertise was presented in a publication by the United Cerebral Palsy Association and cited by Golightly (1987). She described the six "role transitions" as follows:

> First, role extension entails designing and implementing instructional objectives within one's own discipline. Second, role enrichment involves designing instructional objectives to include strategies from other disciplines. Third, role expansion involves deriving information from the deliberate pooling of knowledge and skills among team members. Fourth, role exchange permits carrying out the intervention strategies learned from other team members. Fifth, role release involves effectively imparting disciplinary skills to others and providing follow through to ensure appropriate application. Sixth, role support, used in complex interventions, entails using consultative back-up when extensive disciplinary expertise is needed. (p. 128)

An example of how role release was realized in a preschool program involving teachers and physical and occupational therapists was presented by Mather and Weinstein (1988). These authors noted that when the sharing of expertise began, mutual trust was established and the professionals became committed to designing the best program for the students, instead of being concerned with protecting their own "turf." Role release is especially important when teachers are working with the inclusion of students with special needs in general education settings (cf. Salend, 1998; Smith, 1998; Tiegerman-Farber & Radziewicz, 1998; and Wood, 1998).

Awareness of the Individuality of Team Members

Team members must be aware of each other's individuality. Persons on interactive teams must be cognizant of and sensitive to factors such as cultural differences, variety of backgrounds and educational experiences, and stages of professional development.

Team members must seek to understand their own cultural values and racial identity, as well as the value systems of the racial and ethnic individuals with whom they will be collaborating (Brown, Pryzwansky, & Schulte, 1998). Helms (1992) advocated the development of an "autonomous racial identity." This approach incorporates a "positive view of one's own race, an integration of information about the characteristics of other racial groups—including their similarities and dissimilarities to one's own race, and a dedication to the abandonment of racism" (Brown et al., 1998, p. 162).

Sue, Arredondo, and McDavis (1995) described several multicultural competencies that are applicable to interactive teaming situations: awareness of one's own assumptions, values, and biases and how they affect culturally diverse clients; understanding the world view of the culturally different client; and developing appropriate intervention strategies. Ramirez, Lepage, Kratchowill, and Duffy (1998) built on the work of Sue and others, and outlined the following competencies: (1) understanding the impact of one's race/ethnicity and culture, (2) valuing and understanding the impact of other races/ethnicities and cultures, (3) adapting a culturally responsive consultation style, and (4) adapting culturally responsive strategies during the problem-solving stages.

Brown and his colleagues (1998) noted that race and ethnicity are variables that influence problem solving and decision making and suggested the following:

> Culturally sensitive consultants who have not already done so need to immerse themselves in the literature and in experiences that will allow them to match their worldviews with those of their consultees and, when the need arises, to help consultees better understand the cultural perspective of the people with whom they work. (p. 164)

However, as Harris (1996) cautioned: "It is best to learn about the cultures of collaborators by learning about them as individuals, rather than members of a cultural group to avoid stereotyping" (p. 356).

In addition to cultural issues, differences in training and approaches to educational services will affect the success of teaming, and such differences need to be explored and addressed. Bruneau-Balderrama (1997) noted that personality factors, teaching philosophy, and classroom management style should be explored by teachers before they embark on any collaborative venture, especially an inclusion model. (See Chapter 4 on roles of team members for additional information.)

Research in the areas of adult learning and professional growth also has implications for interactive teaming. As Fishbaugh (1997) commented, often individuals fail to consider adult stages of development in interactions with coworkers. She stated: "Adults are not finished products. On the contrary, individuals continue to develop throughout their life stages" (p. 133).

Three models useful for understanding adult development are Professional Stages, Career Cycles, and Conceptual Stages. Awareness of these potential differences may enhance a team member's ability to understand another individual's responses and behaviors in certain situations.

Peryon (1982) paralleled the Professional Stages of teachers with the phases of adulthood described by Sheehy (1977). Peryon identified these stages:

1. *New teachers:* They strive to become the ideal and use what they have been taught; they need support, encouragement, and recognition as professionals.

2. *Teachers with 5 to 10 years of experience:* They have confidence and know what works for them; they need to be recognized as competent.

3. *Middle period of teaching:* They often are rethinking old ideas and analyzing their professional goals for the future; they need to be given a chance to grow and be reinforced for new achievements.

4. *Mature period of teaching:* They have reached self-actualization in terms of their careers; they need to be recognized as top professionals and to be needed by others.

Burke, Christensen, and Fessler (1984) presented the concept of Career Cycles. Their model is similar in some ways to the stages described by Peryon; however, it includes induction and both career wind-down and exit. It also incorporates more of a systems view because factors in the personal and organizational environments are included. The Career Cycles are illustrated in Figure 3.4 and described more fully in Figure 3.5. It is important to note that teachers or other professionals do not necessarily proceed through these cycles sequentially according to years of experience, and in fact they may be in two cycles at the same time. Examples of the latter point are beginning professionals (induction) who are competent and growing, or beginners who are experiencing career frustration. (For additional information on adult life stages, see Glickman, 1995.)

The third approach to be discussed is the Conceptual Stages of adults identified by Hunt (1981) and further developed by Sprinthall and Thies-Sprinthall (1983). These researchers contend that adults develop a mode of responding to complex situations such as teaching. Their behaviors and verbal comments may be affected by the conceptual stage at which they are functioning. These stages are not necessarily correlated to years of experience or intelligence; rather they illustrate how a person may respond in a given situation. The conceptual stages are presented in Figure 3.6.

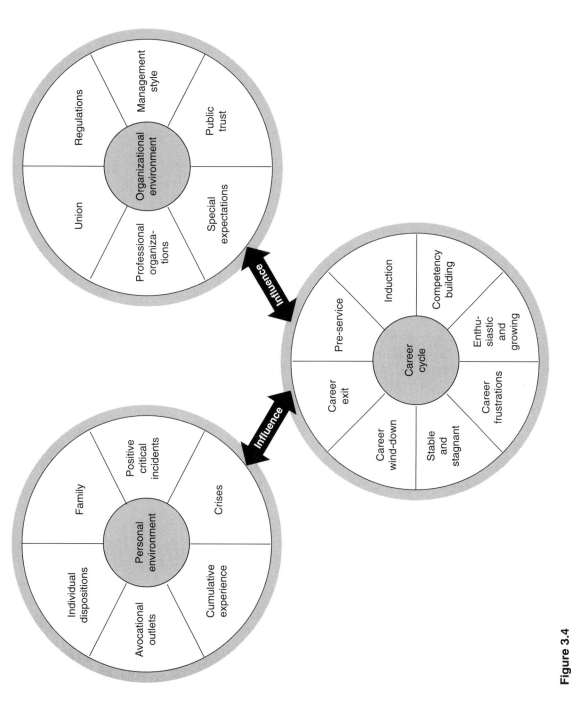

Figure 3.4

A model of the stages of the teacher career cycle and the environmental factors that affect it.

Source: From *Teacher Career Stages: Implications for Staff Development* by P. S. Burke, J. C. Christensen, and R. Fessler, 1984, Bloomington, IN: Phi Delta Kappa Foundation. Reprinted by permission.

The stages of the Career Cycle can be characterized by the following descriptors:

1. **Preservice**
   Preparing initially in a college or university
   Retraining for a new role or assignment through coursework or inservice

2. **Induction**
   Teaching during the first few years
   Shifting to another position, building, or system
   Socializing into the system
   Striving for acceptance by students, peers, supervisors
   Attempting to achieve comfort in dealing with everyday occurrences

3. **Competency Building**
   Improving teaching skills and abilities
   Seeking new materials, methods, and strategies
   Demonstrating receptiveness to new ideas
   Attending workshops and conferences willingly
   Enrolling in college coursework through own initiative

4. **Enthusiastic and Growing**
   Exhibiting high level of competence
   Progressing as professional
   Experiencing high job satisfaction
   Enjoying going to work and interacting with students
   Seeking new ways to enrich teaching
   Helping to identify appropriate staff development activities

5. **Career Frustration**
   Feeling frustration and disillusionment with teaching
   Experiencing waning job satisfaction
   Questioning worth of work
   Feeling "burnout"
   Experienced usually at midpoint of career, but also with new teachers

6. **Stable but Stagnant**
   Putting in "a fair day's work for a fair day's pay"
   Doing only what is expected
   Doing an acceptable job, but not committed to excellence
   Participating only at surface level
   Being a passive consumer of staff development

7. **Career Wind-Down**
   Preparing to leave profession
   Reflecting on positive experiences and looking forward to retirement
   Resenting forced job termination or anxious to get out of unrewarding job

8. **Career Exit**
   Retiring or leaving job for other circumstances
   Being unemployed after involuntary or elective job termination
   Exiting temporarily for child rearing
   Exploring career alternative such as moving to a nonteaching position

Figure 3.5 Descriptors of career cycles. *Source:* From *Teacher Career Stages: Implications for Staff Development* by P. S. Burke, J. C. Christensen, and R. Fessler, 1984, Bloomington, IN: Phi Delta Kappa Foundation. Reprinted by permission.

Stage A

Strong evidence of concrete thinking

Knowledge seen as fixed

Employs a singular "tried–and–true" method

Exhibits compliance as a learner and expects the same from pupils

Low on self-direction and initiative. Needs detailed instructions

Doesn't distinguish between theory and facts

Almost an exclusive reliance on advance organizers

Teaching is "filling the students up with facts"

Stays at Bloom's Level One and Two regardless of student level

Enjoys highly structured activities for self and for pupils

Uncomfortable with ambiguous assignments

Does not question authority

Follows a curriculum guide as if it were carved in stone

Verbalizes feelings at a limited level. Has difficulty recognizing feelings in pupils

Reluctant to talk about own inadequacies; blames pupils exclusively

Stage B

Growing awareness of difference between concrete vs. abstract thinking

Separates facts, opinions, and theories about teaching and learning

Employs some different teaching models in accord with student differences

Evidence of teaching for generalization as well as skills

Some evidence of systematic "matching and mismatching"; can vary structure

Some openness to innovations and can make some appropriate adaptations

Shows sensitivity to pupil's emotional needs

Enjoys some level of autonomy; self-directed learning a goal for self and for the pupils

Employs Bloom's Taxonomy, Levels One through Four, when appropriate

Evaluations are appropriate to assignments

Stage C

Understands knowledge as a process of successive approximations

Shows evidence of originality in adapting innovations to the classroom

Comfortable in applying all appropriate teaching models

Most articulate in analyzing one's own teaching in both content and feeling

High tolerance for ambiguity and frustration. Can stay on task in spite of major distractions

Does not automatically comply with directions—asks examiner's reasons.

Fosters an intensive questioning approach with students

Can use all six levels of Bloom when appropriate

Responds appropriately to the emotional needs of all pupils

Can "match and mismatch" with expert flexibility

Exhibits careful evaluations based on objective criteria according to level of assignment

Figure 3.6

Descriptions of Hunt's conceptual stages—teachers' attitudes toward learning and teaching.

Source: From "Teacher's Adaptation: 'Reading' and 'Flexing' to Students" by D. E. Hunt, 1981. In B. Joyce, C. Brown, and L. Peck (Eds.), *Flexibility in Teaching,* New York: Longman. Reprinted by permission.

The Process of Team Building

One frustration often voiced by members on a newly formed team is "Things aren't happening quickly enough." Two important considerations for interactive team members to recognize are that teams comprise individuals, and those individuals must have time to develop as a unit (cf. Bailey, 1984). Abelson and Woodman (1983) described a model of team building based on the work of Tuckman and Jensen (1977). This model consists of five stages that an interactive team may go through in the process of becoming established:

1. *Forming*: Individuals become oriented to the team; communication networks are started.
2. *Storming*: Conflict and polarization may occur; leadership may be tested.
3. *Norming*: Role relationships are redefined; team goals are established; leadership is defined and accepted.
4. *Performing*: Members work to accomplish the task.
5. *Adjourning*: Members deal with changes in relationships and feelings about self-esteem, depending on whether the task was satisfactorily completed.

Mostert (1998) described a similar model which he labeled the collaborative life cycle. He commented that most collaborative teams undergo a definite progression from initial team formation to final dissolution. He described the phases as (1) initial formulation, (2) conflict and resolution, (3) consensual behavioral norms, (4) optimum performance, (5) evaluation and redirection, and (6) termination and dissolution.

Considering that teams need time to build and for individuals to adjust, team members can understand that immediate efficiency is not always possible. Also, it is useful to remember that people who have served on teams before will usually adapt much more quickly than those who are new to this type of unit.

Attention to Factors that Affect Team Functioning

Three areas frequently mentioned as problematic to team functioning are a lack of involvement of all team members, an increase in interprofessional rivalry instead of collaboration or "boundary crossing," and a lack of structure in decision making (cf. Epstein, 1988; Kabler & Genshaft, 1983; Kaiser & Woodman, 1985; Yoshida, 1983). The implications of those areas for interactive teams will be considered in terms of the factors of goal structures, communication climates, roles in meetings, and consensus-building strategies.

Goal Structures.   Johnson, Johnson, and Holubec (1986) described three types of goal structures that may be held by participants in a group situation. The structures are *cooperative,* in which group members seek outcomes that are beneficial for all members of the group; *competitive,* in which the goals of the participants are linked so that each can win only if the others fail; and *individualistic,* in which no correlation exists between the goals of the group and the individuals. In the cooperative goal structure, the one most advantageous to interactive teams, all members of the group contribute to the design of a common solution to a problem. In the competitive structure, each member strives to win independently. In the individual goal structure, members may work side by side but alone, because they are working to accomplish their own goals.

In their review of the effect of the three types of goal structures on the professional self-esteem, achievement, positive interpersonal relationships, and social support of adults, Johnson and Johnson (1987) found the cooperative structure to be superior in all areas. These effects are illustrated in Figure 3.7.

Communication Climates.   Two distinctly different climates of teams in which interactions may take place have been identified by Gibb (1961), both of which can be readily identified by the behaviors of the participants. In a *defensive climate,* participants may attempt to evaluate the ideas of another in a judgmental manner. In a *supportive climate,* they encourage others to describe events and situations, and they in turn attempt to describe what other speakers have said. In the defensive mode, the participant attempts to control the discussion by dominating or lecturing; in the supportive mode, the person asks others to assist in identifying the problem and possible solutions.

Figure 3.7
Outcomes of collegial learning.

Source: From "Research Shows the Benefits of Adult Cooperation," by D. W. Johnson and R. T. Johnson, 1987, *Educational Leadership, 45*(3), pp. 27–30. Copyright 1987 by the Association for Supervision and Curriculum Development. Reprinted with permission of the Association for Supervision and Curriculum Development, David W. Johnson, and Roger T. Johnson. All rights reserved.

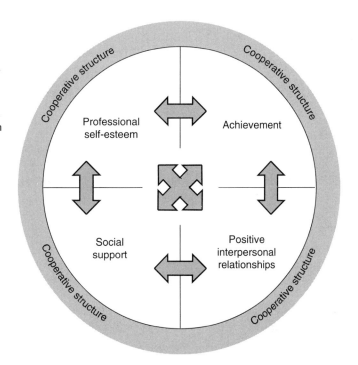

In a defensive climate, team members may enter a meeting with a predetermined strategy designed to manipulate the others into a decision. In a supportive climate, team members have engaged in planning, but their reactions are more spontaneous, depending on the needs of other group members and the situation. They allow others to express concerns and ideas that may not be on "their lists."

In a defensive mode, participants may be neutral, stating, "It doesn't matter to me" or "I don't care—whatever you want is fine." The neutrality of suggesting that anything others want is acceptable indicates this person is defensive by virtue of being uninvolved and unconcerned. In contrast, the supportive team member expresses empathy by restating and attempting to clarify feelings and ideas that may affect the problem.

Superiority is descriptive of the defensive climate, and equality is representative of supportive interactions. The school psychologist who acts as if she knows more than the others in the group, or the special educator who behaves as if general educators are "unspecial" and have nothing to contribute, is expressing superiority. In contrast, the principal who tells a parent that her observations of the child at home are important is emphasizing equality. Each participant is acknowledged as having a contribution to make to understanding the problem; in this case, the mother's expertise in the child's developmental history and home behaviors is given recognition.

Considering the various types of goal structures and communication climates is important for interactive team members who wish to interact effectively with others on the team. The individual who is cooperative—who wants the group goals to be facilitated, as opposed to having his or her own agenda—is more successful in working with others. The individual who is supportive rather than defensive is better able to assist the group in achieving and maintaining a problem-solving focus.

Roles in Team Meetings.   A classic study on the roles members can play in team meetings was conducted by Benne and Sheats (1948). They noted that group participation can be divided into three categories of roles: *task, maintenance,* and *negative.* These roles can be played by both leaders and group members, and all can play several roles during the course of a meeting. Task and maintenance roles are the ones most facilitating to the process of interactive teaming. A summary of the roles adapted from the work by Hybels and Weaver (1997) is included in Figure 3.8.

Consensus Building.   In addition to the goal structures, communication climates, and roles that members can play during meetings, the *decision-making processes* used to reach consensus will affect the team's functioning. If a process is not used, members tend to become frustrated and believe the team is not accomplishing anything, or that their thoughts and ideas are not valued by other team members.

In interactive teaming, participants should strive to work as a team and reach consensus decisions whenever possible. For consensus to be reached, team members must be aware of the needs of all involved and agree on a process for deter-

---

Task Roles

These people help get the task done, assist in coming up with new ideas, and aid in collecting and organizing information:

- *Initiators-expediters* suggest ideas and help keep the group on task.
- *Information givers and seekers* will track down information and enhance the quality of the discussion.
- *Critics-analyzers* look at the good and the bad in the data, detect points that need additional elaboration, discover information that has been left out, and model organized behavior.

Maintenance Roles

The people fulfilling these roles focus on the emotional tone of the meeting and also help keep the meeting going:

- *Encouragers* praise others for their contributions and the group's progress, are active listeners, and help others feel good about what is happening.
- *Harmonizers-compromisers* help resolve conflicts and determine solutions that are acceptable to everyone. They also remind others that group goals are more important than individual agendas.
- *Observers* help further group cohesiveness, and are sensitive and aware of the needs of each person.

Negative Roles

The individuals who are playing these roles slow the group down and interfere with progress:

- *Aggressors-resistors* attack others to make themselves look superior.
- *Recognition-seekers* and *self-confessors* call attention to themselves and make contributions that are off-task or lengthy.
- *Help seekers* join groups to meet their own needs and use the group to further their own agendas.
- *Withdrawers* make no contributions and may appear bored or shy.

Figure 3.8
Roles in team meetings.
Source: From *Communicating Effectively* (pp. 240–244) by S. Hybels and R. L. Weaver, 1997, New York: McGraw-Hill. Adapted by permission of McGraw-Hill, Inc.

mining team decisions. An example of considering the needs of others was provided by Bailey (1987), who identified five areas of importance when working with families:

> The ability to (1) view a family from a systems perspective; (2) systematically assess relevant family needs; (3) use effective listening and interviewing techniques; (4) negotiate values and priorities to reach a joint solution; and (5) act as "quality advisors" in helping families match needs with available community resources. (p. 64)

A number of decision-making processes have been identified in the literature. The challenge for team members is selecting the most appropriate one for their situation. Most are similar to the sequence suggested by Doyle and Strauss (1976) and further developed by Margolis and Brannigan (1987). These authors recommended the following steps: (1) Define the problem, (2) analyze the problem and any factors that could be contributing to it, (3) generate possible alternatives, (4) establish and agree on criteria for selecting solutions, and (5) select and evaluate possible solutions.

Two examples of decision-making processes are Problem Resolution Through Communication by Fine, Grantham, and Wright (1979), and the Nominal Group Technique developed by Delbecq, Van de Ven, and Gustafson (1975) and summarized by Kaiser and Woodman (1985). Problem Resolution Through Communication stresses listening and communication skills, and it includes considerations of feelings and taking another's point of view (Figure 3.9). Nominal Group Technique is especially useful in ensuring that all team members participate in the decision-making process and that the decision reflects a consensus of the group. The steps in the Nominal Group Technique are listed in Figure 3.10.

Leadership Styles

Leadership behaviors, styles, and beliefs are integral to the success of an interactive team. As will be explained in Chapter 6, any member of the team can serve as the leader, but someone must assume that role for the team's work to be completed. Fishbaugh (1997) noted, "Team members assume or release leadership responsibilities within the team as appropriate for their individual expertise in any given situation" (p. 138). Katzenbach and Smith (1999) commented that the leader's role was to build commitment, fill gaps, and shift the leadership role as appropriate.

Administrators such as principals, directors, or division heads do not have to function as team leaders in interactive teaming situations, but they can assist the team's work in other ways. Gerber (1991) noted that administrators need to provide program advocacy and promote the goals of collaborative efforts. He also stated that they should visibly participate because this enhances credibility, and they should provide support for maintenance and durability of collaboration. Garner (1995) stated that the administrator in a team model works to create an environment in which team members feel empowered, and noted that such a leader must have self-confidence and trust in others. Fuller (1998) had similar observations noting that the leader must be someone who can provide guidance but who will let the team operate without undue interference. In their study on teacher assistance teams, Kruger, Struzziero, Watts, and Vacca (1995) found that administrator support variables accounted for more than 50% of the variance in consumers' satisfaction.

Leadership styles affect how team meetings are conducted, the views others may have toward the person in the role of leader, and the opinions of the success of a model or system being implemented. The beliefs leaders have about what they consider to be the "rules of the game" also will affect the functioning of the team.

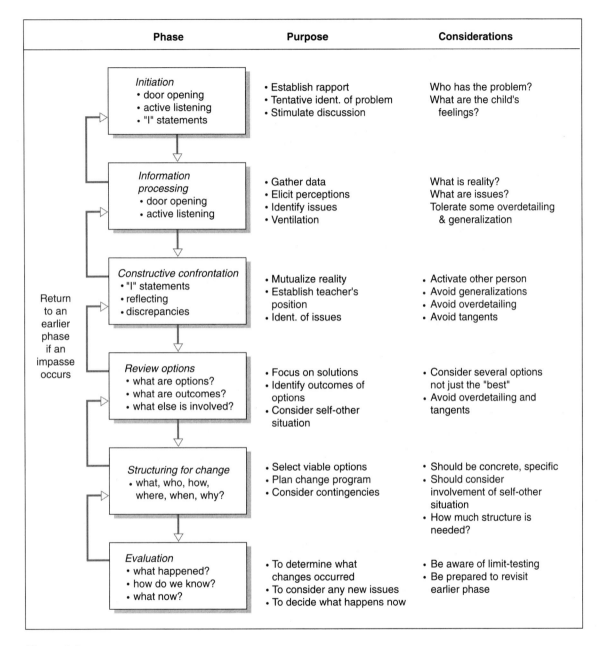

| Phase | Purpose | Considerations |

Initiation
- door opening
- active listening
- "I" statements

- Establish rapport
- Tentative ident. of problem
- Stimulate discussion

Who has the problem?
What are the child's feelings?

Information processing
- door opening
- active listening

- Gather data
- Elicit perceptions
- Identify issues
- Ventilation

What is reality?
What are issues?
Tolerate some overdetailing & generalization

Constructive confrontation
- "I" statements
- reflecting
- discrepancies

- Mutualize reality
- Establish teacher's position
- Ident. of issues

- Activate other person
- Avoid generalizations
- Avoid overdetailing
- Avoid tangents

Review options
- what are options?
- what are outcomes?
- what else is involved?

- Focus on solutions
- Identify outcomes of options
- Consider self-other situation

- Consider several options not just the "best"
- Avoid overdetailing and tangents

Structuring for change
- what, who, how, where, when, why?

- Select viable options
- Plan change program
- Consider contingencies

- Should be concrete, specific
- Should consider involvement of self-other situation
- How much structure is needed?

Evaluation
- what happened?
- how do we know?
- what now?

- To determine what changes occurred
- To consider any new issues
- To decide what happens now

- Be aware of limit-testing
- Be prepared to revisit earlier phase

Return to an earlier phase if an impasse occurs

Figure 3.9
Problem Resolution Through Communication.

Source: From "Personal Variables That Facilitate or Impede Consultation" by M. J. Fine, V. L. Grantham, and J. G. Wright, 1979, *Psychology in the Schools, 16,* p. 537. Reprinted by permission of the publisher.

Step 1—Silent generation of ideas in writing. Each member is asked to write down key ideas related to the issue under consideration silently and independently. The benefits of this step are that members can think/reflect freely, interruptions are avoided; undue focusing on a particular idea or content area is minimized; competition, status pressure, and conformity are avoided; the group remains problem-centered; and the group avoids selecting a choice prematurely.

Step 2—Round-robin recording of ideas. Each member is asked sequentially to provide one idea until all ideas are processed. The group leader records each item on a blackboard or flip chart. Benefits include: equal participation, increase in problem-mindedness, depersonalization—the separation of ideas from personalities, an increase in the ability to deal with a larger number of ideas, tolerance for conflicting ideas, encouragement of hitchhiking (generating new ideas from presented ideas), and the development of a written record.

Step 3—Serial discussion for clarification. Each idea is discussed in turn. During this process, each item can potentially receive adequate discussion/clarification, logic can be provided behind arguments and disagreements, and differences of opinion can be recorded without undue argumentation. It is important to stress here that steps 2 and 3 are solely for idea generation and clarification and not evaluation.

Step 4—Preliminary vote on item importance. Each member independently rank orders, in his or her opinion, the most salient items. Typically, a limit is placed (e.g., each member's top five). Independent listing minimizes status, personality characteristics, and conformity pressures. From the total list, the most salient items emerge, ranked in order, based on the total frequency of each item.

Step 5—Discussion of the preliminary vote—(optional). Each member is allowed a brief period to comment on the selected items. This allows the group to examine inconsistent voting patterns and also allows for discussion of items that received unusually high or low rankings.

Step 6—Final vote. The group combines individual judgment into a group decision using a mathematical procedure. This allows for a sense of closure, accomplishment, and documentation. It is important to note that the mathematical resolution may take the form of a rank ordering, a system of rating each item, or the selection of a single best item based on the frequency of votes for each item. The procedure should fit the group's needs.

Figure 3.10
Nominal Group Technique.
Source: From "Multidisciplinary Teams and Group Decision-Making Techniques: Possible Solutions to Decision-Making Problems" by S. M. Kaiser and R. W. Woodman, 1985, *School Psychology Review, 14,* pp. 464–465. Reprinted by permission of the publisher.

Hybels and Weaver (1997) identified three leadership styles in conducting team meetings: authoritarian, democratic, and laissez-faire. The *authoritarian* leader is definitely in charge and controls who talks and what they discuss. Under this type of leadership, individuals may not feel free to contribute or to share their honest opinions. The *democratic* leader ensures that all points of view are recognized and that all members are involved in contributing to a decision. This type of leadership generally results in increased motivation for team members and more creativity in decisions generated. The *laissez-faire* leader does not require or actually assume a responsibility for leading the group. As a result, typically very little is accomplished. The type of leadership style most appropriate for interactive teaming is the democratic style; however, if time for decision making is limited, the authoritarian style may have to be implemented on a short-term basis, but contributions from all members should still be encouraged. The laissez-faire style would not be suitable unless the purpose of the meeting is simply interaction without the necessity of accomplishing a task or making a decision.

Beliefs about the "rules of the game" when serving as a team leader will affect how one fulfills the role. The rules listed in Figure 3.11 are derived from literature, interviews with leaders, and personal experiences. Some are stated humorously, not because they should be taken lightly, but rather because "many a truth is stated in jest."

IMPLEMENTATION OF INTERACTIVE TEAMING

Implementation Procedures

The actual procedures involved in implementing the interactive teaming process should and will vary depending on such factors as the age of the child, severity of the problem, and types of professionals available. The steps presented in Figure 3.12 are generic ones that will need to be adapted to specific situations (cf. Aldinger, Warger, & Eavy, 1991; Fishbaugh, 1997; Gutkin & Curtis, 1990; Jayanthi & Friend, 1992; Mostert, 1998; Voltz, Elliott, & Harris, 1995). Additional information on implementing these procedures for different types of students is provided in Chapters 9 through 13.

Guidelines to remember when implementing the steps are (1) encourage everyone to contribute during the discussion, including the person presenting the situation; (2) reach consensus on the definition of the problem before discussing possible interventions; and (3) consider all factors that could be relevant to the problem or possible interventions. These factors could include materials, teaching techniques, antecedents and consequences of behaviors, criterion level of performance expected, classroom and home environments, and mastery of prerequisite skills.

Interactive team members also need to remain focused on the mutual and reciprocal sharing of ideas throughout the process, and guard against the team becoming dominated by one individual. O'Shea et al. (1998) noted:

> Collaborative approaches can easily become expert systems unless participants consciously work to prevent this from happening. Because of professional role designations (e.g., administrator, school psychologist, special educator), specialty skills cer-

1. **Always do right. This will gratify some people and astonish the rest.**
   This rule can seldom be violated, even by those with established power. *Right* is defined in different ways by various societies and cultures, so it is essential that the leader learn the values of the culture or society. An entry-level leader must project and possess absolute integrity in the conduct of all affairs, and must understand that the standards are applied more rigorously to his or her conduct than to the conduct of others

2. **Rose-colored glasses never come in bifocals.**
   This is another way of saying that there are no knights in shining armor who go around righting all wrongs with a stroke of the sword. The behaviors of a leader are often less than "perfect" in the judgement of others who do not have the total perspective that would enable them to understand the rationale for decision making. Sometimes a leader may have to struggle with what is "right" and balance it with what is essential to help someone save face or to comply with political realities that will allow a different "right" to occur in the future.

3. **If you mess up, 'fess up!**
   Everyone makes errors. Experienced leaders who don't admit and learn from their mistakes are bound to repeat them. Potential leaders who don't admit and learn from their mistakes will not be given an opportunity to repeat them. Successful leaders try to anticipate and prevent errors; when they have erred, they make sure they don't repeat them. They do this by rehearsing and planning, so that possible events are anticipated whenever possible.

4. **Criticism is a compliment.**
   The inability to accept and to profit from constructive criticism often prevents people from becoming successful leaders. Using the comments of others to one's own benefit can help a person grow in a role and be able to fulfill self- and others' expectations.

5. **If you yell at the umpire, you get thrown out of the game.**
   Experienced leaders know that you should not confront authority figures in public or cause them to lose face in front of others, even if they are wrong. They know that when you have an honest disagreement with the authority person, you should go to that person's office and close the door for your discussion. When you emerge, you should support the commonly agreed upon position.

Figure 3.11
Rules of the game.

tain members may possess, and/or past experiences working together, "experts" within problem-solving groups may emerge. Teams committed to professional collaboration need to remember to: (a) establish a reliable, problem-solving format, (b) utilize effective communication skills, (c) periodically discuss their fundamental assumptions of effective collaboration, and (d) monitor their team's interactions on an ongoing basis to ensure the process is working effectively. (p. 339)

6. **Don't go off half-cocked until you have all the facts.**
   Overreaction is a common error, particularly among first-time leaders who might think they need to assert their authority. It can be costly, particularly if an action is taken before the whole picture is assessed.

7. **If I didn't laugh, my heart would break.**
   If the role of leader is taken seriously all the time, it is easy to become tense and discouraged and eventually become ineffective. Sometimes the best way to deal with a situation is to laugh and relieve some of the tension.

8. **Follow the invisible leader—the common purpose.**
   The most effective leaders have learned how to generate group support for their ideas by instilling within the group a sense of "ownership" for the ideas. They begin by listening carefully to what others have to say and by analyzing the effect of a particular plan on other team members.

9. **Speak softly but carry a big stick.**
   Some people who aspire to become leaders or who find themselves in leadership roles think they have to prove they are powerful by being pushy. This behavior usually has the opposite effect of turning people away from their leadership. Those who are successful have learned the value of using a soft, polite tone rather than acting every role as if they were starring in a tough-guy movie.

10. **It ain't over 'til it's over.**
    Going back into the game to try again, even in the face of an apparent defeat, is the mark of a champion. All experienced leaders know that you win some and you lose some. It isn't important, or possible, to win them all. Keeping your perspective is a matter of understanding that the score at the end of the game is more important than the score at the half, and that the win/loss record at the end of the season is the record that counts. Effective leaders are persistent in the face of obstacles. When they fail to win their points, they come back to pursue the issue in a different way or at another time.

Figure 3.11, *continued*

Commitment to Common Goals

The final dimension necessary for an interactive team to be a successful and effective operating unit is shared commitment to common goals. The primary goal is to meet the needs of students. To accomplish this within an interactive teaming framework, team members must believe that collaboration, teaming, and integrating services are viable and vital ways to meet students' needs. As Mostert (1998) commented:

Most societies and organizations operate on the understanding that, at least for part of the time, it is necessary for members to collaborate for the good of a common goal—a goal that most or all members agree is worth attaining. The necessity of col-

The following steps need to be adapted to specific situations, including whether this is a first meeting, a follow-up meeting, or a meeting to make a specific decision such as determination of placement.

1. The person designated as leader or chairperson should *notify the other members* of a meeting time and place, and distribute any available background information to be read before the discussion.

2. At the beginning of the meeting, the leader should make sure everyone has met the others and *state the purpose* and agenda items.

3. The person who requested the meeting should *describe the problem(s).* Other group members should ask questions for clarification, if necessary, and also contribute their own observations to corroborate or contrast with the problem being described.

4. The group should reach consensus on a specific, measureable, and observable *definition of the problem.* (For example, if the problem presented is "Gerry has a bad attitude about school," group members should ask questions and discuss the situation to determine if this means she does not start assignments when directions are given, is not making passing grades on tests, is not submitting her homework, or has been truant.)

5. If more than one problem is identified, each should be discussed, and then all should be *prioritized in terms of importance* to child's and adult's well-being, *and in terms of severity levels.* The desired level of performance (e.g., 75% or better on tests, no more than two absences per month) also should be determined.

6. The *history and frequency* of the problem should be determined (e.g., the problem has occurred 17 times in the last four weeks).

7. Any *previous interventions attempted* should be discussed, and their success or lack of success should be presented. This is an important step to keep from continually suggesting ideas that have been attempted, and it is also an opportunity to build on strategies that have proved effective.

Figure 3.12
Implementation procedures.

laboration should not eliminate the need for competition or individualism, but should rather be viewed as one tool for achieving certain goals that may be untenable in any other way. For example, collaborative efforts in certain circumstances may often achieve much more than any individual effort: many positive benefits are derived from working with others, and collective ownership and responsibility in professional work are often seen as preferable to individual risk-taking. (p. 15)

Consistent with this belief, those involved in interactive teaming must recognize that the "whole is greater than the sum of the parts"; that is, professionals

8. All team members should *brainstorm possible interventions*. Consensus should be reached on which interventions should be attempted in which order and by whom. Consistency in applying reinforcers and consequences should be a primary consideration. If consensus is not readily obtainable, one of the strategies described in Chapter 5 on communication skills, such as the Nominal Group Technique, should be used.

9. Procedures for *collecting data* should be established. It is important to have a data collection system and to implement it to be able to decide on the effectiveness or failure of an intervention. The major criteria for the data collection system are that it measures the target behavior accurately, is easy to implement, and does not interfere with teaching (cf. Tawney & Gast, 1984; Wolery, Bailey, & Sugai, 1988).

10. The *data decision rules* should be determined (i.e., how long will an intervention be attempted before switching to another one). An important consideration is that the intervention needs to be applied consistently and on consecutive days for at least three to five days before a decision can be made on whether it is having the desired effect. An additional consideration is that for some behaviors such as talk-outs, an intervention that involves removal of attention (e.g., ignoring) may result in the behavior getting worse before it gets better.

11. The *responsibilities* for each team member should be clarified. If one or more members are going to provide information or materials, conduct additional observations, consult with others, or serve as reinforcers or people who will deliver negative consequences, these expectations should be clear to everyone.

12. A *timeline for activities* and a follow-up meeting to assess progress should be scheduled.

13. The team should meet regularly to *evaluate the interventions* to determine if changes or modifications need to be made.

14. Members of the team should meet as needed to provide *consultative and collaborative* assistance to each other.

15. Team members should *evaluate team effectiveness* periodically and determine if any changes need to be made in operating procedures, team composition, or other areas.

Figure 3.12, *continued*

and parents can achieve better results working together than when they operate as individuals or separate disciplines (Dunn, 1989; Garner, 1995; Gutkin, 1996; Pugach, 1988). The services provided will be more comprehensive and less fragmented, multiple interventions can be implemented simultaneously, and the chances of behaviors being learned and generalized are greatly increased (Adamson, Cox, & Schuller, 1989; Golightly, 1987; Idol, Nevin, & Paolucci-Whitcomb, 1994).

A secondary goal, which follows from the first, is the support of the concepts of professional development and role release. Professionals and parents must be willing to share ideas and techniques with others, and support their fellow team members in implementing what has been learned. Such sharing may require "paradigm shifts" to better understand one another (Lopez, Dalal, & Yoshida, 1993), and taking responsibility for one's own learning as well as the learning of others (Skrtic, 1991).

If the commitment to students rather than "turf" or the commitment to assisting fellow team members is missing, the team concept will not succeed. If the commitment and the other dimensions are present, the interactive team can be effective. As illustrated in Figure 3.13, the effective team is unified in working toward a shared goal, and the ineffective team is bogged down.

We next examine two descriptions of a team meeting, one unsuccessful and the other successful. In the first example, the leader does not seem aware of the necessary dimensions of teaming. He is not aware of the individuality of team members, does not attend to the process of team building, uses an inappropriate sequence of procedures, and exhibits an ineffective leadership style. Note how these factors interplay to produce an unsuccessful, dysfunctional teaming session.

◇ ◇

Application: Unsuccessful Teaming

At the beginning of the first meeting of the team, the leader stated that this session needed to be "short and sweet" because he had a more important meeting to attend in 30 minutes. The foster mother for Angelina was immediately angered by the comment. She emphatically stated that she was not interested in participating in a meeting that people did not consider important. The social worker tried to calm her down, and suggested that the meeting proceed but that they could schedule additional time if needed. The leader then said, "Well, we all know that Angelina has been abused, and her biological mother is a crack cocaine addict. Now who has some ideas on what can be done?" The psychologist said he would like to share test results, but the special educator broke in and said she needed to know how to handle this child in her classroom tomorrow, because she had displayed very aggressive behaviors for the past 2 days. The foster mother began to describe how she used time-out at home, but the leader said, "I'm sorry to interrupt, but I really must leave for my next meeting. When would you like to meet again?"

◇ ◇

In the second example, the leader ensures that the competencies of team members are recognized and their roles are clear. He allows time for the team to build and follows a sequence of steps to lead the group through the meeting. He also promotes the concept of role release. Notice how these factors promote successful teaming.

AN EFFECTIVE TEAM	AN INEFFECTIVE TEAM
A team is a unified group of people who join in a cooperative problem-solving process to reach a shared goal.	• Goals are unclear • Members are unprepared • Leadership is poor • Commitment to task is lacking

EFFECTIVE	INEFFECTIVE
Participation and leadership are distributed among all members.	Participation is unequal, leadership is delegated and based on authority.
Goals are cooperatively formed to meet individual and group needs.	Members accept imposed goals.
Ability and information determine influence and power.	Position determines influence; obedience to authority is stressed.
Two-way communication.	Communication about ideas is one-way; feelings are ignored.
Decision-making steps are matched with situation; consensus is sought for important decisions.	Decisions are made by highest authority with minimal member involvement.
Conflict is brought out and resolved.	Conflict is ignored, avoided, or denied.

Figure 3.13

Characteristics of effective and ineffective teams.

Source: From "An Inservice Program for Improving Team Participation in Educational Decision-Making" by L. S. Anderlini, 1983, *School Psychology Review, 12,* p. 163. Reprinted by permission of the publisher.

◇ ◇

Application: Successful Teaming

At the beginning of the first meeting of the team, the leader asked all the members to introduce themselves and describe their roles and relationships to Angelina. After this was accomplished, the leader suggested that each person share any observations or assessment data that had been completed at the time. He also encouraged team members to ask questions as each individual gave his or her report. Next, he asked everyone to identify what he or she considered to be the primary problems in this case.

After a discussion that included the history and frequency of the problems, the group was able to reach consensus that the two top-priority problems were Angelina's kicking others and hitting herself on the head. The leader asked if anyone had identified interventions that were successful for either of these behaviors. The foster mother described how she had used time-out, and the special educator discussed how she had used selective attention and praised Angelina when she interacted appropriately. The counselor suggested including Angelina in a peer group that she conducted for abused and acting-out students. The adapted physical educator discussed games he could share with the special educator that developed cooperation skills.

The leader recommended closing the meeting and scheduling the next meeting in 2 weeks to discuss Angelina's progress and how the interventions of time-out and selective attention were working in the other settings. He also recommended that individual group members continue their discussions in the intervening time so information on particular strategies could be shared. The counselor agreed to contact the foster mother about the groups, and the special educator and adapted physical educator agreed to meet the next day to continue their discussion on cooperative games.

◇ ◇

SUMMARY

Consideration of the research of models and programs with components of interactive teaming suggests that 10 dimensions must be present for the model to be effective:

◆ Legitimacy and autonomy.
◆ Purpose and objectives.
◆ Competencies of team members and clarity of their roles.
◆ Role release and role transitions.
◆ Awareness of the individuality of team members.

◆ Process of team building.

◆ Attention to factors that affect team functioning.

◆ Leadership styles.

◆ Implementation procedures.

◆ Commitment to common goals.

Factors considered to be possible barriers to interactive teaming—such as a lack of role understanding and communication skills, leadership problems, and a lack of awareness of cultural and family considerations—are addressed in the next section of this text.

ACTIVITIES

1. Interview a professional involved in service delivery to at-risk children or students with special needs. Ask how role release is accomplished in his or her job. Also ask which aspects of the role are difficult to release, and which aspects should not be attempted by someone who does not have professional training in that area.

2. Identify your Professional Stage, Career Cycle, and Conceptual Stage. How are they alike and how are they different? Which experiences and educational opportunities do you think have contributed to your cycle and stages?

3. Observe a team meeting and analyze the *goal structures, communication climates,* and *roles* that occur. What contributed to each? Were people consistent or did they change during the course of the meeting?

4. Interview four professionals who have been on teams. Ask them how the team was established and maintained. Also ask them to identify the decision-making processes and implementation procedures used by their teams. Finally, ask them to classify the leadership style of the person in charge of the team as authoritarian, democratic, or laissez-faire.

REFERENCES

Abelson, M. A., & Woodman, R. W. (1983). Review of research on team effectiveness: Implications for teams in schools. *School Psychology Review, 12,* 125–136.

Adamson, D. R., Cox, J., & Schuller, J. (1989). Collaboration/consultation: Bridging the gap from resource room to regular classroom. *Teacher Education and Special Education, 12,* 46–51.

Aldinger, L. E., Warger, C. L., & Eavy, P. W. (1991). *Strategies for teacher collaboration.* Ann Arbor, MI: Exceptional Innovations, Inc.

Anderlini, L. S. (1983). An inservice program for improving team participation in educational decision-making. *School Psychology Review, 12,* 160–167.

Bailey, D. B. (1984). A triaxial model of the inter-disciplinary team and group process. *Exceptional Children, 51*, 17–25.

Bailey, D. B. (1987). Collaborative goal-setting with families: Resolving differences in values and priorities for services. *Topics in Early Childhood Special Education, 7*(2), 59–71.

Benne, K. D., & Sheats, P. (1948). Functional roles of group members. *Journal of Social Issues, 4,* 41–49.

Berry, T. H. (1991). *Managing the total quality transformation.* New York: McGraw-Hill.

Blankstein, A. M. (1992). Lessons from enlightened corporations. *Educational Leadership, 49,* 71–74.

Blanton, L. P., Griffin, C. C., Winn, J. A., & Pugach, M. C. (Eds.) (1997). *Teacher education in transition: Collaborative programs to prepare general and special educators.* Denver, CO: Love Publishing Co.

Brown, B., Pryzwansky, W. B., & Schulte, A. C. (1998). *Psychological consultation: Introduction to theory and practice.* Needham Heights, MA: Allyn & Bacon.

Bruneau-Balderrama, O. (1997). Inclusion: Making it work for teachers, too. *The Clearing House, 70*(6), 328–330.

Burke, P. S., Christensen, J. C., & Fessler, R. (1984). *Teacher career stages: Implications for staff development.* Bloomington, IN: Phi Delta Kappa Foundation.

Courtnage, L., & Healy, H. (1984). Interdisciplinary team training: A competency- and procedure-based approach. *Teacher Education and Special Education, 7,* 3–11.

Covey, S. R. (1991). *Principle-centered leadership.* New York: Simon & Schuster.

David, J. L. (1989). Synthesis of research on school-based management. *Educational Leadership, 46*(8), 45–58.

Delbecq, A. L., Van de Ven, A. H., & Gustafson, D. H. (1975). *Group techniques for program planning: A guide to nominal group and delphi processes.* Glenview, IL: Scott, Foresman.

Deming, W. E. (1986). *Out of the crisis.* Boston: MIT Center for Advanced Engineering Studies.

Doyle, M., & Strauss, D. (1976). *How to make meetings work: The new interaction method.* Chicago: Playboy Press.

Dunn, W. (1989). Integrated related services for preschoolers with neurological impairments: Issues and strategies. *Remedial and Special Education, 10*(3), 31–39.

Elliot, S. N., & Sheridan, S. M. (1992). Consultation and teaming: Problem solving among educators, parents, and support personnel. *The Elementary School Journal, 92,* 315–338.

Epstein, L. (1988). *Helping people: The task centered approach.* New York: Merrill/Macmillan.

Fine, M. J., Grantham, V. L., & Wright, J. G. (1979). Personal variables that facilitate or impede consultation. *Psychology in the Schools, 16,* 533–539.

Fishbaugh, M. S. E. (1997). *Models of collaboration.* Needham Heights, MA: Allyn & Bacon.

Fuller, G. (1998). *Win/win management: Leading people in the new workplace.* Paramus, NJ: Prentice Hall Press.

Garner, H. G. (1995). *Teamwork models and experience in education.* Boston, MA: Allyn & Bacon.

Gerber, S. (1991). Supporting the collaborative process. *Preventing School Failure, 35*(4), 48–52.

Gibb, J. R. (1961). Defensive communication. *Journal of Communication, 11,* 141–148.

Glickman, C. D. (1995). *Supervision of instruction* (4th ed.). Boston: Allyn & Bacon.

Golightly, C. J. (1987). Transdisciplinary training: A step forward in special education teacher preparation. *Teacher Education and Special Education, 10,* 126–130.

Goodlad, J. I. (1997). *In praise of education.* New York: Teachers College Press.

Gutkin, T. B. (1996). Core elements of consultation service delivery for special service personnel: Rationale, practice, and some directions for the future. *Remedial and Special Education, 17*(6), 333–340.

Gutkin, T. B., & Curtis, M. J. (1990). School-based consultation: Theory, techniques, and research. In T. B. Gutkin and C. R. Reynolds (Eds.), *The handbook of school psychology* (2nd ed.), (pp. 577–611). New York: Wiley.

Hanson, M. J., & Widerstrom, A. H. (1992). Consultation and collaboration: Essentials of integration efforts for young children. In C. A. Peck, S. L. Odom, and D. D. Bricker (Eds.), *Integrating young children with disabilities into community programs: Ecological perspectives on research and implementation* (pp. 149–168). Baltimore, MD: Paul H. Brookes.

Harris, K. C. (1996). Collaboration within a multicultural society: Issues for consideration. *Remedial and Special Education, 17*(6), 355–362, 376.

Harrison, C. R., Killion, J. P., & Mitchell, J. E. (1989). Site-based management: The realities of implementation. *Educational Leadership, 46*(8), 55–58.

Hasazi, S. B., Furney, K. S., & DeStefano, L. (1999). Implementing the IDEA transition mandates. *Exceptional Children, 65*(4), 555–566.

Helms, J. (1992). *A race is a nice thing to have.* Topeka, KS: Content Communications.

Hudson, P. J., Correa, V. I., Morsink, C. V., & Dykes, M. K. (1987). A new model for preservice training: Teacher as collaborator. *Teacher Education and Special Education, 10,* 191–193.

Hunt, D. E. (1981). Teachers' adaptation: "Reading" and "flexing" to students. In B. Joyce, C. Brown, & L. Peck (Eds.), *Flexibility in teaching.* New York: Longman Publishers.

Hybels, S., & Weaver, R. L. (1997). *Communicating effectively* (5th ed.). New York: McGraw-Hill.

Idol, L., Nevin, A., & Paolucci-Whitcomb, P. (1994). *Collaborative consultation* (2nd ed.). Austin, TX: Pro-Ed.

Jayanthi, M., & Friend, M. (1992). Interpersonal problem solving: A selective literature review to guide practice. *Journal of Educational and Psychological Consultation, 3*(1), 39–53.

Johnson, D. W., & Johnson, R. T. (1987). Research shows the benefits of adult cooperation. *Educational Leadership, 45*(3), 27–30.

Johnson, D. W., Johnson, R. T., & Holubec, E. (1986). *Circles of learning: Cooperation in the classroom* (rev. ed.). Edina, MN: Interaction Book Company.

Johnson, L. J., Pugach, M. C., & Devlin, S. (1990). Professional collaboration: Challenges of the next decade. *Teaching Exceptional Children, 22*(2), 9–11.

Kabler, M. L., & Genshaft, J. L. (1983). Structuring decision-making in multidisciplinary teams. *School Psychology Review, 12,* 150–159.

Kaiser, S. M., & Woodman, R. W. (1985). Multidisciplinary teams and group decision-making techniques: Possible solutions to decision-making problems. *School Psychology Review, 14,* 457–470.

Katzenbach, J. R., & Smith, D. K. (1999). *The wisdom of teams: Creating the high-performance organization.* Boston: Harvard Business School Press.

Kruger, L. J., Struzziero, J., Watts, R., & Vacca, D. (1995). The relationship between organizational support and satisfaction with teacher assistance teams. *Remedial and Special Education, 16*(4), 203–211.

Larson, C. E., & LaFasto, F. M. J. (1989). *Teamwork.* Beverly Hills, CA: Sage.

Laycock, V. K., Gable, R. A., & Korinek, L. (1991). Alternative structures for collaboration in the delivery of special services. *Preventing School Failure, 35*(4), 15–18.

Lezotte, L. W. (1989). School improvement based on the effective schools research. In D. K. Lipsky & A. Gartner (Eds.), *Beyond separate education: Quality education for all.* Baltimore, MD: Paul H. Brookes.

Lopez, E. C., Dalal, S. M., & Yoshida, R. K. (1993). An examination of professional cultures: Implications for the collaborative consultation model. *Journal of Educational and Psychological Consultation, 4,* 197–213.

Lyon, S., & Lyon, G. (1980). Team functioning and staff development: A role release approach to providing integrated educational services for severely handicapped students. *Journal of the Association for the Severely Handicapped, 5,* 250–263.

Maher, C. A., & Hawryluk, M. K. (1983). Framework and guidelines for utilization of teams in schools. *School Psychology Review, 12,* 180–185.

Margolis, H., & Brannigan, G. G. (1987). Problem solving with parents. *Academic Therapy, 22,* 423–425.

Mather, J., & Weinstein, E. (1988). Teachers and therapists: Evolution of a partnership in early intervention. *Topics in Early Childhood Special Education, 7,* 1–9.

Mostert, M. P. (1998). *Interprofessional collaboration in schools.* Needham Heights, MA: Allyn & Bacon.

National Commission on Teaching and America's Future (1996). *What matters most: Teaching for America's future.* New York: National Commission on Teaching and America's Future.

Orelove, F. P., & Sobsey, D. (1991). *Educating children with multiple disabilities: A transdisciplinary approach* (2nd ed.). Baltimore, MD: Paul H. Brookes.

Orlich, D. C. (1989). Education reforms: Mistakes, misconceptions, miscues. *Phi Delta Kappan, 70,* 512–517.

O'Shea, L. J., O'Shea, D. J., & Algozzine, R. (1998). *Learning disabilities: From theory toward practice.* Upper Saddle River, NJ: Merrill/Prentice Hall.

Peryon, C. D. (1982). Systematic development of special educators as facilitators of mainstreaming. *Journal of Special Education Technology, 5*(3), 31–36.

Phillips, V., & McCullough, L. (1990). Consultation-based programming: Instituting the collaborative ethic in schools. *Exceptional Children, 56,* 291–304.

Pugach, M. C. (1988). Restructuring teaching. *Teaching Exceptional Children, 21,* 47–50.

Quigney, T. (1998). Collaborative teacher training for special and general educators: Rationale and recurring themes. *B. C. Journal of Special Education, 21*(3), 20–32.

Ramirez, S. A., Lepage, K. M., Kratchowill, T. R., & Duffy, J. L. (1998). Multicultural issues in school-based consultation: Conceptual and research considerations. *Journal of School Psychology, 36*(4), 479–509.

Salend, S. J. (1998). *Effective mainstreaming: Creating inclusive classrooms* (3rd ed.). Upper Saddle River, NJ: Merrill/Prentice Hall.

Salvia, J., & Ysseldyke, J. E. (1988). *Assessment in special and remedial education* (4th ed.). Boston: Houghton Mifflin.

Sheehy, G. (1977). *Passages—Predictable crises in adult life.* New York: Bantam Books.

Siders, J. A., Riall, A., Bennett, T. C., & Judd, D. (1987). Training of leadership personnel in early intervention: A transdisciplinary approach. *Teacher Education and Special Education, 10*(4), 161–170.

Skrtic, T. M. (1991). The special education paradox: Equity as the way to excellence. *Harvard Educational Review, 61,* 148–191.

Smith, J. D. (1998). *Inclusion: Schools for all students.* Belmont, CA: Wadsworth Publishing Company.

Sprinthall, N. A., & Thies-Sprinthall, L. (1983). The teacher as an adult learner: A cognitive-developmental view. *National Society for the Study of Education, 82nd Yearbook.* Chicago: The University of Chicago Press.

Sue, D. W., Arredondo, P., & McDavis, J. R. (1995). Multicultural counseling competencies and standards: A call to the profession. In J. G. Ponterotto, J. M. Casas, L. A. Suzuki, and C. M. Alexander (Eds.), *Handbook of multicultural counseling* (pp. 624–644). Thousand Oaks, CA: Sage.

Tawney, J. W., & Gast, D. L. (1984). *Single subject research in special education.* New York: Merrill/Macmillan.

Tiegerman-Farber, E., & Radziewicz, C. (1998). *Collaborative decision making: The pathway to inclusion.* Upper Saddle River, NJ: Merrill/Prentice Hall.

Tuckman, B. W., & Jensen, M. A. C. (1977). Stages of small group development revisited. *Group and Organization Studies, 2,* 419–427.

Turnbull, R., & Cilley, M. (1999). *Explanations and implications of the 1997 amendments to IDEA.* Upper Saddle River, NJ: Merrill/Prentice Hall.

United Cerebral Palsy Association. (1976). *Staff development handbook: A resource for the transdisciplinary process.* New York: Author.

Voltz, D. L., Elliott Jr., R. N., & Harris, W. B. (1995). Promising practices in facilitating collaboration between resource room teachers and general education teachers. *Learning Disabilities Research and Practice, 10*(2), 129–136.

Walton, M. (1990). *Deming management at work.* New York: G. P. Putnam's Sons.

Wangemann, P., Ingram, C. F., & Muse, I. D. (1989). A successful university–public school collaboration: The union of theory and practice. *Teacher Education and Special Education, 12,* 61–64.

West, J. F., & Cannon, G. S. (1988). Essential collaborative consultation competencies for regular and special educators. *Journal of Learning Disabilities, 21*(28), 56–63.

Wolery, M., Bailey, D. B., & Sugai, G. M. (1988). *Effective teaching: Principles and procedures of applied behavior analysis with exceptional students.* Boston: Allyn & Bacon.

Wood, J. W. (1998). *Adapting instruction to accommodate students in inclusive settings* (3rd ed.). Upper Saddle River, NJ: Merrill/Prentice Hall.

Yoshida, R. K. (1983). Are multidisciplinary teams worth the investment? *School Psychology Review, 12,* 137–143.

Facilitating Factors

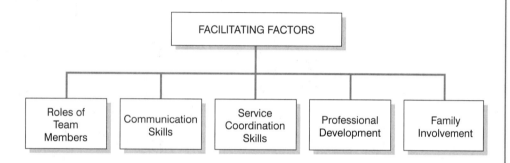

OVERVIEW

The chapters in this part describe the facilitating factors that contribute to effective team functioning. Chapter 4 on the roles of team members provides descriptions of the roles of special educators, related professionals, and para-professionals. The chapter also illustrates how team members can provide direct services and serve as collaborators. In Chapter 5 communication is defined, and factors to consider in communication are explained. The verbal and nonverbal forms of communication are described, and strategies for managing conflict and resistance are presented.

Chapter 6 includes a definition of service coordination skills; in this chapter, essential parameters for the leadership of professionals are identified and guidelines for the procedures that team leaders should implement are explained. Chapter 7 includes a description of power and empowerment, and illustrates three types of professional development. The final chapter in this part, Chapter 8, contains descriptions of factors that have influenced changes in attitudes about family involvement and outlines how family members can assist in providing services to their children as they fulfill vital roles as interactive team members.

4 Understanding Roles and Perspectives of Team Members

Topics in this chapter include:

- Overview of the problems and promises of teaming with professionals who have different goals, training, and perspectives.
- Description of the changes in the composition and functions of the team, as determined by the complexity of the problem and the type of facility within which it operates.
- Descriptions of the roles of each team member, both as direct service provider and as collaborator or consultant, and discussion of the overlapping functions of certain roles.
- Application of the interactive teaming model to a case in which the special education teacher and speech-language therapist collaborate to help a special student with language development, and application of the model in a hospital setting, in which the pediatric nurse serves as team leader.

◇ ◇

Darrell, a 12-year-old middle school student with a moderate cognitive disability, was the subject of a team meeting to plan his instructional program. Darrell went to live with his maternal grandmother after his mother died in childbirth. He was placed in a compensatory education program when he entered school as a 6-year-old, then placed in a part-time special education resource room a year later. In the current meeting to plan his instructional program, the team was to focus on moving Darrell into the regular education classroom part time, while continuing the support he and his family were receiving in the form of remedial reading, speech-language therapy, behavior modification, and nutritional counseling. His grandmother, who was elderly and unemployed, was receiving public assistance for herself and for Darrell.

The school psychologist said, "Darrell is functioning within the range of mild to moderate cognitive disability. His academic achievement scores, according to the WRAT, are significantly below his grade level but consistent with expectations given his mental age. He exhibits passive-aggressive behavior with adults, while becoming more openly hostile with his peers."

The speech-language therapist said, "His primary disability is a moderate developmental delay in language acquisition, which impedes his social and academic functioning. I need to conduct a current language assessment, with particular emphasis on his MLU."

The dietitian said, "His nutritional intake may be a contributing factor to his attention deficit disorder. I suggest that he receive a more balanced diet, emphasizing complex carbohydrates, while limiting the number of exchanges in saturated fats and synthetic sugars."

The social worker said, "He is eligible for related special services such as speech therapy and nutritional counseling, which could be supported by third-party payments."

Darrell's grandmother, who was totally confused, simply nodded her head and smiled.

Darrell's case illustrates dramatically the differences in the roles, perspectives, and vocabularies of professionals on the interactive team. Because each person is a highly trained professional, he or she has specialized knowledge to contribute to the solution of problems. This professional training can be a major asset to the functioning of the team when the professional's knowledge is recognized and translated in a meaningful way. Or it can become a barrier, leading to misunderstanding, territoriality, and conflict.

In this chapter, the differences in the roles and perspectives of team members are described. The changes in the composition and functions of the team are explained according to the context in which it operates—the program for students who are culturally different, who have mild disabilities, or who have severe disabilities. The contributions of each team member, both as a service provider and as a collaborator, are defined. The interactive teaming model is applied to Darrell's case, described above, in an example showing consultation and collaboration between two members of the team, the special education teacher and the speech-language therapist. The model is also applied to cases involving short-term hospital-related programs coordinated by the pediatric nurse.

ROLES AND PERSPECTIVES OF TEAM MEMBERS

The first major task in establishing interactions among team members is recognizing that these individuals have widely disparate roles, vocabularies, and perspectives as a result of their highly specialized professional training. These differences can lead to misunderstanding and bickering among participants (Pipho, 1997). These differences, however, can also be viewed as potential strengths if they are respected by all members of the team and used appropriately by the leader.

Collaboration among professionals is particularly difficult when it involves members of the education and the allied health professions. Eggers (1983) described their difficulties as follows:

> Imagine a sporting event with doctors, nurses, therapists and other health professionals competing against educators and developmental psychologists. Each team insists that the game be played on their field by their rules—impossible conditions for productive, organized competition. . . . The silliness of the image fades and is replaced by an image of a child being pulled in multiple directions by different types of professionals while bewildered, frustrated parents pace the sidelines. (p. 2)

The differences among members of the health-related and education professions are real. In health-related professions, specialists call the people they serve "patients" or "clients"; they provide "treatment" as short-term health care, usually in response to a crisis. Education-related professionals call the people they serve "students" and they provide "treatment" as long-term instruction from a developmental perspective.

In addition, the range and nature of the advocacy groups, organizations, and regulations with which each group must deal are different. While educators function within organizations dependent on public funds and regulated by legislative mandates, health professionals often receive reimbursement from third parties such as insurance companies, Medicaid, and the Social Security system, each having its own set of forms and payment schedules. Each group of professionals has its own perspective, as well as multiple layers of subspecialties. Collaboration becomes increasingly difficult as the layers of subspecialties increase.

TEAM COMPOSITION AND FUNCTIONS

The team's composition and functions are affected by new trends in service delivery which have increased the number of programs available at the preschool and postschool level, the presence of larger numbers of students with disabilities in regular classrooms, and the expansion of health-related and justice system services for students with severe disabilities. Changes in the composition and functions of the team are also resulting from the fact that the number of persons on the team is variable, depending on the nature of the problems it addresses.

TRENDS IN SERVICE DELIVERY

Two trends in service delivery for special needs students have implications for team composition and functions. One of these trends is the expansion of educational programs into preschool, postschool, and regular classroom settings. The other involves changes in the health care system.

Expansion into New Settings

The expansion of educational programs increases the need for professionals to interact with others outside of their traditional groups. For example, McLesky, Henry, and Hodges (1998) documented a 60% increase in the number of students with disabilities placed in general education classrooms from 1988–1989 to 1994–1995. Interactions frequently extend into the related professions of human and social services, including the juvenile justice system, making coordination both more important and more complicated. Professionals across agencies are required to advocate for children and help the families of these children negotiate the multiple bureaucracies that provide service delivery (Davenport, 1990).

Although it is difficult to work across these boundaries, preliminary data indicate that such efforts can be productive (National Center for Schools and Communities, 1998; O'Neil, 1997). Many of these programs extend school services into communities, providing after-school activities, legal, and health assistance (Frischkorn, 1997), social services through family centers (Bush & Wilson, 1997) and comprehensive shelters for homeless families (Nunez & Collignon, 1997). Yale researchers, summarizing the results of 72 collaborative programs for children and their families, have concluded that interagency links have provided both program quality and cost effectiveness (Kagan & Rivera, 1990). They cited (1) training for caregivers and teachers, (2) consistent regulations based on joint planning, and (3) parental involvement among the practices they identified as promising.

New preschool programs reflect the growing emphasis on early intervention for children who have disabilities or are at risk (Magna Awards, 1998). Team members will need to be aware that it is especially important to promote active social interactions between children, particularly in situations that can facilitate improved play behaviors (Esposito & Koorland, 1989; Guralnick & Groom, 1988).

Increased family involvement will also be essential in preschool, postschool, and extended services programs. Successful service delivery will be based on understanding of new family styles, diversity, and their adverse conditions (Vincent & Salisbury, 1988). Team members will need to include parents as full partners in decision making, de-emphasizing traditional views of "dominant and submissive" roles (Wells, 1997; Darling, 1989). They will also need to remain sensitive to the family's needs for privacy (Krauss, 1990), as well as "after-hours" meeting times (Meyer, 1997).

Preschool services also extend to the provision of services for infants as required by Public Law 99-457. Larger numbers of infants will survive as medical science advances and many of them will require special education services (Bartel & Thurmond, 1992; Odom & Warren, 1988). Team members will need to consider services for these infants and toddlers as noncategorical (Mack, 1988). Decision makers will also need to consider the new research findings, which indicate that with intensive, high-quality instruction, a low student–teacher ratio, and establishment of a predictable environment, it is possible that even drug-exposed babies can score normally on developmental tests by the age of 2 (Bellisimo, 1990; Rist, 1990). Effective programs, however, will require collaborative planning among agencies.

Team members also need to design programs for postschool students who are transitioning between traditional schooling and employment. Among the issues these teams will confront are the following:

◆ More people with disabilities are now employed. There is increasing employer awareness that, as a group, workers with disabilities are above average in dependability and job stability (Chamberlain, 1988). New regulations in the Americans with Disabilities Act require employers to analyze the essential functions of jobs and to make necessary modifications for workers with disabilities.

◆ Transition teams will design and coordinate training that enables students to succeed in the workforce. These training factors have been identified through research (Roessler, Brolin, & Johnson, 1990). A need has been identified for curriculum change (Halloran & Ward, 1988), placement in community-based programs (McDonnell, Hardman, & Hightower, 1989), and supported employment (Gemmel & Peterson, 1989) to facilitate transition to adult life for individuals with severe disabilities.

◆ Collaborative, interagency planning will be among the most important factors in the success of transition programs (Sileo, Rude, & Luckner, 1988).

Changes in the Health Care System

The context for changes in the health care system are summarized by Kristin J. Young, R.N., and reprinted with her permission, as follows:

> As recently as 20 years ago, people were hospitalized for what would now be considered minor illnesses. Children, in particular, would stay for many days in a hospital ward, frightened by the equipment and the strangers around them. Their parents would not be permitted to stay at their bedsides except during visiting hours, and they would be required to leave the room any time a procedure was to be done, forcing children to endure it alone. This emotional stress could interfere with the healing process and prolong the child's stay. The nurses assigned to these wards were expected to care for as many as 22 patients. After dispensing medications, changing dressings, emptying bedpans, and administering other treatments, the nurse had little time to address comfort concerns or see to the special needs of those who were physically, mentally, or behaviorally challenged. When children were released from the hospital, their parents were expected to care for them, without receiving much training from the hospital staff. If parents had difficulty providing care, the children were sent to extended care facilities, often located far from their homes, to be cared for by strangers in stark white uniforms.
>
> A number of factors, however, have had an impact on the way health care is delivered in the United States today. Giant steps have been made in the treatment of diseases and in the development of drugs. New requirements for insurance payments have resulted in diagnostic tests being conducted on an outpatient basis, with many illnesses now treated at home. State-of-the-art scanners and imagers can help physicians identify problems that previously required exploratory surgery. Television and the Internet have affected health care by providing ways to communicate and educate the public about health issues. Patient awareness and early detection are the surest ways of maintaining health and preventing complications. Consequently, our overall population is stronger, healthier, and living longer, including our children with special needs.
>
> Children with special needs who must be admitted to the hospital are usually very ill, cannot be treated at home, and must stay for a long time. Their acuity level is high, requiring more skilled care. Doctors give less direct patient care; they oversee their patients' welfare with daily exams and change or write new orders to promote a good outcome, which the nurses carry out. Nurses have fewer patients, but they must now give a greater amount of care. Usually intravenous drug therapy is involved, which means the nurse is responsible for starting and maintaining the IV, something only doctors did in the past. Nurses are also responsible for coordinating the care a patient needs. That is where collaboration comes in.

Education professionals who work with P–12 students have become increasingly aware of and more involved in health-related issues in their classrooms. Demographic changes cited in Chapter 1 have led to increases in the numbers and complexity of health-related problems in school-aged students. Teachers are encouraged, for example, to become more aware of and more responsive to health problems such as asthma (Anderson & Luong, 1997). At the same time, schools with limited budgets are hiring health aides rather than registered nurses as school nurses, in an effort to save money (Cowell, 1998).

A number of health care issues related to the education of students with disabilities made national news in early 1999:

◆ On February 9, NBC-TV Nightly News reported that school nurses, now required in 17 states, were becoming primary care providers for many children with working parents. Now expected to do more than test vision and dispense bandages, the nurses are administering ritalin, teaching dental care, and helping to identify the victims of child abuse (NBC, 1999).

◆ On March 3, the Associated Press reported nationwide on the Supreme Court decision for Cedar Rapids, Iowa, finding that the daily health care by a registered nurse, for a high school sophomore who was quadriplegic and ventilator dependent, was essential for his access to integrated education, and should be financed by the school district under the Individuals with Disabilities Education Act (IDEA) (Associated Press, 1999).

◆ On August 3, *USA Today* reported on the recommendations from the American Academy of Pediatrics that physicians use a "media history" quiz with parents during their children's medical exams. The quiz would focus on children's television, movie and video viewing, video/computer game, and Internet use, radio/CD/tape listening habits, as well as child–parent interactions with books; it would also identify parental concerns about their children's use of tobacco, alcohol and drugs, sexuality and aggressive behavior (Elias, 1999).

These examples are but a few of the many related to the scope and magnitude of changes in health care systems, which continue to impact methods of service delivery for students with disabilities.

CHANGES IN TEAM COMPOSITION AND FUNCTIONS

As indicated in Chapter 1, an interactive team can consist of as few as two members or as many as are required to provide the specialized knowledge and skills for the student in question. The number of people on the team increases with the complexity and nature of the problem. Not all members are present at every meeting, and not every meeting of the team is formal. Professionals may interact informally as required to maintain communication and provide follow-up for the decisions made by the larger group.

It is also important to note that each team member has two functions: to provide direct services and to serve as a collaborator. *Direct services* are offered as individual "hands-on" activities with the special needs student and family. *Collaboration* falls under *indirect services,* that is, consultation on subjects in which he or she has expert knowledge, or team efforts to plan, implement, and evaluate the student's program.

Effective use of the specialized knowledge and skills of each member of the team requires an understanding of the knowledge and skills that other individuals have acquired through their professional training. It also requires appropriate application of these skills to the tasks for which the team has responsibility: planning, implementation, and evaluation of the special needs student's program.

The knowledge and skills of persons most often found on interactive teams are highlighted briefly in this chapter. In addition to the special educator, these teams can include family members, an administrator, classroom teacher, school psychologist, counselor, social worker, speech-language therapist, English as a second language (ESL) or bilingual education specialist, migrant or compensatory education teacher, school nurse, physical therapist, occupational therapist, and other health-related professionals.

Team members may also interact with specialists in adaptive technology, adaptive physical education, behavior analysis, juvenile justice, and vocational or transition education, and they may be responsible for the supervision of paraprofessionals. As indicated earlier, the number of people on a given team is dependent on the nature and complexity of the student's problems. In addition, the number of people available and the degree to which they serve as specialists or as generalists depends on factors such as the size of the school district or clinical facility and whether it is in a rural, suburban, or urban area. These factors can affect a district's or facility's financial resources and availability of specialized personnel.

ROLES OF SPECIAL EDUCATORS

The role of the special educator changes according to the context in which service is offered. Services may be provided for students who are culturally different or who have mild or severe disabilities. The roles of the special educator in each of these three contexts are outlined as follows and presented in greater detail in Chapters 9 through 12.

Role When Serving Culturally Different Students

The special or remedial educator who serves culturally different students interacts primarily with the student's family members, the school administrator, and classroom teachers. When the student speaks another language, the special educator also interacts with professionals trained in teaching bilingual education or ESL. In this capacity, the special educator is both a service provider and a collaborator.

Role as Service Provider. The knowledge and skills needed by the special educator who works with this population of students have been specified in detail by Fradd, Weismantel, Correa, and Algozzine (1988) and by Fox, Kuhlman, and Sales (1988). It is generally agreed that this professional should be aware of the problems inherent in teaching culturally different students and should demonstrate knowledge about cultural differences, as well as the ability to apply this knowledge in the instructional setting (Fox et al., 1988; Wlodkowski & Ginsberg, 1995). It is further recognized that the teacher of culturally different students needs some knowledge about language development, language assessment, and multicultural education systems (Fradd et al., 1988).

Role as Collaborator.   The team member who works with culturally different students also needs to be an effective collaborator. The understanding of one's own culture and cultural biases is an important step in the development of the flexibility and open-mindedness that characterize effective collaborators. Specific guidelines for these skills are presented in greater detail in Chapter 9 on cultural diversity.

Role When Serving Students with Mild Disabilities

The special or remedial educator who serves students with mild disabilities—those who are classified as having a learning disability, behavior disorder, or some mild cognitive, physical, or sensory disability—deals largely with the student's parents and with other members of the education profession. These people include the school administrator, school psychologist, counselor or social worker, behavior specialist, adaptive technology specialist, speech-language therapist, classroom teacher, adaptive physical educator, and paraprofessional. In most cases, the student with a mild disability will be served much of the time in a regular classroom.

Role as Service Provider.   The special or remedial educator who works with students with mild disabilities most often functions in a school-based setting, operating a resource, itinerant, or team-teaching program to provide part-time intervention for students with specific academic and behavioral difficulties. The primary functions of this role are student assessment, program evaluation, and the provision of instruction.

For the student who has had difficulties, the special educator may conduct an educational assessment, administering a series of tests to determine the student's current levels of functioning and specific deficits in academic areas such as reading, math, and study skills. The special educator may also observe the student in the regular classroom or evaluate the student's behavioral characteristics, using checklists and interviews with parents and teachers to collect data related to program eligibility and placement.

When the student's educational program is planned by the team, the special educator presents the data that were obtained. The special educator may also discuss the difficulties that typically characterize students in the specific category for which this student is being considered and present program placement options that seem most appropriate. This may happen less formally during pre-referral discussions.

When the instructional program has been implemented, the special educator measures the effectiveness of the program that has been designed, using continuous measurement techniques. These procedures enable the specialist to chart the student's performance on specific academic and behavioral objectives, and to obtain data that are useful both in making appropriate modifications and in communicating with other members of the team (Deno & Mirkin, 1977; Wesson, Fuchs, Tindal, Mirkin, & Deno, 1986).

The special educator's primary responsibility is to provide instructional services in an intensive (one-to-one or small group) short-term program. Usually this student receives services within the context of the regular classroom, frequently from the classroom teacher (Morsink & Lenk, 1992). The competencies needed by special educators of students with mild disabilities have been studied in depth and will be summarized in Chapter 11.

Role as Collaborator.   In addition to providing direct services to the student, the special educator has an important role as a collaborator on the related services team. The special educator provides information about the special student's learning needs and characteristics, and about special strategies and materials that have been found to be effective for students with certain difficulties. When providing this information, the special educator is a consultant to others.

The special educator also often functions collaboratively with others to collect additional data on the child's needs, during prereferral or before placement in a special program. Following the guidelines in the IDEA, the team that conducts the assessment is the same one that designs the student's Individual Education Program (IEP) (Turnbull & Cilley, 1999). Sometimes a behavior specialist and/or adaptive technology specialist is included on the team. Historically this group might be called the *teacher assistance team*, which functions to identify educational problems and develop interventions to be implemented by the referring classroom teacher (Campbell, 1987b). Teacher assistance teams have worked effectively to help teachers implement interventions for students with academic or behavior problems (Chalfant, 1989; Chalfant, Pysh, & Moultrie, 1979), and they have been discussed in Chapter 2.

Similarly, a prereferral intervention model based on an indirect, consultative model of service delivery has been successful in preventing future student problems. In the prereferral intervention model, the regular classroom teacher and special education consultant work together to increase the teacher's ability to individualize instruction for heterogeneous groups of students (Graden, Casey, & Christenson, 1985). Additional information on this topic is presented in Chapter 11.

Role When Serving Students with Severe Disabilities

The special educator who serves students with severe disabilities also fulfills the dual roles of service provider and collaborator. The service provided is—on a continuum—more nearly that of developmental/medical than educational/remedial assistance. The special education collaborator, in this case, is more closely aligned with members of the allied health professions than with classroom teachers and other general education personnel.

Role as Service Provider.   The student with severe disabilities often has multiple disabling conditions. These include physical and sensory disabilities, in addition to some degree of cognitive or neurological impairment. Also, these students may have manifestations of behavior disorders with a resultant need for behavior modification. And, because this student may take medications, suffer from seizures, or have special needs for medical equipment such as tracheotomy tubes or catheters, the special educator should have knowledge about the safe and legal use of procedures that may be required. Specialized competencies for teachers of students with physical and multiple disabilities have been studied in depth by Dykes, Brenner, and Lee (1985) and are presented in greater detail in Chapter 12. These generic techniques are required so that special education teachers are able to position, lift, and transport students; monitor use of medications and prosthetic devices; manage seizures; and modify aberrant behaviors.

The major function of the special educator who serves students with severe disabilities is to teach them and to synthesize their special related services. Because of the multiple disabilities involving related services of a medical nature, however, the teaching function may appear to be of secondary importance. The special educator plans, implements, and monitors an instructional program based on the student's current educational-developmental level. This program is most often based on the student's development of functional skills such as self-care, daily living, communications, and vocational skills. It should not, however, be based on the assumption of need for custodial care; instead, it should focus on the development of skills that maximize the student's opportunities for full participation in society, with consideration for the quality of life. A few programs that serve students with severe disabilities are in special classrooms or center schools; for students who require a continuous level of special instruction and an integrated educational/medical program, this type of placement may be appropriate. For most others, however, placement in regular schools may be workable and beneficial (Biklen, 1988).

Regardless of the setting in which the student with severe disabilities is placed, the role of the special educator also includes teaching students the skills of "normalization"—how to act and speak "normally" (Wolfensberger, 1972). Normalization strategies have been used to gain community acceptance of group homes for persons with cognitive impairment (Heal, Haney, & Novak Amado, 1988). Similarly, it has been found that the same strategy—emphasizing the disabled student's abilities and developing behaviors valued by the norm group—is instrumental in gaining acceptance for students with severe disabilities placed in regular classrooms (Biklen, 1988; Littlejohn, 1989). Recent studies show the positive effects of socialization experiences for students with disabilities on the attitudes of their high school classmates (Ferguson, 1997).

Finally, the teacher will want to become familiar with and seek resources for the implementation of new technology, particularly that related to computer use (Burkhead, Sampson, & McMahon, 1986; Morsink, 1984), which may enable individuals with disabilities to function independently and to participate more fully in the new information/service society (Naisbitt, 1982).

Role as Collaborator.   The special educator often functions as a collaborator in the position of team leader or *"educational synthesizer"* (Campbell, 1987a, p. 107). In this leadership position, the teacher uses an accepted functional curriculum to identify the content to be mastered by the student. Then the special educator coordinates the activities of related services professionals who design assessment and instructional procedures to accommodate the student's movement, vision, hearing, and postural limitations. The team leader coordinates the educational program through group meetings and review of the student's performance data, collected by the professionals who implement various aspects of the program. After reviewing these data, the coordinator determines whether the student is acquiring targeted skills and then communicates these findings to various team members, who subsequently make appropriate adjustments in the program.

The special educator who serves students with severe disabilities is often confronted with the need for *role release* (Bailey, 1984), as described in Chapter 3, in which team members share expertise and often more than one person on the team performs the same function. The professional development function is also important on the interactive team. At times this involves sharing information from one's own discipline with others who need to understand it to implement their component of the program effectively; at other times it requires the ability to respect and accept the consultation of parents and other professionals who are specialists in various aspects of the student's care program (Bailey, 1984).

◊ ◊

Application: Informational Interview

This application is based on the original work of Beach (1985) and is used here with her permission. Jean Beach is the special educator (SE) who works with Darrell, the student presented in the vignette at the beginning of this chapter, in the middle school special education resource room. Jean has made some observations of Darrell's language functioning in the resource room, and she is concerned that he has speech and language difficulties that are out of her area of expertise. She arranges for an *informational interview* with a team member, the speech-language therapist (SLT) who assists other students at the middle school. Jean is interested in observing the speech and language development program, in obtaining information about the referral process and screening/testing procedures, and in learning how to help Darrell and other students in her classroom who exhibit problems in language development.

She arranges to observe the SLT's language development group, which includes three other students from the special education resource room, during her planning period. Jean observes as the SLT directs activities in which the students learn analogies (e.g., "Pine trees have pine cones; apple trees have. . . . Trucks have wheels, dogs have. . . ."). Then she watches the SLT work with the group on articulating sounds in the initial, middle, and ending positions, using visual images presented as picture cards. Finally, she observes as the SLT administers a language test to another student, to determine his difficulties in phonology, syntax, semantics, memory, word finding, and retrieval. Jean makes notes on her observations, organizes the data she has collected on her observations of Darrell in the special education resource room, and arranges to meet with the SLT the next day to discuss what she has seen and request assistance with Darrell.

The conference begins with small talk about the school and their common training at the university where they both obtained their degrees, and it continues with Jean thanking the SLT for letting her observe the language development group and testing session the previous day. Then Jean addresses her concerns about Darrell's language difficulties.

SE: I have a student named Darrell in my resource room, who seems to have a lot of difficulties in language development. According to his cumulative folder, he was in the speech program once before—he has a structural deficit (some sort of hole in the speech mechanism itself)—but he received help in articulation and then was dismissed. He isn't having articulation problems like those of the other students I observed yesterday, but he certainly would have trouble with the analogies. I believe he has a more general language deficit, and I'm interested in referral to you for further testing. How do I proceed?

SLT: Here is a simple form. You just put the student's name and the date on the top line; then add a one-line description of your reason for the referral. I do testing one day a week. I would start with a screening test to determine if there is a need for further testing, and then—if more testing is necessary—we would get parent permission for a complete evaluation, including articulation, language development, voice, and fluency. After testing, I would meet with you and the parents to give you the results of what has been done and to make suggestions for future programming.

SE: I wasn't sure about the district's policy on testing. Do we need parent permission for routine screening?

SLT: No, but we would need permission for a complete evaluation and, of course, for placement if that is needed.

SE: When I observed your group yesterday, I saw that another student in my resource room, who is paired with Darrell for some language activities, was having a lot of trouble with the analogies. Both of these students read at the preprimer level, although they're in sixth grade. I find that a tape recorder is quite helpful in working with them on their reading vocabulary words. If you think the recorder would help with some of the other language development activities in my classroom, I could help you put words on tape, and then both of these students could listen to them to get a little more practice.

SLT: That's a really good idea. It is much more meaningful to students receiving special help if they can do some of the same language development activities in their own classroom. The coordination and repetition makes the special program more effective.

SE: When I work with both of these students in reading, I use a language experience approach that includes modified phonetics. Right now they are practicing the sh digraph in the initial position of words, such as ship, show, shine, and so on. Their words are pronounced on tape, while the student circles the picture showing the correct sound, given a choice of two pictures. I've been correcting their papers for the past two weeks and I've picked up certain consistent errors which I've charted on graph paper. Would you be interested in seeing the graph?

SLT: Oh, yes! That would be very helpful. If we're both picking up the same error patterns, then we can work together more effectively to help the students.

SE: I also work with Darrell in a general language arts class, and I notice that it is really difficult for him to respond appropriately during group activities. I know what he is trying to say, but it comes out wrong. He'll say "ain't got no" or something, and then the group laughs. How can I help him?

SLT: When you ask him to make a verbal response, do you use picture cards or some other kind of visual cues? Or do you just use words?

SE: I would be using a verbal format, with questions and answers.

SLT: It may be that he needs some additional visual cues to get the answers right. I have some syntax programs on picture cards; I'd be happy to let you borrow them to see if they might help.

SE: That would be great! I'll try that for a week or so and let you know how it works out. Listen, I know your planning period is over, and so is mine. But thanks again for letting me watch your groups yesterday and letting me watch you give the clinical evaluation of the language functions test that you might use with Darrell if needed. You've been really helpful in assisting me in working with him.

SLT: Thank you for giving me such precise data and descriptions of his problems. It will really help me in determining whether or not he needs additional testing and assistance. Since the copy machine is right next to my office and you use it a lot, maybe we can catch each other for a few minutes at a time to share information about Darrell and other students.

This conference between team members was highly productive for several reasons. Each acknowledged and respected the specialized training of the other. Both came together with the attitude that they shared a common goal of providing a better program for a student. Both shared and respected each other's expertise, showed a genuine interest in the other's program, and both expressed a willingness to continue the dialogue. Although the initial meetings were time consuming—the meetings lasted between 20 and 30 minutes—subsequent meetings could be brief, and each team member could make the other's job easier by sharing materials and expertise focused on their common goal.

ROLE DESCRIPTIONS OF OTHER TEAM MEMBERS

As indicated earlier, the number of people on a team will vary, as determined both by the nature and severity of the student's problem, and by the size and resources available in the school district or clinical program. The roles of other team members are described in clusters, which include those with related or overlapping functions. These include the following: the program administrator; the classroom teacher; the behavior specialist, school psychologist, counselor, or social worker; the speech-language therapist, the teacher of bilingual education or ESL; the physical therapist, occupational therapist, adaptive physical educator, and adaptive technology specialist; the vocational or transition specialist; the teacher of migrant or Chapter 1 programs; and the school nurse and other health-related professionals. The roles of family members and paraprofessionals are presented separately, in Chapters 8 and 6, respectively.

Program Administrator

The contributions and specialized knowledge of the administrator are considered first because it is important to emphasize that the person with this title is not ordinarily the team leader. The organization's administrator, recognizing the team's value, delegates responsibility for its coordination to a team leader. The role of the leader will be described in more detail in Chapter 6. It should be noted that, although the administrator is not ordinarily the team's leader, it is essential that the administrator support the concept of teaming, and see the team's function as supportive of the organization's overall mission.

Those who have implemented school-based teacher assistance teams have learned that the administrator, who is typically responsible for teacher evaluation, often is not the best person to serve as the team leader because team members may be reluctant to share concerns about their effectiveness with the person who will evaluate them. The role of the administrator, therefore, is proposed as that of overall management of the school or clinic and its programs, but not necessarily as a leader of the interactive team.

The administrator is charged with overall fiscal, legal, and programmatic responsibility for the unit in which the team functions. This unit is usually a school, and its administrator is a principal when the team serves students from culturally diverse backgrounds or those with mild disabilities. It may be a clinic or specialized organization with a director when the team serves students with severe disabilities. Because the administrator has overall responsibility for the unit, she must give permission for the team to function as a decision-making body, as well as provide it with the necessary information and support to implement its decisions. Also, because the administrator has overall responsibility for the unit, she must balance the budget and see that all legal mandates and protections are observed while attending to the needs of all constituencies. The administrator's priority is the welfare of the entire unit, rather than personal advocacy for the special needs of any one student or program.

The specialized areas of knowledge of the administrator or director include but are not limited to the following: leadership and change; professional development and relations; planning and evaluation; public and community relations; personnel management; and knowledge about budgets, law, educational and medical programs, resources, and facilities. In some cases, the school administrator is the instructional leader for the unit, although observations of what elementary and secondary principals actually do seem to suggest that this activity represents less than 20% to 30% of their time (Howell, 1981; Morsink, 1999). And, in clinical settings, it is unlikely that the director is trained in both education and the allied health professions in addition to having expertise in administration.

For the team to function effectively, however, it is particularly important for the administrator to understand and convey to the public that she values this team and has delegated to it decision-making authority for the programs of special needs students. It is equally important for the administrator to provide the members of the team with information about the legal policies and procedures within which they are authorized to operate, and to provide them with information about the fiscal and instructional resources available to them in program implementation. After having established the team, however, the administrator steps down from the direct leadership role and delegates responsibility for the team's functioning to the team itself.

Classroom Teacher

Since the 1997 amendments to the IDEA, it has become increasingly likely that the classroom teacher will be a key member of the team, since his or her presence is often required (Turnbull & Cilley, 1999). The classroom teacher has unique skills and knowledge that may be applied to the development, evaluation, and implementation of the special student's instructional program. The classroom teacher is more often involved when the student is culturally different or has a mild disability, although in many cases the student with severe or multiple disabilities may also be served at least part time in the regular school program.

The classroom teacher has been trained as a specialist in "normal" human growth and development. This team member is, therefore, in an excellent position to observe the special needs student's interactions with peers who demonstrate age- and grade-appropriate behaviors. Such observations are not possible in the special classroom, where this student is separated from peers who set the *norms* for age-appropriate learning and behavior. The classroom teacher who observes a first grader reversing letters knows that other "normal" 6-year-olds sometimes do the same thing. The classroom teacher who observes a moody, hostile adolescent recognizes that all adolescents are moody and may occasionally appear to be hostile or withdrawn. The classroom teacher, by comparing the individual's behavior with the group norms, is also able to determine that a 9-year-old who frequently reverses letters or an adolescent who is consistently hostile or withdrawn may have special needs. It is of primary importance that the classroom teacher make data-based observations of these behaviors, comparing the target student's performance with that of others in the group, to determine the nature and severity of the problem. In making such observations, the teacher should take care to define the behavior precisely, specify the conditions for observation, and ensure that the observations are made under consistent environmental conditions (Haring & Phillips, 1972; Morsink, 1984). Classroom teachers who make such observations will be much more effective members of the team because they are able to communicate the precise nature of the student's problems in coping with the school curriculum and the classroom environment. Some schools will have specialists in behavior analysis and/or adaptive technology to make or assist with these observations.

The classroom teacher is also a specialist in the academic subject matter or scope and sequence of the curriculum for particular grade levels or subjects. This team member's primary responsibility is to implement the academic curriculum in the classroom. Peterson (1988) has pointed out that the role of the teacher is now viewed primarily as that of a "thoughtful professional," one who understands the relationship between teaching and learning and is able to enhance the student's cognitive functioning in a specific academic area. Others (Gensante & Matgouranis, 1989; Ross, 1989; Williams, 1996) have referred to effective teachers as those who use "reflective teaching," describing what they do and its effect on learners, and using this information to improve their instruction.

The classroom teacher's most important role with the student who has special needs, both before and after referral (if the student is placed), focuses on the provision of appropriate learning experiences. Wang, Haertel, and Walberg (1997), Nevin and Thousand (1986), and Villa and Thousand (1988) have summarized a number of strategies that have been found effective in accommodating the special student in the classroom environment. These include outcomes-based strategies such as peer tutoring, cooperative learning, mastery learning, and applied behavior analysis. In addition, it is important for the classroom teacher to establish an effective environment in which all students can learn: one that has a positive classroom climate and that includes adapted teacher-directed instruction, followed by opportunities for students to practice their skills under supervision, with teacher feedback (Larrivee, 1985; Morsink, Thomas, & Smith-Davis, 1987; Rosenshine & Stevens, 1986; Wang et al., 1997).

Other members of the team need to realize that classroom teachers are trained to accommodate students in groups, rather than to tutor them individually. It is the classroom teacher's primary responsibility to provide academic instruction for all members of the group, not only to enhance the learning of individuals with special needs. This professional is in the best position to assist the special needs student in working with the group, learning to follow routines and complying with accepted standards of group behavior. The classroom teacher, however, is not as effective as the special educator in providing intensive one-on-one or small-group instruction on specific academic skills or behavior management. The same characteristics that enhance the teacher's effectiveness in whole-group instruction may limit the ability to deal with individuals who have diverse needs, particularly when teachers lack the technological and human support to implement simultaneously a variety of diverse teaching strategies (Gerber, 1988). It is possible, however, for a classroom teacher, in a school with a principal who supports full inclusion, to accommodate the special needs of diverse students, as shown in the Chapter 1 application in this book.

Behavior Specialist, School Psychologist, Counselor, or Social Worker

Because the roles of these four professionals often overlap, we describe their roles in tandem. Large, affluent school districts may have all four of these individuals in every school, but those that are smaller or sparsely populated may have only one per school or per district.

Behavior Specialist.   The behavior specialist is a possible member of IEP teams that are considering the special needs of students whose behavior interferes with their own learning or with the learning of others in the classroom. A behavioral assessment and intervention plan are required for any student who has been removed from any placement for 10 or more school days. The behavior specialist, trained in applied behavior analysis, gathers information by making data-based observations of the student in the classroom environment; conducting interviews with the student, teachers, and others; generating behavior support plans; and assisting in the implementation and monitoring of the plan's outcomes.

This team member needs skill in the identification of problem behaviors and the ability to define them in concrete ways that lead to development of plans. Successful behavior intervention plans include positive strategies, curricular modifications, and the use of supplementary supports to enable students to use appropriate behaviors. Therefore, it is essential for this team member to have in-depth knowledge of the possible causes and functions of behavior problems, as well as an understanding of the curriculum, the selection and use of assessment instruments, and the ability to develop, implement, and monitor objective interventions based on direct measurement techniques. While some preparation programs for school psychologists and counselors may include at least some of these skills, many special education programs offer degrees in applied behavior analysis and behavior intervention strategies. School districts might also contract with external public or private agencies to provide these services

Psychologist.   The person trained as a school psychologist is a psychoeducational specialist certified to administer formal tests of intellectual and interpersonal functioning. The school psychologist is also trained in the selection, administration, and interpretation of certain standardized and informal tests used to determine the student's eligibility for special programs and to assist in planning those programs (Frisbee, 1988; Larsen, 1984). In small districts, the psychologist may conduct the entire assessment, whereas in larger districts, other specialists may be part of the assessment team as necessary for individual cases—physicians or audiologists for evaluating hearing, physicians or vision specialists for conducting an assessment of visual functioning, and so on. Because assessment is of such importance in the referral and placement of the special student, it is particularly important that the school psychologist select instruments that are free from bias and are administered in the student's own language, with adaptations for physical and sensory disabilities, and according to legally approved procedures (Larsen, 1984; Reid, 1987; Turnbull & Cilley, 1999).

Counselor.   The school counselor may also conduct observations or collect assessment data during the referral stage of program decision making, although this professional is more highly trained in the assessment of social and emotional skills than in the measurement of cognitive functioning. The counselor frequently consults with teachers and parents to design individual and group programs that assist students in developing their interpersonal skills and in coping with their emotions (Tobias, 1988). Frequently in secondary and middle schools, the counselor is also responsible for designing and coordinating the student's class schedule, and assisting students with making decisions about their future plans for higher education or vocational careers. Often, especially in small districts that do not have a social worker, the counselor also functions as a liaison with personnel from a variety of community agencies.

Social Worker.   The social worker is the professional who collects information about the student's home background and history. This person is familiar with the variety of community resources and related services that may be used to help the special needs student and the family, and serves as the liaison with professionals in these agencies. A school social worker may be involved as a person who can interface with the public assistance and justice systems for students in foster homes or who may be the recipients of social security or welfare funds. The social worker may also conduct observations of the student in the home or classroom, and may administer assessment instruments or implement programs to assist the teacher, the student, and the family in coping with the behavior of difficult students (Ryberg & Sebastian, 1981).

Overlapping Functions.   Either the psychologist, counselor, or social worker may collect information from the student's home, locate resources, or serve as a liaison with community agencies (Ryberg & Sebastian, 1981). The behavior specialist, psychologist, social worker, and counselor are all trained to observe the student in the classroom and then consult with teachers, parents, and other personnel in the design of programs to manage the student's behavior or to enhance learning ability. This team member is often trained in child advocacy, counseling, group process skills, and consultation. The professional organizations for school psychologists and counselors have urged that their members expand their roles beyond the assessment of problems to their prevention (American Association for Counseling and Development, 1984; National Association of School Psychologists, 1974). For example, these professionals are frequently called on to provide schools with assistance in dealing with or preventing school violence, as shown in the following application.

The following application is reprinted with permission from its developers, Anne Kemmerer, Amanda Szurek, and Diane Carion. It illustrates another way in which university faculty members and students in preparation for careers in education and related professions can and should be part of interactive teams.

◊ ◊

Application: A Timely Workshop

Only hours after the tragic incident in Littleton, Colorado, a very timely program was initiated here at Slippery Rock University. Wednesday, April 21, was the culmination of a year's worth of planning. The School Collaboration Center, in conjunction with the Counseling Educational Psychology Department, College of Education, hosted 200 seventh-grade students from the Grove City Middle School. The topic: "Bullying and Teasing: Laying the Groundwork for Conflict Resolution." The goal: Making Grove City Middle School a bully-free zone. The principal, Ms. Kelly, and the guidance counselor, Mr. Wise, welcomed the program with open arms.

Twenty SRU graduate students, most of them future guidance counselors, facilitated a hands-on workshop for the 200 students. The workshop, planned by Dr. Anne Kemmerer, Dr. Pamela Soeder, and graduate student Amanda Szurek, gave the students an intense 3.5 hours of training that gave examples of defining "bullying," what makes a victim, recognizing the difference between "tattling" and "reporting," and teaching the skills to identify an adult in the school system that they can trust for reporting incidents.

The general program was a huge success. The real success will be determined when one of these students takes on an assertive and active role when faced with this issue because of the information shared at this workshop.

◊ ◊

In larger districts, the behavior specialist, psychologist, social worker, or counselor may be able to provide follow-up consultation, conduct group or individual counseling sessions, or work with parents. Some larger districts have been able, for example, to offer group counseling sessions in areas such as substance abuse, divorce, and test anxiety, which help prevent the increase in referrals for special programs (Bernstein & Simon, 1988). In small districts this team member may be serving several schools; fragmentation in job location may limit the position's functions to the administration and interpretation of psychological tests. In some instances, small districts are not able to employ a behavior specialist, psychologist, counselor, or social worker. The person who serves in this capacity may be employed by a social services agency, or as a private consultant, working under contract with the school district.

The behavior specialist, psychologist, social worker, and counselor are heavily involved in the delivery of sensitive information, and they are often required to explain technical terms or to make suggestions for changes in the status quo. In this role, it is particularly important that they use terminology that is clear, understandable, and inoffensive (Courtnage & Healy, 1984; Larsen, 1984; Tobias, 1988). These professionals' explanations should include information about the limitations of test data and of classification procedures. These explanations should also emphasize findings derived from multiple sources of information, as opposed to conclusions based on a single data point, such as the numerical score on a particular test.

The professional in this role frequently has the perspective of *child advocacy* as a first priority (Sigmon, 1987). The perspective of child advocate may appear, at times, to conflict with the perspective of the administrator or classroom teacher, and it may not seem to be compatible with the overall goals of the organization or the particular needs of the child's family. This possibility of conflict in perspective is also one to which team members need to remain sensitive.

Speech-Language Therapist and ESL or Bilingual Specialist

The people who assume these three roles have some functions and characteristics in common, yet their training is also highly specialized. Both their specializations and their common functions are presented.

Speech-Language Therapist.   The person trained as a speech-language therapist is an educational-medical professional certified by the American Speech-Language and Hearing Association (ASHA). For the student whose difficulties include speech or language development, the speech-language therapist (SLT) is an essential member of the professional team. The SLT is trained to diagnose and remediate expressive and receptive communication disorders to ensure the development of communication skills that are the foundation of all language-related learning (Morsink, 1983). This team member is in the best position to evaluate and treat a student who has difficulty with the content and form of language, or with the way language is transmitted through sounds (phonology), words (morphology), or word order (syntax), according to Bloom and Lahey (1978). This student is often one whose speech is immature or difficult to understand, and who has apparent inability to understand directions or difficulty expressing ideas verbally (Culatta, Page, & Culatta, 1981).

One of the most important functions of the SLT is to administer a series of formal and informal tests to determine the nature and extent of the language difficulty. The therapist might, for example, administer one or more tests of concept development, language production, and articulation. One of the most commonly used, and most practical measures of the student's language ability is the language sample, through which the SLT obtains the student's *mean length of utterance* (MLU), the average number of words per sentence or sentence fragment. For a student with a mild disability, the SLT may be particularly interested in obtaining a language sample to determine the way this student uses language in everyday situations. For a student with a severe disability, the language assessment may focus on the student's ability to use and interpret gestures and to make basic needs understood.

When the student is from a culturally different background, it is particularly important for the SLT to determine whether the student's language is simply different as a result of culturally determined patterns or whether it is deficient (Westby, 1985). The SLT may be asked to assist when the student's oral reading performance is characterized by numerous dialect differences, indicative of common language patterns that occur in black English or in students for whom another language (e.g., Spanish) is the first language. It is important for all who work with the student to recognize these patterns and distinguish them from language deficits (Spache & Spache, 1986).

ESL or Bilingual Specialist.   The student with performance deficits caused solely by the fact that English is the second language should *not* be classified as eligible for special education, according to the 1997 IDEA amendments, although this student may be eligible for assistance in ESL or bilingual education. Conversely, the ESL student may not be denied special education services on the basis of his or her home language. When English is the second language for the student, the SLT should collaborate with a specialist in that language. Large districts may have specialists in ESL or in bilingual education. In small districts, it may be necessary to seek assistance from a community volunteer or a professional at a nearby university who is a native speaker of the language. It is also important for school districts to provide information to parents in a language they can understand, to assess students using instruments in their own language, and to provide uniform procedures for students to register for school, regardless of the country of their birth.

Overlapping Functions.   There are five areas in which it is particularly important for the SLT and bilingual teacher or foreign language specialist to collaborate; these have been summarized by Fradd and Weismantel (1988):

1. *Student identification.* Data combined from both specialists can be used to confirm or refute a label, such as "learning disability," as determined by the language assessment.
2. *Assessment and diagnosis.* Language dominance needs to be established, and the label "disabled" is applied only when the student is deficient in measures of intelligence, academics, or social behavior, as measured in the dominant language.
3. *Placement.* It is desirable to place the student in an integrated group, including both bilingual and general education students when possible.
4. *Instructional planning.* For the bilingual student, this includes a dual language plan for instruction in the academic and social skills, as well as a model for providing these services.

5. *Achievement review.* The annual review should include new language samples and work samples from the academic areas being remediated, as well as progress in the direction of mainstreaming.

To avoid conflicts, gaps, or overlapping functions, it may be useful to further delineate the specific training and roles of the ESL and bilingual education resource teachers. These have been specified in detail by Fradd and Weismantel (1988). The ESL teacher provides instruction focused on whole language and cognition including grammar and linguistics. The bilingual teacher provides instruction first in the non-English language and culture; the sequence of this instruction begins with affective skills and progresses to cognition and finally to academics. In large districts, there may be specialists in both ESL and SLT, whereas in smaller districts, these functions may be filled by the same individual or contracted by the school to an external specialist.

When the student's major difficulty is language development and use, it is of greatest importance for all adults to provide consistent models and to have common expectations. For the learner who is culturally different and also has a severe disability, it may be more important to communicate in the student's native language and in gestures or universal signs, when it is not feasible to provide instruction in the use of English as a second language. The SLT and the ESL or bilingual specialist are the people on the team who can best provide information on the type of program that is most appropriate for a given student.

Physical Therapist, Adaptive Physical Educator, Occupational Therapist, and Adaptive Technology Specialist

There are some commonalities and some differences between and among the functions and training of these professionals. Their roles are presented separately, and the overlapping functions then discussed.

Physical Therapist.   The physical therapist (PT) is a link between medicine and education, because the PT understands students' medical problems as well as the importance of movement in learning (Morsink, 1983). This specialist intervenes when education alone cannot fulfill the needs of the client because there is an inability to move, a discontinuity in the normal growth process, or a physical rather than a cognitive barrier to learning. The specific contributions of the physical therapist at differing points in the client's lifetime are expressed by Eggers (1983), as follows:

> For infants, the therapist can effect changes in potential for development, through good therapy and intervention, since the young child is adaptable even with severe damage. With preschool and young children, the therapist can intervene to prevent irreversible change. During the school years, the physical therapist can help the

teacher to provide carry-over and generalization activities in the classroom, and can make the learning environment more conducive to learning by assisting with correct positioning and the use of adaptive equipment. (p. 5)

The physical therapist works to develop a program of assessment and intervention after the physician has referred the client for these services. Assessment of the disability includes a determination of the strength and range of movement, and the relationship between the movement and the individual's ability to learn or to perform learning-related functions.

Because it is important to continue the physical therapy program on a regular basis, the PT often works collaboratively with the special educator, classroom teacher, and parents, who are responsible for carrying out some of the program in the therapist's absence. The nature and type of program designed for the student with severe disabilities may include assistance with basic functional skills, such as feeding, self-care, and walking.

Adaptive Physical Educator.   This professional is trained in physical education, exercise physiology, and in the special needs of students with mild or severe disabilities. Those providing adapted physical education are trained to provide remediation in the areas of physical and motor fitness, psychomotor skills, leisure and recreation skills, and affective development. In addition, the adaptive physical educator can collaborate with other team members in designing cooperative games and motor development activities that enhance the child's physical skills, self-concept, and interactions with peers. Sometimes this professional works with community agencies to design special physical education programs, such as horseback riding or swimming for students with physical, emotional, or sensory limitations.

Occupational Therapist.   The occupational therapist (OT) assists the client, family, and team members in the design of specialized equipment and the retraining of skills that will enable the student with special needs to function in the classroom or on the job. The role of the OT is described by Barker (in Morsink, 1983), as follows:

> . . . to facilitate, promote and maintain optimum independence of the student through adaptive skills and effective functioning in the school and social environments. The OT, utilizing a medical knowledge base, evaluates and plans goal-directed, developmentally sequenced activities as treatment for the correction of perceptual, sensory, psychosocial, motor or self-care deficits. (p. 6)

The OT is often engaged in the creation or modification of special devices to assist the person with physical or sensory disabilities in sitting, walking, eating, writing, reading, and so on. These include, for example, special devices to enable the person with poor motor skills to grip a pencil or the amputee to drive a car.

Adaptive Technology Specialist.   In the computer-based society, the adaptations required for full functioning may be those that enable the person with physical limitations to use new technology, such as computers. Some adaptive technology specialists are trained to develop computer hardware and software that can be used by individuals with disabilities. Computers may be modified so they can be operated by an individual using a stick attached to the forehead or foot; they may also be programmed to synthesize speech or to translate speech into print or Braille. Adaptive technology specialists are also highly trained in the selection and design of software, which emphasizes programmed or errorless learning, to enable the student with learning difficulties to practice and master complex skills. Their skills are valuable to the team that serves students with mild disabilities, as well as those with severe disabilities.

The adaptive technology specialist is a new potential team member. This person may be trained in instructional technology, computer science, with specialization in the adaptation of technology for students with special needs, or may be a special educator with advanced training in instructional technology. Adaptations are essential when their use will enable the student with special needs to learn and/or function in the least restrictive environment. The adaptive technology specialist may, upon receiving a referral on a student, observe or evaluate that student either in school, the home, or in a specialized technology lab. This team member may also read student records, interview the student, teachers, and parents, and complete a community-based assessment. The technology specialist allows for input from these persons before making a recommendation on the use of specific equipment, then reports recommendations back to the IEP team for decision making.

The adaptive technologist relies on classroom teachers to provide input on the students' skills and specific needs in reading, writing, and language, listening and problem-solving skills, his or her work habits, and needs to produce printed output. Teachers and related services personnel also provide the adaptive technologist with information about concerns related to mobility, vision, hearing, speech-language, cognitive, or behavioral performance with which the student might receive assistance from adaptive technology. The technology specialist acquires information about the availability of existing hardware and software used and needed in the classroom or community environment. It is important for the adaptive technology specialist to have knowledge about exceptionalities and about the use and availability of the newest hardware, software, and special devices for augmentative communication and mobility, as well as the technical skills required to adapt existing devices to special needs. This specialist makes an effort to find the simplest—often lowest "tech"—solution, since adaptations do not necessarily improve in value just because they increase in cost.

Overlapping Functions.   Although the physical therapist, occupational therapist, and adaptive physical educator may all provide assistance with the development and use of motor skills, the PT is the only one whose assistance requires referral from a physician. The PT is more concerned with the development of basic motor skills, whereas the OT is more often concerned with the use of these skills in classroom and vocational settings. Both the PT and the adaptive physical educator are concerned with motor development; however, the PT works with clients individually and the adaptive physical educator also works with students in groups.

Both the OT and the adaptive technology specialist may have the training to design adaptive equipment for use with computers; the OT, however, usually does not have training in the development of programmed software for use with computer-assisted instruction or the selection of software appropriate for specific areas of the curriculum. These individuals may work together in large districts; in smaller, remote areas, one of these individuals may perform several functions if the team does not have access to all types of specialists.

Vocational or Transition Specialist

The professional who is a vocational educator is specially trained in preparing students for specific types of vocations which include a variety of careers related to service industries in agriculture, food services, manufacturing, installation, and repair. Each vocational specialist is a professional trained in a highly specific area, who teaches this specialty in high schools or vocational schools. Although the vocational educator is knowledgeable in his or her area of training, this person does not always have training in adapting the vocational training program to the special needs of students with disabilities.

The transition specialist is more often an individual with generic training in vocational education and specialized knowledge in the training needs of adolescents and adults with disabilities. This professional assists the student, the family, and the school personnel in making the transition from the world of school to work. The transition specialist helps the team plan for the student's continuing vocational/educational training, home and community participation (e.g., where to live, how to obtain transportation), family relationships, financial support, recreation and leisure, as well as physical and emotional health (Boone, 1990). Planning for transition into the adult world is more difficult than planning for school-related programs, because there is no single agency to coordinate all aspects of the student's services.

Either the vocational educator or the transition specialist, or both, may work with the school and related community agencies to assess the skills of the student and match them with the requirements of a particular job. These professionals may be responsible for providing the special needs student with prevocational training and for conducting on-the-job support services such as job coaching, which ensure that the student will have the communications and interpersonal abilities, as well as the vocational skills, to succeed in the world of work (Bell, 1989).

Migrant Education or Chapter 1 Teacher

School districts and communities that have a large number of people classified as migrant workers or as having incomes below the poverty level may have one or more specialists in migrant or remedial education. The specialist in migrant education has acquired knowledge about the particular problems of the migrant worker's family, including residential instability and educational discontinuity.

The teacher in a Chapter 1 program serves the children of families whose incomes are below the poverty level. These are the children whose caregivers are eligible for aid to dependent children. Often, they are from single-parent families. The Chapter 1 specialist is trained to provide enrichment activities and remedial training to students who are not achieving well in school and who have low levels of motivation or low expectation for success. Federal programs now provide additional funding for whole schools with a high percentage of students who qualify for Chapter 1 funding. This Fund for the Improvement and Reform of Schools and Teaching (FIRST) Program (1989) enables the entire school to engage in collaborative efforts to effect school improvement.

School Nurse and Other Health-Related Professionals

In larger school systems, or in cases that involve clients with severe or multiple disabilities, a school nurse or other health-related professionals may be members of the team. When there is a medical problem, a physician will be involved in the diagnosis and in consultation or making recommendations for treatment, although the physician ordinarily interacts with the student's parents or other health-related professionals, rather than serving as a regular team member at school-based meetings.

School Nurse.   The school nurse may assist others in planning for educational programs that involve wellness, substance abuse, and prevention of disease. More recently, school nurses are assuming additional responsibilities (NBC, 1999; Associated Press, 1999) for the increasing numbers of students with disabilities and those at risk. The nurse takes on an increasingly important function in the implementation of a program for a student who suffers from AIDS (Reed, 1988). In some districts, school policies or bargaining agreements require that the nurse oversee particular health-related procedures, such as dispensing of medications. Each member of the team should request information regarding these policies. Some schools do not have school nurses, although services have to be provided for students with disabilities somewhere in the district.

Pediatric Nurse.   Many children are hospitalized at some time, either for a short-term stay or for prolonged time periods, with more of their care delegated to the pediatric nurse. This health care provider can be viewed as a potential team member, particularly in the role of consultant to the school and parents, but also as a team leader within the hospital setting. The role of this team member is presented in greater depth in the section on interactive teaming in hospital settings.

Dietitian.   A dietitian or nutritional specialist may function as a consultant for students who, because of diabetes or other metabolic disorders, need assistance in planning and monitoring their diets. This specialist evaluates the individual's diet and nutritional status to determine the overall nutritional intake, as well as special needs such as those related to lower caloric intake or the reduction of sugar or sodium. The dietitian may work with the student's family, in addition to consulting with school and related services personnel, and may advise the team about special devices to assist with feeding or to monitor the intake of particular elements.

Other health-related professionals may serve as consultants or collaborators on the team as needed. In every case, each of these specialists has particular knowledge in an area that may be of primary importance to the student's treatment.

Physician's Role as Consultant

The physician contributes to the interactive team largely as a consultant. It is unlikely that, unless the student has severe and multiple disabilities, the physician will be directly involved in the educational program. The role of the physician has been addressed in detail by Ross (1984), who outlines the procedures for conducting an evaluation of the student. This evaluation focuses on a case history, including a description of the current illness, past history, review of systems, and family or social history. When appropriate, the physician may also conduct a neurological or sensory examination.

Students are most often referred to the physician because of symptoms such as hyperactivity, hearing loss, or seizures. When the physician's diagnosis is a condition such as epilepsy, cerebral palsy, muscular dystrophy, or developmental disability the team will need to develop a complete plan that extends over a lifetime and allows such individuals to develop to their fullest potential.

Input from the physician is provided most often in the form of a written report, detailing the medical findings of an examination and making recommendations that may be implemented by others on the team. As noted earlier, recent recommendations from professional associations may lead to an expanded role in violence prevention for the physician (Elias, 1999).

Roles of Family Members and Paraprofessionals

Family members often have perspectives that differ from those of the other team members, particularly when they represent different cultural backgrounds. Their role, knowledge, and perspectives are discussed in Chapters 7 and 8. Chapter 8 presents the new emphasis on family systems and on the role of the parent or other family member as an equal member of the team.

The roles of paraprofessionals will be presented in Chapter 6; these individuals are subordinate to the other team members, and their duties are delegated and monitored by others.

INTERACTIVE TEAMING IN HOSPITAL SETTINGS

This section was adapted from the work of Kristin J. Young, R.N., with her permission. The section is focused on the role of the pediatric nurse as a member of the hospital-based care team. It includes information about children and young adults who are eligible for services under IDEA and those who are sick but do not necessarily have disabilities. Special educators should be aware that the "rules" are different for each of these groups. Also, the special educator should be aware that if a child who is eligible for special education is hospitalized long term, the district may provide a teacher or use district funds to help support the hospital-paid teacher to continue this child's education.

The role of the pediatric nurse, who spends more time with the patient than does any other health care provider in the hospital, is presented here in greater depth. The nurse will witness changes in condition and report these changes to the physician so the care plan can be altered if necessary. The nurse is the patient's advocate, and must be diligent in her efforts to obtain the most appropriate treatment. Patient care conferences are held informally throughout the day, during which the nurse, patient, family, and physician discuss options and give feedback regarding the viability of each option. Conferences also include pharmacists, respiratory therapists, physical therapists, X-ray technicians, recreational therapists, and teachers.

The nurse may work extensively with parents and other family members. Parents now are encouraged to stay with their children for the duration of their illness in many hospitals, and in some cases siblings and grandparents are also allowed to stay. This allows the family to continue to function as a unit; stress is reduced because the patient is not made to stay alone and the parents do not feel so helpless. As family members observe the nursing care their children are receiving, they become familiar with the procedures and learn to perform the simpler tasks themselves. Family members also provide insight into the child's character and response to certain treatments so that the staff can approach them in a way that is the least threatening to them.

The nurse also stays in touch with other hospital caregivers. Some hospitals employ teachers and child development specialists to provide learning, recreation, and stress management for their pediatric patients. The teacher often confers with the child's regular teacher to get assignments and identify learning needs. The teacher then works with children in a one-to-one situation during a time of treatment when they are most able to concentrate on schoolwork. If a child becomes too tired or too ill to continue working, the teacher may leave homework for the child to do later or make arrangements to come back at another time, thereby promoting the child's overall learning experience by responding positively to the child's needs.

The child development specialists provide informal teaching, recreation, and stress management. They are often referred to as "play ladies" because they have a storeroom full of toys, games, and crafting supplies. For example, a premature infant, who requires stimuli to keep his mind active, may respond to cassette tapes, crib mobiles, and infant exercisers brought in by the play ladies when the nurse cannot take time to play with them. Older children are encouraged to express themselves through artwork. The play ladies commission young artists to design Christmas cards which are sold to the public; the profits enable the hospital to purchase supplies, equipment, and more toys. One year a young cancer patient designed a card with a menagerie of elves, all of whom were bald to resemble herself in chemotherapy. Later, she gave them wigs so they wouldn't feel so out of place in the world. The play ladies also encourage the use of games to occupy time and provide diversion from the reality of hospitalization. The game "Chutes and Ladders" is very popular among chronically ill children because it demonstrates the ups and downs of their diseases and treatments.

The pediatric nurse also collaborates with social service and home care agencies when patients need assistance obtaining services. The family of a child diagnosed with leukemia, for example, will feel overwhelmed by the seriousness of the illness, not to mention the enormous bills and time lost at work when they choose to spend precious time with their child. Social workers, who interact closely with families, help them obtain medical benefits, clothes, transportation, and even living quarters when necessary. In other cases, there may be a suspicion of child abuse or neglect. At those times, the social worker investigates the situation and helps to determine whether the child's best interest is served by remaining in the current household or by being removed. When families need assistance performing specific health-oriented tasks, the social worker may arrange for the families to attend special classes or arrange for a home health care agent to visit the family for home visits.

In all of these situations, the nurse caring for the patient coordinates the different services. In many hospitals the "primary nursing model" is followed, which means one nurse is primarily responsible for seeing that all needed tests, care, and services are given before the patient is discharged. She is assigned to that patient every day and is involved in every aspect of his or her care. If she is not working on the day of discharge, she will often make preparations for home care or follow-ups prior to that day. In a managed care setting, however, every nurse is expected to give total care to every patient on any given day. In this way all nurses become more experienced in a wider variety of ailments, rather than focusing on one or two "primaries." They become more adept at problem solving and no longer rely on the "primary nurse" to do all the work. In this model, the primary nurse may delegate duties to other staff, but overall care is enhanced because more than one person is familiar with the patient's special needs.

An example of the work of a pediatric nurse is given in the following application.

◇ ◇

Application: Caring for James
A Day in the Life of a Pediatric Nurse

6:45 p.m.   I arrive on my nursing unit to take my assignment for the next 12 hours. It is Thursday evening and I am expecting to have mostly patients who are postoperative or who are receiving chemotherapy or IV antibiotics. I am not disappointed. My assignment consists of two children who had appendectomies that day, a young cancer patient just finishing her current round of chemo, and James, a 15-year-old with failing kidneys who is being admitted after an attempt to place an arteriovenous fistula for dialysis has failed. Ordinarily this would not require admission, but the doctors wish to try again tomorrow, and James lives several hours away from the hospital. As I sit at the table to take report on these patients, I am thinking the assignment is rather light, and I should have plenty of time to catch up on some paperwork tonight.

8:00 p.m.   I have checked on all of my patients, given their scheduled medications, and seen to their comfort for the evening. I am now waiting for James to arrive on the floor from the recovery room. The recovery room nurse has told me that the procedure itself went fine, but that the dialysis catheter they tried to place in his forearm does not work properly. This is a problem occasionally, because many of these patients have scar tissue along their veins and arteries from multiple needle sticks occurring when blood samples are drawn or IVs placed. James's kidneys are still functioning enough that his life is not in peril, but he will need dialysis very soon. He has a history of noncompliance with his recommended treatment program, so he is losing his kidneys faster than he should lose them. He is awake from the anesthesia, and appears to be in an irritable mood. The recovery room orderly will find his family in the waiting area before they bring him up to the unit.

8:20 p.m.   James arrives on the floor on a stretcher. He is complaining loudly about being in the hospital and is already threatening to leave. After an orderly gets him situated in his room, I check his vital signs and do a quick physical assessment to ascertain that he is in no distress. Then I must ask him and his family members about his medical history and personal routines so that we may make his stay as comfortable and problem-free as possible. I learn that he is from a remote rural area of our state and lives with his grandparents, who have had legal custody since he was a toddler. His mother is minimally involved in his care and sees him only a few times a year. She is reported to be a drug and alcohol abuser, and is believed to have indulged heavily during her pregnancy with James. I notice that he has some mild characteristics of fetal alcohol syndrome, including a flat upper lip and wide-set eyes. His family tells me he has had trouble in school all his life, does not learn well, and acts out frequently. His aunt fears for his grandmother, saying she is not able to control his behavior, and he is sometimes violent. I also learn that he smokes cigarettes, and he is now quite verbose in his annoyance that he has been prevented from smoking since early that morning. Again he threatens to leave the hospital. I tell him that since he is a minor, he cannot leave without his grandmother's permission. If he escapes, police will be sent to bring him back. He says he doesn't care, and he doesn't believe me. I tell him it is the truth, but if he is desperate to get out of his bed and go for a walk, I will allow it as long as a family member or staff member is with him at all times. He is agreeable to these terms, and his aunt and uncle agree to go with him for a stroll outside.

9:00 p.m.   James is back in his room and is in a more pleasant mood. I have completed admission paperwork and am ready to proceed with his care for the remainder of my shift. As I change the dressing on his arm, he begins to talk to me about his personal life. As he talks, he seems to look through me in his conversation, as if he were talking to an imaginary person behind me, rather than to me. His voice is calm as he tells me about the many people he hates and how he would shoot them in the head if his grandfather would give him the right kind of gun. Then he decides he doesn't need a gun; he can cut their heads off with a long knife instead. His aunt, the only family member left in the room now, tells him not to say things like that. He rolls his eyes and shrugs. His aunt may not have custody of him, but she seems intelligent and obviously cares about him. I am glad she is there. I leave the room to check on my other patients and call his doctor to notify him of this behavior.

9:30 p.m.   I have called the physician to tell him the situation and convey my concerns about James's emotional well-being. He is also concerned, but does not know James personally, because he is covering for his regular doctor for the night. He tells me to keep things low key for the night and let him know if the behavior gets any worse. I agree. I spend as little time in his room as possible, but keep observing him even though it makes me nervous. I ask my charge nurse and hospital security to listen for trouble, in case he is truly unstable. I can't stop the images of newspaper headlines from flashing through my mind.

12:00 a.m.   James has been watching TV in his room for a couple of hours. His aunt remains at his bedside. She suggests he should try to sleep now but he says he can't sleep. His aunt and I agree that he should not be given any narcotics to help him sleep. I call the pharmacy, asking them to recommend a non-narcotic sleep aid for a teenager. She suggests Benadryl, which will cause drowsiness without any adverse side effects. I phone the doctor to get an order for the Benadryl.

12:30 a.m.   When I get to James's room with the Benadryl, he appears to be dozing. His aunt is dozing in the cot beside him. I leave the room again, taking the Benadryl with me. I can give it to him later if he awakens and becomes restless.

3:00 a.m.   James is awake and wants to talk again. This time he has questions about his own mortality. He asks if I think he will go to hell if he dies. I ask him if he wants to speak to the chaplain. No, he'll try to go back to sleep. He doesn't want the Benadryl.

4:30 a.m.   James has been restless in his bed. Now he wants to speak to the chaplain. He is very demanding in his request. He seems totally unconcerned that most people are asleep at this hour. I promise to call the chaplain closer to daybreak. He is unhappy and grumbles "okay." He curses that he doesn't want the Benadryl—it doesn't work.

6:00 a.m.   I call the chaplain and explain James's disturbing behavior and his request. The chaplain, who also has a degree in psychology, states he will come in as soon as he can.

7:00 a.m.   The chaplain is in James's room now, discussing James's beliefs and assessing his behavior. By this time, his doctor is there also, as well as the pediatric social worker, the hospital dietician, the nurse for the upcoming shift, and some other family members. After the chaplain and I fill them in on the events of the night, the team recommends that permission be obtained for James to be evaluated by a psychologist. They feel that his condition should be closely monitored, since he may need to receive emotional, as well as medical support, and that special education may be needed. They express hope that various caregivers will col-laborate to support his family members, to give him the care he needs in and near his home, where he feels comfortable, rather than in a distant residential environ-ment. They discuss the possibility that a social worker might make arrangements for James to be home schooled. A home health nurse will monitor his physical con-dition and report any changes to his doctor. Ideally, she and a psychologist might introduce him and his family to behavior modification techniques to make him more compliant with his medications and diet. A dietician will help create a menu he can follow with special attention focused on his kidneys' ability to process foods, fluids, and electrolytes. The chaplain says he wants to call James from time to time to check on his spiritual well-being. The team believes that James will benefit from this collaborative effort. If James can learn that he must follow guidelines to maintain his health, he can be put on a list for a kidney transplant. With appropriate help, the team believes that James should have a good chance of living a long, happy life as a normal, functioning member of society.

   7:30 a.m.   I leave the hospital for the day, feeling that I have had a significant part in making a young man's life better than it was yesterday.

◊ ◊

SUMMARY

Members of the interactive team are highly trained professionals, each with spe-cialized knowledge and skills that may contribute to the joint solution of prob-lems. The team may consist of as few as two persons or it may be much larger; the team's size depends on the nature and complexity of the student's problems and the size and resources of the facility.

New trends in service delivery and changes in the health care system have been summarized.

The roles of team members have been described; for the special educator, the roles differ somewhat, according to:

◆ The type of student: one who is culturally different, one who has a mild dis-ability, or one who has severe, multiple disabilities.
◆ The SE's function as service provider or as collaborator.

The roles of other team members have been described, clustered by common and sometimes overlapping functions:

◆ The program administrator.
◆ The classroom teacher.
◆ The behavior specialist, school psychologist, counselor, or social worker.

◆ The speech-language therapist, English as second language or bilingual specialist.

◆ The physical therapist, adaptive physical educator, occupational therapist, and adaptive technology specialist.

◆ The vocational or transition specialist.

◆ The migrant education or Chapter 1 teacher.

◆ The school nurse and other health-related professionals.

◆ The physician, as a consultant to the team.

The interactive team functions most effectively when each member understands and respects the expertise of others, and when all work together to accomplish their common goal: provision of the best possible program for a given student with special needs. The communication skills needed by diverse professionals in reaching their common goal are presented in the next chapter.

ACTIVITIES

1. Imagine you are a member of a team. Conduct an informational interview with one of the professionals on the special education team, using the guidelines presented here:

    a. Plan for the meeting by collecting data and writing down the questions you want to ask the other team member.

    b. Start the meeting by establishing rapport and finding areas of common interest or understanding.

    c. State the purpose of your meeting.

    d. Share the information you have collected for the other team member.

    e. Ask the questions you have prepared to elicit specific information.

    f. Summarize what you have accomplished and make plans for follow-up meetings in the future.

2. Write a series of questions to present to members of a panel who represent the professionals identified in this chapter. You might, for example, want to ask about their specialized training, previous experiences with other professionals, or suggestions for working together more effectively.

3. Construct a table summarizing the major role each direct service provider plays and describing the collaborative contributions that could be made by each professional on the team.

REFERENCES

American Association for Counseling and Development. (1984). Primary prevention in schools [Special issue]. *The Personnel and Guidance Journal, 62,* 443–495.

Anderson, A., & Luong, C. (1997). Health: Facing down asthma. *NEA Today, 15,* (7), 23.

Associated Press. (1999, March 3). Court ruling extends rights of disabled.

Bailey, D. (1984). A triaxial model of the interdisciplinary team and group process. *Exceptional Children, 51,* 17–26.

Bartel, N., & Thurmond, K. (1992). Medical treatment and educational problems in children. *Phi Delta Kappan, 74,* 57–61.

Beach, J. (1985). *Interaction with speech-language therapist.* Unpublished paper, University of Florida, Department of Special Education, Gainesville.

Bell, F. (1989). *Potential training sites for severely handicapped persons in Alachua County.* Unpublished master's thesis, University of Florida, Gainesville.

Bellisimo, Y. (1990). Crack babies: The schools' new high risk students. *Thrust, 19,* 23–26.

Bernstein, R., & Simon, D. (1988). A stitch in time: The role of the school psychologist. *Counterpoint, 8*(4), 6–7.

Biklen, D. (1988). *Regular lives.* Washington, DC: WETA-TV Department of Educational Activities.

Bloom, L., & Lahey, M. (1978). *Language development and language disorders.* New York: Wiley.

Boone, R. (1990). The development, implementation, and evaluation of a preconference training strategy for enhancing parental participation in and satisfaction with the individual transition conference (Doctoral dissertation, University of Florida, 1989). *Dissertation Abstracts International, 51*(3), 618-A.

Burkhead, E., Sampson, J., & McMahon, B. (1986). The liberation of disabled persons in a technological society: Access to computer technology. *Rehabilitation Literature, 47*(7), 162–168.

Bush, M., & Wilson, C. (1997). Linking schools with youth and family centers. *Educational Leadership, 55*(2), 38–41.

Campbell, P. (1987a). The integrated programming team: An approach for coordinating professionals of various disciplines in programs for students with severe and multiple handicaps. *Journal of Association for Persons with Severe Handicaps, 12*(2), 107–116.

Campbell, P. (1987b). Teacher assistance teams. In B. Algozzine (Ed.), *Behavior problem management: Educator's resource service.* Rockville, MD: Aspen Publishers.

Chalfant, J. (1989). Learning disability policy issues and promising approaches. In F. Horowitz & M. O'Brien (Eds.), Knowledge base, research agenda, and social policy application [Special issue]. *American Psychologist, 44*(2), 392–398.

Chalfant, J., Pysh, M., & Moultrie, R. (1979). Teacher assistance teams: A model for within-building problem solving. *Learning Disabilities Quarterly, 2*(3), 85–97.

Chamberlain, M. (1988). Employer's ranking of factors judged critical to job success for individuals with severe disabilities. *Career Development for Exceptional Individuals, 11*(2), 141–147.

Courtnage, L., & Healy, H. (1984). *A model in team building.* Cedar Falls, IA: University of Northern Iowa College of Education.

Cowell, J. (1998). Health: Is the school nurse a nurse? *The American School Board Journal, 185*(2), 45–46.

Culatta, B., Page, J., & Culatta, R. (1981). *Improving language functioning: A manual for language clinicians and teachers working in regular education settings.* Lexington: University of Kentucky Dean's Grant Project.

Darling, R. (1989). Using the social system perspective in early intervention: The value of a sociological approach. *Journal of Early Intervention, 13*(91), 24–35.

Davenport, S. (1990). The child with multiple congenital anomalies. *Pediatric Annals, 19*(1), 23–33.

Deno, S., & Mirkin, P. (1977). *Data-based program modification: A manual.* Minneapolis: University of Minnesota Leadership Training Institute.

Dykes, M. K., Brenner, J., & Lee, J. (1985). *Consensus study on motor disabilities competencies.* Unpublished manuscript, University of Florida, Department of Special Education, Gainesville.

Eggers, N. (1983, November). In C. V. Morsink (Ed.), *Context for generic guidelines for allied health and education professionals who serve persons with disabilities.* Synthesis of proceedings for Training Alliances in Health and Education meeting of the American Society of Allied Health Professionals (USDOE, OSERS, Grant G008301774). Philadelphia: American Society of Allied Health Professionals.

Elias, M. (1999, August 3). Pediatricians defend media exam. *USA Today,* p. 10D.

Esposito, B., & Koorland, M. (1989). Play behavior of hearing impaired children: Integrated and segregated settings. *Exceptional Children, 55,* 412–419.

Ferguson, J. (1997). What students say about mainstreaming. The *American School Board Journal, 184*(12), 18–19.

Fox, C., Kuhlman, N., & Sales, T. (1988). Cross-cultural concerns: What's missing from special education training programs? *Teacher Education and Special Education, 11,* 155–161.

Fradd, S., & Weismantel, J. (1988). Developing and evaluating the program. In S. Fradd & J. Weismantel (Eds.), *Meeting the needs of linguistically and culturally different students: A handbook for educational leaders.* Boston: Little, Brown and Company.

Fradd, S., Weismantel, J., Correa, V., & Algozzine, B. (1988). Developing a personnel training model for meeting the needs of handicapped and at-risk language-minority students. *Teacher Education and Special Education, 11,* 30–38.

Frisbee, C. (1988). *The role of the school psychologist with handicapped and at-risk students.* Unpublished manuscript, University of Florida, College of Education, Gainesville.

Frischkorn, D. (1997). Families and communities: You know you've been successful when. . . . *NEA Today, 15*(7), p. 21.

Fund for the Improvement and Reform of Schools and Teaching (FIRST). (1989, May 2). *Federal Register, 54*(83). (CFDA No. 84. 211A)

Gemmel, S., & Peterson, M. (1989). Supported employment and provision of on-going support services: A pilot project. *Career Development for Exceptional Individuals, 12,* 123–128.

Gensante, L., & Matgouranis, E. (1989). The more I see, the better I teach. *Educational Leadership, 46*(8), 28.

Gerber, M. (1988). Tolerance and technology of instruction: Implications for special education reform. *Exceptional Children, 54,* 309–314.

Graden, J., Casey, A., & Christenson, J. (1985). Implementing a pre-referral intervention system: Part I, the model. *Exceptional Children, 51,* 377–384.

Guralnick, M., & Groom, J. (1988). Peer interactions in mainstreamed and specialized classrooms: A comparative analysis. *Exceptional Children, 54,* 415–425.

Halloran, W., & Ward, M. (1988). Improving transition programming: Changing special education's focus. *The Pointer, 32*(2), 43–46.

Haring, N., & Phillips, E. (1972). *Analysis and modification of classroom behavior.* Englewood Cliffs, NJ: Prentice Hall.

Heal, L., Haney, J., & Novak Amado, A. (1988). *Integration of developmentally disabled individuals into the community* (2nd ed.). Baltimore: Paul H. Brookes.

Howell, B. (1981). Profile of the principalship. *Educational Leadership, 39,* 333–336.

Kagan, S., & Rivera, M. (1990). *Collaborations in action: Reshaping services for young children and their families.* New Haven, CT: Yale University, Bush Center in Child Development and Social Policy.

Kemmerer, A., Soeder, P., Szurek, A., & Carion, D. (1999). *A timely workshop.* Slippery Rock, PA: SRU College of Education School Collaboration Center.

Krauss, M. (1990). New precedent in family policy: Individualized family service plan. *Exceptional Children, 56*, 388–395.

Larrivee, B. (1985). *Effective teaching for successful mainstreaming.* New York: Longman Publishers.

Larsen, J. (1984). The school psychologist and the teacher. In C. V. Morsink (Ed.), *Teaching special needs students in regular classrooms* (pp. 72–74). Boston: Little, Brown and Company.

Littlejohn, B. (1989). *A change strategy for mainstreaming severely handicapped students into the regular classroom.* Unpublished paper, University of Florida, Department of Special Education, Gainesville.

Mack, F. (1988). Future trends in early childhood special education. *Reading Improvement, 25,* 132–145.

Magna Awards (1998). A jump start for at-risk kids. *The American School Board Journal, 185*(4), A26.

McDonnell, J., Hardman, M., & Hightower, J. (1989). Employment preparation for high school students with severe handicaps. *Mental Retardation, 27,* 396–404.

McLesky, J., Henry, D., & Hodges, D. (1998). Inclusion: Where is it happening? *TEACHING Exceptional Children, 31*(1), 4–10.

Meyer, W. (1997). A turn down the harbor with at-risk children. *Phi Delta Kappan, 87,* 312–316.

Morsink, C. V. (Ed.). (1983, November). (With contributors E. Ellis, N. Eggers, J. Wittenmyer, G. Meyer, T. Barker, H. Johnson, J. Anderson, B. Stone, H. Garner, B. Gellman, B. Simon, & C. Del Polito). *Context for generic guidelines for allied health and education professionals who serve persons with disabilities.* Synthesis of proceedings for Training Alliances in Health and Education meeting of the American Society of Allied Health Professionals (USDOE, OSERS, Grant G008301774). Philadelphia, PA: American Society of Allied Health Professionals.

Morsink, C. V. (1984). *Teaching special needs students in regular classrooms.* Boston: Little, Brown and Company.

Morsink, C. (1999). *21st century teachers for a better future.* Final Report to Howard Heinz Endowment. Slippery Rock, PA: SRU College of Education.

Morsink, C. V., & Lenk, L. (1992). The delivery of special education programs. *Remedial and Special Education, 13*(6), 33–43.

Morsink, C. V., Thomas, C., & Smith-Davis, J. (1987). Noncategorical special education programs: Process and outcomes. In M. Wang, M. Reynolds, & H. Walberg (Eds.), *Handbook of special education: Research and practice* (Vol. 1, pp. 287–312). Oxford, England: Pergamon.

Naisbitt, J. (1982). *Megatrends.* New York: Warner Books.

National Association of School Psychologists. (1974). The changing role of the school psychologist: Primary prevention. *School Psychology Digest, 3*(4), 4–25.

National Center for Schools and Communities. (1998). Community schools in the making. In *Conversations: Supporting children and families in the public schools.* New York: Fordham University Center.

NBC. (1999). School nurses. *Nightly News,* February 9, 1999.

Nevin, A., & Thousand, J. (1986). What the research says about limiting or avoiding referrals to special education. *Teacher Education and Special Education, 9,* 149–161.

Nunez, R., & Collignon, K. (1997). Creating a community of learning for homeless children. *Educational Leadership, 55*(2), 56–60.

Odom, S., & Warren, S. (1988). Early childhood special education in the year 2000. *Journal of the Division of Early Childhood, 12,* 263–271.

O'Neil, J. (1997). Building schools as communities: A conversation with James Comer. *Educational Leadership, 54*(8), 6–10.

Peterson, P. (1988). Teachers' and students' cognitional knowledge for classroom teaching and learning. *Educational Researcher, 17*(5), 5–14.

Pipho, C. (1997). The possibilities and problems of collaboration. *Phi Delta Kappan, 78,* 261–262.

Reed, S. (1988). Children with AIDS: How schools are handling the crisis [Special report]. *Phi Delta Kappan, 69,* K1–K12.

Reid, W. (1987). *Assessment and the Hispanic American*. Gainesville: University of Florida Project on Bilingual Special Education.

Rist, M. (1990, January). The shadow children. *The American School Board*, 19–24.

Roessler, R., Brolin, D., & Johnson, J. (1990). Factors affecting employment success and quality of life: A one year follow-up of students in special education. *Career Development for Exceptional Individuals, 13*(2), 95–107.

Rosenshine, B., & Stevens, R. (1986). Teaching functions. In M. C. Wittrock (Ed.), *Handbook of research on teaching* (3rd ed., pp. 376–391). New York: Macmillan.

Ross, D. (1989). First steps in developing a reflective approach. *Journal of Teacher Education, 40*(2), 22–30.

Ross, J. (1984). The physician and the teacher. In C. V. Morsink (Ed.), *Teaching special needs students in regular classrooms* (pp. 77–83). Boston: Little, Brown and Company.

Ryberg, S., & Sebastian, J. (1981). The multidisciplinary team. In M. Hardman, M. Egan, & E. Landau (Eds.), *What will we do in the morning?* (pp. 12–29). Dubuque, IA: William C. Brown.

Sigmon, S. (1987). Present roles and future objectives for school psychology. *Journal of Social Behavior and Personality, 2*, 379–382.

Sileo, T., Rude, H., & Luckner, J. (1988). Collaborative consultation: A model for transition planning for handicapped youth. *Education and Training in Mental Retardation, 23*, 333–339.

Spache, G., & Spache, E. (1986). *Reading in the elementary school* (5th ed.). Boston: Allyn & Bacon.

Tobias, A. (1988). *The role of the school counselor with handicapped and at-risk students*. Unpublished paper, University of Florida, College of Education, Gainesville.

Turnbull, R., & Cilley, M. (1999). *Explanations and implications of the 1997 amendments to IDEA*. Upper Saddle River, NJ: Merrill/Prentice Hall.

Villa, R., & Thousand, J. (1988). Enhancing success in heterogeneous classrooms and schools: The powers of partnership. *Teacher Education and Special Education, 11*, 144–154.

Vincent, L., & Salisbury, C. (1988). Changing economic and social influences on family involvement. *Topics in Early Childhood Special Education, 8*(1), 48–59.

Wang, M., Haertel, G., & Walberg, H. (1997). *What do we know: Widely implemented school improvement programs*. Philadelphia: Mid-Atlantic Educational Lab at Temple University.

Wells, K. (1997). Professional development for parents. *The American School Board Journal, 184*(1), 38–39.

Wesson, C., Fuchs, L., Tindal, G., Mirkin, P., & Deno, S. (1986). Facilitating the efficacy of ongoing curriculum-based measurement. *Teacher Education and Special Education, 9*, 166–172.

Westby, C. (1985). Learning to talk—talking to learn: Oral-literature language differences. In *Communication skills and classroom success* (Vol. 1, pp. 181–213). San Diego: College Hill Press.

White, S. (1997). Family friendly schools. *The American School Board Journal, 184*(3), 31–33.

Williams, A. L. (1996). Enacting constructivist transactions. In J. Henderson (Ed.), *Reflective teaching: A study of your constructivist practices* (2nd ed., pp. 105–120). Englewood Cliffs, NJ: Merrill/Prentice Hall.

Wlodkowski, R., & Ginsberg, M. (1995). A framework for culturally responsive teaching. *Educational Leadership, 53*(1), 17–21.

Wolfensberger, W. (1972). *The principal of normalization in human services*. Toronto: National Institute on Mental Retardation.

5 Enhancing Communication Skills

Topics in this chapter include:

- Description of a model of communication.
- Characteristics of communication in interactive teaming.
- Factors to consider in communication.
- Forms of communication.
- Strategies for managing conflict.
- An application illustrating effective and ineffective communication.

Principals and central office personnel have circulated the following example of what can happen as people try to communicate with each other. The original source of this communiqué is not known.

Halley's Comet

A school superintendent told the assistant superintendent the following: "Next Thursday at 10:30 a.m. Halley's Comet will appear over this area. This is an event that occurs only once every 75 years. Call the school principals and have them assemble their teachers and classes on their athletic fields and explain this phenomenon to them. If it rains, cancel the day's observation and have the classes meet in the auditorium to see a film about the comet."

The memo from the assistant superintendent to the principals stated: "By order of the superintendent of schools, next Thursday at 10:30 Halley's Comet will appear over your athletic field. If it rains, then cancel the day's classes and report to the auditorium with your teachers and students. You will be shown films, a phenomenal event which occurs only once every 75 years."

The principals announced to the teachers: "By order of the phenomenal superintendent of schools, at 10:30 next Thursday Halley's Comet will appear in the auditorium. In case of rain over the athletic field, the superintendent will give another order—something which occurs once every 75 years."

Teachers told their students: "Next Thursday at 10:30 the superintendent of schools will appear in our auditorium with Halley's Comet, something which occurs every 75 years. If it rains, the superintendent will cancel the comet and order us all out to our phenomenal athletic field."

Students reported to their parents: "When it rains next Thursday at 10:30 over the school athletic field, the phenomenal 75-year-old superintendent will cancel all classes and appear before the whole school in the auditorium accompanied by Bill Halley and the Comets."

In Chapter 4, the roles of parents and various professionals were described. Interactions among people who may have different perspectives in a team or consultative setting are affected by how well those involved are able to use a variety of communication skills to share and receive information and to resolve conflicts. The humorous Halley's Comet example illustrates how important accuracy and clarity are in preventing misunderstandings that may result when people in different roles attempt to communicate with one another.

The importance of communication skills for consultants and team members has been strongly supported in the literature. In fact, many people believe expertise in communication may be the most vital skill the individual can possess. Gutkin and Curtis (1982) stated:

> At the heart of all consultation methodology is the consultant's ability to establish a helping relationship and communicate effectively with the consultee. At its most basic level, consultation is an interpersonal exchange. As such, the consultant's success is going to hinge largely on his or her communication and relationship skills. (p. 822)

Pugach and Johnson (1995) commented:

> Perhaps the most important skill of effective collaborators is the ability to communicate ideas effectively. Communication is the foundation of all interactions between humans. Without the ability to communicate, our lives would be barren. (p. 49)

Communication skills also have been identified through research studies and inclusion in training programs as required areas for development and expertise. In her study on the consultation skills needed by resource teachers, Friend (1984) surveyed principals, regular classroom teachers, and resource teachers. The educators said they placed much importance on such skills as establishing a climate of trust, explaining perceptions of a problem, defining problems, interviewing, resolving conflicts by using strategies to minimize hard feelings, and using specific strategies to facilitate interpersonal communication.

Similar results were obtained by West and Cannon (1988) in their study of collaborative consultation strategies needed by regular and special educators. Their results included the description of competency statements in the areas of personal characteristics, interactive communication, and collaborative problem solving—all of which relate to communication as a facilitating factor in interactive teaming. Dieker and Barnett (1996) observed, "The overall success of co-teaching hinges on one major factor: communication between teachers" (p. 7). Bruneau-Balderrama (1997) described important elements in implementing inclusion, and noted: "Probably the most important factor in the success of any collaborative endeavor is open and frequent communication" (p. 329).

This chapter includes a description of a communication model and a discussion of vital characteristics of communication involved in interactive teaming. Factors to consider in communication are explained. The nonverbal, listening, and verbal forms of communication are described, along with skills to be developed and barriers that can be present. The final section of the chapter deals with procedures for managing conflict and resistance.

COMPONENTS OF THE PROCESS OF COMMUNICATION

Definition of Communication

Communication can be defined as a dynamic and ongoing process in which people share ideas, information, and feelings. The skills involved in communication are "not ends in themselves, but means or instruments that must be placed at the service of helping outcomes in order to be meaningful" (Egan, 1986, p. 73).

McKenna (1998) noted that the purpose of communication is to share information, and what is said is "only as effective and informative as how it's heard" (p. 10). Martin and Nakayama (2000) defined communication as a "symbolic process whereby reality is produced, maintained, repaired, and transformed" (p. 78), and commented that communication "occurs whenever someone attributes meaning to another person's words or actions" (p. 61). These authors also delineated the complexity of intercultural communication by describing it as "both cultural and individual, personal and contextual, characterized by differences and similarities, static and dynamic, oriented to the present and the past, and characterized by both privilege and disadvantage" (p. 49).

ELEMENTS OF THE COMMUNICATION PROCESS

The communication process comprises several elements, as shown in Figure 5.1. Hybels and Weaver (1997) described these elements as follows: *Senders-receivers* are the people who are sending and receiving the messages. Typically, people are senders and receivers at the same time because they are both initiating communication and receiving another's responses simultaneously. The *message* is composed of the ideas and thoughts being transmitted through verbal and nonverbal forms of communication. The *channel* is the route traveled by the message, which typically involves both sound and sight because we look at people's facial expressions as well as hear their words. *Feedback* is the response of the senders-receivers to each other, and as in the message, feedback can be both verbal and nonverbal. Feedback enables the sender to gauge whether or not the receiver understood the message as it was intended. *Noise* is the physical (e.g., loud voices, truck passing) or psychological (e.g., daydreaming, planning a trip) interference that prevents the message from being accurately comprehended. The *setting* is the location where the communication is taking place. Because settings can be formal (e.g., office or auditorium) or informal (e.g., comfortable room, restaurant), they can affect the feelings people have while they are communicating. Another variable to consider is whether the location represents someone's "territory," such as the director or principal's office, and whether that location intentionally or unintentionally intimidates the others involved in the communication (cf. Dettmer, Thurston, & Dyck, 1993; Idol, Paolucci-Whitcomb, & Nevin, 1986; Martin & Nakayama, 2000; McKenna, 1998).

Figure 5.1
Elements of the communication process.

Source: From *Communicating Effectively,* 5th ed. (p. 13) by S. Hybels and R. L. Weaver, 1997, New York: McGraw-Hill. Reprinted by permission of The McGraw-Hill Companies, Inc.

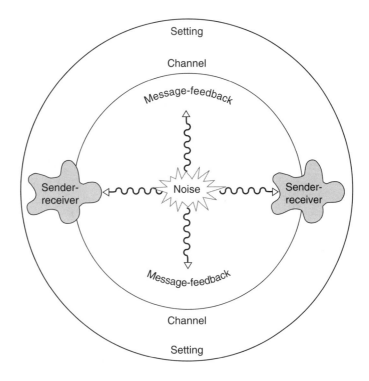

CHARACTERISTICS OF EFFECTIVE COMMUNICATION IN INTERACTIVE TEAMING

In addition to being cognizant of the various elements of communication, team members need to be sensitive to the characteristics of effective interactions. Lang, Quick, and Johnson (1981) noted that good communication is *purposeful,* with an intent clear to all parties; *planned,* in terms of thinking through what should be transmitted; *personalized,* according to the receiver's background; *open,* in terms of people's being able to express feelings; and *clear,* in that the words used are part of the other's language. On the latter point of clarity, Ehly and Eliason (1983) cautioned professionals in the fields of education and psychology to be aware of their use of jargon and "psychobabble" (e.g., IEP, BEH, PDP, CAT testing), which can interfere with understanding.

Fishbaugh (1997) cited the importance of personal characteristics such as *open-mindedness, acceptance,* and *flexibility* to ensure positive individual interactions. Katzenbach and Smith (1999) listed the following significant interpersonal skills: *risk taking, helpful criticism, objectivity, active listening, giving the benefit of the doubt, support,* and *recognizing the interests and achievements of others.*

Turnbull and Turnbull (1990) identified two prerequisites to effective communication that are vital to the teaming process: *knowing ourselves* and *developing respect and trust.* Gaining and maintaining the respect of others are obviously vital to the success of interactive team members. Establishing rapport can be accomplished by being willing to share information and learn from others (i.e., role release), treating others with respect, sharing credit for ideas, participating in activities beyond the scope of one's job (e.g., extracurricular and social functions), and demonstrating credibility by being aware of the domains of team members, such as showing an understanding of the dynamics of a regular classroom (Fishbaugh, 1997; Heron & Harris, 1987; Idol et al., 1986; Lopez, Dalal, & Yoshida, 1993; Spodek, 1982; Vargo, 1998).

Two final characteristics of communication required in teaming have been described previously in this text, but they merit repetition because of their importance: *confidentiality* and *sensitivity to cultural differences*. The willingness to protect the confidentiality of information shared in the collaboration and consultation of teaming interactions is vital (Gutkin, 1996). A person involved in such situations has only to be let down once by a consultant's or team member's breaking a confidence for him or her to be reluctant to participate again. Similarly, people from various cultures who receive adverse feedback on their communication skills or who are rebuffed by people who are unaware or uncaring about communication norms in their culture may learn to be defensive or unresponsive as a coping strategy.

FACTORS TO CONSIDER IN COMMUNICATION

Several factors affect the communication process as it occurs in the consultation and collaboration of teaming. These factors are related to personal characteristics; cultural differences; attitudes and experiences; the existence of backup support, such as data; and context and situational variables. Each of these factors is described in the following sections.

Personal Factors

The qualities identified by Rogers (1961) as most important for people in helping roles were empathy, genuineness, and unconditional positive regard. *Empathy* is the ability to understand the world of others by "walking a mile in their shoes." Empathy is not the same as sympathy, which involves feeling sorry for someone; rather, it is placing oneself in the situation to examine how that person feels (Brown, Pryzwansky, & Schulte, 1998; Egan, 1986). In his review of the literature, Gladstein (1983) noted that two forms of empathy were described: emotional empathy, or the ability to be affected by someone else's emotional feelings; and role-taking empathy, which involves the ability to understand another's frame of reference or point of view.

Genuineness is the ability to be "real" in caring for others, instead of dealing with them in a superficial manner. Gutkin and Curtis (1982) referred to genuineness as the "cardinal rule" of effective communication, though as Turnbull and

Turnbull (1990) recognized, this level of caring is not always as easy as it may appear: "On the contrary, many go through life seeking to develop this quality in themselves. It requires hard work to awaken this quality in ourselves and inspire it in others" (p. 114). *Unconditional positive regard* is the ability to accept others without prejudice or bias, and to realize that they are entitled to their opinions.

Two other qualities named by Hybels and Weaver (1997) as contributing to or detracting from communication are initiative and assertiveness. *Initiative* involves taking the lead, as appropriate, to facilitate the process. *Assertiveness* is the ability to stand up confidently for what one thinks or feels. Assertiveness is often confused with aggressiveness, but the latter refers to an attempt to establish power and control even at the expense of the feelings of others. An aggressive team member may speak and act as though he is not concerned with the emotions or positions of other members, and this may set up a confrontational relationship. In her study of the contrasting behaviors of assertiveness, nonassertiveness, and aggressiveness, Arab (1985) noted that those who are assertive are effective collaborators, whereas those who exhibit characteristics of the other two behaviors are not.

Fine, Grantham, and Wright (1979) compiled another set of personal factors that can play a role in the effectiveness of people in collaborative or consultative roles. These factors are predominantly concerned with how the person in a helping role attends to his or her own needs and how that process facilitates or impedes consultation. They cited the following considerations:

1. The consultant's identity remains the same; that is, his or her own orientation and feelings about life and self cannot be separated from the consultation process.

2. The consultant needs to adhere to his or her own needs to be able to help others; that is, stress management and rejuvenation are vital to be able to continue to give to others.

3. The problem belongs to the consultee, not to the consultant; that is, consultants should be facilitators and assist in problem solving, but they should not "own" the problem.

4. The consultant must be willing to let go of feelings about "the way it is supposed to be"; that is, remember the purpose is to help another person grow and develop skills, rather than force him or her to follow a certain program or become a "clone."

5. Lack of closure in this process is acceptable; the problems to be resolved will take time and cannot be forced or speeded up.

6. The consultant should not try to carry the burden alone; others in the system should be called on to share their expertise.

7. The perceptions and expectations of all concerned should be made explicit; that is, people in helping positions should clarify roles and responsibilities.

8. Alternatives should be offered to the consultee; that is, when a person is willing to try different interventions that have been suggested, the consultant

should permit the person to select the one that seems most viable, and then support him or her in attempts to implement it.

9. People involved should view this as a problem-sovling process; the solutions will take time, rather than being immediate answers. Also, a number of problem-solving approaches can be used.

10. A broad skill repertoire is essential; that is, people in helping roles must be familiar with a variety of strategies and techniques.

11. Success must be considered as a value judgment; that is, all possible outcomes of the helping process—such as changes in the child, system, parents, and other professionals—must be considered, rather than determining success or failure based on one indicator.

Cultural Differences

As Ramirez, Lepage, Kratchowill, and Duffy (1998) noted: "School consultants almost inevitably provide services to individuals who are different from themselves in their culture of origin" (p. 479). Awareness of and sensitivity to cultural differences in communication and decision-making processes are vital for interactive team members. Jackson and Hughley-Hayes (1993) observed that the ability to acknowledge cultural differences in communication and relationships enhances the potential for success in interactions (cf. Martin & Nakayama, 2000).

Because teams and families include members with diverse cultural norms and different interaction skills, it is important for interactive team members to develop expertise in *cross-cultural* or *intercultural communication skills* (cf. Martin & Nakayama, 2000). If such skills are not developed, conflicts among professionals and between professionals and the families they serve are likely to occur.

The primary differences in cultural norms among diverse ethnic groups identified by Hallman, Bryant, Campbell, McGuire, and Bowman (1983) related to how individuals perceive self, family, religion, sex roles, society, human nature, nature, and the supernatural. Belton-Owens (1999) noted that differences of all kinds, including race, religion, economics, and many forms of social behaviors, may be barriers between home and school.

According to Lynch and Hanson (1992), it is important for collaborators to "engage in cross-cultural interactions that explore differences openly and respectfully, interactions that dispel myths and open doors to understanding" (p. 50). Roberts, Bell, and Salend (1991) identified the following abilities as important to develop:

(a) understanding and appreciating cultural differences in verbal and nonverbal communication styles,

(b) determining whether organizational mores tend to privilege or silence different groups of people,

(c) developing a common set of meanings among collaborators, and

(d) analyzing the language used by collaborators and changing linguistic practices that are disabling to the collaborators (as summarized in Harris, 1996, p. 357).

Harris (1996) commented: "People who are effective cross-cultural communicators tend to respect individuals; make continued and sincere attempts to take others' points of view, be open to learn, and be flexible; have a sense of humor; and tolerate ambiguity well" (p. 357). Harris also described generic and specific interpersonal and communication skills for a multicultural society. These skills are included in Table 5.1.

Individuals from the nondominant culture who aspire to become professionals in special services programs and serve on interactive teams will confront some conflicts as they encounter the differences between what they value and the behaviors expected of "good" students and families in traditional schools. It may take more time, energy, and commitment on the part of professionals from different cultural backgrounds to develop a level of shared understanding, common knowledge, and communication skills that will provide them with a basis for collaboration. However, intercultural communication and collaboration of professionals with families allows all members of the team to contribute to the development of effective instructional programs for students from diverse backgrounds.

Attitudinal and Experiential Factors

Closely linked with personal qualities and cultural differences are attitudinal and experiential factors that are the result of how team members feel about themselves, others, and the consultation or teaming process based on the experiences they have had. The factors can be examined individually from every team member's perspective, but for brevity's sake, in this chapter they are described from the viewpoints of the consultant, consultee, and parents, because team members tend to fit into one of these three categories.

Weissenburger, Fine, and Poggio (1982) conducted a study on consultant and teacher characteristics as they related to the outcomes of consultation. They cited six teacher attitudes that may interfere with interventions suggested by a consultant (based on the work of Grieger, 1972). Those attitudes were "(a) the child needs fixing, (b) it is wrong to express negative feelings, (c) children must not be frustrated, (d) children 'should-ought' to behave in certain ways, (e) children are blameworthy for their misdeeds, and (f) the child 'makes me' feel that way" (p. 263).

The study by Weissenburger et al. (1982) yielded several other attitudes that can affect communication and the teaming process. They found that consultant facilitativeness as perceived by teachers was positively related to problem resolution, as well as teacher attitudes of "I'm OK—you're OK." Teacher dogmatism, or holding tightly to one's own beliefs rather than trying to learn from others, was found to hinder the desired outcomes of consultation.

Parents' attitudes also are affected by their previous experiences. Turnbull and Turnbull (1990) cited the following areas that can positively or negatively affect

Table 5.1

Generic and Specific Interpersonal and Communication Skills for a Multicultural Society

Generic	Specific
Exhibit the following **interpersonal** skills:	
Be caring	Make continued and sincere attempts to understand the world from others' points of view
Be respectful	
Be empathetic	Respect individuals from other cultures
Be congruent	Have a sense of humor
Be open	Tolerate ambiguity
Show positive self-concept	Approach others with a desire to learn
Show enthusiastic attitude	Be prepared and willing to share information about yourself
Show willingness to learn from others	
Be calm	Identify needed multicultural knowledge base
Try to live stress-free	Move fluidly between the roles of giver and taker of information
Be a risk taker	
Be flexible	
Be resilient	
Manage conflict and confrontation	
Manage time	
Exhibit the following **communication** skills:	
Listening	Work effectively with an interpreter or translator
Acknowledging	Use nontechnical language as an aid in equalizing differences between collaborators
Paraphrasing	
Reflecting	Acknowledge cultural differences in communication- and relationship-building
Clarifying	
Elaborating	Use communication to create systems of meaning among collaborators
Summarizing	Identify language practices that are disabling and change them
Grasping overt meaning	
Grasping covert meaning	Ensure that problem identification does not conflict with cultural beliefs
Interpreting nonverbal communication	
Interviewing effectively	Use information regarding socially hidden aspects of power that privilege or silence culturally diverse groups in problem solving
Providing feedback	
Brainstorming	
Responding nonjudgmentally	

Source: From "Collaboration Within a Multicultural Society: Issues for Consideration" by K. C. Harris, 1996, *Remedial and Special Education, 17*(6), 355–362, 376. Copyright 1996 by PRO-ED, Inc. Reprinted by permission.

communication: parents' past experiences in dealing with professionals, personalities and values, and expectations and stereotypes. In addition, Bailey (1987) noted that often parents and professionals' priorities for education or treatment are different. He also commented that parents may appear to lack motivation if they do not understand the relevance of requests, or they may lack the time, skill, energy, or resources to follow up on recommendations. Professionals may not understand the needs of the family or may be unable to motivate family members, all of which contribute to the attitudes of both sides regarding future communication (Bailey, 1987).

Pruitt, Wandry, and Hollums (1998) studied 73 families that included children or adolescents who were receiving special education services. They found that the overwhelming majority of parents recommended that educators should realize that parents know and understand their children, and recognize that the contributions and suggestions of parents are valuable and should be respected. The parents also urged that educators use a more humane demeanor when discussing their children, listen more, interact in an honest manner, and treat individuals with dignity and respect.

Additional attitudinal considerations related to how perceptions can "color one's vision" are concerned with how parents may be categorized by professionals. Sonnenschien (1984) described how professionals can view parents in negative ways and thereby diminish effective communication. Sonnenschien stated that professionals can consider parents as vulnerable clients, patients, the cause of the problem, adversaries, less observant, hostile, less intelligent, resistant, denying, or anxious. Any of these views may have a negative effect on expectations for success or the development of a productive relationship with parents.

Two final considerations are the use of emotion-laden words and the lack of common experiences. On the former point, it is important to realize that parents will be particularly sensitive to words that describe their child in terms such as *retarded, handicapped,* or *disturbed.* Although it may be necessary to use these labels in program placement, professionals should take care to explain their meanings, as well as their tentative status and limitations. Also, the negative effect may be softened if professionals introduce such terms to parents in a private setting, rather than using them first in a team meeting (Losen & Losen, 1985).

The lack of common experiences is particularly evident in cases such as a childless professional who cannot understand the fatigue experienced by a working single parent who is asked to implement speech and physical therapy follow-up every night with a child who has multiple disabilities. The parent may lack the professional's understanding of the importance of this follow-up in successful therapy. Open communication on the part of both parties can help bridge this gap. Interactive team members should remember to treat each situation individually and, as much as possible, to avoid stereotyping parents and other professionals based on previous experiences.

Backup Support Factors

A source of backup support for communication interactions is the existence of data. Each team member will be able to provide different types of data depending on the area of expertise. For example:

◆ Parents will be able to describe developmental milestones and home behaviors.
◆ Regular classroom teachers can contribute data on curriculum, achievement tests, and group teaching strategies.
◆ Psychologists can delineate the interpretation of intelligence tests.
◆ Special educators can outline teaching techniques and strategies for individualizing.
◆ Adaptive physical educators and physical therapists can demonstrate movement limitations and modifications.
◆ Counselors and social workers can share perspectives on emotional factors.
◆ Assistive technology specialists can provide options for adapted microcomputers or other communication devices.

To provide these different types of data, team members will use observation as well as appropriate data collection strategies unique to their professional fields, such as single-subject designs (Tawney & Gast, 1984; Zirpoli & Melloy, 1993), achievement and intelligence tests (Overton, 2000; Venn, 2000), or statistical interpretations of other types of tests (Kerlinger, 1986; Sax, 1997).

One strategy for collecting and sharing data that is useful at the beginning of a team or consultative process is the *informational interview* (Hudson, 1987), which was illustrated in one of the Application sections in Chapter 4. Any team member can use this strategy to establish rapport and share information with another. The six steps in the informational interview are these: (1) preplanning, (2) establishing rapport, (3) stating the purpose, (4) providing information, (5) using specific questions to obtain information, and (6) summarizing and planning a follow-up. These steps are illustrated in Figure 5.2.

Data collection is particularly important for the team as members attempt to identify problems, determine appropriate interventions, and evaluate the effectiveness of strategies that have been implemented. Team members will need to take the initiative in gathering appropriate data, organizing the data, and then sharing the results with others in an understandable manner.

Context or Situational Factors

The final set of factors that can affect communication are those related to the context or situation in which the interactions will occur. Hudson (1987) described two types of situations: proactive and reactive. In a *proactive* situation, parents and professionals meet to establish a positive relationship and share information. In

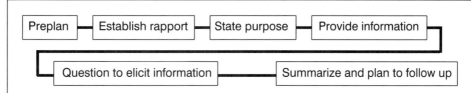

Steps:

1. *Preplan*—formalize an appointment, review any background material, and decide on questions to be asked.

2. *Establish rapport*—at the beginning of the meeting, talk briefly about nonprofessional interests that people may have in common. In Hawaii, this is called "talk story." On the mainland, it is often called "small talk."

3. *State purpose*—clarify the purpose of the meeting by stating that you are attempting to establish some common ground and to get to know each other in ways that will enable you to work together more productively.

4. *Provide information*—discuss yourself as a professional. Talk about your "philosophy" of education if you are talking with another educator. You may have a diagnostic-prescriptive philosophy that emphasizes the importance of individual differences which may be in contrast with the mainstream teacher's focus on group learning approaches. Or you may have an educational, as contrasted to a medical, orientation to treatment which differs from that of some health-related professionals. Share your ideas in a way that suggests you are trying to identify areas of commonality. Share samples of the child's work or some supportive data if you are talking with a parent.

5. *Use specific questions to elicit information*—ask questions about the other person's role, background, and philosophy. The focus here should be on ways in which you can work together. Search for commonalities in comparing what this person tells you and the information you provided to them.

6. *Summarize and plan to follow up*—stress the idea that this is the first step in what you hope will be a long and productive relationship. Thank the other person for their time and effort and indicate that you will be contacting them again. If you have a specific time or purpose, state it and try to arrange a common meeting time.

Figure 5.2 Informational interview.

Source: From *Proactive and Reactive Consultation: A Model for Preservice Training* by P. Hudson, 1987. Unpublished manuscript, University of Florida, Department of Special Education, Gainesville. Adapted by permission.

this context they can be more relaxed, because they are meeting to anticipate and prevent problems. In a *reactive* situation, the team is meeting as a result of a problem being manifested, and therefore members may be more emotional. In a reactive context, the emphasis in communication must shift from information sharing to listening, supporting, and discussing possible interventions.

FORMS OF COMMUNICATION

All the factors previously described can affect both forms of communication— nonverbal and verbal—and listening, which is a "bridge" between the two forms. *Nonverbal* behaviors include attending to what is being said and encompass what is commonly referred to as "body language." *Listening* involves understanding the message and indicating that understanding to the sender. *Verbal* behaviors include such strategies as descriptive statements, paraphrasing, and questioning. Each set of skills is now described in more detail.

Nonverbal Behaviors

Most communication messages are transmitted in ways other than the use of words alone. In fact, it has been suggested that up to 90% of the content of a message may be transmitted through nonverbal behaviors and vocal inflections. Pugach and Johnson (1995) commented that nonverbal communication is very powerful, and often the nonverbal messages are a more accurate representation of the actual intent of the communication than what is verbally transmitted.

Body Language and Attending Skills.   Body language often is the transmitter of silent messages, such as when a speaker diverts his eyes or covers part of his face (Nierenberg & Calero, 1971). Cramer (1998) noted that learning to "read" body language can help assess one's effectiveness as a speaker. She commented that the body language of the listener can signal the acceptance or understanding of what is being said, or it can indicate lack of comprehension or rejection of the message of the speaker.

Closely related to body language are *attending skills*. These behaviors indicate that the listener or receiver is psychologically and emotionally present and listening. Egan (1986) summarized five attending behaviors: (1) facing the person squarely or turning toward the person with whom you are communicating, (2) having an open posture instead of crossing arms and legs, (3) leaning toward the other person at times to indicate attentiveness, (4) maintaining eye contact, and (5) appearing relaxed and interested instead of fidgeting or looking at your watch. He cited the following advantages to the effective use of attending behaviors: (1) They let people know you are "with them" instead of thinking about or responding to other things in the environment, (2) the behaviors assist in establishing and maintaining good rapport, and (3) using these strategies puts the person in the position of being an effective listener.

Interpreting Nonverbal Messages.   Egan (1986) noted that nonverbal messages can modify a verbal message in the following ways: confirm, deny, confuse, emphasize, or control. In certain situations, however, "negative" nonverbal signals can be sent to understanding or familiar listeners without penalty. If certain team members appear to be bored, when in reality they are simply tired, it is probable that the understanding listener will forgive them. In contrast, if they send the same signal to a team leader who is sensitive to the need for respect, inattentiveness may be interpreted as rudeness or hostility. It is permissible for the team member to assume a relaxed posture—leaning back, with hands clasped behind neck—with an old friend, but the team member who portrays this nonverbal image to a parent or a newly introduced professional peer risks being thought of as uninterested and unwilling to modify professional beliefs. Obviously, the danger of misinterpretation of nonverbal signals is more acute at the beginning of a relationship than after it has been established and people know how to "read" others' signals.

Team members must be able to pick up on nonverbal signals for two important reasons. First, they can avoid sending messages that may hinder communication in the sense that they are perceived negatively by the receiver. Second, people who are able to accurately "read" their listeners' nonverbal behaviors can use this feedback to enhance their communications. When receivers send negative signals, the perceptive sender changes the verbal or nonverbal message being sent. Ignoring the signals can have disastrous consequences, whereas reading them and responding accordingly can have great benefits (Losen & Losen, 1985).

Considerations.   As Martin and Nakayama (2000) observed, nonverbal communication is symbolic, governed by rules that are contextually determined, and developed through cultural experiences. Interactive team members must be cognizant of the fact that nonverbal communication behaviors differ among cultural groups. For example, in the mainstream culture of the United States, it is considered important for the sender and receiver to receive feedback by looking at each other's eyes. However, this may not be true in every culture; in many Asian cultures, too much direct eye contact is a signal of disrespect, particularly when given by a person in a position of lower status. The appropriateness of touch and physical proximity also varies according to cultural standards, with people in Hispanic cultures tending to touch more and stand closer than those in Asian cultures. Smiling, which usually signals happiness and acceptance in the dominant cultural groups in the United States, may reflect embarrassment or even anger in some Asian cultures. In high context cultures, such as African-American, there is less reliance on verbal communication, so nonverbal communication and interpretation are very important (Miranda, 1993).

For the successful team member, it is also important to remember that the word *culture* can have a very general meaning. In the broadest sense, a culture is any group that has a history and comes together around a set of common goals, standards, and language. The teaching profession is a culture, and it is different from the cultures of physical therapy and social work. Each school or agency often has its own culture, just as each family has its own set of standards and customs. The team member who is not aware of those nonverbal behaviors that are expected in a particular professional culture is well advised to behave conservatively; for example, be careful about invading another's personal space or using extended direct eye contact. This sensitivity to nonverbal communication differences is especially important for all team members at the early stages of their interactions in a new group.

Listening

Listening can be considered a "bridge" between the nonverbal and verbal forms of communication because it incorporates elements of both and affects both. Listening also is a way to understand thoughts and needs as well as to demonstrate empathy. As Covey (1989) stated: "Seek first to understand, then to be understood" (p. 235).

Egan (1986) said:

> The art of listening has three parts: (1) listening to and understanding nonverbal behavior; (2) listening to and understanding verbal messages; and (3) listening to and understanding the person. (p. 79)

Importance of Listening.   According to Hybels and Weaver (1997), listening makes up more than half of the time devoted to the various communications skills (see Figure 5.3). Despite its importance, however, Bolton (1979) commented that very few people are truly good listeners. Based on the research available, he found that even at the purely informational level it is estimated that 75% of what is heard is ignored, misunderstood, or quickly forgotten. McKenna's (1998) estimate of the amount of time spent listening was much higher than Hybels and Weaver indicated. She stated that people spend up to 80% of each day listening. She also commented: "Listening is our most frequently used communication skill, yet we often feel that it requires no effort on our part" (p. 30).

Styles of Listening.   Gordon (1970) described two styles of listeners: active and passive. Turnbull and Turnbull (1990) stated that most people tend to prefer one

Figure 5.3
Percentage of time devoted to various communication skills.

Source: From *Communicating Effectively*, 5th ed. (p. 13) by S. Hybels and R. L. Weaver, 1997, New York: McGraw-Hill. Reprinted by permission of The McGraw-Hill Companies, Inc.

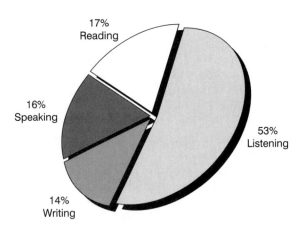

17%
Reading

16%
Speaking

53%
Listening

14%
Writing

style or another, but effective listeners use both styles depending on the situation. *Passive listeners* often are silent, but they remain involved in the interaction by demonstrating attending behaviors and giving words of encouragement. This style of listening is particularly appropriate when a team member needs to "vent" and share emotions.

In *active listening* the receiver is much more involved and animated. The listener frequently makes comments, asks questions, and shares his or her own experiences (Turnbull & Turnbull, 1990). Gordon (1970) believed this style of listening encourages people to express thoughts, assists in building relationships, and helps in finding solutions to problems. McKenna (1998) described this type of listening as *reflective listening*. She noted that reflective listening allows the listener to focus on the central points of the issue, and encourages the speaker to describe his or her feelings and position on the topic.

Active or reflective listening also communicates to other team members basic attitudes about how a receiver or listener feels toward and may react to another person. Gordon (1970) delineated these attitudes as follows:

1. You must *want* to hear what the other person has to say.
2. You must sincerely want to help the person with his/her problem.
3. You must genuinely be able to accept the other person's feelings, no matter how different they are from your own.
4. You must trust the other person's capacity to handle, work through, and find solutions to his/her own problems.
5. You must realize and appreciate that feelings are transitory in nature; consequently you need not fear them.
6. You must view the other person as separate from yourself with alternative ways of perceiving the world (summarized in Turnbull & Turnbull, 1990, p. 131.)

Listening Skills.   In implementing active listening, Gordon (1974) recommended the following three steps:

1. The receiver should listen carefully to what is being said.
2. After hearing the expression of strong feelings, the receiver should restate the feelings.
3. After restating those feelings, the receiver should infer the reason for the feelings. The statement is "You feel . . . (angry) because. . . . "

This strategy can be used effectively in conversations among good friends or between a therapist and a client in a private meeting. There is, however, a certain amount of risk involved with using the "you" message in a team meeting, because the statement that one individual knows how and why another feels a certain way may be considered arrogant or rude. The suggested modification for use by team members is to soften the inference about feelings and to eliminate the use of the word *because*. This type of feedback is more appropriately used in a group discussion, particularly one in which the participants are relatively unknown to each other. The empathy statement in this case would be "It sounds as if you are angry about this. . . . "

Other skills to indicate a person is listening and to clarify what has been heard have been described by Brammer (1988). *Paraphrasing* involves responding to basic messages being sent by another person. *Clarifying* includes restating points or requesting restatements to ensure understanding. *Perception checking* is a strategy to determine the accuracy of the feelings or emotions detected. These skills, along with examples to illustrate how they can be used, are summarized along with verbal skills in Figure 5.4, provided in the next section.

Verbal Behaviors

Like nonverbal and listening skills, verbal signals are critical for team members who wish to send and receive messages accurately. The elements of verbal skills to be discussed are paralanguage, content-level sequences, verbal skills, and roadblocks.

Paralanguage.   The way people say things is referred to as *paralanguage*. Hybels and Weaver (1997) identified the components of paralanguage as *rate* (speed), *pitch* (high or low), *volume* (loudness), and *quality* (pleasing or unpleasing). Each of these components can affect the meaning and interpretation of what is being said.

Another important component of paralanguage is *intonation*. Often intonation (i.e., *how* it is said rather than *what* is said) is a more powerful and more primitive conveyor of meaning than are words. The intonations in language convey warmth or disapproval to an infant, even before there is an understanding of words. When used by speakers of a foreign language, intonation also is effective in communicating meanings in the absence of specific word comprehension. The effective receiver or listener uses verbal intonation in a way similar to a handwriting analysis—to determine deeper meanings. Eisenhardt (1972) developed a series of examples that illustrate the point. She asked how many different ways can the word *please* be said and have it mean something different each time? A teacher might say "Please!" to a child tapping his pencil annoyingly. A friend says "Please" to another friend when begging for a favor. In each example the word remains the same, but the elements of intonation convey different meanings. Those elements are *stress, pitch,* and *juncture* (pause).

The three elements of intonation can be used effectively by team members to communicate assertiveness, neutrality, or empathy, depending on the situation and the previous responses of others in the group. For example, suppose the team member assuming the role of leader needs to communicate emphatically that the group will not make a decision on the basis of a single, biased test. The intonation of the message would communicate assertively, "We will not violate this child's right to a multidimensional assessment, nor to the parent's right to due process!" The words "not" and "right" would receive stress; a pause for emphasis would be placed between the words "assessment" and "nor," and the pitch would be lowered decisively at the end of the sentence.

Conversely, the team member who had just been told by a divorced mother that her ex-husband had refused to pay child support would use a different into-nation to convey empathy. The response, "Things must be really tough for you right now" would be characterized by softer inflections: a wavy pitch without distinct juncture, and stress on either the word "tough" or "you," depending on the focus of the conversation. (For additional information on these constructs, see McKenna, 1998, or Martin & Nakayama, 2000.)

Content-Level Sequence.   Fong (1986) has shown that there are different levels in the emotional content of verbal messages, each of which is appropriate at a different point in the sequence of developing a relationship with another person. It is possible to share feelings with a close associate, but not with a stranger; it is easier to criticize a friend than an enemy. Each of these situations illustrates the importance of using the appropriate level of emotional content in communication. According to Fong (1986), there are four levels: (1) small talk, (2) communicating an interest in common work or other experiences, (3) sharing some information about self, and (4) intimacy, the "you and I" relationship and feelings.

The first level, *small talk,* is characterized by impersonal contact, such as might be used with a total stranger in the supermarket. The topics of conversation that would be appropriate to use with a person standing in the checkout line include the weather, prices, and headlines. All of these are impersonal topics that can be shared superficially with someone sharing a temporary environment. If the com-ments are too lengthy or personal, the listener likely will turn away in discomfort. On first meeting, to tell another person about a death in the family is the verbal counterpart of throwing one's arms around a total stranger. This may seem an extreme and unlikely example, but consider an IEP conference at which a school psychologist begins the meeting by telling a father—who is a total stranger—that his third-grade son cannot read and is being considered for placement in a class called "learning disabilities." In the absence of prior conversations in which these two people have built some type of relationship, this statement would be totally out of sequence and could have long-term effects on future interactions.

At the second level, the two communicators *discuss common interests* that have to do with their work environments or past experiences. The communication begins with some impersonal questioning, in which one or both people try to find out something that is shared. One person may say, "Where did you go to school?" The other answers, "I went to the University of Kentucky." The first rejoins, "No kidding, my brother went there, too. Are you as big a basketball fan as he is?" If it turns out that there is a link, the communication will continue, and a higher level of communication can be established.

In level three, *sharing information about self,* the communicators attempt to exchange some thoughts, but not feelings. The initiator of the conversation would share his or her thoughts first, and solicit feedback on similar thoughts from the receiver. For example, a special education teacher and a regular classroom teacher are conversing in the lounge. The classroom teacher says, "Jose seems to be having some trouble hearing in my class. Does he have that same problem when he works with you?" The response would remain on the informational/thought level, with the objective of common problem solving. There are no feelings expressed, but there is a sharing of a high level of thought. A conversation at this level would be much more difficult and less productive, however, for two individuals who had not shared the first two levels, "Isn't this weather great?" and "I enjoy camping, too."

At the highest level, *intimacy,* team members find it possible to share feelings that have to do with the "I" and "you" relationship. Conversations at this level are concerned with impressions, the way people feel about one another, and their reactions. At this level it is advisable to be cautious, even when people think they know each other well. Feeling-level conversations between people of the opposite sex or from different cultural backgrounds are particularly difficult, because they can be easily misunderstood or misinterpreted.

In any event, conversations at this level should not be attempted prematurely. After their relationship was well established through the three previous levels, two team members who were having difficulty might approach each other at this level. For example, a speech therapist had designed an outstanding program in language development for a child, but the program was not succeeding because the special education teacher was not providing follow-up in the resource room. The speech therapist could say, "I feel so discouraged by my efforts to teach Charles to speak in complete sentences. I'm getting the impression that this is an intervention program you do not support. Since I only have Charles for 30 minutes a week, the follow-up in your room is very important." Notice the use of "I" messages rather than "you" messages as an attempt to keep the other person from becoming immediately defensive and to better the chances for an open discussion.

Verbal Skills.   Brammer (1988) described four sets of verbal communication skills, in addition to the listening skills that have been discussed. Those sets of skills are leading, reflecting, summarizing, and informing. *Leading skills* include direct and indirect leads, focusing, and questioning. The purposes of leading skills are to encourage the persons involved to get a conversation going, keep it on track, and encourage elaboration. *Reflecting skills* involve "mirroring" back feelings and content to the sender to communicate an understanding of one's frame of reference and feelings. *Summarizing skills* are designed to pull ideas together and ensure a common understanding of items that have been discussed and agreed on. *Informing skills* provide information based on experience, knowledge, and background. The two types of informing skills are advising and informing. The latter is preferable in most instances, because some people are insulted when they are given "advice" by another. These skills and corresponding examples are described in more detail in Figure 5.4.

One other important set of verbal skills relates to statements designed to provide feedback. These statements can be phrased as descriptive or judgmental.

1. **Listening Skills**

   Paraphrasing—responding to basic messages

   "You are feeling positive about this intervention, but you are confused as to the best way to implement it."

   Clarifying—restating a point or requesting restatement to ensure understanding.

   "I'm confused about this. Let me try to state what I think you have said."

   Perception checking—determining accuracy of feeling or emotion detected

   "I was wondering if the plan you chose is really the one you want. It seems to me that you expressed some doubt; did I hear correctly?"

2. **Leading Skills**

   Indirect leading—getting a conversation started

   "Let's start with you describing how things are going with the first strategy."

   Direct leading—encouraging and elaborating discussion

   "What do you mean when you say there is no improvement? Give me a recent example of an incident in class."

   Focusing—controlling confusion, diffusion, and vagueness

   "You have been discussing several problems with Tommy's behavior in class. Which of these is most important to you? To Tommy?"

   Questioning—inquiring about specific procedures in an open-ended way

   "Please explain the behavior management system you are currently using" not "Do you have any type of management system?"

3. **Reflecting Skills**

   Reflecting feelings—responding to the emotions expressed

   "It sounds as if you are feeling very frustrated with this situation."

   Reflecting content—repeating ideas in new words for emphasis

   "His behavior is making you wonder about your effectiveness as a teacher."

4. **Summarizing Skills**

   Summarizing—pulling themes together

   "Let's take a look at what we have decided thus far. We have agreed to try peer tutoring and a different reinforcement system."

5. **Informing Skills**

   Advising—giving suggestions and opinions based on experience

   "Based on my 14 years as a teacher, I can tell you that idea will not work!"

   Informing—giving information based on expertise, research, training

   "I attended a workshop on the jigsaw technique. Perhaps that strategy would help make the groups in your room more effective."

Figure 5.4

Communication skills.

Source: From *The Helping Relationship: Process and Skills,* 4th ed. (pp. 66–67) by L. M. Brammer, 1988, Englewood Cliffs, NJ: Prentice Hall. Adapted by permission of Prentice-Hall, Inc.

Descriptive statements are based on data. Whenever possible, the descriptive statement should indicate a measured quantity and time frame, and it also should indicate the source of the data. For example, after observing in a teacher's classroom, the counselor might say, "I noticed that John and Jennifer responded to five out of the eight questions you asked during the 20 minutes I was in your room yesterday." This type of statement described exactly what was seen, when, for how long, and where the observation took place. *Judgmental* statements are based on feelings, which can come across positively or negatively. The same situation could be described in a judgmental way as "It seemed to me that John and Jennifer answered most of the questions yesterday." This statement could be interpreted positively that John and Jennifer are doing well in class, but it also could be interpreted negatively if the implication was that the teacher primarily called on John and Jennifer because they knew the answers and that the teacher ignored the other students. As a rule, team members should use descriptive statements to avoid the chance that the message will be interpreted in a negative way.

Barriers.   Gordon (1974) identified a number of "roadblocks" to effective verbal communication. These *roadblocks* are barriers to interactions among individuals or in team situations. Examples of roadblocks are provided in Figure 5.5.

USING AND MISUSING FORMS OF COMMUNICATION

As team members use nonverbal, listening, and verbal skills, there are several considerations to keep in mind:

1. The verbal and nonverbal signals should match; otherwise, the message may be misinterpreted. Usually the nonverbal message will be interpreted more strongly and will have the greater impact. For example, the team member who says to another, "Tell me how that intervention is going" and then looks at her watch is adding the message, "I am interested if you can give me your answer very quickly, because I have somewhere else to go."

2. Listeners should respond to the signals and paralanguage of others and modify behaviors as necessary. This includes being sensitive to cultural differences (e.g., Martin & Nakayama, 2000; Miranda, 1993) and gender differences (c.f. Gray, 1992; Tannen, 1990).

3. Team members should be sensitive to the context and change roles accordingly (e.g., from leader to listener).

4. The verbal levels of communication should be implemented in the proper sequence so that respect is given to the extent or depth of the relationship, and familiarity is not rushed or assumed.

5. Consideration must be given to using the appropriate verbal skills without injecting roadblocks, employing stereotyped responses (e.g., using paraphrasing repeatedly), or jumping in with too many strategies too soon.

6. Team members should be sensitive to the real intent of a message (i.e., hearing what is really meant). Several tongue-in-cheek examples of statements and their "real" meanings are contained in Figure 5.6.

Technology offers new avenues for communication among interactive team members. The Internet and World Wide Web offer rapid communication possibilities and accessibility to a variety of resources that can contribute to teaming and

---

1. **Ordering, Commanding**
Can produce fear or active resistance.
Invites "testing."
Promotes rebellious behavior, retaliation.
"You must . . ."; "You have to . . ."; "You will. . . ."

2. **Warning, Threatening**
Can produce fear, submissiveness.
Invites "testing" of threatened consequences.
Can cause resentment, anger, rebellion.
"If you don't, then . . ."; "You'd better, or. . . ."

3. **Moralizing, Preaching**
Creates "obligation" or guilt feelings.
Can cause others to "dig in" and defend their positions even more ("Who says?").
Communicates lack of trust in other's sense of responsibility.
"You should . . ."; "You ought to . . ."; "It is your responsibility. . . ."

4. **Advising, Giving Solutions**
Can imply other is not able to solve own problems.
Prevents other from thinking through a problem, considering alternative solutions and trying them out for reality.
Can cause dependency or resistance.
"What I would do is . . . "; "Why don't you . . ."; "Let me suggest. . . ."

5. **Persuading with Logic, Arguing**
Provokes defensive position and counterarguments.
Often causes other to "turn off," to quit listening.
Can cause other to feel inferior, inadequate.
"Here is why you are wrong . . . "; "The facts are . . ."; "Yes, but. . . ."

6. **Judging, Criticizing, Blaming**
Implies incompetency, stupidity, poor judgment.
Cuts off communication over fear of negative judgment or "bawling out."
Child often accepts judgments as true ("I am bad"); or retaliates ("You're not so great yourself!").
"You are not thinking maturely . . ."; "You are lazy. . . ."

Figure 5.5   *(continued)*
Roadblocks to communication.
Source: From *Teacher Effectiveness Training* by T. Gordon, 1974, New York: David McKay Co.
Adapted by permission.

7. **Name-Calling, Ridiculing**
Can cause other to feel unworthy, unloved.
Can have devastating effect on self-image of other.
Often provokes verbal retaliation.
"Crybaby"; "Okay, Mr. Smarty. . . ."

8. **Analyzing, Diagnosing**
Can be threatening and frustrating.
Other can feel trapped, exposed, or not believed.
Stops other from communicating for fear of distortion or exposure.
"What's wrong with you is . . ."; "You're just tired"; "You don't really mean that."

9. **Reassuring, Sympathizing**
Causes other to feel misunderstood.
Evokes strong feelings of hostility ("That's easy for you to say!").
Other often picks up messages such as "It's not all right for you to feel bad."

10. **Praising, Agreeing**
Implies high expectations as well as surveillance of other's "toeing the mark."
Can be seen as patronizing or as a manipulative effort to encourage desired behavior.
Can cause anxiety when other's perception of self doesn't match praise.
"Well, I think you're doing a great job!"; "You're right—that teacher sounds awful!"

11. **Probing, Questioning**
Because answering questions often results in getting subsequent criticisms or solutions, others often learn to reply with nonanswers, avoidance, half-truths, or lies.
Because questions often are unclear as to what the questioner is driving at, the other may become anxious and fearful.
Other can lose sight of his or her problem while answering questions spawned by concerns.
"Why . . ."; "Who . . ."; "What did you . . ."; "How. . . ."

12. **Diverting, Sarcasm, Withdrawal**
Implies that life's difficulties are to be avoided rather than dealt with.
Can imply other's problems are unimportant, petty, or invalid.
Stops openness when a person is experiencing a difficulty.
"Let's talk about pleasant things . . ."; "Why don't you try running the world!" Remaining silent; turning away.

Figure 5.5, *continued*

collaboration efforts. Communication via electronic mail can reduce time and scheduling difficulties since individuals do not have to be in the same place at the same time (Cramer, 1998). Chat rooms and video conferencing offer real-time text-based interactions, and allow team members including parents to communicate simultaneously without being assembled in the same location (cf. Grabe & Grabe, 2000). Interactive team members are encouraged to use technology-based communication tools as one of the avenues of communication; however, they also need to recognize that many persons still prefer face-to-face meetings.

Judith Martin, who writes about manners, points out some of the meanings behind metatalk:

How do you do? How are you? Both of these mean *Hello.* The correct question, when you want to know how someone's digestion or divorce is getting along, is *Tell me, how have you really been?*

Call me. This can mean *Don't bother me now—let's discuss it on office time,* or *I would accept if you asked me out* or *I can't discuss this here* or *Don't go so fast.*

I'll call you. This has opposite meanings, and you have to judge by the delivery. One is *Let's start something* and the other is *Don't call me.*

Let's have lunch. Among social acquaintances, this means *If you ever have nothing to do on a day I have nothing to do, let's get together.* Among business acquaintances, it means *If you have something useful to say to me I'll listen.*

Let's have dinner. Among social acquaintances, it means *Let's advance this friendship.* Among business acquaintances, it means *Let's turn this into a friendship.*

Please stop by some time and see me. Said to someone who lives in the same area, it means *Call me if you'd like to visit me.* Genuine dropping in disappeared with the telephone, so if you want to encourage that, you have to say *I'm always home in the mornings. Don't bother to call; just drop by.*

Please come and stay with me. Said to someone from another area, this means *I would consider extending an invitation at your convenience if it coincides with my convenience.*

We must get together. Watch out here, because there are several similar expressions. This one means *I like you but I'm too busy now to take on more friendships.*

We really must see more of each other. One of the tricky ones, this actually means *I can't make the time to see you.*

We must do this more often. Another variation. This one is really *This was surprisingly enjoyable, but it's still going to happen infrequently.*

Yours truly, Yours sincerely. The first is business, the second distant social. Both mean *Well I guess that's all I've got to say so I'll close now.*

Is all that clear? Oh, one last thing. People who say *I only say what I really mean,* really mean *I am about to insult you.*

Figure 5.6   Metatalk.

Source: From *Miss Manners' Guide to Excruciatingly Correct Behavior* by J. Martin, 1982, New York: Atheneum Publishers, an imprint of Macmillan Publishing Company. Copyright © 1979, 1980, 1981, 1982 by United Features Syndicate, Inc. Reprinted by permission.

MANAGING CONFLICT

Even when decision-making processes are being implemented, factors are being considered, and appropriate communication behaviors are being used, conflicts may still arise. Two important considerations regarding conflict are that it is a naturally occurring phenomenon in groups or organizations, and that it may actually result in improved functioning in the system. Owens (1987) made several comments related to the former point that have implications for interactive teams:

Conflict in organizations is now seen as inevitable, endemic, and often legitimate. This is because the individuals and groups within the human social system are inter-dependent and constantly engaged in the dynamic processes of defining and redefining the nature and extent of their interdependence. Important to the dynam-ics of this social process is the fact that the environment in which it occurs is, itself, constantly changing. (p. 246)

Fishbaugh (1997) reached a similar conclusion in her description of conflict in educational settings:

Just as change is not an event but a process, so conflict resolution is an ongoing process. The lack of conflict may indicate a lack of progress. How conflict is sup-ported and resolved is as important as avoiding unnecessary interpersonal misun-derstanding. Providing an environment that prevents superfluous conflict while supporting meaningful conflict resolution will allow creative tension to move educa-tion or other human services institutions forward in the implementation of innova-tion. (p. 161)

Figure 5.7
Benefits of conflict.

Source: From *Organizational Behavior in Education,* 3rd ed. (p. 249) by R. G. Owens, 1987. Upper Saddle River, NJ: Prentice Hall. Copyright © 1987 by Prentice-Hall, Inc. Reprinted by permission.

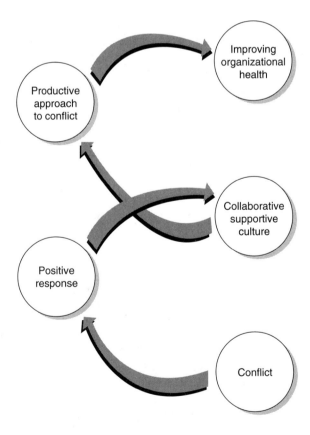

The benefits of conflict that may result in improvements in the organization have been cited by Filley (1975) and Owens (1987). Filley pointed out that conflicts often stimulate the search for new solutions or facts, thus resulting in an improvement in group cohesion and performance. Owens noted that if a positive response is made to the conflict, people may be encouraged to search out effective ways of dealing with it, and improved organizational functioning (e.g., clarified relationships and clearer problem solving) may result. This cycle is illustrated in Figure 5.7. Note that the professionals are using active listening when communicating with other team members.

Conflict also may result in negative consequences, such as hostility and destructiveness on the part of group members (Owens, 1987). In such cases, team members may have to deal with a subset of the group or single individuals who are being resistant or defensive. Strategies follow for each of these types of situations.

CONFLICTS WITHIN THE GROUP

When conflicts occur within a team or group, the people involved need to remind themselves to consider problems from a systems perspective (i.e., the whole child or organization) and not to focus on or attempt to change individual members (Turnbull & Turnbull, 1990).

Weider-Hatfield (1981) suggested a process that may be useful:

1. Examine the problem intrapersonally and ask, "Why am I feeling this way? Why are the others feeling differently?"
2. Try to get an interpersonal and common definition of the problem and differences other group members perceive.
3. Discuss the goals everyone shares.
4. Generate possible resolutions collaboratively.
5. Weigh goals against resolutions.
6. Evaluate the resolutions after time has passed.

Walther-Thomas, Korinek, and McLaughlin (1992) developed a process for conflict resolution using the acronym RESOLVE. Their model is outlined in Table 5.2.

McKenna (1998) noted that the first goal in resolving conflict should be dealing with emotions. She stressed the importance of treating the other person with respect, listening until you experience the other side, and stating your views, needs, and feelings. Martin and Nakayama (2000) offered similar suggestions for dealing with conflict:

Table 5.2
RESOLVE: Managing Conflict in Team Situations

Before conflicts develop:
- Cultivate mutual trust, respect, and role parity among team members.
- Use effective problem-solving and communication skills.
- Anticipate others' needs, interests, and positions.
- Develop effective conflict management skills.

When conflicts occur:
- Stay calm, breathe deeply, and listen with an open mind.
- Separate the problem from the person presenting it.
- If the problem cannot be adequately discussed at the present time, schedule a convenient time within the next 24 hours to do so.
- Schedule an appropriate location and sufficient time to discuss the issue fully.

In conflict situations use RESOLVE:

Respond verbally and nonverbally to the other person's feelings and ideas. Use body basics of good communication (e.g., eye contact, body language, attending behaviors, breathing, facial expressions, vocal tone).

Encourage the other person to share his or her perceptions and feelings, and to propose solutions that will be good for all parties.

Stay focused on finding an appropriate solution—don't get sidetracked by other issues.

Organize your thoughts carefully before the meeting. Be prepared.

Listen responsively (e.g., reflecting, clarifying, paraphrasing) to try to understand the other person's position and try to think of the other person's position.

Voice your belief that conflicts are opportunities to increase understanding and improve relationships. Thank the person(s) for his or her willingness to work with you to resolve this conflict.

End on a positive note with a written plan for implementation, monitoring, and follow-up.

After a conflict has been RESOLVEd:
- Follow through on commitments that you make during the conflict resolution session.
- Self-evaluate your own behaviors in handling the conflict, and
- Make changes to increase personal and professional effectiveness.

Source: From *Managing Conflict in Team Situations: RESOLVE* by C. S. Walther-Thomas, L. Korinek, and V. K. McLaughlin, 1992. Unpublished training materials. Williamsburg, VA: College of William and Mary. Reprinted by permission.

(1) stay centered and do not polarize; (2) maintain contact; (3) recognize the existence of different styles; (4) identify your preferred style; (5) be creative and expand your conflict style repertoire; (6) recognize the importance of conflict context; and (7) be willing to forgive. (p. 308)

The outcomes of conflicts within a group can be classified in three ways, depending on the results. Filley (1975) described these outcomes as:

1. *Win/lose:* Some group members win, while others believe they have lost.
2. *Lose/lose:* Both groups are disappointed in the outcomes.
3. *Win/win:* All members are satisfied with the outcomes.

Filley stated that win/win outcomes can be achieved through a process known as *integrative decision making* (IDM). In IDM, participants consider relationships, perceptions, and attitudes that may be affecting the situation. They discuss and agree on a definition of the problem, and then generate possible solutions. The final step is reaching consensus or at least majority agreement on the best alternative(s) to resolve the problem. Another strategy for negotiating agreement was described by Fisher, Ury, and Patton (1991). They listed the following considerations: (1) separate the people from the problem; (2) focus on interests, not positions; (3) invent options for mutual gain; and (4) insist on using objective criteria.

DEALING WITH RESISTANCE

Karp (1984) defined *resistance* as "the ability to avoid what is not wanted from the environment" (p. 69). Piersel (1985) said that resistance can occur for a number of reasons: The person may not know what to do or expect; the person may have different expectations about what should be occurring; or the person may have no intent or need to problem solve due to previous unsuccessful results, an inability to recognize alternatives, or a need to avoid failure or the appearance of being unsuccessful or incompetent. Fishbaugh (1997) noted that resistance may result from defensiveness on the part of the consultee to a consultant's attitude of superiority.

Nine types of resistance have been identified by Karp (1984). They are the *block, rollover, stall, reverse, sidestep, projected threat, press, guilt trip,* and *tradition.* The general considerations in dealing with resistance presented by Karp include allowing it to come to the surface by asking people for their feelings, showing that the resistance is honored by making eye contact and restating points, openly exploring the resistance by identifying how people feel, and rechecking with the people involved to make sure the understanding is accurate. Karp also recommended asking "what" or "how" questions rather than "why" questions, because the latter type tends to put people on the defensive. Another suggestion was to use "I" statements rather than "you" statements, because these also tend to make people respond defensively. Examples and strategies for dealing with the nine types of resistance are illustrated in Table 5.3.

Final considerations in dealing with people who are resistant are concerned with the behaviors team members demonstrate in the situation. As Turnbull and Turnbull (1990) stated, individuals who want to help others cease being resistant must demonstrate a willingness and openness to accept a mutual commitment toward resolving the problem. Fuller (1998) stressed the importance of being flexible and encouraging individuals to express their ideas. Aldinger, Warger, and

Table 5.3
Karp's Strategies for Dealing with Resistance

Type of Resistance	Example	Explanation	Possible Response
THE BLOCK	"I don't want to" or "I'd rather not!"	Most obvious form of authentic resistance. Easiest to work with. The resister is clear about what the demander wants.	"What are some of your objections?"
THE ROLLOVER (passive resistance)	"Tell me exactly what you want me to do."	Least common and one of the most difficult to identify and work with. Frequently the resister does not know role, what he/she is resisting. Expressed by minimal compliance with the letter of the demand and no compliance with the spirit of the demand.	"Are you clear about what is being asked of you?" "How do you think this will change your role?"
THE STALL	"I'll get on it first thing Thursday," or "I'll try to rearrange my schedule for that."	Difficult to distinguish between a stall and an honest response to present conditions. Knowledge of how a person usually responds to requests or demands will make the distinction.	"What things may prevent you from starting this tomorrow or in the near future?"
THE REVERSE	"Wow! What a great idea!"	A very subtle form of resistance and practically impossible to identify without knowing the resister well. Occurs as a statement of enthusiastic support when what you were expecting from this individual was a hard time. The resister tells you what you want to hear—and then immediately forgets about it.	"I'm pleased with your response. What aspects do you like best?"
THE SIDESTEP	"Let Sally try it first; then I'll try it."	Expressed as a counterdemand to get someone else to do the desired thing. The appeal is to your sense of fairness. "How come you didn't tell Pam she had to do this?" This then puts you on the defensive to justify your choice.	"I understand your concern; what can I expect from you?"

Type of Resistance	Example	Explanation	Possible Response
THE PROJECTED THREAT	"The (teachers) won't like it."	The resistance expressed here is in terms of an implied threat that someone else with some power won't approve of your demand. The third party's view may or may not be positive.	"I appreciate your concern and will check it with the others. In the meantime, what are your plans for . . .?"
THE PRESS	"You owe me one."	An authentic resistance. The resister does not want to cooperate and is calling in an old debt to get off the hook. It is your decision whether this is an appropriate time to pay back a debt.	"I realize I may owe you one; however, what are you planning on doing to implement . . .?"
THE GUILT TRIP	"See what you are making me do."	Guilt is a common tactic in shaping behavior. The resister's problem with what you want is his/her problem, not yours. It's good to work with the problem but not to shoulder it.	"I'm sorry this is a problem for you; however, what do you plan on doing . . .?"
THE TRADITION	"But we've always done it this way."	The most time-honored/traditional approach. This approach really is an appeal to safety, not effectiveness. Most who rely on this approach are those who are unwilling to take risks and have a low opinion of their own creativity and resourcefulness.	"I agree that the old approach has merits, but what could we do to adapt it to this new approach?"

Source: From "Working with Resistance" by H. Karp, 1984, *Training and Development Journal, 38*(3), pp. 69–73. Adapted by permission.

Eavy (1991) emphasized the need for collaborators to provide support for strategies suggested and communicating respect for others' expertise in order to build self-esteem. Brammer (1988) and Piersel (1985) both noted that a consultant must model, shape, and reinforce problem solving and reduction of resistance. The importance of these strategies was reiterated by Fine et al. (1979) when they said, "If we are asking teachers to be nondefensive, to consider different facets of a situation, and to risk making choices without complete data, then our best ally may be the behavior we model for them" (p. 539).

◇ ◇

Application of Communication Strategies

In Table 5.4, two illustrations of ineffective communication and desired communication in interactive teaming are provided. In the first example, the psychologist is using several acronyms (e.g., CAT, EMH, BEH) with which the parent may not be familiar. In addition, several emotionally laden words such as "obvious reading and

Table 5.4
Contrasting Communication Strategies

Ineffective Communication	Desired Communication in Interactive Teaming
1. Psychologist to parent: "On the CAT your son was in the 10th percentile for his grade level. We think a placement in EMH class with an appropriate IEP would meet his needs. He has obvious reading and language deficits and his communication development is delayed. We suspect that he may also have BEH tendencies due to the frustration he has experienced in academic settings."	"I would like to explain the results of recent testing to you. Your son took a test in the areas of reading, language, and math. This chart illustrates how he did compared with others of his grade level. The types of questions he was responding to included (examples given). The results show that he has difficulty with reading comprehension, or understanding the meaning of what he has read. Have you noticed similar patterns as you read with him at home? Given this performance, what do you think would be the best plan for your child?"
2. Program administrator to special educator and parents: "The numbers in our programs for multi-disabled are low this coming year so we can't really justify having two classes at the elementary level. Therefore, we have decided to place the 15-year-old child at the high school level and move the other students into other classes. Jackie is verbal and does not need an augmentative communication system, so she does not need to be placed in the elementary nonverbal class. We want her to learn vocational and functional skills and continue to work on range of motion in PT. In addition, we do not think she needs APE any longer; instead we can have her work on computer literacy with the specialist and the OT."	"We are considering the best placements for our students with multiple disabilities for next year and wanted your input. One possibility is placing Jackie at a middle or high school level. This will enable her to have access to the computer lab and the classes on homemaking and work skills. What are your ideas on this?"

language deficits" are used but not explained. In the desired communication column, the psychologist tries to explain testing results and provides examples of questions. In addition, she asks for the parent's comments about a placement instead of presenting it as a decision that has been made without the parent's input.

In the second example, the program administrator presents a decision based on numbers rather than on what individual students need. In describing a program for Jackie, he does not state whether a high school placement is in the best interest of the child's overall development, nor does he request the parents or special educator's input into the decision. Jargon such as "augmentative," "functional," and "APE" are used without explanation. In the desired communication column, the administrator presents a possibility for a placement, describes the potential benefits, and asks for ideas from the special educator and parents.

◊ ◊

SUMMARY

An understanding of communication skills is an essential facilitating factor in interactive teaming. The areas encompassed in this understanding include the following:

◆ Awareness of a communication model that includes senders-receivers, messages, channels, feedback, noise, and setting.

◆ Sensitivity to characteristics of communication in interactive teaming.

◆ Consideration of personal, attitudinal, and experiential factors; backup support factors; and context or situational factors.

◆ Implementation of effective nonverbal, listening, and verbal skills.

◆ Knowledge of ways to manage conflicts in groups and strategies for dealing with resistant people.

The next chapter describes leadership skills for individuals on interactive teams. The strategies contained in Chapter 6 are vital to facilitate the teaming process.

ACTIVITIES

1. Observe an interaction between a professional and a parent. Were respect and trust evident or missing? Was rapport established and maintained? Were cultural differences understood and accepted? Did verbal and nonverbal messages match?

2. Observe a team meeting among professionals. Was the situation proactive or reactive? What content-level sequences were used? Was jargon explained? Which verbal and listening skills were implemented? Were any judgmental statements or roadblocks evident? If so, what were the responses to them? If a conflict arose, how was it handled?

3. Conduct an informational interview with a parent or professional. Write your overall assessment of the interview. Also write an analysis of your use and the interviewee's use of effective communication strategies.

4. Design a checklist or rating scale of the behaviors you think are necessary for effective communication. Evaluate yourself on the behaviors. Observe a meeting and consider how the participants interact. If you think some people in the meeting are better at communicating than others, identify what behaviors or skills you think give them an advantage.

REFERENCES

Aldinger, L. E., Warger, C. L., & Eavy, P. W. (1991). *Strategies for teacher collaboration.* Ann Arbor, MI: Exceptional Innovations, Inc.

Arab, C. (1985, May). *Getting what you deserve: Assertive, aggressive, and non-assertive behavior.* Paper presented at the Florida Academy of School Leaders, Daytona Beach.

Bailey, D. B. (1987). Collaborative goal-setting with families: Resolving differences in values and priorities for services. *Topics in Early Childhood Special Education, 7*(2), 59–71.

Belton-Owens, J. (1999). Multicultural issues confronted by parents and families. In G. Boutte (Ed.), *Multicultural education: Raising consciousness* (pp. 232–260). Belmont, CA: Wadsworth Publishing.

Bolton, R. (1979). *People skills.* Upper Saddle River, NJ: Prentice Hall.

Brammer, L. M. (1988). *The helping relationship: Process and skills* (4th ed.). Upper Saddle River, NJ: Prentice Hall.

Brown, B., Pryzwansky, W. B., & Schulte, A. C. (1998). *Psychological consultation: Introduction to theory and practice* (4th ed.). Needham Heights, MA: Allyn & Bacon.

Bruneau-Balderrama, O. (1997). Inclusion: Making it work for teachers, too. *The Clearing House, 70*(6), 328–330.

Covey, S. R. (1989). *The 7 habits of highly effective people: Powerful lessons in personal change.* New York: Simon & Schuster.

Cramer, S. F. (1998). *Collaboration: A success strategy for special educators.* Needham Heights, MA: Allyn & Bacon.

Dettmer, P., Thurston, L. P., & Dyck, N. (1993). *Consultation, collaboration, and teamwork for students with special needs.* Boston: Allyn & Bacon.

Dieker, L. A., & Barnett, C. A. (1996). Effective co-teaching. *Teaching Exceptional Children, 29*(1), 5–7.

Egan, G. (1986). *The skilled helper: A systematic approach to effective helping.* Monterey, CA: Brooks/Cole.

Ehly, S. W., & Eliason, M. (1983). Communicating for understanding: Some problems in psychology and education. *Journal for Special Educators, 19*(3), v–ix.

Eisenhardt, C. (1972). *Applying linguistics to the teaching of reading and the language arts.* Columbus, OH: Merrill.

Filley, A. C. (1975). *Interpersonal conflict resolution.* Glenview, IL: Scott, Foresman.

Fine, M. J., Grantham, V. L., & Wright, J. G. (1979). Personal variables that facilitate or impede consultation. *Psychology in the Schools, 16,* 533–539.

Fishbaugh, M. S. E. (1997). *Models of collaboration.* Needham Heights, MA: Allyn & Bacon.

Fisher, R., Ury, W., & Patton, B. (1991). *Getting to yes: Negotiating agreement without giving in.* New York: Penguin Books.

Fong, M. (1986). *The levels of communication in personal relationships.* Unpublished manuscript, University of Florida, Department of Counselor Education, Gainesville.

Friend, M. (1984). Consultation skills for resource teachers. *Learning Disability Quarterly, 7,* 246–250.

Fuller, G. (1998). *Win/win management: Leading people in the new workplace.* Paramus, NJ: Prentice Hall Press.

Gladstein, G. A. (1983). Understanding empathy: Integrating counseling, developmental, and social psychology perspectives. *Journal of Counseling Psychology, 30,* 467–482.

Gordon, T. (1970). *Parent effectiveness training.* New York: Wyden.

Gordon, T. (1974). *Teacher effectiveness training.* New York: David McKay.

Grabe, M., & Grabe, C. (2000). *Integrating the Internet for meaningful learning.* Boston, MA: Houghton Mifflin.

Gray, J. (1992). *Men are from Mars, women are from Venus.* New York: HarperCollins.

Grieger, R. M. (1972). Teacher attitudes as a variable in behavior modification consultation. *Journal of School Psychology, 10,* 279–287.

Gutkin, T. B. (1996). Core elements of consultation service delivery for special service personnel: Rationale, practice, and some directions for the future. *Remedial and Special Education, 17*(6), 333–340.

Gutkin, T. B., & Curtis, M. J. (1982). School-based consultation: Theory and techniques. In C. R. Reynolds & T. B. Gutkin (Eds.), *The handbook of school psychology.* New York: Wiley.

Hallman, C. L., Bryant, W. W., Campbell, A., McGuire, J., & Bowman, K. (1983). *U.S. American value orientations* (Cultural Monograph No. 4). Gainesville: University of Florida, College of Education, Bilingual Multicultural Education Training Project.

Harris, K. C. (1996). Collaboration within a multicultural society: Issues for consideration. *Remedial and Special Education, 17*(6), 355–362, 376.

Heron, T. E., & Harris, K. C. (1987). *The educational consultant: Helping professionals, parents, and mainstreamed students.* Austin, TX: Pro-Ed.

Hudson, P. (1987). *Proactive and reactive consultation: A model for preservice training.* Unpublished manuscript, University of Florida, Department of Special Education, Gainesville.

Hybels, S., & Weaver, R. L. (1997). *Communicating effectively* (5th ed.). New York: McGraw-Hill.

Idol, L., Paolucci-Whitcomb, P., & Nevin, A. (1986). *Collaborative consultation.* Rockville, MD: Aspen.

Jackson, D. N., & Hughley-Hayes, D. (1993). Multicultural issues in consultation. *Journal of Counseling & Development, 72,* 144–147.

Karp, H. (1984). Working with resistance. *Training and Development Journal, 38*(3), 69–73.

Katzenbach, J. R., & Smith, D. K. (1999). *The wisdom of teams: Creating the high-performance organization.* New York: HarperCollins.

Kerlinger, F. N. (1986). *Foundations of behavioral research* (3rd ed.). New York: Holt, Rinehart & Winston.

Lang, D. C., Quick, A. F., & Johnson, J. A. (1981). *A partnership for the supervision of student teachers.* DeKalb, IL: Creative Educational Materials.

Lopez, E. C., Dalal, S. M., & Yoshida, R. K. (1993). An examination of professional cultures: Implications for the collaborative consultation model. *Journal of Educational and Psychological Consultation, 4,* 197–213.

Losen, S. M., & Losen, J. G. (1985). *The special education team.* Boston: Allyn & Bacon.

Lynch, E. W., & Hanson, M. J. (Eds.). (1992). *Developing cross-cultural competence: A guide for working with young children and their families.* Baltimore, MD: Paul H. Brookes.

Martin, J. N., & Nakayama, T. K. (2000). *Intercultural communication in contexts* (2nd ed.). Mountain View, CA: Mayfield Publishing Company.

McKenna, C. (1998). *Powerful communication skills: How to communicate with confidence.* Franklin Lakes, NJ: Career Press.

Miranda, A. H. (1993). Consultation with culturally diverse families. *Journal of Educational and Psychological Consultation, 4,* 89–93.

Nierenberg, G., & Calero, H. (1971). *How to read a person like a book.* New York: Hawthorn Books.

Overton, T. (2000). *Assessment in special education: An applied approach* (3rd ed.). Upper Saddle River, NJ: Merrill/Prentice Hall.

Owens, R. B. (1987). *Organizational behavior in education* (3rd ed.). Upper Saddle River, NJ: Prentice Hall.

Piersel, W. C. (1985). Behavioral consultation: An approach to problem solving in educational settings. In J. R. Bergan, *School psychology in contemporary society: An introduction.* Columbus, OH: Merrill.

Pruitt, P., Wandry, D., & Hollums, D. (1998). Listen to us! Parents speak out about their interactions with special educators. *Preventing School Failure, 42*(4), 161–166.

Pugach, M. C., & Johnson, L. J. (1995). *Collaborative practitioners, collaborative schools.* Denver, CO: Love Publishing Company.

Ramirez, S. Z., Lepage, K. M., Kratchowill, T. R., & Duffy, J. L. (1998). Multicultural issues in school-based consultation: Conceptual and research considerations. *Journal of School Psychology, 36*(4), 479–509.

Roberts, G. W., Bell, L. A., & Salend, S. J. (1991). Negotiating change for multicultural education: A consultation model. *Journal of Educational and Psychological Consultation, 2*(4), 323–342.

Rogers, C. R. (1961). *On becoming a person: A therapist's view of psychotherapy.* Boston: Houghton-Mifflin.

Sax, G. (1997). *Principles of educational and psychological measurement and evaluation* (4th ed.). Belmont, CA: Wadsworth Publishing.

Sonnenschien, P. (1984). Parents and professionals: An uneasy relationship. In M. L. Henniger & E. M. Nesselroad (Eds.), *Working with parents of handicapped children: A book of readings for school personnel.* Lanham, MD: University Press of America.

Spodek, B. (1982). What special educators need to know about regular classrooms. *Educational Forum, 46,* 295–307.

Tannen, D. (1990). *You just don't understand: Women and men in conversation.* New York: Ballantine Books.

Tawney, J. W., & Gast, D. L. (1984). *Single subject research in special education.* New York: Merrill/Macmillan.

Turnbull, A. P., & Turnbull, H. R. (1990). *Families, professionals, and exceptionality: A special partnership* (2nd ed.). Upper Saddle River, NJ: Merrill/Prentice Hall.

Vargo, S. (1998). Consulting teacher-to-teacher. *Teaching Exceptional Children, 30*(3), 54–55.

Venn, J. (2000). *Assessment in special education: An applied approach* (3rd ed.). Upper Saddle River, NJ: Merrill/Prentice Hall.

Walther-Thomas, C. S., Korinek, L., & McLaughlin, V. K. (1992). *Managing conflict in team situations: RESOLVE.* Unpublished training materials. Williamsburg, VA: College of William and Mary.

Weider-Hatfield, D. (1981). A unit in conflict management communication skills. *Communication Education, 30,* 265–273.

Weissenburger, J. W., Fine, M. J., & Poggio, J. P. (1982). The relationship of selected consultant/teacher characteristics to consultation outcomes. *Journal of School Psychology, 20*(4), 263–270.

West, J. F., & Cannon, G. S. (1988). Essential collaborative consultation competencies for regular and special educators. *Journal of Learning Disabilities, 21*(1), 56–63, 28.

Zirpoli, T. J., & Melloy, K. J. (1993). *Behavior management: Applications for teachers and parents.* Upper Saddle River, NJ: Merrill/Prentice Hall.

6 Developing Service Coordination Skills

Topics in this chapter include:

- Discussion of essential skills for leadership of professionals.
- Description of the initial tasks of the team leader.
- Guidelines for procedures needed by subsequent team leaders, who serve as quality advisers: coordinating services, delegating responsibility, providing follow-up, and guiding paraprofessionals or volunteers.
- Application of the interactive teaming model to a situation in which the quality adviser delegates to and provides follow-up with a paraprofessional.

At their first meeting, the team discussed the educational and social needs and placement options for Juan, an 11-year-old Hispanic boy with diabetes, who was having difficulties in reading achievement and social adjustment. The first meeting was attended by Juan's mother, his sixth-grade teacher, the special educator [a learning disabilities (LD) resource teacher], the speech-language therapist, and the school nurse; it was chaired by the school counselor. After hearing the parent and teacher's descriptions of Juan's reading difficulties, the counselor noted that it was late and recommended gathering more information about Juan's diet, his classroom behavior, and his language abilities in English, his second language. When the team met again two weeks later, the LD teacher was the only person who had gathered additional information.

As the counselor attempted to initiate problem solving at the second meeting, he was puzzled by the group's reactions. He first noted that Juan's mother was not participating, even when she was asked to speak. Then he noted that the sixth-grade teacher responded with hostility to the report on classroom observations by the LD teacher, while the nurse and speech-language therapist completed unrelated paperwork. The second meeting ended as the first one had, with the counselor suggesting that the group still needed additional information. The parent walked quietly away, while several other participants muttered protests about wasted time.

This team had no goals and no operating procedures. The team suffered from a lack of direction because the counselor was viewed merely as a facilitator who convened the meeting and encouraged the discussion. Everybody was assumed to be working together but nobody was "in charge." The leader neither delegated responsibility nor conducted follow-up activities. The special educator, who took nondelegated initiative for conducting a classroom observation, was viewed by the classroom teacher as an intruder. Juan's mother, who had assumed that she was to be the hostess for a social visit from the school nurse, had not been contacted. The counselor, who did not understand the essential skills and procedures for team leadership, had apparently assumed that everyone on the team would just "collaborate."

In this chapter, the essential skills for team leaders are presented from the perspective that they involve the management of tasks rather than people. The initial tasks of the team leader are described, and the procedures used subsequently by the leader in service coordination are discussed in detail. To avoid confusion, we will call the subsequent leaders who coordinate services the "quality advisers." Finally, the interactive teaming model is applied to the procedures for leadership in service coordination through an example of how a team leader can delegate to and provide follow-up on the activities of a paraprofessional.

ESSENTIAL SKILLS FOR LEADERSHIP OF PROFESSIONALS

For an interactive team to function effectively, it needs a special kind of leadership. The management of professionals (such as those who make up the interactive team) is much more complex than the management of workers. It is collegial rather than directive and needs to occur within an organization that is performance oriented rather than authority oriented (Black, 1998; Peterson & Deal, 1998).

In the interactive teaming model, the role of leader can be filled by any member of the team. The leader is selected by the program administrator, who delegates responsibility for coordination of services to this leader. The team leader is a service coordinator who maintains the continuity of the team over time and across meetings that focus on the special needs of individual students. For each individual student, the team also uses as its quality adviser the person with greatest knowledge of the services or content expertise about the case. While the adviser changes with each case, the leader remains constant.

To be effective, the leader needs to be supportive of others as they carry out their tasks and must assume accountability for the overall effectiveness of the program. The team leader is aware of the different roles and perspectives of team members as described previously, and is able to select, from among the expertise presented by members of the team, the best person(s) to whom to delegate responsibility for coordinating a particular student's program. The leader needs to demonstrate all the skills, attributes, and behaviors of effective leaders in organizations. These skills, attributes, and behaviors are now summarized as a synthesis of the research on effective leadership.

Research on Leadership

Effective leaders can help professionals with different backgrounds and vocabularies to focus on a common set of future goals (Covey, 1990; Deming, 1986; Jarvis & Chavez, 1997; Juran, 1992; Nanus, 1992). Research on leadership has been responsible for an evolution in understanding of its components.

Early investigators observing leaders in diverse contexts have identified two broad dimensions of leadership. They determined that the effective leader needs to initiate *structure* and demonstrate *consideration*. To initiate structure is to establish patterns, methods, and procedures for accomplishing tasks. To demonstrate consideration is to develop trust, warmth, and respect with the staff.

Some early students of leadership described leaders as either task oriented or relationship oriented (McGregor, 1960), although Hersey and Blanchard (1974) were among those who questioned the dichotomous view. In their categorization of styles, Hersey and Blanchard suggested also that the effective leader had a range of styles and that the ability to adapt style to the situation was an important dimension of effectiveness. Further expansion of the concept of adaptation in leadership was proposed by Bennis (1989) and Covey (1990).

The extension of Hersey and Blanchard's work into studies of effective school principals showed that these school leaders had a variety of styles, but all demonstrated that they were able to encourage staff collaboration and develop innovative practices (DeBevoise, 1984; Hall, Rutherford, Hord, & Huling, 1984). According to the research of Clifton and his associates (SRI, 1980), the effective school leader develops positive relationships with colleagues and is capable of creating an open, supportive environment. Covey (1990) emphasizes that caring and integrity must be genuine and integral to the leader's being, as opposed to superficially acquired techniques. Sergiovanni (1992) views school leadership as a form of stewardship: relating to individuals, honoring their values. He terms this a "servant leadership" based on trust and mutual respect.

The concept of *power* was widely discussed as a dimension of leadership in the early literature. Effective leaders are able to use power for organizational good, as opposed to personal gain (McClelland, 1975). The most productive exercise of power in the leadership of professionals comes through participatory management, which empowers others (Powers & Powers, 1983). This concept is discussed further in Chapter 7. These leadership concepts, inherent in Deming's (1986) total quality management (TQM) process, were originally initiated in business and industry. The TQM leadership concepts are based on teamwork, and focus on team members as participants in decisions that seek continuous improvement in response to feedback from "customers," clients, or constituents. While some authors caution that schools are not corporations (Black, 1998), these concepts have been extended to applications in educational institutions (Bonstingl, 1992; Tribus, 1992). The TQM principles have been applied also to school restructuring as it relates to programs for special students by Audette and Algozzine (1992).

The team leader should keep in mind that the team's goal is continuous improvement. Deming (1986), who emphasized the importance of "constancy of purpose," indicated that the critical steps in the continuous improvement cycle are (1) plan, (2) do, (3) check, and (4) act. He suggests that improvement of the system, or process, is the way to obtain results. This point of view enables team members to focus on a common goal, and to identify and eliminate barriers to achieving this goal. A mind-set for long-range planning, with continuous improvement, is essential for the team leader, who can then encourage flexibility, risk taking, and innovation.

Wilson (1993) summarizes several studies of characteristics and behaviors of empowered teacher-leaders, which are similar to those ascribed to effective leaders in general: They are hard working and creative; they collaborate with others to provide assistance. In defining the characteristics of effective teacher-leaders,

Wilson also cites the work of Kouzes and Posner (1990), who conducted a major study of managers in public and private organizations. Their research supports earlier conclusions of others with regard to effective leadership that empowers team members: Leaders take risks, challenge the existing system, communicate the shared vision, engage in teamwork, and support and inspire others. Effective leaders coach and encourage their teams, while serving as role models and planners. These teacher-leaders are more comparable to the team leaders described in this text. They do not seek full "leadership" roles as administrators; instead, they function as team leaders in collegial settings.

Recent studies have lent support to the earlier descriptions of the skills and characteristics of effective leaders, both in businesses and in school environments. For example, *Investor's Business Daily,* through an ongoing series based on extensive analysis of leaders, has identified 10 traits that characterize successful leaders. Their list begins with "How you think is everything: Always be positive. Think success, not failure. Beware of a negative environment." The final trait is "Be honest and dependable; take responsibility. Otherwise numbers 1–9 won't matter" (see, for example, Richman, 1999a, 1999b). The list goes on to highlight many of the qualities identified in earlier research: planning and implementing goals, being a continuous learner, hard worker, and innovator, analyzing feedback, and communicating effectively. Kelley (1991) indicates that the quality of a company is heavily dependent on the quality of its "worklife" and that teamwork, which requires skills in both leadership and followership, is increasingly important.

Similarly, the leaders in effective schools are found to have skills and attributes that are characteristic of all effective leaders. Peterson and Deal (1998) stress the importance of the school leader in shaping the culture by communicating core values and traditions, speaking about mission, honoring the school "heroes" and celebrating their accomplishments. Jarvis and Chavez (1997) add a dimension they call "roles" (creator of context, seeker and initiator of communication, promoter of possibilities, and guardian of morale) to the traditional model of leader behaviors that focuses on responsibilities and relationships. Goldman (1998) shows that the leader's style and value system are evident in almost every component of the school's personality, or culture.

The growing body of research on effective leaders and successful organizations, including schools, places an increasing emphasis on the importance of a positive culture and the leader's part in establishing that culture. Peterson and Deal (1998) define culture as " . . . the underground stream of norms, values, beliefs, traditions, and rituals that has built up over time as people work together, solve problems, and confront challenges" (p. 28). These authors define "toxic cultures" as those with negative values and disgruntled staff, where oppositional groups dominate, leading both faculty and students to a sense of hopelessness. This type of toxic culture appears similar to the school environment described by large numbers of school leavers interviewed in the longitudinal study by Altenbaugh, Engel, and Martin (1995).

Several authors have given examples of positive school cultures, with high levels of student and staff satisfaction and achievement. Peterson and Deal (1998) describe schools in which staff have a shared sense of mission, with norms that emphasize collegiality, caring, and concern for student growth. Glasser (1997) has named these environments "quality schools," in which staff have demonstrated the power of showing care for students while giving them choices, and of empha-

---

1. **Initiating Structure**
   This is the leader's task-oriented behavior of stating the organization's purpose, establishing the mechanisms and procedures, and defining the roles of members, through which the organization may obtain its results (Bennis, 1997; Gersten, Carnine, & Green, 1982; Heskett & Schlesinger, 1996). It has a "power" dimension, focused on the use of power for corporate as opposed to personal uses (Covey, 1990; Deming, 1986; McClelland, 1975), and for the educational leader, it includes a personal commitment to a cause that can benefit others (SRI, 1980).

2. **Facilitating Goal Achievement**
   These are the leader's acts of implementation that enable the team members to collaborate in the fulfillment of their common purpose (Bennis, 1989; Drucker, 1992; Schlecty, 1997; Senge, 1990; SRI, 1980). These acts include translating the organization's mission into specific goal statements, delegating tasks, and reinforcing excellence (Blanchard & Johnson, 1982; Gersten et al., 1982).

3. **Demonstrating Consideration**
   This is the leader's relationship-oriented behavior, which emphasizes the social and personal aspects of working with people in the organization and building positive, supportive relationships with team members (SRI, 1980). It focuses heavily on providing the work group with support and demonstrating to them that they are respected, trusted, and valued (Covey, 1990; Glasser, 1997; Maxwell, 1995; Peterson & Deal, 1998).

4. **Showing Adaptability**
   This is the leader's proactive and reactive behavior that may be classified as situational. It is based in part on Hersey and Blanchard's (1974) concept that leaders have not only a dominant style (task oriented or relationship oriented) but that effective leaders also have a range of supporting styles from which they can select, depending on the situation (Kelley, 1991; Wasley, et al., 1997). It is dependent on skill 5.

5. **Using Direct Feedback**
   This is the skill of listening and being available that shows the leader believes the organization's mission, its workers, and its constituents are important (Glasser, 1997; Peters & Austin, 1985). It includes the leader's assessment of the actions, needs, and viewpoints of patrons, faculty, and students, and the use of this insight in decision making (Covey, 1996; Deming, 1986; Juran 1992; Scholtes, 1988; SRI, 1980).

6. **Encouraging Innovations**
   This is the behavior through which the leader builds in provisions for growth, change, and development, both for individuals and for the organization (Joyce & Showers, 1995; Kotter, 1996). It includes support of risk taking to encourage the development of a better service or product (Covey, 1990; Fullan, 1993; Tribus, 1992;). For the leader of the interactive team, this service or product is related to the program developed for the student with special needs.

Figure 6.1
Summary of essential skills for leaders of professionals.

sizing the importance of seeking continuous improvement. Wasley, Hampel, and Clark (1997) also provide examples of high schools in which the staff has attempted to bring about whole-school change that emphasized a positive culture with student growth. They have identified seven interrelated clues to the success of schools in achieving this change, finding two critical considerations: civil discourse among participants, and rigorous analysis of inside and outside feedback. These descriptors are supportive of the earlier research on effective schools, adding emphasis on the variables that comprise interactive teaming.

Summary of Skills for Team Leaders

In summary, leadership has been defined as behavior that facilitates change. It has a dimension of power, which focuses on the strength necessary to accomplish goals that are believed to promote the common good. Effective leadership includes both an emphasis on fulfilling the organization's mission and on the development of trust and respect between the leader and group. From a synthesis of the behaviors, skills, and attributes found in the leaders and in the organizations that meet the criteria of excellence, six generic constructs that describe the effective leadership of professionals are proposed. Their definitions are presented in Figure 6.1.

As can be seen in Figure 6.1, the leader of professionals needs special skills to maintain the careful balance between directing the activities of the group and allowing competent professionals the autonomy they require to function effectively. As indicated earlier, in reaching this balance, it is important for the leader to understand that his or her role is to manage tasks, rather than manage people. Finally, the team leader should understand that complexity, conflict, and ambiguity are to be expected. Bennis (1989) emphasizes that "sooner or later, each of us has to accept the fact that complexity is here to stay and that order begins in chaos" (p. 113).

INITIAL TASKS OF THE TEAM LEADER

The team leader's initial tasks set the stage for effective collaboration. These activities include (1) setting up the team, (2) identifying resources, and (3) establishing operating procedures. Each of these tasks is described briefly.

Setting up the Team

The interactive team is a new and flexible group that is not a part of the established administrative structure within the school or clinical program. In the Chapter 4 discussion of the role of the administrator, it was pointed out that the administrator has overall fiscal and legal responsibility for the unit's program. This administrator—the principal or program director—does not usually function as the team leader and therefore needs to *delegate* to the team leader the authority to plan, implement, and evaluate programs for special needs students. This is how the administrator gives the team its legitimacy and autonomy, as described in Chapter 3. It is also another way of showing that the team leader has the administrator's "permission" to accomplish the team's tasks, an essential part of delegating responsibility, described later in this chapter.

Glatthorn and Newberg (1984), in their discussion of the team approach for instructional leadership at the secondary school level, have outlined a four-stage process that describes how the person designated by the administrator can establish a team with this type of authority. Their guidelines may be adapted for use as initial procedures for setting up the interactive team, as outlined in Figure 6.2. These initial steps are taken to ensure that the current official leader—the administrator of the unit—is involved and supportive, and that all members of the staff understand that specific responsibilities, which are consistent with the organization's overall goals, have been delegated to the interactive team. From that point on, the leadership is vested in the team itself, to be exercised by its designated leader.

It is important to emphasize that a formal team is not created immediately for every student about whom a teacher, parent, or other service provider has a concern. Formal assessment for the purpose of determining whether or not special education is required occurs only after the classroom teacher has attempted to make ongoing changes in an existing program to improve the academic performance and/or social behavior of a given student. If performance does not

Figure 6.2
Sequence of initial steps for setting up an interactive team.

1. Conduct observations and interviews with administrator and staff to obtain answers to these questions:
   - What is the administrator's leadership style?
   - Which individuals are currently performing leadership functions?
   - Which individuals are believed to be capable of leadership?
2. Meet with the administrator to obtain answers to this question:
   - Which leadership function does he or she wish to perform and which functions can—given the organizational constraints—be delegated to others?
3. Ask the administrator in a general meeting of the organization's entire staff to address two issues:
   - Explain how the team's duties are consistent with the overall goals of the organization.
   - Delegate functions to be carried out by the team, under the direction of its leader, with the support of the administrator.

improve as a result of applying the strategies and procedures used routinely by all teachers to enhance the performance of any student, then the teacher may call for assistance. The request would be made initially to a grade level or schoolwide team that is designed to meet the school's mission of academic improvement for all students. This team might be called the "high-performance" or "student success" team. The teacher with a concern would request assistance from other team members, who would offer suggestions. In requesting assistance, the teacher might summarize the problem by using information collected during observations in the classroom, usually made by a supportive colleague. The observations would include:

◆ Academic skills or behaviors of the student that seemed to interfere with learning, such as a lower level of performance, motivation, or interactions.

◆ Academic skills or behaviors that seemed to enhance learning, such as special interests or talents, leadership skills, insight, and so on.

In addition, the concerned teacher would provide a review of work samples completed by the student of concern, indicating any aspects of the problem as well as documenting any special skills that might be considered strengths. The team, working as a problem-solving unit, would suggest strategies that might further assist the teacher who presented the concern. This teacher, usually with help from a colleague, would implement the strategies recommended, documenting their effect on the student. If paraprofessionals or students-in-training are part of the classroom, one of these individuals might assist in making the observations and participate in the problem-solving team meeting's follow-up. Frequently, these informal procedures—characteristic of the things good teachers do on a regular basis—may enable the student to succeed without need for further intervention. These procedures are consistent with the goals of the Individuals with Disabilities Education Act (IDEA) in the sense that they try to prevent students at risk from failure that would require special education services.

When prevention strategies do not solve the problem, a formal referral is made, and the legal requirements for parental notification and permission are followed for the procedures that include diagnosis, placement, implementation, and follow-up. The school administrator should keep IDEA requirements in mind when setting up the team and delegating responsibility to the team leader. The law requires that the team developing the Individual Education Program (IEP) for a student must include those persons who conducted this student's diagnosis and made placement decisions.

The team includes the following members:

◆ A representative of the local education agency (LEA) who is qualified to provide, or to supervise, special education programs, in addition to being knowledgeable about the general curriculum and the availability of resources. This individual must be able to make commitments of resources on behalf of the LEA.

◆ The student's parents or guardian.

◆ A regular education teacher.

◆ A special educator.

◆ An individual who can provide instructional interpretation of the diagnostic evaluations.

◆ The child with the disability, when appropriate.

If the team is considering the services for a student with transition needs, representatives of the agencies likely to provide or pay for these services would also be team members. A behavior specialist, bilingual educator, or adaptive technology specialist would be included if the student's needs were related to these areas of expertise. Other members may, of course, be added if needed in an individual case.

Identifying Resources

The initial team leader will want to take steps to identify the human and fiscal resources that are available for the team's use. These steps include analyzing the expertise of potential team members, identifying the available fiscal resources that might be used to support the team's efforts, and organizing information about community resources that are available. These steps are illustrated in Figure 6.3.

As a first step, the team leader will find it useful to analyze and prepare a brief outline of the professional training and expertise of potential team members, such as that provided in Chapter 4. This analysis will help team members understand the types of knowledge and skills they and others can contribute to the solution of a given student's problems. It will also be useful in helping the team identify the person who should serve as *major service coordinator*—described in TQM terms as the *quality adviser*—for each student's program planning, implementation, and evaluation.

Outline expertise of members

Identify budgeted funds

List community resources

Figure 6.3
Initial steps for identifying resources available to the team.

Second, the team leader should obtain from the organization's administrator an outline of the *fiscal resources* that have been budgeted for use by the team. This outline is useful for preventing misunderstandings, such as assuming the budget is unlimited or not knowing that funds are available for particular purposes.

Finally, the team leader should obtain a list of community, state, and national resources (advocacy groups, professional organizations, and service agencies) that might contribute their expertise to the cases addressed by the team. It is useful, during the initial stages of establishing the team's workscope, to compile a reference guide of these resources. This step is the leader's way of showing that people are viewed as major resources, and that the team is concerned with helping people do their jobs effectively.

The types of resources that might be available include general and specialized health care providers, day care facilities, and welfare and social service agencies.

Wittenmyer (1983) has outlined a systematic procedure for identifying these resources, which are available in any community. She suggests that several resources are available within any community, including the following:

◆ Public interest law firms.

◆ Jaycees/Chamber of Commerce school–business partners.

◆ Big Brother/Big Sister groups.

◆ Foster homes/group homes.

◆ Special groups: ARC, CP, LD, and so on.

Establishing Operating Procedures

The team will function more effectively if it has a set of operating procedures that is understood by all members. This involves outlining the legal requirements, establishing the mission, and conducting effective meetings.

Outlining Legal Requirements.   It is important for the team leader to coordinate the legal requirements for procedures as team members work through the decision points of prereferral, screening, services, instructional planning, and evaluation. The leader will find it particularly useful to provide each team member with a written summary of required legal procedures under which the team needs to operate. Because the legal requirements for the classification and placement of students as "disabled" are the most rigorous, they will be summarized briefly. These requirements include, but are not limited to, information on *informed consent*, *due process*, and, when appropriate, *participation* in the regular education program. A document explaining these procedures, as required by the jurisdiction in which the organization operates, is always available from the organization's administrator.

Specific procedural guidelines are also required during the team meeting for planning the special student's instructional program. A checklist of these procedures may serve as a guide to essential procedures during the program-planning

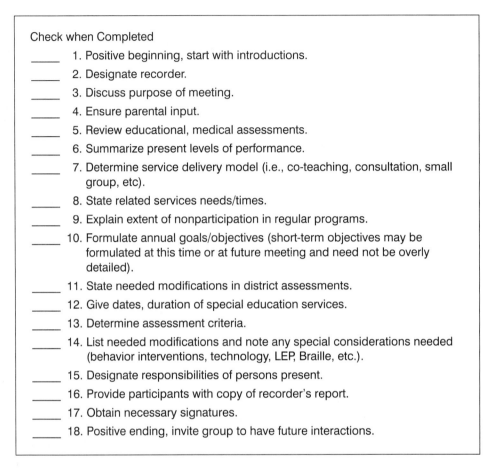

Check when Completed

_____ 1. Positive beginning, start with introductions.

_____ 2. Designate recorder.

_____ 3. Discuss purpose of meeting.

_____ 4. Ensure parental input.

_____ 5. Review educational, medical assessments.

_____ 6. Summarize present levels of performance.

_____ 7. Determine service delivery model (i.e., co-teaching, consultation, small group, etc).

_____ 8. State related services needs/times.

_____ 9. Explain extent of nonparticipation in regular programs.

_____ 10. Formulate annual goals/objectives (short-term objectives may be formulated at this time or at future meeting and need not be overly detailed).

_____ 11. State needed modifications in district assessments.

_____ 12. Give dates, duration of special education services.

_____ 13. Determine assessment criteria.

_____ 14. List needed modifications and note any special considerations needed (behavior interventions, technology, LEP, Braille, etc.).

_____ 15. Designate responsibilities of persons present.

_____ 16. Provide participants with copy of recorder's report.

_____ 17. Obtain necessary signatures.

_____ 18. Positive ending, invite group to have future interactions.

Figure 6.4
Procedures for use in team meeting to plan student's instructional program.

meeting. A brief version of this checklist is shown in Figure 6.4. These legal procedures must be followed in the event of official referral for placement in special education programs.

Establishing Team Mission.   Every team has a mission. The mission of the team responsible for planning and monitoring the program for a special needs student is predetermined and defined by law in the IDEA 1997 amendments. During its early meetings, the team leader should clarify its mission. For the team that considers the instructional needs of many students, or meets regularly to propose solutions for building-wide problems, a mission statement will have to be developed. The group mission, if stated as a focused and relatively narrow purpose, will help the team direct its actions and set reachable goals. The team leader assists the group in seeing its mission as a clear statement of a problem to be solved. The problem statement guides decisions about what the team wants to accomplish, the information it needs to collect, and the strategies it should select (Scholtes, 1988).

In establishing the mission, the team might use interactive discussions designed to help groups reach consensus. Although many strategies are available, only one is outlined here for illustrative purposes.

The procedures focus first on a *brainstorming* technique, modified from the outline by Dunn and Dunn (1970), which includes a series of questions to help the group focus. In implementing this technique, the leader poses written questions, which alternate from positive to negative and back again; for example, "What is the ideal mission of our team? What might prevent us from reaching this ideal? In what ways might we begin to solve the problems that confront us? What might prevent us from succeeding? What are our next steps?" The idea behind brainstorming is to allow the members to state, in a series of rapid responses, all possible ideas that might help them define their group mission, before narrowing down their focus to the most realistic set of guidelines.

The second part of the initial procedures for consensus building uses a concept outlined by Powers and Powers (1983) to facilitate ownership by all members of the team. After obtaining information from the group during a brainstorming session, the leader summarizes the statements that were made, giving credit to the individuals who suggested them. The leader then returns this summary to the group for review and feedback on its accuracy. This material thus represents the group's thinking, rewritten in a way to facilitate consensus building. The team leader may find that when a group disagrees or is simply unsure about what course to take, the techniques of brainstorming and consensus building are instrumental in maintaining the focus on mission.

During the initial stages of operation, the leader will also want to guide the group in deciding how it will reach consensus in the event of disagreement (Glatthorn & Newberg, 1984). For example, will they vote and be guided by majority rule? Or will they defer to the opinion of the person with the highest degree of knowledge about the issue? On a team in which professionals have specific types of expertise, intensive training, and strong opinions, it is difficult to establish meaningful interactions. The team's leader, by establishing effective operating procedures, can enable this group to function as a unit. Figure 6.5 lists some suggested operating rules for teams.

Conducting Effective Team Meetings.   Scholtes (1988) has listed a detailed set of guidelines to help teams conduct effective meetings. The modified components of selected guidelines that apply most directly to the interactive school-based team are summarized here:

1. *Premeeting preparation:* The preparation for a meeting begins when members collect information on the nature of the problem to be discussed. Those who plan to present obtain data and organize it to support their description of the current situation:

Figure 6.5
Sample operating rules for teams.

> The team for problem-solving and special program planning at Prairie Marsh Elementary School developed the following operating rules for their team.
>
> 1. Meetings will start and end on time.
> 2. Members will arrive on time, with assignments completed, prepared to contribute, using researched information and data whenever possible.
> 3. Confidentiality will be honored.
> 4. Every member will listen attentively and question respectfully when clarification is needed. No side conversations.
> 5. Decisions will be made by consensus; that is, all group members will agree that they can "live with" the decision and will support it following the meeting.

◆ When, how often, and under what conditions does the problem occur?

◆ How does the current situation compare with the goal, ideal situation, or problem solution?

2. *Presentation/discussion:* Each team member who has relevant information prepares a brief presentation, taking care to communicate in jargon-free language. The procedures for effective communication within teams have been presented in previous chapters.

3. *Agenda development:* A meeting agenda should be circulated in advance. Scholtes suggests that it include the topic, time for each item, presenter, and item type (discussion item or announcement). A well-designed agenda can double as a record of the meeting, and be used as a presentation outline for the team to communicate with the organization's administrator, funding agency, and others. Ideally, the final agenda item involves drafting the next meeting's agenda.

4. *Documentation procedures:* When item follow-up is required, it should be documented so each member's responsibilities are clear. A standard form might be developed for recording progress, using the meeting's agenda as an outline. Scholtes suggests that the record include a description of topics, each followed by a summary of main points, decisions/conclusions, and next steps. Most useful of all in documenting procedures is the picture book format, developed by Scholtes and associates (see Figure 6.6). Its designers suggest that the team leader or quality adviser complete the three entries in the left column before the meeting.

5. *Evaluation procedures:* The most effective meetings are those that are evaluated by participants. This procedure helps the team leader make continuous improvements in the meeting process.

The first three segments of a Picture Book are standard:

Project

Enter a brief description of the project.

Reason selected

Summarize the issues that led to selection of this project, including its importance to customers.

Situation analysis

Summarize any data and include any flowcharts (probably at least a top-down flowchart) or cause-and-effect diagrams that show what the team learned about the status of the process or problem at the beginning of the project. (This box may take up a page or more if you have detailed records.)

Other segments will depend on your project. Some typical items included (not necessarily in this order) are:

Data collection

Show charts or graphs of data the team collects.

Data analysis

Show conclusions from data analysis. Include charts or graphs as appropriate.

Goal

State the goal of the next phase of the project.

Actions

Summarize the actions taken during a certain phase of the project. With a slight twist, a similar box could state actions the team recommends to follow up on its project.

Evaluation

Present summary data and conclusions from the project. Include evaluation of the project, especially what actions or decision were most and least effective, and things the team could improve on next time.

Description: The picture book format displays the milestones in a project through a series of flowchart-like entries. The project team leader and/or quality adviser should fill in the first two or three entries prior to the team's first meeting.

Figure 6.6
Picture book format for documenting team procedures.
Source: From *The Team Handbook* (pp. 4–14) by P. Scholtes, 1988, Madison, WI: Joiner Associates. Copyright 1988 by Joiner Associates, Inc. Reprinted with permission of the author.

Those who have served as team leaders in large-group settings offer additional suggestions for the conduct of effective meetings. Facilitation specialist Tyree (1997), for example, has suggested that successful facilitators understand and explain to the group the "triad" in each situation: (1) the context—task and people variables of the problem, (2) the content—task or goal being addressed, and (3) the process—method used to address the content. For those situations in which the context is complex, either because the task or the people present unusual difficulties, it may be useful to separate the roles of the leader into two parts, one to deal with the process (an outside, neutral facilitator) and the other to manage the content (an insider, with special knowledge of the problem). Tyree also suggests that the facilitator monitor the progress of the meeting by checking frequently for consensus, using "thumbs up/down" votes on particular options or flagging with stickers any written items that they feel will require additional discussion.

Irvine (1998), a former school board chair, has provided additional suggestions for the team leader who operates in the public eye. She suggests that—prior to the public meeting—the leader initiate and maintain working relationships with members of the press, as well as parent and professional organizations, agencies, and interest groups. Her tips for running meetings smoothly include having ground rules for limiting speakers to 2 minutes each, maintaining eye contact with board members to ensure their understanding of items on which they are voting, and conducting orientation meetings for new members.

SERVICE COORDINATION PROCEDURES FOR QUALITY ADVISERS

The functions of the team leader, who organizes and facilitates the team's operations, differ from those of another member of the team who also fills a leadership role. We will call this second individual the *quality adviser,* a term borrowed from the literature on total quality management. The quality adviser, in Tyree's term, deals with the *content* piece of the team's agenda, while the team leader or facilitator manages the team's *process,* or method of operating. While the team leader is the same person throughout the team's existence, the quality adviser changes according to the case being handled by the team. The quality adviser—who might be the special educator, school counselor, a parent, or someone else—is the member with the greatest expertise in this particular case, and therefore is its major content adviser in coordination of services.

The quality adviser fills a leadership role originally called *care manager* (Young, 1987) or *case manager.* Case management is defined as "a set of logical steps and a process of interaction within a service network which assure that a client receives needed services in a supportive, effective, and cost effective manner" (Weil, Karls, & Associates, 1985, p. 2).

The *quality adviser,* who manages a specific case, has four major responsibilities:

1. Coordinating the services needed by the student/client and family.
2. Delegating responsibility for providing those services to the individuals best able to provide them.
3. Providing follow-up to ensure that goals are being met.
4. Guiding the contributions of paraprofessionals and volunteers who assist on the case.

Each of these responsibilities will be discussed briefly.

Coordinating Needed Services

Each quality adviser needs to coordinate the special student's program by inter-acting with other team members and agencies. Because the team will be working with individuals and groups from agencies outside its own organization, it is important for the quality adviser to follow established guidelines for *interagency collaboration*. If the initial tasks of the team leader have been completed, each qual-ity adviser will find that the team has access to a resource file showing the agen-cies with which the team may need to interact to obtain necessary services.

The quality adviser will need to make certain the file includes all necessary information about the agency's services and its procedures for referral. This file might take the form of a set of index cards, on which the following information is recorded:

◆ The name, address, and phone number of the contact person.
◆ Days and times information about new referrals is taken.
◆ Type of information required (birth certificate, test data, etc.).
◆ Type of release form the agency requires, and its confidentiality.
◆ Type of service responsibilities the agency has.
◆ The agency's available funding options and constraints.

The Regional Resource Center Task Force on Interagency Collaboration (1979) has suggested that this information be organized at the state level into a common format so that the services of each agency can be readily compared with those of other potential providers. A modified version of their format is shown as Figure 6.7.

In addition to coordinating the student's program through interagency collab-oration, the quality adviser should maintain records of the decisions the team has made, the dates they were made, and the people responsible for their implemen-tation. These records will enable the quality adviser to track the progress of the case and request additional assistance from one or several members of the team as necessary.

Two additional areas require consideration by the quality adviser. These are the increasing use of technology and the importance of time management.

The uses of technology for education are growing at a pace and in a manner unimaginable even a decade ago. Adaptive equipment that ranges from wheel-chairs able to traverse rough terrain to affordable voice-operated computers now enables persons with disabilities to participate more fully in every aspect of daily life. Through wireless networks and telephone and cable alliances, instant global communication is becoming a reality. The barriers that exist in educational uses of technology are largely related to the ability of individuals to accept the rapid pace of change, and of institutions to provide the essential training for its use (Garcia, 1998). Increasing numbers of new professionals, including administrators, are receiving training in the application of computer technology to their career

Agency Name _____

Service Description _____

Operates Under Which State/Federal Laws? _____

Client Eligibility (age, income, disability, other) _____

Early and Multidisciplinary Assessment

Early Identification? _____

Types of Assessments Checklist

_____ Medical	_____ Academic performance
_____ Vision	_____ Adaptive behavior
_____ Hearing	_____ Motor abilities
_____ Speech and language	_____ Prevocational
_____ Social history	_____ Vocational
_____ Psychological	_____ Other
_____ General intelligence	

Where Services Are Delivered Checklist

_____ Regular program	_____ Home-based
_____ Part-time special program	_____ Group home facilities
_____ Full-time special program	_____ Work-training center
_____ Long-term residential facility	_____ Job placement
_____ Short-term medical facility	_____ Job coaching
_____ Clinics	_____ Other

Types of Services Checklist

_____ Case management	_____ Recreation
_____ Academic instruction	_____ Client counseling
_____ Independent living skills	_____ Parent training
_____ Speech and language development	_____ Family, genetic counseling
_____ Social/sexual training	_____ Nutrition services
_____ Prevocational/career training	_____ Respite care
_____ Vocational training	_____ Income maintenance
_____ On-the-job training	_____ Transportation
_____ Psychological services	_____ Protective services
_____ Physical or occupational therapy	_____ Crisis intervention
_____ Medical and dental services	_____ Other

Figure 6.7
Common format for comparison of agency programs.

Source: Adapted from *Interagency Collaboration on Full Services for Handicapped Children and Youth,* by Regional Resource Task Force on Interagency Collaboration, 1979, Washington, DC: U.S. Department of Health, Education, and Welfare, Bureau of Education for the Handicapped.

fields—web browsers to locate home pages, Power Point for group presentations, HTML for creation of home pages, spreadsheets for surveys and data analysis (Sharp, 1998). However, large numbers of practicing professionals are in need of additional assistance with the educational applications of technology. The quality adviser who coordinates a given student's special program would be well advised to seek the assistance of the educator responsible for the school's technology program or an area business person with technology expertise. The team may find that it can communicate efficiently and effectively, for example, through use of e-mail to track student progress on a regular basis without calling too many time-consuming meetings. In addition, teams that collaborate across distance barriers, such as those that include members from a school and a university or service agency, may be able to talk face to face using cost effective interactive video equipment such as PictureTel (Morsink, 1999).

The overload of tasks and information has caused many persons with roles such as that of team leader to seek better ways of managing time. At the school level, faculty members have found that they can manage time more effectively by scheduling common time blocks for committee meetings (Shanklin, 1997) and by consolidating the number of committees or teams on which they serve (Morsink, 1999). Team members who complete similar kinds of paperwork tasks across cases will find that common recording forms are useful, not only for saving time, but also for ensuring compliance with laws. In the business arena, consultants are often hired to serve as "productivity coaches" who teach others how to manage time; a monthly advisory letter entitled the "Organized Executive" provides ongoing assistance (Palmer, 1997). Some of their recommendations are applicable to the school environment, including skimming through large amounts of information in a short time, while controlling interruptions, long meetings, and e-mail overload. Learning to delegate and to say "no" are among the solutions to time management across settings. Time can be saved on teams by using the strategies for conducting meetings outlined earlier in this chapter. The chapter's application provides an example of effective delegation.

Delegating Responsibility

Since no quality adviser has either the time or the expertise to implement personally all aspects of the student's program, he or she needs to be able to delegate responsibilities to others. The process of *delegating* is most productive when it is guided by the leader's knowledge of each team member's task strengths and preferences (SRI, 1980). The quality adviser who is most effective in delegating understands the importance of providing resources, encouragement, and supportive feedback (Gersten et al., 1982).

Delegating refers to the assignment of part of the duties to another person who will assist with this task. The following guidelines for effective delegating are derived from the work of Developmental Dimensions (1981) for school teams and of Milch (1984) for teams of health-related professionals; they have been modified to fit the role of the quality adviser as service coordinator. In delegating responsibility, the quality adviser should:

1. *State the task clearly and objectively to the person who will do it.*
2. *Tell this person why the task is important.*
3. *Give "permission."* Others in the work environment need to know who has been delegated authority to accomplish the task so they will give full cooperation rather than resistance.
4. *Clarify the expected results.* It is important to tell the designee what to accomplish, but not how to do the job.
5. *Allow for interaction.* Make certain the task and its results are clear by asking the designee to restate what is to be done.
6. *Agree on follow-up.* Be sure to set a time and place to meet after the task is completed to monitor the results. It is not adequate to say, "Let's get together *sometime* and talk about it *some more*."

Throughout these steps, the effective quality adviser—as team leader—is communicating clearly, showing high expectations for results, and expressing confidence in both the importance of the task and the ability of the person to whom it is delegated. In the vignette that introduced this chapter, the team leader made major errors in delegating responsibility. He neither stated expectations clearly nor clarified the results that were required. Not granting "permission" to the special education teacher to conduct observations in the regular classroom was another major error, which resulted in the classroom teacher's feeling that the special educator was interfering. Moreover, he did not establish guidelines for follow-up, so team members did not know they were expected to do more than just talk about the problem.

In explaining the importance of stating the task clearly, Milch (1984) indicates that an unclear task statement may cause the team member to spend a large amount of time and effort, only to be told that "this is not what was expected." It is easy to see how such misunderstanding can foster frustration and even resentment among the team members. Milch also elaborates on the importance of clarifying the results that are expected, as opposed to specifying the exact procedures to be used. When the leader clarifies results, the person to whom the task is delegated feels free to apply professional knowledge and skill in determining how to achieve these results. Conversely, when the leader prescribes the details by which the task is to be accomplished, there is no respect shown for the person to whom the task is delegated. This type of delegating is a "put down," likely to be met with the (usually unspoken) response, "Well, if you know so much about my job, why don't you do it yourself?" Most people have experienced this type of delegating, which is illustrated in Figure 6.8.

Providing Follow-Up

We have emphasized throughout the chapter that the quality adviser who assumes the leadership position is not an authoritarian: The quality adviser develops the goals and objectives the team wishes the student to meet in collabo-

Figure 6.8
Ineffective delegating and follow-up.

ration with other team members. It is the quality adviser, however, who delegates specific responsibilities and then follows up by monitoring the progress of these assignments. The quality adviser gives both positive and corrective feedback during follow-up to the people to whom responsibility has been delegated. The cartoon in Figure 6.8 illustrated not only ineffective delegating, but also highly insensitive follow-up on the part of the special educator.

While providing follow-up, the quality adviser needs to use the key principles that have been shown to motivate staff to improve their performance: enhancing self-esteem, expressing empathy, and asking for help (Developmental Dimensions, 1981). The quality adviser continually seeks information about the progress and problems of those to whom specific responsibility is delegated. Using a calendar with time lines for follow-up, the quality adviser initiates contact with other members of the team. It is important for this leader to provide *supportive feedback* to all members of the group (Gersten et al., 1982). Supportive feedback is based on guidelines that enhance future interactions, and it includes the expression of willingness to help the team member who encounters difficulty in completing delegated tasks. The guidelines that seem most appropriate for the quality adviser's provision of feedback are adapted from the work of Developmental Dimensions (1981) and incorporate some of the strategies suggested by Blanchard and Johnson (1982). They include the following:

1. *Describe the problem clearly.* This is done by the member of the team who has experienced the problem. The team member who has made a direct observation that includes data-based input should use the data to describe the problem.

2. *Ask for the person's help in solving the problem.*

3. *Talk about causes of the problem.* The quality adviser should initiate this part of the discussion as an expression of empathy for the team member. The quality adviser should take care, however, not to let the discussion of causes become a dead-end explanation of why nothing can be done to solve the problem. The discussion should be kept short, then shifted to solutions.

4. *Brainstorm possible solutions.* The quality adviser requests possible solutions, saying, "Let's list some solutions we might try." The quality adviser writes them down, using phrases to describe each idea. When three or four potential solutions have been written, the quality adviser and team member look at them again and pick the one that has the best chance of initial success.

5. *Agree on the action and a follow-up discussion time.* Decide what role each person will play in the implementation of this solution. For example, the quality adviser might say, "OK, then, you're going to . . . and I'm going to help you by. . . . Let's meet again Friday at 2 o'clock to talk about how well this solution is working."

Positive Feedback.   When providing feedback to the person to whom a task has been delegated, the quality adviser hopes to be able to acknowledge the job's having been done well, thank the person, and praise the person's efforts. Praise is easier to provide than corrective feedback, although adults sometimes find it difficult to praise other adults in a sincere, helpful manner. It is easier to provide praise when the team has an established pattern in which the person to whom the adviser has delegated a task expects feedback on performance (Milch, 1984). *Positive feedback* is most effective when it is delivered immediately, or as soon after task completion as feasible. It should be brief and highly specific, specifying the results that were accomplished (Blanchard & Johnson, 1982; Milch, 1984). The quality adviser should also thank the person for helping and encourage the continuation of efforts on behalf of the team (Developmental Dimensions, 1981). An illustration of effective praise between professionals is as follows:

The school psychologist, as quality adviser, has delegated to the classroom teacher the task of implementing a behavior modification program for a boy named Tracy, who has been engaging in disruptive, off-task conversations during academic instruction. The psychologist, coming in to observe the effects of the program, notices great improvement in the boy's behavior because of the teacher's implementation of the plan. The psychologist says, "You really kept Tracy on task during math class today! When he started talking about his favorite TV show, you just ignored him and called on Barbara. Preventing him from going off on a tangent increased the accuracy of the whole group on their math facts. Thanks for sticking with me on this. I know it's hard to ignore off-task behavior, but it pays off!"

This kind of specific feedback relates the teacher's contribution to the team's results, thus showing the effect of the new program. It heightens the feeling that the person being praised has accomplished something of importance and lessens the possibility that the praise will sound phony or exaggerated, as it would if the quality adviser simply had said, "You're doing just great!"

Corrective Feedback.   It is less pleasant for the quality adviser to give *corrective feedback* to a person whose work has not supported the team's efforts. But without corrective feedback, tasks lack clarity, and positive feedback eventually loses its meaning. Corrective feedback should be specific, including descriptions of both the behavior and its negative effect on the situation (Blanchard & Johnson, 1982; Developmental Dimensions, 1981; Milch, 1984). Beyond this, the quality adviser should show a desire to be helpful, rather than appear punitive or vengeful. The quality adviser can demonstrate helpfulness by asking for reasons for the lack of effective contributions and by listening to the reasons with empathy, but without accepting them as excuses for continued ineffectiveness. The quality adviser can focus on problem solving by saying, "What can we do to prevent this problem from recurring?" The quality adviser and team member engage in some collaborative problem solving; then they agree on a follow-up to determine whether the proposed solution is working. Finally, and most important of all, the quality adviser expresses confidence in the person's ability to contribute increasingly to the team's efforts.

The emphasis in corrective feedback is on task completion that enables the team to reach its goal, rather than on the personal performance of the team member. The quality adviser's role is to work collaboratively with the person in need of assistance to design the solution to a shared problem. Although the leader is a collaborator, he or she is also the person in charge, the one who will follow up on the strategy and retain ultimate responsibility for its effectiveness. It is important in this role to maintain a careful balance between being too directive and too "friendly." The overly directive quality adviser allows the team member to avoid assuming ownership or responsibility for the problem; the overly friendly leader appears too weak to provide the follow-up necessary for task completion.

Guiding Paraprofessionals and Volunteers

The team member who functions as quality adviser may also have the task of coordinating the work of *paraprofessionals, preservice trainees,* and *volunteers* who assist the team members in their roles as service providers or collaborators. In a number of school districts and clinical programs, paraprofessionals, who have some training but less than full certification in their field, are employed as assistants for the professionals in special programs. In many other programs, people with expertise in their own fields volunteer their time to help school or health-related personnel. The team member's role in recruiting, training, and coordinating the work of these people is becoming increasingly important.

Paraprofessionals.   The role of the paraprofessional is to supplement the instructional or other support services provided to the special needs student, under the supervision of the teacher or other professional responsible for those services. For the purpose of this discussion, the preservice trainee, who may be a student teacher or health professions-related intern, is considered a paraprofessional, because this person is not yet certified to conduct the duties of a professional. According to O'Shea and Hendrickson (1987), the paraprofessional in the classroom most often engages in activities such as the following:

◆ Provides follow-up tutoring.

◆ Circulates throughout the room to check students' progress.

◆ Provides students with drills and reviews.

◆ Prepares instructional materials and games.

◆ Reads stories to students.

◆ Conducts small-group noninstructional activities.

◆ Corrects homework and workbook assignments.

◆ Arranges learning centers, demonstrations, bulletin boards.

In a classroom for students with physical disabilities, the paraprofessional also assists students with functional skills such as dressing and eating, with the use of braces and other prosthetic devices, and with lifting and transferring, as from a wheelchair to a toilet. The paraprofessional may also help other members of the team, such as the computer specialist and the physical or occupational therapist.

O'Shea and Hendrickson (1987) suggest that the professional can guide the paraprofessional most effectively by using certain interpersonal and management strategies, modified in Figure 6.9. O'Shea and Hendrickson stress the importance of working with paraprofessionals in a team relationship, in which the professional is the leader. The teacher, related professional, or quality adviser assumes the role of helping the paraprofessional develop additional skills. Through observation, supervision, and specific feedback, the professional with good communication skills can promote positive growth in the paraprofessional, ensuring that this individual will be a more effective member of the interactive team.

Volunteers.   Volunteers have assisted in schools on an organized basis since the National School Volunteer Program began in 1950. In 1981, leaders in business and industry joined the efforts to provide assistance to school programs through the creation of the Advisory Council on Private Sector Initiatives (National Association of Partners in Education, 1988). NAPE has combined the two groups of volunteers, the school volunteers and the school–business partnerships. Volunteer support for schools by business and industry now involves at least 17% of the nation's schools and 9 million of our children (Greer, 1989).

1. **Praise** the paraprofessional for specific tasks that are well done.
2. **Provide** corrective feedback privately, not in the presence of students or clients.
3. **Teach** the paraprofessional to use the disciplinary system designed by the professional, with rules that are consistent, as agreed upon by all.
4. **Encourage** the paraprofessional to handle discipline problems, but provide support when needed.
5. **Remind** the paraprofessional to set a good example, to show respect and courtesy to others.
6. **Discuss** the importance of fairness to all.
7. **Stress** the importance of using the school day for worthwhile tasks, not busy work.
8. **Stress** the necessity of not being overly friendly with students.
9. **Demonstrate** how to select students who get along well together when organizing committees and work groups.
10. **Encourage** the paraprofessional to keep a sense of humor!

Figure 6.9
Effective guidance of paraprofessionals.
Source: From *Training Module: Using Teacher Aides Effectively* by D. O'Shea and J. Hendrickson, 1987, Gainesville: University of Florida, Multidisciplinary Diagnostic and Training Program. Adapted by permission.

School volunteers may be specialists in their own fields—writers, researchers, vice presidents, designers, marketing personnel, physicians, attorneys, photographers—some of whom are actively involved in their professions, and some of whom are retired. Several schools have used volunteers to assist with programs in literacy, dropout prevention, and drug abuse prevention. These volunteer partners represent a rich resource of knowledge and support for the interactive team. Volunteers may engage in activities such as the following:

◆ Tutoring students with special needs.
◆ Serving as mentors for students who lack adult role models.
◆ Sponsoring training, demonstrations, and tours for students.
◆ Assisting with projects or judging contests.
◆ Providing work internships for students.
◆ Donating equipment and materials.

It is important for team members to work within the overall system of their organization to identify and coordinate the efforts of volunteers, and to assist in the design of a training program that will enable volunteers to work effectively

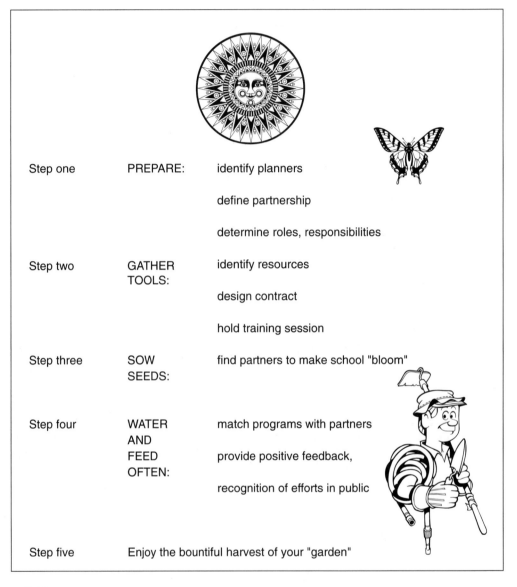

Step one	PREPARE:	identify planners
		define partnership
		determine roles, responsibilities
Step two	GATHER TOOLS:	identify resources
		design contract
		hold training session
Step three	SOW SEEDS:	find partners to make school "bloom"
Step four	WATER AND FEED OFTEN:	match programs with partners
		provide positive feedback,
		recognition of efforts in public
Step five	Enjoy the bountiful harvest of your "garden"	

Figure 6.10
Building and managing educational partnerships with volunteers.

Source: Adapted from a chart presented by B. McCauley at a conference sponsored by the Florida Department of Education and the Florida Chamber of Commerce, March 1989.

with students who have special needs. These volunteers will appreciate guidance about the rules of the organization and the instructional and management techniques that are effective with the type of special students to whom they are assigned. They will also appreciate both positive and constructive feedback when it is delivered sensitively, although the team leader is not in the position of serving as a "supervisor" of their efforts.

McCauley (1989), who has suggested that the nurturing of *school–community partnerships* is like growing a garden, has developed guidelines for the successful use of volunteers and business partners. These guidelines are adapted in Figure 6.10. Both paraprofessionals and volunteers should be provided with guidance that recognizes their contributions and allows them to become respected members of the interactive team. The quality adviser is the team member in the best position to ensure that this occurs.

Application

The following application illustrates the correct way for the team leader or quality adviser to delegate a task to a paraprofessional and to provide effective feedback while monitoring the completion of the task. The task is presented as a series of examples, with comments on their appropriateness.

The quality adviser is a classroom teacher. The task is to conduct a follow-up review for a special needs student on a lesson the teacher has taught in reading.

Step 1: State the Task Clearly

Clear	Unclear
I'd like you to help Jimmy master these five words he missed in reading today.	I'd like you to help Jimmy in reading for about 20 minutes.

In the unclear example, the task is unclear and unfocused; in addition, the element of time is specified objectively, but the task is not.

Step 2: Tell Why the Task Is Important

Nobody likes the feeling of being delegated a task because it is unimportant or unworthy of the attention of the "boss."

Clear	Unclear
It's really important for him to have extra practice because it takes a lot of time and repetition for him to learn.	It's really important for him to learn to read.

The unclear example states something so obvious that it sounds as if the teacher is talking down to the paraprofessional. In the first example, the paraprofessional is addressed in a way that shows respect for his or her skill. The teacher is sharing knowledge about the nature of the student's difficulty and relating it to the task delegated, which heightens the importance of the task.

Step 3: Give Permission

Others in the work environment need to know that the "boss" has delegated task authority to someone else so that they will give full cooperation rather than resistance. In our example, the child with whom the paraprofessional will work needs to know that this person is the "acting teacher." Assurance of permission would be given to the paraprofessional in the child's presence.

Clear	Unclear
I've told Jimmy that you're going to be his reading teacher for the next 20 minutes and that I expect him to work just as well for you as he does for me.	You have my permission to use this reading book to work with Jimmy.

The word *permission* is used here to mean that the delegator confers an "acting in my place" title upon the person to whom responsibility is being delegated. It is important that knowledge of this permission be shared with the individual over whom the paraprofessional has been delegated responsibility.

Step 4: Clarify Results

It is important for the delegator to tell the designee what is to be accomplished, but not how to do the job. In the cartoon shown as Figure 6.8, the special educator delegated the details on how to do the task of making flashcards. The effect was predictable: The paraprofessional gave the job back to him.

Clear	Unclear
Mastery of each word means he can read it correctly within five seconds and that he gets it right three times in a row.	Use these flashcards instead of letting him practice writing the words or playing a game.

The unclear example suggests that the quality adviser—the teacher—does not trust the paraprofessional to make decisions about how the task is accomplished. The quality adviser also gives no guidance on what is expected as a result of the efforts—the behavior expected or product to be completed.

Step 5: Allow for Interaction

The quality adviser should make certain the task and its results are clear by asking the paraprofessional to restate what is to be done.

Clear	**Unclear**
Let's be sure we're both clear on what is to happen. Can you summarize what I'd like you to do?	Do you have any questions about what you are to do?

In the unclear example, the quality adviser will not know whether the task is understood, because it is unlikely that the paraprofessional will ask any questions.

Step 6: Agree on Follow-Up

The quality adviser should set a time and place to meet after the task is completed to monitor the results. This will allow her to thank the paraprofessional for assistance and to include the paraprofessional in deciding whether the task should be modified to increase its effectiveness with the student.

Clear	**Unclear**
Could we meet at 3 o'clock today in my office to analyze the progress Jimmy has made?	If Jimmy has trouble, let's get together and talk about it some more.

In the unclear example, the plan for monitoring effectiveness is so open that nothing further will happen.

All the way through these steps, the effective leader is communicating clearly, showing high expectations for results, and expressing confidence in both the importance of the task and the ability of the person to whom it is delegated. By using these procedures, it is more likely that the paraprofessional will become a valued and valuable member of the interactive team.

Step 7: Conduct Follow-Up

The effective leader gives both positive and corrective feedback during follow-up of delegated activities. The specific substeps for conducting follow-up to encourage improved performance were outlined earlier in the chapter. In this application, only the most important of the substeps—describing the problem, discussing possible causes, listing alternative solutions, and agreeing on next steps—are illustrated.

The paraprofessional (PP) who has worked with Jimmy describes a problem during the scheduled follow-up conference with the quality adviser, the teacher/ leader (TL):

PP: Jimmy mastered three of the five words I taught him, but he is still having trouble reading the other two words.

TL: What do you think caused this problem?

PP: I'm not sure. It could be that the two words were so much alike that they were confusing to him. The words were *horse* and *house.*

TL: Yes, those words do look a lot alike. That's a good observation. Do you have any other ideas?

PP: It was close to the end of the 20 minutes when I presented those words. He might have been more tired then. He seemed to be looking around at the other kids instead of concentrating.

TL: That's certainly consistent with what we know about Jimmy's behavior and attention span. Let's list a few ideas about how we might modify the task next time you work with him to make it more effective.

The paraprofessional and the teacher/leader list four possible alternatives for task modification:

1. Reduce practice time from 20 minutes to 10 minutes at a time; repeat practice twice a day.
2. Remove Jimmy from his desk during work on reading; place him in a quiet corner away from distractions.
3. Use practice alternatives that are more motivating, such as word games or computer-assisted instruction on the troublesome words.
4. Highlight the differences between the words *horse* and *house,* either by printing the contrasting letter in red; or pairing each word with a picture illustrating its meaning, to help Jimmy develop his own device for learning the differences between the two words.

TL: Which of these alternative ways of changing the task do you think would be most effective the next time you work with Jimmy?

PP: I'd like to try the last one—helping him develop some kind of trick for learning the differences in the two words.

TL: That sounds as if it might help him—not just for the next practice time, but over the long term—to develop a strategy for telling the difference between words that look alike. Why don't you design a set of materials that highlight the differences in these words and their meanings? Then try it with him tomorrow and see whether he masters all five words, including *horse* and *house.* Let's get together again after school at this time tomorrow to see how well our new plan worked.

In this example of follow-up, the teacher serving as quality adviser provided an opportunity for the paraprofessional to function as an important part of the interactive team. The emphasis in follow-up was on the task, rather than on the performance of the paraprofessional. It was possible for the two team members to function well together because they focused on solution of the problem—designing a task that was more effective in helping their shared student learn the target words. Moreover, although the professional was clearly "in charge" of the conference, the paraprofessional's observations, ideas, and contributions were important. This is how the team leader can obtain maximum efforts from all members of the interactive team.

◊ ◊

SUMMARY

There are two types of team leaders. The person who calls and conducts meetings, collects and distributes information on resources, and maintains records is the official, designated, ongoing team leader. The temporary leader, called the quality adviser, changes with each case; this leadership role is given to the person with the greatest knowledge about the specific case being considered by the team. Both types of team leaders need special skills in the leadership of professionals:

◆ Skills that are similar to the skills, attributes, and behaviors of effective leaders in other organizations, including business and industry.
◆ Skills that focus on the management of tasks, rather than of individuals.

The ongoing, designated team leader has three tasks that set the stage for the effective functioning of the team in the future:

◆ Set up the team within the context of the organization.
◆ Identify resources for use by the team.
◆ Establish operating procedures.

Each designated leader, called a quality adviser, is responsible for overall coordination of a case that involves a specific special needs student. The quality adviser is responsible for:

◆ Coordinating the services provided to the student or client.
◆ Delegating responsibility to other team members.
◆ Providing follow-up on the effectiveness of delegated tasks.
◆ Guiding the activities of paraprofessionals and volunteers who assist the team.

In this chapter, the work of the team leader has been outlined. The emphasis of the chapter has been on the use of the leader as a collaborator who can encourage the full participation of each team member to reach the team's goal: the best possible program for a given student.

In the next chapter, the dimension of leadership as a facilitating factor will be explored further. The discussion will focus on ways in which professional development can be used to empower team members in their efforts to bring about long-term systematic change, which enhances the effectiveness of programs for students with special needs.

ACTIVITIES

1. Using the six steps presented in the chapter, write or act out the conversation you would use to delegate a teaching task to a practicum student in your classroom or clinical program. (Use any task of your choice.)

2. Explain the difference between listening with empathy to the reasons for a paraprofessional's problem in completing a task and accepting those reasons as excuses for failure to complete the task.

3. Using the guidelines presented in the chapter, write or act out the conversation you would use in giving your paraprofessional corrective feedback during follow-up on a task you had delegated. (Use any situation of your choice.)

4. Using the guidelines presented in this chapter, delegate a task to a paraprofessional or practicum student in your program, observe that person completing the task, and provide feedback on the task performance during a follow-up conference.

Using directories, knowledgeable people, the phone book, and other resources you can muster, prepare a resource card file.

Card Entry Format

1. Upper right—name of agency or service
2. Left margin, line two—address and phone number
3. Left margin, line three—service description
4. Back of card, line one—hours of operation
5. Back of card, line two—area served
6. Back of card, line three—fee charged and financial notes
7. Back of card, line four—name of contacts

Example:

1. County Office of Child Services 2. 429 Elm Street 307-4569 3. Assigns case worker to home of child who has been abused. Makes referrals or gives shelter when necessary.	4. M–Sa, 8 a.m.–6 p.m. and 24 hours emergency 5. Whole County 6. No Charge 7. George Bundy
Front	Back

Figure 6.11
Community resources card file.

5. Use directories, interviews, and other sources of information to develop a card file of community resources that might be used by an interactive team in your area. The sample shown in Figure 6.11 provides a useful format for this activity.

REFERENCES

Altenbaugh, R., Engel, D., & Martin, D. (1995). *Caring for kids: A critical study of urban school leavers.* London: Falmer Press.

Audette, B., & Algozzine, G. (1992). Free and appropriate education for all students: Total quality and the transformation of American public education. *Remedial and Special Education, 13*(6), 8–18.

Bennis, W. (1989). *Why leaders can't lead: The unconscious conspiracy continues.* San Francisco: Jossey-Bass.

Bennis, W. (1997). 21st century leadership: Do you have what it takes? Edited by E. Wakin. *Beyond Computing, 6*(4), 38–43.

Black, S. (1998). Research: A different kind of leader. *The American School Board Journal, 185*(6), 32–35.

Blanchard, K., & Johnson, S. (1982). *The one minute manager.* New York: William Morrow.

Bonstingl, J. (1992). The quality revolution in education. *Educational Leadership, 50*(3), 4–9.

Covey, S. (1990). *The 7 habits of highly effective people.* New York: Simon & Schuster.

Covey, S. (1996). Three roles of the leader in the new paradigm. In F. Hesselbein, M. Goldsmith, & R. Beckhard (Eds.), *The leader of the future.* San Francisco: Jossey-Bass.

DeBevoise, W. (1984). Synthesis of research on the principal as instructional leader. *Educational Leadership, 41*(5) 14–20.

Deming, W. E. (1986). *Out of the crisis.* Boston: MIT Center for Advanced Engineering Studies.

Developmental Dimensions. (1981). *Interaction management system.* Pittsburgh: Author.

Drucker, P. (1992). *Managing for the future: The 1990's and beyond.* New York: Truman Talley Books.

Dunn, R., & Dunn, K. (1970). *Practical approaches to individualizing instruction.* West Nyack, NY: Parker.

Fullan, M. (1993). *Change forces.* London: Falmer Press.

Garcia, R. (1998). Hang-ups of introducing computer technology. *THE Journal, 26*(2), 65–66.

Gersten, R., Carnine, D., & Green, S. (1982, March). *Administrative supervisory support functions for the implementation of effective educational programs for low income students.* Paper presented at the annual meeting of the American Educational Research Association, New York.

Glasser, W. (1997). A new look at school failure and school success. *Phi Delta Kappan, 78,* 596–603.

Glatthorn, A., & Newberg, N. (1984). A team approach to instructional leadership. *Educational Leadership, 39*(3), 60–63.

Goldman, E. (1998). The significance of leadership style. *Educational Leadership, 55*(7), 20–22.

Greer, J. (1989). Partnerships: What is our contribution? *Exceptional Children, 55,* 391–393.

Hall, G., Rutherford, W., Hord, S., & Huling, L. (1984). Effects of three principal styles on school improvement. *Educational Leadership, 41*(5), 22–31.

Hersey, P., & Blanchard, K. (1974). So you want to know your leadership style? *Training and Development Journal, 28*(2), 22–36.

Heskett, J., & Schlesinger, L. (1996). Leaders who shape and keep performance-oriented cultures. In F. Hesselbein, M. Goldsmith, & R. Beckhard (Eds.), *The leader of the future*. San Francisco: Jossey-Bass.

Irvine, J. (1998). My life as a chair. *The American School Board Journal, 185*(10), 45–46, 55.

Jarvis, M., & Chavez, C. (1997). Leadership and the triangle of success. *Phi Kappa Phi Journal, 77*(1), 35–37.

Joyce, B., & Showers, B. (1995, May). Learning experiences in staff development. *The Developer*, p. 3.

Juran, J. (1992, July 29). *Managing for world class quality*. Keynote address at the Third Annual Symposium: Quality in Action in Academe, Lehigh University, PA.

Kelley, R. (1991). *The power of followership*. New York: Doubleday.

Kotter, J. (1996). *Leading change*. Boston: Harvard Business School.

Kouzes, J., & Posner, B. (1990). *The leadership challenge: How to get extraordinary things done in organizations*. San Francisco: Jossey-Bass.

Maxwell, J. (1995). *Developing the leaders around you: How to help others reach their full potential*. Nashville, TN: Thomas Nelson, Inc.

McCauley, B. (1989, March). *Creating and managing an educational partnership program*. Presentation to Partners in the Business of Education, a Joint Conference by the Florida Department of Education and the Florida Chamber of Commerce, Ft. Lauderdale, FL.

McClelland, D. (1975). *Power: The inner experience*. New York: Irvington.

McGregor, D. (1960). *The human side of enterprise*. New York: McGraw-Hill.

Milch, E. (1984). *Delegating and monitoring staff performance*. Gainesville, FL: Alachua General Hospital.

Morsink, C. (1999). *21st century teachers for a better future*. Final Report to Howard Heinz Endowment. Slippery Rock, PA: SRU College of Education.

Nanus, G. (1992). *Visionary leadership*. San Francisco: Jossey-Bass.

National Association of Partners in Education. (1988). *1988 Annual report*. Alexandria, VA: Author.

O'Shea, D., & Hendrickson, J. (1987). *Training module: Using teacher aides effectively*. Gainesville: University of Florida, Multidisciplinary Diagnostic and Training Program.

Palmer, D. (1997, June). How America's most successful executives accomplish so much in so little time. *Executive Focus*, pp. 23–24.

Peters, T., & Austin, N. (1985). *A passion for excellence: The leadership difference*. New York: Warner Books.

Peterson, K., & Deal, T. (1998). How leaders influence the culture of schools. *Educational Leadership, 56*(1), 28–30.

Powers, D., & Powers, M. (1983). *Making participatory management work*. San Francisco: Jossey-Bass.

Regional Resource Center Task Force on Interagency Collaboration. (1979). *Interagency collaboration on full services for handicapped children and youth*. Washington, DC: U.S. Department of Health, Education, and Welfare, Bureau of Education for the Handicapped.

Richman, M. (1999a, February 16). IBD's 10 secrets to success. *Investor's Business Daily*, p. A8.

Richman, M. (1999b, August 30). IBD's 10 secrets to success. *Investor's Business Daily*, p. A4.

Schlecty, P. (1997). *Inventing better schools: An action plan for education reform*. San Francisco: Jossey-Bass.

Scholtes, P. (1988). *The team handbook*. Madison, WI: Joiner Associates.

Senge, P. (1990). *The fifth discipline: The art and practice of the learning organization*. New York: Harper & Row.

Sergiovanni, T. (1992). *Moral leadership*. San Francisco: Jossey-Bass.

Shanklin, N. (1997). A run-away horse: Reining in committee work. In R. Benton (Ed.), *Partnerships for learning: Real issues and real solutions* (TECSCU Monograph Series, Vol. II, pp. 160–163). Oshkosh, WI: Poesch Printing.

Sharp, W. (1998). School administrators need technology too. *THE Journal, 26*(2), 75–76.

SRI. (1980). *Administrator perceiver technical manual.* Lincoln, NE: Selection Research.

Tribus, M. (1992, July 30). *Quality management in education.* Third Annual Symposium: Quality in Academe, Lehigh University, PA.

Tyree, R. (1997, May*). Introductory facilitation training.* Presentation to Department Chairs, College of Education, Slippery Rock University of Pennsylvania.

Wasley, P., Hampel, R., & Clark, R. (1997). The puzzle of whole-school change. *Phi Delta Kappan, 78,* 690–697.

Weil, M., Karls, J., & Associates. (1985). *Case management in human service practice.* San Francisco: Jossey-Bass.

Wilson, M. (1993). The search for teacher leaders. *Educational Leadership, 50*(6), 24–27.

Wittenmyer, J. (1983). Unit five: Referral, coordination, and management of services. In C. M. Del Polito & J. G. Barresi (Eds.), *Alliances in health and education: Serving youngsters with special needs* (pp. 115–133). Washington, DC: American Society of Allied Health Professions.

Young, T. (1987). Therapeutic case advocacy: A summary. *Focal Point, 1*(3), 1–5.

7

Empowering Team Members Through Professional Development

Topics in this chapter include:

- Discussion of the terms *power* and *empowerment* as they relate to professional development and the process of change.

- Description of the best practices for professional development summarized from the research.

- Description of three types of professional development for teams: sharing knowledge, building skills, and developing the team.

- Guidelines and examples for implementing knowledge sharing and skill development.

- An application, showing how the level of a team's development might be viewed from the perspective of the leader's style.

The team that had met to evaluate and place students with special needs in exceptional children's programs at the elementary school was having difficulty implementing its programs. The students they had identified and placed were functioning well, but teacher referrals had increased by 25%. The school psychologist found that teachers were asking for her help in placing problem students in pull-out programs, but that her services as a consultant to others in the building were not welcomed. Three classroom teachers who had been involved in the team were cooperative, but most of their colleagues seemed confused about how to use prereferral programs for students who were having learning or behavior problems.

Together, the special education teacher, the school psychologist, and two of the classroom teachers approached the school principal, who was new in the district and eager to establish her school as a model program for serving students with a variety of special needs. The team agreed to support the principal's efforts in professional development by presenting inservice training on the potential contributions and limitations of their roles. They also agreed to serve, along with selected classroom teachers, as "mentors" who would conduct follow-up observations and assist in program planning and the coaching of teachers who wished to implement alternative learning strategies for the students with special needs in their classrooms.

The team members, under the direction of the school principal, conducted a needs assessment to determine the types of problems school personnel were having with their students with special needs and the areas in which they felt least effective in assisting these students. They learned that teachers were most concerned about managing the behavior of special needs students during large-group instruction and providing students with academic instruction that would enable them to master the basic skills. With this information in hand, the team members began to design a plan for professional development to assist all members of the school staff in working more effectively with students with special needs.

A group representing the leadership in the school's teachers' union and the PTA was asked by the principal to design a formal evaluation of the professional development program's effectiveness and to conduct this evaluation one year after its implementation. The evaluation plan was to focus on the decrease in student referrals to special programs, while also considering the effects of professional development on the whole school's sense of "mission" and teachers' and parents' satisfaction with the program. Evaluation during the second year of implementation was to include an analysis of the effect of the program on the average student's academic achievement, as well as individual learning and behavior changes in students with special needs.

Read between the lines of this case to see why an attempted change first faltered, then flourished. Experienced change agents understand that school improvement occurs best when it is based on empowerment, rather than on rule enforcement. In this chapter, the guidelines for use of professional development as a facilitating factor are outlined. Power is defined, and the distinction is drawn between power and empowerment. The best practices for empowering team members through professional development are outlined, and the relevant research on team development in business and industry is summarized. Three levels of professional development—sharing knowledge, developing skill, and developing the team— are described. Applications of each level are given as the use of professional development as a facilitating factor in interactive teaming is explained.

POWER, EMPOWERMENT, AND CHANGE

Team members who recognize the need for a change in the behavior of others or in the culture of the organization in which they work often wish they had the power to implement this change. Professional development is one of the most effective ways to bring about change. Such development has the greatest effect when it is implemented by people who understand how it relates to the change process by empowering people rather than by imposing power on them.

Cuban (1998) and Bennis (1989) have pointed out that effective leaders manage conflict creatively, encouraging both innovation and challenges presented as divergent points of view. Covey (1990) added that the leader's power is based on the group's respect for his or her credibility and genuineness, as opposed to the leader's ability to act out superficial behaviors that give the appearance of power.

Responsible and Effective Use of Power

The term *power* is used here to mean the ability to accomplish the goals of the team in providing the best possible program for each student with special needs. The use of power is discussed along two dimensions: (1) understanding the positive aspects of power and (2) recognizing and using established power. Each of these dimensions is discussed briefly.

Understanding the Positive Aspects of Power.   It should be emphasized that power is equated with strength or effectiveness, but is not used as a synonym for autocratic leadership. As shown in Chapter 6, power is essential in the exercise of leadership that facilitates change.

Several types of power are available to the team member who wishes to be a change agent. The types of power include coercive, reward, legitimate, expert, and charismatic power. *Coercive power,* which involves the use of threat or punishment, is used least often by leaders who wish to obtain cooperation; likewise, *reward power* is of only temporary value in facilitating behavioral or organizational change. Glasser (1997) has shown that coercive and reward power, in fact, have a negative effect on school climate and may interfere with change. *Legitimate power,* which is based on the group's acceptance of a common purpose, requires that the leader conform to this purpose and fit the group's concept of how their leader should behave. The use of legitimate power is the most desirable within the interactive team, although this is not the only type of power available to the team leader.

The leader who is perceived to have *expert power* is felt to have knowledge, insight, and vision. For the interactive team, expert power can also be appropriately used to initiate the changes necessary to implement a student's program. The expert is viewed as the one who can solve the problem or make something happen. The person who demonstrates expert power in a group is the one who comes prepared with facts and information. The data collected may take the form of charts and graphs, showing the student's responses to various types of programs; historical information, including test scores and work samples; or a summary of the research on a particular program that has been found effective. The team member with data is the individual most likely to be perceived by others as having the necessary expert power to bring about desired change.

Recognizing and Using Established Power.   The team member who wishes to bring about positive change does not always have the power—either legitimate or expert—to do so. In this case, it is important for the person who wishes to facilitate change to recognize and use *established power* within the organization. Tucker (1972) has developed a key to planning change based on an understanding of power. This key is presented as a flowchart, which follows a series of questions. In Question 1, team members who wish to be *change agents* are asked to determine whether they have power. If they answer "yes," they have no obstacle and can go all the way through the flowchart, even skipping steps to accomplish their change. (There may be later consequences to skipping steps, because they may not have "institutionalized" the changes.)

If the change agents have no power, they must decide whether to behave as revolutionaries or to "communicate the importance of that change to persons in power" (Tucker, 1972, p. 2). In most instances, team members do not have power and must propose their change through a third party who is known and respected by the power structure in the organization. Tucker pointed out that this sharing of power involves both risk and compromise, but he suggested that it is the most effective strategy for the powerless beginner. Tucker's key for planning change has been adapted for use by the interactive team member and is presented as Figure 7.1. The "change" presented in the flowchart is the new program, which the interactive team wishes to implement to improve the services

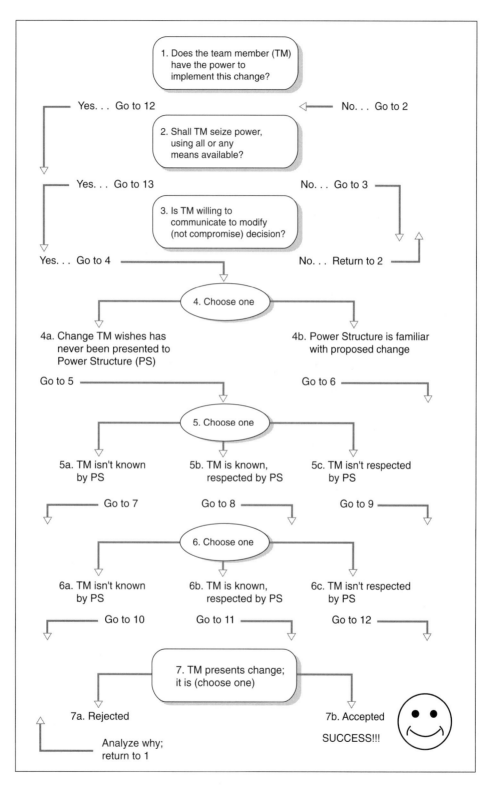

Figure 7.1 A flowchart for planning change. *Source: From A Plan to Achieve Change* by J. Tucker, 1972, Austin: University of Texas, Department of Special Education. Adapted by permission.

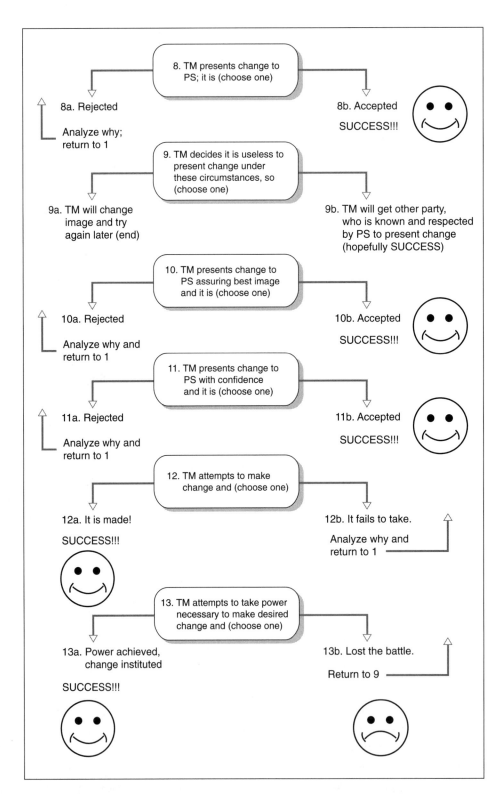

Figure 7.1, *continued*

offered to students with special needs. The team members responsible for implementing this program are "change agents" who work within the *power structure* of the organization to be sure the changes required by this program will be accepted by members of the organization.

In the flowchart, the team member asks a series of questions, in which the key issues are the following:

◆ Does the member have the power to bring about the desired change? If not, shall power be seized, or should the team member "give" the change idea to another person who may be more successful?

◆ Is the member willing to discuss the change with others, knowing that the proposal will be modified in the process of discussion?

◆ Is the team member known and respected by the power structure? If not, should the team member try to gain respect or, alternatively, "give" the change to a known and respected person for implementation?

As shown in Figure 7.1, the team member who is established within or respected by the power structure of the organization will be able to get necessary program changes accepted more readily than a person who is rejected by the power structure or is new to the organization. This strategy is particularly important for first-year teachers or new team members. In the latter instance, the team member will find that the most effective way to implement changes is by *giving ideas away to an established person who is respected and accepted by the power structure.* This concept is key to the understanding of how to use power by sharing it; this is called *empowerment.* Empowerment is essential in the process of change.

Bringing About Change

One might assume that when there is a compelling need for change, it would be easy to implement this change. Those who study the change process caution that this is not so (Bennis, 1989; Cuban, 1988; Fullan, 1993; Fullan, Galluzzo, Morris, & Watson, 1998; Gartner & Lipsky, 1987; Skrtic, 1987). The difficulties in implementing change are shown in the following application.

◇ ◇

Application

The faculty at Woodside Elementary School had worked for five years to develop its mission and strategies for enabling all students to succeed. After extensive discussions, involving the entire faculty and representatives from the community and local university, the school created a learning community with a model for full inclusion of all students. Students worked together to solve problems, teachers adapted instruction to the special needs and learning styles of every student, and used authentic assessments such as projects and portfolios to document student success. Although the school became known for its effectiveness in using innovative strategies, there remained a disquieting skepticism on the part of the district's central administrators who were concerned about the lack of improvement in standardized test scores. Then the principal, who had been the instructional leader, left. The district selected a new principal who believed in the traditional model, emphasizing basic academic skills, with effectiveness measured by standardized tests. The whole-school changes that had been in effect for the past several years began to disappear.

◊ ◊

From both successful and unsuccessful attempts at change, one can abstract the importance of a supportive climate created by an internal team, and endorsed by the organizational power structure. The prospective *change agent* or developer needs to understand that successful change can occur only when both internal and external people or groups directly responsible for problems are involved in the design and implementation of the *change strategy*. The preceding application shows a change that flourished, then faltered.

Two ways of viewing change have been selected as most relevant to the design of an educational change strategy. The first is a theory based on the study of change as a process, which takes place at the personal level; the second is a perspective on the "new paradigm."

The Change Process.   The first way of viewing change is through studies that emphasize change as a process rather than a single event which takes place at a very personal level. Recent studies of the change process in education and related settings provide new guidance on the way to manage successful change. Fullan (1997) points out that no single model can predict or facilitate change and that conflict and resistance are essential components of change, to be managed productively. Fullan views change as a highly personal, emotional event which requires careful management as opposed to suppression of resistance. He emphasizes the role of vision as critical in the sense that all participants need to have the same vision in order to effect the change. Fullan suggests that change related to the simultaneous improvement of schools and teacher preparation programs requires restructuring, beginning with an emphasis on redefining the culture of the school. Changes in the use of time also may be essential, following the emphasis on reculturing. Team training, peer coaching, mentoring and the use of action research are among the strategies he recommends for school improvement.

Du Four (1998) has also provided a series of practical applications for managing the change process. He concurs with Fullan that the change agents should not pay too much attention to resisters by "putting them down" and therefore driving them underground. Instead, he recommends that they be brought into the team through focus on the common mission of helping all students to learn, and by emphasis on the positive ways to make this occur. A faculty team might begin the change process with a review of the literature on what is known about effective schools using this information to design the common mission. All participants can contribute to the common database with shared descriptions of the activities they use that are successful. The team specifies milestones to measure its progress, and promotes public celebrations of success in specific classrooms.

Because change is a process rather than a single event, changes may be jeopardized by changes in personnel. The discrepancy in knowledge or commitment between long-term team members and persons who are new to the organization can become a barrier in the process of change. Mentoring programs are essential both for school leaders and for other personnel in order to prevent newcomers from ignoring the shared mission and allowing the culture to revert to old patterns. Strategies for mentoring successors include regular discussions of problems and issues, sharing the secrets for unwritten social skills and "rules of the game," provision of essential training opportunities, and delegating. These strategies enable new leaders to replace those currently in power without disruption of the organization's mission. Successful schools mentor leaders, new teachers, students, and their parents.

Extensive studies have been conducted of change in educational organizations (Fullan, 1997; Hall, George, & Rutherford, 1977; Hall, Loucks, & Newlove, 1976). Hall and his colleagues believe change is a process rather than a single event, and that change takes place slowly, at the personal rather than the system level. They have designed two frameworks for analyzing change. The first is based on the individual's stages of concern for the change (Hall et al., 1977). These levels range from awareness to refocus, and they indicate the individual's readiness for acceptance of change. Individual teachers faced with change progress through the levels of basic awareness to concern about how the innovation will affect them, how they are going to manage the change, and then concern for the effect of the innovation on the entire class.

Ultimately, people incorporating change progress to a concern for collaboration with others and then to refocusing—thinking about how the innovation might be used to modify the whole system. This conceptual framework also includes a set of strategies through which the change agent or developer can affect individuals who are at different levels of concern. According to this theory, the effectiveness of interventions will be determined by the change agent's understanding of the stage of the "client's" concern about the change.

Hall et al. (1976) have also looked at the effect of change as measured by the levels of use by individuals within the system. Studying several innovations over a 15-year period, they have determined that 40% of the teachers remain at the routine level of innovation, even 3 or 4 years after the innovation has been implemented. Hall, Rutherford, Hord, and Huling (1984) also found that the principal's style determines whether an innovation remains. They classified school principals as responders (those who do what central office asks), managers (those who take an innovation and adapt it to their own school), or initiators (those who start with analysis of their own district and teachers, then design their response to change around the analysis of what needs to occur within their context). These researchers concluded that changes are of a higher quality and quantity in schools where the leader is classified as an initiator.

The New Paradigm.   The kinds of changes that have occurred recently in schools can be viewed through the perspective of a "paradigm shift." The term *paradigm shift* has been widely discussed during the past decade. The new paradigm applies to the way leadership is viewed, the way teaching and learning are conceptualized, and the way schools are organized.

Keller (1998) summarizes 20 years of research on school leaders, showing that the descriptions of the effective leader have changed from "strong leader" to "facilitator." This emphasis is on power sharing, with a team approach to problem solving. McAdoo (1998) adds that the team approach faces many barriers, even with external financial support and extensive time investment. Contentions from professional organizations on the roles of teachers, prohibiting too much involvement in "administration," may result in barriers to networking. Teams may meet for extensive periods of time to develop documents that are not used. McAdoo concludes that new concepts of leadership are needed, with new definitions of the roles of participants.

For the purpose of the interactive team, the paradigm shift is also examined within the learning environment—the classroom itself. Lasley (1998) has shown that the popularized teachers in recent movies have demonstrated this shift in their thinking. It is a shift in the understanding of how students learn, a shift from an instructional paradigm to a learning paradigm. Lasley explains that this is a shift from an understanding of "this is what I taught" to "this is what the students learned (or did not learn)," almost as if the teacher could get inside of the students' minds. Lasley cautions that there is risk in use of the learning paradigm, since the bureaucracy demands compliance with the instructional paradigm, and schools in which the learning paradigm is practiced are "messy" places—not quiet and orderly with desks in straight rows and red marks on test papers. Teachers using the learning paradigm need time for planning, both alone and together; they also need creative ability to reach outside of legislative mandates and to move beyond the use of canned commercial programs to creation of experiences that engage students in depth.

The new paradigm is also a change from an individualized to a collaborative learning community, an environment in which individuals assist one another to make learning happen for all participants. Du Four (1998) has provided guidance for school leaders on how to create this type of learning community. The leader is encouraged to lead "from the center," by helping staff create a shared mission, engage in collective inquiry with an experimental mindset, and develop a results orientation that emphasizes continuous improvement. Leading for change presents a number of conflicts for the change agents; many may find it easier to continue their traditional practices. Nanus (1992) points out that the only way to keep people from reverting to the old ways is to persuade individuals that this change is better for themselves and for the organization.

Newman and Wehlage (1995) have summarized 5 years of research on school change that results in improved student learning, emphasizing the importance of this new paradigm, the professional learning community, which provides teachers with opportunities to collaborate for a common purpose. They indicate that the factors explaining successful reform included the shared vision of student learning, changes in teaching practices that support this vision, the school's organizational structure, and support from external sources. A related summary by McLaughlin and Schwartz (1998) indicates that failing schools have no vision, goals, or positive leadership; success is found in those schools where rules-driven models have been replaced by missions to improve performance through improvement in teaching and learning for all students. Professional development was found to be a major factor in improvement, using outside consultants and "coaches" based in the school who team teach and assist one another.

Wang (1998) points out that failing schools can become successful when their staff is able to collaborate and that professional development leading to high expectations for students, adaptive teaching strategies for individual students, and links to the community are factors in success. The approach is developed around a comprehensive, coordinated team. Glasser (1997) also has described a paradigm shift in the successful school, away from the concept of a charismatic or powerful leader to that of a community of learners with a common mission that emphasizes genuine caring for all students. The new paradigm, then, is comprehensive—it shifts from teaching to learning, from individuals to teams, and from a charismatic powerful leader to a community of learners.

Implementation Strategies.   Tucker (1984) has analyzed change in higher education and suggested guidelines for selecting strategies to implement change. These guidelines are adapted here to focus on change in special programs provided by interactive teams. Guidelines include selecting the focus for change, determining who to involve, and deciding how to intervene.

The first guideline for the developer is to determine the *focus for change.* Exactly what needs to be modified or developed? Tucker (1984) lists six factors to consider in selecting the change focus:

1. Change will occur more easily when it is *timely* and appropriate.
2. The developer should determine whether the innovation has a *reasonable chance* of success.
3. The developer should select the *least drastic* solution as the answer to the problem.
4. Plans for change are more effective when they are designed with built-in *responses to the personal needs* of those affected by the change.
5. In addition to communicating with those affected by the change, the developer must also remember to *communicate with those within the system who must approve the change.*
6. The developer should remain *sensitive to the values* of those for whom the change is implemented.

Bennis (1989) has added suggestions for some ways to avoid disastrous conflicts and counterproductive efforts to bring about needed changes. For the purpose of the interactive school team, we have selected only a few of these, then modified and adapted them for the team's consideration, as follows:

◆ Discuss the proposed change honestly, rather than overselling its potential benefits.

◆ Avoid involving those with fanatical positions on a team that plans change strategy.

◆ Focus on action, rather than depending on rhetoric.

◆ Be cautious about proposals that would "turn off" the key people in the organization.

Two examples of initial strategies to facilitate change—one successful and one not successful—are given as follows:

Example 1

Eager to minimize the problem of student absences from class and armed with funds from a small grant, the school improvement team decided to take a proactive stance, changing from former punitive responses to truancy to a system including positive reinforcement for students with perfect attendance. The team decided to notify parents when students had perfect attendance, then to enter the names of students with perfect attendance in a drawing through which some would win gift certificates. The proposed change made the headlines of the local paper, with a negative report that students were being paid for attendance and a promise from the school board to punish those teachers who had suggested this illegal use of public money.

Example 2

A new special education teacher, whose resource room served students with multiple and severe disabilities, was eager to promote the inclusion of her students into schoolwide activities. She volunteered to sponsor the student council and the cheerleading club, as well as attending numerous school social and athletic activities. As she became known to the faculty and students as a whole-school supporter and participant, she provided information about the nature of various special abilities and disabilities. She also provided the school administrator with positive information about inclusion to share with the local paper. Gradually, with administrative and parental permission, she encouraged several student leaders to sign up for a "buddy" in her classroom. The student leaders visited her classroom and, by the end of the year, had begun to accompany their new buddies to schoolwide activities.

These examples include some of the highlights for selecting the change focus.

Next, it is useful to *determine who to involve* in the design of the change strategy. These individuals may be labeled *change agents*. Every group has influential people who must be involved if change is to occur. Even if the developer does not conduct a systematic study of the "real power" people, the developer can identify some people who need to be involved as change agents in any change strategy (Tucker, 1984). Certainly the developer must include the individuals with administrative titles who have responsibility for the program to be changed. Those who make decisions about the spending of funds will need to be consulted when money is involved. Elected or appointed representatives of particular constituencies must also be included. Individuals in the system with knowledge about the particular topic need to be involved (e.g., the school nurse when the education of children with AIDS is the issue; the building director when the change involves designing classrooms that are free of architectural barriers). It is important to remember that anyone who will be affected by the change should be involved in some way in its design.

In trying to select specific individuals to involve as change agents in a planning group, the developer should consider the characteristics of the people themselves. How will they react to the proposal? Will they be able to function with others in the group? The group should include people who may oppose the change so a sense of ownership can be developed among diverse constituencies. This concept of extending ownership was implemented quite effectively by Pelfry (1988), who selected a planning committee for a change that involved the extensive acquisition of computers. He included on this committee a board member who had previously opposed all changes that required substantial expenditures, thus converting a potential opponent into a strong ally.

After deciding on a focus and the people who will be involved, the developer decides *how to intervene* to facilitate the change. Tucker (1984) has suggested seven generic *change strategies*:

1. Call attention to a contradiction.
2. Use research.
3. Lower the situational conflict (involve persons in social interactions).
4. Adopt two or more options.
5. Identify the alternative solutions, citing the probable consequences.
6. Apply a historical approach.
7. Appeal to values and traditions.

Those who are involved in or affected by the proposed change need to have a sense of ownership of the new plan. Their sense of ownership is established by joint participation in planning for, developing, implementing, and evaluating the plan.

Application of Change Strategy

In designing a change strategy, the developer first considers the generic intervention plans and determines the individuals who need to be involved as change agents. Then the developer plans the sequence of steps to be taken in facilitating the change. The following guidelines for designing these steps have been synthesized from the work of J. Tucker (1972), A. Tucker (1984), Grosenick and Reynolds (1978), and Losen and Losen (1985).

1. *Identify real and potential supporters.* These may be friends or colleagues who share the belief in a need for change. Or they might be people who, with additional information, could become supporters. Losen and Losen (1985) suggest that special educators may be able to engage the school board attorney as an ally by providing this individual with the latest information on school law as it relates to students with disabilities. The attorney, who is obligated to remain current in a range of topics related to school law, may appreciate this highly specialized information. The special educator, who can obtain this information from current journals and professional societies, is able to develop a dimension of expert power by providing this technical knowledge.

2. *Test the waters.* The developer might visit someone else's classroom or office and say, "I have an idea that I think might improve the program. I don't even know whether it's feasible, but this is what it is. . . . What do you think about it? What are the chances we might be able to do that? Who else might be interested in this idea? Who would be against it? What problems might we face if we really wanted to do it?" In this manner, the developer talks informally with as many people as possible, modifying the plan as others make important suggestions. The individual who skips this step and presents the entire, new idea to the group will frequently find that the idea is rejected (Tucker, 1984). Individual contacts enable the developer to count the votes and incorporate the ideas of many persons who subsequently develop ownership in the plan.

3. *Translate the change into language that others can understand.* For advocates, the language of change is based on values, such as "equal opportunity" and "student rights." For policy makers, the language of change is directly related to dollars and cents. Successful change agents may convince even a conservative administration that special education makes sense in terms of cost effectiveness, because it is cheaper to provide preventive programs to children in school than to institutionalize them for a lifetime, during which they would drain, rather than contribute to, the tax base.

4. *Identify additional sources of support that may be used to supplement the regular budget.* Both governmental agencies and charitable foundations often fund special projects through grants. Service clubs, which exist in every community, are always looking for worthy projects. Lions Clubs give glasses to needy children; Shriners help build hospitals. Locate some other sources of funding that may help to get the project "off the ground."

5. *Ask for technical assistance.* If the proposal for change is technical or complex, ask for help from experts. On a public health issue, help may be available from the public health department or the public information office of the local hospital. When proposing a change that involves computer use, involve business

and industry personnel who are prominent in computer technology. Be sure that these people and their organizations are recognized for their contributions—through media exposure and letters of appreciation to their superiors—so they will share ownership of the new idea. Failing to ask for help may be a serious error, because those who could be your strongest allies may become opponents if they think they are being bypassed or that the change agent is setting up a program that is competitive with theirs.

6. *Share information on success.* When students in a new reading program improve their achievement scores or work-study students receive excellent reports from their employers, let the media know. Pictures of successful students and human interest stories can enhance the public relations of the organization. Again, the "power people" (school principal or program director) should share in the good press so they can develop an even stronger sense of commitment to continue the innovative program.

Team members who attempt to bring about change will encounter false starts, resistance, and the need to go "back to the drawing board" many times before real progress can be made. The task requires patience and perseverance, as well as an understanding of the theories and strategies for facilitating change. The individual who follows these guidelines, however, may be able to minimize the discouragement and negative personal consequences of repeated failure.

Empowering Others

The discussion of empowerment in this chapter is focused on providing team members with both *legitimate power* through decision sharing and *expert power* through information sharing. Both types of empowerment are based on professional development, and their purpose is to enable team members to accomplish changes that benefit special needs students.

Empowerment as Power Sharing.   Empowerment is illustrated in the way the team leader—a person with power—shares this power with others who can help to implement the necessary change (Du Four, 1998; McLaughlin & Schwartz, 1998; Newman & Wehlage, 1995). Powers and Powers (1983) have shown how *participatory management* can be used successfully by leaders who are perceived as powerful. Participatory management includes the use of consultation (in a process that emphasizes information exchange), coalition building, task orientation, conflict resolution, and flexibility. Many of these techniques have been presented earlier in the discussions on consultation and communication skills. Powers and Powers show also that, although the participatory structure operates more slowly, it is no less decisive, and that the leader who is effective within this framework sets clear goals that have a greater chance for successful implementation because they are based on group consensus. Those who wish to establish their leadership on behalf of educational teams will be interested in developing the shared power more descriptive of participatory rather than of autocratic management.

Leaders in business and industry have long been concerned with this type of empowerment. The development of individual skills and group cohesiveness among members of their organization's staff, which culminates in the building of an organizational team, has been summarized by Ends and Page (1984) and by Scholtes (1988). It is worthwhile to note that these procedures have much in common with those suggested as the best practices for professional development in educational organizations.

In the business and industry model for team building, summarized by Ends and Page (1984), the organization's manager is the team builder who initially has power. The word *power* is defined as "the ability to influence the behavior of others" (p. 53). These authors describe the process of team building as a sequence in which the leader learns to influence the behavior of individuals, then develops small- and large-group leadership skills, and finally demonstrates the ability to allow members of the group to influence group decisions in an interactive manner. Their point is clear and consistent with the entire body of literature on change: People do not become involved in activities over which they have no influence. They point out that this interaction is important both in allowing team members to have influence in the group, and in seeing that the group leader has used their ideas to influence those above this group in the organization's power structure. Once the team is functioning as a unit, there is a sense of pride among group members in their belonging to a winning team. In effective schools, this same sharing of common goals and pride in teamwork is present (Audette & Algozzine, 1992; Du Four, 1998; Levine, 1985; Newman & Wehlage, 1995).

Empowerment also takes on a dimension of personal development within the context of group growth. Covey (1990) emphasizes the importance of each individual's attention to his or her own personal energy needs, and suggests replenishment, inspiration, and stress reduction as forms of personal empowerment. Some of this inspiration and stress reduction that facilitate personal empowerment can result from the provision of a supportive work environment and of respect and recognition for each member's contributions to the team effort (Jackman, 1991). Jackman, who has assisted in the analysis of successful teams in business and industry, emphasizes the importance of shared respect and support among members of the winning team. Jackman indicates that the "key player" is one who values consensus based on shared goals and that a "star team" is one in which all members are nurturing and enthusiastic about each other's contributions to the group effort. The team is more effective, then, when each member is empowered, and when the team itself has developed as a mature, supportive unit.

Empowerment as Knowledge Sharing.   Empowerment also involves the development of expert power or knowledge among members of the staff. In the interactive team, knowledge acquisition begins with information sharing among team members. Individuals engage in a type of professional development based on the sharing of the specialized knowledge about their roles with other members of the team (Lyon & Lyon, 1980). Such information sharing has been illustrated in the Chapter 4 application showing an informational interview between a special educator and a speech-language therapist.

Ends and Page (1984) emphasized that the process of organizational team building begins with the development of skills in individual team members. They indicated that the process must be nonthreatening and that the change needs to be consistent with the individual's self-image. If these conditions are met, the team member goes through a four-stage process of change in learning the new behavior: recognizing the need to change, knowing what to change, desiring to learn, and practicing until the new behavior is acquired. These authors indicated clearly that the strongest teams are those in which individual members possess knowledge and skill.

In the educational literature, the acquisition of knowledge and skill that results in empowerment is referred to as *professional development*. The educational organizations that are most effective in implementing needed changes are those in which a large number of individuals have been involved and have developed a sense of ownership for the new program (Glatthorn & Newberg, 1984; Lieberman, 1988; Sickler, 1988; Wang, 1998). These organizations are characterized by a sense of shared understanding about the changes that are necessary (Du Four, 1998; Newman & Wehlage, 1995). Finally, Wang, Haertel, and Walberg (1997) and Stedman (1987), summarizing the school effectiveness research, have shown that the best schools for students with special needs are those in which the entire staff and the community share a sense of ownership for and a belief in the ability of low-functioning students. This sense of shared purpose originates in the development of knowledge and skills through professional development.

An example of professional development for a new teacher is found in the following application:

◊ ◊

Application

Several parents in the district approached the director of special education to express their concern about a first-year teacher who was having difficulty in the classroom. One of the parents complained that her son, who had been suspended for hitting and kicking his teacher, had never done things like that before. The parent indicated that the new teacher seemed unable to control the classroom and that, when there was a problem, she went straight to the principal. Others stated that the children had responded much more positively to last year's teacher, and wondered what could be done. The director talked with the teacher and learned that this child was running out of the room and that she had tried to restrain him, but felt that she was unable to manage his behavior. After suggesting to the teacher that she attend the forthcoming professional development programs on behavior management, and also asking the district's behavior specialist to make follow-up observations and provide assistance in the classroom, the director was pleased to hear that both the teacher and children had been helped by this assistance.

◇ ◇

SUMMARY OF BEST PRACTICES

The process of professional development in educational organizations was originally summarized by the National Inservice Network (NIN), a governmental agency active in the 1970s (Hutson, 1979). More current summaries of effective practices and their relationship to school improvement have been completed by Darling-Hammond (1998), Wang et al. (1997), Showers and Joyce (1996), Showers, Joyce, and Bennett (1987), Joyce, Showers, and Rolheiser-Bennett (1987), and by Schmoker and Wilson (1993).

Current research on professional development supports the newer models of networks, teacher academies, and professional development schools. Teaching teams, study groups, and action research projects within schools were found to be particularly effective, especially when they were related to teachers' work with students and to subject matter, when they focused on problem solving, were grounded in research, and extended over time through mechanisms such as discussion and peer coaching (Darling-Hammond, 1998). Wang et al. (1997) have identified 12 research-based comprehensive change models that have resulted in growth in student achievement, all of which would seem appropriate for professional development programs. The practices identified that result in student growth include the following: high student expectations, frequent student–teacher and student–student interactions, student-directed learning, direct instruction, small-group instruction, cooperative learning, positive classroom climate, adaptive instructional strategies, and teacher, paraprofessional, or peer tutoring. From among the research-based programs, the Community for Learning, formerly known as ALEM (Wang et al., 1997) is the only one that features instruction for the inclusive school.

Other research on professional development highlights the importance of teacher input into decisions about professional development, including visits to other sites with successful programs, and subsequent development of plans for application of these practices at their own sites (Renji, 1996). Renji further points out that many districts have increased the available time for professional development through extended school years, team teaching, and block scheduling which free up time for teacher teams to plan and learn together. Previously promoted best practices that have been supported by newer research include provision of released time or building in time during the school day, reimbursement for expenses, and the collaborative development of goals and strategies by teams of teachers and administrators; common current topics for professional development include educational technology, student assessment, and cooperative learning (Teacher Education Reports, 1998). Teacher-to-teacher networking (Pennell & Firestone, 1998) and new teacher induction programs were found to be particularly helpful (Du Four, 1998), while the creation of a community of learners has proven especially challenging at the high school level (Wineburg & Grosman, 1998).

The explosion of technology leads both to an intensified need for staff development in the use of technology and an expanded opportunity for its use in delivery of new information. Rapid advances in technology are creating a dynamic environment for tomorrow's students. McGroddy (1997) paints part of this picture in his description of wireless identification chips placed inside of shoes that enable purchase prices to be read at the door of a store for payment; distance capabilities that enable workers to live in Japan while working in Philadelphia; lab imaging systems that revolutionize health care; computers that enable sports teams to "mine" data on opponents in preparation for the next play. McGroddy explains that learning will be enhanced by technology simulations which enable learners to see things that—in actuality—are too small, experience things that are too far away, and experiment with concepts that are too dangerous. In addition, he cites current examples of student teams from different schools, creating on-line tutorials for one another, changing the role of teacher from one of knowledge dispenser to facilitator of learning. The role of technology in staff development cannot be overemphasized.

Teachers have also begun to use technology for connections that enhance their professional development opportunities. Teacher resources can be located as a category in a web search, with additional sites being added on a daily basis. Teacher resources include teaching tips, lesson plans, information about the availability of grants, workshops, and courses, as well as library reference tools and opportunities to talk with other educators about common problems. Teachers can also locate television resources, science projects, museum displays, summaries of learning theories and their potential applications in the classroom on web sites. Some sites provide daily updates, while others enable teachers to put their own information on a home page and connecting to parents or students at home.

Statewide networks, such as "Learn North Carolina" (www.learnnc.org, Learners' and Educators' Assistance & Resources Network), are beginning to emerge. The web site, sponsored by the University of North Carolina, is open to all teachers within the state. It includes information on topics such as professional development opportunities which teachers can access through their local schools, and teaching resources, such as model lesson plans contributed by teachers. This format holds great promise.

The content presented in a professional development program is focused directly on the behavior of teachers and indirectly on the behavior of students. The best kind of professional development will affect student behavior because it results in the enhancement of teacher competency. Wang et al. (1997) and Joyce et al. (1987) have shown evidence that professional development programs for several models of teaching result in higher student achievement. The developer should know that these models have proved their effectiveness with students and would, therefore, be appropriate for use in whole-school professional development programs. The decision about content for professional development should also take into consideration the need of participants to obtain a basic level of knowledge about a program before they are able to "buy into" it (Showers et al., 1987).

There are three other special considerations for professional developers who wish to implement best practices. First, activities that are effective with one group may not be appropriate for others. That is, it may be important to design programs that are responsive to differences in the language and culture of various groups, such as providing evening sessions with supper and child care (Boone, 1990) or assisting participants in environments closer to their homes (Padilla, 1989), rather than requiring them to attend meetings at school. Second, developers should conceptualize the total plan for professional development, rather than view it as a single event in which all participants assemble to be lectured for an hour and then go back to their classrooms where nothing will change. The positive effects of continued support after the initial presentation of the idea have been impressive (Glatthorn, 1987; Showers et al., 1987) and the applications of a new team model for "coaching" have been especially strong (Showers & Joyce, 1996). These will be discussed in greater detail later in the chapter. Finally, developers should be aware that certain individual traits or characteristics may influence the effectiveness of professional development programs. These include the probability of more positive responses by those who exhibit flexibility in thinking, and the effect of what the teacher believes about teaching and the way he or she teaches (Showers et al., 1987). Developers who wish to bring about change through empowerment of team members will be aware of these and other findings identified earlier as "best practices."

STRATEGIES FOR PROFESSIONAL DEVELOPMENT

Three of the most widely used types of professional development for teams are (1) knowledge sharing, (2) skill development through coaching/reflection, and (3) team development. One way to empower team members is to provide them with new knowledge or skills in formal, scheduled learning activities. This is usually done through traditional professional development activities in which team members share knowledge that enhances their colleagues' understanding. Skill development can be accomplished through a combination of peer coaching and individual reflection during which team members observe each other and incorporate new learning into their existing structure of knowledge and skills. Finally, professional development can become an ongoing activity through which the team itself matures as a unit capable of functioning effectively. In the following discussion, strategies for professional development through formal knowledge sharing and coaching with reflection will be presented along with a summary of the extended teams operating in professional development schools. The chapter's application will provide an activity for identifying the team's maturity level and need for professional development as a unit.

Sharing Knowledge

Two aspects of knowledge sharing will be discussed: (1) the importance of determining the knowledge or content to be shared through a needs assessment, and (2) the guidelines for presentation. This discussion is directed at the formal sharing of knowledge through professional development activities. Informal knowledge sharing, which occurs more frequently, has been described in the informational interview, Chapter 4, and in the Chapter 5 description of communication skills.

Needs Assessment.   NIN researchers summarizing best practices suggest that content should be based on a needs assessment. That is, the content is selected on the basis of a survey of the staff members who will receive the new information. In the survey, they have been asked what they need to know, have stated their major problems, and have suggested needs for further training. Through this needs assessment, those who share their knowledge determine the information that should be presented. An example of a needs assessment instrument, developed by members of a team of special educators who serve children with mild learning disabilities, is presented as Figure 7.2. This needs assessment was used to plan the content for a professional development program in which these team members participated. A modified version of the instrument was used as a post-test to determine the effect of the knowledge sharing program on its participants.

Guidelines for Presentation.   The effective presenter of the professional development program establishes expert power by demonstrating knowledge and speaking with confidence. This person uses visual aids to help focus information on the topic, establishes eye contact with other members of the group, and sits or stands in a position that is higher than others while presenting information. When the presenter is a newcomer or is younger than others in the group, it is particularly important for him or her to acquire the knowledge necessary for establishing the impression of expert power and to use effective presentation skills to enhance this image. A person who is highly respected by the group might help establish the newcomer's credibility by indicating that this person is an expert in the field and by showing some relationship between the experience of the presenter and that of the participants.

Information presenters should communicate clearly through correct use of media and an understanding of the most effective ways of presenting information. Effective use of media involves both its selection and its use. The first tendency of planners may be to overuse media, thinking that more is always better, as was shown tongue-in-cheek in the comic strip, *Beetle Bailey*. In the strip, General Half-track was once shown conducting an inservice for his troops. He began by giving a progress report: "Enlistments are down," said the general as he pushed a button and a big foot clamped down on the floor, "while discharges are up." The general shot off a rocket. "The picture looks cloudy," he said as smoke poured out of the

For each item, please circle the number that shows the degree to which you feel you can demonstrate the skill (**1 = low, 5 = high ability** to perform).

1. Establish positive motivational strategies that can be used with students with varying learning styles and ages.

    1   2   3   4   5

2. Analyze materials according to appropriateness for students.

    1   2   3   4   5

3. Develop lesson plans that assist my students in learning the skills I want to teach.

    1   2   3   4   5

4. Develop a schedule that allows me to work effectively with the variety of students in my classroom.

    1   2   3   4   5

5. Respond appropriately to the learning needs of students from different cultures.

    1   2   3   4   5

6. Resolve behavioral difficulties between students with emotional disabilities and other exceptionalities.

    1   2   3   4   5

7. Develop a plan of intervention for deviant behaviors.

    1   2   3   4   5

8. Identify specific teaching materials to meet needs of a given exceptionality.

    1   2   3   4   5

9. Create positive public relations within the community regarding my classroom.

    1   2   3   4   5

10. What is your major problem in your classroom at this time? Describe it briefly.

11. What change would you most like to make in your classroom, if you had the authority to make this change? Describe what you would change.

Figure 7.2
Pretest/assessment of skills for teachers.

chart. "Original estimates have been shot full of holes." You can picture his demonstration of a shower of bullets. "There is nothing to do but pick up the pieces and start over," he said as little bits of paper were tossed into the room by a small catapult. The result was that people left the meeting whispering, "I could do without some of the visual aids." The point, of course, is for the presenter to consider whether visual aids will enhance or distract the audience from the message.

Visual aids are important because they help the presenter to focus the attention of the audience, enhancing the presenter's image as one with expert power. Transparencies, charts, and slides are the most frequently used types of visual aids. To be effective, the visual aid should focus on key words, while the presenter elaborates on each point. If the presenter wishes to provide the audience with details on the information being presented, handouts would be more effective than a transparency or chart. An attempt to provide these factual details without handouts would result in an overload of verbal information, thus increasing the chances for misunderstanding. The type of media selection, then, should fit the purpose of sharing knowledge as outlined in the presenter's objectives.

Knowledge sharing is also enhanced when the presenter uses *summative*, rather than redundant or interfering, *media combinations* (Deterline, 1968). A summative combination combines auditory and visual input in a complementary way. Suppose the presenter is teaching an audience about hearing impairments and is describing "how we hear." The speaker using summative media combinations would use a visual presentation that enhances, summarizes, and clarifies the auditory description of the concept. Thus, the speaker might present a model of the route that sound waves travel while saying, "We hear when sound waves are transmitted through the ear to the brain." The summative media combination is illustrated in Figure 7.3.

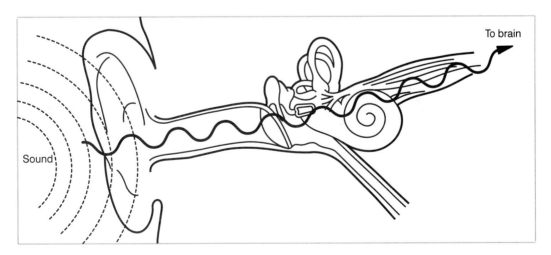

Figure 7.3
Summative media combination: how we hear.

In a *redundant* media combination the leader would say, "We hear when sound waves are transmitted through the ear to the brain," while showing a transparency with just those words. The redundant use of media is boring, because the audio and visual components repeat rather than enhance each other. Such redundancy may even encourage the audience to tune out either the auditory or the visual component of the message.

The *interfering media combination* presents a visual that goes beyond the image of the auditory and distracts the audience from the major message. Thus, presenting the auditory description of how we hear with a visual showing a child with a hearing aid (Figure 7.4) is an interfering use of media combinations. Rather than helping the audience to visualize the route or even repeating the verbal message, this visual causes the audience to focus on an external aid to hearing and the boy's raised hand, thus making processing the verbal message more difficult.

The use of summative media combinations that clarify information being presented is one way to enhance the professional development program. Effective presenters also employ other ways to enhance knowledge sharing in professional development programs. The following presentation guidelines have been modified from the work of LeRoux (1984)[1]:

1. Establish credibility through demonstration of knowledge.
2. Use cue cards for notes, rather than read from a script.
3. Face the audience directly, keeping your weight distributed equally on both feet and standing without hands in pockets.
4. Use gestures to enhance the presentation.
5. To use eye contact effectively, focus for about three seconds on each person.
6. Practice the art of asking questions.
7. Answer questions appropriately.
8. Build rapport with the audience by giving equal recognition to all participants.

LeRoux (1984) elaborates on the correct ways to ask and answer questions, because these are among the most difficult parts of any presentation. He suggests that the presenter begin by giving the audience permission to interrupt with questions and by mentioning that there will be a question-and-answer time at the end of the presentation. When finished, the presenter should say, "Now it's time for questions." The speaker can "warm up" the audience by saying, "First I want to ask you a question." The presenter should ask a simple question that participants can answer by raising hands. The presenter might also prime the audience for questions by saying, "The question most frequently asked is. . . . Now, what are your questions?"

---

[1] From *Selling to a Group* by P. LeRoux, 1984. New York: Harper & Row. Adapted by permission of Harper & Row Publishers, Inc.

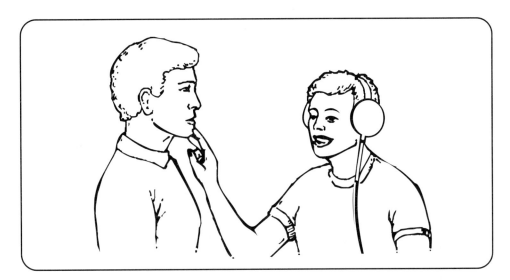

Figure 7.4
Interfering media combination: how we hear.

Finally, the correct way to field a question is to use this three-step process:

1. Indicate whose question you are answering: Point to the person.
2. Give eye contact to the person asking the question.
3. When the person has finished, repeat the question so the entire group can hear it.

LeRoux (1984) also suggests that the presenter try to neutralize negative questions so they do not build up resistance from the audience. For instance, after a presentation on inclusion, a classroom teacher in the audience might ask, "How am I going to have time to work with students with disabilities in my classroom when I have 35 other children?" The presenter could rephrase the question in a neutral way, such as "You're wondering whether you can deal with the increasing demands on your time in the classroom. Let me answer that by giving you some examples of how other teachers who are concerned about all of their students have dealt with this issue. . . . " The presenter is then in a position to give some useful suggestions, rather than being forced into a defensive posture. The answer should be brief, and the presenter should move on quickly to the next question.

Application of Knowledge Sharing.   Suppose the presenter has identified the inability to work effectively with students who have hearing impairments as a major need among members of the staff. She designs a 1-hour presentation aimed at attitude change and knowledge sharing for the whole staff. After a brief introduction and overview that establish her credibility and relate the presentation to the needs identified by the group, she presents:

1. An opening simulation, during which she plays a record of conversations as heard by people with different types of hearing impairments.

2. A group discussion of the feelings and insights experienced by participants as they listened to the record, followed by the development of a group-generated list of the types of difficulties that might be experienced by students with hearing impairments in the classroom.

3. A brief overview of information on hearing impairment which includes the use of summative transparencies such as those shown in Figure 7.3 to illustrate how we hear and to present information about the three major types of hearing impairments.

4. An illustration of one method teachers can use to help students with hearing impairments in the classroom. This part of the presentation incorporates transparencies made from Figure 7.3 and Figure 7.4 which illustrate the value of using summative visual aids to clarify auditory information presented.

5. A small-group activity, during which participants work together to develop a set of lesson materials for use with students with hearing impairments in their classes (these materials would be equally appropriate for use with all of their students). Participants work with others at their grade level to design a set of summative visual aids with an accompanying auditory script for a lesson they might teach in math, science, or social studies. The presenter circulates to give assistance while the participants work and then collects the materials at the end of the session.

6. The presenter hands out a list of other suggestions that teachers might use to increase their effectiveness with students who have hearing impairments. She indicates that the lesson materials developed by each group will be typed and that the visual aids will be redrawn as transparencies by students in the school's art class; these materials will then be distributed to all members of the group for use in their classes.

7. The presenter obtains the participants' opinions about the effectiveness of the professional development program, including (a) how much they enjoyed the presentation, (b) the degree to which they learned how to work more effectively with students with hearing impairments, and (c) whether they planned to use any of the knowledge they had acquired during the session.

This example of a professional development program aimed at knowledge sharing has shown how the presenter can transmit relevant information to a diverse group of individuals. It has also shown how to use professional development activities not only to increase the knowledge of participants, but also to establish a sense of teaming among members of the staff. The provision of follow-up materials, designed by participants, will further enhance the opportunities for continued interaction and cooperation among those who collaborated in their design.

Developing Skills

Team members can empower each other by engaging in activities that enhance their skills. The most effective means are based on knowledge about adults as learners. These include skill development through peer observation and coaching, and opportunities for the learner to reflect on what is learned and to incorporate new learning into one's own existing knowledge structure.

Developing Skills Through Coaching.   Team members can empower each other by developing skills through mutual assistance known as *coaching*. In earlier models of coaching, team members engaged in frequent, ongoing observations of each other's performance, followed by conferences that focused on constructive feedback (O'Shea, 1987). Coaching provides team members with an increased amount and quality of supervised practice, as well as assistance in the transfer of newly developed skills (Ackland, 1991; Joyce & Showers, 1988; Neubert, 1988). Coaching has been used effectively at both the preservice and inservice levels. In one interesting program, special education seniors were coached by teams of mentors, who included special educators, general educators, and university faculty members (Duarte, 1992–93). In preservice education, coaching has been shown to improve the learner's ability to transfer new learning (Peterson & Hudson, 1989; Wynn, 1987, 1988).

Coaching also increases desirable teaching behaviors and decreases undesirable ones (Peterson & Hudson, 1989). Coached teachers also seem to retain information longer and to have a greater effect on the learning improvement of pupils in their classrooms (Showers, 1984). Most significant for team members, it has been found that coaching improves collegiality because it reduces teachers' isolation and provides them with peer support (Wynn, 1987, 1988).

Coaching seems to be most effective when implemented by teacher groups who observe and assist each other as peers. Rogers (1987) has described one of these programs in detail, showing how teachers within the school worked together in teams of two or three to observe and videotape each other's teaching. Members of these teams asked their partners to help them identify a goal for improvement and then engage in observation of teaching performance. This nonjudgmental, supportive observation provided constructive feedback and thus facilitated the goal of self-improvement. Leggett and Hoyle (1987) have developed a program in which preservice students learn to work together as teams, using observation and feedback in a spirit of collegiality for instructional improvement.

Showers and Joyce (1996), summarizing the literature on professional development that leads to student growth, have pointed out that simple exposure to new knowledge results in very low rates of teacher implementation, as low as 10%.

The addition of classroom follow-up, particularly through peer coaching, increases implementation of new practices significantly, in addition to motivating teachers to collaborate with one another. These authors now promote staff development that involves the entire staff of a school site, encouraging developers to work intensively with the staff to plan and organize the procedures. Showers and Joyce caution that peer coaching should not be used as an evaluation procedure. They caution further that when observers deliver verbal feedback, they tend to act as evaluators. Therefore, they have developed new role reversal procedures in which the observer is the member of the team being coached, while the one observed is the coach. Stating that learning occurs during collaborative planning, materials development, and reflection, Showers and Joyce have designed their new staff development programs to model these procedures. The recommendation for building in time for collaboration is high on their agenda. They also recommend that peer coaching teams be formed on the first day of training during which time developers provide opportunities for these teams to work through a sequence for planning long-term activities, monitoring their implementation, and measuring their impact on students.

Sahakian and Stockton (1996) provide an example of the collaborative model of peer observation. These authors argue that the older expectation of the clinical model, that an observer will see all steps followed during a single lesson, is unrealistic. Their new observation model attempts to end the isolation of teachers by forming triads or teams that agree to observe one another regularly, biweekly for a 4-week period every semester. Both peers and administrators are involved in observations. Team meetings led by the administrator focus on questions that enable teachers to analyze the instructional strategies they have observed. The triads develop their own issues for discussion, engaging in thoughtful reflection that leads them to common understandings of curriculum issues, as well as enhancing collegiality.

Developing Skills Through Reflection.   During the process of coaching, the team member is confronted with new information in the form of peer feedback, new research, and data on the performance of students. To increase the effectiveness of existing practices and to make new decisions, the team member needs to be able to synthesize this new information, reflect on its meaning, and incorporate it into his or her current cognitive framework. Because interactive teaming, like teaching, is an involved task that requires problem solving within circumstances lacking certainty, effective team members need to become deliberate and reflective decision makers (Patricia & Lamb, 1990). A considerable body of knowledge exists that supports the value of critical reflection in teacher education (Ross & Krogh, 1988; Roth, 1989; Williams, 1996). During field-based experiences, the intern analyzes relevant research and theory while documenting the process and outcomes of teaching through a format such as a journal. This opportunity allows the intern to formulate possible solutions to classroom problems while linking theory with practice and establishing the relationship between action and reflection (Krutilla & Safford, 1990; Valli, 1989; Zeichner & Liston, 1987).

Professionals who recommend preparing students as active decision makers through the process of reflection on self and data may do so in response to studies which disclose that student teachers become less creative, more rigid, more authoritarian, and less responsive to the needs of pupils when they complete their field-based experiences than when they began (Thies-Sprinthall, 1984). Findings from the work of Johnson (1986) and Goodlad (1990) suggest that student teachers may learn less during the latter part of their field experiences, either believing they have already mastered all they need to know, or that the theory taught earlier has little relevance to classroom practice. Blase (1985) further suggests that over time teachers narrow and routinize their methods, materials, and content to conform with the expectations of the bureaucracy. All of this evidence suggests the need for development of decision-making and problem-solving skills through teachers' critical reflection on personal performance and research data.

It is suggested, then, that the team member can develop and retain new professional skills most effectively when encouraged to reflect on the observations made by a peer during coaching. The use of a database in problem solving has long been advocated in special education programs. It is consistent also with the basic principles of total quality management (Deming, 1986) and with the guidelines for development of effective teams (Scholtes, 1988). Professional development is facilitated both through coaching and by opportunities to develop decision-making skills through reflection on personal performance and student achievement data (Peterson & Hudson, 1989; Showers, 1984; Showers & Joyce, 1996).

Developing the Team

The final type of professional development to be discussed is the development of the team itself as a mature, supportive, effective functional unit. One of the strongest new initiatives in team building takes place through university teacher preparation programs in models known generically as professional development schools. Many groups have recommended closer connections between theory and practice, campus and field in preparation of teachers (Book, 1996; Buck, Morsink, Griffin, Hines, & Lenk, 1992; Darling-Hammond, 1997). Professional development schools with campus-field collaboration have been implemented nationwide providing preservice teachers with opportunities to develop skills in collaboration and simultaneous professional development for current educators. This is particularly important in challenging teaching environments such as inner city schools (Howey, 1997; Ilmer, Snyder, Erbaugh, & Kurz, 1997; Darling-Hammond, 1997). Partnerships between universities and schools in the preparation of new teachers are also recommended by Fullan (1997), since they enable the partners to combine the theoretical with the practical dimensions of research into best practices and provide the mechanisms for development of networks that can involve others. In some programs, current teachers combine professional development opportunities with the acquisition of advanced degrees (Boyer, 1997), while in others preparation represents a dramatic departure from tradition by replacing all on-campus education classes with intensive field-based experiences in schools (Wilmore, 1996).

The efforts at collaboration between university and school district personnel add a new dimension of complexity to team building. Universally, the barriers cited include differences in vocabulary and environmental "cultures" between campus and school sites, as well as the need for extensive personal time investment (Morsink, 1999). Initial data on the effectiveness of collaborative experiences for preservice elementary and special education teachers suggests that field-based problem-solving interactions can enhance students' understanding of both the necessity and the complexity of the teaming process, and that individuals with differing perspectives can learn from one another in joint efforts to assist children (O'Shea, Williams & Sattler, 1999). Among the most promising practices is the involvement of teacher educators as on-site teachers in public school classrooms as a way to enhance their understanding of instructional realities and incorporate them into their preservice programs (Brown, 1997; Williams, 1999; Winograd, 1998).

The team's development is the focus of this entire book, and its importance is highlighted in the basic principles of total quality management (Deming, 1986), particularly those of "constancy of purpose," responsiveness to the "customer," and continuous improvement. Although it is not our intention to review these guidelines at this point, we have selected a summative activity, through which the reader may consider data and reflect on information about the hypothetical team's need for professional development, and the leadership style most effective for teams at varying developmental or maturity levels.

◊ ◊

Application

This activity is based on the early work of Hersey and Blanchard (1974), related to the leadership styles needed for effective management of groups. As indicated in Chapter 6, these authors have described the leader's behavior as either task oriented or relationship oriented. They have further indicated that the maturity of the group determines the degrees of directiveness and personal relationship that are appropriate for leadership of the group. It is important to specify that *maturity*, as used here, refers to the group's maturity as a team, a functional unit (not to the age level or the personality variables that may be synonyms for maturity in other contexts). Classifying leadership into four quadrants, Hersey and Blanchard indicate that the immature group needs the highest level of task direction and the lowest level of personal relationship. Conversely, the most mature group requires neither task direction nor relationship development. The four categories are as follows:

1. Below-average maturity group—high task/low relationship.
2. Average maturity group—high task/high relationship.
3. Average maturity group—low task/high relationship.
4. Above-average maturity group—low task/low relationship.

In the application that follows (Figure 7.5), read each of the 10 situations describing the team's behavior, and make a decision about the team's maturity level as a func-

"You are the group leader. . ."	
SITUATION	ALTERNATIVE ACTIONS
1. Your team members are not responding lately to your friendly conversation and low-key directions. They haven't followed through on I.E.P. assignments.	A. Insist on uniform procedures and task accomplishment. B. Make yourself available for discussion but don't push. C. Talk with team members, then set goals. D. Do not intervene.
SITUATION	ALTERNATIVE ACTIONS
2. The effectiveness of your team is increasing. You have been making sure that all members were aware of their roles and performance expectations.	A. Be friendly, but continue to make sure that all members are aware of their roles and tasks. B. Take no definite action. C. Do what you can to make the members feel important and involved. D. Emphasize the importance of timeliness and tasks.
SITUATION	ALTERNATIVE ACTIONS
3. Members of your team are unable to solve a problem. You have previously left them alone. Group performance and interpersonal relations have been good.	A. Get involved with the group and work with the members in problem-solving. B. Let the group work it out. C. Intervene quickly to correct and redirect. D. Encourage group work on the problem and be available for discussion.
SITUATION	ALTERNATIVE ACTIONS
4. You are considering a major change in referral procedures. Your subordinates have a fine record of accomplishment. They respect the need for change.	A. Allow group involvement in developing the change, but don't push. B. Announce changes and then implement with close supervision. C. Let the group formulate its own direction. D. Incorporate group recommendations, but design change yourself.
SITUATION	ALTERNATIVE ACTIONS
5. The achievement of your group has dropped during the last few months. Members have been unconcerned with meeting objectives, and have continually needed reminding to have their tasks done on time. Redefining roles has helped in the past.	A. Allow group to determine its own direction. B. Incorporate group recommendations, but see that objectives are met. C. Redefine goals and supervise carefully. D. Allow group involvement in setting goals, but don't push.

Figure 7.5 What is your leadership style?

Source: Reprinted from the *Training and Development Journal.* Copyright (February 1974), the American Society for Training and Development. Reprinted with permission. All rights reserved.

SITUATION	ALTERNATIVE ACTIONS
6. You are considering major changes in your team's structure. Members of the group have made suggestions about needed changes. The group has demonstrated flexibility in its day-to-day operations.	A. Define the change and supervise carefully. B. Acquire group's approval on the change and allow members to decide on implementation. C. Be willing to make changes as recommended, but maintain control of implementation. D. Avoid confrontations; leave things alone.
SITUATION	ALTERNATIVE ACTIONS
7. Group performance and interactions are good. You feel somewhat unsure about your lack of direction of the group.	A. Leave the group alone. B. Discuss the situation with the group and then initiate necessary changes. C. Take steps to direct team members toward working in a well-defined manner. D. Be careful of hurting leader-subordinate relations by being too directive.
SITUATION	ALTERNATIVE ACTIONS
8. Your superior has appointed you to head a task force that is far overdue in making requested recommendations for change. The group is not clear on its goals. Attendance at sessions has been poor. Their meetings have turned into social gatherings. The group has the necessary talent.	A. Let the group work it out. B. Incorporate group recommendations, but see that objectives are met. C. Redefine goals and supervise carefully. D. Allow group involvement in setting goals, and don't push.
SITUATION	ALTERNATIVE ACTIONS
9. Your team members, usually able to take responsibility, are not responding to your recent redefining of standards.	A. Allow group involvement in redefining standards, but don't push. B. Redefine standards and supervise carefully. C. Avoid confrontation by not applying pressure. D. Incorporate group recommendations, but see that new standards are met.
SITUATION	ALTERNATIVE ACTIONS
10. Recent information indicates some internal difficulties among team members. The group has a remarkable record of accomplishment. Members have effectively maintained long range goals. They have worked in harmony for the past year. All are well qualified for the task.	A. Try out your solution with subordinates and examine the need for new practices. B. Allow group members to work it out themselves. C. Act quickly and firmly to correct and redirect. D. Make yourself available for discussion, but be careful of hurting leader-member relationships.

Figure 7.5, *continued*

	(1)	(2)	(3)	(4)
1	A	C	B	D
2	D	A	C	B
3	C	A	D	B
4	B	D	A	C
5	C	B	D	A
6	A	C	B	D
7	C	B	D	A
8	C	B	D	A
9	B	D	A	C
10	C	A	D	B
	(1)	(2)	(3)	(4)
	HT/LR	HT/HR	HR/LT	LT/LR

Figure 7.6
Style range.
Source: Reprinted from the *Training and Development Journal.* Copyright (February 1974), the American Society for Training and Development. Reprinted with permission. All rights reserved.

tional group based on this information. Then select one of the four alternative actions, each of which indicates a particular level of the leader's style in task and relationship response.

When you finish, compare your selected actions with those of the designers, using the style range answer chart (Figure 7.6). The answers A, B, C, and D are listed in rows reading across from the situation number. All answers that indicate the response for a particular "style" are found in the columns, reading down. That is:

1. Responses (high task/low relationship) for below-average maturity group
2. Responses (high task/high relationship) OR
3. Responses (high relationship/low task) for average maturity group
4. Responses (low task/low relationship) for above-average maturity group.

Absolute "right" and "wrong" responses are not given, both because we have taken some liberty with the original authors' ideas, and because we think your reflection on these decisions will lead to a lively discussion. From this activity, you should be able to make decisions about the types of behaviors that characterize mature and immature teams, and to formulate some suggestions about the types of professional development activities that might be appropriate for groups that exhibit these behaviors.

◊ ◊

SUMMARY

Members of the interactive team are interested in obtaining *power*, which is defined as the ability to facilitate change that improves programs for special needs students. Power is obtained through empowerment—the provision of knowledge, skill, and change strategies to persons within the organization who serve these students or clients. The empowerment of individuals is accomplished through professional development, designed in accordance with information about the best practices for its use.

Three types of professional development programs, increasing in complexity and effectiveness, are available to members of the interactive team:

◆ Sharing knowledge.

◆ Developing skills.

◆ Developing the team.

Professional development requires an understanding of the process of change and an ability by the developer to design a change strategy that will affect the entire organization in which special needs students are served. Effective professional development increases the power of the team by empowering its members with knowledge and skills that assist them in implementing needed changes. The empowerment of family members, which enables them to function as full members of the interactive team, is described in the following chapter.

ACTIVITIES

1. Compare and contrast the following pairs of terms:
   - ◆ power structure; change agent
   - ◆ inservice training; professional development
   - ◆ power; empowerment
   - ◆ legitimate power; expert power

2. Through observation and discussion, identify one or two professionals in your program who demonstrate excellent skills that might be used by others. Plan a professional development program that includes modeling, demonstration, and follow-up coaching by these exemplary professionals.

3. Conduct or design a needs assessment that might be used in planning a professional development program for your organization.

4. Observe a meeting of a team that is planning a program for professional development. Explain how the leader involves (or does not involve) others in the decision-making process.

5. Design a knowledge-sharing professional development program that meets the following criteria for oral presentation. Present it to members of your group and obtain their evaluation of its effectiveness.
   a. Brief overview/theoretical base presented.
   b. Interesting opener/closing.
   c. Appropriate media and handouts used.
      - ◆ Designed to match purpose.
      - ◆ Audiovisual combinations are summative.
      - ◆ Momentum maintained during handout distribution.
   d. Effective activities.
      - ◆ Designed to match objective(s).
      - ◆ Designed to involve audience.
   e. Effective presentation.
      - ◆ Demonstrated professionalism.
      - ◆ Demonstrated knowledge.
      - ◆ Used notes appropriately.
      - ◆ Used nonverbals effectively (eyes, stance, gestures).
      - ◆ Used verbals effectively (volume, inflections).
      - ◆ Used questions appropriately (eliciting, responding, answering).
      - ◆ Managed audience (developing rapport, managing disruptions).
      - ◆ Used humor and/or examples.
      - ◆ Avoided information overload.

REFERENCES

Ackland, R. (1991). A review of the peer coaching literature. *Journal of Staff Development, 12,* 22–27.

Audette, B., & Algozzine, B. (1992). Free and appropriate education for all students: Total quality and the transformation of American public education. *Remedial and Special Education, 13*(6), 8–18.

Bennis, W. (1989). *Why leaders can't lead: The unconscious conspiracy continues.* San Francisco: Jossey-Bass.

Blase, J. (1985). The socialization of teachers. *Urban Education, 20,* 235–256.

Book, C. (1996), Professional development schools. In J. Sikula, T. Buttery, & E. Guyton (Eds.), *Handbook of research on teacher education* (2nd ed.). New York: Macmillan.

Boone, R. (1990). The development, implementation, and evaluation of a preconference training strategy for enhancing parental participation in and satisfaction with the individual transition conference (Doctoral dissertation, University of Florida, 1989). *Dissertation Abstracts International, 51*(3), 816A.

Boyer, M. (1997). Staff development: Master teachers. *The American School Board Journal, 184*(7), 34–35.

Brown, B. (1997). *University faculty member exchanges places with third grade teacher.* Unpublished manuscript. Slippery Rock, PA: SRU College of Education.

Buck, G., Morsink, C., Griffin, C., Hines, T., & Lenk, L. (1992). Preservice training: The role of field-based experiences in the preparation of effective educators. *Teacher Education and Special Education, 15*(2), 108–123.

Covey, S. (1990). *The 7 habits of highly effective people.* New York: Simon & Schuster.

Cuban, L. (1988). A fundamental puzzle of school reform. *Phi Delta Kappan, 69,* 341–344.

Cuban, L. (1998, October 14). The superintendent contradiction. *Education Week,* pp. 56, 43.

Darling-Hammond, L. (1997). *Doing what matters most: Investing in quality teaching.* New York: National Commission on Teaching and America's Future.

Darling-Hammond, L. (1998, January–February). Teachers and teaching: Testing policy hypotheses from a national commission report. *Educational Researcher,* pp. 5–15.

Deming, W. E. (1986). *Out of the crisis.* Boston: MIT Center for Advanced Engineering Studies.

Deterline, W. (1968). *Instructional technology workshop.* San Rafael, CA: General Programmed Teaching.

Duarte, P. (1992–93). A mentorship program for special education seniors. *National Forum of Applied Educational Research Journal, 6*(1), 54–67.

Du Four, R. (1998). *The principal series, facilitator's guide for tapes 1–3: Creating a collaborative learning community.* Alexandria, VA: Association for Supervision and Curriculum Development.

Ends, E., & Page, C. (1984). *Organizational team building.* Lanham, MD: University Press of America.

Fullan, M. (1993). *Change forces.* London: Falmer Press.

Fullan, M. (1997, April). *Managing change.* Keynote address to the Superintendents' and Deans' Summit on Transformation and Collaboration for Student Success. Philadelphia, PA: Mid-Atlantic Lab for Student Success at Temple University.

Fullan, M., Galluzzo, G., Morris, P., & Watson, N. (1998). *The rise and stall of teacher education reform.* Washington, DC: AACTE.

Gartner, A., & Lipsky, D. (1987). Beyond special education: Toward a quality system for all students. *Harvard Educational Review, 57,* 367–395.

Glasser, W. (1997). A new look at school failure and school success. *Phi Delta Kappan, 78,* 596–603.

Glatthorn, A. (1987). Cooperative professional development: Peer-centered options for teacher growth. *Educational Leadership, 45,* 31–35.

Glatthorn, A., & Newberg, J. (1984). A team approach to instructional leadership. *Educational Leadership, 39*(3), 60–63.

Goodlad, J. (1990). *Teachers for our nation's schools.* San Francisco: Jossey-Bass.

Grosenick, J., & Reynolds, M. (1978). *Teacher education: Renegotiating roles for mainstreaming.* Reston, VA: The Council for Exceptional Children.

Hall, G., George, A., & Rutherford, W. (1977). *Measuring stages of concern about the innovation: A manual for use of the SOC Questionnaire.* Austin: University of Texas, R&D Center for Teacher Education.

Hall, G., Loucks, S., & Newlove, B. (1976). *Measuring levels of use of the innovation: A manual for trainers, interviewers and raters.* Austin: University of Texas, R&D Center for Teacher Education.

Hall, G., Rutherford, W., Hord, S., & Huling, L. (1984). Effects of three principal styles on school improvement. *Educational Leadership, 41*(5), 22–31.

Hersey, P., & Blanchard, K. (1974). So you want to know your leadership style? *Training and Development Journal, 28*(2), 22–36.

Howey, K. (1997, November–December). School-focused teacher education: Issues to address. *Action in Teacher Education, XIX,* 4–5.

Hutson, H. (1979). *Inservice best practices: The learnings of general education.* Bloomington, IN: National Inservice Network.

Ilmer, S., Snyder, J., Erbaugh, S., & Kurz, K. (1997). Urban educators' perceptions of successful teaching. *Journal of Teacher Education, 48*(5), 379–384.

Jackman, M. (1991, July–August). The queen of team. *Executive Female,* pp. 37–40.

Johnson, L. (1986). Factors that influence skill acquisition of practicum students during a field-based experience. *Teacher Education and Special Education, 9*(3), 89–103.

Joyce, B., & Showers, B. (1988). *Student achievement through staff development.* New York: Longman Publishers.

Joyce, B., Showers, B., & Rolheiser-Bennett, C. (1987). Staff development and student learning: A synthesis of research on models of teaching. *Educational Leadership, 45,* 11–23.

Keller, B. (1998, November 11). Research: Principal matters. *Education Week, XVIII,* pp. 25–27.

Krutilla, J., & Safford, P. (1990). Portrait of the shared student teaching experience: Owning reflection and action. *Teacher Education and Special Education, 13*(3–4), 217–220.

Lasley, T. (1998). Paradigm shifts in the classroom. *Phi Delta Kappan, 80*(1), 84–86.

Leggett, D., & Hoyle, S. (1987). Preparing teachers for collaboration. *Educational Leadership, 44,* 58–63.

LeRoux, P. (1984). *Selling to a group.* New York: Harper & Row.

Levine, M. (1985). Excellent companies and exemplary schools: Common goals and characteristics. *NASSP Bulletin, 69*(7), 56–59.

Lieberman, A. (1988). Expanding the leadership team. *Educational Leadership, 45,* 4–9.

Losen, S., & Losen, J. (1985). *The special education team.* Boston: Allyn & Bacon.

Lyon, S., & Lyon, G. (1980). Team functioning and staff development: A role release approach to providing integrated services for severely handicapped students. *Journal of the Association for the Severely Handicapped, 5*(3), 250–263.

McAdoo, M. (1998). Buying school reform: The Annenburg grant. *Phi Delta Kappan, 80,* 364–369.

McGroddy, J. (1997, October). *Transforming the future through technology.* Address to annual meeting of the Teacher Education Assembly, Pennsylvania Association of Colleges and Teacher Educators, Grantville, PA.

McLaughlin, M., & Schwartz, R. (1998). *Strategies for fixing failing public schools.* Cambridge, MA: Harvard Graduate School, Pew Forum.

Morsink, C. (1999). *21st century teachers for a better future*. Final Report to Howard Heinz Endowment. Slippery Rock, PA: SRU College of Education.

Nanus, B. (1992). *Visionary leadership*. San Francisco: Jossey-Bass.

Neubert, G. (1988). *Improving teaching through coaching* (Fastback 277). Bloomington, IN: Phi Delta Kappa.

Newman, F., & Wehlage, G. (1995). *Successful school restructuring*. Madison, WI: Center for Organizing and Restructuring Schools.

O'Shea, D., Williams, L., & Sattler, R. (1999). Collaboration preparation across special education and general education: Preservice level teachers' views. *Journal of Teacher Education, 50*(2), 147–158.

O'Shea, L. (1987). The supervision throughput model: Interpersonal communication skills and problem-solving procedures for effective intern supervision. *Teacher Education and Special Education, 10,* 71–80.

Padilla, S. (1989). *The effect of teacher's home visits on special student's school performance*. Unpublished manuscript, University of Florida, Department of Special Education, Gainesville.

Patricia, L., & Lamb, M. (1990). Preparing secondary special education teachers to be collaborative decision makers and reflective practitioners: A promising practicum model. *Teacher Education and Special Education, 13*(3–4), 228–232.

Pelfry, R. (1988, February). How to sell a school board by really trying. *Electronic Learning,* p. 16.

Pennell, J., & Firestone, W. (1998). Teacher-to-teacher professional development. *Phi Delta Kappan, 80,* 354–357.

Peterson, S., & Hudson, P. (1989). Coaching: A strategy to enhance preservice teacher behaviors. *Teacher Education and Special Education, 12,* 56–60.

Powers, D., & Powers, M. (1983). *Making participatory management work*. San Francisco: Jossey-Bass.

Renji, J. (1996). *Teachers take charge of their learning: Transforming professional development for student success*. Washington, DC: National Foundation for the Improvement of Education.

Rogers, S. (1987). If I can see myself, I can change. *Educational Leadership, 45,* 64–67.

Ross, D., & Krogh, S. (1988). From paper to program: A story from elementary PROTEACH. *Peabody Journal of Education, 65*(2), 19–34.

Roth, R. (1989). Preparing the reflective practitioner: Transforming the apprentice through the dialectic. *Journal of Teacher Education, 40*(2), 31–35.

Sahakian, P., & Stockton, J. (1996). Opening doors: Teacher-guided observations. *Educational Leadership, 53*(7), 50–53.

Schmoker, M., & Wilson, R. (1993). Transforming schools through total quality education. *Phi Delta Kappan, 74,* 389–395.

Scholtes, P. (1988). *The team handbook*. Madison, WI: Joiner Associates.

Showers, B. (1984). *Peer coaching: A strategy for facilitating transfer of training* (Report to the U.S. Department of Education). Eugene, OR: University of Oregon, Center for Educational Policy and Management. (ERIC Document ED 271 849).

Showers, B., & Joyce, B. (1996). The evolution of peer coaching. *Educational Leadership, 53*(7), 12–16.

Showers, B., Joyce, B., & Bennett, B. (1987). Synthesis of research on staff development: A framework for future study and a state-of-the-art analysis. *Educational Leadership, 45,* 77–87.

Sickler, J. (1988). Teachers in charge: Empowering the professionals. *Phi Delta Kappan, 69,* 354–356.

Skrtic, T. (1987). *An organizational analysis of special education reform*. Washington, DC: The National Inquiry into the Future of Education for Students with Special Needs.

Stedman, L. (1987). It's time we changed the effective schools formula. *Phi Delta Kappan, 69,* 215–224.

Teacher Education Reports. (1998). Council stresses link between staff development and reform. *Teacher Education Reports, 20*(24), 1–3. Washington, DC: Author.

Thies-Sprinthall, L. (1984). Promoting the developmental growth of supervising teachers: Theory, research programs, and implications. *Journal of Teacher Education, 35*(3), 53–60.

Tucker, A. (1984). *Chairing the academic department: Leadership among peers* (2nd ed.). New York: American Council on Education–Macmillan.

Tucker, J. (1972). *A plan to achieve change.* Austin: University of Texas, Department of Special Education.

Valli, L. (1989). Collaboration for transfer of learning: Preparing preservice teachers. *Teacher Education Quarterly, 16*(1), 85–95.

Wang, M. (1998, June 24). Comprehensive school reform can debunk myths about change. *Education Week, XVIII*, pp. 39, 52.

Wang, M., Haertel, G., & Walberg, H. (1997). *What do we know: Widely implemented school improvement programs.* Philadelphia, PA: Mid-Atlantic Regional Educational Lab at Temple University.

Williams, A. L. (1996). Enacting constructivist transactions. In J. Henderson (Ed.), *Reflective teaching: A study of your constructivist practices* (2nd ed., pp. 105–130). Upper Saddle River, NJ: Merrill/Prentice Hall.

Williams, A. L. (1999). *Participant responses to a rural university and urban elementary school collaboration around a preservice field-based seminar.* Slippery Rock, PA: SRU College of Education.

Wilmore, E. (1996). Brave new world: Field-based teacher preparation. *Educational Leadership, 53*(7), 59–63.

Wineburg, S., & Grosman, P. (1998). Creating a community of learners among high school teachers. *Phi Delta Kappan, 80*, 350–353.

Winograd, K. (1998). Rethinking theory after practice: Education professor as elementary teacher. *Journal of Teacher Education, 49*(4), 296–305.

Wynn, M. (1987). Student teacher transfer of training to the classroom: Effects of an experimental model (Doctoral dissertation, University of Florida, 1986). *Dissertation Abstracts International, 47*, 3008A.

Wynn, M. (1988, April). *Transfer of training to the classroom by student teachers: Effects of an experimental model.* Paper presented at the annual meeting of the American Educational Research Association, New Orleans, LA. (ERIC Document ED 239 830)

Zeichner, K., & Liston, D. (1987). Teaching student teachers to reflect. *Harvard Educational Review, 57*, 23–48.

8 Enabling and Supporting Families

◊ ◊

Topics in this chapter include:

- The changing view of families of children with disabilities.
- The various roles of professionals supporting families.
- The unique roles of family members collaborating with professionals.
- Strategies for collaborating effectively with families.
- An application for involving families in special education.

Linda is the single mother of a 6-year-old child with disabilities, Miriam, and a 4-year-old child, Carlos. Linda lives in Miami with her mother, a native Cuban, who speaks very little English. Linda has fought many battles in the past six years. Physicians told her that Miriam would not live to see her first birthday, ophthalmologists reported that the girl was totally blind, and physical therapists said she would never walk.

In spite of the gloomy prognosis, Linda was committed to making Miriam's life the best that it could be. Linda searched for early intervention services when Miriam was 18 months old. They attended early intervention clinics; Linda spoke with other parents of infants with disabilities. Linda placed Miriam in public school programs for toddlers with disabilities. She and Miriam attended summer camps for children with visual impairments and their families. Linda learned physical therapy techniques needed to help Miriam with motor control and eating.

If there is a typical story of a parent of a child with disabilities, this may be one. But Linda brings a new twist to the story. Linda is currently running her own advocacy consultation business. She collaborates with professionals and parents in school districts around Florida in an effort to meet the needs of children with visual and multiple disabilities. She serves as an advocate in due process hearings, and makes presentations at legislative hearings and many special education national conferences. Linda continues her battles for appropriate services for her daughter, and fights for better services for other children with disabilities. She is a distinct kind of parent, well versed in legal and educational issues, articulate in presenting her opinion, and an equal partner on the special education team.

During the last 25 years, much has been written about families of students with disabilities. With the passage of Public Law 94-142 in 1975, and subsequent reauthorization of the Individuals with Disabilities Education Act (IDEA) in 1997, the role of the family as an integral part of the special education process was recognized. Special education personnel became aware of the need to develop skills in supporting and involving families. Although families were encouraged to participate in the development of their children's educational programs, the attempts to achieve such involvement yielded mixed results.

Parental involvement usually was limited to attending IEP conferences and approving program and placement decisions made by special education personnel (Meyers & Blacher, 1987). Parents were merely consumers of services and typically were passive participants in the educational process. Furthermore, school administrators discouraged the involvement of parents in school functions (Fuqua, Hegland, & Karas, 1985) for fear that agitated and unsatisfied parents would instigate due process hearings and lawsuits. If school personnel did encourage *family-centered involvement,* it usually was regarded as more of a kindhearted or paternalistic gesture.

However, much has changed. Today, families are being asked to be collaborators and partners with schools. Additionally, the members of the partnership are not only the parents but all members of the family, including extended family members and non-blood relatives. Grandparents, brothers, sisters, godparents, and even close family friends are recognized as vital sources of support for the family (Turnbull & Turnbull, 1997). They often can influence the outcomes of students with disabilities and should be included in any discussion of home–school collaboration. Today, families are respected as experts on their children and are valued for their equal and full partnership in the educational process.

The purpose of this chapter is to present the factors that influenced the changing attitudes of professionals about involving families in home–school collaboration and understanding families of children with disabilities. A contemporary view of the role of the professional and family in a collaborative partnership is also described in this chapter. A discussion of the importance of understanding families from culturally and linguistically diverse backgrounds is given and strategies for involving the families of these types of students are discussed.

CHANGES IN THE FAMILY STRUCTURE AND PARENTAL INVOLVEMENT

American families have changed dramatically during the last few decades. The sociocultural conditions that influence the American family have implications for professionals working with families today (Lynch & Hanson, 1998; National Parent–Teacher Association, 1998). Although the majority of families in the United States still form the typical two-parent middle-class household, atypical family structures and diverse economic and educational conditions in U.S. families are becoming more common. Reports from the U.S. Census Bureau (1997a, 1997b, 1998a) on the diverse structures and demographic profiles of today's families indicate the following:

◆ The proportion of children under 18 years of age living with two parents declined from 85% in 1970 to 69% in 1995.

◆ White children are less likely to be living with one parent than are black children, or children of Hispanic origin.

◆ In 1995, 8.8% of the U.S. population was foreign born, with the largest group from Mexico and the Philippines. Most of the other foreign-born persons came from Canada, China, Cuba, the Dominican Republic, El Salvador, Jamaica, Korea, Germany, Great Britain, and Poland.

◆ In 1993, 30% of preschoolers in the United States were cared for in organized child care facilities. There has also been an increase in child care by fathers.

◆ Among whites, 83% have at least a high school degree, compared with 74% for blacks, and 53% for persons of Hispanic origin.

◆ In 1995, the number of people below the official government poverty level was 13.8% of the nation's population. Twenty-one percent of American children under age 18 lived in families with incomes below the poverty level. In 1995, the poverty rate for children under 6 years of age was 23.7%.

◆ In the United States in 1995, 15.4% of Americans were without health insurance, of which the majority were poor.

◆ In 1995, 15% of the nation's children were in households receiving cash assistance or food stamps.

◆ In 1996, 4% of children lived with neither parent, up from 3% in 1970. Some lived with grandparents or other relatives; others lived with nonrelatives, for example, as foster children.

◆ In 1996, 28% of children lived in one-parent families, up from 12% in 1970.

◆ In 1996, 19% of children lived with a parent or guardian who had not graduated from high school.

◆ In 1998, 56% of the adult population were married and living with their spouse.

◆ Among people age 25 to 34 years old, 34.7% had never been married. For blacks, in this age group, 53.4% had never been married.

◆ Of all children under 18, 5.6% lived in the household of their grandparents.

Additionally, other reports indicate the condition of the family unit in the United States:

◆ Cohabitation has become a common family form, replacing the old stepfamily structure (Levin, 1993).

◆ In 1990, one in ten Florida babies was born to an unmarried teen mother (Florida Kids Count, 1993).

◆ An estimated 100,000 children are homeless (Children's Defense Fund, 1991; Hanson & Lynch, 1992).

◆ Most homeless women are "mothers, are under 35 years, are members of a minority group, have not completed high school, and have experienced more than one episode of homelessness in their lifetimes" (Milburn & D'Ercole, 1991, p. 1161).

◆ More than 46% of children under the age of 5 receive care outside the home from a nonfamily caregiver (Hayes, Palmer, & Zaslow, 1990).

◆ More same-sex partners are now raising children (Lynch & Hanson, 1998).

◆ By the year 2000, one fourth to one third of the U.S. population will be African-American, Asian, and Hispanic (Williams, 1992).

◆ In 1998, 38% of the homeless population in 30 American cities was comprised of families. These proportions are likely to be higher in rural areas. Twenty-six percent of all requests for emergency shelter went unmet due to lack of resources (U.S. Conference of Mayors, 1998).

Today, school personnel are being called on to serve diverse families and their student populations. The patterns of change in family structure and sociocultural influences indicate that the current needs of families are indeed diverse, requiring heightened sensitivity to effective ways to interact and engage families in a collaborative relationship. Researchers are clear that parent and family involvement is a wise investment for schools truly concerned about student outcomes. It is critical to understand that families represent the most powerful and pervasive influence that a child will ever experience and families who devote attention to the child may contribute more to the child's development than any extrafamilial factor (Fox, Dunlap, & Philbrick, 1997). The research on parent involvement during the past 20 years documents the profound benefits for students, families, and schools when family members become participants in their children's education and their lives (National Parent–Teacher Association, 1998). The findings listed in Table 8.1 summarize the powerful influence families have on student outcomes.

UNDERSTANDING FAMILIES OF CHILDREN WITH DISABILITIES

In recent years, the idea that families of children with disabilities function normally and that the child exerts positive influences on family members has been stated definitively (Dunst, Trivette, & Deal, 1988; Powell & Gallagher, 1993; Turnbull & Turnbull, 1997). The role of the family and their involvement with school personnel have improved significantly. Factors that may have influenced these changes are in the areas of legislation, theory development, and improved research on family adjustment.

Legislative Factors

The passage of P.L. 99-457 in 1986 and the reauthorization of IDEA in 1997 considerably influenced the roles and responsibilities of the parent and the professional in meeting the educational needs of children with disabilities. For families receiv-

Table 8.1
Research on Parent and Family Involvement in Schools

Parent and Family Involvement and Student Success

1. When parents are involved, students achieve more, regardless of socio-economic status, ethnic/racial background, or the parents' educational level.

2. When parents are involved in their students' education, those students have higher grades and test scores, have better attendance records, and complete homework more consistently.

3. Students whose parents are involved in their lives have higher graduation rates and greater enrollment rates in postsecondary education.

4. In programs that are designed to involve parents in full partnerships, the student achievement of low-income children not only improves, it can reach levels that are standard for middle-class children. In addition, the children who are farthest behind make the greatest gains.

5. The most accurate predictor of a student's achievement in school is not income or social status, but the extent to which that student's family is able to (1) create a home environment that encourages learning; (2) communicate high, yet reasonable, expectations for their children's achievement and future careers; and (3) become involved in their children's education at school and in the community.

Parent and Family Involvement and School Quality

6. Schools that work well with families have improved teacher morale and higher ratings of teachers by parents.

7. School programs that involve parents outperform identical programs without parent and family involvement.

8. Schools where children are failing improve dramatically when parents are enabled to become effective partners in their child's education.

Parent and Family Involvement and Program Design

9. For low-income families, programs offering home visits are more successful in involving parents than programs requiring parents to visit the school. However, when parents become involved at school, their children make even greater gains.

10. Parents are much more likely to become involved when educators encourage and assist parents in helping their children with their schoolwork.

Source: From *National Standards for Parent/Family Involvement Programs* (pp. 7–9), 1998, Chicago, IL: National Parent–Teacher Association. Adapted by permission.

ing services under Part C early intervention programs, the Individualized Family Service Plan (IFSP) is required under this legislation. The intent of the service plan is similar to that of an IEP for a child. However, the IFSP is designed to focus on generating individualized goals and services for meeting the needs of the families and young children with disabilities being served in early intervention programs. Those needs may include parent support, counseling services, or parent education. Although Part C mandates services for families of young children with disabilities, the implications of the IFSP will ultimately be to older children with disabilities and their families.

IDEA 1997 emphasized the parent's role in working with schools. In particular, it requires that parents be provided a copy of their child's IEP and that a parent has the right to ask for revisions of the child's IEP or to invoke due process procedures if the parent feels the child is not making adequate progress toward meeting the goals and objectives outlined in the document. Furthermore, states are required to offer mediation to parents as a voluntary option for resolving disputes. Mediation, however, cannot be used to delay or deny a parent's right to due process.

Furthermore, legislation under IDEA 1997 provided continued support for Parent Training and Information centers (PTIs) across the states and territories. Parent centers in each state provide training and information to parents of infants, toddlers, school-aged children, and young adults with disabilities and the professionals who work with their families. This assistance helps parents participate more effectively with professionals in meeting the educational needs of children and youth with disabilities. To reach the parent center in your state, contact the Technical Assistance Alliance for Parent Centers at http://www.pacer.org/natl/natl.htm. Four regional PTI centers exist in the west (Navato, California), midwest (Marion, Ohio), south (Beaumont, Texas), and northeast (Concord, New Hampshire).

Theoretical Factors

Various theoretical points of view related to families of children with disabilities have been presented in recent literature. One of the most applicable is the *family systems theory* (Carter & McGoldrick, 1980; Minuchin, 1974; Turnbull & Turnbull, 1997). Theorists maintain that the underlying structure of the family can be conceptualized into four *family subsystems: marital, sibling, parental,* and *extrafamilial.*

The ability of the family to function effectively depends on how clearly the boundaries and rules of the family are defined and how cohesive and flexible the family is during life cycle changes. The underlying premise is that life events, such as the birth of a child with disabilities, will affect not only the parents but also the siblings, grandparents, and friends. The implications of this theoretical framework are that interventionists are a part of the extrafamilial subsystem and therefore affect each member of the family, even though they may be involved directly with only one member, usually the mother. The traditional view of parent involvement and training with only mothers of children with disabilities must be broadened to include fathers, siblings, grandparents, and others who share in the care of these children.

Literature on theoretical approaches for understanding families provides professionals with a wealth of information. The social support perspective (Dunst, Cooper, Weeldreyer, Snyder, & Chase, 1988; Dunst, Trivette, & Cross, 1986), cognitive coping approach (Turnbull et al., 1993), stress and adaptation theory (McCubbin & Patterson, 1983), feminist family theory (Osmond & Thorne, 1993), and ethnocultural application of family theories (Dilworth-Anderson, Burton, & Johnson, 1993) provide a range of perspectives for understanding diverse families and families of children with disabilities. Various approaches to understanding families give professionals many more tools to assess family functioning and adaptation to children with disabilities.

Research Factors

The idea that families have a difficult time adjusting to the presence of a child with disabilities has been a major concern of professionals working in special education. Dunst (1985) stated that the traditional view of families of children with disabilities was based on a deficit model in which much attention was placed on the pathology in families. In the traditional view, the goal of the professional was to remediate the deficits by helping families come to grips with the problems of having a child with disabilities. Families were viewed as overly emotional; family members were rejecting or struggling with the acceptance of the child with disabilities. These families were viewed as dysfunctional in contributing to their child's general welfare and educational program. Traditionally, the image of the family with a child with disabilities was one of chronic sorrow, severe depression, and emotional turmoil.

No longer is the family viewed as pathological and unhealthy. Instead, the family is portrayed positively. During the past few years, researchers have reported on studies supporting the notion that families are not necessarily adversely affected by the presence of a child with disabilities (Dunst, 1985; Dunst et al., 1988; Powell & Gallagher, 1993; Turnbull et al., 1993; Turnbull & Turnbull, 1997; Zeitlin, Williamson, & Rosenblatt, 1987). In fact, some researchers found that families of children with disabilities are as well adjusted as families with nondisabled children (Dunlap, Ondelacyt, & Sells, 1979; Gallagher, Cross, & Scharfman, 1981; O'Halloran, 1995; Salisbury, 1987). The availability of *multifaceted family assessment* procedures—including survey instruments, rating forms, natural observation, and interviews—has yielded more sensitive data on families of children with disabilities (Bailey & Simeonsson, 1988).

Some studies, however, report increased amounts of *family stress* when family members are coping with children with disabilities (Crnic, Friedrich, & Greenberg, 1983; Gallagher, Beckman, & Cross, 1983). How families cope with this stress influences their interaction with professionals in special education and other related fields. For example, Shuster, Guskin, Hawkins, and Okolo (1986) reported that mothers were reluctant to share information about their infants with disabilities with medical and early intervention personnel if the mothers were stressed, felt devalued, or lacked respect for the service provider. Thus, the goal of family intervention is to help families expand internal and external resources to meet the challenges and take advantage of the opportunities of family life (Zeitlin & Williamson, 1988). Providing families with support networks that help them adjust to caring for a child with disabilities should be one goal of general and special education professionals.

Golan (1980) stated that families should be viewed as "normal people with normal troubles engaged in developmental processes of change and adaptation" (p. 266). Moreover, through support networking and advocacy efforts, parents are educated to be equal partners with educators. Many families have become sophisticated in working with school personnel by taking on a more active role in the educational process. Clearly, the relationship of the family and the professional has changed from coexistence to collaboration. In the next sections, the roles and responsibilities of professionals and parents within the collaborative partnership are delineated.

ROLE OF THE PROFESSIONAL

School personnel are responsible for initiating and maintaining a positive, interactive, and facilitative relationship with families of children with disabilities. In this regard, the role of the professional is multifaceted. Many school personnel feel comfortable with the more traditional responsibilities of providing information on student progress, results of diagnostic evaluations, inclusive educational placement strategies, and schedules of upcoming school events.

But the role of the professional has expanded to include parent education and advocacy, medical report interpretation, active listening, and working with culturally diverse students and their families. The family's needs can range from information about due process hearings to help obtaining transportation, welfare payments, and food stamps. School personnel may take on the shared roles of social worker, attorney, physician, therapist, psychologist, clergy, and friend. The professional should not assume all these jobs without assistance or training, however.

Collaboration, role sharing, and role release are required for special educators and other team members to be successful in their expanded job responsibilities. Although many professionals may be willing to expand their roles in encouraging family involvement, few are trained to assume the added responsibilities. The various roles and responsibilities of the special education team members as collaborators are discussed next.

Providing Basic Information

The traditional role of the professional working with families has been as information provider. Teachers of students with mild disabilities, for example, usually provide the family with information on academic and emotional/social progress. The teachers and therapists of students with severe disabilities provide information on developmental progress, self-care skills, communication, and progress on related therapies such as occupational, physical, and speech. As educators and families move toward more inclusive settings for students with disabilities, the educator will need to provide information on students' integration into general education classrooms. Both general and special educators will need to be involved in information dissemination.

Information has been provided to families in many ways. Formal staffing and IFSP or IEP meetings are the most common arenas for professionals and families to interact. In some cases, special educators contact family members by phone,

---

How to Get Ready

_____ 1. Make a list of questions and concerns.
_____ 2. Ask your child if he/she has questions for the teacher.
_____ 3. Arrange for a babysitter for small children.

Questions You May Want to Ask

_____ 1. In which subjects does my child do well? Is my child having any trouble?
_____ 2. Does my child get along with other children?
_____ 3. Does my child obey the teacher?
_____ 4. How can I help at home?

Questions the Teacher May Ask You

_____ 1. What does your child like the best about school?
_____ 2. What does your child do after school? (What are his/her interests?)
_____ 3. Does your child have time and space set aside for homework?
_____ 4. How is your child's health?
_____ 5. Are there any problems that may affect your child's learning?
_____ 6. What type of discipline works well at home?

At the Conference

_____ 1. Arrive on time.
_____ 2. Discuss your questions and concerns.
_____ 3. Share information that will help the teacher know your child better.
_____ 4. Take notes if you wish.

After the Conference

_____ 1. If you have more questions or you ran out of time, make another appointment.
_____ 2. Tell your child about the conference.
_____ 3. Plan to keep in touch with the teacher.
_____ 4. If you were satisfied with the conference, write a note to the teacher.

Figure 8.1
Parent checklist for IEP meetings.

Source: From *Strategies for Communicating with Parents of Exceptional Children: Improving Parent–Teacher Relationships* (pp. 283–284) by R. L. Kroth and D. Edge, 1997, Denver, CO: Love Publishing Company. Reprinted by permission.

share daily logs with parents, or send notes home informing the family of the child's program.

Generally, it is helpful for professionals to provide parents with a checklist to help them prepare for the IEP conference. Figure 8.1 is an example of such a checklist. For more detailed information on preparing for the IFSP/IEP conference, see Turnbull and Turnbull (1997). Informal meetings provide professionals with time to share information with parents related to early developmental intervention, academic changes, behavioral problems, and therapy prescriptions.

Reporting Evaluation Results

The role of the team has been to interpret results of diagnostic evaluations to families. Providing diagnostic feedback is frequently the responsibility of a school psychologist or special education teacher. Informing family members about their child's educational or physical disabilities can be extremely sensitive and requires skills typically associated with problem solving, collaborating, and counseling. The professional who reports evaluation results in a sensitive way may still have families who are discouraged and, at times, shocked by the results of the evaluation.

Guidelines for providing families with test results have been stated in various sources (Teglasi, 1985; Turnbull & Turnbull, 1997). Additionally, Fish (1990) and Margolis and Branningan (1990) provide educators with strategies for interacting with angry parents, including active listening, empathizing, establishing trust, and systematic problem-solving techniques. Team members should adhere to the following when providing diagnostic feedback:

◆ Provide feedback in a private, safe, comfortable environment.

◆ Keep the number of professionals to a minimum.

◆ Begin by asking parents their feelings about the child's strengths as well as weaknesses.

◆ Provide the evaluation results in a *jargon-free* manner, using examples of test items and behavioral observations throughout.

◆ Provide parents results from a variety of assessment activities, including standardized tests, criterion-referenced tests, direct behavioral observations, play-based or community-based assessment, and judgment-based approaches.

◆ Be sensitive to viewing the child as an individual and a "whole" child when reporting various evaluation results.

◆ Allow the parent time to digest the results before educational planning begins.

◆ Be sensitive to linguistically different families and the use of interpreters.

◆ Prepare for the session with other team members, clarifying any possible conflicts before the meeting.

◆ Use conflict resolution strategies to clarify any possible conflicts with families.

Understanding and Gathering Family Information

The role of the professional working with students with disabilities has expanded significantly in the area of assessment instruments and analysis. No longer are team members asked to assess only the student's needs; they are now being asked to assess the family's concerns, priorities, and resources as well. Educational teams must understand the complex family system and know how to match intervention with the service needs of individual families. As mentioned earlier, the linear view of the child with disabilities and the parent (most typically the mother) has been replaced with a systemic view of *family subsystems* (parental, marital, sibling, and extrafamilial) (Turnbull & Turnbull, 1997). Bailey and Simeonsson (1988) stated that conducting family assessments:

◆ Helps the professional understand the child as part of a family system.

◆ Identifies the family's service needs.

◆ Specifies the family's strengths and adaptations.

◆ Expands the efficacy of services and intervention.

Some of the most commonly used instruments and checklists for assessing family functioning, needs, and supports includes the Family Needs Survey (Bailey & Simeonsson, 1990), Parent Needs' Survey (Seligman & Darling, 1989), Parenting Stress Index (Abidin, 1986), and the Family Support Scales (Dunst, Trivette, & Jenkins, 1988). Additionally, professionals can use informal procedures for gathering information on the family support network by using the ECOMAP (Hartman, 1978), a one-page visual representation of the family's relationships. Lines and circles are drawn to represent relationships with extended family and kin, friends and neighbors, church and coworkers, and schools and professional services represented by individuals or organizations. In addition to the existence of such relationships, participants describe the nature, strength, and reciprocity of their relationships indicated via various coding conventions. Figure 8.2 illustrates an ECOMAP for a single Puerto Rican mother with a child who has Down syndrome. It shows a concise and convenient mapping of the current relationships and interactions maintained by the family.

Although these instruments and procedures have been recommended by experts in the field, professionals must keep several cautions in mind when using the instruments. Many assessment tools involve personal questions, which some families might consider overly intrusive. The responsibility for administering such instruments may fall on a psychologist or social worker, neither of whom usually has the time to conduct such assessments. Special education teachers may find the instruments too detailed for use in the school setting. Furthermore, professionals may not have received training in administering many of the assessment tools and shaping their results into concrete family plans (Bailey & Simeonsson, 1988).

Research by Garshelis and McConnell (1993) found that individual professionals on interdisciplinary teams did not do well in matching the family's needs with

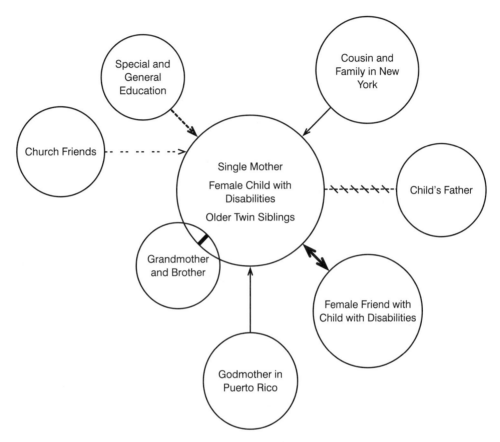

Figure 8.2
An ECOMAP.

the mothers' perceptions of family needs. The collaborative teaming process helped professionals come to consensus and more closely match the parents' perceived needs. The researchers concluded that professionals should allow parents to provide the team with perceived family needs, and should use those needs to guide the interventions developed with the family. Professionally directed assessments of family needs may not be accurate.

Professionals must be cautious when using family surveys with families of children with disabilities. Some of the instruments lack validity and reliability and have small norming populations (L'Abate & Bagarozzi, 1993; McGrew, Gilman, & Johnson, 1992). Furthermore, professionals should be overly cautious when using the surveys with families from culturally and linguistically diverse backgrounds (Behar, Correa, & Beverly, 1993). Few family instruments have been normed on culturally or linguistically diverse families, and the families' cultural values and beliefs might not be taken into consideration when interpreting the results. Professionals should keep in mind that each family of a child with a disability has unique characteristics and should be evaluated on an individual basis.

Providing Instruction to Families

Professionals in special programs frequently are involved in educating parents to implement educational programs at home. The educational objectives can vary from teaching parents specific strategies such as learning strategies for increasing word recognition to teaching parents time-out procedures for decreasing tantrum behavior. An abundance of research is available that supports the efficacy of educating parents in skills related to teaching students with disabilities (Turnbull & Turnbull, 1997).

However, more recent trends in family literature indicate that the concept of parents as teachers and of professionals as parent trainers is questionable. Professionals must understand that although parents are effective in teaching and reinforcing behavior in their children, their role as teachers can be an added burden and source of stress for the family. Turnbull and Turnbull (1997) pointed out that families often do not have the time outside of their work and household responsibilities to "teach" their children. In many families the stress of daily intervention with their children can have detrimental effects on family members' interactions. Dunst, Leet, and Trivette (1988) found that adequacy of family resources and personal well-being affected the family's ability to adhere to prescribed interventions for the child. They concluded that some families did not follow through on prescribed interventions because they had to invest time and energy in meeting other family needs. Families with inadequate resources and social support did not carry out child treatments. To presume these families are resistant, uncooperative, or noncompliant is a grave error in professional judgment.

The following vignette illustrates these issues:

Mrs. Green has a 4-year-old daughter, Kinesha, with severe visual and motor disabilities and mental retardation requiring extensive supports. At a recent IEP meeting, the special education professionals recommended that Mrs. Green continue the physical therapy interventions at home. The techniques prescribed involve 30 to 40 minutes a day of range-of-motion exercises and movement facilitation techniques to enhance posture and movement. Kinesha cries during much of the therapy sessions conducted at school and may vomit when she gets extremely upset. In addition, the special education teacher has asked Mrs. Green to provide Kinesha with 10 to 15 minutes of language stimulation a day to enhance her understanding of simple labels for familiar objects. The teacher provides the mother with a simple data collection sheet for the object labeling program. She also recommends that Mrs. Green spend extra time during meals to encourage Kinesha to feed herself. Lastly, the school psychologist is concerned about Kinesha's tantrums and vomiting and would like the mother to implement a time-out procedure for the next few months and report Kinesha's progress at the end of each week. Mrs. Green leaves the meeting with four training programs to be conducted each day at home. On a follow-up visit to the school, Mrs. Green is asked to report on the progress of all the programs. She is embarrassed and says she has been unable to conduct the programs at home.

The professionals involved with Mrs. Green have good intentions for Kinesha's educational program, but they have not made a thorough assessment of the family's needs. Before recommending family intervention programs, professionals should have asked about other family members, working responsibilities of both parents, and daily routines and schedules of the family. The family systems approach acknowledges the right of Mrs. Green and other family members to identify their own priorities for Kinesha. Professionals must consider individualizing their approach to providing families with information about intervention strategies, resources, and advocacy (Dunst, Leet, & Trivette, 1988; Turnbull & Turnbull, 1997). Specific suggestions for providing parents with information are discussed in the last part of this chapter on involvement strategies. Providing information is especially difficult when families are culturally and linguistically different from mainstream school professionals.

Understanding Culturally Diverse Families

Statisticians indicate that by 2050 about 53% of the U.S. population will be non-Hispanic white, 15% black, more than 24% Hispanic, almost 9% Asian and Pacific Islander, and just over 1% American Indian, Eskimo, and Aleut (U.S. Census Bureau, 1998b). It is projected that by 2050 the black population will nearly double its present size; the Asian and Pacific Islander population will increase 3.5 times its 1995 level; and the Hispanic-origin population will increase by 3.5 times its 1995 level. The Hispanic-origin population will show the largest numeric increases of any other race or ethnic group. Additionally, 1 in 10 people in the United States is foreign born, with the largest country of birth of the foreign-born population being Mexico.

Because of the increased numbers of culturally and linguistically diverse populations in many school districts, educators are required to work with students and families from diverse cultural groups. Although most studies of families of children with disabilities have been directed toward Anglo-American families in the mainstream culture, an increasing number of studies have described families from culturally and linguistically diverse groups (Bailey, Skinner, Correa, et al., 1999; Bailey, Skinner, Rodriguez, et al., 1999; Behar et al., 1993; Blanes, Correa, & Bailey, 1999; Hanline & Daley, 1992; Harry, 1992; Heller, Markwardt, Rowitz, & Farber, 1994; Lynch & Hanson, 1998; Shapiro & Simonsen, 1994; Skinner, Bailey, Correa, & Rodriguez, 1999). The culturally diverse family—that is, the family from a cultural background other than Anglo-American—may not understand the special education needs of their child. Often because of language barriers, the family may not understand the nature of the child's disability, the educational services available for the child, or the expectations of professionals working with the child and family (Bailey, Skinner, Rodriguez, et al., 1999; Harry, 1992; Heron & Harris, 1987; Lynch & Hanson, 1998). Nevertheless, the professional must view the culturally diverse family as having different values and beliefs that are positive (Behar et al., 1993; Correa, 1989). The belief system held by the family may actually be a strength for coping with and caring for the child with a disability.

The role of the professional working with the culturally diverse family is multi-faceted. Professionals must first assess their own biases toward different ethnic groups. Second, they must make an effort to understand the family. At the same time, the culturally and linguistically diverse family must be helped to understand and participate in the traditional culture of schools. Acculturation into school life is a two-way process in which professionals and families collaborate. "Professionals who are hoping to make a difference for children must be willing to take the initiative in building a bridge between the cultures of diverse families and the culture of schools" (Harry, Kalyanpur, & Day, 1999, p. 7). Harry et al. outline four steps that are essential in building cultural reciprocity among families and school personnel. The four steps involve:

1. Identifying the cultural values that are embedded in our interpretation of a student's difficulties or in the recommendations for services such as independence and individuality.
2. Recognizing whether the family being served understands and values the interpretations we as service providers place on the student's difficulties and, if not, having the family share why their values differ from ours.
3. Respecting the differences identified between the family and the school.
4. Determining the most effective way of adapting the professional's interpretation or recommendation to the value system of the family.

Guidelines for professionals making home visits (Wayman, Lynch, & Hanson, 1990) and developing IFSPs (Bennett, Zhang, & Hojnar, 1998) are useful in working with families. Some additional strategies for professionals working with culturally diverse families include the following:

◆ Empowering families with skills for adapting and coping with a school system that may be very different from what they are accustomed to.
◆ Enabling families to reinforce educational programs at home in natural and functional ways.
◆ Assisting families through the transition from their native culture to the mainstream school culture, understanding that the native culture can be heterogeneous within groups such as Hispanics and Asians.
◆ Serving as *culture brokers* by providing a link between the majority and minority cultures.
◆ Linking with community leaders from the ethnic or racial group to help enhance the collaborative home–school relationship.
◆ Serving as mediators and advocates for the ethnic and racial group.
◆ Removing barriers such as cultural differences and linguistic and communication differences to enhance interaction between professionals and families.

◆ Assessing the family in terms of their experiences in their native country; the role of extended family members and siblings; the amount of community support available; religious, spiritual, and/or cultural beliefs; and parenting practices (e.g., discipline, independence).

◆ Providing information, written and oral, in ways that enable families to comprehend. Language and communication can be one of the biggest barriers to providing services to families from linguistically diverse groups.

Interpreting Information

For many families of children with disabilities, the information given to them about their child's disability can be overwhelming. In particular, medical information can be difficult to understand and interpret. Professionals in special programs are typically the only people families can turn to when deciphering medical, psychological, and insurance reports. Interpreting information in terminology that a family understands is an appropriate role for the professional. Special educators and other school-based professionals may be more available than physicians to families seeking information.

Special educators, particularly school counselors and teachers of students with severe disabilities, can be greatly helped when team members, such as school nurses and public health officials, provide relevant medical information. Additionally, teachers of students with severe disabilities should have access to reference guides (e.g., *Merck Manual; Physicians' Desk Reference;* medical dictionaries; ophthalmology, ontology, anatomy, and physiology textbooks) that may help in the interpretation of medical reports.

The following vignette illustrates the role of the special education professional in translating information and the difficulty that may arise from that role.

Ms. Long, the early intervention teacher, and Mr. Franks, the physical therapist, make a home visit to inform Ms. Hupp, the single parent of Tina, a child with motor disabilities, of a new form of spinal surgery, "selective dorsal root rhizotomy." The PT explains the procedure to Tina's mother in clear terms. The procedure, although still in experimental stages, has significantly reduced hypertonicity in some young children with cerebral palsy. A rhizotomy involves cutting of selected spinal nerves that control the tone of certain muscles in the body. Mr. Franks uses pictures of the spinal area to help illustrate the procedure. Ms. Hupp is grateful for the information but confused about whether to pursue the surgical evaluation. She finally asks the teacher, Ms. Long, what she thinks of the procedure. Ms. Long says she herself is uncomfortable advising the mother on the surgery but refers her to a local physical therapist who has worked with children who have had the rhizotomy surgery. Ms. Long comforts the mother and says she understands how difficult it is for parents to have to make decisions about experimental surgery such as rhizotomy. She asks the mother if there are family members who can help her make the decision and suggests that she speak with the surgeon at length about the advantages and disadvantages of the procedure. The mother says she will talk to her sister, call the surgeon, and get back in touch with the PT.

Parents often ask teachers to help them make decisions regarding medical, financial, or personal family matters. Parents who are young, inexperienced, less educated, or from diverse ethnic cultures often turn to school personnel for such help. Although this situation indicates that the parent trusts the professional, professionals may be uncomfortable with advising the parent on decisions involving an issue that is outside of their expertise. Professionals should provide as much information as possible and allow the parents to share their feelings. However, professionals must make it clear that the final decision lies with the family.

Furthermore, professionals are frequently put in the role of interpreting special education information for families who do not speak English or who cannot read. Using interpreters for non-English-speaking families can be a major help. Unfortunately, many interpreters used in the schools are not knowledgeable about special education terminology.

Providing parents with information and support may appear basic to school professionals. The task becomes a challenge when families lack basic information on special education, legal, medical, financial, and psychological information.

Communicating Effectively

As illustrated in the previous section, the importance of being sensitive to the language and culture of parents is a prerequisite to effective communication with families of children with disabilities. There are other prerequisites to developing positive communication between families and professionals. Turnbull and Turnbull (1997) outlined three major skills needed:

1. Professionals must understand themselves and appreciate the personalities and behaviors of others.
2. Professionals and families must have mutual respect for and trust in each other.
3. Both families and professionals must view their relationship as a partnership and work collaboratively.

In their effort to communicate openly with parents, professionals must use good interpersonal communication skills. A comprehensive discussion of interpersonal communication including both verbal and nonverbal skills has been outlined in Chapter 5. When working with families, the professional's most important communication attributes are empathy, genuineness, and unconditional positive regard.

As professionals expand their roles and responsibility in family involvement, they will most likely come across difficult parents, who for various reasons may be angry, resistant, pushy, adversarial, or noncaring. Sonnenschein (1984) warns that professionals may label parents inaccurately based on the parents' behaviors. Parents may be accurate in their feelings and perceptions of certain situations and factors that affect their children. Roos (1985) further warns that professionals often yield to the temptation to blame, compete with, or undermine parents of children with disabilities. Those who react to "difficult" parents by becoming defensive and fighting back will soon find that the foundation for developing a partnership will be weak. As mentioned earlier, Fish (1990) and Margolis and Branningan (1990) provide strategies for interacting with angry parents and resolving conflicts.

Communicating with families from diverse cultural and linguistic backgrounds can also be challenging to professionals. Several guidelines have been provided specifically to aid interpersonal communication with diverse families (Gersten & Woodward, 1994; Lynch & Hanson, 1998; Wittmer, 1992). In particular, professionals should be sensitive to issues of nonverbal communication (e.g., eye contact, facial expressions, gestures, proximity, touching) among diverse cultural groups.

Professionals must understand that most families have strengths (Behar et al., 1993; Dunst, Trivette, & Deal, 1988; Turnbull & Turnbull, 1997; Webster, 1977) and that many parents are emotionally stronger as a result of having a child with disabilities in the family (Skinner et al., 1999; Turnbull et al., 1993; Wikler, Wasow, & Hatfield, 1983). It is critical for professionals to refrain from viewing parents of children with disabilities as dysfunctional and to respect their involvement on the educational team. The roles and responsibilities of professionals in creating a positive partnership with families are extensive. Nonetheless, it is not a one-sided association. The next section relates to the family's role in the establishment of the education team.

ROLE OF THE FAMILY

As the term implies, a partnership involves families becoming equal and active in the association with educators. For most families, the role of a collaborative partner is foreign and uncomfortable. Therefore, the responsibility for initiating the partnership may fall on the professional. However, for the relationship to be maintained, the parent must commit to helping professionals meet the unique needs of their children by providing information, reinforcing school programs at home, asserting and advocating for quality services, and understanding the professionals' role.

Providing Information

For professionals in special programs to understand their students' educational, medical, and emotional needs, comprehensive information is often required. The family is usually in the best position to provide teachers and other professionals with such information. First, parents should feel comfortable releasing consent to the schools to obtain medical information on their children, especially in the areas of vision, hearing, and neurological status. If such information takes some time to be received by the professionals, the parent should try to keep the teacher and related service staff informed of any medical information that may indirectly or directly affect the child's physical and educational needs. The following vignette illustrates how one set of parents designed a practical way of informing teachers and other school personnel about the medical and educational history of their child with emotional disabilities.

In September, Mr. and Mrs. Bell, the parents of Michael, a 7-year-old boy with autism, came to school to visit with the special education teacher. Mrs. Bell brought a three-ring notebook with comprehensive information on Michael's disability. She had divided the notebook into five sections: medical, psychiatric, educational, financial, and resources. In addition, the Bells had included yearly pictures of Michael and samples of his drawings and preacademic work. During the conference, the Bells shared information on Michael's last school placement and on current psychiatric reports. The teacher appreciated the information, because she was still waiting for Michael's school folders to be transferred. She was unaware that Michael had been diagnosed with infantile autism at the age of 3 and was currently taking Ritalin. Mr. and Mrs. Bell signed consent for release of information forms for the teacher and left the teacher with copies of the most relevant reports.

In this case, Michael's parents were able to provide professionals with a comprehensive compilation of information on his medical and educational history. To help organize the numerous documents gathered over the years, the Bells assembled a notebook. For parents of children with medical needs and severe disabilities, keeping track of medical and educational information is critical. However, professionals must respect the fact that family history or social work reports may be too sensitive to release. If parents do not provide the teacher with important information, the teacher may become frustrated when trying to obtain the information from physicians, therapists, and other professionals.

Furthermore, families should provide education personnel with their beliefs and values related to child-rearing practices and discipline. Particularly for families from diverse cultural backgrounds, the values they hold about child development, behavior problems, and discipline techniques may be extremely important as educators match services with family concerns, priorities and needs.

For Mrs. Gonzalez, requiring her child to use a spoon and fork during mealtimes was difficult. The educational team had suggested that she encourage independence in feeding for her 5-year-old daughter with hydrocephaly. Mrs. Gonzalez said it was difficult to maintain the behavioral program outlined by the team, because she didn't want her child to go hungry or suffer. After consulting with other families from Nicaragua, the teachers realized that independence was not necessarily valued in children under the age of 7. The team adapted the feeding program with Mrs. Gonzalez, requiring that part of the meal be eaten with a spoon and fork and that the rest could be finger fed. Over time, Mrs. Gonzalez saw her daughter's feeding skills improve and began to increase the use of the utensils at meals.

Other information parents can provide to teachers involves family activities that may affect the child's behavior or assist in supplementing educational programs. For example, families can tell teachers about vacations; relatives or friends the child cares about; and favorite restaurants, TV shows, or games the family enjoys. Teachers can relate the child's home experiences to educational activities at school. In particular, parents should keep professionals informed of any changes in the health of the child or family situations that may affect emotional behavior.

Reinforcing the School Program at Home

Many families are under added pressures with both parents regularly working outside of the home or single parents needing to work full time. Professionals must understand that parents often have to take care of family priorities before they can attend to school responsibilities. All children need unstructured time with their parents for fun, play, and sharing. It is easy for school personnel to so burden families with "ought to's" that parents feel guilty about taking time to simply play with their children. The parent must be viewed as a parent, not as another teacher.

Professionals can provide parents with intervention programs that can be easily integrated into normal family routines without making the family feel guilty for not being able to spend more time "teaching" their child. If math is an area that teachers think should be reinforced at home, they can ask parents to have their children add items at the grocery store or check the bill at a fast-food restaurant. For children with more severe disabilities, parents and siblings can usually help in activities such as teaching table setting, recognizing photographs of familiar objects, and even stimulating vision or hearing. Only if the family is willing should teachers provide families with sophisticated educational lessons requiring data collection or lengthy practice. Home programs often will not be effective if they are time consuming or complex.

If possible, parents should try to attend school events involving their child's program. It may be helpful for them to meet and talk with other families. The school can often provide helpful information on various topics. Parents do not attend school meetings for many reasons. Meetings are often scheduled at a time that interrupts work (e.g., 3 p.m.) or during mealtimes. Meetings take place in school buildings that may be far from home, in unfamiliar surroundings. For families from diverse backgrounds, schools may be threatening places. School desks are uncomfortable, no drinks are offered, nor are babysitting services provided. Topics may be of no interest, or they may be subjects that some families consider inappropriate. Speakers may use jargon or present complicated concepts. Professionals and middle-class Anglo parents may dominate discussions.

Culturally diverse parents who do not attend meetings may actually use their time more effectively at home with their children. Effective programs can be developed by asking a sample of parents from different groups within the school population what topics they want information about, when to schedule meetings, and where to have the meetings. Interpreters may be needed in some locations.

Advocating for Quality Services

As mentioned earlier, the professional who is competent in collaborating with others on the educational team must develop skills in assertive communication. This holds true for parents as well. The traditional role of parents involved in their child's educational program has been either passive, submissive behavior or aggressive, hostile behavior. These behaviors are exhibited in reactions to what families perceive as intimidation and control by school professionals. In turn, submissive or aggressive parental behaviors fail to earn respect from school professionals. Parents as well as professionals need to learn how to communicate effectively, showing respect for others while stating facts and opinions based on evidence in such a way that listeners do not become defensive. Training in advocacy and assertiveness is important for parents and other family members. The responsibility for this training can fall on either the school or national parent organizations such as Parent to Parent and Parent Training and Information Centers. The following narrative illustrates why it is important for parents to communicate their expectations and goals assertively to professionals working with their children.

Mrs. Avila, a native Puerto Rican mother of an 18-year-old daughter with mild disabilities, attended an IEP meeting at which her daughter's transition program was discussed. Mrs. Avila was asked if she would consent to her daughter's attending the local sheltered workshop for vocational training in assembling packages of ballpoint pens. Mrs. Avila's first reaction was to ask the professionals if those were realistic expectations for her daughter's future. The transition specialist said it was an excellent opportunity for the daughter and presented retainment and productivity statistics on the workshop. Mrs. Avila was intimidated by the professionals and consented to the transition program without further discussion. During the following six months, her daughter developed aggressive behaviors, appeared to lose motivation in school, and regressed in her social and communication skills. Mrs. Avila became depressed and angry about the school's decision to place her daughter in the sheltered workshop. She had higher expectations for her daughter and wanted her to work in the community. Mrs. Avila did not know how to work with the professionals on changing the transition program. She felt a loss of power and control over her daughter's training.

Mrs. Avila's situation clearly exemplifies what many families experience when working with professionals. Mrs. Avila believed that it was important to respect educational experts and not question their knowledge or authority. Turnbull and Turnbull (1997) explained that parents' diminished sense of status and power in decision making is common. Families are usually outnumbered by professionals and made to feel less important in the educational process.

Families should not settle for second best. They should understand the limitations of the school system, but still push for quality programming. Families with skills in assertive communication and knowledge of the IFSP/IEP process are able to represent their child's interest in securing the best possible educational services (Turnbull & Turnbull, 1997). While their child is receiving services, families should remain involved and assertive. They should provide professionals in special programs with regular feedback on the educational program. Telling teachers what their goals, priorities, and expectations are for their child is important. If a problem arises, the parent should respect the chain of command and begin by speaking directly with the professional responsible for the child. If the problem cannot be resolved at that level, the parent should contact the teacher's supervisor, principal, and finally the superintendent for action. Most problems, however, can be resolved when an open, honest relationship exists between families and professionals at the school level.

Understanding the Professional's Perspective

If a collaborative partnership is to be maintained, families must understand the professionals' perspective and the limitations the system places on their ability to act. With some insight into school policies such as teacher accountability, teachers' contracts, and teachers unions, families can begin to understand the conditions under which the teacher functions. Employers, on one hand, expect the teacher to advocate on behalf of the school district. Families, on the other hand, need the teacher to advocate for better services for their children. If there is a conflict in providing the services, the teacher is often caught in between. External mediators serve a critical role in solving conflicts between families and schools.

Schools today are under extreme pressure from state education departments, and many face lawsuits from parents regarding appropriate services for students with disabilities. Moreover, state and local communities are under pressure to provide better services with diminishing funds and personnel. Teachers are now under the microscope for ensuring that students pass state standards examinations and are being held accountable to the scores of the children in their classrooms. Families must understand the complexities of school systems and put themselves in the shoes of the professional. Many authors provide useful information for both professionals and parents who want to advocate for quality services for children in the areas of due process (Brock & Shanberg, 1990; Sussan, 1990), conflict resolution (Margolis & Brannigan, 1990; Fish, 1990; Fisher & Ury, 1991), advocacy (Friesen & Huff, 1990; Mlawer, 1993), and parent involvement (Katsiyannis & Ward, 1992).

Joyce Epstein (1995) has suggested that schools create partnership action teams that focus specifically on family participation and school improvement. She suggests action teams develop 3-year plans that identify the school's strengths, needed area for changes, expectations, and links to student goals.

Parents need to see professionals as people who may become extremely emotionally attached to a child, typically acting as if they were the child's prime experts. Parents must remember that professionals can become protective of students and sometimes may not behave objectively. Professionals with special programs have a vested interest in their students' programs and are committed to getting the best possible services for their students. It is sometimes difficult for special education team members to remain completely objective about students. Both parents and professionals need to balance caring and objectivity.

A professional may wear a cloak of objectivity to hide feelings. But objectivity without caring is not desirable. It is not an error or a weakness to *care* or show authentic feelings. It is an error to allow feelings to overcome objectivity. Team members can help each other maintain this delicate balance, rather than scorning the member who errs in either direction. Together parents and professionals can foster an excellent relationship if they remember that the goal of the partnership is to improve services to children with disabilities.

STRATEGIES FOR SUPPORTING FAMILIES

The major roles and responsibilities of professionals and families have now been outlined. How professionals establish collaborative relationships with families is a concern that education professionals will have for years to come. There are no simple guidelines for involving families in the educational program of their children with disabilities. However, Patrikakou, Weissberg, Hancok, Rubenstein, and Zeisz (1997) recommend four essential ingredients to building healthy communication between school and home. These ingredients are the four P's:

1. *Positive.* Remember to communicate praise and encouragement not just concerns and problems.
2. *Personalized.* Parents will appreciate a personal note jotted on a school memo. Correspondence sent to parents can also be decorated by the student.
3. *Proactive.* Keep parents informed of upcoming events, class rules, school policies, and expectations; also, let them know immediately if there is a problem before it gets more severe.
4. *Partnership.* Encourage parents to respond to school notes by leaving space for comments or have them respond to a few quick questions.

Establishing effective interactions between families and professionals takes a commitment of time, energy, financial resources, and sensitivity from school administrators, direct service providers and related service personnel. In Figure 8.3, practical strategies to meet the needs of families in special education programs are presented.

1. *Establish an advisory committee with parents and professionals* to outline and monitor the "family-professional" goals of the school. Have the committee follow a systematic plan for implementing parent training, advocacy, and information exchange (Epstein, 1995).

2. *Gather extensive information on the families' concerns, priorities, strengths, and needs.* Use a variety of informal and formal assessment instruments to gather information. Emphasize information gathered through family interviews. For special education teachers, formal psychosocial instruments may be too detailed. Use personal future's planning techniques such as the MAPs to better understand the student's and families priorities and needs (Falvey, et al., 1994).

3. *Identify family needs and preferences for school involvement.* The Family Information Preference Inventory (Turnbull & Turnbull, 1997) can be adapted to provide school personnel with information on the needs of parents in the areas of teaching the child at home, advocacy and working with professionals planning for the future, coping with family stress, and using resources.

4. *Develop school manuals on school policies and procedures, curriculum, and transition.* Manuals for parents are available from many parent organizations such as PACER centers (http://www.pacer.org/natl/natl.htm). However, individualizing manuals for each school district is advantageous because policies and procedures may be different across states, and curriculum, transition, and resource information may be specific to a school district.

5. *Provide parents with videotapes, films, and slide-tape presentations that provide instruction and support to families.* A resource center for such materials has been established by the Young Adult Institute, 4602 34th Street, New York, NY 10001. A variety of Internet sites (National Parent Information Network, http://npin.org/index.html; National Information Center for Children and Youth with Disabilities, http://www.nichcy.org/; and National Parent Network on Disabilities, http://www.npnd.org/) provide valuable information for families on educating children with disabilities. In addition, establish a materials lending library for families and a toy lending library for parents of young children.

Figure 8.3   *(continued)*
Strategies for involving families.

Application

An Individualized Family Service Plan (IFSP) was developed for the family of Rachel, a 2-year-old with disabilities. Rachel was premature and evidenced retinopathy of prematurity (retinal damage that left her with only light perception), motor impairment, and cognitive delays. The development of this plan involved all the skills described in interactive teaming. The parent, Janet Howe, a single mother with two children, was asked to provide the team with goals and needs relevant to her own family.

6. *Involve parents in individual classroom projects* such as publishing family recipe calendars in which each family has a favorite recipe printed. Also, publish a classroom newsletter in which current activities and news on each student or family can be distributed among the families. Design home–school diaries for the purpose of sharing individual information with families daily or weekly. Include photographs and charts that illustrate examples of the children's progress. Provide a system for distributing feedback on the child's behavior and progress using "happy-grams," classroom web page, e-mail, phone calls, or videotape.

7. *Develop a survival vocabulary list in the native language(s) of your families* for use with parents and school personnel. Include basic special education terminology, greetings, body parts, action words, calendar words, etc. Silberman and Correa (1989) have published a Spanish survival vocabulary list for use with children with physical disabilities and their families.

8. *Provide parents with a current listing of respite care and babysitting services for children with disabilities.* Keep a list of other resources on a bulletin board near the entrance of the classroom, such as announcements on family group meetings, weekend workshops, state or national conferences, television programs pertaining to special education, and handouts on preparation for IFSP or IEP meetings.

9. *Include parents* in transition planning, discussing the expectations of the next environment, issues of inclusion, materials or equipment necessary for the next environment. Have parents visit potential receiving classrooms. Provide team meetings with both exiting and receiving classroom personnel and families.

10. *Make extra efforts to include hard-to-reach families.* Provide single parents, fathers, and parents who live at a far distance from the school an opportunity to share in their child's learning by organizing activities that do not require them to come to the school building (Brand, 1996; Flynn & Wilson, 1998; Weiss, 1996).

11. *Organize a telephone tree for families in the classroom.* Use the telephone tree to remind parents of upcoming events including classroom learning units, field trips, holiday celebrations, and open-house meetings (Patrikakou et al., 1997).

12. *Communicate personally with the family.* Contact parents at least once a month through e-mail, a phone call, or quick "home note" that suggests ideas for home learning activities (Patrikakou et al., 1997). Provide the parent a place to respond to encourage two-way communication. Periodically, ask parents what the most effective form of communication would be for them.

Figure 8.3, *continued*

The parent, early intervention teacher, psychologist, school counselor, and physical therapist attended the initial planning meeting. The meeting took place at the local community day-care center, where the early intervention program is located. Ms. Howe began the meeting by stating her perceptions of Rachel's educational needs as well as the family's needs. Table 8.2 is an example of the goals developed

Table 8.2
Sample of an Individualized Family Support Plan

Area of Need	Suggested Goals
1. Ms. Howe needs babysitting once a week to attend the infant program's parent support group.	1. The local high school has developed a respite care program for parents in the community who need babysitting or homecare. The group will be contacted to provide Ms. Howe with volunteer babysitting services every week. The early interventionist will consult with the high school volunteer, orienting her to Rachel's special physical and cognitive needs.
2. Ms. Howe wants help in interpreting and understanding the ophthalmologist's reports.	2. The local itinerant vision teacher will be contacted to help Ms. Howe understand the effects of visual impairment on Rachel's overall development. Additionally, the vision teacher will sit down with Ms. Howe and review tape-recorded sessions of Ms. Howe's visits to the ophthalmologist. The ophthalmologist has agreed to be available to school personnel for added explanation of Rachel's condition on a consultative basis.
3. Ms. Howe is concerned about Rachel's language development. In particular, Rachel is using echolalia when engaged in communication.	3. The early interventionist and physical therapist will consult with the local university speech clinic/laboratory in an effort to improve their skills in early language development. The speech-and-language therapist will conduct a staff development workshop for all the personnel at the early intervention program on how to stimulate language in young children. If necessary a formal referral will be made to the speech clinic.
4. Ms. Howe reports that her other child, Ricky, age 10, is exhibiting resentment toward Rachel by not helping around the house and refusing to watch Rachel while mother is cooking dinner. Ms. Howe would like some suggestions as to what to do.	4. The school counselor has arranged a sibling support group for brothers and sisters of children with disabilities attending the early intervention program. A family therapist, Mr. Dodd, himself a sibling of an adult with disabilities, conducts the groups once a month at the day-care center.

based on Ms. Howe's family concerns, priorities, and needs. Ms. Howe and all the team members will meet every 6 months to discuss progress on the IFSP.

◊ ◊

SUMMARY

This chapter has presented the issues related to establishing a partnership among professionals and families of children with disabilities. Developing a collaborative relationship is not simple.

Professionals and parents must understand their roles and responsibilities in the partnership. The association involves a two-way commitment.

Many families are unable to find the time or energy to get actively involved with the school program. Families may feel powerless and insignificant in the education of their child. They may be timid and nonassertive about their feelings, especially if they come from a diverse cultural background.

Professionals must not mistake a family's lack of involvement or shyness as not caring. Instead, they should find creative ways to keep parents informed and make families feel as though the "door is always open" to involvement.

Education professionals clearly serve a role in empathizing with families who are coping with and adjusting to having a child with a disability. They must identify the strengths the family brings to the collaborative relationship.

Providing families with the tools (support services) to cope with the care of a child with disabilities becomes the major role of professionals. Support can come from many parts of the family subsystem, but for professionals it includes providing them with information and resources or services for their children.

The professional must view the family as being the child's best expert. Families frequently report that professionals make them feel as if they do not understand their own child's problems. Families know and understand their children better than any professional can. Likewise, professionals working with children with disabilities have expertise in specialized areas that parents may not realize. The mutual knowledge and expertise of both parents and professionals can be shared, and the result is quality services for children with disabilities. Professionals must view the parents as equal and valued team members.

Clearly, professionals today see the value of involving families in the educational process. However, professionals may lack the skills needed to establish the parent–professional relationship. This chapter has attempted to provide education personnel with insight into the skills that are needed for the partnership. As stated by Will (1988), "professionals must be flexible, and be willing to 'go the extra mile,' in spite of limited resources, to provide family members with the tools necessary to live and work cohesively as a unit. This is not an easy task, but it is one which will yield tremendous results" (p. 2).

ACTIVITIES

1. Generate a list of informational interview questions to ask families of children with disabilities. Make sure the questions are stated in a manner that shows respect for the families. Practice asking the questions in a simulated role-play situation.

2. Make a home visit with someone at the local school (e.g., special education teacher, psychologist, social worker, counselor). Observe how the home visit is conducted. Be prepared to ask some general information questions about the child. For example, ask family members (e.g., parent, sibling, extended family member) to describe things the child likes to do at home.

3. Attend a local community family support group. Observe the group interactions. Write a brief reaction to the meeting, listing the activities that were most effective and those that were least effective during the meeting.

4. Analyze published videotapes on the reaction of families to having a child with disabilities. Discuss how the videotapes depict the strengths and the needs of the families of children with disabilities.

5. Review selected articles from the journal *Exceptional Parent*. Abstract the articles selected for their portrayal of the family experiences associated with caring for a child with disabilities.

REFERENCES

Abidin, R. R. (1986). *Parenting stress index* (2nd ed.). Charlottesville, VA: Pediatric Psychology Press.

Bailey, D. B., & Simeonsson, R. J. (1990). *Family needs survey*. Chapel Hill: University of North Carolina, Frank Porter Graham Child Development Center, FAMILIES Project.

Bailey, D. B., Jr., & Simeonsson, R. J. (1988). Assessing the needs of families with handicapped infants. *Journal of Special Education, 22,* 117–127.

Bailey, D., Skinner, D., Correa, V., Arcia, E., Reyes-Blanes, M., Rodriguez, P., Vázquez-Montilla, E., & Skinner, M. (1999). Needs and supports reported by Latino families of young children with developmental disabilities. *American Journal on Mental Retardation, 104,* 437–451.

Bailey, D., Skinner, D., Rodriguez, P., Gut, D., & Correa, V. (1999). Awareness, use, and satisfaction with services for Latino parents of young children with disabilities. *Exceptional Children, 65,* 367–381.

Behar, L., Correa, V. I., & Beverly, C. (1993). *Family functioning analysis of Hispanic families of young children with disabilities: Implications for P.L. 99-457 and personnel preparation.* Manuscript submitted for publication.

Bennett, T., Zhang, C. & Hojnar, L. (1998). Facilitating the full participation of culturally diverse families in the IFSP/IEP process. *The Transdiciplinary Journal, 8*(3), 227–248.

Blanes, M., Correa, V., & Bailey, D. (1999). Perceived needs of and support for Puerto Rican mothers of young children with disabilities. *Topics in Early Childhood Special Education, 19*, 54–63.

Brand, S. (1996). Making parent involvement a reality: Helping teachers develop partnerships with parents. *Young Children, 51(2)*, 76–81.

Brock, K. A., & Shanberg, R. (1990). Avoiding unnecessary due process hearings. *Journal of Reading, Writing, and Learning Disabilities International, 6*, 33–39.

Carter, E. A., & McGoldrick, M. (Eds.). (1980). *The family life cycle: A framework for family therapy.* New York: Gardner Press.

Children's Defense Fund. (1991). *The state of America's children 1991.* Washington, DC: Author.

Correa, V. C. (1989). Involving culturally diverse families in the education of their limited English proficient handicapped and at risk children. In S. Fradd & M. J. Weismantel (Eds.), *Bilingual and bilingual special education: An administrator's handbook* (pp. 130–144). San Diego: College-Hill Press.

Crnic, K. A., Friedrich, W. N., & Greenberg, M. T. (1983). Adaptation of families with mentally retarded children: A model of stress, coping, and family ecology. *American Journal of Mental Deficiency, 88(2)*, 125–138.

Dilworth-Anderson, P., Burton, L., & Johnson, B. (1993). Reframing theories for understanding race, ethnicity, and families. In P. G. Boss, W. J. Doherty, R. LaRoss, W. R. Schumm, & S. K. Steinmetz (Eds.), *Sourcebook of family theories and methods: A contextual approach* (pp. 627–649). New York: Plenum.

Dunlap, W. R., Ondelacyt, J., & Sells, E. (1979). Videotape involves parents. *Journal of American Indian Education, 19(1)*, 1–7.

Dunst, C. J. (1985). Rethinking early intervention. *Analysis and Intervention in Developmental Disabilities, 5*, 165–201.

Dunst, C. J., Cooper, C. S., Weeldreyer, J. C., Snyder, K. D., & Chase, J. H. (1988). Family needs scales. In C. J. Dunst, C. M. Trivette, & A. G. Deal (Eds.), *Enabling and empowering families: Principles and guidelines for practice.* Cambridge, MA: Brookline Books.

Dunst, C. J., Leet, H. E., & Trivette, C. M. (1988). Family resources, personal well-being, and early intervention. *The Journal of Special Education, 22*, 108–116.

Dunst, C. J., Trivette, C. M., & Cross, A. H. (1986). Mediating influences of social support: Personal, family and child outcomes. *American Journal of Mental Deficiency, 90(4)*, 403–417.

Dunst, C. J., Trivette, C. M., & Deal, A. G. (1988). *Enabling and empowering families: Principles and guidelines for practice.* Cambridge, MA: Brookline Books.

Dunst, C. J., Trivette, C. M., & Jenkins, B. (1988). Family support scales. In C. Dunst, C. Trivette, & A. Deal (Eds.), *Enabling and empowering families* (pp. 155–157). Cambridge, MA: Brookline Books.

Epstein, J. (1995). School/family/community partnerships: Caring for the children we share. *Phi Delta Kappan, 76*, 701–712.

Falvey, M. A., Forest, M., Pearpoint, J., & Rosenberg, R. (1994). Building connections. In J. S. Thousand, R. A. Villa, & A. L. Nevin (Eds.), *Creativity and collaboration learning: A practical guide to empowering students and teachers* (pp. 347–368). Baltimore: Paul H. Brookes.

Fish, M. C. (1990). Family-school conflict: Implications for the family. *Journal of Reading, Writing, and Learning Disabilities International, 6*, 71–79.

Fisher, R., & Ury, W. (1991). *Getting to yes: Negotiating agreement without giving in* (2nd ed.). Boston: Houghton Mifflin.

Florida Kids Count (1993). *Key facts about the children: A report on the status of Florida's children.* Tallahassee, FL: Florida Center for Children and Youth [or Washington, DC: The Center for the Study of Social Policy].

Flynn, L., & Wilson, P. G. (1998). Partnerships with family members: What about fathers? *Young Exceptional Children, 2(1)*, p. 21–28.

Fox, L., Dunlap, G., & Philbrick, L. A. (1997). Providing individual supports to young children with autism and their families. *Journal of Early Intervention, 21*, 1–14.

Friesen, B. J., & Huff, B. (1990). Parents and professionals as advocacy partners. *Preventing School Failure, 34,* 31–35.

Fuqua, R. W., Hegland, S. M., & Karas, S. C. (1985). Processes influencing linkages between preschool handicapped classrooms and homes. *Exceptional Children, 51,* 307–314.

Gallagher, J. J., Beckman, P., & Cross, A. H. (1983). Families of handicapped children: Sources of stress and its amelioration. *Exceptional Children, 50*(1), 10–19.

Gallagher, J. J., Cross, A., & Scharfman, W. (1981). The father's role. *Journal of the Division for Early Childhood, 3,* 3–14.

Garshelis, J. A., & McConnell, S. R. (1993). Comparison of family needs assessed by mothers, individual professionals, and interdisciplinary teams. *Journal of Early Intervention, 17,* 36–49.

Gersten, R., & Woodward, J. (1994). The language-minority student and special education: Issues, trends, and paradoxes. *Exceptional Children, 60,* 310–322.

Golan, N. (1980, May). Intervention at times of transition: Sources and forms of help. *Social Casework,* 259–266.

Hanline, M. F., & Daley, S. E. (1992). Family coping strategies and strengths in Hispanic, African-American, and Caucasian families of young children. *Topics in Early Childhood Special Education, 12,* 351–366.

Hanson, M. J., & Lynch, E. W. (1992). Family diversity: Implications for policy and practice. *Topics in Early Childhood Special Education, 12,* 283–306.

Harry, B. (1992). *Cultural diversity, families, and the special education system: Communication and empowerment.* New York: Teachers College Press.

Harry, B., Kalyanpur, M., & Day, M. (1999). *Building cultural reciprocity with families: Case studies in special education.* Baltimore: Paul H. Brookes.

Hartman, A. (1978). Diagrammatic assessment of family relationships. *Social Casework, 59,* 465–476.

Hayes, C. D., Palmer, J. L., & Zaslow, M. J. (1990). *Who cares for America's children? Child care policy for the 1990s.* Washington, DC: National Academy Press.

Heller, T., Markwardt, R., Rowitz, L., & Farber, B. (1994). Adaptations of Hispanic families to a member with mental retardation. *American Journal of Mental Retardation, 99,* 289–300.

Heron, T. E., & Harris, K. C. (1987). *The educational consultant: Helping professionals, parents, and mainstreamed students.* Austin, TX: Pro-Ed.

Katsiyannis, A., & Ward, T. J. (1992). Parent participation in special education: Compliance issues as reported by parent surveys and state compliance reports. *Remedial and Special Education, 13,* 50–55.

L'Abate, L., & Bagarozzi, D. A. (1993). *Sourcebook of marriage and family evaluation.* New York: Brunner/Mazel.

Larsen, D., Attkisson, C., Hargreaves, W., & Nguyen, T. (1979). Assessment of client patient satisfaction: Development of a general scale. *Evaluation and Program Planning, 2,* 197–207.

Levin, I. (1993) Family as mapped realities. *Journal of Family Issues, 14,* 82–91.

Lynch, E. W., & Hanson, M. J. (1998). *Developing cross-cultural competence: A guide for working with young children and their families* (2nd ed.). Baltimore: Paul H. Brookes.

Margolis, H., & Brannigan, G. (1990). Calming the storm. *Learning, 18,* 40–42.

McCubbin, H. I., & Patterson, J. M. (1983). Family stress and adaptation to crises: A Double ABCX Model of family behavior. In D. Olson & B. Miler (Eds.), *Family studies review yearbook* (pp. 87–106). Beverly Hills, CA: Sage Publications.

McGrew, K. S., Gilman, C. J., & Johnson, S. (1992). A review of scales to assess family needs. *Journal of Psychoeducational Assessment, 10,* 4–25.

Meyers, C. E., & Blacher, J. (1987). Parents' perceptions of schooling for severely handicapped children: Home and family variables. *Exceptional Children, 53,* 441–449.

Milburn, N., & D'Ercole, A. (1991). Homeless women. *American Psychologist, 46,* 1161–1169.

Minuchin, S. (1974). *Families and family therapy.* Cambridge, MA: Harvard University Press.

MIS Report (1991–1992). Tallahassee: Florida Department of Education.

Mlawer, M. A. (1993). Who should fight? Parents and the advocacy expectation. *Journal of Disability Policy Studies, 4*(1), 105–115.

National Parent–Teacher Association. (1998). *National standards for parent/family involvement programs* (pp. 7–9). Chicago, IL: Author.

O'Halloran, J. M. (1995). The celebration process [fact sheet]. In *Parent articles 2* (pp. 195–196). Phoenix, AZ: Communication Skill Builders/ The Psychological Corporation.

Osmond, M. W., & Thorne, B. (1993). Feminist theories. In P. G. Boss, W. J. Doherty, R. LaRoss, W. R. Schumm, & S. K. Steinmetz (Eds.), *Sourcebook of family theories and methods: A contextual approach* (pp. 591–625). New York: Plenum.

Patrikakou, E., Weissberg, R., Hancock, M., Rubenstein, M., & Zeisz, J. (1997). *Positive communication between parents and teachers* [online]. Philadelphia, PA: Laboratory for Student Success (LSS). Available: www.temple.edu/LSS.

Powell, T., & Gallagher, P. A. (1993). *Brothers and sisters: A special part of exceptional families* (2nd ed.). Baltimore: Paul H. Brookes.

Roos, P. (1985). Parents of mentally retarded children—misunderstood and mistreated. In H. R. Turnbull & A. P. Turnbull (Eds.), *Parents speak out: Then and now* (pp. 245–260). Columbus, OH: Merrill.

Salisbury, C. L. (1987). Stressors of parents with young handicapped and nonhandicapped children. *Journal of the Division for Early Childhood, 11,* 154–160.

Seligman, M., & Darling, R. B. (1989). Parent needs survey. In M. Seligman, & R. Benjamin Darling (Eds.) *Ordinary families, special children: A systems approach to childhood disability.* New York: Guilford Press.

Shapiro, J., & Simonsen, D. (1994). Educational/ support group for Latino families of children with Down syndrome. *Mental Retardation, 32*(6), 403–415.

Shuster, S., Guskin, S., Hawkins, B., & Okolo, C. (1986). Views of health and development: Six mothers and their infants. *Journal of the Division for Early Childhood, 11,* 18–27.

Silberman, R., & Correa, V. I. (1989). Spanish survival words and phrases for professionals who work with students who are bilingual and severely/multiply handicapped and their families. *Journal of the Division of Physically Handicapped, 10,* 57–88.

Skinner, D., Bailey, D., Correa, V., & Rodriguez, P. (1999). Narrating self and disability: Latino mothers' construction of meanings vis-à-vis their child with special needs. *Exceptional Children, 65,* 481–495.

Sonnenschein, P. (1984). Parents and professionals: An uneasy relationship. In M. L. Henniger & E. M. Nesselroad (Eds.), *Working with parents of handicapped children: A book of readings for school personnel* (pp. 129–139). Lanham, MD: University Press of America.

Sussan, T. A. (1990). How to handle due process litigation effectively under the Education for All Handicapped Children Act of 1975. *Journal of Reading, Writing, and Learning Disabilities International, 6,* 63–70.

Teglasi, H. (1985). Best practices in interpreting psychological assessment data to parents. In A. Thomas & J. Grimes (Eds.), *Best practices in school psychology* (pp. 415–430). Kent, OH: National Association of School Psychologists.

Turnbull, A. P., & Turnbull, H. R. (1997). *Families, professionals, and exceptionality: A special partnership* (3rd ed.). Upper Saddle River, NJ: Merrill/ Prentice Hall.

Turnbull, A. P., Patterson, J. M., Behr, S. K., Murphy, D. L., Marquis, J. G., & Blue-Banning, M. J. (1993). *Cognitive coping, families, and disabilities.* Baltimore: Paul H. Brookes.

U.S. Census Bureau. (1997a). *America's children at risk.* Washington, DC: Author.

U.S. Census Bureau. (1997b). *How we're changing: Demographic state of the nation: 1997.* Washington, DC: Author.

U.S. Census Bureau. (1998a). *Marital status and living arrangements: March 1998 (Update)*. Washington, DC: Author.

U.S. Census Bureau. (1998b). *1997 Population Profile of the United States*. Washington, DC: Author.

U.S. Conference of Mayors. (1998). *A status report on hunger and homelessness in America's cities: 1998* [online]. Washington, DC: Author. Available: www.nch.ari.net/who.html.

Wayman, K., Lynch, E., & Hanson, M. (1990). Home based early childhood services: Cultural sensitivity in a family systems approach. *Topics in Early Childhood Special Education, 10,* 56–75.

Webster, E. J. (1977). *Counseling with parents of handicapped children: Guidelines for improving communication*. New York: Grune & Stratton.

Weiss, H. (1996). Family-school collaboration: Consultation to achieve organizational and community change. *Human Systems: The Journal of Systemic Consultation and Management, 7,* 21–235.

Wikler, L., Wasow, M., & Hatfield, E. (1983). Seeking strengths in families of developmentally disabled children. In L. Wikler and M. P. Keenan (Eds.), *Developmental disabilities: No longer a private tragedy* (pp. 111–114). Silver Spring, MD: National Association of Social Workers.

Will, M. (1988, Spring). Family support: Perspectives on the provision of family support services. *Focal Point, 2,* 1–2.

Williams, B. F. (1992). Changing demographics: Challenges for educators. *Intervention in School and Clinic, 3,* 157–163.

Wittmer, J. (1992). *Valuing diversity and similarity: Bridging the gap through interpersonal skills*. Minneapolis, MN: Educational Media Corporation.

Zeitlin, S., & Williamson, G. (1988). Developing family resources for adaptive coping. *Journal of the Division for Early Childhood, 12,* 137–146.

Zeitlin, S., Williamson, G. G., & Rosenblatt, W. P. (1987). The coping with stress model: A counseling approach for families with a handicapped child. *Journal of Counseling and Development, 65,* 443–446.

Implementation of Interactive Teaming

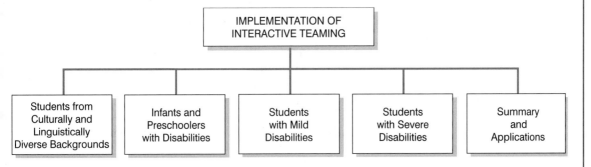

OVERVIEW

In Part II, the facilitating factors that contribute to the effective implementation of interactive teaming were examined. All the factors described affect in various ways the implementation of services for students who are at risk or have one or multiple disabilities.

Regardless of the category or label of students, all interactive teams operate within a common framework of problem identification, intervention design and implementation, and evaluation of effectiveness. Other similarities include the necessity of collaboration among all members, role release in the sharing and use of the professional expertise of others, and the need for constant and clear communication among team members so that comprehensive and coordinated services can be provided to children and adolescents with special needs.

Some differences among the categories also exist. The roles of team members will vary in scope, levels of involvement, and the amounts and forms of

direct (i.e., teaching) and indirect (i.e., consultation) services provided. In addition, there may be differences in the educational focus, such as academics versus self-care skills, and in the types of interventions that team members design and implement.

Implementation with culturally diverse students is examined in Chapter 9. How interactive teaming can be implemented and considerations and roles of service providers working with infants and preschoolers with disabilities are delineated in Chapter 10. The implementation of interactive teaming with students with mild disabilities and students with severe disabilities is described in Chapters 11 and 12, respectively. Student characteristics, considerations for meeting educational needs, and a description of professional roles are presented in each chapter. The concluding chapter is comprised of a summary and extended case study illustrating the implementation of the interactive teaming model. Current trends and promising practices for the future also are included.

9

Implementation with Students from Culturally and Linguistically Diverse Backgrounds

Topics in this chapter include:

- The various educational needs of students from diverse backgrounds.
- Teaching strategies for working with students from diverse backgrounds.
- The unique roles of professionals working with students from diverse backgrounds.
- An application for team involvement in educational planning for students from diverse backgrounds.

Helena, a 10-year-old Salvadoran child, has become a problem for her fourth-grade teacher, Ms. Harris. She has been in the United States for eight months and is receiving English instruction from Mrs. Garcia, the ESOL (English for Speakers of Other Languages) teacher. However, Ms. Harris reports that Helena is distracted during the day and is not paying attention in class and cannot complete even the simplest first-grade worksheets. She has observed the other children in her fourth-grade class teasing her and calling her names. She understands that Helena's parents are Spanish speakers and because she does not speak Spanish has not communicated directly with the family. Ms. Harris reports that she has adapted instruction to implement a token reward system for compliance, but Helena continues to fall behind in her academics and social interactions. She suspects Helena may have a learning disability that warrants special education services. Ms. Harris has told the school psychologist that she feels it would be best for Helena to be placed in a resource room for most of the day with ESOL pull-out.

Frustrated with the situation, Ms. Harris has decided to let Helena work independently during the day and no longer requires her to participate in class lessons or student group projects. She has decided to wait until the prereferral and referral process is completed and does not seek any help from other professionals.

The education of students and families from linguistically and culturally different backgrounds in today's public schools is a critical and specialized area within general education and special education because of the dramatically changing demographics of the United States. Large numbers of foreign-born and U.S.-born children from culturally diverse populations are entering public schools. Although this chapter focuses on students from ethnically or linguistically diverse backgrounds, it is important to note that today a broader definition of cultural diversity must be understood. The word *culture* is used here in its broadest sense. It includes any group of people with a common set of values and a language. "Culture represents the encompassing expression of a person's life ... that subsumes racial and ethnic rituals, symbols, language, and general ways of behaving" (Dilworth-Anderson, Burton, & Johnson, 1993, p. 628). Culture provides the blueprint that determines who we are: how we think, feel, and behave (Gollnick & Chinn, 1998). Culture is also dynamic and ever changing as people learn to accommodate their environmental conditions.

Some might assume that any discussion about *cultural diversity* relates to His-panic, African-American, Native American, or Asian (the groups most often given the term *minority*). But for purposes of this chapter, cultural diversity can encom-pass groups such as the Amish, Mormons, Appalachians, Jews, armed forces, homosexuals, the homeless, and the poor. These groups often are underrepre-sented in discussions of diversity. Although some of these groups may experience less economic or political subordination and may be more assimilated to the dom-inant culture (Ogbu, 1985; Tharp, 1989), they still possess distinct group identity and should be respected for their diversity. Overlooking the influences culture has on students and families who are not of color, have not immigrated to the United States, do not have an ethnic surname, or do not speak a native language other than English is an error in understanding cultural diversity.

Many students live in situations that may place them at risk for school discrim-ination or school failure. Some of these at-risk situations include the following:

◆ Students who are gay or lesbian.
◆ Students who come from migrant families.
◆ Students who live in poor inner city or rural areas.
◆ Students who are homeless.
◆ Students who have HIV or AIDS.
◆ Students who are victims of child abuse or live in violent environments.
◆ Students who live with relatives, guardians, or foster parents.
◆ Students who are latchkey and unsupervised at home (Salend, 1998).

The interactive team of professionals working with this special population must have a strong knowledge base in understanding differences (e.g., cultural, linguistic, religious, environmental, lifestyle) and in preparing these students for successful experiences in inclusive general education. Educators who do not understand the similarities and differences among and within groups can inad-vertently marginalize students from culturally diverse backgrounds from the mainstream, often resulting in poor educational outcomes for students. Profes-sionals must develop cultural competence and culturally responsive practices when working with these students and their families.

The vignette about Helena is an example of what might happen if profession-als are not sensitive to the special needs of students from diverse cultures and if collaboration with other professionals is not sought. Ms. Harris should have con-tacted other professionals for consultation on Helena's learning and behavioral problems. With the help of other professionals knowledgeable about Salvadoran students, an appropriate assessment of the situation and plan of action could have been implemented.

The purpose of this chapter is to highlight the specific needs of students from culturally and linguistically diverse backgrounds and to delineate the various roles of the professionals working with these students. First, a brief overview of cultural and linguistic differences will illustrate characteristics of students from culturally and linguistically diverse backgrounds. Some of these students are limited English proficient (LEP) students, which may put them at risk for special education services. Second, a short discussion of the educational needs of students from culturally and linguistically diverse backgrounds is presented to suggest various service delivery options available for these students. Within the description of the educational needs of these students, assessment techniques and modified teaching strategies used for students from diverse backgrounds will be delineated. Third, the role of the professionals involved in the education of students from culturally and linguistically diverse backgrounds is presented. Cultural insensitivities can be found in all aspects of educating students from diverse backgrounds. The key to overcoming these insensitivities is to have a culturally competent interactive team available for instruction and collaboration.

UNDERSTANDING THE NEEDS OF STUDENTS FROM CULTURALLY AND LINGUISTICALLY DIVERSE BACKGROUNDS

Students from culturally diverse populations are at risk for placement into special education due in part to their linguistic differences, their culturally determined behavioral characteristics, and their socioeconomic status (Artiles & Trent, 1994; Artiles & Zamora-Duran, 1997; Gollnick & Chinn, 1998; Harry, 1992, 1994; Patton, 1998). If placed in special education, they are often not provided support in their native language, which can have an even greater effect on their linguistic and academic development (Artiles & Trent, 1994; Briscoe, 1991; Correa & Tulbert, 1991; Figueroa, Fradd, & Correa, 1989; Harry, 1992, 1994; Saville-Troike, 1991). Similarly, some students from culturally and linguistically diverse backgrounds are underrepresented in programs for gifted students (Patton, 1997; Rhodes, 1992). Although the dilemma of disproportionality of students from culturally diverse background is complex and controversial, it is important to note that the interactive team plays a key role in reducing inappropriate placements in special education programs (Artiles & Zamora-Duran, 1997; Harry, 1994; Harry & Anderson, 1994; Heller, Holtzman, & Messick, 1982; MacMillan & Reschley, 1998; Patton, 1998; Oswald, Coutinho, Best, & Singh, 1999). Errors in referrals to special education begin with the general education teacher and proceed to the prereferral and referral process. Bias in assessment and poor assessment procedures can place the student from a culturally diverse background on a track to special education that may not be reversible.

The interactive team is responsible for distinguishing actual learning problems and giftedness from problems associated with learning English as a second language (ESL) or other linguistic differences, being in the process of acculturation to the mainstream Anglo school culture, or lacking educational experiences because of impoverished home environments. The following sections discuss characteristics that may be associated with students from diverse backgrounds. However, it is important to emphasize that the following descriptions of diverse students are not stereotypical of these students' overall personal characteristics. Regardless of the cultural background from which students come, each should be regarded as an individual possessing unique traits that must be considered if adequate educational services are to be provided.

Culture is a dynamic process, full of changes. Students and their families from culturally and/or linguistically diverse backgrounds change as they come into contact with the mainstream culture and their community's culture. Glenn (1989) warns that "we need an approach to education that takes seriously the *lived culture* of children and their families, not the fiestas and folklore that had meaning for their grandparents but are not part of the lives of families coming to terms with the losses and gains of immigration" (p. 779). Therefore, professionals must not assume that culture is an imprint that can be used with all individuals from that culture. To say that a child from Cuba lives the Cuban culture, thinks a certain way, and experiences a family structure particular to Cubans would be wrong. Given these cautions, the following sections outline characteristics that may place the student at risk for receiving appropriate educational services.

Language Characteristics

Many students from culturally diverse backgrounds have linguistic differences that affect their ability to succeed in an English-dominant school system. It is often critical to understand these linguistic differences so that professionals can accurately discriminate an actual language disorder from the natural progression of *second language acquisition* and acculturation. All aspects of language and speech development must be considered. These students often exhibit the usual problems associated with learning a second language, such as poor comprehension, limited vocabulary, grammatical and syntactical mistakes, and articulation difficulties (First, 1991; Winzer & Mazurek, 1994). Ambert (1982) discusses how the identification of a language problem in English could be explained by understanding aspects of the child's native language. Table 9.1 shows some examples.

There is evidence that many linguistically diverse students are identified as having a language disorder, usually related to articulation, when in fact they are exhibiting normal characteristics of second language acquisition (Ortiz & Polyzoi, 1988). Table 9.2 outlines the stages of second language acquisition described by Clarke (1991) as cited in Winzer and Mazurek (1994). Therefore, it is critical for professionals working with students who are limited English proficient to know the differences between an actual language disorder and that of second language acquisition. A child who has a language disorder will evidence the problem in the native language as well. For example, a Hispanic child who has a problem with the omission of initial sounds will say "mida" for *comida* (food) or "anjo" for *banjo* (bathroom). Assessing students in their native language becomes a critical component of a culturally responsive educational process.

Furthermore, Cummins (1985) states that students learning a second language learn basic interpersonal communication skills (BICS) more easily than cogni-

Table 9.1
Examples of Limited English Proficient Students' Language Differences

Language Area	Example
Phonology	A Hispanic child may say "choo" for the English word *shoe*, because the *sh* sound is not found in Spanish.
Semantics	When shown a picture of an umbrella and asked to tell the teacher what you use it for, a Haitian child might state that it is used for the sun. In Haiti, the meaning or use of an umbrella is for protection from both the intense tropical sun and the rain.
Morphology	Chinese children indicate plural by placing a number in front of the noun. Therefore, a child who is asked to tell the teacher how many arms and legs he has, may respond by saying "two arm" and "two leg."
Syntax	In Spanish, an adjective follows a noun it is describing. Therefore, a child who comments on the teacher's dress as being pretty may say "the dress pretty."

Source: From "The Identification of LEP Children with Special Needs," by A. N. Ambert, 1982, *Bilingual Journal*, 7(1).

tive/academic language proficiency (CALPS). Social language usually develops within 2 years; however, cognitive and academic language could take up to 5 to 7 years to learn, requiring extended instruction in the student's native language.

Additionally, students who speak with a *nonstandard dialect,* but are competent in English frequently are discriminated against by professionals and peers (Gollnick & Chinn, 1998; Manning & Baruth, 2000; Salend, 1998). For example, it is estimated that between 80% and 90% of African-Americans in the United States use some form of black English (Smitherman, 1985) or Ebonics (Schnaiberg, 1997). Anokye (1997) believes that African American Vernacular English (AAVE) is a valid language that is not inferior but simply linguistically different, like other dialects. Chicano, Puerto Rican, and African-American students with nonstandard English dialects might be considered inferior by classmates and teachers. Teachers may have negative attitudes toward students and lowered expectations of these students' linguistic abilities (Anokye, 1997; Harry, 1992). This comes at a time when the use of nonstandard English dialect among the youth culture is becoming more popular (Salend, 1998). Many may be referred to special education merely because the professionals believe that nonstandard English dialects convey an inability to function in a mainstream classroom. Professionals should respect these students and encourage bidialectal use of language, teaching students when to use standard English and when to use other dialects (Anokye, 1997; Gollnick & Chinn, 1998; Salend, 1998).

Table 9.2
The Stages of Second Language Acquisition

Stage 1: Early Phase (Preproduction)

- May make contact with another child in the group.
- May show a silent period but use nonverbal gestures to indicate meaning, particularly needs, dislikes, and likes.
- Watches other children and may repeat words and phrases.
- May join others in a repetitive story or song.
- Responds to actions of songs.

Stage 2: Early Production, Emergence of Speech

- Starts to name other objects and other children; uses single verbs such as *come, look, go,* and adverbs such as *here* and *there.*
- Begins to put words together into phrases such as "Where find it?" or "Me put it."
- Enjoys sharing activities with children who speak a common language.
- May choose to speak only in the first language.
- Responds to stories, poems, and rhymes in English.

Stage 3: Familiarity with English

- Shows confidence in using English.
- Shows ability to move between the first and the second language.
- Can join conversations in English with peers.
- Shows confidence in taking part in small groups with staff and other children.
- Begins to sort out small details, such as he and she distinctions.
- More interested in communicating meaning than in grammatical correctness.
- Understands more English than he or she uses.
- Expands vocabulary for naming objects and events; begins to describe in more detail, such as by color, size, and quantity; uses simple adverbs.
- Shows confidence in initiating interaction.
- Continues to rely on support and friends.

Stage 4: Becoming Confident in English

- Shows great confidence in using English in most social situations; enjoys having fun with language.
- Has growing command of the grammatical system of English, including complex verbal meanings and more complex sentence structures.
- Uses pronunciation very like that of a native speaker.
- Has an extensive vocabulary.
- Continues to use own first language in groups.

Source: From *Special Education in Multicultural Contexts* (p. 360) by M. Winzer and K. Mazurek, 1994, Upper Saddle River, NJ: Merrill/Prentice Hall. Reprinted by permission.

Cultural Characteristics

Various learning and behavioral characteristics associated with students from culturally diverse populations are provided in this section. In general, professionals should avoid negative stereotypes or overgeneralizations when considering this information. There is, however, sufficient literature to support the differences in children's learning and behavioral styles, depending on their socioeconomic backgrounds and the individual child's cultural dominance.

Learning Styles.   Many authors have written about the diverse learning styles of students. Although no particular style fits a particular cultural group, it is important to know that students may need multiple approaches to learning. In particular, students from multicultural backgrounds may require special attention to matching the teaching style with their individual learning styles (Irving & York, 1995). According to Salend (1998), dimensions of learning styles instruction include the following:

◆ Environmental considerations such as background noise levels, lighting, temperature, and seating arrangements.
◆ Emotional considerations such as individual levels of motivation, persistence, conformity, responsibility, and need for structure.
◆ Grouping considerations such as learning alone or in groups, and with or without adults present.
◆ Physical considerations such as learning modality preferences, time of day, and need for food, drink, and mobility while learning.
◆ Psychological considerations such as approaching a task globally or analytically.

Salend (1998) described high-context cultures as those in which cooperation is encouraged, time schedules are flexible, and less authoritarian approaches are emphasized. In a low-context culture, competition, individualization, and strict adherence to time are the norm.

The current Anglo middle-class culture of schools must be flexible enough to accommodate the diverse learning styles of all students, including students from diverse cultures. Alternative learning environments have been recommended for culturally diverse students (Cuban, 1989; Fradd & Weismantel, 1989; Gilbert & Gay, 1985; Gollnick & Chinn, 1998; Salend, 1998; Westby & Rouse, 1985). Classroom environments should include activities that are group negotiated, controlled, noncompetitive, and relatively unrestricted in terms of time. Activities that actively involve students in the learning process—such as field trips, art projects, experience stories, and pretend play—would provide a better match for the needs of high-context learners.

The learning styles of students also have been described as falling into two areas: (1) *field-sensitive* or *field-dependent behavior* and (2) *field-independent behavior* (Castañeda & Gray, 1974; Gollnick & Chinn, 1998). Field-sensitive learners are concerned with social environment. They react to support or doubt from others, prefer more personal relationships with teachers, and work cooperatively with others. Field-independent learners are task oriented, more independent of external judgment, prefer formal relationships with teachers, and work independently and for individual recognition.

For students who evidence field-dependent behaviors, teaching should more closely relate to a personalized and humanized curriculum that emphasizes the interests and experiences of the students. Teachers should display physical and verbal expressions of approval and warmth together with providing lessons that encourage cooperation, informal class discussions, and the development of group feelings. A balance between both field-independent and field-dependent curricula should be maintained by professionals when working with students from diverse cultural and linguistic backgrounds. *However, educators must realize that no two students are alike and, therefore, each educational program must be based on individual student needs rather than on stereotyped learning styles.*

Behavioral Styles. Culturally and linguistically different students are often referred to special education because of certain behavioral characteristics that appear abnormal in U.S. classrooms (Hoover & Collier, 1985, 1991; Ishii-Jordan, 1997; McIntyre, 1999). However, the behaviors exhibited by students from different cultures may be culturally appropriate in their native culture or may be normal reactions in the process of adjusting to culture shock or acquiring a second language.

Uri, a newly arrived 15-year-old Chechen student, has been referred to the school psychologist for counseling. His teacher describes Uri as severely withdrawn, not making eye contact or speaking to her when she talks to him. She is concerned that Uri may be unable to survive in the mainstream classroom. The school psychologist contacts the social worker for the state Department of Human Resources. Uri was recently placed in foster care. Before his arrival in the United States, he had been living in a refugee camp with other Chechen orphan children. Although Uri's records did not clearly state his history, it was suspected that Uri had been traumatized by the war and was experiencing post-traumatic stress disorder. He arrived severely malnourished and with little if any educational experience.

An interactive team will need to collaborate with people who have recently immigrated from Chechnya to obtain information that might provide them with some insight into Uri's withdrawn behavior. Providing Uri with a school buddy and contacting a local college student who studied Russian and Chechen to volunteer to work with Uri a few hours a week might reduce Uri's anxiety and resistance to the school environment. Careful follow-up of Uri's behavior in the classroom and close interactions with Uri's foster parents should be carried out by all team members. If his behavior does not change after school counseling and tutoring intervention programs have been implemented in the general education classroom, a referral would be warranted.

Professionals working with culturally diverse students must obtain information about the conditions in which these students have lived. Many abnormal behaviors, including withdrawal, defensiveness, disorganization, and aggression, may be attributed to various sociocultural influences (Hoover & Collier, 1985; Ishii-Jordan, 1997; McIntyre, 1999). In 1993, the United Nations Children's Fund (UNICEF) estimated that "10 million children worldwide suffer psychological trauma from wars," (Boyden, 1993, p. 122). Students adjusting to being refugees of war-torn countries and entering a new culture will most probably experience some degree of social trauma and emotional problems (DeBlassie & Franco, 1983; Lynch & Hanson, 1998), often described as post-traumatic stress disorders (Carlin & Sokoloff, 1985).   Working closely with family members, the team can begin to ameliorate the impact of culture shock often associated with immigration (Foner, 1997; Lynch & Hanson, 1998). Interactive teams also can carefully conduct functional behavioral analyses over time to separate the more subtle behaviors of second language acquisition and cultural adjustment from behaviors related to emotional problems (Fradd, Barona, & Santos de Barona, 1989; Ishii-Jordan, 1997; McIntyre, 1999).

Socioeconomic Characteristics

Some culturally and linguistically diverse students who have had extensive training in both public and private schools are from middle-class or upper-class families. A large percentage of culturally and linguistically diverse students come from poor homes and have had little preparation for school (Gollnick & Chinn, 1998; Winzer & Mazurek, 1994). Although the poverty rate had decreased by the end of the 1990s, the child poverty rate remained significantly higher than the rates for working-age adults and the elderly (U.S. Census Bureau, 1999). Children continue to represent a large share of the poor population (39%) even though they were only about 26% of the total population and there is an increase of children who now fall under the "extreme poverty" line (living below half of the poverty line) (Children's Defense Fund, 1999). In 1998 of the 34.5 million people who were below the poverty level, 45.8% were white, non-Hispanics; 22.2% were white, Hispanics; 26.4% were blacks; and 5.6% were other races, making whites the largest group of poor in the United States (U.S. Census Bureau, 1999). Table 9.3 illustrates the impact of child poverty on America.

Furthermore, it is estimated that more than 1 million children are homeless (Linehan, 1992; O'Connor, 1989) and about 28% of the homeless students are not attending school (Pear, 1991). "Half of the homeless are now families, and one-third of the residents of homeless shelters are children" (Gollnick & Chinn, 1998, p. 46). These students suffer from poor health, have no transportation to school, and do not retain important records and forms for school files. Many poor and culturally different students have been placed in special education or have dropped out of school (Gollnick & Chinn, 1998; Ortiz & Garcia, 1988; Salend, 1998). Dropout rates for migrant students are estimated between 45% and 57%, and between 40% and 50% for rural students (Grossman, 1995). For special edu-

Table 9.3
Impact of Poverty on America's Children

Poverty matters profoundly to the 14.5 million U.S. children—more than one in every five—who live below poverty line.

- Poor children's troubles include increased risk of stunted growth, anemia, repeated years of schooling, lower test scores, and less education, as well as lower wages and lower earnings in their adult years.

- Poverty is a greater risk to children's overall health status than is living in a single parent family.

- A baby born poor is less likely to survive to its first birthday than a baby born to an unwed mother, a high school dropout, or a mother who smoked during pregnancy.

- Poverty puts children at a greater risk of falling behind in school than does living in a single parent home or being born to teenage parents.

- Reasons for poor children's problems appear to include their families' inability to afford adequate housing, nutritious food, or adequate child care, as well as lead poisoning, limited learning opportunities at home, and severe emotional stress and family breakup caused by economic strains on the parents.

Source: From Arloc Sherman, *Poverty Matters: The Cost of Child Poverty in America* (p. 1). Washington, DC: Children's Defense Fund, 1998. Reprinted by permission.

cation students it is estimated that the dropout rate is 50% higher than the average 25% rate for all students in the United States. The highest dropout rates for ethnically diverse students are for Hispanic students at over 40% and Native Americans at over 48% (Grossman, 1995).

Some professionals view the lack of achievement by poor students as a problem inherent in the student, and they often assume that the families have failed to prepare their children for school and do not teach them the value of education (Cuban, 1989; Manning & Baruth, 2000). Teachers may fail to recognize that economic differences affect cognitive and learning styles of students, causing them to respond differently to instruction (Gollnick & Chinn, 1998; Ortiz & Garcia, 1988). Further, studies have shown that teachers pay more attention to students who are attractive, well dressed, and well behaved, whereas they may ignore or discriminate against students who may have unwashed and worn clothing or who are not so well groomed (Harry, 1992). Incidences of racism still exist in schools. Murray and Clark (1990) identified the following eight patterns of racism in school: hostile and insensitive acts toward others; bias in the use of punishment; bias in giving attention to students; bias in curriculum materials; inequality in the amount of instruction; bias in attitudes toward students; failure to employ educational professionals from various cultural backgrounds; and denial of racist acts. Obviously, the attitudes of educators must change if students from poor environments and from culturally and linguistically diverse backgrounds are to survive in school.

Cuban (1989) provides an alternative way to frame the problem of poor and at-risk students in schools today. He states that the reason students fail in school is that the school culture ignores and devalues the students' own cultural backgrounds and seldom adapts to students' individual differences. Cuban further states that "instead, schools seek uniformity, and departures from the norm in achievement and behavior are defined as problems. Social, racial, and ethnic discrimination are embedded in the routine practices of schools and districts" (p. 781).

The need for reforming schools to accommodate the special needs of students from poor and culturally diverse populations is urgent. Around the nation many school leaders are recognizing the need for more family and community input, teacher-run schools, alternative schools, dropout prevention programs, and other innovative ways to adapt to the changing school population. Manning and Baruth (2000) and Bennett (1999) provide examples of promising practices in multicultural education, including suggestions for effective curriculum development, assessment alternatives, community and family programs, and instructional practices. Additionally, Slavin and Fashola (1998) outline the most recent proven and promising practices for educational programs in America. Innovative programs are crucial to the success of culturally and linguistically diverse students in today's schools.

MEETING EDUCATIONAL NEEDS

A major function of the team serving students from culturally and linguistically diverse backgrounds is to prepare these students for acculturation to the mainstream American culture without unwarranted stripping away of their linguistic and cultural characteristics. Many researchers believe that children should strive to develop bicultural competence by having the ability, the volition, and the capacity to negotiate comfortably two sets of cultural assumptions, patterns, beliefs, and behaviors (Gollnick & Chinn, 1998; Rotheram-Borus, 1993; Winzer & Mazurek, 1994). Children who comfortably "code-switch" between the home dialect on the playground and standard English in the classroom are practicing bicultural competence. Each member of the interactive team must work cooperatively to assess and develop intervention programs that prepare students for their roles in their native community and in the larger mainstream communities. The educational needs of students from culturally and linguistically diverse backgrounds are complex in the areas of service delivery options, assessment, program design, and teacher competencies. The following section addresses these needs.

Service Delivery Options

Various service delivery models are being used with students from culturally and linguistically diverse backgrounds. Most schools are providing students who are significantly limited English proficient (LEP) with alternative programs such as bilingual education (use of native language and English) or *English to speakers of other languages* (ESOL) (use of English only). Although very controversial, bilingual education programs have been criticized as holding students back from learning English and some research indicates that students taught in an English-only immersion program perform academically better than students in a transitional program (Porter, 1997). Others report successful gains in English language and academic skills with bilingual programs (Baca, 1998; Gollnick & Chinn, 1998). However, if the LEP student evidences learning problems warranting special education, a combination of language and special education services must be provided. Preferably ESOL and special education services should be provided using a consultant teacher assistance model within an inclusive general education classroom.

Perhaps the most important issue is to find a set of program components that works well in a given unique community or school (August & Hakuta, 1997). Keeping a student in the general education classroom for the majority of his or her instruction is the goal for inclusion, and pull-out programs such as bilingual education, ESOL, or special education should be kept to a minimum (Walther-Thomas, Korinek, McLaughlin, & Williams, 2000). It is the responsibility of the transdisciplinary team to work collaboratively to provide integrated service for students in the inclusive classroom. Methods for successful inclusion have been described by Salend (1998), Gollnick and Chinn (1998), and Baca and Cervantes (1998).

Assessment and Curricular Design

The most startling effect of cultural and linguistic differences on children occurs when professionals assume that students from culturally and linguistically diverse backgrounds appear to be developmentally delayed, learning disabled, emotionally disabled, or mentally disabled (Artiles & Zamora-Duran, 1997; Harry, 1992, 1994; Harry & Anderson, 1994; Heller et al., 1982; MacMillan & Reschly, 1998; Oswald et al., 1999; Salend, 1998). As mentioned previously, overrepresentation of culturally and linguistically diverse students in special education has been reported extensively. The issues are complex and specifically involve judgmental or biased decisions in the prereferral and referral process along with inappropriate assessment procedures (Artiles & Trent, 1994; Harry, 1994; MacMillan & Reschly, 1998).

Students from diverse backgrounds taking standardized tests are hindered by their native language, their lack of familiarity with the tests' content and with test-taking skills, and possible bias of test administrators when attempting to understand the social and cultural factors associated with the assessment process (Salend, 1998). The school psychologist is in a particularly sensitive position when it comes to the use of standardized assessment instruments to place students from culturally and linguistically diverse backgrounds in special programs. This professional, more than any other member of the team, needs to take special care in assessing students using procedures for measuring first and second language proficiency, examining achievement and intelligence testing in students' primary languages, and documenting students' language use in natural environments (Rueda, 1997).

By not understanding the cultural values of students and their families, professionals may erroneously assess students' abilities, refer them to special education, and implement special programs ineffectively. Conversely, a professional who believes a student's learning difficulties are related only to the child's adjustment to the dominant culture may underestimate a true learning problem. Teachers in general, special, ESOL, and bilingual education, together with speech and language professionals, and school psychologists must understand the cultural and linguistic context of the student's behavior and language when they observe the child to determine whether a true learning problem exists. Good observations of the child's behavior and native language in school and at home will help the professionals make these difficult decisions. Teamwork is critical in this process. Collaboration with families, communities, and related service professionals will be necessary for making an appropriate special education placement decision.

Many of the standardized tests are available in Spanish, but few are available in other languages, such as Haitian Creole, Russian, Vietnamese, Korean, Chinese, or Japanese. These languages are prevalent in schools with a high enrollment of culturally diverse students. Although the list in Table 9.4 is not exhaustive, it can guide professionals in providing a comprehensive battery of tests when assessing limited English proficient students. Readers are referred to recent publications (De Valenzuela & Cervantes, 1998; Hargett, 1998; Navarrett, Wilde, Nelson, Martinez, & Hargett, 1990; O'Malley & Pierce, 1996; Pierce & O'Malley, 1992; Rueda, 1997; Valdes & Figueroa, 1994) for further guidance in selecting assessment and curriculum instruments.

Additionally, other forms of evaluation are necessary with this population. Informal assessment procedures—including authentic assessment, portfolio assessment, sampling language, direct observation, anecdotal records, videotapes, and writing samples—have been extremely effective in providing the interactive team with information on the culturally diverse students' abilities (Gollnick & Chinn, 1998; Reschly, Tilly, & Grimes, 2000; Rueda, 1997). Procedures for collecting oral *language samples* usually involve tape-recording a sample of the student's conversations for 15 to 30 minutes on three occasions. A language sample provides the education professional with data on aspects of the student's language such as subject–verb agreement, past and future tenses, and vocabulary. It also samples the child's knowledge of various experiences within his or her own cultural and linguistic framework. Written language samples provide information about students' level of achievement in writing ability. Samples should be taken in both the students' own language and English. Analysis of the samples provides a basis both for assessment of students' skills and for planning instructional programs. Table 9.5 outlines several alternatives to traditional assessment that have been proposed for students from culturally and linguistically diverse backgrounds (Duran, 1989; Guerin & Maier, 1983; McLoughlin & Lewis, 1990; Rueda, 1997; Hargett, 1998; Navarrett et al., 1990; O'Malley & Pierce, 1996; Pierce & O'Malley, 1992; Valdes & Figueroa, 1994).

Table 9.4
Tests Frequently Used with Limited English Proficient Students

TEST AREA: LANGUAGE

Test Name	Reference
Boehm Test of Basic Concepts—3rd Ed.	Boehm (1999)
Dos Amigos Verbal Language Scales	Critchlow (1996)
Language Assessment Scales	DeAvila & Duncan (1990)
Pictorial Test of Bilingualism and Language Dominance	Nelson, Fellner, & Norrell (1975)
Test of Auditory Comprehension of Language —3rd Ed. (English/Spanish)	Carrow-Woolfolk (1985)
Test of Language Development—Primary (TOLD—P3)	Newcomer & Hammil (1996)
Woodcock Language Proficiency Battery	Woodcock (1991)

TEST AREA: ACADEMICS

Wide-Range Achievement Test—Revised	Jastak & Wilerson (1993)
Bateria Woodcock Psycho-Educativa en Español	Woodcock (1982)
Peabody Individual Achievement Test	Markwardt (1997)
Brigance Assessment of Basic Skills—Spanish Edition	Brigance (1983)

TEST AREA: INTELLIGENCE

Wechsler Intelligence Scale for Children—Revised	Wechsler (1974)
Bateria de Evaluación de Kaufman para Niños	Torrijos (1997)
Kaufman Assessment Battery for Children	Kaufman & Kaufman (1983)
System of Multicultural Pluralistic Assessment	Mercer & Lewis (1978)
Leiter International Performance Scale—Revised	Roid & Miller (1997)
Raven's Progressive Matrices	Court & Raven (1986)
Universal Nonverbal Intelligence Test	Bracken & McCallum (1998)

Table 9.5
Alternative Assessments Used with Limited English Proficient Students

Alternative Assessment Strategies	Description
Culture-Free/-Fair Tests	Measure aspects of growth presumed to be unrelated to culture. However, no test is completely culture-free.
Culture-Specific Tests	Measure knowledge and competence within a nondominant culture. Tests are limited in measuring school learning.
Test Translations	English-language tests translated into the student's dominant language. Translations do not remove the bias in the test items.
Pluralistic Assessment	Measures student's medical status, social performance, and learning potential normed on diverse students.
Adaptive Behavior Assessment	Measure student's ability to cope with social and cultural demands. Does not measure academic abilities.
Dynamic Assessment	Employs test-train-test procedures providing information on what instruction is needed for a student to acquire skills.
Curriculum-Based Assessment	Tests whether students have mastered material taught in the classroom curriculum and uses direct daily measurement of progress
Portfolio Assessment	Uses a continuous collection of student work, projects, essays, records of progress, and other demonstrations of accomplishments.

Instructional Strategies

A number of instructional strategies have been reported to be effective with students from culturally and linguistically diverse backgrounds (Adams & Hamm, 1991; Baca & Cervantes, 1998; Correa & Tulbert, 1991; Gollnick & Chinn, 1998; Manning & Baruth, 2000; Putnam, 1998; Salend, 1998; Voltz & Damiano-Lantz, 1993; Wigg, Freedman, & Secord, 1992; Winzer & Mazurek, 1994). The basic components for teaching culturally diverse students are the same components for teaching *all* students. Good instruction is good instruction for all students. Some interventions, however, work more effectively than others (Forness, Kavale, Blum, & Lloyd, 1997; Lloyd, Forness, & Kavale, 1998). According to these researchers, interventions that were not very effective included special class placement, perceptual training, the Feingold diet, modality-based instruction, and social skills training. Interventions that may be effective are psychotropic drugs, class size, psycholinguistic training, peer tutoring, computer-assisted instruction, and stimulant drugs. The interventions that were found to be most effective included early intervention, formative evaluation, cognitive-behavioral modification, direct instruction, behavior modification, reading comprehension instruction, and mnemonic training. Additionally, interventions with culturally and linguistically diverse students should (1) match the learning style of the student, (2) provide opportunity for the student to use native and English language skills, (3) include the student's native heritage and culture as a context for designing curricula, (4) promote confidence and elevate self-esteem in the student, (5) encourage student-to-student interactions, and (6) prepare the student for inclusion into the dominant school culture.

Overall, teachers need to employ reciprocal interaction teaching models that foster empowerment and learning through verbal and written exchanges between families, students, and teachers, and among students (Cummins, 1985; Harry, Kalyanpur, & Day, 1999). Fradd and Bermudez (1991) suggest that teachers use the POWER model, which includes process-oriented instruction, whole language, cooperative learning, cognitive mapping, and reading and writing across the curriculum.

The *whole-language approach* has influenced language instruction for LEP students (Fradd et al., 1989; Freeman & Freeman, 1993). The whole-language approach provides the student with language arts activities that focus on the students' language and experiences in and out of school to increase their reading and writing abilities (Weaver, 1991). This approach also gives non-English-speaking students reading and language arts instruction while they are developing the background to understand and apply formal language rules (Fradd et al., 1989). Students are encouraged to use all sensory modes to learn and appreciate language, including music and movement. Whole-language materials are being adapted for use with LEP students.

Additionally, strategies for teaching students with mild disabilities have potential application for students from culturally and linguistically diverse backgrounds. Numerous strategies have been used with students with mild disabilities, including direct instruction (Carnine, Silbert, & Kameenui, 1997; Gernsten & Keating, 1987; Morsink, Thomas, & Smith-Davis, 1987; Ornstein, 1987), peer tutoring (Maheady, Sacca, & Harper, 1988), and precision teaching (White & Haring, 1976). Some of these strategies will be discussed in Chapter 11, as they relate to working with students with mild disabilities. Because it is beyond the scope of this chapter to describe instructional strategies in detail, readers are referred to the referenced publications for further guidance in implementing the strategies. However, two strategies in particular merit discussion in view of their applicability to working with culturally diverse students. They are *cooperative learning* (Johnson & Johnson, 1999; Putnam, 1998; Slavin, 1999) and *learning strategies* (Deshler, Schumaker, & Harris, 1999).

Cooperative Learning.   Cooperative learning involves students helping one another in small-group instruction and provides an opportunity for students to develop academic as well as social skills. The major elements of cooperative learning include positive interdependence, individual accountability, collaborative skills, and face-to-face interactions (Johnson & Johnson, 1999; Slavin, 1999). To implement cooperative learning structures, teachers should arrange classrooms to facilitate cooperation, assign two to six students to a group, and plan an instructional activity. Students are responsible for working cooperatively in groups to acquire the skills of the activity assigned.

Students can be evaluated on both an individual and group basis for successful completion of assignments. For example, if an educator wants LEP students to learn how to use English vocabulary words needed for ordering at a fast-food restaurant, the following procedures could be implemented:

1. Assign a set of words for each member of the group to define and learn to pronounce.
2. Get the small groups together to share and discuss the words.
3. Allow the students to take a group quiz, where they can interact and review the words.
4. Provide an individual quiz for students to reinforce individual accountability.
5. Take the students to a fast-food restaurant to practice their new vocabulary words.

Cooperative learning improves the students' motivation and raises self-esteem, while freeing the teacher from direct instruction, drill, and classroom management. Additionally, for LEP students, interaction with English-speaking group peers enhances language development and socialization. Cooperative learning is also a successful tool for promoting social relations between culturally different students (Adams & Hamm, 1991). Readers should refer to Slavin (1999), Manning and Lucking (1991, 1993), and Whittaker (1991) for more detailed guidelines on implementing cooperative learning activities.

Learning Strategies.   Learning strategies enable students to meet immediate academic requirements successfully and to generalize those skills to novel situations and settings. Examples of learning strategies developed at the University of Kansas (Deshler et al., 1999) include paraphrasing, sentence writing, error monitoring, self-questioning, and paragraph and theme writing. For example, the use of a learning strategy for spelling words, reported by Graham and Freeman (1986), can be adapted for working with LEP students who are learning to spell English words associated with a basic anatomy lesson. The words the students would need to spell are associated with body organs, such as *stomach, heart, lungs, brain,* and *kidney.* The following procedures would be implemented:

1. Teach the student to say the word.
2. Write and say the word.
3. Check the word.

4. Trace and say the word.

5. Write the word from memory.

Pictures or mnemonics can be used to facilitate the students' learning of the body organ words. Learning strategies have been shown to improve academic achievement in mathematics, reading, writing, and spelling in students who had been low achieving (Deshler et al., 1999). The strategies appear to be excellent learning tools for students from culturally and linguistically diverse backgrounds, as well.

In general, the instructional strategies discussed have been limited to application with students with mild disabilities. However, many of the strategies have been adapted for use with students from culturally and linguistically diverse backgrounds. Some effective instructional practices generated for these students are outlined in Figure 9.1.

---

1. Allow students to develop ownership in learning by involving them in classroom management (Voltz & Damiano-Lantz, 1993).

2. Use cultural referents and student experiences during instruction (Salend, 1998).

3. Facilitate understanding of new words and phrases through use of rephrasing, pictorials, and pantomimes, and by writing key words (Salend, 1998).

4. Use storytelling to encourage use of oral language skills (Maldonado-Colon, 1990).

5. Develop a reward system, using group or companion contingencies (Echevarria-Ratleff & Graff, 1988).

6. Present daily rehearsal of student expectations (Fradd & Tikunoff, 1987).

7. Offer a buddy or peer tutorial system (Salend, 1998).

8. Use an assortment of culturally appropriate teaching materials (Manning & Baruth, 2000).

9. Use children's literature that represents cultural diversity (e.g., ethnic groups, gender differences, diverse family structures, gay & lesbian families) (Manning & Baruth, 2000).

10. Arrange a variety of high-context teaching activities (e.g., field trips, cooking activities, plays) (Westby & Rouse, 1985).

11. Develop cultural reciprocity by involving families in educational programs and using community, family, and home cultural information to promote engagement in instructional tasks (Correa & Tulbert, 1992; Harry et al., 1999).

12. Use active learning techniques by which students can collaboratively share alliances (Adams & Hamm, 1991; Fradd & Bermudez, 1998).

13. Develop student's language competence through use of art forms, drama, simulations, role plays, music, and games (Salend, 1998).

Figure 9.1
Classroom interventions successful with LEP students in inclusive classrooms.

Instructional strategies are effective tools for the educator involved with students from culturally and linguistically diverse backgrounds. Additionally, today's educator must incorporate the concept of multicultural education into all aspects of the classroom curriculum. Banks (1994a, 1994b) and Bennett (1999) provided excellent texts for implementing a multicultural curriculum that encourages understanding and respect of *all* students.

Selecting the appropriate curricula to meet the diverse needs of all students in today's classrooms remains a critical aspect of the educator's responsibility. Unfortunately, a paucity of curriculum materials is available for students from culturally and linguistically diverse backgrounds (Manning & Baruth, 2000; Salend, 1998). By collaborating with other team members, the job of designing effective instruction for students from diverse backgrounds becomes less arduous.

ROLES OF PROFESSIONALS INVOLVED WITH STUDENTS FROM CULTURALLY AND LINGUISTICALLY DIVERSE BACKGROUNDS

Professionals involved with educating students from culturally diverse backgrounds must understand the complex aspects of cultural influences on the student and the family. Often interactive teaming revolves around the general education teacher and the bilingual education teacher. However, for students with limited English proficiency the roles of the school psychologist and the speech-language therapist become critical, and if the student evidences any potential learning or behavioral problems, the special education professional must be involved.

The general roles of professionals were outlined in Chapter 4. Some specialized contributions of team members who work with students from culturally and linguistically diverse backgrounds are presented in Table 9.6.

◇ ◇

Application

In the vignette at the beginning of the chapter, Ms. Harris, Helena's teacher, had decided that the best way to cope with a limited English proficient student was to not make many demands on her and refer her to special education. Unfortunately, for Helena to succeed in an inclusive educational environment, she will eventually need to attend to large-group instruction and stay on task. Providing her with individual worksheets will not prepare her for the next environment, fifth grade. The following solution to this problem exemplifies the interactive team approach.

Interactive Team Plan for Improving Helena's Attention to Task

The general education teacher, Ms. Harris, arranges a series of cooperative planning meetings. She asks each specialist to outline the concerns and needs for Helena's success in an inclusive classroom. Ms. Harris takes on the role of services

Table 9.6
Roles of Professionals and Others Involved with Culturally and Linguistically Diverse Students

Personnel	Direct Service Provider	Team Member
Bilingual Educator	• Assess language development in student's native language. • Provide academic instruction using native and English language, and native heritage/cultural context. • Communicate with family in native language or with interpreters.	• Serve as culture broker. • Conduct staff development on bilingualism/biculturalism. • Collaborate on bilingual techniques with other team members. • Integrate regular and special education curriculum into bilingual program.
Teacher of English to Speakers of Other Languages (ESOL)	• Instruct in English as a second language, minimizing the pull-out approach. • Communicate with family in native language or with interpreters.	• Serve as culture broker. • Conduct staff development on factors affecting second language acquisition and language development. • Consult with team members on effective techniques for teaching student English.
General Educator	• Conduct curriculum-based assessment to develop appropriate academic program. • Provide peer tutoring or a buddy system for adjustment into classroom. • Provide intervention that includes the student's cultural experiences. • Collect data and make referrals to bilingual education or special education when necessary.	• Integrate bilingual and/or special education techniques into general academic program. • Report on progress with inclusion in all areas including social/emotional adjustment. • Use native languages aides, volunteers, parents to assist in classroom program. • Integrate a multicultural education program into the daily curriculum that promotes an understanding and respect for diversity and work closely with librarian or media specialist to ensure a vast array of multicultural literature.
Special Educator	• Conduct nondiscriminatory assessment in the areas of achievement and language. • Communicate cross-culturally with student and family. • Adapt teaching materials according to the needs of student. • Develop IEP in cooperation with general and bilingual educators. • Role release to general and bilingual educators effective teaching strategies including direct instruction, cooperative learning, learning strategies, and behavior management techniques.	• Serve as culture broker. • Accept shared responsibilities with bilingual/ESOL/general educators. • Interpret assessment results. • Conduct staff development on special education and remediation techniques

Table 9.6, *continued*

Personnel	Direct Service Provider	Team Member
Title 1 Teacher	• Instruct young children who qualify for Title 1 federal funds (low SES, LEP).	• Share instruction techniques with special educator. • Prepare team for student's entry into general education. • Serve as culture broker.
Migrant Teacher	• Provide instruction that prepares the child for inclusion in the general education curriculum. • Visit migrant camps or communities and communicate with family.	• Provide team with information on migrant conditions of the family. • Maintain records with the Migrant Students Record Transfer System (MSRTS) • Encourage alternative methods of earning credits toward graduation. • Provide on-site tutoring programs. • Serve as culture broker.
School Psychologist	• Conduct nondiscriminatory assessment in the areas of intelligence/achievement. • Maintain current cumulative records on students.	• Interpret test results. • Conduct staff development on working with culturally diverse families. • Explain all school procedures, policies, legal mandates. • Participate in prereferral process.
Speech-Language Therapist	• Conduct assessment in both English and native language in the areas of language and speech development. • Conduct individual, group, or integrated therapy with students.	• Role release therapy techniques that can be integrated into all educational programs. • Interpret test results.
Guidance Counselor/ Social Worker	• Assess student in the areas of adaptive behavior and vocational planning. • Provide individual or group therapy sessions to work on self-concept and self-esteem. • Communicate with families. • Establish families' concerns, needs, and priorities.	• Interpret results of testing and progress in counseling sessions. • Make home visits and report findings of family status. • Serve as liaison with other non-school agencies.

Table 9.6, *continued*

Personnel	Direct Service Provider	Team Member
Administrator	• Manage all aspects of school programs. • Assure that all programs are meeting the unique needs of LEP students. • Evaluate staff performance.	• Provide team with guidance on legal and district-wide policies and procedures. • Serve as meeting manager. • Support team in acquiring materials and resources necessary to deliver quality services. • Be available to meet with families and parent groups. • Encourage a multicultural approach to all aspects of school life.
Parents/ Family Members	• Support school programs and assist in enhancing the child's development of English. • Support bicultural instruction.	• Provide team with information on language and cultural background. • Support parent organizations and parent education efforts by the school or community.

coordinator by taking charge of coordinating all information shared by the interactive team.

Mrs. Garcia, the ESOL teacher, is invited to visit Ms. Harris's classroom and make an anecdotal record of Helena's conduct. Both share their concern that Helena is having difficulty adjusting to the school environment and is behaving much like a child who does not understand the language and is in the initial stages of second language acquisition. They decide to use the prereferral team at the school, which includes the school psychologist, speech-language therapist, social worker, and the special education teacher for suggesting instructional and behavioral strategies to use in the fourth-grade classroom. Both Ms. Harris and Mrs. Garcia agree that Helena should be pulled out from the classroom only if necessary for ESOL instruction. In addition, Mrs. Garcia will begin to visit Helena's classroom and integrate her instruction into Helena's daily classroom routine. Ms. Harris has also agreed to observe other limited English proficient students, and to get ideas for classroom adaptations.

Ms. Harris contacts the school psychologist, the social worker, the special education teacher, and the speech-language therapist. These professionals also visit Helena's classroom and collect analysis data on Helena's academic and behavioral performance. Each professional graphs those data and presents them at the prereferral meeting arranged by Ms. Harris. The speech-language therapist assesses Helena's ability to understand both Spanish and English.

During the prereferral meeting, all team members are present. Additionally, Helena's parents and an interpreter attend. The special education teacher provides the team with suggestions for instructional strategies to use with Helena and a behavior management program that uses social praise as a reinforcer. All team members agree to participate in Helena's intervention programs to the degree appropriate. Everyone agrees that Helena would benefit from a buddy-system program with another student.

Each team member speaks empathetically with the parents about Helena. Her parents are made to feel comfortable and are asked throughout the meeting if they have any questions or suggestions. They help the team understand the experiences they had when they immigrated to the United States from El Salvador and explain Helena's previous school experiences. Helena's father says his daughter likes to listen to music and that music seems to bring her out socially. The father will bring a few of Helena's favorite cassettes to school, so they can be shared with the other students and be available to Helena when she wants some time away from the stresses of the classroom.

Mrs. Garcia agrees to give Ms. Harris some strategies that can be integrated into the inclusive classroom. She will visit Helena in the classroom twice a week and facilitate the instructional strategies. The school psychologist is interested in

Table 9.7
Interactive Team Plan for Helena

1. Mrs. Garcia, the ESOL teacher, will work closely with Ms. Harris to assist in developing appropriate adaptations to Helena's instruction. Mrs. Garcia will meet weekly with Ms. Harris to integrate the teaching units into Helena's ESOL instruction.

2. Ms. Harris, Mrs. Garcia, and the school psychologist will make a home visit. They will gather information on Helena's educational history in El Salvador and understand the families' concerns, priorities, and needs for Helena's education. They will introduce the family to other Hispanic families in the community and involve the community outreach program to make sure that Helena and her family receive the support they need.

3. Ms. Harris will begin to embed multicultural instruction into her daily teaching units. She will have a unit on families and talk to the children about differences related to language and the Hispanic culture. She will have students do book reports on Hispanics and other ethnic groups to teach them about cultural acceptance and friendships. Each student will conduct a home interview to understand their own cultural heritage. If Helena's family is comfortable with the idea, she will invite them to come to class to talk (with the use of an interpreter) about El Salvador.

4. Ms. Harris will work with the prereferral team to outline specific strategies for improving Helena's academic as well as behavioral outcomes. She will also increase opportunities to read aloud to the students, and have Helena participate in small-group speaking situations and choral speaking with audiotaped books and songs. She will reduce worksheet work and encourage cooperative learning activities.

5. Mrs. Garcia will administer an "interest inventory" to learn more about Helena's interests, likes, and dislikes, then share those results with Ms. Harris and the prereferral team to plan instruction and communication accordingly.

6. The principal at the school will provide inservice training (and other training in diversity) for teachers by Latino experts from the community who know Latinos' cultural backgrounds, strengths, and challenges.

Helena's adjustment to the "culture shock" of moving to the United States and offers to spend 15 minutes once a week with Helena, observing her adjustment to school. The family also agrees to participate in the plan and is given simple and functional ideas for home intervention.

The special education teacher will serve as a consultant to the team. If Helena is officially placed in special education, the teacher will take a more active role in intervention. Objectives are developed during the meeting, and various team members share responsibility for conducting the interventions outlined. The chart in Table 9.7 provides an overview of the various strategies that are implemented on behalf of Helena and her family. Team members agree to reconvene within 6 weeks to discuss Helena's progress. If progress is not seen within the 6 weeks, a formal referral to special education will be made.

◊ ◊

SUMMARY

Culture often plays a significant role in educators' differential treatment of students in students' interaction with peers and adults. Professional expectations for various groups or types of students, definitions of what constitutes "appropriate," and tolerable behaviors and reactions to student behaviors are often based on cultural beliefs, values, and norms. When students' expressed values, attitudes, and behaviors are different from those of the profession in charge, these differences are often judged to be deficits, problems, or deviance rather than differences (Walther-Thomas et al., 2000).

The data on the prevalence of students from linguistically and culturally diverse backgrounds who are at risk for school failure indicate that school personnel must acquire the skills necessary to understand and work with this population. Interactive teaming is the most efficient way to meet the special needs of these students.

By consulting and collaborating with others on the team, school personnel can design educational programs that are sensitive to the students' cultural backgrounds and specific learning styles. This chapter has provided an overview of what research shows are the best practices in working with students from diverse backgrounds. The major points discussed are as follows:

◆ Students from diverse backgrounds are a heterogeneous population, and negative stereotypes should be avoided when learning about cultural characteristics associated with their native cultures.

◆ Certain learning, behavioral, and socioeconomic characteristics related to students from diverse backgrounds place these students at risk for success in schools.

◆ A variety of service delivery options is available for students from diverse backgrounds. The goal, however, is to provide services that ensure inclusion into the general education program and protect the student from long-term placement in segregated programs.

◆ Comprehensive and nondiscriminatory assessment practices, involving both formal and informal procedures, will assist in deciding whether a student evidences a significant learning problem or evidences characteristics associated with second language acquisition and cultural assimilation.

◆ A variety of instructional strategies can be used in working with students from diverse backgrounds, including strategies developed for students with mild disabilities. Cooperative learning and learning strategies are two strategies that can be adapted to working with students from diverse backgrounds.

◆ The various roles of school personnel involved with students from diverse backgrounds are focused on enhancing students' use of English, providing a learning environment that promotes inclusion into the mainstream, developing confidence and self-esteem in students, and providing family involvement in a manner that is sensitive to the native culture.

ACTIVITIES

1. Play a cultural simulation game such as *BaFá BaFá* (Shirts, 1977). Help the class acknowledge the diverse feeling of interacting with a different culture. Transcribe their feelings on transparencies as they are discussed.

2. Facilitate a cultural journey (Lynch & Hanson, 1998). Ask students to describe their own culture, beliefs, traditions, foods, and holidays. Have students describe family stories depicting their families' experiences in the United States. Ask students if they have ever experienced discrimination due to their cultural background.

3. Conduct an informational interview with a professional who is involved in the educational programs of students from diverse cultural backgrounds. Use the guidelines provided in Chapter 4.

4. Tour a school program serving limited English proficient students. Observe the students' activities and schedules. Note if any special adaptations or curricula are being used. Observe any bilingual instruction occurring, and note the personnel who are proficient in two or more languages.

5. Volunteer in an after-school program for bilingual students, at-risk students, or immigrant adults. Note the characteristics of the students as related to their cultural backgrounds. Tutor non-English-speaking students in English. Find topics related to their culture to use as conversation warm-ups.

6. Obtain a language sample from a limited English proficient student. Consult with a speech-language therapist or a bilingual teacher regarding the gram-

matical language structures used by the student. Evaluate the child's proficiency in English.

7. Compile a resource file of materials for your classroom that promote multicultural education. Order catalogs that have multicultural educational materials such as books, dolls, crayons, and construction paper.

REFERENCES

Adams, D., & Hamm, M. (1991). Diversity gives schools infinite learning possibilities. *School Administrator, 48*(4), 20–22.

Ambert, A. (1982). The identification of LEP children with special needs. *Bilingual Journal, 7,* 17–22.

Anokye, A. D. (1997). A case of orality in the classroom. *The Clearing House, 70*(5), 229–231.

Artiles, A. J., & Trent, S. C. (1994). Overrepresentation of minority students in special education: A continuing debate. *The Journal of Special Education, 27*(4), 410–437.

Artiles, A. J., & Zamora-Duran, G. (1997). Disproportionate representation: A contentious and unresolved predicament. In A. J. Artiles & G. Zamora-Duran (Eds.), *Reducing disproportionate representation of culturally diverse students in special and gifted education* (pp. 1–6). Reston, VA: The Council for Exceptional Children.

August, D., & Hakuta, K. (1997). *Improving schools for language-minority children: A research agenda* [online]. Washington, DC: National Academy Press. Available: books.nap.edu/hal2/0309054974/gifmid/R1.gif.

Baca, L. (1998). Bilingualism and bilingual education. In L. Baca & H. Cervantes, *The bilingual special education interface* (3rd ed.), pp. 26–45. Upper Saddle River, NJ: Merrill/Prentice Hall.

Baca, L., & Cervantes, H. (1998). *The bilingual special education interface* (3rd ed.). Upper Saddle River, NJ: Merrill/Prentice Hall.

Banks, J. A. (1994a). *An introduction to multicultural education*. Boston: Allyn & Bacon.

Banks, J. A. (1994b). *Multiethnic education: Theory and practice* (3rd ed.). Boston: Allyn & Bacon.

Bennett, C. I. (1999). *Comprehensive multicultural education: Theory and practice* (4th ed.). Needham Heights, MA: Allyn & Bacon.

Boehm, A. E. (1999). *Boehm test of basic concepts—3rd edition*. San Antonio: Psychological Corporation.

Boyden, J. (1993). *Families: Celebration and hope in a world of change*. London: Gaia Books Limited.

Bracken, B., & McCallum, R. (1998). *Universal nonverbal intelligence test (UNIT)*. San Antonio, TX: The Psychological Corporation.

Brigance, A. H. (1983). *Brigance diagnostic assessment of basic skills, Spanish edition*. North Billerica, MA: Curriculum Associates.

Briscoe, D. B. (1991). Designing for diversity in school success: Capitalizing on culture. *Preventing School Failure, 36*(1), 13–18.

Carlin, J., & Sokoloff, B. (1985). Mental health treatment issues for Southeast Asian refugee children. In T. Owan (Ed.), *Southeast Asian mental health: Treatment, prevention, services, training, and research* (pp. 91–112). Washington, DC: U.S. Department of Health and Human Services.

Carnine, D., Silbert, J., & Kameenui, E. (1997). *Direct instruction reading* (3rd ed.). Upper Saddle River, NJ: Merrill/Prentice Hall.

Carrow-Woolfolk, E. (1985). *Test for auditory comprehension of language: 3rd Edition*. Chicago: DLM/Riverside Publishers.

Castañeda, A., & Gray, T. (1974). Bicognitive processes in multicultural education. *Educational Leadership, 32*(3), 203–207.

Children's Defense Fund. (1999). *Extreme child poverty rises by more than 400,000 in one year.* [Online]. Available: http://www.childrensdefense.org/release990822.html.

Clarke, P. (1991, May). Does your programme support the development of English as a second language? *Resource Newsletter of the FKA Multicultural Resource Center*, pp. 4–5.

Correa, V., & Tulbert, B. (1991). Teaching culturally diverse students. *Preventing School Failure, 35(3)*, 20–25.

Court, J. H., & Raven, J. (1986). *Manual for Raven's progressive matrices and vocabulary scales (section 2): Colored progressive matrices (1986 ed. with U.S. norms)*. London: Lewis.

Critchlow, D. C. (1996). *Dos amigos verbal language scale*. Novato, CA: Academic Therapy.

Cuban, L. (1989). The at-risk label and the problem of urban school reform. *Phi Delta Kappan, 10(70)*, 780–784, 799–801.

Cummins, J. (1985). *Bilingualism and special education: Issues in assessment and pedagogy*. San Diego: College-Hill.

DeAvila, E., & Duncan, S. E. (1990). *Language assessment scales*. Monterey, CA: CTB/McGraw Hill.

DeBlassie, R. R., & Franco, J. N. (1983). Psychological and educational assessment of bilingual children. In D. R. Omark & J. G. Erickson (Eds.), *The bilingual exceptional child* (pp. 55–68). Boston: College-Hill.

Deshler, D., Schumaker, J. B., & Harris, K. (1999). *Teaching every adolescent every day: Learning in diverse middle and high school classrooms (Advances in teaching and learning)*. Cambridge, MA: Brookline Books.

De Valenzuela, J. S., & Cervantes, H. (1998). Procedures and techniques for assessing the bilingual exceptional child. In L. Baca & H. Cervantes, *The bilingual special education interface* (pp. 169–178). Upper Saddle River, NJ: Merrill/Prentice Hall.

Dilworth-Anderson, P., Burton, L., & Johnson, B. (1993). Reframing theories for understanding race, ethnicity, and families. In P. G. Boss, W. J. Doherty, R. LaRoss, W. R. Schumm, & S. K. Steinmetz (Eds.), *Sourcebook of family theories and methods: A contextual approach* (pp. 627–649). New York: Plenum.

Duran, R. P. (1989). Assessment and instruction of at-risk Hispanic students. *Exceptional Children, 56(2)*, 154–159.

Echevarria-Ratleff, J., & Graff, V. L. (1988). California bilingual special education model sites (1984–1986): Programs and research. In A. Ortiz & B. A. Ramirez (Eds.), *Schools and the culturally diverse exceptional student: Promising practices and future directions* (pp. 104–111). Reston, VA: Council for Exceptional Children.

Figueroa, R. A., Fradd, S. H., & Correa, V. I. (1989). Bilingual special education and this special issue. *Exceptional Children, 56*, 174–178.

First, J. (1991). *The common school: Making the vision work for all children*. Boston: National Coalition of Advocates for Students.

Foner, N. (1997). The immigrant family: Cultural legacies and cultural changes. *International Migration Review, 31(4)*, 961–974.

Forness, S. R., Kavale, K. A., Blum, I. M., & Lloyd, J. W. (1997). Mega-analysis of meta-analyses: What works in special education and related services. *Teaching Exceptional Children, 29*, 4–9.

Fradd, S., Barona, A., & Santos de Barona, M. (1989). Implementing change and monitoring progress. In S. Fradd & M. J. Weismantel (Eds.), *Meeting the needs of culturally and linguistically different students: A handbook for educators* (pp. 63–105). Boston: College-Hill.

Fradd, S. H., & Bermudez, A. B. (1991). POWER: A process for meeting the instructional needs of handicapped language-minority students. *Teacher Education and Special Education, 14(1)*, 19–24.

Fradd, S., & Tikunoff, W. (1987). *Bilingual education and bilingual special education: A guide for administrators*. Boston: College-Hill.

Fradd, S., & Weismantel, M. J. (1989). *Meeting the needs of culturally and linguistically different students: A handbook for educators*. Boston: College-Hill.

Freeman, D. E., & Freeman, Y. S. (1993). Strategies for promoting the primary languages of all students. *Reading Teacher, 46*, 552–558.

Gernsten, R., & Keating, T. (1987). Long-term benefits from direct instruction. *Educational Leadership, 44(6)*, 28–31.

Gilbert, S. E., & Gay, G. (1985). Improving the success in school of poor black children. *Phi Delta Kappan, 67*, 133–137.

Glenn, C. L. (1989). Just schools for minority children. *Phi Delta Kappan, 10*(70), 777–779.

Gollnick, D. M., & Chinn, P. C. (1998). *Multicultural education in a pluralistic society* (5th ed.). Upper Saddle River, NJ: Merrill/Prentice Hall.

Graham, S., & Freeman, S. (1986). Strategy training and teacher-vs.-student controlled study conditions: Effects on LD students' spelling performance. *Learning Disability Quarterly, 9*, 15–21.

Grossman, H. (1995). *Special education in a diverse society*. Boston: Allyn & Bacon.

Guerin, G. R., & Maier, A. S. (1983). *Informal assessment in education*. Palo Alto, CA: Mayfield.

Hargett, G. R. (1998). *Assessment in ESL and bilingual education: A hot topics paper* [online]. Portland, OR: Northwest Regional Educational Laboratory's Comprehensive Center, Region X. Available: www.nwrac.org/pub/hot/assessment.html.

Harry, B. (1992). *Cultural diversity, families, and the special education system: Communication and empowerment*. New York: Teachers College Press.

Harry, B. (1994). *The disproportionate representation of minority students in special education: Theories and recommendations*. Alexandria, VA: National Association of State Directors of Special Education.

Harry, B., & Anderson, M. (1994). The disproportionate placement of African American males in special education programs: A critique of the process. *Journal of Negro Education, 63*, 602–619.

Harry, B., Kalyanpur, M., & Day, M. (1999). *Building cultural reciprocity with families: Case studies in special education*. Boston: Paul H. Brookes.

Heller, K. A., Holtzman, W. H., & Messick, S. (1982). New approaches to assessment and instruction. In K. A. Heller, W. K. Holtzman, & S. Messick (Eds.), *Placing children in special education: A strategy for equity* (pp. 92–117). Washington, DC: National Academy Press.

Hoover, J. J., & Collier, C. (1985). Referring culturally different children: Sociocultural considerations. *Academic Therapy, 20*, 503–509.

Hoover, J. J., & Collier, C. (1991). Meeting the needs of culturally and linguistically diverse exceptional learners: Prereferral to mainstreaming. *Teacher Education and Special Education, 14*(1), 30–34.

Irving, J. J., & York, E. D. (1995). Learning styles and culturally diverse students: A literature review. In J. A. Banks & C. A. McGee Banks (Eds.), *Handbook of research on multicultural education*. New York: Macmillan.

Ishii-Jordan, S. R. (1997). When behavior differences are not disorders. In A. J. Artiles & G. Zamora-Duran (Eds.), *Reducing disproportionate representation of culturally diverse students in special and gifted education* (pp. 27–46). Reston, VA: The Council for Exceptional Children.

Jastak, J. F., & Wilerson, G. S. (1993). *The wide range achievement test: Revised*. Wilmington, DE: Jastak Associates.

Johnson, D., & Johnson, R. (1999). *Learning together and alone: Cooperative, competitive, and individualistic learning*. Boston: Allyn & Bacon.

Kaufman, A. S., & Kaufman, N. L. (1983). *Kaufman assessment battery for children*. Circle Pines, MN: American Guidance Service.

Linehan, M. F. (September, 1992). Children who are homeless: Educational strategies for school personnel. *Phi Delta Kappan, 74*(1), 61–66.

Lloyd, J. W., Forness, S. R., & Kavale, K. A. (1998). Some methods are more effective than others. *Intervention in School and Clinic, 33*, 195–200.

Lynch, E. W., & Hanson, M. J. (1998). *Developing cross-cultural competencies: A guide for working with children and their families* (2nd ed.). Baltimore: Paul H. Brookes.

MacMillan, D. L., & Reschly, D. J. (1998). Overrepresentation of minority students: The case of greater specificity or reconsideration of the variables examined. *Journal of Special Education, 32*, 15–24.

Maheady, L., Sacca, M. K., & Harper, G. (1988). Classwide peer tutoring with mildly handicapped high school students. *Exceptional Children, 55,* 52–59.

Maldonado-Colon, E. (1990). Development of second language learners' linguistic and cognitive abilities. *The Journal of Educational Issues of Language Minority Students, 9,* 37–48.

Manning, M. L., & Baruth, L. G. (2000). *Multicultural education of children and adolescents.* Needham Heights, MA: Allyn & Bacon.

Manning, M. L., & Lucking, R. (1991). The what, why, and how of cooperative learning. *The Clearing House, 64,* 152–165.

Manning, M. L., & Lucking, R. (1993). Cooperative learning and multicultural classrooms. *The Clearing House, 67,* 12–16.

Markwardt, F. C. (1997). *Peabody individual achievement test—Primary.* Circle Pines, MN: American Guidance Service.

McIntyre, T. (1999). The culturally sensitive disciplinarian [On-line]. Available: http://maxweber. hunter.cuny.edu/eres/docs/eres/EDSPC715_MC INTYRE/C_SenDiscip.html.

McLoughlin, J. A., & Lewis, R. B. (1990). *Assessing special students* (2nd ed.). New York: Merrill/ Macmillan.

Mercer, J. R., & Lewis, J. F. (1978). *System of multipluralistic assessment.* Cleveland, OH: Psychological Corporation.

Morsink, C. V., Thomas, C., & Smith-Davis, J. (1987). Noncategorical special education programs: Process and outcomes. In M. Wang, M. Reynolds, & H. Walberg (Eds.), *Handbook of special education: Research and practice* (Vol. 1, pp. 287–312). Oxford, England: Pergamon.

Murray, C. B., & Clark, R. M. (1990). Targets of racism. *The American School Board Journal, 177(6),* 22–24.

Navarrett, C., Wilde, J., Nelson, C., Martinez, R., & Hargett, G. (1990, summer). *Informal assessment* (ERIC Document Reproduction Service No. ED 337 041)

Nelson, D., Fellner, M. J., & Norrell, C. L. (1975). *Pictorial test of bilingualism and language dominance.* Corpus Christi, TX: South Texas Testing Service.

Newcomer, P. L., & Hammil, D. (1996). *Test of language development—primary-3rd edition.* Austin, TX: Pro-Ed.

O'Connor, K. (1989). *Homeless children.* San Diego, CA: Lucent.

Ogbu, J. U. (1985). Research currents: Cultural-ecological influences on minority school learning. *Language Arts, 62,* 860–869.

O'Malley, J. M., & Pierce, L. V. (1996). *Authentic assessment for English language learners: Practical approaches for teachers.* Reading, MA: Addison Wesley Longman.

Ornstein, A. C. (1987). Emphasis on student outcomes focuses attention on quality of instruction. *NASSP Bulletin, 71(495),* 88–95.

Ortiz, A., & Garcia, S. (1988). A prereferral process for preventing inappropriate referrals of Hispanic students to special education. In A. Ortiz & B. A. Ramirez (Eds.), *Schools and the culturally diverse exceptional student: Promising practices and future directions* (pp. 6–18). Reston, VA: Council for Exceptional Children.

Ortiz, A., & Polyzoi, E. (1988). Language assessment of Hispanic learning disabled and speech and language handicapped students: Research in progress. In A. Ortiz & B. A. Ramirez (Eds.), *Schools and the culturally diverse student: Promising practice and future directions* (pp. 32–44). Reston, VA: Council for Exceptional Children.

Oswald, D., Coutinho, M., Best, A. & Singh, N. (1999). Ethnic representation in special education: The influence of school-related economic and demographic variables. *The Journal of Special Education, 32,* 194–206.

Patton, J. M. (1997). Disproportionate representation in gifted programs: Best practices for meeting this challenge. In A. J. Artiles & G. Zamora-Duran (Eds.), *Reducing disproportionate representation of culturally diverse students in special and gifted education* (pp. 59–85). Reston, VA: The Council for Exceptional Children.

Patton, J. M. (1998). The disproportionate representation of African Americans in special education: Looking behind the curtain for understanding and solutions. *The Journal of Special Education, 32(1)*, 25–32.

Pear, R. (1991, September 9). Homeless children challenge schools. *The New York Times*, p. A10.

Pierce, L. V., & O'Malley, J. M. (1992). *Performance and portfolio assessment for language minority students* (Program Information Guide Series 9). Washington, DC: National Clearinghouse for Bilingual Education.

Porter, R. O. (1997). The politics of bilingual education. *Society, 34(6)*, 31–39.

Putnam, J. (1998). *Cooperative learning and strategies for inclusion: Celebrating diversity in the classroom.* Baltimore: Paul H. Brookes.

Reschly, D. J., Tilly, W. D., III, & Grimes, J. P. (2000). *Special education in transition: Functional assessment and noncategorical programming.* Longmont, CO: Sopris West.

Rhodes, L. (1992). Focusing attention on the individual in identification of gifted black students. *Roeper Review, 14(3)*, 108–110.

Roid, G. H., & Miller, L. J. (1997). *Leiter international performance scale—revised.* Wood Dale, IL: Stoelting.

Rotheram-Borus, M. J. (1993). Biculturalism among adolescents. In M. Bernal & G. Knight (Eds.), *Ethnic identity* (pp. 81–102). Albany, NY: SUNY Press.

Rueda, R. (1997). Changing the context of assessment: The move to portfolios and authentic assessment. In A. J. Artiles & G. Zamora-Duran (Eds.), *Reducing disproportionate representation of culturally diverse students in special and gifted education* (pp. 7–25). Reston, VA: The Council for Exceptional Children.

Salend, S. J., (1998). *Effective mainstreaming: Creating inclusive classrooms* (3rd ed.). Upper Saddle River, NJ: Merrill/Prentice Hall.

Saville-Troike, M. (1991). *Teaching and testing for academic achievement: The role of language development.* Washington, DC: National Clearinghouse for Bilingual Education.

Schnaiberg, L. (1997). "Ebonics" vote puts Oakland in maelstrom. *Education Week.* [On-line]. Available: http://www.edweek.org/ew/vol-16/17ebon.h16.

Sherman, A. (1997*). Poverty matters: The cost of child poverty in America.* Washington, DC: Children's Defense Fund.

Shirts, G. (1977). *Bafá Bafá: A cross cultural simulation.* Del Mar, CA: Simille II.

Slavin, R. (1999). *Educational psychology: Theory and practice/A practical guide to cooperative learning.* Boston: Allyn & Bacon.

Slavin, R., & Fashola, O. (1998). *Show me the evidence! Proven and promising programs for America's schools.* Thousand Oaks, CA: Corwin Press.

Smitherman, G. (1985). What go round come round: King in perspective. In C. K. Brooks (Ed.), *Tapping potential: English and language arts for the black learner* (pp. 41–62). Urbana, IL: National Council for Teachers of English.

Tharp, R. G. (1989). Psychocultural variables and constants: Effects on teaching and learning in schools. *American Psychologist, 44*, 349–359.

Torrijos, E. C. (1997*). Batería de evaluación de Kaufman para niños.* [On-line]. Available: http://www.geocities.com/Athens/Aegean/2190/materi.htm.

U.S. Census Bureau. (1999). *Poverty in the United States: 1998.* Washington, DC: Author.

Valdes, G., & Figueroa, R. (1994). *Bilingualism and testing: A special case of bias.* Norwood, NJ: Ablex Publishing.

Voltz, D. L., & Damiano-Lantz, M. (1993). Developing ownership in learning. *Teaching Exceptional Children, 25(4)*, 18–22.

Walther-Thomas, C., Korinek, L., McLaughlin, V., & Williams, B. (2000). *Collaboration for inclusive education: Developing successful programs.* Boston: Allyn & Bacon.

Weaver, C. (1991). Whole language and its potential for developing readers. *Topics in Language Disorders, 11*, 28–44.

Wechsler, D. (1974). *Wechsler intelligence scale for children: Revised.* Cleveland: Psychological Corporation.

Westby, C. E., & Rouse, G. R. (1985). Culture in education and the instruction of language learning-disabled students. *Topics in Language Disorders, 5*, 15–28.

White, O., & Haring, N. (1976). *Exceptional teaching: A multimedia training package*. Upper Saddle River, NJ: Merrill/Prentice Hall.

Whittaker, C. R. (1991). *The cooperative learning planner*. Ann Arbor, MI: Exceptional Innovations.

Wigg, E. H., Freedman, E., & Secord, W. A. (1992). Developing words and concepts in the classroom: A holistic-thematic approach. *Intervention in School and Clinic, 27*(5), 278–285.

Winzer, M., & Mazurek, K. (1994). *Special education in multicultural contexts*. Upper Saddle River, NJ: Merrill/Prentice Hall.

Woodcock, R. W. (1982). *Bateria Woodcock psico-educativea en Español*. Allen, TX: DLM Teaching Resources.

Woodcock, R. W. (1991). *Woodcock language proficiency battery: Revised*. Chicago: DLM/Riverside Publishers.

10 Implementation with Infants and Preschoolers with Disabilities

Topics in this chapter include:

- The characteristics associated with young children and their families.
- The various developmental and service delivery needs of young children and their families.
- The unique roles of professionals working with young children and their families.

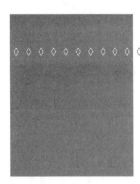

Nicholas, a 4-year-old with cerebral palsy, attends a faith-based preschool in his local community. The public school program provides him with services from an itinerant early childhood special education teacher twice a week. The preschool teacher and the early interventionist work closely on (1) adapting the preschool environment for his motor needs, including positioning equipment, bathroom accommodations, and adaptive feeding utensils; (2) providing him with a computer and augmentative communication aides; (3) facilitating social interaction with same-age peers; (4) integrating his special language, cognitive, and physical therapy goals into a developmentally appropriate program; and (5) designing a data-collection system for monitoring his developmental progress.

All team members are briefed about Nicholas's family background. Although Nicholas's grandparents have legal custody of him, his mother, an unwed teenager living in another state, does take a role in his life when possible. Nicholas's speech and physical therapists and his service coordinator at the local children's medical center meet monthly with his grandparents and the early intervention teachers to discuss his progress, the family's needs, and preparations for Nicholas's transition to the kindergarten program in the local public school.

Interactive teaming may never be more important than when working with children like Nicholas and his family. With the passage of P.L. 99-457 in 1986 and the subsequent Part C services under the Individuals with Disabilities Education Act (IDEA) in 1997, early childhood personnel are realizing that skills in coordination of services, consultation with related personnel, and collaboration with families are critical. The services provided by these regulations should be multidisciplinary, coordinated, family centered, and provided in settings where children without disabilities are served (Harbin, 1998). Transdisciplinary teaming approaches are necessary in serving young children because of the large numbers of professionals involved in early intervention (Landerholm, 1990). Full-service programs for young children with disabilities and their families involve professionals from health, education, and human services.

Part C of IDEA also mandates the expansion of interagency collaboration. States and local agencies serving infants and toddlers (birth to age 3) with disabilities developed interagency collaboration councils (ICC) as mechanisms for coordination of services. Never has interagency collaboration been taken more seriously by professionals in special education (Brown, Thurman, & Pearl, 1993; Stegelin & Jones, 1991). Successful interagency collaboration requires all the interactive teaming skills outlined in Part II of this book.

This chapter focuses on the specific components of early intervention that incorporate interactive teaming skills. First, a brief overview of the various conditions that make children eligible for early intervention services is provided to acquaint the reader with the increasing numbers of young children who are at risk. Second, a discussion of the intervention needs of young children with disabilities suggests various service delivery options available for these children and their families. Within the description of the intervention needs of these children, assessment techniques and intervention strategies used for young children will be delineated. Third, the role of the professionals involved in intervention with young children and their families is presented. The key to providing a successful early intervention program requires that an interactive team be available for intervention, consultation, and collaboration.

CHARACTERISTICS OF YOUNG CHILDREN WITH DISABILITIES AND THEIR FAMILIES

Regulations under Part C of the IDEA provide eligibility criteria for three subgroups receiving early intervention: *established conditions, developmental delays,* and *at risk.* Some states serve all three subgroups of children while other states with large numbers of at-risk children have elected to use the criteria for established conditions and developmental delays.

The term *established conditions* refers to young children who have a genetic disorder, congenital malformation, or a neurologic disorder that has a high probability of resulting in a developmental delay. The term *developmental delays* refers to young children who evidence a certain percentage of difference between their performance level and chronological age or a certain number of standard deviations below their chronological age based on quantitative and/or qualitative assessment. For a child to be eligible for services under the *at-risk* group, "children may currently demonstrate no abnormality, but have biological or environmental factors associated with their medical history or home context that increase the risk of delay in the future" (Brown et al., 1993, p. 30).

The numbers of young children who could be eligible for early intervention services is dramatically increasing (Anastasiow & Harel, 1993; McNab & Blackman, 1998). Perhaps one of the most alarming statistics of risk factors facing American children today is that children living in poverty are more likely to have disabilities than their peers who live in middle- and upper-income families (Janko-Summers & Joseph, 1998). The factors that put poor children at risk include "neglected prenatal care, inadequate nutrition, lack of access to preventive health care, caregiver's mental and physical health problems and a host of other difficult life circumstances" (Janko-Summers & Joseph, 1998, p. 207).

Furthermore, increased numbers of infants suffering from fetal alcohol syndrome and fetal alcohol effects challenge early interventionists. These children may have lifelong disabilities caused by prenatal neurologic damage resulting in cognitive and language delays as well as the presence of challenging behaviors (Burgess & Streissguth, 1992; Howard, Williams, & McLaughlin, 1994; Streissguth, 1997). Similarly, children exposed to cocaine and other drugs pose a challenge to early intervention programs. Although the initial sensationalized problems of these children are not substantiated by current research, some research indicates that about one third of cocaine/polydrug-exposed children evidence some delays in language, problems in attention, and self-regulation (Griffith, 1992; Hanson, 1994; Sparks, 1992). The practice of categorizing these children as a new breed of disability or designing special programs for cocaine/polydrug-exposed children is not supported by professionals in the field (Griffith, 1992; Schutter & Brinker, 1992). However, intervention does require (1) a collaborative effort with medical, educational, and therapeutic programs; (2) treatment of the mothers' addiction; and (3) parental involvement, empowerment, and education.

Other groups of young children who are entering the early intervention arena include students exposed to lead poisoning. Needleman (1992) reported that 16% of all American children have blood lead levels in the neurotoxic range, placing them at risk for impaired neurobehavioral functioning. Most of those children are inner city African-Americans living in poverty. Delays in development have been noted in these children including inattentiveness and mild learning disabilities.

Furthermore, a growing number of children are homeless or living in violent environments. Homeless young children may be at risk for developmental delays due to their transitory state and lack of access to basic resources such as food and medical care (Gollnick & Chinn, 1998; Linehan, 1992; Salend, 1998). The effects of violence on young children also place the child at risk for normal development. Children who are abused can suffer significant emotional delays. However, current research indicates that children who witness violence and live in unsafe and stressful environments are also affected adversely, sometimes evidencing posttraumatic stress disorder symptoms such as emotional withdrawal, aggression, and inattentiveness (Craig, 1992; McCormick & Holden, 1992).

Finally, the number of children affected by medical conditions such as prematurity, cancer, medically fragile status (Bartel & Thurman, 1992), or human immunodeficiency virus (HIV) (Landry & Smith, 1998; Seidel, 1992) have needs that challenge early interventionists. Collaboration with medical personnel as well as social service personnel will be necessary. Personnel will need knowledge and understanding of the issues related to terminal illness, death, and dying. Collaboration with families whose young children are dying may be extremely difficult for early interventionists not prepared in these areas. Consulting with social workers, family therapists, and other mental health professionals may be an important first step for the interventionists.

The discussion of the increasing numbers of children at-risk illustrates the changing causes of developmental delays today. By adding these at-risk children to the existing numbers of children with established conditions, one can better understand the enormous challenges that face early interventionists. Further complicating the challenges is the fact that families no longer comprise a working husband, a wife who stays at home, and siblings. Instead, today's family can include custodial grandparents, foster parents, same-sex partners, cohabitating couples, teen parents, parents with disabilities, and single parents.

Furthermore, legislative reforms such as the Omnibus Personal Responsibility and Work Opportunity Act (American Public Welfare Association, 1996) present added challenges to early intervention as the infrastructure and resource base for many programs that supported families from poor backgrounds have been shifted (e.g., Medicaid, Supplemental Security Income, Temporary Assistance to Needy Families, child care). These welfare reforms have left complex gaps in support services for poor families with children who have disabilities (Harbin, 1998; Janko-Summers & Joseph, 1998; Ohlson, 1998). Meeting the intervention needs of young children and their families finds today's early intervention team engaged in an extremely complex and sometimes very frustrating enterprise.

INTERVENTION NEEDS OF YOUNG CHILDREN WITH DISABILITIES

The needs of young children with disabilities are different from the needs of elementary- or secondary-age children. Early intervention programs serving children from birth to age 5 *should not* involve teaching a lower extension of the elementary education curriculum. Early intervention programs should be family centered; include coordinated service delivery options that promote inclusion; use transdisciplinary play-based assessment approaches; and provide the child with individually and developmentally appropriate intervention.

Family-Centered Approaches

Family-centered early intervention has been defined as an approach to intervention that "recognizes the child in the context of the family, responding to family concerns and priorities, working in partnership with families and enabling families to use resources to meet their needs" (McWilliam et al., 1998, p. 69). The major goal of this approach is to support families in their natural caregiving roles by building on unique individual and family strengths, and to enable and empower families to meet their own needs in ways that create self-competence (Bailey, McWilliam, & Winton, 1992; Bailey, Palsha, & Simeonsson, 1991; Caro & Derevensky, 1991; Mahoney & Bella, 1998; McWilliam et al., 1998). The following nine essential elements characterize family-centered care:

1. Recognizing the family as a constant in the child's life and intervention settings as temporary.
2. Facilitating parent/professional collaboration in the care of the child, in the child's program, and in intervention policy.
3. Sharing information about the child in an unbiased, supportive manner.
4. Implementing comprehensive intervention programs that include emotional and financial services for families, as well as child-directed services.
5. Recognizing the individuality of families, including their strengths and patterns of coping and adjusting.
6. Incorporating the unique developmental needs of young children into the service delivery system.
7. Encouraging parent-to-parent support systems.
8. Designing intervention systems that are flexible, accessible, and responsive to the unique needs of different families.
9. Recognizing and respecting cultural and linguistic difference (Association for the Care of Children's Health, 1989).

Mahoney and Bella (1998) warn that although the IFSP has included family needs, concerns, and priorities, service providers must be responsible for monitoring the impact of services on the family. Unless the impact of family-centered practices on specific child and family outcomes is monitored, "we may fail to meet the goals of family-centered services—enhancing the effectiveness of families in nurturing and caring for their children" (p. 92). Furthermore, the IFSP document should be written in language that is clear and simple, be positive in describing the child's strengths, contain nonjudgmental statements, provide specific and functional outcomes for everyday routines, provide for services in natural environments, and encourage professionals working together (McWilliam et al., 1998). For further information on writing an IFSP, the reader is referred to Olson and Kwiatkowski (1995) and Woods (1995).

Although somewhat controversial, the debate on the merits of parent education exists. (For more information, see the topical issue of *Topics in Early Childhood Special Education*, 1999, Volume 19, No. 3.) Mahoney et al. (1999) believe that parent education should be a critical component of family-centered early intervention and advocate for a renewed emphasis on formal parent education activities (e.g., training parents on explicit instructional strategies; management of problem behaviors, parent–child interaction strategies).

Service Delivery Options

Meeting the complex needs of today's young children and families requires the involvement of multiple agencies and programs. Most children who have significant disabilities due to established conditions or developmental delays receive services from the state's lead agency for Part C of the IDEA. These services can involve various agencies. Espe-Sherwindt (1991) estimated that the average number of agencies involved with families receiving Part C services was 4.7. The agencies included primary physician/health clinics, the Special Supplemental Food Program for Women, Infants, and Children, educational and therapeutic services for the child, protective services, mental health services, and case management services. Young children who are at risk are served by other agencies such as Head Start, Medicaid, Maternal and Child Health Block Grants, Title 1 Programs, social services block grants, or state appropriations programs. The high number of agencies and programs available for young children with disabilities or at-risk children necessitates interactive teaming efforts by all personnel and the family.

Perhaps one of the most impressive models of interactive teaming can be found in the establishment of local interagency collaborative councils (LICCs) (Morgan, Guetzloe, & Swan, 1991; Peterson, 1991; Stegelin & Jones, 1991; Swan & Morgan, 1993). LICCs were first mandated by P.L. 99-457 and are now operating in all communities serving young children with disabilities or at-risk populations. The following vignette helps illustrate the function of an LICC.

The case of Ryan, a 2.5-year-old diagnosed with lead poisoning, is discussed at the February meeting of the Jones County ICC. At the LICC meeting are Ryan's mother and his health care provider, the service coordinator for Part C, the Part C early interventionists, the director from First Start, the school district's prekindergarten special education supervisor, the school psychologist, the Head Start director, the supervisor for the elementary education program, the director of the regional resources center, and the social services worker. The service coordinator introduces the mother to the team and provides some background on Ryan's intervention needs. The boy receives services from the Part C early interventionists, but has been tested by the school psychologist and found to be ineligible for special education services when he turns 3 years old. The service coordinator would like to make sure Ryan remains in an early intervention program until he is 4, when he can attend Head Start.

The mother and health care provider provide the team with information on how Ryan is progressing. His major IFSP goals are in increasing his attention and engagement with toys and adult–child interactions. He has been improving since he started receiving early intervention services at home. The mother wants to earn her GED and get off government assistance by working part time. But she fears the home visit program will be discontinued. The First Start director believes Ryan would qualify for First Start services until he turns 4. She asks the mother if she would be interested in placing Ryan in a home-care provider program on the days she is working. The mother says she would like to visit the program first but is interested in the option. The First Start parent liaison would provide support to the home-care provider and make home visits in the evenings when the mother comes home from work.

The First Start director would like to work closely with the Part C early interventionist to transition the IFSP to First Start. Head Start is now alerted to Ryan's referral when he turns 4, and the school district will monitor his progress as he nears kindergarten. The service coordinator suggests scheduling an IFSP transition meeting for all interested. The resource materials director offers office space for the meeting and reminds the First Start director that she may check out any early childhood materials Ryan might need in the home-care program. The school's prekindergarten special education consultant offers to help the home-care provider on a short-term basis. The social services worker mentions that his agency can provide transportation for Ryan to the home-care program if necessary. They will continue to provide Ryan and his mother with transportation to his health care provider.

Interagency coordinating councils integrate services for young children and their families. Cooperation, collaboration, and a genuine desire to share information are requirements for successful councils. The LICC has the potential of providing seamless services to young children and their families. Swan and Morgan (1993) provide an excellent guide for creating effective local interagency coordinating councils. They outline the following eight basic premises of LICC collaboration:

1. One agency alone cannot provide all the services needed for a young child with disabilities or at high risk and his or her family.
2. With limited resources and categorical focus, agency programs must coordinate efforts to avoid waste, unnecessary duplication, and service gaps.
3. There is nothing to be gained by competition. The agency that provides the service is not as important as the fact that the child and family are appropriately served.
4. The differences across agency programs represent a strength, not a weakness or problem to be eliminated.
5. The service delivery system must consist of a variety of options from which families may choose.
6. Agency programs are "equal" in importance.
7. Agencies must provide mutual support and assistance to one another. Favorable trade-offs exist.
8. A structured system of interagency collaboration must exist (Swan & Morgan, 1993, p. 15).

Once an LICC is created, service delivery options can be expanded. For example, if the LICC had not been working cooperatively, Ryan may have gone without services for a year and his mother might have felt pressured to stay at home, opting to remain on government assistance and not earn her GED. The absence of early intervention between ages 3 and 4 may have placed Ryan at risk for further developmental delays and placement into special education.

Service delivery options vary depending on the age and special needs of the young child. For newborns and infants with significant disabilities service delivery begins in a *hospital-based program.* An understanding of the complex residual medical complication of critically ill newborns in neonatal intensive care units

(NICUs) is extremely important for early intervention professionals (McNab & Blackman, 1998). NICUs are graded by level of care provided with the Level 1 NICU providing the most significant treatment for infants with severe illness. The Level 2 and 3 NICUs provide care for newborns with a moderate degree of illness or newborns with illnesses that are complex or difficult to diagnose (Brown et al., 1993). NICU programs have expanded to encompass a range of professionals, including pediatricians; neonatologists; NICU nurses; social workers; physical, occupational, speech-language, and respiratory therapists; audiologists; and infant developmental specialists (i.e., early childhood special educators). Most NICU programs focus on family support, including programs that encourage social interactions and environments of the infants and their caregivers. A family-centered approach is most critical in the NICU where the emotional and psychological needs of families are emphasized (Long, Artis, & Dobbins, 1993; McNab & Blackman, 1998). Another goal of NICU-based programs is preparing families for the transition from hospital to home. IFSP plans can be designed with families and professionals during the infant's stay in the NICU and follow the child to the Part C community or home-based program once he or she is discharged.

Infants being discharged from NICU are often linked to *developmental follow-up programs*. The purposes of this service delivery option include (1) to provide ongoing support for families, (2) to smooth the transition for the infant and families, (3) to direct the family toward appropriate community resources, and (4) to provide ongoing secondary care of infants (Brown et al., 1993, p. 224). Professionals involved with developmental follow-up programs must be closely linked with community services and the LICC. Follow-up programs are important for infants with established conditions as well as infants who are at risk for developmental delays. Examples of specific follow-up program models are described in Brown et al. (1993).

Home-based programs are most appropriate for infants and toddlers with disabilities who are younger than 18 months. Home-based programs require that professionals be competent in working with families within their home environment. This model of service delivery reinforces family-centered versus child-centered intervention; however, intervention is provided less frequently. Related service personnel must be careful to coordinate services with the quality adviser or home visitor to ensure that families are not overwhelmed by home visits and intrusion into their private lives. Transdisciplinary models of teaming are critical in home-based programs, where the home visitor has knowledge of all aspects of the infant's intervention program. Other team members serve as consultants to the home visitor.

For some toddlers and preschoolers ages 18 months to 3 years, *center-based programs* can be beneficial. For younger toddlers, half-day center-based programs may be more appropriate. Although contact with families may be less frequent, professionals must continue providing a family-centered approach to center-based services. Evening or weekend parent support programs can be established to meet the needs of some families. Additionally, early interventionists should collaborate with community child care center providers to ensure that natural

environments (i.e., those in which typically developing children would participate) are made available to preschoolers with disabilities and their families
(Bricker, 1995; Bricker, Pretti-Frontczak, & McComas, 1998; Hanline & Hanson,
1989). Interestingly, a recent study by Sewell, Collins, Hemmeter, and Schuster
(1998) reports that 34% of the services provided by early intervention clinicians
occurred in community-based settings (e.g., child care sites, family center,
churches, other service agencies, libraries) as compared to reports from the early
1990s that indicated that the majority of services were provided in either home-
or clinic-based settings (Kochanek & Buka, 1998). The shift from segregated settings to community and neighborhood settings is positive and implies the need
for more collaborative relationships across service providers. Consulting and collaborating with child care providers, faith-based program providers, and other
community-based providers becomes one of the most important roles of early
childhood special educators as community-based settings become an available
option for service delivery.

Several itinerant service delivery models have been described by Odom et al.
(1999) including these:

1. *Itinerant-direct service model:* The specialized professionals work directly with
   the children with disabilities and are responsible for delivering the individual
   services.

2. *Itinerant teaching-collaborative/consultative model:* Differs from the direct service
   model in that the role of the specialized professional is to work with the classroom teacher to establish activities and experiences in the program without
   support

3. *Team teaching model:* An early childhood teacher and special education
   teacher both teach in the same classroom.

4. *Early childhood teacher model:* An early childhood teacher has the primary
   responsibility for planning, implementing, and monitoring classroom activities and has little contact with specialized professionals.

5. *Early childhood special education model:* A reverse mainstreaming model where
   a special education teacher serves as the lead teacher and usually works with
   an assistant teacher.

6. *Integrative inclusive activity model:* Children with disabilities are enrolled in an
   early childhood special education class, and typically developing children are
   enrolled in an early childhood classroom. Both classes are located in the same
   building. For a part of the day, and for certain activities, the two classes merge
   for integrative-inclusive experiences.

While these six models have been reported as some of the most common examples
for serving young children with disabilities, other researchers have reported over
22 different classroom patterns for early intervention (Dunst, Bruder, Trivette, Raab,
& McLean, 1998). No matter what model is employed, however, each requires some
degree of collaboration and interactive teaming among professionals.

The transition from Part C to Part B usually occurs when the child reaches his or her third birthday. The IDEA regulations require that a transition plan be developed no later than 90 days prior to the child's third birthday. The plan should outline the process that will be incorporated in selecting and preparing the receiving program for enrollment of the child. Most communities offer Part B programs for 3- to 5-year-old children with disabilities in local elementary schools. In those cases, family members are encouraged to visit the receiving program and coordinate the transition of the child into the public school. This can often be a difficult transition for families who have become indoctrinated to a more personal family-centered approach and now face a more child-centered and public school bureaucratic system. The child's IFSP can be used as the transition document, however, some school districts prefer to reevaluate the child and develop a new IEP. Because transition services occur across agencies and are sometimes extremely complex, collaboration is essential. To establish a community-wide transition systems, professionals and families should seek technical assistance, and sample policies and procedures should be used to develop local transition models (see Rous, Hemmeter, & Schuster, 1999, for a description of a technical assistance project on transition training).

Assessment Techniques

An important component of early intervention programs involves assessment of young children and their families. The IFSP should address both child needs and outcomes as well as family concerns, priorities, and needs requiring professionals to understand comprehensive ecological assessment techniques.

Arena assessments have become one of the most promising approaches to child assessment. These assessments require interactive teaming skills from each professional. Working together with the family, early intervention professionals provide a natural play environment in which to observe the infant interacting with toys, objects, adults, and peers. Linder (1997) describes a transdisciplinary play-based assessment technique that involves multiple professionals observing the abilities of young children through play. The play facilitator interacts with the child, providing opportunities for other team members to observe developmental skills in the language, cognition, motor, and social/emotional domains. Planning the play activities is an important initial step for the transdisciplinary assessment team. A parent facilitator is selected to work with the family member present during the play session and gather information on the family's needs and concerns. After the assessment, team members review the videotaped assessment and work together to interpret the results and plan the intervention. The arena model of assessment encourages collaboration and consultation from all team members.

Intervention Strategies

Effective early intervention programs provide individualized and developmentally appropriate practices to young children with disabilities (Bredekamp, 1991;

Bredekamp & Copple, 1997; Bredekamp & Rosengrant, 1995; Carta, 1995; Fewell & Oelwein, 1991; Odom, 1994). For some children, specialized instructional strategies may be required. The following list highlights some recommended strategies for early intervention:

1. Structure the physical space to promote play, engagement, and learning (Bailey & Wolery, 1992; Cook, Tessier & Klein, 2000).
2. Structure the social environment by using models, proximity, and responsive adults to promote engagement and learning (Bailey & Wolery, 1992; Bricker et al., 1998).
3. Use children's preferences to promote learning (Bailey & Wolery, 1992).
4. Structure routines using violation of expectancy, naturalistic time delay, and transition-based teaching (Walker & Shea, 1999).
5. Use structured play activities (Cook et al., 2000; Trawick-Smith, 1994).
6. Use differential reinforcement, response shaping, and correspondence training (Walker & Shea, 1999).
7. Use peer-mediated strategies to promote communication and social skills (Kohler & Strain, 1999).
8. Use naturalistic or milieu teaching strategies to promote communication and social skills (Bricker et al., 1998; McCormick, Loeb, & Schiefelbush, 1997).
9. Use response prompting procedures and stimulus modification (Bailey & Wolery, 1992; Walker & Shea, 1999).

Many of these instructional strategies will have to be understood by families, paraprofessionals, and general early childhood educators serving young children with disabilities in their early childhood programs. Special education personnel will help educators integrate these strategies into an early childhood program that supports developmentally appropriate practices (DAP). The following guidelines characterize DAP:

1. Activities should be integrated across developmental domains.
2. Children's interests and progress should be identified through teacher observation.
3. Teachers should prepare the environment to facilitate children's active exploration and interaction.
4. Learning activities and materials should be concrete, real, and culturally relevant to the lives of young children.
5. A wide range of interesting activities should be provided.
6. The complexity and challenge of activities should increase as children understand the skills involved (Bredekamp & Copple, 1997).

No single philosophical approach to early intervention meets the needs of the diverse population. A combination of individualized and adapted instructional strategies with a DAP approach is the ideal model for early intervention.

Much attention has been placed on early literacy development (Hockenberger, Goldstein, & Haas, 1999; Rush, 1999) and linguistic performance (Crain-Thoreson & Dale, 1999) in young children with disabilities and children at risk for learning. Early interventionists should focus a majority of their instructional programs on developing children's early literacy skills such as listening, speaking, reading, and writing. Literacy is an integral part of the learning process and requires a strong partnership with family members at home.

Essential features of effective early intervention services include family-centered approaches, coordinated service delivery options, transdisciplinary assessments, and individualized and developmentally appropriate practices of instruction. Professionals from many disciplines are involved in providing effective services to young children and their families. Their roles and responsibilities are critical to the success of early intervention programs. The next section addresses the various roles of early intervention professionals.

THE ROLE OF THE PROFESSIONALS

"Multidisciplinary coordination between personnel was mandated for early intervention services because no single agency, group, or discipline could meet all of the needs of eligible children and their families" (Brown & Rule, 1993, p. 246). Part C of the IDEA specified 11 disciplines to be actively involved in early intervention services in every state. The general roles of professionals have been outlined in Chapter 4. Specialized contributions of team members who work with infants, toddlers, and preschoolers with disabilities are outlined in this chapter.

Delineating the roles of each of the team members within the educational and community setting is a first step in clarifying each group's function on the team. Table 10.1 outlines the various roles and responsibilities in both direct service and team involvement.

Although family members are not delineated as one of the 11 disciplines in the Part C legislation, they play one of the most important roles on the interactive team. Families can do the following: (1) Reinforce developmental and therapeutic programs in the home and community setting, (2) inform team members of the results of health-related appointments and treatment recommendations, and (3) provide team members with information on medical, behavioral, and family issues. Also, families should be respected if they choose not to be actively involved because of external or family stresses (e.g., work schedules, family crisis) (LeLaurin, 1992).

Other team members that may participate in interactive teams are agency or school administrators and paraprofessionals. Administrators may (1) support inclusive early education programs by providing resources and materials for

Table 10.1
Roles of Professionals and Others Involved with Infants, Toddlers, and Preschoolers with Disabilities and Their Families

Personnel	Direct Service Provider	Team Member
Audiologists	• Determine auditory function and characteristic of hearing losses • Assess and monitor middle ear infections • Determine relationship of auditory function and communication development • Recommend appropriate amplification or assistive devices	• Interpret all auditory function reports to family and professionals • Provide team members with instruction on hearing loss and use of amplification or assistive devices
Early Childhood Special Educators	• Conduct screening and child-find programs • Assess children's developmental competence • Develop an individualized IFSP or IEP for each child and family • Assess family needs and strengths • Implement family support services or parent education • Evaluate program effectiveness • Advocate for children and families	• Coordinate interdisciplinary services • Integrate and implement interdisciplinary team recommendations • Coordinate services from multiple agencies • Provide consultation to other professionals, families, and other caregivers • Support inclusive early intervention by serving as itinerant/consultant to the early childhood educators
Early Childhood General Educators	• Develop learning environments and activities that promote DAP philosophy • Develop learning environments and activities that promote social interactions of children with and without disabilities • Integrate multicultural education into all aspects of program • Provide families with information and support related to enhancing the development of the child • Evaluate program effectiveness • Advocate for children and families	• Integrate interdisciplinary team recommendations • Collaborate with ECSE on instructional strategies and social integration for children with disabilities • Provide consultation to other professionals, families, and other caregivers
Nutritionists	• Develop nutrition care plans through assessments of nutritional status, food intake, eating behavior, and feeding skills	• Coordinate nutrition services • Provide consultation and technical assistance to parents and team members • Provide preventive nutrition information, services, guidance • Make referrals to community resources

Personnel	Direct Service Provider	Team Member
Nurses	• Assess physiological, psychological, and developmental characteristics of the child and family • Plan and implement interventions to improve the child's health and developmental status • Develop medical plans to treat underlying causes of medical or developmental problems • Administer medications, treatments, and regimens prescribed by a licensed physician • Monitor complex medical procedures (tracheotomy suctioning, catheterization procedures, G–tube feeding, mechanical ventilation, etc.)	• Collaborate with caregivers and team members to meet basic health and daily-care needs of the child • Assist in interpreting all medical information and reports • Make referrals to community resources
Occupational Therapists	• Assess children's developmental levels, functional performance, sensory processing, and adaptive responses • Assess family–infant interactions • Recommend, select, design, and fabricate assistive seating and orthotic devices • Prevent secondary impairments	• Provide consultation to other professionals, families on the child's functioning and integrate therapy recommendations • Consult with caregivers and team members on adaptive or assistive devices
Physicians	• Provide services to the child, including assessment, comprehensive medical care, diagnosis, treatment, and referral	• Provide consultation and instruction to parents and team members • Consult with community settings to provide diagnostic and treatment services
Psychologists	• Administer psychological and developmental tests and other assessment procedures • Plan a program of psychological services, including family counseling, parent training, and child development	• Integrate and interpret assessment information to parents and team members • Coordinate psychological services • Collaborate with team members on family needs and strengths

Table 10.1, *continued*

Personnel	Direct Service Provider	Team Member
Physical Therapists	• Assess for motor skills, neuromotor, neuromusculoskeletal, cardiopulmonary, oral motor, and feeding • Implement environmental modifications and recommend adaptive equipment and mobility devices	• Provide consultation to teach handling, positioning, and movement techniques to facilitate motor functioning and posture • Collaborate on methods for integrating therapy into the child's program
Social workers	• Make home visits to evaluate a child's living conditions and patterns of parent–child interaction • Assess psychosocial development of the child within the family context • Provide individual or group counseling for family members	• Build partnerships with the family • Consult with team members on family needs and strengths • Coordinate community services • Consult with team members on the impact of culture on the family, and how to provide culturally competent intervention
Speech-Language Pathologists	• Assess communication and oral-motor abilities • Plan and implement appropriate therapeutic programs • Design augmentative communication systems including manual sign language, computerized communication devices, or picture/symbol systems	• Provide consultation to caregivers and team members regarding communication and oral-motor therapy programs • Refer children to medical or other professional services necessary
Vision Specialist	• Conduct assessment of functional vision • Determine the relationship of development and visual loss • Provide early orientation and mobility programs • Recommend assistive or low-vision devices	• Interpret visual functioning to caregivers and team members • Consult and refer children to medical or other professional services necessary • Collaborate on designing environments that accommodate the child's visual loss • Teach caregivers and team members sighted-guide techniques • Assist caregivers and team members with pre-Braille or low-vision instruction

Source: Adapted from Bailey (1989).

those programs, (2) provide professional development to team members, and (3) advocate for the program. Paraprofessionals and volunteers can (1) ensure that the environment is ready and safe for young children, (2) provide follow-up to instructional programs throughout the day, and (3) assist in all early intervention activities by valuing child-directed and child-initiated responses. It is important for the teacher to outline the job task descriptions for the classroom assistant as well as to think carefully about his or her role relationship philosophy. Cook et al. (2000) outline a range of role relationships philosophies that go from an authoritative style to one that involves coaching. The three philosophies range in assistance and supervision as follows:

◆ The teacher is the authority who makes all decisions; issues directives. Paraprofessionals given little or no freedom are dependent on teacher to tell what to do, when, and how, since only the teacher's way is "right."

◆ The teacher asks for suggestions; discusses child-instructional issues. Paraprofessionals have some involvement with teacher in planning and moderate autonomy to perform tasks within the general guidelines.

◆ The teacher serves in a counseling, support role when needed. Paraprofessionals are assigned broad tasks and are trained and coached by teacher to function independently in planning and carrying out activities consistent with educational philosophy.

These authors further describe methods for recruiting paraprofessional services, communicating expectations, providing constructive feedback, and evaluating paraprofessional services. Paraprofessionals and volunteers are often from the children's community culture and can serve as cultural mediators to the team.

The role of the *quality adviser* or *service coordinator* can vary with individual children and families. A paradigm of service coordination has emerged under Part C that emphasizes family-driven versus agency-driven practices (Cook et al., 2000; Dunst & Trivette, 1989; Swan & Morgan, 1993). Two levels of service coordination have been defined in the literature (Swan & Morgan, 1993). One level is coordination of community services and the other level is coordination of child and family services. The interagency coordinating councils are the primary vehicles for the community level of service coordination. The service coordinator's role is to organize comprehensive services and mobilize resources when necessary. It is important to note that family members can serve as their child's primary service coordinator under Part C regulations. At the family level, the service coordinator assists specific families in the ongoing process of coordinating and monitoring services across the various providers. The individual service coordinator helps the family identify short-term and long-term outcomes and support services needed and helps the family gain access to these services (Cook et al., 2000; Swan & Morgan, 1993). If services do not exist, the service coordinator mobilizes resources and services required.

The role of each team member is critical to the success of providing coordinated and appropriate services to young children and their families. In previous chapters we have discussed the importance of developing interactive teams. Professionals and family members often do not possess the knowledge and skills necessary to collaborate and work effectively in teams. In early childhood, models of inservice that emphasize an interactive team approach to learning and implementing recommended practices have been effective (Olson, Murphy, & Olson, 1998; Palsha & Wesley, 1998). For example, in the Building Effective Successful Teams (BEST) inservice model, the team, not separate individuals, is responsible for completing and applying information from inservice training materials (Olson et al., 1998), therefore creating a stronger connectedness among the individuals in the team. Three self-study packages were developed for inservice training areas: (1) team building, (2) activity-based programming, and (3) building partnerships with families. Figure 10.1 describes one of the team building exercises used for evaluating how well teams communicate.

Although, interactive teaming is highly effective in working with young children and their families, it requires more than direct intervention from an array of experienced professionals. Developing effective early childhood interactive teams takes training, time, trust, and commitment. The efforts being done in early child-

---

The Ball of Yarn Game

Directions: You will all be sitting on the ground in a circle or around a table. Only the person holding the ball of yarn may speak. The person with the ball must keep it until someone signals nonverbally that he or she wishes to have it. The person who is passing the yarn holds on to an end of it so that a pattern starts to emerge as the yarn unwinds.

The individual holding the ball may refuse to give it to a member who requests it. The discussion should last for 10 minutes, at the end of which time there will be an elaborate pattern of yarn on the ground between the participants from all the times the yarn was passed from hand to hand. Start your discussion by deciding what to discuss. The individual who starts this discussion can ask the questions, "O.K. What shall we discuss?" After completing the game, discuss what the yarn "interaction-o-gram" tells you. Then answer the following questions.

• What do the patterns you see tell you about your team?

• What does this tell you about active or silent members?

• What did it feel like to hold the ball or to want the ball when you couldn't have it?

• How does this game reflect the real communication patterns on your team?

Figure 10.1
Example exercise from the BEST Inservice Project.

Source: From *Journal of Early Intervention, 21,* 333–349. Copyright © 1998 by the Division of Early Childhood, Council for Exceptional Children, Jennifer Olson, Cari Lee Murphy, and Phillip D. Olson. All rights reserved.

hood special education toward this end are commendable. General educators and special educators of school-age children might benefit from adopting or adapting the unique features of early intervention collaboration outlined in this chapter.

◇ ◇

Application

In this section, we follow Anthony, a 5-year-old with developmental disabilities, through the various service agencies he and his parents have used during the past 5 years. Anthony's parents have worked with personnel from the local hospital, follow-up clinic, early intervention program, child care center, and school district during the past 5 years as they have been transitioned from one service agency to another. They say the transitions have been smooth and the personnel supportive and collaborative. The following describes the various steps and strategies that were used during each of the transitions. The *assess–plan–implement–evaluate* framework for transition planning was used by each sending and receiving program or agency (Rosenkoetter, Hains, & Fowler, 1994; Wesley & Buysee, 1996).

Hospital Transition

Anthony was born 3 months premature and weighed less than 4 pounds. He stayed in a Level 1 NICU for 3 months while physicians monitored bleeding in his head, respiratory problems, and severe jaundice. During that time, Anthony's parents connected with the NICU family support program. The program team consisted of a social worker who specialized in working with NICU families, a developmental psychologist, Anthony's primary physicians, a nurse, and a service coordinator from the hospital's neonatal follow-up program.

Team members met regularly to discuss Anthony's progress with the family, and extended family members were encouraged to participate in these sessions. The social worker invited the parents to attend an NICU parent support group, which met in the evenings once a week. Anthony showed much improvement during his stay in the NICU and was moved to a Level 2 NICU after 3 months.

The team began to prepare the family for the first transition: taking Anthony home. The nurse provided the family with instructions for Anthony's heart monitor, medication regimen, and dates for home visits. The service coordinator provided the family with information on the follow-up clinic and scheduled their first appointment. The developmental psychologist reported her findings from neurobehavioral and developmental assessments. Anthony appeared to have some moderate developmental delays. Early stimulation and intervention strategies were discussed with the family. The social worker invited the parents to attend the 1-year reunion for families that had been part of the support group. A discharge conference was scheduled with the family and the team and an IFSP was created. All the information on the transition activities, programs, and agencies, phone numbers, and scheduled appointments were given to the parents in the transition notebook.

Neonatal Follow-Up Transition

Anthony was home at 5 months and was being followed up by the nurse and service coordinator. The primary concerns and intervention program were focused on

Anthony's medical stability and early development. After 3 months, the family and service coordinator met with the home-based teacher from the local Part C early intervention center (EIC). A new transition team was formed consisting of the home-based teacher, family therapists, and center psychologist. They met for a few evenings to discuss the transition from follow-up clinic to the home visitation program.

Anthony had improved medically and was to be monitored by the follow-up clinic annually. The team discussed Anthony's continued delay in gross motor and cognitive skill development and his IFSP was updated. The family concerns and outcomes were focused on providing an early stimulation program and finding a support group for the mother, who was feeling isolated from other parents.

Home-Based and Center-Based Early Intervention Transition

The home-based teacher visited the family every week, providing them with activities for developmental stimulation. The EIC began providing monthly physical therapy and speech therapy services. The teacher and parents, however, were shown the therapeutic programs to integrate into Anthony's daily routines. His mother began attending a support group at the EIC.

When Anthony turned 15 months, the home-based teacher initiated the transition plan for him to enter a local child care program serving children with and without disabilities in a natural environment. The parents and home-based teacher observed the classroom and evaluated what would be necessary for him to attend. The parents attended the IFSP transition meeting and three new members joined the team: the child care classroom teacher, the nutritionists, and the occupational therapist. A plan was developed that included scheduling transportation, ordering positioning equipment and feeding utensils, and scheduling a phase-in period. Three months later Anthony began to attend the local child care center. Anthony's parents linked up with the center-based family support group. The parents and team met every 6 months to review the IFSP.

When Anthony turned 28 months old, another transition meeting was scheduled. This time the child care center teacher and parents went to the local school district prekindergarten program. They evaluated the environment, and talked with the principal, teacher, and school psychologist. The school's early childhood teacher also visited Anthony in his EIC classroom. He was referred to the special education program and a psychological assessment was completed. The child care center team (sending agency) and the school district team (receiving agency) met to plan for the transition to the prekindergarten program at the elementary school. The plan included (1) a sending and receiving agency communication plan, (2) a plan to expand the IFSP outcomes to IEP goals, and (3) a plan to evaluate Anthony's transition.

School District Transition

The receiving agency implemented the specified objectives in the transition plan and prepared the environment to meet his needs. When Anthony turned 3, the parents and team met once again and evaluated if the school district was ready to receive Anthony. All documents were transferred to the early childhood teacher, including data collection and anecdotal progress notes. The parents were linked with the school's parent support group and were introduced to all school staff. The first day of school, Anthony's child care center teacher stayed with him in the classroom. The transition was smooth, and Anthony adapted well to his new program.

Observations

In less than 3 years, Anthony's family dealt with more than 13 professionals. Each transition brought the parents stress and anxiety. However, the team members were sensitive to the needs of the family adjusting to an infant with disabilities. The family-centered approach was evident throughout the process. Parents were included in all meetings when they were able to attend. No decisions were made without them. They were empowered to assess–plan–implement–evaluate each of the programs before the transitions. Each team member was treated with equal respect and openness. Documentation was provided for the family at each step of the way. For programs serving young children with disabilities to be seamless in the delivery of services, professionals and parents must communicate, collaborate, and consult.

◊ ◊

SUMMARY

Collaboration and teaming are integral components to serving young children with disabilities and their families. Legislative backing for cooperation and integration of a system that has typically been fragmented has created a great opportunity to improve services to these individuals. The diverse characteristics of the young children receiving services in early intervention programs further justifies the need for interactive teaming. More and more children live in environments or suffer from physiological conditions that put them at risk for developmental delays. Additionally, personnel must understand that the advantages of family-centered approaches far outweigh the agency-driven or child-centered approaches of yesterday's programs.

A continuum of service delivery options is necessary to meet the needs of infants, toddlers, and preschoolers with disabilities and their families. However, those options and array of services must be closely coordinated and monitored. Intervention strategies must be individualized and developmentally appropriate for all children, and transdisciplinary arena assessments should be supported by the team. The family should be empowered to take an active role in deciding what they need and how they want those needs met. The roles of professionals on the early intervention team should be formed around the family, enabling the family to make informed decisions. As equal partners, each team member can offer valuable information and skills development to the team. Collaboration and consultation among early interventionists can result in high-quality services for young children and their families.

ACTIVITIES

1. Conduct an informational interview with a professional who is involved in early intervention programs for young children with disabilities or at risk. Use the guidelines provided in Chapter 4.

2. Attend a local interagency coordinating council meeting. Observe the teaming and collaboration skills among the professionals.

3. Volunteer at a local day-care center, an early childhood prekindergarten program, a Head Start classroom, or NICU "cuddle program." Use child-directed approaches to play and develop social interactions.

4. Invite family members of young children with disabilities to participate in class lectures about family-centered intervention.

5. Invite neonatologists, nurses, or developmental psychologists to visit the class to talk about how parents are involved in the care of infants in an NICU and get information on how the hospital deals with drug-addicted or HIV-infected babies.

6. Attend tours of schools and community agencies serving young children with disabilities or children at risk. Note the goal and mission of the various agencies as related to the quality of services provided to the children and their families.

7. Play the "Ball of Yarn Game" in class over a topic familiar to the small group of students in class.

REFERENCES

American Public Welfare Association. (1996). *The Personal Responsibility and work opportunity reconciliation act of 1996*. Issue Brief [online]. Washington, DC: Author. Available: www.apwa.org/reform/analysis/htm.

Anastasiow, N. J., & Harel, S. (1993). *At-risk infants: Interventions, families, and research*. Baltimore: Paul H. Brookes.

Association for the Care of Children's Health. (1989, Spring). *Family support bulletin*. Bethesda, MD: Author.

Bailey, D. B. (1989). Case management in early intervention. *Journal of Early Intervention, 13*, 120–134.

Bailey, D. B., McWilliam, R. A., & Winton, P. S. (1992). Building family-centered practices in early intervention: A team-based model for change. *Infants and Young Children, 5*(1), 78–82.

Bailey, D. B., Palsha, S. A., & Simeonsson, R. J. (1991). Professional skills, concerns, and perceived importance of work with families in early intervention. *Exceptional Children, 58*(2), 156–165.

Bailey, D., & Wolery, M. (1992). *Teaching infants and preschoolers with disabilities* (2nd ed.). Upper Saddle River, NJ: Merrill/Prentice Hall.

Bartel, N. R., & Thurman, S. K. (1992). Medical treatment and educational problems in children. *Phi Delta Kappan, 74*(1), 57–61.

Bredekamp, S. (1991). *Guidelines for appropriate curriculum content and assessment in programs serving children ages three through eight*. Washington, DC: National Association for the Education of Young Children.

Bredekamp, S., & Copple, C. (1997). *Developmentally appropriate practices in early childhood programs* (rev. ed.). Washington, DC: National Association for the Education of Young Children.

Bredekamp, S., & Rosengrant, T. (Eds.). (1995). *Reaching potentials: Transforming early childhood curriculum and assessment* (Vol. 2). Washington, DC: National Association for the Education of Young Children.

Bricker, D. (1995). The challenge of inclusion. *Journal of Early Intervention, 19*, 179–194.

Bricker, D., Pretti-Frontczak, K, & McComas, N. (1998). *An activity-based approach to early intervention* (2nd ed.). Baltimore: Paul H. Brookes.

Brown, W., & Rule, S. (1993). Personnel and disciplines in early intervention. In W. Brown, S. Thurman, & L. E. Pearl (Eds.), *Family-centered early intervention with infants and toddlers: Innovative cross-disciplinary approaches* (pp. 245–268). Baltimore: Paul H. Brookes.

Brown, W., Thurman, S. K., & Pearl, L. E. (1993). *Family-centered early intervention with infants and toddlers: Innovative cross-disciplinary approaches*. Baltimore: Paul H. Brookes.

Burgess, D. M., & Streissguth, A. P. (1992). Fetal alcohol syndrome and fetal alcohol effects: Principles for educators. *Phi Delta Kappan, 74*(1), 24–30.

Caro, P., & Derevensky, J. L. (1991). Family focused intervention model: Implementation and research findings. *Topics in Early Childhood Special Education, 11*(3), 66–80.

Carta, J. (1995). Developmentally appropriate practice: A critical analysis as applied to young children with disabilities. *Focus on Exceptional Children, 27*, 1–14.

Cook, R. E., Tessier, A., & Klein, M. D. (2000). *Adapting early childhood curricula for children in inclusive settings* (5th ed.). Upper Saddle River, NJ: Merrill/Prentice Hall.

Craig, S. E. (1992). The educational needs of children living with violence. *Phi Delta Kappan, 74*, 67–68, 70–71.

Crain-Thoreson, C., & Dale, P. (1999). Enhancing linguistic performance: Parents and teachers as book reading partners for children with language delays. *Topics in Early Childhood Special Education, 19*, 28–39.

Dunst, C. J., Bruder, M. B., Trivette, C., Raab, M., & McLean, M. (1998). *Increasing children's learning opportunities through families and communities*. Early Childhood Research Institute, Year 2 Progress Report, Submitted to the U.S. Department of Education Office of Special Education Programs, Washington, DC.

Dunst, C. J., & Trivette, C. M., (1989). An enablement and empowerment perspective of case management. *Topics in Early Childhood Special Education, 8*(4), 87–102.

Espe-Sherwindt, M. (1991). The IFSP and parents with special needs/mental retardation. *Topics in Early Childhood Special Education, 11*(3), 107–120.

Fewell, R. R., & Oelwein, P. L. (1991). Effective early intervention: Results from the model preschool program for children with Down syndrome and other developmental delays. *Topics in Early Childhood Special Education, 11*(1), 56–68.

Gollnick, D. M., & Chinn, P. C. (1998). *Multicultural education in a pluralistic society* (5th ed.). Upper Saddle River, NJ: Merrill/Prentice Hall.

Griffith, D. R. (1992). Prenatal exposure to cocaine and other drugs: Developmental and educational prognoses. *Phi Delta Kappan, 74*(1), 30–34.

Hanline, M. F., & Hanson, M. J. (1989). Integration considerations for infants and toddlers with multiple disabilities. *Journal of the Association for Persons with Severe Handicaps, 14*(3), 178–183.

Hanson, M. (1994). Substance abuse and early intervention. *Topics in Early Childhood Special Education, 14*(2), 1–291 (entire issue).

Harbin, G. (1998). Welfare reform and its effect on the system of early intervention. *Journal of Early Intervention, 21*, 211–215.

Hockenberger, E. H., Goldstein, H., & Haas, L. S. (1999). Effects of commenting during joint book reading by mothers with low SES. *Topics in Early Childhood Special Education, 19*, 15–27.

Howard, V. F., Williams, B. F., & McLaughlin, T. F. (1994). Children prenatally exposed to alcohol and cocaine: Behavioral solutions. In R. Gardner, D. M. Sainato, J. O. Cooper, T. E. Heron, W. L. Heward, J. Eshleman, & T. A. Grossi (Eds.), *Behavior analysis in education: Focus on measurably superior instruction* (pp. 131–146). Belmont, CA: Brooks/Cole.

Janko-Summers, S., & Joseph, G. (1998). Making sense of early intervention in the context of welfare to work. *Journal of Early Intervention, 21,* 207–210.

Kochanek, T. T., & Buka, S. (1998). Patterns of early intervention service utilization: Child, maternal, and provider factors. *Journal of Early Intervention, 21,* 217–231.

Kohler, F. W., & Strain, P. S. (1999). Maximizing peer-mediated resources in integrated preschool classrooms. *Topics in Early Childhood Special Education, 19,* 92–102.

Landerholm, E. (1990). The transdisciplinary team approach in infant intervention programs. *Teaching Exceptional Children, 22*(2), 66–70.

Landry, K., & Smith, T. (1998). Neurocognitive effects of HIV infection on young children: Implications for assessment. *Topics in Early Childhood Special Education, 18,* 160–168.

LeLaurin, K. (1992). Infant and toddler models of service delivery: Are they detrimental for some children and families? *Topics in Early Childhood Special Education, 12,* 82–104.

Linder, T. W. (1997). *Transdisciplinary play-based assessment: A functional approach to working with young children.* Baltimore: Paul H. Brookes.

Linehan, M. F. (1992). Children who are homeless: Educational strategies for school personnel. *Phi Delta Kappan, 74*(1), 61–66.

Long, C. E., Artis, N. E., & Dobbins, N. J. (1993). The hospital: An important site for family-centered early intervention. *Topics in Early Childhood Special Education, 13*(1), 106–119.

Mahoney, G., & Bella, J. M. (1998). An examination of the effects of family-centered early intervention on child and family outcomes. *Topics in Early Childhood Special Education, 18,* 83–94.

Mahoney, G., Kaiser, A., Girolametto, L., MacDonald, J., Robinson, C., Safford, P., & Spiker, D. (1999). Parent education in early intervention: A call for a renewed focus. *Topics in Early Childhood Special Education, 19,* 131–140.

McCormick, L., & Holden, R. (1992). Homeless children: A special challenge. *Young Children, 47,* 61–67.

McCormick, L., Loeb, D., & Schiefelbush, R. I. (1997). *Supporting children with communication difficulties in inclusive settings.* Boston, MA: Allyn & Bacon.

McNab, T. C., & Blackman, J. A. (1998). Medical complications of the critically ill newborn: A review for early intervention professionals. *Topics in Early Childhood Special Education, 18,* 197–205.

McWilliam, R. A., Ferguson, A., Harbin, G., Porter, P., Munn, D., & Vandiviere, P. (1998). The family-centeredness of individualized family service plans. *Topics in Early Childhood Special Education, 18,* 69–82.

Morgan, J. L., Guetzloe, E. C., & Swan, W. (1991). Leadership for local interagency coordinating councils. *Journal of Early Intervention, 15,* 255–267.

Needleman, H. L. (1992). Childhood exposure to lead: A common cause of school failure. *Phi Delta Kappan, 74*(1), 35–37.

Odom, S. (1994). Developmentally appropriate practice, policies, and use for young children with disabilities and their families. *Journal of Early Intervention, 18,* 346–348.

Odom, S., Horn, E., Marquart, J., Hanson, M., Wolfberg, P., Beckman, P., Lieber, J., Li, S., Schwartz, I., Janko, S., & Sandall, S. (1999). On the forms of inclusion: Organizational context and individualized service models. *Journal of Early Intervention, 22,* 185–199.

Ohlson, C. (1998). Welfare reform: Implications for young children with disabilities, their families, and service providers. *Journal of Early Intervention, 21,* 191–206.

Olson, J., & Kwiatkowski, K. (1995). *Planning family goals: A systems approach to the IFSP.* San Antonio, TX: Communication/Therapy Skill Builders.

Olson, J., Murphy, C. L., & Olson, P. D. (1998). Building effective successful teams: An interactive teaming model for inservice education. *Journal of Early Intervention, 21,* 339–349.

Palsha, S., & Wesley, P. W. (1998). Improving quality in early childhood environments through on-site consultation. *Topics in Early Childhood Special Education, 18,* 243–253.

Peterson, N. L. (1991). Interagency collaboration under part H: The key to comprehensive, multidisciplinary, coordinated infant/toddler intervention services. *Journal of Early Intervention, 15,* 89–105.

Rosenkoetter, S. E., Hains, A. H., & Fowler, S. (1994). *Bridging early services for children with special needs and their family.* Baltimore: Paul H. Brookes.

Rous, B., Hemmeter, M. L., & Schuster, J. (1999). *Journal of Early Intervention, 22,* 38–40.

Rush, K. L. (1999). Caregiver–child interactions and early literacy development of preschool children from low-income environments. *Topics in Early Childhood Special Education, 19,* 3–14.

Salend, S. J., (1998). *Effective mainstreaming: Creating inclusive classrooms* (3rd ed.). Upper Saddle River, NJ: Merrill/Prentice Hall.

Schutter, L. S., & Brinker, R. P. (1992). Conjuring a new category of disability from prenatal cocaine exposure: Are the infants unique biological or caretaking casualties? *Topics for Early Childhood Special Education, 11,* 84–111.

Seidel, J. F. (1992). Children with HIV related developmental difficulties. *Phi Delta Kappan, 74*(1), 38–40, 56.

Sewell, T. J., Collins, B. C., Hemmeter, M. L., & Schuster, J. W. (1998). Using simultaneous prompting within an activity-based format to teach dressing skills to preschoolers with developmental delay. *Journal of Early Intervention, 21,* 132–145.

Sparks, S. (1992). *Children of prenatal substance abuse.* San Diego, CA: Singular Press.

Stegelin, D. A., & Jones, S. D. (1991). Components of early childhood interagency collaboration: Results of a statewide study. *Early Education and Development, 2*(1), 54–67.

Streissguth, A. (1997). *Fetal alcohol syndrome: A guide for families and communities.* Baltimore: Paul H. Brookes.

Swan, W. W., & Morgan, J. L. (1993). *Collaborating for comprehensive services for young children and their families: The local interagency coordinating council.* Baltimore: Paul H. Brookes.

Trawick-Smith, J. W. (1994). *Interactions in the classroom: Facilitating play in the early years.* Upper Saddle River, NJ: Merrill/Prentice Hall.

Walker, J. E., & Shea, T. M. (1999) *Behavior management: A practical approach to education.* Upper Saddle River, NJ: Merrill/Prentice Hall.

Wesley, P. E., & Busse, V. (1996). Supporting early childhood inclusion: Lessons learned through a statewide technical assistance project. *Topics in Early Childhood Special Education, 16,* 476–499.

Woods, J. J. (1995). *A family's guide to the Individualized Family Service Plan.* Baltimore: Paul H. Brookes.

11 Implementation for Students with Mild Disabilities

Topics in this chapter include:

- Characteristics of students with mild disabilities.
- Educational needs of students with mild disabilities.
- Service delivery options.
- Teacher competencies and selected teaching strategies.
- Description of roles of interactive team members.
- An application illustrating team members working together to meet the needs of a student with mild disabilities.

Andy, a personable 13-year-old, has become increasingly difficult to manage in Ms. Baker's eighth-grade math class. Although Andy repeated third grade, he is still behind in mathematics compared with his classmates. He is aware of the difficulties, and lately he has been acting out as a way of avoiding assignments. Rather than begin his seatwork when Ms. Baker gives an assignment, he gets up out of his seat to sharpen a just broken pencil, or he turns to another child to talk. If he does get started on an assignment and has to erase a mistake, he angrily wads up the paper and begins again. Because of his poor math skills and the avoidance behaviors, he is falling further behind each day.

Ms. Rhodes, Andy's mother, is a single parent holding down two part-time jobs to support Andy and his older brother, Gregory. She is aware of his problems and is concerned, but when she has time to help him with his homework, he often demonstrates the same behaviors he does at school.

Andy was referred for testing in the middle of third grade, and by the end of the year, he was placed in a resource room for students with learning disabilities. In her summary of the psychological assessment, Dr. Eaddy noted Andy's low tolerance for frustration and his reluctance to attempt tasks because he did not want to fail.

Ms. Rodriquez, the resource teacher, has begun to work with Andy on his math and reading skills for 45 minutes each day. He seems to look forward to coming to the resource room because there are only six other students in the class, and he receives more individual attention. Even in this small setting, though, he glances around to see if other students are watching his struggles with math.

Ms. Rodriquez and Ms. Baker have asked the speech-language therapist for assistance in developing Andy's vocabulary and other types of language activities in which he can be successful. Mr. Morrow, the therapist, provided a number of activities that Andy seemed to enjoy initially, but he now appears to be growing wary of doing them because none of the other students is doing similar assignments.

Andy's strongest suit is his skill in sports. Lately he has become increasingly competitive because this is the only outlet in which he thinks he can do better than his peers. The emphasis on winning has alienated two of his friends, who have chosen to play with others because Andy seems so intent on winning rather than having fun or participating as a team player. The adapted physical education teacher, Ms. DiCicco, has suggested that dur-

ing the PE period the teachers involve all the students in cooperative games so the interactions among the students will be more positive.

This vignette illustrates the complex array of problems that many students with mild disabilities or those considered "at risk" often face in school settings. This complexity presents real challenges to interactive team members in their roles as collaborators with other professionals and as direct service providers. In cases like Andy's, the interactive teaming model requires cooperation, commitment, and coordination of efforts among all the personnel involved to ensure continuity and comprehensive academic, social, and behavioral programming.

This chapter includes a discussion of the characteristics and needs of students with mild disabilities. Service delivery options, teacher competencies, and selected strategies also are presented. The last section of the chapter contains information on the roles of the professionals who may be involved in programming for children and adolescents with mild disabilities.

CHARACTERISTICS OF STUDENTS WITH MILD DISABILITIES

As discussed in the first chapter, this country is experiencing a dramatic increase in the number of students considered at risk for school difficulties or failure. Many of these students will eventually be labeled "mildly disabled" at some point in their school years; that is, they will be identified as learning disabled, mentally retarded, or mildly emotionally disturbed/behaviorally disordered. Currently, these students make up almost 90% of the school-age population identified as having disabilities, and they often have similar characteristics and needs (Mercer & Mercer, 1998; Morsink, Thomas, & Smith-Davis, 1987).

The term "mild disabilities" can also include students with sensory disabilities (i.e., vision and hearing), physical or health impairments, (e.g., cerebral palsy or epilepsy), and communication disorders (e.g., speech and language problems). These students can be considered to have a mild disability if the severity of their disability and the extent of their educational needs are such that they are appropriately served in a general education classroom for at least part of the day. In addition, these students would be provided other types of services, such as speech-language therapy or remediation from a special educator, as needed.

Brief descriptions are provided to highlight characteristics of students in each area. Although this information will be familiar to special educators, school psychologists, and other personnel who received training on learners with exceptional needs as part of their programs, it is included here as reference material for interactive team members who may not have this knowledge or who need to update their information. The references cited in each area will be of further assistance to those who need more information. Additional material on pupils whose sensory, physical, or intellectual disabilities are more severe is provided in the next chapter.

Learning Disabilities

Mercer (1997) noted that many authorities in the field of learning disabilities consider the discrepancy between estimated ability and actual academic performance to be the "common denominator" in defining this area of exceptionality. Specific academic difficulty areas typically include oral language, reading skills and comprehension, written expression, and mathematics calculation and reasoning. Other characteristics that may be present are visual and auditory perceptual disorders; lack of metacognitive strategies; social-emotional problems, including lack of motivation and hyperactivity; memory difficulties; motor disorders; and attention problems and hyperactivity (O'Shea, O'Shea, & Algozzine, 1998). Hallahan, Kauffman, and Lloyd (1999) observed that persons with learning disabilities also exhibit wide interindividual and intraindividual differences, and they often have other disabilities as well.

Certain central nervous system dysfunctions often related to learning disabilities include attention deficit disorder (ADD) and attention deficit hyperactivity disorder (ADHD). The exact relationship between learning disabilities and ADD or ADHD continues to be investigated, and is often the subject of debate among educators and medical professionals and parents. A distinction between the terms was described by Silver (1990) who stated that a learning disability affects the brain's ability to learn, and the presence of attention deficit disorders interferes with one's availability for learning.

Mental Retardation

The definition of mental retardation has evolved from one focusing primarily on significantly subaverage intelligence and associated adaptive behavior impairments to one that stresses interaction among the major dimensions of the capabilities of an individual, the environments in which the person functions, and the need for varying levels of support (Beirne-Smith, Ittenbach, & Patton, 1998).

The definition adopted by the American Association on Mental Retardation (AAMR) in 1992 follows:

> Mental retardation refers to substantial limitations in present functioning. It is characterized by significantly subaverage intellectual functioning, existing concurrently with related limitations in two or more of the following applicable adaptive skill areas: communication, self-care, home living, social skills, community use, self-direction, health and safety, functional academics, leisure and work. Mental retardation manifests before age 18. (p. 1)

The needed levels of support are based on four dimensions: (1) intellectual functioning and adaptive skills, (2) psychological/emotional considerations, (3) physical health/etiology considerations, and (4) environmental considerations. The four levels of needed support identified by the American Association on Mental Retardation (1992) are intermittent, limited, extensive, and pervasive.

Emotional Disturbances/Behavior Disorders

Kauffman (1997) commented: "Defining an emotional or behavioral disorder is unavoidably subjective, at least in part" (p. 21). He noted that conceptual models, complexities of measurement systems for emotions and behaviors, the relationships among behavioral problems and other exceptionalities, and the transience of problems during developmental stages also compound the difficulty in determining accurate definitions. Another issue is the subjectivity of standards for determining a behavior disorder because expectations may vary by sex, age, subculture, community, and economic conditions (Cullinan & Epstein, 1994).

Identification procedures vary from state to state, but the most frequently cited characteristics are school learning problems (not due to mental retardation), difficulty in establishing and maintaining satisfactory interpersonal relationships, inappropriate feelings and manifestations of behaviors, unhappiness or depression, and in some cases the existence of physical problems influenced by personal or school situations. Emotionally disturbed children frequently are impulsive, distractible, and hyperactive.

Visual Impairments

Finkelstein (1989) noted that students with visual impairments may have sight that is useful for some purposes, while others are blind or have such profound visual impairments that their vision is not usable as an educational medium. These students may have difficulty with concept development and social problems due to the limitations of their vision and the ways they are treated by others. They often need assistance with orientation and mobility (i.e., moving around in their environment), daily living skills, and language development, in addition to other academic needs (Shea & Bauer, 1994).

Hallahan and Kauffman (2000) described educational definitions of blindness based on the method of reading instruction. They noted that individuals who have such severe impairments that they must use Braille or other aural methods such as audiotapes are considered blind, and those who can read print with or without magnifying devices as having low vision.

Hearing Impairments

Hearing impairments range from mildly hard of hearing to profoundly deaf (Wray, Flexer, & Ireland, 1988). In the population with hearing impairments, two groups typically are described: (1) *deaf* people, whose loss is so great that their hearing is not functional for everyday life; and (b) *hard-of-hearing* people, who have some degree of functional hearing with or without a hearing aid. The two predominant types of hearing impairments are *conductive,* which occurs in the outer or middle ear, and *sensorineural,* which occurs in the inner ear.

Students with hearing losses may experience difficulties in academics, because so much is learned through listening, or social and personal adjustment problems due to a feeling of isolation and a reduced ability to communicate (Kirk, Gallagher, & Anastasiow, 1997). In addition to academics and social adjustment, students with hearing impairments may need help with listening skills and other forms of communication such as speech-reading, cued speech, and sign language (cf. Moores, 1996).

Physical Impairments

Physical impairments and special health care needs were defined in P.L. 94-142 and restated in amendments to the Individuals with Disabilities Education Act (IDEA). Three areas are included: orthopedic impairment, other health impairment, and traumatic brain injury.

Orthopedic impairments include such congenital abnormalities as clubfoot, impairments caused by diseases such as poliomyelitis, and impairments resulting from other causes such as cerebral palsy. The impairments may range from mild to severe, and they *may or may not* be accompanied by other disabling conditions such as mental retardation or sensory deficits. Students with orthopedic impairments may need training in daily living and social skills, assistive technology devices to aid them in communication, and modifications for written assignments and tests. They also may require services to help them with physical flexibility and movement, or medication and special diets (Hill, 1999).

Other health impairments include chronic or acute problems such as asthma, hemophilia, epilepsy, AIDS, or diabetes that adversely affect educational performance. Traumatic brain injury is an acquired injury to the brain resulting in total or partial functional disability or psychosocial impairments. For students in both of these categories, modifications of instructional and service delivery options will be required and should be reviewed on a regular basis to ensure consistency with the child or adolescent's current functioning level (Heward, 2000).

Communication Disorders

Communication disorders often overlap with other types of disabling conditions such as hearing impairments, mental retardation, cerebral palsy, or learning disabilities (Kirk et al., 1997; Wiig & Semel, 1984). Communication problems may take the form of a speech impairment, language disorder, or both. *Speech impairments* include articulation problems (e.g., substitutions or distortions of sounds), voice disorders (e.g., inappropriate quality or loudness), or fluency disorders (e.g., stuttering). *Language disorders* can be classified as receptive (i.e., problems in understanding language) or expressive (i.e., difficulties in producing language, such as limited vocabulary). In addition to remediation on the specific type of deficit, a student with a speech or language disorder may need help in an academic area such as reading, or with social interactions with peers including the possible use of an augmentative communication device (cf. Shames, Wiig, & Secord, 1998).

Considerations

Several considerations regarding students with mild disabilities are worthy of mention at this point. The first is that not all of the students within a category will exhibit all of the characteristics cited at any given time. Second, students may have combinations of conditions, such as behavior and speech disorders, that warrant a variety of services. Third, professionals should try to ensure that the difficulties or disorders being identified are not due to the cultural differences discussed in Chapter 9. Finally, labeling should be kept to a minimum because of the possible adverse reactions of parents or students. Instead, interactive team members should focus on students' strengths and specific needs, such as reading comprehension or interacting appropriately with peers, rather than on categorical labels.

MEETING EDUCATIONAL NEEDS

Based on the preceding description of characteristics of students who may be considered to have mild disabilities, the educational needs that emerge can be put into five major categories: (1) academic remediation, (2) social interactions, (3) self-concept and motivation, (4) behavior management, and (5) special education and support services (e.g., orientation and mobility, counseling, physical therapy, etc.). To consider ways of addressing these needs, four programmatic areas are discussed: (1) the process of identifying problems and designing interventions, (2) service delivery options, (3) teacher competencies, and (4) selected teaching strategies.

Although the emphasis in this section is on teachers and teaching strategies, many of the principles can be implemented by team members with other areas of expertise, such as psychology, adapted physical education, assistive technology, and speech-language therapy. These principles should be viewed as supplementary and complementary to existing literature on competencies and effective strategies in each individual field, not as replacements for them. Also, these competencies are in addition to those already discussed as necessary for functioning as a successful team member.

Problem Identification and Designing Interventions

The actual steps used in problem identification and intervention design should be based on the sequence described in Chapter 3. These steps ensure *understanding and clarity of the problem, discussion of previous interventions, identification of data collection procedures and data decision rules, consensus on interventions to be attempted,* and *procedures for evaluating effectiveness and making modifications as necessary.*

These procedures can be beneficial in programming for students with mild disabilities at various times or decision points. First, for at-risk students, the procedures can be viewed as preventive and prereferral measures. Second, if difficulties persist, team members may decide to proceed with a referral for screening, but they can continue to meet to discuss interventions and provide ideas and support to each other. Third, if the child is placed in a special program or is receiving other types of services, the team members should continue to consult and collaborate to ensure that the child's total program is cohesive. Fourth, if the child is mainstreamed for academic or social skills, the teachers should collaborate on identifying desired student behaviors and appropriate teaching or management strategies. Evaluation should be ongoing during all of these situations; that is, team members should be assessing the effectiveness of the interventions, as well as their consultation and collaboration skills, and assisting one another to make whatever modifications are deemed appropriate (Fishbaugh, 1997; Jayanthi & Friend, 1992; Mostert, 1998). The focus should be development of school-based teams working toward comprehensive, integrated, and programmatic approaches to students' problems (Adelman & Taylor, 1998).

As illustrated in the vignette about Andy, a number of personnel may be involved in the interactive teaming situation and also in follow-up consultation with other team members. Role release will need to occur in all these contexts, along with sensitivity to cultural differences, attention to the perspectives of others, expertise in communication, and effectiveness in leadership strategies.

Service Delivery Options

Students with mild disabilities receive services in several settings, depending on the severity of their problems and where the people involved in placement decisions believe their needs can be best met. If the child or adolescent evidences severe difficulties in all five of the areas of need previously identified, he/she will likely be placed in a more restrictive setting, such as a full-time special class or in a special class with part of the day spent in a general education classroom. If the difficulties are evidenced primarily in one area such as academic problems, the child may spend the majority of the day in the general classroom with assistance from a resource teacher or a speech-language therapist. Those whose problems are considered very mild may be in general education settings all day, although the teacher will consult as needed with other professionals (e.g., special educator, speech-language therapist, adaptive physical educator). According to the 15th Annual Report to Congress (1993), 69.3% of special education students were in regular classrooms more than 40% of the time during the 1991–1992 school year. The continuum of options for service delivery is illustrated in Figure 11.1.

Variations and combinations of the services illustrated on the continuum have been used to meet the needs of students with mild disabilities. Most, if not all, rely on some level of collaboration or teaming among teachers. Simpson and Myles (1990) described a general education collaboration model that incorporated flexible departmentalization and classroom modifications that support mainstreaming. Laycock, Gable, and Korinek (1991) noted that collaborative approaches can provide early intervention for at-risk learners and facilitate access to accommodations in the regular classroom for students with mild disabilities.

Pull-in programs, in which the specialist teaches in the regular classroom, were described by Meyers, Gelzheiser, and Yelich (1991). They found that compared with pull-out programs, the teachers in pull-in situations had more collaborative meetings, focused more on specific instructional issues, and learned more instructional techniques. Gable, Hendrickson, and Rogan (1996) examined the use of middle school collaborative teams to support a "stay-put" program for at-risk stu-

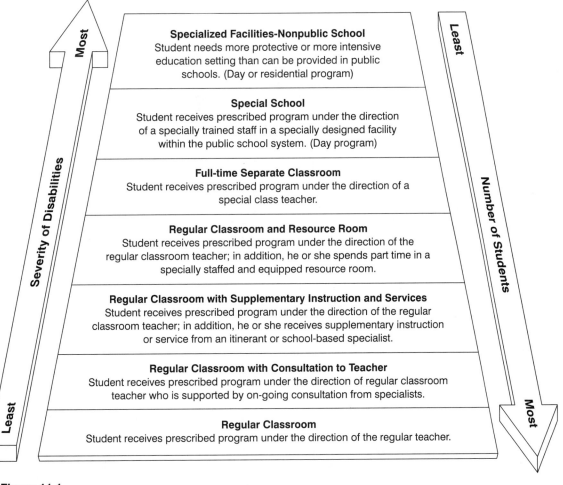

Figure 11.1
Continuum of educational services for students with disabilities.
Source: From EXCEPTIONAL CHILDREN: AN INTRODUCTION TO SPECIAL EDUCATION 6/E by Heward, William L., 2000. Reprinted by permission of Prentice-Hall, Inc., Upper Saddle River, NJ.

dents and those with mild disabilities. Their program utilized a regular classroom accommodation model based on the concept of a "class within a class." Morsink and Lenk (1992) commented on four promising strategies for integrating students with mild disabilities in regular classrooms using collaboration among teachers: adapting learning environments with augmentative technology, learning strategies, peer tutoring, and cooperative learning. They observed that for students at the secondary level, collaborative planning is a major need for transition program delivery. Sileo, Rude, and Luckner (1988) outlined the need for such collaboration among specialists, regular and vocational teachers, and family members to provide transition planning that focuses on relevant life development activities.

The use of teams to conduct functional behavior assessments mandated by P.L. 105-17 was outlined by Vaughn, Hales, Bush, and Fox (1998). Todd, Horner, Sugai, and Sprague (1999) described the use of teams to provide a systems approach to behavioral support services. They outlined four patterns of problems and intervention systems: schoolwide, nonclassroom or specific settings, classroom settings, and individual students with chronic behavior problems. Implementation of teaming approaches after crises such as student suicides was presented by Roberts, Lepkowski, and Davidson (1998). The focus of these teams is to create comprehensive postvention plans to handle crises that impact groups of students or an entire school.

Bauwens, Hourcade, and Friend (1989) described cooperative teaching or co-teaching approaches in which regular and special educators coordinate ways to teach academically and behaviorally heterogeneous groups of students. They described three cooperative teaching options: (1) complementary instruction, in which the regular educator maintains primary responsibility for teaching subject matter and the special educator focuses on the students' mastery of academic survival skills; (2) team teaching, in which the teachers jointly plan and deliver instruction; and (3) supportive learning activities developed by the special educator to supplement the content delivered by the regular educator.

Cook and Friend (1995) identified a set of questions teachers should consider in order to create a collaborative working relationship in a co-teaching model. These questions are included in Table 11.1. Bauwens and Hourcade (1997) expanded on their earlier work and noted that the critical feature in cooperative teaching is that two educators possessing distinct sets of skills are working in a coordinated fashion to teach academically heterogeneous students in a general education classroom. They provided descriptions and pictorial representations of co-teaching arrangements.

Gable and Manning (1997) also described similar service delivery models which they labeled *cooperative teaching options* and *collaborative instructional options*. These options are summarized in Table 11.2. Dieker and Barnett (1996) outlined steps to prepare school teams for implementation of co-teaching at the elementary and middle school levels. Boudah, Schumacher, and Deshler (1997) examined the collaborative instruction model at the secondary level, and commented that in such arrangements strategy instruction needs to be integrated with enhanced content instruction in order for students to be successful in general education settings.

Table 11.1
Questions for Creating a Collaborative Working Relationship in Co-Teaching

Topic	Questions
Instructional beliefs	• What are our overriding philosophies about the roles of teachers and teaching, and students and learning? • How do our instructional beliefs affect our instructional practice?
Planning	• When do we have at least 30 minutes of shared planning time? • How do we divide our responsibilities for planning and teaching? • How much joint planning time do we need? • What records can we keep to facilitate our planning?
Parity signals	• How will we convey to students and others (for example, teachers, parents) that we are equals in the classroom? • How can we ensure a sense of parity during instruction?
Confidentiality	• What information about our teaching do we want to share with others? • What information should not be shared? • Which information about students can be shared with others? • What information should not be shared?
Noise	• What noise level are we comfortable with in the classroom?
Classroom routines	• What are the *instructional* routines in the classroom? • What are the *organizational* routines for the classroom?
Discipline	• What is acceptable and unacceptable student behavior? • Who is to intervene at what point in student's behavior? • What are the rewards and consequences used in the classroom?
Feedback	• What is the best way to give each other feedback? • How will you ensure that both positive and negative issues are raised?
Pet peeves	• What aspects of teaching and classroom life do each of us feel strongly about? • How can we identify our pet peeves so as to avoid them?

Source: From "Co-Teaching: Guidelines for Creating Effective Practices" by L. Cook and M. Friend, 1995, *Focus on Exceptional Children, 28*(3), pp. 1–16. Reprinted by permission of Love Publishing Company.

Vaughn, Schumm, and Arguelles (1997) presented five models of co-teaching and lesson plan formats, as well as discussing major issues such as grading, classroom management, and time. Salend and his colleagues (1997) noted that cooperative teaching brings academic instruction and supportive services to students in the environment where the need exists. Their article addressed important concerns about cooperative teaching such as respecting skill differences and recognizing mutual strengths of all individuals involved, confronting differences, creating a sense of community, changing language, noting changes in students, and receiving administrative support (Salend et al., 1997).

A final service delivery option currently receiving much attention among educators who teach students with mild disabilities is full inclusion. Many promote the need for integrating regular and special services to provide high-quality edu-

Table 11.2
Cooperative Teaching Options and Collaborative Instructional Options

---

Cooperative Teaching Options

• *Shadow Teaching*
General educator is primarily responsible for teaching specific subject matter, while the special educator works directly with one or two target students on academics and/or behavior

• *One Teach/One Assist*
General educator is primarily responsible for teaching specific subject, while the special educator circulates around the classroom and offers individual students assistance

• *Station Teaching*
General educator is primarily responsible for teaching specific subject matter to subgroups of students, who rotate among the learning stations

• *Complimentary Teaching*
General educator is primarily responsible for teaching specific subject matter, while the special educator assumes responsibility for teaching associated academic skills (e.g., note taking, test taking) or school survival skills (e.g., sharing, self-control)

• *Parallel Teaching*
General educator and special educator divide the class into two smaller groups to provide more individualized instruction

• *Supplementary Teaching Activities*
General educator is primarily responsible for teaching specific subject matter, while the special educator assumes responsibility for giving students content-specific assistance (e.g., reinforcing content through small-group activities or outside assignments)

• *Team Teaching*
General and special educator share equal responsibility for planning, carrying out and evaluating the lesson

• *Alternative Teaching*
General educator is responsible for teaching majority of students, while the special education teacher assumes the responsibility for teaching a select group of students who require significant curricular accomodations

---

cation for all students (e.g., Goodlad & Lovitt, 1993), and others have described successful inclusion programs that provide many positive benefits (e.g., Jakupcak, 1993). As the debate continues over the appropriateness of full inclusion for students with mild disabilities, professional organizations reiterate the need for a continuum of services as mandated by the IDEA (National Joint Committee on Learning Disabilities, 1993), and leaders in the field call for strengthening the conceptual foundations and empirical base (Kauffman, 1993) and for pragmatic approaches toward redefining relationships with regular education (Fuchs & Fuchs, 1994).

Walther-Thomas, Bryant, and Land (1996) noted that the popularity of inclusive models is growing, and cited U.S. Department of Education data that indi-

Table 11.2, *continued*

Collaborative Instructional Options

• *Same*
Students with special needs participate in regular class instruction and pursue the same content objectives within the same instructional material. When teaching all students the same content, consider team teaching, station teaching, parallel teaching or supplemental teaching.

• *Multi-level*
Students with special needs participate in regular class instruction, but pursue different content objectives, based on their individual needs.

Example: The majority of students will use a 4th-garde textbook for health instruction, while selected students with special needs follow along in 2nd-grade level material, using study guides. During class discussion, special needs students are asked basic questions about the content and/or parallel textual material (e.g., health content from a 2nd-grade book, IEP-related questions).

• *Curriculum Overlapping*
Students with special needs participate in the same large-group instruction, but pursue objectives from different academic and/or social areas.

Example: In a cooperative team learning activity, the majority of students have a content-specific assignment, while selected students with special needs serve as timekeepers (e.g., to work on telling time), or are paired with two students without disabilities who model and reinforce attention-to-task, positive socialization and/or responses to basic content objectives. When teaching different yet complementary content, consider complementary teaching, shadow teaching or a parallel teaching arrangement.

• *Alternative*
Students with special needs pursue different activities/content objectives from the rest of the class.

Example: While the majority of class completes a writing assignment, students with special needs receive instruction in an unrelated area from another person (e.g., peer tutor or special education teacher). When teaching separate content, consider an alternative teaching arrangement.

Source: From "The Role of Teacher Collaboration in School Reform" by R. A. Gable and M. L. Manning, 1997, *Childhood Education, 73*(4), pp. 219–223. Reprinted by permission.

cated this trend is likely to continue. Rainforth and England (1997) commented that when collaborating for inclusion, individuals become members of a team and assume many team roles. They also provided descriptions of the values and skills required for collaboration and guidelines for collaborative teaching approaches. Hobbs and Westling (1998) listed the following schoolwide and in-class components necessary for successful inclusion:

Schoolwide Components

◆ Administrative leadership.

◆ Inservice training or technical assistance.

◆ Adequate time for meeting and planning among professionals and parents.

◆ Parent and family support.

◆ Community support.

◆ Access to journals and information.

◆ Reduced class sizes.

In-Class Components

◆ Integrated related-therapy services, medical support, and behavior management support.

◆ Appropriate physical layout of class.

◆ Adapted curricula and materials.

◆ Use of volunteer personnel.

◆ Use of paraprofessional personnel.

◆ Cooperative teaching or collaborative consultation between teachers.

◆ Cooperative learning.

◆ Peer tutoring.

◆ Collaborative problem solving (Hobbs & Westling, 1998, p. 14).

Additional information on inclusion can be found in texts such as those by Salend (1998), Smith (1998), Tiegerman-Farber and Radziewicz (1998), and Wood (1998).

Teacher Competencies

A sampling of research in the past 20 years in regular and special education on competencies for general and special education teachers reveals that the skills identified often are quite similar. Researchers such as Brophy (1979), Good (1979), and Stevens and Rosenshine (1981) stressed teacher behaviors that included a teacher-controlled approach, activities with an academic focus, sufficient time for instruction, an emphasis on classroom management, practice opportunities for student responses, material taught in small steps, and frequent testing of student learning with appropriate feedback.

Englert (1984) identified competencies in the areas of classroom organization; teaching and maintaining rules and procedures; allocated and engaged time; and lesson introduction, demonstration, practice, and evaluation. Morsink et al. (1987) suggested that four generic sets of competencies were suitable for teachers of students with mild disabilities. Those competencies are (1) teacher-directed instruction, (2) provision for students to engage in active academic responding with teacher feedback, (3) contingent reinforcement of appropriate student behaviors, and (4) adaptive instruction, geared to individual needs for differences such as longer learning time, simplified language, or concrete materials. Wolery, Bailey, and Sugai (1988) listed the areas of child development, curriculum content, disabling conditions, principles of learning and behavioral procedures, and instructional monitoring and evaluation procedures as essential knowledge and skills for teachers.

In a research synthesis by the Northwest Regional Education Laboratory (1990), the following recommendations were developed based on effective teacher practices:

◆ Use a preplanned curriculum with learning goals and objectives sequenced to facilitate student learning.

◆ Form instructional groups based on student achievement levels and review and adjust group membership as skill levels change.

◆ Use classroom management strategies that minimize disruptive behaviors.

◆ Hold students accountable for appropriate behavior and achievement and give help immediately when they experience problems.

◆ Provide additional learning time on priority objectives.

Simmons and Kameenui (1991) described the importance of teachers using principles of instructional design, information analysis, and taxonomies of knowledge. Algozzine and Ysseldyke (1992) designed a conceptual model for effective instruction that included four components: (1) planning instruction (e.g., deciding what and how to teach), (2) managing instruction (e.g., preparation and establishing a positive environment), (3) delivering instruction (e.g., motivation, feedback, and active involvement), and (4) evaluating instruction (e.g., monitoring student understanding and making decisions about performance). Examples of application of their model are provided in a special focus section on effective instruction in *Teaching Exceptional Children* (see Algozzine, Ysseldyke, & Campbell, 1994).

Based on their review and synthesis of the effectiveness research, Mercer and Mercer (1998) identified four sets of instructional variables related to student learning: (1) focus on time for learning, (2) ensure high rates of student success, (3) provide positive and supportive learning environments, and (4) plan and maintain a motivational environment.

SELECTED TEACHING STRATEGIES

In terms of teaching techniques, the team members will need to consider the academic and behavioral problems presented by the student. Only a selected number of strategies will be cited to illustrate the range of possibilities that might be appropriate for students with mild disabilities. More detailed information on teaching methods for specific academic and behavioral problems is available in a number of textbooks, such as those by Bos and Vaughn (1998), Churton, Craston-Gingras, and Blair (1998), Hallahan et al. (1999), Jensen and Kiley (2000), Lasley and Matczynski (1997), Lovitt (1995), Mercer and Mercer (1998), Olson and Platt (2000), O'Shea et al. (1998), and Sabornie and deBettencourt (1997). Additional information can be obtained on web sites such as www.ldonline.org, www.nclearn.org, or www.cec.sped.org.

Most students with mild disabilities will need to be taught general strategies for *how* to learn (Deshler & Schumaker, 1986) or explicit strategies, such as decision trees used in problem-solving exercises in computer simulations (Hollingsworth & Woodward, 1993). Others may need to be taught classroom discourse strategies to promote literacy development (Englert, Raphael, & Mariage, 1994); specific strategies for reading comprehension, such as semantic mapping (Sinatra, Berg, & Dunn, 1985) or reciprocal questions (Manzo & Manzo, 1993); or techniques for written expression (Thomas, 1996; Thomas, Englert, & Gregg, 1987).

Students who are experiencing difficulties in mathematics need to acquire a cognitive strategy for solving different types of problems (cf. Montague & Bos, 1986), as well as self-monitoring strategies (Frank & Brown, 1992). Students with sensory impairments may need help developing residual hearing and listening skills. Students with physical disabilities or communication disorders may need help with alternative communication strategies.

Nevin and Thousand (1986) identified a number of promising practices that can be used in regular classroom settings: (1) curricular adaptations, (2) mastery learning, (3) individualized learning, (4) peer tutoring, (5) accelerated learning systems, and (6) applied behavior analysis. Henley, Ramsey, and Algozzine (1993) described several approaches and strategies that have received attention in recent years including integrated teaching, whole language, the Adaptive Learning Environment Model, skillstreaming, and direct instruction. Bos and Vaughn (1998) provided an overview of the use of cognitive behavior modification, modeling and demonstration strategies, reflective thinking, information processing and schema techniques, and microcomputers and multimedia systems. Other methods that have been shown to improve academic functioning, as well as social interactions, are cooperative learning strategies, such as the jigsaw technique (cf. Aronson, Blaney, Stephan, Sikes, & Snapp, 1978; Johnson, Johnson, Warring, & Maruyama, 1986; Lloyd, Crowley, Kohler, & Strain, 1988; Putnam, 1993). Learning styles instruction (Carbo, 1990) and teaching school survival skills to adolescents (Schaeffer, Zigmond, Kerr, & Farra, 1990) also can enhance achievement.

Schumm, Vaughn, and Harris (1997) advocated the use of a "Planning Pyramid" that considers the following aspects of instruction: teacher, topic, content, student, and instructional practices. Orkwis and McLane (1998) described universal design principles that apply to content, goals, methods, and manner of assessment. They defined universal design as "the design of instructional materials and activities that allows the learning goals to be achievable by individuals with differences" (p. 9).

Kling (1997) asked teachers to rate preferred strategies based on specific children's behaviors. Their ratings appear in Table 11.3. Burke, Hagan, and Grossen

Table 11.3
Preferred Strategies Used with Specific Children's Behaviors

Behavior	Strategy Used	Rating
1. Hyperactivity/ Distractibility	daily home reports	5
	individualized instruction	5
	timer	5
	sticker charts	5
	time recording on papers	5
	* organizational folders	4
	praise	4
	humor	4
	copy cards at desk	4
	opportunity for movement	4
	teacher/pupil conference	4
	self-monitoring charts	3
	teacher monitoring work	3
2. Disorganization	self-monitoring chart	5
	positive reinforcement	5
	** one paper at a time	5
	assignment pads	5
	parent signing homework	4
	folders for papers	3
3. Talkative	parent conferences	5
	teacher prompts/signals	4
	seating in front of room	4
	read story geared to problem	4
4. Disruptive behavior	daily home communication	5
	student explanation of behavior	5
	positive reinforcement	5
	nonverbal skills	4
5. Unmotivated	positive reinforcement	5
	parent signature of homework	5
6. Belligerent behavior	positive reinforcement	5
	provide leadership role	4
7. Socially immature	consistency	5
	firm expectations	3
8. Slow worker	modify amount of work	5
	clock to budget time	4
9. Academic problems	reinforcement and repetition	5
	one-to-one instruction	5
	concrete materials	5
	smaller quantities of work	5
	provide tests in segments	5
	self-monitoring charts	5
	visual aids to show directions	5
	peer tutoring	5
	study guides	5
	home/school reinforcement	5
	change course requirements	4
	oral or untimed tests	4

Note: Ratings indicate how 26 teachers rated each strategy's *usefulness*, after 1 year of trial, on a Likert scale from 1 to 5, with 1 being the least effective and 5 being the most effective.

Sample expansions of strategies:

*Organize folders: File folders of different colors were provided for each student. Some teachers established a notebook for the folders so that papers would be in one place. Teachers provided reinforcers for papers for students so that torn papers would not fall out of the notebook.

** One paper at a time: Teachers used several methods, such as baskets in a designated place, where students could return a completed assignment and collect a new paper. The strategic placement of these baskets was important. Some students needed the opportunity for movement, but it was essential to place them in an area where they would not disturb others. Some teachers found it was effective to number assignments in order and place "work to do" in a folder in students' desk to reduce clutter.

Source: From "Empowering Teachers to Use Successful Strategies" by B. Kling, 1997, *Teaching Exceptional Children,* 30(2), pp. 20–24. Reprinted by permission.

(1998) described the use of big ideas, conspicuous strategies, primed background knowledge, mediated scaffolding, judicious review, and strategic integration as ways to accommodate diverse learners. A summary of their work is included as Table 11.4, and additional information can be found at the following web site: http://darkwing.uoregon.edu/~ncite/index.html. Swanson (1999) investigated the effectiveness of interventions such as sequencing, segmentation of information, modeling problem-solving steps, presenting cues to prompt strategies use, and directed response/questioning of students. His results indicated that a combined strategy and direct instruction model was the most effective intervention. Additional strategies to address academic difficulties are listed in Table 11.5.

Considerations

In trying to determine which strategies to recommend or attempt to implement in a particular situation, several considerations should be kept in mind. Knight (1976) noted that in working with other professionals it is particularly important to inform them that their role is important (whether it is one of providing service or following up on a skill), to ensure them that they will be helped rather than judged, and to clarify which procedures will be used in evaluation. Hasbrouck and Christen (1997) described an instrument to help special education peer coaches observe classroom teachers' skills, strategies, and techniques, and provide feedback.

Additional considerations on making suggestions to regular classroom teachers about behavior problems were identified by Martens, Peterson, Witt, and Cirone (1986). They noted that teachers classify strategies in terms of effectiveness, ease of use, and frequency of use. They cautioned consultants to be aware of the extent to which the interventions they suggest are similar to those a teacher may already be using, and the degree to which a teacher's behavior will have to change in order to implement an intervention.

Guskey (1990) provided a framework for synthesizing diverse instructional strategies: (1) instructional strategies should share common goals, (2) strategies should complement each other, (3) time should be taken to experiment and adapt strategies to individuals and classrooms, and (4) educators should recognize that the combined beneficial effects of several strategies will surpass the effects of any single strategy. A final set of considerations are the procedural principles identified by Idol, Nevin, and Paolucci-Whitcomb (1994) designed to facilitate performance of learners with special needs in inclusive classrooms:

1. Procedural principles designed to facilitate teaching and learning of difficult-to-teach learners must be easy to implement in inclusive classrooms.

2. Teaching and learning procedures should be designed for use with any student who is achieving poorly, rather than for a single learner with special needs.

3. Teaching and learning procedures need to be based on the use of classroom curricula.

Table 11.4
Ways to Accelerate Student Learning

The National Center to Improve the Tools of Educators (NCITE) has identified six features of instruction that effectively accommodate and accelerate student learning.

1. Big Ideas

Big ideas are concepts and principles that facilitates the most efficient and broadest acquisition of knowledge across a range of examples.

A social studies example of a big idea: Human rights problems are associated with the need to achieve religious freedom; freedom of speech; equal protection under the law; and equal rights for women, minorities, and different social classes.

2. Conspicuous Strategies

Conspicuous strategies are an approximation of the steps experts follow covertly to solve complex problems and difficult tasks.

For example, the steps in the strategy for science inquiry are (a) identify the variable to test, (b) create a condition that changes that variable, (c) keep the other variables the same, (d) gather data, and (e) interpret the outcome.

3. Primed Background Knowledge

Before understanding of new information can occur, necessary background knowledge must be taught or "primed." This requires teaching component steps and concepts that allow an in-depth understanding of a big idea or strategy.

For example, in writing instruction, if students are to write good narrative explanations, they should have some knowledge of words indicating chronology, such as *first, then, next, after,* and *finally.*

4. Mediated Scaffolding

Scaffolding refers to the guidance, assistance, and support that a teacher, peer, or task provides to a learner.

For example, in teaching reading comprehension, the teacher's frequent interspersed questions are a scaffold that can gradually be reduced as students become able to interact with text on their own.

5. Judicious Review

Judicious reviews should be (a) sufficient for initial learning to occur, (b) distributed over time, (c) varied for generalizability, and (d) cumulative.

An example of judicious review in math is incorporating review of addition, subtraction, multiplication, and division facts even when introducing new knowledge, such as fractions.

6. Strategic Integration

Strategic integration is the process where prior learning is integrated into more complex concepts.

For example, in beginning reading instruction, teachers can provide decodable text as students are learning letter-sound relationships to figure out words.

Source: From "What Curricular Designs and Strategies Accommodate Diverse Learners?" by M. D. Burke, S. L. Hagan, and B. Grossen, 1998, *Teaching Exceptional Children, 31*(1), pp. 34–38. Reprinted by permission.

Table 11.5

Strategies to Help Students Achieve Basic Academic Skills

Strategies That Help	Strategies That Do Not Help
Mostly narrow teacher questions with a "right" answer	Mostly open-ended questions **or** Nonacademic conversation
Calling on nonvolunteers or using patterned turns to select students to answer questions	Selecting only volunteers when calling on students to answer questions
Immediate feedback (as to right or wrong) to students' answers	Not giving clear feedback to students' answers
"Staying with" a student until he or she answers a question	Quickly letting someone else answer; leaving a student with little or no feedback
Short and frequent—rather than long and occasional—paper and pencil activities	Games, art work, many interest centers
Specific praise for good performance	Vague or general praise, or praise when it isn't especially deserved
Covering material thoroughly	Covering a lot of material quickly
Much time spent in teacher questioning, feedback, and supervised practice	Much class time spent in anything else
Time spent in structured learning activities led by the teacher	Time spent in unstructured or free time
Instruction broken down into small steps, short activities sequenced by the teacher	Long, unbroken periods of seatwork or independent work, with students' choice of activities or sequences
Plenty of practice (repetition) with frequent correction and praise	Little practice **or** Independent practice without prompt feedback
A lot of supervision and help, in whole-class or group settings	Individualized, self-paced instruction; independent work
Continuous teacher direction of student behavior and activity	Situations calling for much pupil self-control or self-direction
Materials or questions at a level of difficulty at which students have a high rate of success	Challenging materials or questions, or work in which students are not likely to know most of the answers
Many opportunities and much encouragement to answer teacher questions	Few opportunities or little encouragement to answer questions frequently

4. Teaching and learning procedures must include components that teach learners to generalize.

5. Teaching and learning procedures need to be useful for group instruction.

6. Learners must be directly taught the skill areas they are required to master.

Wolfe (1998) made an observation that is important for all interactive team members who are providing direct services and collaborating with other professionals to remember: "Teaching is decision making and the more we know about the science of teaching the better we can artistically apply that knowledge" (p. 64). Schamber (1999) commented that diversity in members of teaching teams is a major benefit since it provides multiple perspectives in dealing with students and other issues.

ROLES OF PROFESSIONALS INVOLVED WITH STUDENTS WITH MILD DISABILITIES

As described in Chapter 4, interactive team members involved in the education of students with mild disabilities can serve in two types of roles: collaborator/consultant and direct service provider. In both roles, the professionals will apply the knowledge from their own areas of specialization; participate actively in planning, decision making, implementation, and evaluation of interventions; and ensure that programming is provided in a comprehensive and coordinated way (Johnson, Pugach, & Devlin, 1990).

In the role of collaborator/consultant, team members should consider the types and degree of services required and determine which academic or behavioral management strategies are warranted based on the student's needs. Donaldson and Christiansen (1990) designed a *collaborative decision-making model* that can be used as a guide to select appropriate options for service delivery, instruction, and behavior management (see Figure 11.2). In this model, team members will need to consult/collaborate by identifying the problems presented, deciding on the appropriate placement in the continuum of services displayed in Figure 11.1, and determining which instructional or behavior management strategies to implement. The final part of the cycle involves evaluating the success of the options or interventions, and deciding what procedures for follow-up or alternative placements are warranted. Additional examples of the types of contributions and activities interactive team members can participate in as direct service providers and collaborators/consultants are provided in Table 11.6.

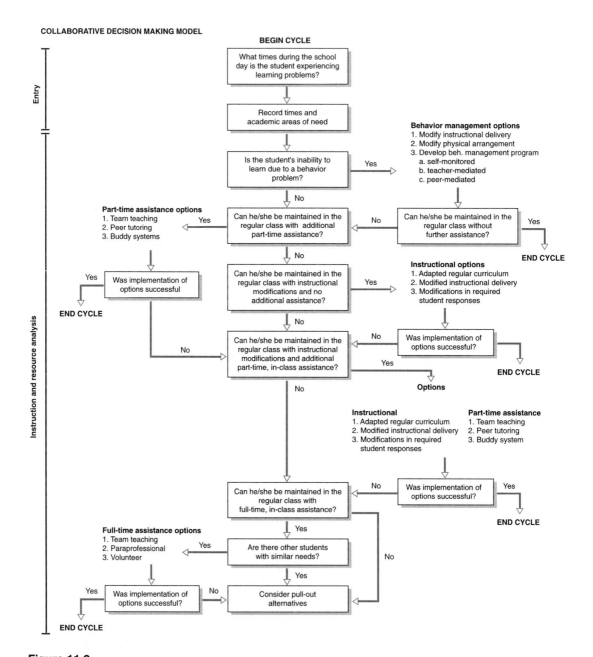

COLLABORATIVE DECISION MAKING MODEL

BEGIN CYCLE

What times during the school day is the student experiencing learning problems?

Record times and academic areas of need

Is the student's inability to learn due to a behavior problem?

Behavior management options
1. Modify instructional delivery
2. Modify physical arrangement
3. Develop beh. management program
   a. self-monitored
   b. teacher-mediated
   c. peer-mediated

Yes

No

Part-time assistance options
1. Team teaching
2. Peer tutoring
3. Buddy systems

Yes

Can he/she be maintained in the regular class with additional part-time assistance?

No

Can he/she be maintained in the regular class without further assistance?

Yes

END CYCLE

Yes

Was implementation of options successful

END CYCLE

No

Can he/she be maintained in the regular class with instructional modifications and no additional assistance?

Yes

Instructional options
1. Adapted regular curriculum
2. Modified instructional delivery
3. Modifications in required student responses

No

No

Can he/she be maintained in the regular class with instructional modifications and additional part-time, in-class assistance?

No

Was implementation of options successful?

Yes

END CYCLE

No

Options

Instructional
1. Adapted regular curriculum
2. Modified instructional delivery
3. Modifications in required student responses

Part-time assistance
1. Team teaching
2. Peer tutoring
3. Buddy system

No

Can he/she be maintained in the regular class with full-time, in-class assistance?

Was implementation of options successful?

Yes

END CYCLE

Full-time assistance options
1. Team teaching
2. Paraprofessional
3. Volunteer

Yes

Yes

Are there other students with similar needs?

No

Yes

Yes

Was implementation of options successful?

No

Consider pull-out alternatives

END CYCLE

Entry

Instruction and resource analysis

Figure 11.2
Collaborative decision-making model.

Source: From "Consultation and Collaboration: A Decision-Making Model" by R. Donaldson and J. Christiansen, 1990, *Teaching Exceptional Children, 22*(2), pp. 22–25. Reprinted by permission of the authors and the Council for Exceptional Children.

Table 11.6
Role of Professionals and Others Involved with Students with Mild Disabilities

Personnel	Direct Service Provider	Team Member
Special Educator	• Assess educational achievement. • Design instructional program. • Implement academic/behavioral strategies. • Follow up on skills taught by others.	• Serve as case manager. • Interpret assessments. • Observe in other settings. • Consult on individualizing instructional techniques.
Regular Educator	• Implement academic/behavioral strategies. • Assist in social integration.	• Consult on curriculum. • Consult on group management techniques.
Parent	• Reinforce academic and behavioral programs at home.	• Provide background information. • Consult on possible interventions.
Administrator	• Reinforce appropriate behavior.	• Provide information on services available in school and community. • Assist with scheduling and class size.
Psychologist	• Assess psychological functioning.	• Interpret test results. • Collaborate in designing interventions and data collection strategies.
Speech-Language Therapist	• Assess speech-language development. • Remediate speech-language disorders in individual or small group sessions.	• Interpret test results. • Provide follow-up materials for other team members. Consult on strategies to use.
Counselor	• Provide counseling on self-concept, getting along with adults and peers, etc.	• Collaborate with others about emotional or behavioral situations.
Physical and Occupational Therapist	• Assess physical and occupational needs. • Provide physical therapy. • Provide occupational therapy.	• Interpret test results. • Collaborate with others on ways to enhance physical development or classroom modifications.
Hearing and Vision Specialists	• Assess hearing and vision. • Teach strategies such as auditory training, listening skills, orientation and mobility.	• Interpret test results. • Teach others how to use special equipment or materials.
Adapted Physical Educator	• Assess psychomotor skills. • Remediate areas of physical fitness.	• Collaborate in designing cooperative games and motor development activities.

Application

The vignette about Andy at the beginning of this chapter contains descriptions of several behaviors that an interactive team could target for change. However, in a team meeting the professionals and Andy's mother agreed that the most problematic behavior in all settings (e.g., general education classroom, resource room, home, playground) was his unwillingness to begin tasks on time. Instead, Andy used a variety of avoidance tactics, including breaking pencils and arguing, to keep from starting his assignments.

The team members decided that a behavior management system using a contingency contract might help modify Andy's behavior. Because Andy enjoys sports, the adapted physical educator, Ms. DiCicco, agreed to allow him to be her "assistant" when she coached the soccer team if he met the conditions of the contract.

The regular classroom teacher, Ms. Baker, said she would like to focus on math seatwork for purposes of the contract. Ms. Rodriquez, the resource teacher, identified writing journal assignments as the area of concern in her classroom. Mr. Morrow, the speech-language therapist, cited oral language practice activities as a goal, and noted that this should be assessed in all settings because Andy received speech therapy only once a week. Andy's mother, Ms. Rhodes, said she wanted him to begin his homework assignments promptly. The objectives and personnel involved in Andy's program are listed in Table 11.7.

The team members discussed the level of performance that should be required for Andy to earn the privilege of being Ms. DiCicco's assistant with the soccer team and decided that a success rate of 60% (i.e., three out of five assignments) for three consecutive days would be a good starting point. They based this decision on a

Table 11.7

Interactive Team Plan for Andy

Objectives	GenEd	SpEd	Parent	APE
1. Andy will begin his math seatwork within 2 minutes of the assignments being given.	x			
2. Andy will request help within 5 minutes of the directions being provided instead of crumpling up his paper.	x	x	x	
3. Andy will begin his homework within 2 minutes of his mother's request to start.			x	
4. Andy will distribute equipment for the soccer team within 2 minutes of the request by the adapted physical educator or coach.				x

desire for Andy to experience success and receive the reinforcement early in the program so that he would be motivated. They agreed to gradually increase the percentage and the number of days as his behavior improved.

Ms. Rhodes said she would like to be the one to explain the program to her son, and everyone else supported this idea. Then the team members discussed a system for collecting and sharing their data with Ms. Baker, who would determine if the criteria had been met and notify Ms. DiCicco that Andy was eligible for the reward. The team members agreed to meet again in 2 weeks to evaluate the effectiveness of the program, and discuss any needed modifications.

◊ ◊

SUMMARY

The characteristics of students with mild disabilities often are similar. Their needs can be categorized into five areas:

◆ Academic remediation.

◆ Social interactions.

◆ Self-concept and motivation.

◆ Behavior management.

◆ Special education and support services.

To meet these needs, interactive team members should implement a process for problem identification and designing interventions, use appropriate service delivery options, demonstrate competencies, intervene with effective teaching strategies, and evaluate and adapt programs as necessary.

A number of personnel are involved in the education of students, both as direct service providers and as team members who serve as collaborators/consultants. It is essential that all of these people work together in a cohesive and coordinated manner, keeping students' needs as the focus of attention, in order to provide effective programs. Chapter 12 describes how professionals and parents serve as interactive team members for students with severe disabilities.

ACTIVITIES

1. Conduct informational interviews with a regular educator, resource teacher, and parent about the characteristics of a child with a mild disability. Compare their comments on the child's academic and behavioral needs.

2. Volunteer to tutor or provide a special activity for a child with a mild disability. Describe your observations of the child's behaviors and interests.

3. Observe a child in three different settings, such as regular and special education classrooms and speech-language therapy. What similarities and differences did you notice in the child's behavior and performance?

4. Attend a school-based committee or teacher-assistance team meeting. Based on your observations of the meeting, answer the following questions: Who attended the meeting, and did everyone participate? How was information presented? What characteristics and needs were mentioned? Which academic and behavior management strategies were discussed? How were decisions made?

REFERENCES

Adelman, H. S., & Taylor, L. (1998). Involving teachers in collaborative efforts to better address the barriers to student learning. *Preventing School Failure, 42*(2), 55–60.

Algozzine, B., & Ysseldyke, J. E. (1992). *Strategies and tactics for effective instruction.* Longmont, CO: Sopris West.

Algozzine, B., Ysseldyke, J. E., & Campbell, P. (1994). Strategies and tactics for effective instruction. *Teaching Exceptional Children, 26,* 34–36.

American Association on Mental Retardation (1992). *Mental retardation: Definition, classification, and systems of supports* (9th ed.). Washington, DC: Author.

Aronson, E., Blaney, N., Stephan, C., Sikes, J., & Snapp, M. (1978). *The jigsaw classroom.* Beverly Hills, CA: Sage Publications.

Bauwens, J., & Hourcade, J. J. (1997). Cooperative teaching: Pictures of possibilities. *Intervention in School and Clinic, 33*(2), 81–85, 89.

Bauwens, J., Hourcade, J. J., & Friend, M. (1989). Cooperative teaching: A model for general and special education integration. *Remedial and Special Education, 10*(2), 17–22.

Beirne-Smith, M., Ittenbach, R., & Patton, J. R. (1998). *Mental retardation* (5th ed.). Upper Saddle River, NJ: Merrill/Prentice Hall.

Berdine, W. H., & Blackhurst, A. E. (1985). *An introduction to special education* (2nd ed.). Boston: Little, Brown.

Bos, C. S., & Vaughn, S. (1998). *Strategies for teaching students with learning and behavior problems* (4th ed.). Needham Heights, MA: Allyn & Bacon.

Boudah, D. J., Schumacher, J. B., & Deshler, D. D. (1997). Collaborative instruction: Is it an effective option for inclusion in secondary classrooms? *Learning Disability Quarterly, 20*(4), 293–316.

Brophy, J. E. (1979). Teacher behavior and its effects. *Journal of Educational Psychology, 71,* 733–750.

Burke, M. D., Hagan, S. L., & Grossen, B. (1998). What curricular designs and strategies accommodate diverse learners? *Teaching Exceptional Children, 31*(1), 34–38.

Carbo, M. (1990). Igniting the literacy revolution through reading styles. *Educational Leadership, 48*(2), 89–92.

Churton, M. W., Craston-Gingras, A. M., & Blair, T. R. (1998). *Teaching children with diverse abilities.* Needham Heights, MA: Allyn and Bacon.

Cook, L., & Friend, M. (1995). Co-teaching: Guidelines for creating effective practices. *Focus on Exceptional Children, 28*(3), 1–16.

Cullinan, D., & Epstein, M. H. (1994). Behavior disorders. In N. G. Haring, L. McCormick, & T. G. Haring (Eds.), *Exceptional children and youth* (6th ed.). New York: Merrill/Macmillan.

Deshler, D. D., & Schumaker, J. B. (1986). Learning strategies: An instructional alternative for low-achieving adolescents. *Exceptional Children, 52,* 583–590.

Dieker, L. A., & Barnett, C.A. (1996). Effective co-teaching. *Teaching Exceptional Children, 29*(1), 5–7.

Donaldson, R., & Christiansen, J. (1990). Consultation and collaboration: A decision-making model. *Teaching Exceptional Children, 22*(2), 22–25.

Englert, C. S. (1984). Measuring teacher effectiveness from the teacher's point of view. *Focus on Exceptional Children, 17*(2), 1–14.

Englert, C. S., Raphael, T. E., & Mariage, T. V. (1994). Developing a school-based discourse for literacy learning: A principled search for understanding. *Learning Disability Quarterly, 17*(1), 2–32.

15th Annual Report to Congress on the Implementation of the Individuals with Disabilities Education Act (1993). Washington, DC: U.S. Department of Education, Office of Special Education Programs.

Finkelstein, D. (1989). *Blindness and disorders of the eyes.* Baltimore: The National Federation for the Blind.

Fishbaugh, M. S. E. (1997). *Models of collaboration.* Needham Heights, MA: Allyn & Bacon.

Frank, A. R., & Brown, D. (1992). Self-monitoring strategies in arithmetic. *Teaching Exceptional Children, 24*(2), 52–54.

Fuchs D., & Fuchs, L. S. (1994). Inclusive schools movement and the radicalization of special education reform. *Exceptional Children, 60*(4), 294–309.

Gable, R. A., Hendrickson, J. M., & Rogan, J. P. (1996). TEAMS supporting students at risk in the regular classroom. *Clearing House, 69*(4), 235–238.

Gable, R. A., & Manning, M. L. (1997). The role of teacher collaboration in school reform. *Childhood Education, 73*(4), 219–223.

Good, T. L. (1979). Teacher effectiveness in the elementary school. *Journal of Teacher Education, 30,* 52–64.

Goodlad, J. I., & Lovitt, T. C. (1993). *Integrating general and special education.* New York: Merrill/Macmillan.

Guskey, T. R. (1990). Integrating innovations. *Educational Leadership, 47*(5), 11–15.

Hallahan, D. P., & Kauffman, J. M. (2000). *Exceptional learners: Introduction to special education* (8th ed.). Boston: Allyn & Bacon.

Hallahan, D. P., Kauffman, J. M., & Lloyd, J. W. (1999). *Introduction to learning disabilities* (2nd ed.). Boston: Allyn & Bacon.

Hasbrouck, J. E., & Christen, M. H. (1997). Providing peer coaching in inclusive classrooms: A tool for consulting teachers. *Intervention in School and Clinic, 32*(3), 172–177.

Henley, M., Ramsey, R. S., & Algozzine, R. (1993). *Characteristics of and strategies for teaching students with mild disabilities.* Boston: Allyn & Bacon.

Heward, W. L. (2000). *Exceptional children: An introduction to special education* (6th ed.). Upper Saddle River, NJ: Merrill/Prentice Hall.

Hill, J. L. (1999). *Meeting the needs of students with special physical and health care needs.* Upper Saddle River, NJ: Merrill/Prentice Hall.

Hobbs, T., & Westling, D. L. (1998). Promoting successful inclusion through collaborative problem-solving. *Teaching Exceptional Children, 31*(1), 12–19.

Hollingsworth, M., & Woodward, J. (1993). Integrated learning: Explicit strategies and their role in problem-solving instruction for students with learning disabilities. *Exceptional Children, 59*(4), 444–455.

Idol, L., Nevin, A., & Paolucci-Whitcomb, P. (1994). *Collaborative consultation* (2nd ed.). Austin, TX: Pro-Ed.

Jakupcak, J. (1993). Innovative classroom programs for full inclusion. In J. W. Putnam (Ed.), *Cooperative learning and strategies for inclusion: Celebrating diversity in the classroom.* Baltimore: Paul H. Brookes.

Jayanthi, M., & Friend, M. (1992). Interpersonal problem solving: A selective literature review to guide practice. *Journal of Educational and Psychological Consultation, 3*(1), 39–53.

Jensen, R. A., & Kiley, T. J. (2000). *Teaching, leading, and learning: Becoming caring professionals.* Boston: Houghton Mifflin.

Johnson, D. W., Johnson, R. T., Warring, D., & Maruyama, G. (1986). Different cooperative learning procedures and cross-handicap relationships. *Exceptional Children, 53,* 245–252.

Johnson, L. J., Pugach, M. C., & Devlin, S. (1990). Professional collaboration. *Teaching Exceptional Children, 22*(2), 9–11.

Kauffman, J. M. (1993). How we might achieve the radical reform of special education. *Exceptional Children, 60*(1), 6–16.

Kauffman, J. M. (1997). *Characteristics of emotional and behavioral disorders of children and youth* (6th ed.). Upper Saddle River, NJ: Merrill/Prentice Hall.

Kirk, S. A., Gallagher, J. J., & Anastasiow, N. J. (1997). *Educating exceptional children* (8th ed.). Boston: Houghton Mifflin Company.

Kling, B. (1997). Empowering teachers to use successful strategies. *Teaching Exceptional Children, 30*(2), 20–24.

Knight, N. (1976). Working relationships that work. *Teaching Exceptional Children, 8,* 113–115.

Lasley, T. J., & Matczynski, T. J. (1997). *Strategies for teaching in a diverse society: Instructional models.* Belmont, CA: Wadsworth Publishing.

Laycock, V. K., Gable, R. A., & Korinek, L. (1991). Alternative structures for collaboration in the delivery of special services. *Preventing School Failure, 35*(4), 15–18.

Lloyd, J. W., Crowley, E. P., Kohler, F. W., & Strain, P. S. (1988). Redefining the applied research agenda: Cooperative learning, prereferral, teacher consultation, and peer-mediated interventions. *Journal of Learning Disabilities, 21,* 43–52.

Lovitt, T. C. (1995). *Tactics for teaching* (2nd ed.). Upper Saddle River, NJ: Merrill/Prentice Hall.

Manzo, A. V., & Manzo, M. C. (1993). *Literacy disorders: Holistic diagnosis and remediation.* Fort Worth, TX: Harcourt Brace Jovanovich.

Martens, B. K., Peterson, R. L., Witt, J. C., & Cirone, S. (1986). Teacher perceptions of school-based interventions. *Exceptional Children, 53,* 213–223.

Mercer, C. D. (1997). *Students with learning disabilities* (5th ed.). Upper Saddle River, NJ: Merrill/Prentice-Hall.

Mercer, C. D., & Mercer, A. R. (1998). *Teaching students with learning problems* (5th ed.). Upper Saddle River, NJ: Merrill/Prentice Hall.

Meyers, J., Gelzheiser, L. M., & Yelich, G. (1991). Do pull-in programs foster teacher collaboration? *Remedial and Special Education, 12*(2), 7–15.

Montague, M., & Bos, C. S. (1986). The effect of cognitive strategy training on verbal problem solving performance of learning disabled adolescents. *Journal of Learning Disabilities, 19,* 26–33.

Moores, D. (1996). *Educating the deaf: Psychology, principles, and practices* (4th ed.). Boston: Houghton Mifflin.

Morsink, C. V. (1984). *Teaching special needs students in regular classrooms.* Boston: Little, Brown.

Morsink, C. V., & Lenk, L. L. (1992). The delivery of special education programs and services. *Remedial and Special Education, 15*(6), 33–43.

Morsink, C. V., Thomas, C. C., & Smith-Davis, J. (1987). Noncategorical special education programs: Process and outcomes. In M. C. Wang, M. C. Reynolds, & H. J. Walberg (Eds.), *Handbook of special education: Research and practice* (Vol. 1). New York: Pergamon Press.

Mostert, M.P. (1998). *Interprofessional collaboration in schools.* Needham Heights, MA: Allyn & Bacon.

National Joint Committee on Learning Disabilities (1993). *A reaction to "full inclusion": A reaffirmation of the right of students with learning disabilities to a continuum of services.* Washington, DC: Author.

Nevin, A., & Thousand, J. (1986). What the research says about limiting or avoiding referrals to special education. *Teacher Education and Special Education, 9,* 149–161.

Northwest Regional Educational Laboratory (1990). *Effective schooling practices: A research synthesis 1990 update.* Portland, OR: Author.

Olson, J. L., & Platt, J. M. (2000). *Teaching children and adolescents with special needs* (3rd ed.). Upper Saddle River, NJ: Merrill/Prentice Hall.

Orkwis, R., & McLane, K. (1998). *A curriculum every student can use: Design principles for student access.* ERIC/OSEP Topical Brief. Reston, VA: The Council for Exceptional Children.

O'Shea, L. J., O'Shea, D. J., & Algozzine, R. (1998). *Learning disabilities: From theory toward practice.* Upper Saddle River, NJ: Merrill/Prentice Hall.

Putnam, J. W. (1993). *Cooperative learning and strategies for inclusion: Celebrating diversity in the classroom.* Baltimore: Paul H. Brookes.

Rainforth, B., & England, J. (1997). Collaborations for inclusion. *Education and Treatment of Children, 20*(1), 85–104.

Riegel, R. H. (1983). Mainstreaming equals cooperative planning. *Academic Therapy, 18,* 285–298.

Roberts, R. L., Lepkowski, W. J., & Davidson, K. K. (1998). After a student suicide, the TEAM approach. *Education Digest, 64*(2), 50–55.

Sabornie, E. J., & deBettencourt, L. U. (1997). *Teaching students with mild disabilities at the secondary level.* Upper Saddle River, NJ: Merrill/Prentice Hall.

Salend, S. J. (1998). *Effective mainstreaming: Creating inclusive classrooms* (3rd ed.). Upper Saddle River, NJ: Merrill/Prentice Hall.

Salend, S. J., Johansen, M., Mumper, J., Chase, A. S., Pike, K. M., & Dorney, J. A. (1997). Cooperative teaching: The voices of two teachers. *Remedial and Special Education, 18*(1), 3–11.

Schaeffer, A. L., Zigmond, N., Kerr, M., & Farra, H. E. (1990). Helping teenagers develop school survival skills. *Teaching Exceptional Children, 23*(1), 6–9.

Schamber, S. (1999). Surviving team teaching's good intentions. *Education Digest, 64*(8), 18–24.

Schumm, J. S., Vaughn, S., & Harris, J. (1997). Pyramid power for collaborative planning. *Teaching Exceptional Children 29*(6), 62–66.

Shames, G. H., Wiig, E. H., & Secord, W. A. (1998). *Human communication disorders* (5th ed.). Boston: Allyn & Bacon.

Shea, T. M., & Bauer, A. M. (1994). *Learners with disabilities: A social systems perspective of special education.* Madison, WI: Brown & Benchmark Publishers.

Sileo, T. W., Rude, H. A., & Luckner, J. L. (1988). Collaborative consultation: A model for transition planning for handicapped youth. *Education and Training in Mental Retardation, 23*(2), 333–339.

Silver, L. B. (1990). Attention deficit-hyperactivity disorder: Is it a learning disability or a related disorder? *Journal of Learning Disabilities, 23,* 394–397.

Simmons, D. C., & Kameenui, E. J. (1991). Knowing what you teach: A first step in instructional design. *LD Forum, 17*(1), 23–26.

Simpson, R. L., & Myles, B. S. (1990). The general education collaboration model: A model for successful mainstreaming. *Focus on Exceptional Children, 23*(4), 1–10.

Sinatra, R. C., Berg, D., & Dunn, R. (1985). Semantic mapping improves reading comprehension of learning disabled students. *Teaching Exceptional Children, 17*(4), 310–314.

Smith, J. D. (1998). *Inclusion: Schools for all students.* Belmont, CA: Wadsworth.

Stevens, R., & Rosenshine, B. (1981). Advances on research in teaching. *Exceptional Education Quarterly, 2*(1), 1–9.

Swanson, H. L. (1999). Instructional components that predict treatment outcomes for students with learning disabilities: Support for a combined strategy and direct instruction model. *Learning Disabilities Research and Practice, 14*(3), 129–140.

Thomas, C. C. (1996). Helping students with learning difficulties develop expressive writing skills. *Reading and Writing Quarterly: Overcoming Learning Disabilities, 12*(1), 59–75.

Thomas, C. C., Englert, C. S., & Gregg, S. (1987). An analysis of errors and strategies in the expository writing of learning disabled students. *Remedial Education and Special Education, 8,* 21–30, 46.

Tiegerman-Farber, E., & Radziewicz, C. (1998). *Collaborative decision making: The pathway to inclusion.* Upper Saddle River, NJ: Merrill/Prentice Hall.

Todd, A. W., Horner, R. H., Sugai, G., & Sprague, J. R. (1999). Effective behavior support: Strengthening school-wide systems through a team-based approach. *Effective School Practices, 17*(4), 23–33.

Vaughn, K., Hales, C., Bush, M., & Fox, J. (1998). East Tennessee State University's "Make A Difference" Project: Using a team-based consultative model to conduct functional behavioral assessments. *Preventing School Failure, 43*(1), 24–30.

Vaughn, S., Schumm, J. S., & Arguelles, M. E. (1997). The ABCDEs of co-teaching. *Teaching Exceptional Children, 30*(2), 4–10.

Walther-Thomas, C., Bryant, M., & Land, S. (1996). Planning for effective co-teaching: The key to successful inclusion. *Remedial and Special Education, 17*(4), 255–64, Cover 3.

Wiig, E. H., & Semel, E. (1984). *Language assessment and intervention for the learning disabled* (2nd ed.). Columbus, OH: Merrill.

Wolery, M., Bailey, D. B., & Sugai, G. M. (1988). *Effective teaching: Principles and procedures of applied behavior analysis with exceptional students.* Boston: Allyn & Bacon.

Wolfe, P. (1998). Revisiting effective teaching. *Educational Leadership, 56*(3), 61–64.

Wood, J. W. (1998). *Adapting instruction to accommodate students in inclusive settings* (3rd ed.). Upper Saddle River, NJ: Merrill/Prentice Hall.

Wray, D., Flexer, C., & Ireland, J. (1988). Mainstreaming hearing-impaired children: Typical questions posed by classroom teachers. *Hearsay* (Fall), 76–79.

12 Implementation for Students with Severe Disabilities

Topics in this chapter include:

- The characteristics associated with students who have severe disabilities.
- The various educational needs of students with severe disabilities.
- Selected teaching strategies for working with students who have severe disabilities.
- The unique roles of professionals involved with students who have severe disabilities.
- An application for team involvement in educational planning for students with severe disabilities.

Mr. and Mrs. Fredricks arrive at their daughter's elementary school for their annual IEP meeting. Sally, 7, has been diagnosed with severe neurological impairment due to spinal meningitis contracted at age 2. Sally is an attractive child who appears to react positively by smiling at and using a variety of vocalizations to communicate with her family, teachers, and peers. She enjoys participating in group activities involving a touch screen on a computer, and she loves to swim in the local YWCA swimming pool twice a week. However, Sally evidences severe seizure disorders requiring anticonvulsant medication and is currently fed through a gastrointestinal tube (G-tube).

Additionally, Sally has been diagnosed with cortical blindness, although she is able to track a brightly colored object 2 feet from her eyes. Although she has no severe maladaptive behavior at this point, Sally has required behavioral management procedures to decrease eye poking, which frequently occurs during transition periods throughout the day. Sally has one older brother, who attends the same elementary school. She spends most of her day in an inclusive classroom with her first-grade peers.

As her parents enter the principal's conference room, Sally's first-grade teacher, the special education teacher, the school psychologist, the school counselor, and the principal greet them. At first glance it appears to be a typical reunion in a typical school setting. However, within the next 10 minutes the room slowly fills with the following team of professionals: a physical therapist, an occupational therapist, a school nurse, a pediatric neurologist, a speech/hearing clinician, an itinerant vision teacher, an orientation and mobility specialist, a representative from the Commission for the Blind, the behavioral specialist, and the school district's special education director. The Fredricks have also invited a parent advocate and their personal lawyer. Now, with 19 people in the room, the school counselor begins the meeting by asking all members of the team to introduce themselves. One and a half hours later, the meeting comes to a close with Mr. and Mrs. Fredricks expressing satisfaction with the decisions made on behalf of Sally's educational services.

Although this scenario does not happen frequently, scenes similar to it occur in many U.S. schools serving students with severe and multiple disabilities. Such service is perhaps idealistic, but it is warranted by the nature of the students for whom individual educational plans must be developed. The education of students with severe and multiple disabilities requires of professionals an extraordinary amount of cooperation, collaboration, and interaction. In fact, Rainforth and York-Barr (1997) have written a text devoted to the topic of collaboration and teaming for students with severe disabilities.

In the vignette, Sally has special educational as well as medical needs that must be met by the educational system. In her case interactive teaming is the *core* of her educational program. This chapter introduces the specific needs of students with severe and multiple disabilities and delineates the various roles of the professionals working with these students. Within the descriptions of the students and of the roles of the professionals working with these students, strategies and techniques used for students with severe or multiple disabilities are presented. More than any group of at-risk students, the group evidencing severe impairments requires a comprehensive interactive team approach.

Before discussing the role of the professionals involved in the education and treatment of students with severe disabilities, this chapter first describes the general characteristics and needs of these students. Brief descriptions are provided to highlight characteristics of students in each area. Although information on characteristics of students with severe disabilities will be familiar to special educators, school psychologists, and other personnel who have received training about these students, it is included here as reference material for interactive team members who may not have this knowledge or who need to update their information. The references cited in each area will be of further assistance to those who need more information.

CHARACTERISTICS OF STUDENTS WITH SEVERE DISABILITIES

Although students with severe disabilities are a fairly heterogeneous group, they have some common characteristics and educational and medical needs. The abilities of this population are sometimes overlooked when a description of their disabilities is presented. In fact, the definition of the population has shifted from a deficit approach to more valuing descriptions that affirm the growth potential and unique capacities of individuals with disabilities (Rainforth & York-Barr, 1997). The Association for Persons with Severe Handicaps (TASH, 1991) considers persons with severe disabilities as

> . . . individuals of all ages who require extensive ongoing support in more than one major life activity in order to participate in integrated community settings and to enjoy the quality of life that is available to citizens with fewer or no disabilities. Support may be required for life activities such as mobility, communication, self-care, and learning as necessary for independent living, employment, and self-sufficiency. (p. 30)

Similarly, the American Association on Mental Retardation (AAMR, 1992) has revised their definition of mental retardation as follows:

Mental retardation refers to substantial limitations in present functioning. It is characterized by significantly subaverage intellectual functioning, existing concurrently with related limitations in two or more of the following applicable adaptive skills: communication, self-care, home living, social skills, community use, self-direction, health and safety, functional academics, leisure, and work. Mental retardation manifests before age 18.

The AAMR revised definition also describes the intensities of support, which range from intermittent, limited, extensive, to pervasive (see Table 12.1). Most individuals with severe disabilities would require limited, extensive, or pervasive supports (Westling & Fox, 2000).

According to the 1994–1995 U.S. Census, nearly 26 million of the 53.9 million individuals with disabilities would be classified as having severe disabilities. They represent 9.9% of all Americans or about 1 in every 10 (McNeil, 1997).

Students with severe disabilities have much to offer society. The types of students considered as having severe disabilities vary from state to state. For purposes of this chapter, students with severe disabilities may have the following traditional classifications or medical diagnoses:

Table 12.1
AAMR Definition of Intensities of Supports

Intermittent
Support on an "as-needed basis." Characterized by episodic nature, person not always needing the support(s), or short-term supports needed during life-span transitions (e.g., job loss or an acute medical crisis). Intermittent supports may be high or low intensity when provided.

Limited
An intensity of supports characterized by consistency over time: time limited but not of an intermittent nature; may require fewer staff members and less cost than more intense levels of support (e.g., time-limited employment training or transitional supports during the school to adult provided period).

Extensive
Supports characterized by regular involvement (e.g., daily) in at least some environments (such as work or home) and not time limited (e.g., long-term support and long-term home living support).

Pervasive
Supports characterized by their constancy, high intensity; provided across environments; potential life-sustaining nature. Pervasive supports typically involve more staff members and intrusiveness than do extensive or time-limited supports.

Source: From *Mental Retardation: Definition, Classification, and Systems of Supports* (9th ed.) by the American Association on Mental Retardation, 1992, Washington, DC: Author. Reprinted by permission.

◆ Moderate, severe, or profound mental disabilities.

◆ Physical and health impairments due to cerebral palsy, spina bifida, traumatic brain injury, or other neurological damage.

◆ Visual impairment associated with other disabilities.

◆ Hearing impairment associated with other disabilities.

◆ Deaf/blindness.

◆ Autism.

Students with severe disabilities have been described as having learning challenges, including (1) acquiring new skills rapidly, (2) retaining skills they have learned, (3) generalizing skills from one situation to another, (4) synthesizing skills learned separately into meaningful and functional routines, and (5) multiple and complex needs related to medical, health, orthopedic, sensory, and affective conditions (Rainforth & York-Barr, 1997). The following discussion provides additional descriptions of some of the characteristics found in this population. However, it is important to remember that all students are individuals with unique capabilities. Generalizations of these characteristics to all students with severe disabilities would be inaccurate. The information helps establish the need for medical, social, and educational collaboration when providing services to them.

Physical and Sensory Impairments

Students with severe disabilities frequently evidence orthopedic and sensory disabilities (Sailor, Gee, Goetz, & Graham, 1988; Westling & Fox, 2000). In the United States, approximately one child in five with multiple disabilities appears to have hearing impairments, and about two in five appear to have vision impairments (Orelove & Sobsey, 1996, p. 414). The numbers of children with multiple and sensory impairments, however, could be increasing due to improved medical advances for the treatment of premature and/or low birth weight infants. Many of these students evidence severe motor impairments due to cerebral palsy. Students with both physical and sensory impairments have a number of needs. Appropriate intervention requires attention from medical personnel in the areas of physical and occupational therapy, as well as neurology, ophthalmology, and audiology.

Challenging Behavior

Students with severe disabilities often have associated *excessive behaviors* such as self-injury, stereotypy, aggression, or social isolation. Students need treatment in these areas if their behaviors appear to be interfering with school and community functioning. With the most severe behaviors, professionals will usually need to form a committee to assist in monitoring treatment and progress and to ensure that the rights of the individual are respected.

A comprehensive and functional analysis of what may be causing the behavior is important (Horner, Albin, Sprague, & Todd, 2000; Iwata, Dorsey, Slifer, Bauman, & Richman, 1982; O'Neil, Horner, Albin, Sprague, Storey, & Newton, 1997). Understanding the communicative function of excessive behavior is a promising approach to intervention (Donnellan, Mirenda, Mesaros, & Fassbender, 1984; Durand, 1990; Durand & Crimmins, 1992).

In some of the most severe situations, medical professionals are likely to be involved in the intervention of the most severe behavior problems if medication is required, such as Tegritol (an *anticonvulsant* used to tranquilize), Haldol, Mellaril, or Prolixin (*antipsychotic/neuroleptic* drugs). Other medication, such as Cogentin, Artane, or Benadryl, is given to counter the side effects of the neuroleptic drugs. Considered anticholinergic and anti-Parkinson medications, these drugs combat the tremors and rigidity often associated with the neuroleptic drugs (A. L. Correa, personal communication, 2000). Sobsey and Cox (1996) provide a list of the most commonly used anticonvulsants with an explanation of untoward reactions and side effects.

Medical Conditions

Students with the most severe disabilities often have associated medical problems such as the need for *tracheostomy suctioning, gastrostomy feeding, oxygen supplementation, seizure monitoring,* or *clean intermittent catheterization* (CIC) (Ault, Graff, & Rues, 1993; Heller, Fredrick, Best, Dykes, & Cohen, 2000). The ability to administer routine medical and emergency procedures will be required of all professionals working directly with the student who has complicated medical needs. Additionally, the increased numbers of students with traumatic brain injuries, fetal alcohol syndrome, and prenatal exposure to polydrug use challenge medical, social, and school personnel.

Certification in procedures such as cardiopulmonary resuscitation (CPR) and first aid should be required of all professionals working with this population. Additionally, special education personnel should know about infection control procedures associated with communicable diseases such as infectious hepatitis, herpes, cytomegalovirus (CMV), and acquired immune deficiency syndrome (AIDS). Students with severe disabilities may also be taking anticonvulsant medication such as phenobarbital, Dilantin, Mysolin, and Tegritol to control seizure activity. Professionals must understand their side effects (e.g., drowsiness, lethargy, and impaired vision) and their influence on student performance (Ault, Guy, Guess, & Rues, 1991; Sobsey & Cox, 1996).

The characteristics associated with students with severe disabilities are numerous, complex, and often not consistent among the population. By assessing and analyzing these students' strengths and weaknesses, team members can develop appropriate instructional programs. The complex nature of these students' disabilities make program development a challenge.

MEETING EDUCATIONAL AND COMMUNITY NEEDS

A major function of the team serving students with severe disabilities is to help them reach their optimal potential for independence and community living with nondisabled people. Interactive teams in special education are being challenged by the continuing movement toward inclusive education (National Association of School Boards [NASB], 1993), including inclusion of students with the most severe disabilities into general education (Hobbs & Westling, 1998; Sailor, Gee, & Karasoff, 2000; Snell & Janney, in press; Westling & Fox, 2000). Early participation in inclusive classrooms can prepare students to function successfully in their home communities. The most effective school practices for serving the needs of students with severe disabilities are "(a) inclusion, (b) collaborative teams, (c) integrated therapy, (d) systematic, activity based instruction, (e) data-based decision making and (f) positive behavior supports" (Snell & Brown, 2000a, p. 116). If schools support these practices, three major student outcomes can be achieved. Billingsly, Gallucci, Peck, Schwartz, and Staub (1996) and Staub, Schwartz, Gallucci, and Peck (1994) outline the three desirable outcomes for students in inclusive settings as follows:

1. The *skills outcome* encompasses the abilities that an individual needs to acquire (e.g., functional academics and useful social, motor, and communication skills).
2. The *membership outcome* encompasses belonging to a group and being treated as a group member (e.g., developing peer affiliations and peer groups during and after school).
3. The *relationship outcome* includes ongoing, familiar, social interactions with others (e.g., play, companionship, friendship).

Meyer and Eichinger (1994) developed Program Quality Indicators (PQIs) to evaluate effectively the outcomes of inclusive programs and provide guidance in program development for students with severe disabilities. The PQI checklist contains 38 items in the areas of local agency district indicators, building indicators, educational and placement and related services indicators, and individual student and program indicators. Teams of school personnel can use this instrument to make decisions about educational programming and services.

The educational needs of students with severe disabilities are complex in the areas of support services, assessment, program design, and teacher competencies. The following section addresses these needs.

SUPPORT SERVICE OPTIONS

The nature of support services provided to students with severe disabilities does *not* typically include academic instruction (Izen & Brown, 1991), but instead focuses on functional life routines necessary for community life (Snell & Brown, 2000a). The interactive team that promotes inclusive education comprises parents, members from allied health professionals, general and special education personnel, and vocational and community personnel. However, some programs serving students with severe and multiple impairments have been segregated from regular education programs. In fact, residential programs serving students who are deaf-blind, visually impaired, or hearing impaired still exist in many regions of the United States. Segregated programs have made it easier for allied health professionals such as physical therapists and occupational therapists to serve a large population of students with disabilities in one central location.

However, a strong campaign has been under way to move programs serving even students with the most severe disabilities into general education settings (NASB, 1993; Sailor et al., 2000; Westling & Fox, 2000). This campaign has left many professionals in a quandary about how best to provide support services such as physical therapy to students in their home-schools. In a recent study by Strong and Sandoval (2000), several concerns surfaced from families, students, and general education teachers about including students with neuromuscular diseases into general education classrooms. For families, the concerns related to communication with schools, talking about death, and the need to be empowered. For students, the concerns related to a sense of belonging, learning about the disease, self-concept as the disease progressed, and ongoing loss of abilities. For general education teachers, the concerns related to communicating with parents, fears and attending to medical needs of the student, support in the classroom/collaboration, setting appropriate expectations, and the need for flexibility and adaptability. Although the study focused on students with neuromuscular disease, the concerns about inclusion and solutions for better collaboration and communication are clear for many students with severe disabilities.

A transdisciplinary team model is critical and allows the general and special educator the opportunity to integrate therapy techniques throughout the student's daily program. Table 12.2 describes four different team support approaches for instructing students with severe disabilities in inclusive educational settings.

Ultimately, the optimal inclusive placement for a student would be in a chronological-age-appropriate school setting, with the natural proportion of students with disabilities to students without disabilities, and incorporating community-referenced programming that incorporates aspects of building friendships and quality of life (Orelove & Sobsey, 1996; Snell & Brown, 2000b; Westling & Fox, 2000). Under the mandates of the reauthorization of the IDEA in 1997, creative placement options have also been proposed for young preschoolers with disabilities and young adults with disabilities under *transition* programs. For infants and preschoolers, service can be provided in home-based or center-based programs in the most natural environments. Placing early intervention programs in regular child care or Head Start settings is strongly supported by many school districts. A transition plan for moving the services from Part C (birth to 3 intervention) to Part B must be developed at least 90 days prior to the child's third birthday.

Similarly, secondary transition programs are being developed in many middle and high schools. The Individual Transition Plan (ITP) is written as part of the IEP

Table 12.2
Team Support Approaches

- *General education teacher with team planning and consultation from special education:* The student with disabilities is taught with peers using the same or adapted methods, but with no extra staff support.

- *Collaborative teaching (also called team teaching or co-teaching):* Two or more team members plan and teach the entire class (students with and without disabilities) cooperatively, usually for part of the day.

- *Pull-in with collaborative teaming:* Special education teacher or another team member (e.g., related service staff) teaches or provides support to the student(s) with disabilities in the context of a general education classroom or school activity. Classmates typically are involved in the same or similar activities as the students with disabilities and may participate together in small or large groups or alongside.

- *Pull-out with collaborative teaming (also called alternative activities):* Support is provided by special education staff or other team members (e.g., related services staff, vocational teacher) to the student, with disabilities in a setting away from the general education classroom for a particular reason identified by the team (e.g., to give privacy, more space, access to materials not in the classroom). Other classmates may accompany the student who is removed from the general education setting. Any use of pull-out depends on team collaboration to be effective and needs to be regularly reevaluated.

Source: From "Development and Implementation of Educational Programs," by M. E. Snell & F. Brown, 2000, in M. E. Snell & F. Brown (Eds.), *Instruction of Students with Severe Disabilities* (5th ed., p. 132), Upper Saddle River, NJ: Merrill/Prentice Hall. Reprinted by permission.

as early as the student's 14th birthday and a required statement of community agency responsibilities and goals must be written by the time the student is 16 years old. Close collaboration with families, educators, and adult services agencies such as state human service agencies (e.g., vocational rehabilitation, development disability) and private organizations (e.g., the Arc, formerly the Association for Retarded Citizens) is critical for successful transition to postschool life (Moon & Inge, 2000; Westling & Fox, 2000).

Assessment and Program Design

Assessment and program development for students with severe disabilities are not simple processes. The interactive team must be prepared to provide *multifaceted assessment* of students in the areas of vision, hearing, sensorimotor development, functional/ecological inventories, and family functioning. Several researchers provide an excellent description of the assessment process and procedures recommended for developing an appropriate and functional IEP for students with severe disabilities (Brown & Snell, 2000; Rainforth & York-Barr, 1997; Westling & Fox, 2000). Furthermore, there is growing support for the use of authentic assessment approaches that include portfolios documenting what the student actually learns through various methods (e.g., videotapes, audiotapes, interviews, observational data, social validation, permanent products of student work, medical and physical evaluations, curriculum-based assessment, ecological inventories, and functional assessments) (Siegel-Causey & Allinder, 1998). In fact, some states have begun to use the *Alternate Portfolio* as a way to meet statewide educational assessments and accountability systems for students with severe disabilities (Kleinert, Kearns, & Kennedy, 1997).

The reauthorization of IDEA in 1997 also mandated the use of functional behavioral assessments and the development of behavioral intervention plans of support for students with behavior problems, such as self-injury, aggression, and property damage. The positive behavior support plan should include the following:

◆ A rationale for the comprehensive support plan.

◆ Operational definitions of the problem behaviors.

◆ Summary (hypothesis) statement from the functional assessment.

◆ An overview of the general approaches selected for intervention.

◆ Emergency or crisis procedures.

◆ A detailed implementation plan.

◆ An evaluation plan.

This approach to behavioral intervention should require team consensus and guide new support members who must learn and implement the comprehensive plan at later points in time (Horner et al., 2000).

The number of published assessments and curricula for students with severe disabilities is limited. Some of the most widely used materials for program development are the *Syracuse Community-Referenced Curriculum Guide* (Ford, Schnorr, Meyer, Davern, Black, & Dempsey, 1989), *Choosing Options and Accommodations for Children (COACH)* (Giangreco, Cloninger, & Iverson, 1998), and the *Activities Catalog* (Wilcox & Bellamy, 1987). *Perkins Activity and Resource Guide*, a curriculum for students who are deaf-blind, would also be beneficial for some students who have severe disabilities but are not sensory impaired (Cushman, Heydt, Edwards, Clark, & Allon, 1992). Additionally, Brown and Lehr (1993) and Brown, Evans, Weed, and Owen (1987) have described an assessment-curriculum model for designing intervention programs for students. The *Component Model of Functional Life Routines* offers an assessment and curriculum model for generating skills that are functional, structured, and comprehensive in the domain areas of personal management, vocational school, leisure, and mobility. Additionally, Brown and Snell (2000) described the *ecological inventory*, which generates skills by breaking down the domains into environments, subenvironments, activities, and skill sequences. Table 12.3 illustrates the functional analysis conducted in assessing the various ecological domains for a 13-year-old student with severe multiple disabilities.

Table 12.3
Analysis of Functional Domains for Luis (Age 13)

Domain	Environment	Subenvironment	Activity	Skill Sequence
Vocational	School	Library	Attaching cards to books	1. Open book front cover. 2. Paste back of card folder. 3. Place folder inside front page. 4. Slip library card into folder.
Community	Post office	Mail drop-off slot	Taking school mail to post office	1. Pick up mail at school office. 2. Enter school van. 3. Exit school van and enter post office. 4. Approach drop-off slot. 5. Deposit mail in drop-off slot.
Recreation	School	Pep rally	Participating in weekly pep rally	1. Enter gym. 2. Get pom-pom from usher. 3. Find seat in bleachers. 4. Respond by clapping hands, shaking pom-pom, stomping feet, and cheering appropriately. 5. Exit gym.
Domestic	School	Kitchen	Preparing microwavable frozen meal	1. Remove meal from freezer. 2. Remove from box. 3. Remove foil. 4. Place in microwave. 5. Turn timer to spot marked by tape. 6. Wait during cooking. 7. At sound of bell, remove meal. 8. Prepare to eat. 9. Eat meal. 10. Dispose of container.

As outlined in Chapter 10, an abundance of assessment/curriculum models is available for use with young children with disabilities. The most recent and promising materials for use with children birth to age 6 are the *Assessment Evaluation Programming System* (AEPS) and its curriculum guide (Bricker, 1993; Cripe, Slentz, & Bricker, 1993).

Several curriculum materials for transition planning that emphasize student involvement have been described by Rusch and Chadsey (1998), including *Choice-Maker Self-Determination* (Martin & Marshall, 1995); *Whose Future Is It Anyway?* (Wehmeyer & Kelchner, 1995); *Next S.T.E.P.: Student Transition and Educational Planning* (Halpern, Herr, Wolf, Lawson, Doren, & Johnston, 1997); and *TAKE CHARGE for the Future* (Powers, Sowers, Turner, Nesbitt, Knowles, & Ellison, 1996). Two programs that focus specifically on career planning are the MAPS (Falvey, Forest, Pearpoint, & Rosenberg, 1992) and the PATH (Pearpoint, O'Brien, & Forest, 1993). For example, in the PATH process a group facilitator takes the team (usually with the student involved) through an eight-step process that includes:

1. The dream.
2. Sensing the goal, positive and possible.
3. Grounding in the now.
4. Who do we enroll?
5. Recognizing ways to build strength.
6. Charting actions for the next 3 months.
7. Planning the next month's work.
8. Committing to the next steps.

The goals for many of these programs involve preparing the student for postschool goals, such as integration into the community both through *group-home* or supported-living arrangements, supported employment, and community-based vocational programs.

Specialized Curriculum Components

A variety of domain areas have been proposed for students with severe disabilities. For younger students a developmental model has been used most frequently. For school-age and older students an ecological or functional model has been proposed. The following sections cover a few of the components included in an IEP for a student with severe disabilities.

Physical Management Component.   Although a large percentage of students with severe disabilities may have physical impairments, some of these students may not need specialized equipment or physical management. However, for those who have physical disabilities, specialized equipment (e.g., wheelchairs, walkers, positioning equipment, prone standers, and adapted bathroom seating) is often required for use in the classroom and at home.

The student with severe impairments often is unable to maintain proper body alignment and posture. Without a stable body, the student will be unable to perform even minimal tasks such as eating, bathing, brushing his teeth, or going to the bathroom. Teachers and parents need basic skills in relaxing the *hypertonic* (spastic/high muscle tone) student to dress the student or change diapers. Additionally, for students with *hypotonic* muscle tone, the physical therapist (PT) or the occupational therapist (OT) can instruct the special education staff and parents on how to alert the child's neurological and motor system to provide the child with appropriate stimulation.

The physical therapist develops a program of assessment and intervention after the physician has referred the student for these services. Assessment of the disability includes a determination of the strength and range of movement, and the relationship between the movement and the individual's ability to learn or perform learning-related functions. Because it is important to continue the physical therapy program regularly, the PT and OT often work collaboratively with special educators, classroom teachers, and parents, who are responsible for carrying out some of the programs in the therapist's absence. The nature and type of program designed for the student with movement disabilities may include the following:

◆ Neurodevelopmental treatment.

◆ Lifting, transferring, carrying, and positioning techniques.

◆ Adaptive equipment (e.g., rolls, wedges, standing boards, corner chairs, scooter boards, TumbleForm positioning aids, wheelchairs, and transport chairs) (Campbell, 2000).

Assistive technology has contributed significantly to students' ability to participate in typical environments. One of the most significant technologies available for some students with physical impairments is speech recognition systems such as IBM's ViaVoice and Dragon Systems' Naturally Speaking (Bowe, 2000). Educational teams need to be aware of available technology and often an assistive technology expert can help the interactive team with its understanding of the hardware and software needs for individual students.

Sensory Enhancement Component.   Technology for students with sensory disabilities is also enhancing the access to educational information and increasing quality of life for many. With students who have visual or hearing impairments, *sensory aids* such as glasses, contact lenses, hearing aids, or FM systems may be necessary. For students with visual impairments, the advent of speech synthesis technology has made print media easily accessible (Bowe, 2000). Additionally, special *mobility aids* such as the traditional long cane, the Mowat Sensor, Pathsounder or Sonicguide, prescribed by an *orientation and mobility specialist,* may be needed for students with multiple disabilities who are blind (Hill, 1986; Joffee & Rikhye, 1991). Functional orientation and mobility techniques have also been developed for students with more significant disabilities (Gee, Graham, Oshima, Yoshioka, & Goetz, 1991; Gee, Harrel, & Rosenberg, 1987; Joffee & Rikhye, 1991).

In some cases, if the student is deaf-blind, a *communication system* such as the Tandom and/or manual signing systems is essential. Interventions with aids such as the Tellatouch (Silberman, 1986) or vibrotactile devices (Niswander, 1987) have been valuable for deaf-blind students.

Finally, the use of functional vision (Langley, 1980, 1986) and auditory assessment will be a critical part of the initial evaluation of students with multiple disabilities. Additionally, interactive team members must strive to achieve an indi-

Table 12.4
Environmental Checklist

Environmental Checklist

Name of Student _____ Date _____

SECTION I - THERAPEUTIC POSITIONING
1. Overall Body Positioning (Sitting)
_____ a. Student is upright, or reclined slightly, with hips, knees, and ankles at 90-degree angles, or other angle(s) recommended by a therapist.
_____ b. Student's head is neutral and upright, with or without external support.
_____ c. Student's arms are supported by the table top or wheelchair tray so the elbows are flexed between 90 and 120 degrees.

2. Overall Body Positioning (Sidelying)
_____ a. Student is supported correctly (i.e., lower shoulder is forward; head is in alignment with the spine; hips, knees and ankles are flexed; pillows are placed between and below bony prominences).
_____ b. Student is lying on the side that results in the better eye (if known) being on the upper lateral half of the body. (**Note:** *Consultation with the team is recommended to determine whether sidelying on a particular lateral half of the body may be contraindicated.*)

3. Overall Body Positioning (Supported Supine)
_____ a. Student is supported correctly (i.e., head in alignment; chin slightly flexed; shoulders rounded forward slightly; hips, knees, and ankles flexed).
_____ b. Student's head is stable with or without external support.

4. Position of Peers, Adults, and Materials
_____ a. Depending on the student's head control, materials are placed horizontally, vertically, or somewhere in between those points.
_____ b. Peers or adults position themselves at or near the student's eye level during interaction.

vidualized set of environmental adaptations for each student including therapeutic positioning, lighting and contrast, and audition (Sobsey & Wolf-Schein, 1996; Utley, 1993; Westling & Fox, 2000). Table 12.4 provides a checklist for team members to complete when working with students who are deaf-blind (Utley, 1993). However, the checklist can help teams prepare environmental settings for many students with severe disabilities.

Medical Support Component.   The special education team can perform most of the techniques required by students with severe disabilities who are medically fragile. With close supervision from medical staff such as the school nurse, team

Table 12.4, *continued*

SECTION II - LIGHTING

1. Amount and Type of Light (indoors)
   _____ a. A combination of light sources (i.e., natural light plus incandescent light, etc.) is available.
   _____ b. The entire work surface is illuminated evenly (dependent upon specific task requirements).
   _____ c. Supplemental lighting is available (if necessary).

2. Position of Light
   _____ a. Student is positioned so that all sources of natural light (e.g., windows) are behind him rather than behind the instructional/social/communicative partners.
   _____ b. Supplemental light source originates from over the student's head so the shade directs the light on only the task materials (if necessary).

   OR
   _____ c. Supplemental light source originates from behind and over the shoulder of the student (e.g., over the left shoulder for those who use the right hand and vice versa).

   OR
   _____ d. Supplemental light source originates from behind and over the shoulder of the student on the lateral half of the head where the most functional eye is.

3. Glare
   _____ a. Work surface is made of (or covered with) nonreflective material.
   _____ b. Materials are made of nonreflective material (if possible).
   _____ c. The amount of light emitted in the direction of the eye is limited or eliminated.

4. Contrast
   _____ a. For tasks that rely on materials that are black or dark in color, the background surface is lighter to enhance contrast. Light colored materials use a dark background surface.
   _____ b. Select or purchase materials that contrast with the work surface (if possible).

Note: The items listed on the checklist are to be viewed as *preliminary only*. A more thorough assessment should be made by team members according to the knowledge base of their respective disciplines.

Source: From "Assessing the Instructional Environment to Meet the Needs of Learners with Multiple Disabilities Including Students Who Are Deaf-Blind," by B. L. Utley, 1993, *Deaf-Blind Perspective, 1*(2), pp. 5–8. Reprinted by permission.

members can administer complex medical procedures such as tube feeding, suctioning, colostomy care, and clean intermittent catheterization (CIC). However, administration of medication and heart or oxygen monitoring procedures may still be the main responsibility of the school nurse. Yet, reports of school nurses contribute significantly to the problems of service delivery. Some schools are using the states' Nurse Practice Act to delegate some of the specialized health procedures to nursing assistants, health technicians, or other unlicensed assistive personnel (Heller et al., 2000), but caution must be taken with these policies. Clear school district policies and procedures must be outlined to protect students, teachers, and medical personnel from accidents.

In a study by Heller et al. (2000), teachers reported that for the most part they are responsible for implementing medical procedures on a daily basis. A list of the 10 most common health-related procedures needed in school settings is given in Figure 12.1. Ault, Rues, Graff, and Holvoet (2000) describe each of the medical procedures and discuss their use in a classroom. They also outline a sample individualized health care plan that can be used by the interactive team serving children with health care needs.

Interestingly, Heller et al. (2000) reported that only 46% of the respondents lived in states that provided state guidelines outlining who is responsible for performing health care procedures. Nonetheless, most personnel responded that their schools had written procedures for emergency management, dispensing medication, and specialized health care procedures. When asked about training, the respondents reported that nurses provided most of the training, while the child's parent was the next highest source of training. Furthermore, the study reported that students infrequently performed their own specialized care procedures. Training students to partially participate or directly perform their own procedures should be encouraged by educational teams.

Teachers indicated that it would be beneficial if nurses could work in collaboration with the teachers and share the responsibilities of health-related procedures.

Figure 12.1
Ten most common health care procedures needed in the school setting.

Source: From "Specialized Health Care Procedures in the Schools: Training and Service Delivery" by K. W. Heller, L. D. Fredrick, S. Best, M. K. Dykes, and E. T. Cohen, 2000, *Exceptional Children, 66*(2), pp. 173–186.

1. Tube feeding
2. Colostomy/ileostomy care
3. Clean intermittent catherization (CIC)
4. Suctioning
5. Tracheostomy care
6. Ventilator management
7. Inhaler/nebulizer administration
8. Oxygen delivery
9. Insulin injections
10. Blood glucose testing

Additionally, few teachers reported that their districts had written guidelines or procedures to meet the health-related needs of students with severe disabilities. In most schools, medical and educational services may be fragmented and students are still underserved when it comes to their health-related needs. The requirements for coordinated planning, particularly for early intervention services under Part C, are designed to help professionals work together more effectively in the treatment of students with severe or multiple disabilities. As more students who are medically fragile enter the public school system, services for these students will be more clearly defined (Bartel & Thurman, 1992; Bowe, 2000; Izen & Brown, 1991). Students with communicable diseases such as hepatitis, herpes, human immunodeficiency virus, and cytomegalovirus require special disease control procedures in classroom environments (Ault et al., 2000; Bowe, 2000).

Self-Care Component.   A major component of support services for students with severe disabilities is that of developing self-care skills, such as using the toilet, dressing, eating, and personal hygiene. Often, medical professionals and school nurses can provide information as to the readiness of the student for toilet training. Additionally, it is common for feeding programs to be designed for students who are dependent on adult intervention. Often, the OT will design or adapt a self-feeding device to help the student gain independence. Moreover, an OT or speech-language therapist might develop a program for the classroom staff to implement in the area of stimulating the development of *oral-motor skills* such as swallowing, sucking, and chewing.

School personnel will need to provide appropriate facilities for training students in self-care skills such as using the toilet, bathing, and dressing (Campbell, 2000; Dormans & Pellegrino, 1998; Farlow & Snell, 2000; Westling & Fox, 2000). Family involvement is critical and instructional manuals, such as *Steps to Independence* (Baker & Brightman, 1996), can be used to assist families in this area of programming. Additionally, Farlow and Snell (2000) support the use of peers in assisting with certain self-care skills such as grooming and dressing.

Communication Component.   The student with severe or multiple disabilities may be able to communicate using alternative and augmentative communication systems. Students who are unable to use speech as their major communication mode may use gestures, manual signing, communication boards, or electronic devices such as Zygo's Macaw, Prentke Romich's Liberator, and the Dynavox System as an alternative to speech. Augmentative communication systems such as communication boards or electronic speech-output or scanning devices can be designed for individual students by the speech-language therapist and a team of service providers (Bowe, 2000; Miller, 1993). Speech-language therapists, occupational therapists, and special and general educators may all need to understand a simple electronic switch assembly for adapting toys and communication devices (Bowe, 2000; Burkhart, 1980, 1984; Glickman, Deitz, Anson, & Stewart, 1996; Miller, 1993).

For the student with severe or multiple disabilities, the team works on developing language production, concept development, and speech articulation (Langley & Lombardino, 1991). Treating a student who has no formal speech production (verbalizations) and may have a poor prognosis for speech involves developing pragmatic and prelinguistic communication behaviors, such as attending, requesting, rejecting, imitating, turn-taking, and naming (Langley & Lombardino, 1991; Orelove & Sobsey, 1996). Wetherby, Warren, and Reichle (1998) and Siegel and Wetherby (2000) provide guidelines on how to recognize, support, and teach nonsymbolic communicative interactions in the context of daily routines.

The team also may be involved in analyzing the communicative function of a student's excessive behavior, such as hand biting or aggression, and developing an intervention program that provides the student with an alternative means of communicating frustration, boredom, or attention by using gestures or signs (Durand, 1990; Durand & Crimmins, 1992; O'Neil et al., 1997). Whether language takes the form of facial reactions, signing, gesturing, pointing, or verbalizations, teaching students with severe disabilities functional language communication within a social context is a major educational goal.

Community-Based Functional Component.   For school-age students with severe disabilities, the sole use of developmental checklists describing the step-by-step sequence of infant and early childhood development for program implementation is no longer appropriate. As described earlier, a more functional approach to developing curriculum has become the major focus of special education programs. This requires administrative support and resources to develop intervention programs that integrate training in the areas of school, domestic, vocational, community, and leisure skill development (Brown & Snell, 2000; Snell & Brown, 2000a). Simulated school environments can no longer suffice for all-school training and intervention. School personnel must access natural community environments, which contain normal prompts and cues. Such environments benefit the student learning how to wash clothes in a laundromat, shop for food at the grocery store, or ride the bus to a supported employment program every day.

Family and Friends Involvement Component.   Involvement of the family in teaming is critical to the success of educational and vocational intervention with students who have severe disabilities. Because of the nature of the student's disability, the family may have added pressures and stressors that will affect their life adjustment (Beckman, 1983; Bronicki & Turnbull, 1987; Salisbury & Dunst, 1997; Turnbull & Turnbull, 2000). Families often have the medical information about their children that is needed for school programs. Conversely, school professionals can help families obtain and interpret medical information that is necessary for the student. The ultimate responsibility for care and future adjustment of the child with severe disability lies with the family members. Their involvement through training and advocacy will be critical once the public school program has ended.

Friends and peers also are an important part of the lives of students with severe disabilities. Team members should focus on enhancing and facilitating social and friendship relationships among students with severe disabilities and students without disabilities (Strong & Sandoval, 2000). The students with severe disabilities and their friends should be included in many aspects of designing educational programs. Several person-centered planning models have been described in the literature; some are used in conjunction with transition planning described earlier in this chapter (Callahan & Garner, 1997; Kregel, 1998; Miner & Bates, 1997). An excellent method for doing a person-oriented plan is Personal Futures Planning (Mount & Zwernik, 1989). This method serves as a tool for fostering new ways of thinking about students with severe disabilities. When futures planning, a small group of people (e.g., family, peers, neighbors, community leaders, teachers, administrators) agree to meet for mutual support, brainstorming, and strategizing. The goals for this team are to discuss opportunities for the student "to develop personal relationships, have positive roles in community life, increase their control of their own lives, and develop the skills and abilities to achieve these goals" (Mount & Zwernik, 1989, p. 1). Futures planning can complement the development of an IEP process. A similar approach to planning programs for students with severe disabilities is the McGill Action Planning System (Falvey, Forest, Pearpoint, & Rosenberg, 1992; Vandercook, York, & Forest, 1989). MAPS uses support teams in a manner similar to that of Personal Futures Planning to brainstorm and develop goals for the student.

SELECTED TEACHING STRATEGIES

Several strategies are described in this chapter for the purpose of illustrating the types of techniques that can be used for students with severe disabilities. More detailed explanations of the best practices for teaching these students are found in several textbooks, such as Rainforth and York-Barr (1997), Orelove and Sobsey (1996), Westling and Fox (2000), and Snell and Brown (2000b).

One frequently used teaching strategy involves applied behavior analysis. Within the general application of the approach, the teacher selects functional skills for the student and breaks the skill down into small, teachable tasks. Examples of task analyses were outlined in Table 12.3. Once the task sequence has been established, educators must provide a consistent application of prompting and reinforcement procedures. Team members must consider the following components of instructional procedures (Rainforth & York-Barr, 1997):

◆ Setting, grouping, positioning.

◆ Equipment/materials.

◆ Initial instruction and prompt.

◆ Correct response.

◆ Time delay and correction.

◆ Reinforcement.

◆ Frequency to teach.

◆ Frequency of data.

◆ Type of data.

◆ Criterion for change.

A number of *time delay* or *prompting sequences* have been shown to be effective with students with severe disabilities. The sequence of providing *least-to-most prompts* involves allowing wait-time for the student to perform the task step independently before providing help. For example, using the *increasing prompts strategy* for teaching a student to feed himself cereal with a spoon involves first providing the student with the natural cue of the cereal and the spoon. If the student does not respond, a verbal prompt ("Pick up your spoon") might be used. If after a designated time period, the student does not begin the task, a gesture or model can be used, such as picking up the spoon and scooping up some cereal. Again, a wait-time occurs, and if the student has not responded, the teacher might provide the most intrusive prompt—taking the student's hand and guiding him through the task of scooping the cereal.

The other prompting strategy is that of *graduated guidance*. In this strategy the teacher begins with total physical assistance by taking the student's hands and moving him through the complete task of scooping up the cereal. After repeated trials, the teacher would begin to decrease her physical assistance when she judged that the student was becoming more independent. The teacher would decrease the prompts until she was merely shadowing the student's hand as the student ate the cereal.

Additionally, reinforcement procedures would be implemented when necessary. The most natural reinforcers, such as social praise, should be tried first, before more artificial reinforcers (e.g., toys, prizes, or edibles) are used.

Instruction of students with severe disabilities should occur in the environment most natural to the task. If a student is being taught to brush her hair, the teacher should provide the training in the natural environment (e.g., bathroom, dressing table). Often, instruction occurs in simulated settings due to a lack of available natural environments. Although they are not as effective for maintenance and generalization of skills to the natural environments, simulated settings may be necessary.

Furthermore, when teaching students with severe disabilities, use of functional and age-appropriate materials is critical. For example, in teaching a 16-year-old student to operate a tape recorder, the use of a child's toy machine would not be recommended. Instead, a regular tape recorder should be used. A variety of materials and experiences should also be used for training generalization across tasks. For example, if a student is learning to use bathroom facilities at school, she should eventually be instructed to use facilities in other settings, such as her home, fast-food restaurants, and the laundromat. In particular, the various settings may require different skills in flushing toilets, dispensing soap, and drying hands.

Instruction of students with severe disabilities requires ongoing data-based programs, using effective behavior analysis procedures (Snell & Brown, 2000a; Westling & Fox, 2000). Keeping detailed progress of skill sequences helps the teacher make program changes. Additionally, because students with severe disabilities may not progress as quickly as their peers without disabilities, measuring behavior and recording the progress are critical in instruction.

Students with severe disabilities may be limited by physical or sensory impairments; however, their limitations should not exclude them from participating in age-appropriate routines shared by their peers without disabilities. Instruction should be given in inclusive settings with peers without disabilities and involve adaptations when necessary. The *principle of partial participation* (Brown, Branston, Hamre-Nietupski, Pumpian, Certo, & Gruenewald, 1979) affirms that students with severe disabilities can take part to some degree in age-appropriate activities. For example, excluding students from a school play production because they cannot speak clearly would be contrary to the principle of partial participation. Instead, the school play could be adapted so that students who could not speak could use a tape recorder, sign with the use of an interpreter, or play parts that require no speaking.

A variety of teaching strategies has been discussed. Instruction for students with severe disabilities is challenging and complex. As students become more involved in inclusive settings, team members will need specific guidance in instructional procedures for general education classes. Stainback and Stainback (1996), Hunt and Goetz (1997), Giangreco (1996), and Westling and Fox (2000) provide excellent guides for developing instruction in inclusive settings. Repetition and systematic generalization of training are required.

Table 12.5 outlines eight principles that characterize educational team work and influence how teams make decisions about teaching students with severe disabilities (Snell & Brown, 2000a). If programs are not carefully designed and implemented, students, families, and teachers will experience failure and frustration. An interactive team can provide support and contribute creative teaching strategies that are sure to be effective with students. These specific roles and responsibilities are discussed in the next section.

ROLES OF THE PROFESSIONALS INVOLVED WITH STUDENTS WITH SEVERE DISABILITIES

Given the wide range of characteristics of students with severe disabilities, a number of professionals with varying areas of expertise may be needed to plan

Table 12.5
Guiding Team Principles

Educational Programs Are Student Centered
Teams consider students' well-being as their core purpose by giving the student team input; using peer contributions; acknowledging family input; and focusing on a person-centered approach.

Educational Programs Are Team Generated
A cohesive team designs programs.

Educational Programs Are Both Practical and Valid
Teams select goals and objectives that are usable and efficient.

Educational Programs Are Socially Valid
The team asks the question "So what?" Is this change/idea/objective important to the student?

Educational Programs Reflect Functional Priorities
Functional skills are those skills that, if not performed by a student, must be completed for the student by someone else.

Educational Programs Require Active Participation
Student's participation may be partial or complete, but it is best when performance is meaningful and active rather than nonpurposeful and passive.

Educational Programs Foster Self-Determination
Acknowledges that students must make decisions about themselves, attain independence in useful routines, evaluate their own performance, and make adjustments to improve themselves.

Educational Programs Are Individualized
Teaching is tailored to the student's strength, needs, and individual characteristics.

Source: From "Development and Implementation of Educational Programs," by M. E. Snell & F. Brown, 2000, in M. E. Snell & F. Brown (Eds.), *Instruction of Students with Severe Disabilities* (5th ed., pp. 121–124), Upper Saddle River, NJ: Merrill/Prentice Hall. Adapted by permission.

the students' programs. The professionals who serve these students need to coordinate their efforts. Effective leadership, good communication skills, and effective professional development procedures, all of which have been outlined in previous chapters, facilitate coordination. The general roles of professionals are discussed in Chapter 4. Specialized contributions of team members who work with students with severe disabilities are outlined in this chapter.

Delineating the roles of each of the team members within the educational and community setting is a first step in clarifying each group's function on the team. Table 12.6 outlines the various roles and responsibilities in both direct service and team involvement.

Table 12.6

Roles of Professionals and Others Involved with Students with Severe Disabilities

Personnel	Direct Service Provider	Team Member
Special Educator	• Conduct multifaceted assessment in the areas of vision, hearing, sensorimotor development, functional/ecological inventories, family functioning. • Monitor under supervision any medical and behavioral procedures. • Implement computer and augmentative communication systems. • Provide physical management and proper positioning in equipment. • Conduct functional programming emphasizing independence in school and community integration.	• Serve as case manager. • Accept role released responsibilities from related service personnel. • Interpret multifaceted assessments. • Consult on individualized instructional strategies with general educators serving students in inclusive settings. • Advocate for student and family needs.
Physical Therapist	• Assess posture/motor development. • Conduct direct therapy for specific motor problems within an integrated classroom environment. • Order and prepare adaptive equipment. • Monitor use of braces and orthotic devices.	• Conduct staff development on therapy treatment. • Role release the least complex treatment procedures (e.g., range of motion). • Integrate motor goals into daily life routines. • Consult with other medical personnel (orthopedist, neurologist, nurse, etc.).
Occupational Therapist	• Assess fine motor, oral motor, vocational, and leisure skills areas. • Order and modify special devices. • Design feeding programs. • Conduct eye-hand coordination and fine motor skills programs.	• Conduct staff development on therapy treatments. • Role release the least complex treatments (e.g., feeding procedures). • Integrate fine motor goals into daily life routines. • Consult with other medical personnel.
School Nurse/Nutritionist	• Dispense medication. • Monitor complex medical procedures (tracheostomy suctioning, catheterization procedures, G–tube feeding, mechanical ventilation, etc.). • Conduct first aid and minor emergency safety procedures. • Prepare appropriate well-balanced meal plans.	• Conduct staff development on health-related procedures. • Role release the least complex procedures (e.g., postural drainage, gastrostomy feeding, prosthesis care). • Consult with other medical personnel. • Implement and orient staff to emergency procedures involving life-threatening situations. • Contact family for ongoing status of medical/nutritional needs. • Consult staff on side effects of medications.

Table 12.6, *continued*

Personnel	Direct Service Provider	Team Member
School Psychologist	• Assess psychological and adaptive behavior functioning. • Conduct behavior management programs for severe maladaptive behavior.	• Conduct assessments jointly with other team members if special adaptations must be made (e.g., severe vision, motor, hearing impairments). • Interpret test results to team and family. • Conduct staff development on behavior management procedures.
Family	• Reinforce functional/behavioral programming. • Reinforce related services programs (e.g., PT, OT). • Attend all health-related appointments.	• Provide information on medical, behavioral, and family issues. • Accept role release responsibilities for intervention programs (e.g., PT, OT). • Consult with staff on medication, personal care, physical management, and adaptive devices.
School Counselor/ Social Worker	• Provide individual family assessment and counseling. • Provide social service resources. • Make home visits.	• Consult with staff on foster care or public assistance programs. • Provide information on family needs and adjustment. • Serve as liaison with related social service agencies.
Speech-Language Therapist	• Assess and intervene on speech-language impairments. • Conduct functional assessments of hearing. • Design augmentative communication systems. • Intervene on prelinguistic communication behaviors.	• Interpret results of traditional and informal observations of student's speech-language functions. • Provide staff development on alternative speech communication programs, augmentative communication devices, and prelinguistic communication techniques. • Provide integrated therapy programs throughout the student's functional curriculum.
Para-professional	• Conduct health-related and personal hygiene procedures under supervision. • Prepare inclusive classroom for daily activities. • Prepare and assist at mealtimes. • Conduct small group intervention programs.	• Provide information on progress of assigned data-based programs. • Share ideas for effective classroom management. • Attend staff development programs (e.g., basic first aid, physical management).

Table 12.6, *continued*

Personnel	Direct Service Provider	Team Member
Para-professional (cont.)	• Assure that equipment and classrooms are safe and sterile. • Organize students' personal hygiene and clothing materials. • Assist in community-based programming. • Collect basic intervention data, under supervision. • Support students in inclusive settings.	
Administrator	• Reinforce behavioral management procedures. • Encourage involvement of families at whatever level they choose to participate.	• Support staff by providing staff development appropriate to their needs. • Support program by providing adaptive equipment and material. • Provide information on funding resources related to hiring of paraprofessionals and contracting with private agencies for PT or OT services. • Provide financial and transportation support to community-referenced programming. • Coordinate parent advisory councils. • Provide information on due process and legal action issues. • Arrange the school building to maximize interactions between students with and without disabilities. • Arrange school schedule to allow for collaboration and formal staff meetings. • Arrange the school's schedule to avoid reliance on separate pull-out therapy programs.

◊ ◊

Application

The team members who serve students with severe disabilities are often confronted with the need for *role release* (Lyon & Lyon, 1980), in which more than one person on the team performs the same function, such as implementation of a behavior management program. The professional development function, used for related services training, is also important in transdisciplinary teaming. At times this involves sharing information from one's own discipline with others so they can implement their component of the program effectively; at other times it requires the ability to respect and accept the consultation of parents and other professionals who are specialists in various aspects of the student's care program (Bowe, 2000; Bailey, 1984; Rainforth & York-Barr, 1997). Garland, McConigel, Frank, and Buck (1989) (as cited in Orelove & Sobsey, 1996, p. 17) have defined six role transition processes as follows:

1. *Role extension:* Self-directed study and staff development to learn more about your own discipline.
2. *Role enrichment:* Experts in their discipline provide a general overview and understanding of their discipline to other team members.
3. *Role expansion:* Acquiring enough information about other disciplines to make knowledgeable observations and recommendations outside of your own discipline.
4. *Role exchange:* Learning the theory, methods, and procedures of other disciplines and beginning to implement the techniques under supervision of the team member from that discipline.
5. *Role release:* Implementing newly learned techniques into practice with consultation from the team member responsible for that discipline.
6. *Role support:* Informal backup support from other team members when necessary.

The following vignette illustrates the application of the concept of interactive teaming to areas outside of the traditional role responsibilities of the team members.

Becky, a 15-year-old student who has traumatic brain injury from an automobile accident, is receiving services from an occupational therapist, a behavioral specialist, an itinerant vision teacher, a special education teacher, and a speech-language therapist. One of Becky's high school teachers, Ms. Stone, coordinates a conference that all four professionals and the family attend for purposes of professional development and role release. In the conference, the occupational therapist, Ms. Edwards, explains *neurodevelopmental treatment* (NDT) techniques (Bobath & Bobath, 1984; Campbell, 2000) for helping Becky to coordinate her arm and hand function and stabilize her trunk during mealtimes. Ms. Edwards demonstrates these techniques with Becky while she is eating lunch. Ms. Stone and the parent model the facilitation procedure in front of the occupational therapist and ask for feedback on their use of the technique.

Later, in Becky's classroom, the vision teacher shows Ms. Stone and the parent how to present Becky with computer switches in ways that stimulate eye–hand coordination, visual tracking, and information processing. Ms. Stone and the parent now practice both NDT techniques and vision integration activities, and both professionals give them feedback. Finally, the behavior specialists and special education teacher show Ms. Stone and the parent the best ways to help Becky maintain her attention on tasks and organize the tasks in an activity. The special educator incorporates the NDT procedure and the vision activity while modeling and prompting Becky to focus on a computer math game. Once again, Ms. Stone and the parents model all the techniques and ask for feedback.

Becky's mother (with Becky's assistance) shares with the team Becky's favorite hobbies, music preferences, television shows, and the foods she likes and dislikes.

Her mother also updates the team on her medical status, her medication, and the reports from Becky's neurologist. By the end of the session, all four professionals and the parents have shared knowledge of their own disciplines and demonstrated the proper use of the techniques with Becky.

The professionals and parents leave the conference with added knowledge and skills for integrating the techniques into Becky's home, school, and community program. For purposes of checking appropriate use of the procedures and discussing Becky's progress, the team will arrange a monthly follow-up consultation. Within 6 months, the school's transition specialist will join the team on behalf of Becky's transition from school to work. The transition specialists will begin the process of acquiring new knowledge about the other disciplines involved with Becky's educational program and share her expertise through the transdisciplinary role transition process.

The role of the team leader becomes one of service coordinator of an integrated therapy program. Instead of providing Becky with an isolated therapy program in which the related service professional removes her from the inclusive classroom and provides treatment in a private therapy room, the therapist and special education teacher train the general teacher, the family, and paraprofessionals to perform educational, behavioral, and therapy techniques in the classroom, home, and community. Additionally, Becky's friends learn how to best interact with her and support her during activities in the inclusive classroom. In the interactive team approach, the therapist and special education teacher still provide some direct services to the student on a weekly basis. Those services are often provided within the classroom setting, and when appropriate, they are used for demonstration and training of general education staff, families, and peers.

◊ ◊

SUMMARY

The transdisciplinary team serving the needs of students with severe or multiple disabilities comprises a complex group of medical and education professionals.

The team serving students with severe disabilities is at risk for wars over turf. The range of differences in the terminology of the disciplines is enough to cause confusion among the group.

The meetings conducted by this transdisciplinary team often overwhelm the core members of the team, the family. Yet, as much as any group of professionals, the family must work cooperatively for the good of the student.

The nature of the student's condition can be so complex that if collaboration is not established, the student's educational as well as health-related needs will not be met.

Working closely with the families and the students' friends, professionals can orchestrate the delivery of services to students with severe disabilities, whether those services involve physical therapy, occupational therapy, speech therapy, medical interventions, or functional community-based programming.

ACTIVITIES

1. Conduct an informational interview with a professional who is involved in the educational programs of students with severe disabilities. Use the guidelines provided in Chapter 4.

2. Attend a group home or vocational program for individuals with severe disabilities. Observe for skills that will be needed by younger students to function in these future environments.

3. Volunteer to teach a functional skill to a student in a local school program. Offer to take the student into the community to learn this skill. Use a task analytical approach to breaking down the functional skill, and apply intervention strategies to implement the program.

4. Ask people from the community who have multiple disabilities such as cerebral palsy and blindness to speak to the class about their impairments, how they have adapted, problems they have encountered, and the community services available to them.

5. Attend tours of schools and community agencies serving people with severe disabilities. Note the goal and mission of the various agencies as related to the quality of life of people with severe disabilities.

REFERENCES

American Association on Mental Retardation. (1992). *Mental retardation: Definition, classification, and systems of supports* [online] (9th ed.). Washington, DC: Author. Available: www.aamr.org/Policies/faqmentalretardation.html.

Ault, M. M., Graff, J. C., & Rues, J. P. (1993). Special health procedures. In M. Snell (Ed.), *Instruction of students with severe disabilities* (4th ed., pp. 215–247). Upper Saddle River, NJ: Merrill/Prentice Hall.

Ault, M. M., Guy, B., Guess, D., & Rues, J. P. (1991). *Medication information guidelines*. Lawrence, KS: Project ABLE, Department of Special Education, University of Kansas.

Ault, M., Rues, J. P., Graff, J. C., & Holvoet, J. (2000). Special health care procedures. In M. E. Snell & F. Brown (Eds.), *Instruction of students with severe disabilities* (5th ed., pp. 245–290). Upper Saddle River, NJ: Merrill/Prentice Hall.

Bailey, D. (1984). A triaxial model of the interdisciplinary team and group process. *Exceptional Children, 51*, 17–26.

Baker, B. L., & Brightman, A. J. (1996). *Steps to independence: Teaching everyday skills to children with special needs* (3rd ed.). Baltimore: Paul H. Brookes.

Bartel, N. R., & Thurman, S. K. (1992). Medical treatment and educational problems in children. *Phi Delta Kappan, 74*, 57–61.

Beckman, P. J. (1983). Influence of selected child characteristics on stress in families of handicapped infants. *American Journal of Mental Deficiency, 88*, 150–156.

Billingsly, F., Gallucci, C., Peck, C., Schwartz, I., & Staub, D. (1996). "But those kids can't even do math": An alternative conceptualization of outcomes for inclusive education. *The Special Education Leadership Review, 3,* 43–56.

Bobath, B., & Bobath, K. (1984). The neurodevelopmental treatment. In D. Stratton (Ed.), *Management of motor disorders of children with cerebral palsy.* Philadelphia: J. B. Lippincott.

Bowe, F. (2000). *Physical, sensory, and health disabilities: An introduction.* Upper Saddle River, NJ: Merrill/Prentice Hall.

Bricker, D. (1993). *AEPS measurement for birth to three years* (Vol. 1). Baltimore: Paul H. Brookes.

Bronicki, G. J., & Turnbull, A. P. (1987). Family–professional interactions. In M. E. Snell (Ed.), *Instruction of students with severe disabilities* (4th ed.). Upper Saddle River, NJ: Merrill/Prentice Hall.

Brown, F., Evans, I., Weed, K., & Owen, V. (1987). Delineating functional competencies: A component model. *Journal of the Association for Persons with Severe Handicaps, 12*(2), 117–124.

Brown, F., & Lehr, D. (1993). Meaningful outcomes for students with severe disabilities. *Teaching Exceptional Children, 4,* 12–16.

Brown, F., & Snell, M. (2000). Meaningful assessment. In M. E. Snell & F. Brown (Eds.), *Instruction of students with severe disabilities* (5th ed., pp. 67–114). Upper Saddle River, NJ: Merrill/Prentice Hall.

Brown, L., Branston, M. B., Hamre-Nietupski, S., Pumpian, I., Certo, N., & Gruenewald, L. A. (1979). A strategy for developing chronological age appropriate and functional curricular content for severely handicapped adolescents and young adults. *Journal of Special Education, 13,* 81–90.

Burkhart, L. J. (1980). *Homemade battery-powered toys and educational devices for severely handicapped children.* 8503 Rhode Island Ave., College Park, MD 20740.

Burkhart, L. J. (1984). *More homemade battery devices for severely handicapped children—With suggested activities.* 8503 Rhode Island Ave., College Park, MD 20740.

Callahan, M. J., & Garner, J. B. (1997). *Keys to the workplace. Skills and supports for people with disabilities.* Baltimore: Paul H. Brookes.

Campbell, P. H. (2000). Promoting participation in natural environments by accommodating motor disabilities. In M. E. Snell & F. Brown (Eds.), *Instruction of students with severe disabilities* (5th ed., pp. 291–329), Upper Saddle River, NJ: Merrill/Prentice Hall.

Cripe, J., Slentz, K., & Bricker, D. (1993). *AEPS curriculum for birth to three years* (Vol. 2). Baltimore: Paul H. Brookes.

Cushman, C., Heydt, K., Edwards, S., Clark, M. J., & Allon, M. (1992). *Perkins activity and resource guide: A handbook for teachers and parents of students with visual and multiple disabilities.* Boston: Perkins School for the Blind.

Donnellan, A. M., Mirenda, P. L., Mesaros, R. A., & Fassbender, L. L. (1984). Analyzing the communicative functions of aberrant behavior. *Journal of the Association for Persons with Severe Handicaps, 9,* 201–212.

Dormans, J., & Pellegrino, L. (Eds.). (1998). *Caring for children with cerebral palsy.* Baltimore: Paul H. Brookes.

Durand, V. M. (1990). *Severe behavior problems: A functional communication training approach.* New York: Guilford Press.

Durand, V. M., & Crimmins, D. B. (1992). *The motivation assessment scale (MAS) administration guide.* Topeka, KS: Monaco.

Falvey, M., Forest, M. Pearpoint, J., & Rosenberg, R. L. (1992). *All my life's a circle: Using the tools of circles, MAPS, and PATH.* Toronto, Canada: Inclusion Press.

Farlow, L. J., & Snell, M. E. (2000) Teaching basic self-care skills. In M. E. Snell & F. Brown (Eds.), *Instruction of students with severe disabilities* (5th ed., pp. 331–380), Upper Saddle River, NJ: Merrill/Prentice Hall.

Ford, A., Schnorr, R., Meyer, L., Davern, L., Black, J., & Dempsey, P. (Eds.). (1989). *The Syracuse community-referenced curriculum guide for students with moderate and severe disabilities.* Baltimore: Paul H. Brookes.

Garland, C., McConigel, M., Frank, A., & Buck, D. (1989). *The transdisciplinary model of service delivery.* Lightfoot, VA: Child Development Resources.

Gee, K., Graham, N., Oshima, G., Yoshioka, K., & Goetz, L. (1991). Teaching students to request the continuation of routine activities by using time delay and decreasing physical assistance in the context of chain interruption. *Journal of the Association for Persons with Severe Handicaps, 16*, 154–167.

Gee, K., Harrell, R., & Rosenberg, R. (1987). Teaching orientation and mobility skills within and across natural opportunities for travel. In L. Goetz, D. Guess, & K. Stremel-Campbell (Eds.), *Innovative program design for individuals with dual sensory impairments* (pp. 127–157). Baltimore: Paul H. Brookes.

Giangreco, M. E. (1996). *Vermont interdependent services team approach. A guide to coordinating education support services*. Baltimore: Paul H. Brookes.

Giangreco, M. F., Cloninger, C. J., & Iverson, V. S. (1998). *C.O.A.C.H.: Choosing outcomes and accommodations for children* (2nd ed.). Baltimore: Paul H. Brookes.

Glickman, L., Deitz, J., Anson, D., & Stewart, K. (1996). The effect of switch control site on computer skills of infants and toddlers. *American Journal of Occupational Therapy, 50*(7), 545–553.

Halpern, A. S., Herr, C. M., Wolf, N. K., Lawson, J. D., Doren, B., & Johnston, M. D. (1997). *NEXT S.T.E.P.: Student transition and education planning. Teacher's manual*. Austin, TX: Pro-Ed.

Heller, K. W., Fredrick, L. D., Best, S., Dykes, M. K., & Cohen, E. T. (2000). Specialized health care procedures in the schools: Training and service delivery. *Exceptional Children, 66*, 173–186.

Hill, E. W. (1986). Orientation and mobility. In G. T. Scholl (Ed.), *Foundations of education for blind and visually handicapped children and youth: Theory and practice* (pp. 315–340). New York: American Foundation for the Blind.

Hobbs, T., & Westling, D. L. (1998). Promoting successful inclusion through collaborative problem solving. *Teaching Exceptional Children, 31*(1), 12–19.

Horner, R. H., Albin, R. W., Sprague, J. R., & Todd, A. W. (2000). Positive behavior support. In M. E. Snell & F. Brown (Eds.), *Instruction of students with severe disabilities* (5th ed., pp. 207–243), Upper Saddle River, NJ: Merrill/Prentice Hall.

Hunt, P., & Goetz, L. (1997). Research on inclusive educational programs, practices, and outcomes for students with severe disabilities. *Journal of Special Education, 31*(1), 3–29.

Iwata, B. A., Dorsey, M. F., Slifer, K. J., Bauman, K. E., & Richman, G. S. (1982). Toward a functional analysis of self-injury. *Analysis and Intervention in Developmental Disabilities, 2*, 3–20.

Izen, C. L., & Brown, F. (1991). Education and treatment needs of students with profound, multiply handicapping, and medically fragile conditions: A survey of teachers' perceptions. *Journal of the Association for Persons with Severe Handicaps, 16*, 94–103.

Joffee, E., & Rikhye, C.H. (1991). Orientation and mobility for students with severe visual and motor impairment. *Journal of Visual Impairment and Blindness, 85*(5), 211–261.

Kleinert, H. L., Kearns, J. F., & Kennedy, S. (1997). Accountability for all students: Kentucky's alternate portfolio assessment for students with moderate and severe cognitive disabilities. *Journal of the Association for Persons with Severe Handicaps, 22*, 88–101.

Kregel, J. (1998). Developing a career path: Application of person-centered planning. In P. Wehman & J. Kregel (Eds.), *More than a job. Securing satisfying careers for people with disabilities* (pp. 71–91). Baltimore: Paul H. Brookes.

Langley, B. (1980). *Functional vision inventory for the multiple and severely handicapped*. Chicago: Stoelting.

Langley, M. B. (1986). Psychoeducational assessment of visually impaired students with additional handicaps. In D. Ellis (Ed.), *Sensory impairments in mentally handicapped people* (pp. 253–296). San Diego: College-Hill Press.

Langley, M. B., & Lombardino, L. J. (1991). *Neurodevelopmental strategies for managing communication disorders in children with severe motor dysfunction*. Austin, TX: Pro-Ed.

Lyon, S., & Lyon, G. (1980). Team functioning and staff development: A role release approach to providing integrated educational services for severely handicapped students. *Journal of the Association for the Severely Handicapped, 5,* 250–263.

Martin, J. E., & Marshall, L. H. (1995). Choice-Maker: A comprehensive self-determination transition program. *Intervention in School and Clinic, 30,* 147–156.

McNeil, J. (1997). *Americans with disabilities: 1994–1995.* Current Population Reports, P70-61. Washington, DC: U.S. Department of Commerce, Bureau of the Census.

Meyer, L. H., & Eichinger, J. (1994). *Program quality indicators (PQI): A checklist of most promising practices in educational programs for students with severe disabilities* (3rd ed.). Seattle, WA: The Association for Persons with Severe Handicaps.

Miller, J. (1993). Augmentative and alternative communication. In M. Snell (Ed.), *Instruction of students with severe disabilities* (4th ed., pp. 319–346). Upper Saddle River, NJ: Merrill/Prentice Hall.

Miner, C. A., & Bates, P. E. (1997). The effect of person centered planning activities on the IEP/transition planning process. *Education and Training in Mental Retardation, 32,* 105–112.

Moon, M. S., & Inge, K. (2000). Vocational preparation and transition. In M. E. Snell & F. Brown (Eds.), *Instruction of students with severe disabilities* (5th ed., pp. 591–628). Upper Saddle River, NJ: Merrill/Prentice Hall.

Mount, B., & Zwernik, K. (1989). *It's never too early, it's never too late: A booklet about personal futures planning.* St. Paul, MN: Metropolitan Council.

National Association of School Boards (NASB). (1993). *Winners all: A call for inclusive schools* (Monograph). Alexandria, VA: Author.

Niswander, P. S. (1987). Audiometric assessment and management. In L. Goetz, D. Guess, & K. Stremel-Campbell (Eds.), *Innovative program design for individuals with dual sensory impairments* (pp. 99–126). Baltimore: Paul H. Brookes.

O'Neil, R. E., Horner, R. H., Albin, R. W., Sprague, J. R., Storey, K., & Newton, J. S. (1997). *Functional assessment and program development of problem behavior: A practical handbook.* Pacific Grove, CA: Brookes/Cole.

Orelove, F. P., & Sobsey, D. (1996). *Educating children with multiple disabilities: A transdisciplinary approach* (3rd ed.). Baltimore: Paul H. Brookes.

Pearpoint, J., O'Brien, J., & Forest, M. (1993). *PATH: a workbook for planning positive possible futures: Planning alternative tomorrows with hope for school, organizations, businesses, families.* Toronto, Canada: Inclusion Press.

Powers, L. E., Sowers, J., Turner, A., Nesbitt, M., Knowles, E., & Ellison, R. (1996). TAKE CHARGE: A model for promoting self-determination among adolescents with challenges. In L.E. Powers, G. H. S. Singer, & J. Sowers (Eds.), *On the road to autonomy: Promoting self-competence for children and youth with disabilities* (pp. 291–322). Baltimore: Paul H. Brookes.

Rainforth, B., & York-Barr, J. (1997). *Collaborative teams for students with severe disabilities* (2nd ed.). Baltimore: Paul H. Brookes.

Rusch, F. R., & Chadsey, J. G. (1998). *Beyond high school: Transition from school to work.* Belmont, CA: Wadsworth.

Sailor, W., Gee, K., Goetz, L., & Graham, N. (1988). Progress in educating students with the most severe disabilities: Is there any? *Journal of the Association for Persons with Severe Handicaps, 13,* 87–99.

Sailor, W., Gee, K., & Karasoff, P. (2000). Inclusion and school restructuring. In M. E. Snell & F. Brown (Eds.), *Instruction of students with severe disabilities* (5th ed., pp. 1–30). Upper Saddle River, NJ: Merrill/Prentice Hall.

Salisbury, C. & Dunst, C. J. (1997). Home, school, and community partnerships: Building inclusive teams. In B. Rainforth & J. York-Barr (Eds.). *Collaborative teams for students with severe disabilities* (2nd ed., pp. 57–88). Baltimore: Paul H. Brookes.

Siegel, E., & Wetherby, A. (2000). Nonsymbolic communication. In M. E. Snell & F. Brown (Eds.), *Instruction of students with severe disabilities* (5th ed., pp. 409–452). Upper Saddle River, NJ: Merrill/Prentice Hall.

Siegel-Causey, E., & Allinder, R. M. (1998). Using alternative assessment for students with severe disabilities. Alignment with best practices. *Edu-*

cation and Training in Mental Retardation and Developmental Disabilities, 33, 168–178.

Silberman, R. K. (1986). Severe multiple handicaps. In G. T. Scholl (Ed.), Foundations of education for blind and visually handicapped children and youth: Theory and practice (pp. 145–164). New York: American Foundation for the Blind.

Snell, M. E., & Brown, F. (2000a). Development and implementation of educational programs. In M. E. Snell & F. Brown (Eds.), Instruction of students with severe disabilities (5th ed., pp. 115–172). Upper Saddle River, NJ: Merrill/Prentice Hall.

Snell, M. E., & Brown, F. (Eds.). (2000b). Instruction of students with severe disabilities (5th ed.). Upper Saddle River, NJ: Merrill/Prentice Hall.

Snell, M. E., & Janney, R. E. (in press). Practices for inclusive schools: Collaborative teaming. Baltimore, MD: Paul H. Brookes.

Sobsey, D., & Cox, A. (1996). Integrating health care and educational programs. In F. P. Orelove & D. Sobsey (Eds.), Educating children with multiple disabilities: A transdisciplinary approach (3rd ed., pp. 217–251). Baltimore: Paul H. Brookes.

Sobsey, D., & Wolf-Schein, E. (1996). Children with sensory impairments. In F. P. Orelove & D. Sobsey (Eds.), Educating children with multiple disabilities: A transdisciplinary approach (3rd ed., pp. 411–450). Baltimore: Paul H. Brookes.

Stainback, S., & Stainback, W. (1996). Inclusion. A guide for educators. Baltimore: Paul H. Brookes.

Staub, D., Schwartz, I. S., Gallucci, C., & Peck, C. A. (1994). Four portraits of friendship at an inclusive school. Journal of the Association for Persons with Severe Handicaps, 19, 314–325.

Strong, K., & Sandoval, J. (2000). Mainstreaming children with a neuromuscular disease: A map of concerns. Exceptional Children, 65, 353–366.

The Association of Persons with Severe Handicaps (1991). Definition of the people TASH serves (Document 1:1). In L. H. Meyer, C. A. Peck, & L. Brown (Eds.), Critical issues in the lives of people with severe disabilities (p. 19). Baltimore: Paul H. Brookes.

Turnbull, A., & Turnbull, H. R. (2000). Fostering family–professional partnerships. In M. E. Snell & F. Brown (Eds.), Instruction of students with severe disabilities (5th ed., pp. 31–66). Upper Saddle River, NJ: Merrill/Prentice Hall.

Utley, B. L. (1993). Assessing the instructional environment to meet the needs of learners with multiple disabilities including students who are deaf-blind. Deaf-Blind Perspective, 1(2), 5–8.

Vandercook, T., York, J., & Forest, M. (1989). MAPS: A strategy for building vision. Journal of the Association for Persons with Severe Handicaps, 14(3), 205–215.

Wehmeyer, M. L., & Kelchner, K. (1995). Whose future is it anyway? A student directed transition planning process. Arlington, TX: The Arc National Headquarters.

Westling, D. L., & Fox, L. (2000). Teaching students with severe disabilities (2nd ed.). Upper Saddle River, NJ: Merrill/Prentice Hall.

Wetherby, A., Warren, S., & Reichle, J. (Eds.). (1998). Communication and language intervention series: Vol. 7. Transitions in prelinguistic communication. Baltimore: Paul H. Brookes.

Wilcox, B., & Bellamy, G.T. (1987). The activities catalog: An alternative curriculum for youth and adults with severe disabilities. Baltimore: Paul H. Brookes.

13 Summary and Application of the Model in the Future

Topics in this chapter include:

- A summary of the major features of the interactive teaming model.
- An extended case study, showing how the whole model might be implemented.
- Application of the model in the future, with a summary of current trends and predictions for future implementation.

Teachers and related professionals, who once functioned in isolated classrooms and clinical programs, are now encouraged to collaborate as members of an interactive service team. The factors that provide the context and rationale for this change include the following:

◆ Professionals in special programs face conflicting demands to produce students with high levels of achievement and to respond to those with special needs that range from learning and behavior problems to cultural and linguistic differences.

◆ Educators and related professionals are being increasingly pressured to collaborate in the solution of growing education-related problems, because in the future most of our students will have complex special needs. Current programs are ineffective in serving the increasing numbers of students with such needs; previously proposed solutions that do not take into account the body of knowledge about the process of change will also be ineffective.

◆ Those who have summarized the research on effective schools suggest that teachers in these schools are committed to a central mission: maximizing the educational opportunities for their students by working as a team to achieve this goal. Conversely, researchers who have studied teachers' sense of efficacy have identified teachers' feelings of isolation as a major barrier to their believing that they are facilitating growth in their students.

◆ Public Law 94-142, amended in 1990, and again in 1997 as the Individuals with Disabilities Education Act, P.L. 101-476, requires that special education and *related services* be provided for students with disabilities. This requirement suggests that people from many disciplines are potential members of the team. The more effective programs of the future will require collaboration among professionals and between professionals and parents.

◆ Currently, education, medical, and social services professionals are not being prepared as team members. Newly trained professionals in general education and in social services professions lack the ability to address these complex problems and to function as collaborative members of interactive teams.

FEATURES OF THE INTERACTIVE TEAMING MODEL

The model proposed in this book—interactive teaming—is a response to the nation's increasingly complex problems in special needs programs. It incorporates the features of high expectations, teacher empowerment, and parent–professional collaboration, which together characterize effective schools for students with special needs.

The interactive team is an educational and health-related group that functions at the highest professional level, using both consultation and collaboration in its efforts on behalf of students with special needs. Components of this model are used in programs that provide educational, medical, and social services to students with severe disabilities, and in "learning community" programs that are described in the school improvement literature.

This model for interactive teaming has been described in detail in this text. The three sections focus on context and foundations, facilitating factors, and implementation. The context and foundations section includes the framework and rationale, the historical foundations of consultation and teaming, and the dimensions of the interactive team. The facilitating factors are identified as understanding the roles of team members, enhancing communication skills, developing service coordination skills, empowering team members through professional development, and enabling and supporting families. Four types of implementation contexts are presented, including implementation with culturally and linguistically diverse students, infants and preschoolers with disabilities, students with mild disabilities, and students with severe disabilities.

An extended case study, drawing together multiple facets of the model, follows.

◇ ◇

Application: Extended Case Study

Ethan, a minority-group 8-year-old, is both gifted and learning disabled. His mother, who is divorced, is a physician, and Ethan has already decided that he wants to be a lawyer. Born with cerebral palsy that has left him with motor disabilities but without speech impairment, Ethan has an overall measured IQ of 136, with a verbal score that is 40 points higher than his performance score. On the achievement tests measuring basic skills, Ethan scores at the ninth-grade level in reading and at the first-grade level in basic mathematical skills. He also has great difficulty in manuscript handwriting, and he resists his teacher's efforts to instruct him in cursive writing, although all his classmates are beginning to use it and his teacher requires it.

Sometimes Ethan annoys his teachers—the third-grade classroom teacher; the special education resource room teacher; and the music, art, and physical education teachers—because he likes to have them explain their reasons for everything they ask him to do. He is very logical and rule oriented, in addition to being quite good at verbal reasoning. Ethan argues with teachers when they ask him to do something he chooses not to do, and he is becoming disruptive in the classroom. Ethan realizes that each of his teachers has different expectations for classroom behavior and consequences when the rules are broken, and he has become quite effective at playing one adult against another.

Ethan is talkative and cheerful; he has many friends in his third-grade classroom who volunteer to push him around the school in his wheelchair. They also volunteer to help him with his math and handwriting assignments, which are difficult for him. Most recently, several other students in his classroom have begun to use his strategy of arguing with the teacher when they choose not to follow her instructions.

Ethan's classroom teacher, who has taught third grade in this district for 17 years, believes strongly that rules are rules, and that they apply equally to all students in the classroom. She has become frustrated with his behavior, particularly when he fails to turn in his assignments and when he encourages the other students to defy her authority. Ethan's art and PE teachers allow him to do much as he pleases in their classes; they believe he "has physical disabilities and we shouldn't expect much from him in art or physical activities." His music teacher encourages him to express himself verbally whenever he chooses and has made him the master of ceremonies at the school's music programs. His special education teacher, who works with him for one hour a day on math skills, has a strict contingency management program, through which he can earn tokens that accumulate for free time.

Ethan's mother, who is nationally recognized as an authority in her field of medicine, is busy and travels a lot. She adores Ethan and gives him every cultural and material advantage—they go to concerts and lectures together, and she has bought him his own computer with a complete set of games. His mother also makes an effort to work with Ethan on his schoolwork at home, but she thinks the behavior problems he is having at school are the school's responsibility. Ethan's mother is pleasant and cooperative, and she has agreed to support the school's efforts by enforcing a consistent regimen for him at home. She believes, however, that the school personnel should design the school-based program.

The district superintendent is pleased that Ethan's mother does not object to his placement in this school, which contains a large number of low-income students. The superintendent is concerned about the school's attrition rate: It has a largely transient population, and students who enter in the fall rarely remain for the entire school year. He is also concerned about the low level of students' academic achievement and about problems with teacher morale as reported by the president of the professional association. The superintendent is considering making Ethan's school a "magnet," to which residents of the community could choose to send their children because of special programs offered. He is particularly interested in the development of science and computer labs for which he has obtained support from the local Chamber of Commerce in a school-business partnership.

The interactive team that meets to review Ethan's progress in his special program has more than his academic achievement to consider. His case is one in which all the issues of interactive teaming will need to be incorporated.

Step 1

The team meets to review Ethan's progress. Those present are the special educator, classroom teacher, psychologist, music teacher, school principal, and Ethan's mother.

The team follows the steps in program review, shown earlier in Figure 6–4. The special educator will be the team leader, or quality adviser. It is the group's consensus that Ethan should continue in the part-time special education program for help with math. Ethan's mother agrees to make his home use of computer games contingent on his conceptual understanding and mastery of the math facts for addition and subtraction for the numbers 0 through 20. Plans are made for additional testing of Ethan's fine motor skills by a physical therapist and for suggestions on the development of appropriate adaptive handwriting devices by an adaptive technology specialist. After this testing is completed, the special educator and classroom teacher agree that they will meet to plan a program related to his development of handwriting skills. Ethan's classroom teacher expresses a concern that his behavior problems are related, in part, to the fact that the adults in his life have conflicting standards for his behavior; his mother agrees. The principal, recognizing this statement as an opener for his agenda—establishing schoolwide goals for students— suggests that he will follow up on this problem with the entire school staff and with the PTA. Each team member leaves with a written record of the decisions made, the people responsible for implementing each, and the projected date for their next contacts.

Step 2

The physical therapist and the adaptive technology specialist conduct an assessment of Ethan's abilities and limitations in fine motor skills, then discuss their findings with his mother. All conclude that it is unrealistic to expect him to develop cursive handwriting skills at this time and agree that he might be encouraged to develop keyboard skills on the computer, provided it could be equipped with an adaptive device. They report this decision to the quality adviser, the special educator. Together, this subgroup laments that the school has no current resources for obtaining these specialized materials, although they have heard the rumor that the school may be receiving a computer lab.

Step 3

The classroom teacher teams with Ethan's mother to provide a program for at-home computer game use, contingent on mastery of math facts. Deprived of the free use of his computer, Ethan becomes furious and begins to throw tantrums at home and in school. Ethan's mother calls to relate her disappointment with the program. The classroom teacher relates her concern to the special educator, the team leader (or quality adviser), who takes two aspirins and goes to bed.

Step 4

The special educator and the classroom teacher meet the next day. The classroom teacher discusses her concern over Ethan's increased behavior problems, and together the two team members brainstorm possible solutions to their problem, using the problem-solving sequence suggested in Chapter 6. They decide to contact Ethan's mother to request an observation of his home computer setup and to enlist her help with the problem.

Step 5

The special educator, classroom teacher, and Ethan's mother meet briefly in Ethan's home, where he proudly shows his teachers his computer games. Ethan's mother, who has learned about the superintendent's proposed program for school computers, suggests that she might work with the Chamber of Commerce's committee to explore the extension of computers into the school's programs for exceptional students. The special education teacher asks the district's adaptive technology specialist to explore the use of adaptive equipment that might enable Ethan to develop computer skills as a substitute for cursive writing. The classroom teacher agrees to take data on Ethan's behavior in the classroom in an attempt to isolate the variables that intensify his outbursts and lack of compliance with class rules.

Step 6

The principal calls a meeting of the representatives of the school's professional organization to present the superintendent's request for development of a magnet school program in their building and to obtain their input on needs for professional development and the additional resources needed to make the school program a model. Ethan's teacher, who is a member of this committee, discusses her previous interactions with Ethan's mother about the possibility of creating a school–business partnership for the new computer lab.

This news is received with enthusiasm, and several teachers suggest that the school plan a professional development program to provide teachers with additional skills related to the effective use of computers. The music teacher cautions that although new skills in computer use might motivate students and enable teachers to better use technology, the acquisition of computers would not solve the school's basic problem: the increase in students' misbehavior. Ethan's classroom teacher agrees that computers are no panacea and again expresses her concern about the lack of consistency in school rules as a contributing factor to students' misbehavior.

The principal, after listing the teachers' ideas for professional development and school improvement, identifies the need for consistent rules as the group's highest priority. He repeats this process in his meeting with the school's PTA steering committee, and he learns that parents share the teachers' concerns about misbehavior. Then he contacts one of his former professors at a nearby university to help the staff and community develop a uniform set of standards for student behavior.

Step 7

Through a needs assessment, the professor determines that teachers and parents have two major concerns about student behavior:

1. *Poor social behavior:* Students lack the ability to get along together.
2. *Inappropriate academic behavior:* Students fail to raise hands, comply with teacher requests, and complete tasks.

In a schoolwide staff meeting attended by representatives from the PTA, the principal shares the results of this needs assessment as the first step in identifying the school's common goals for student expectations. The professor, who serves as their consultant, organizes the teachers, parents, and other professionals into grade-level clusters. Their first task is to generate a list of positive student behaviors that enable students to get along with others; their second is to generate a list of positive student behaviors that enhance learning. The groups are then asked to rewrite these statements as rules for student behaviors. After grade-level consensus has been reached, the groups meet with those in the grades above and below their own to identify the commonalities in their rule statements. The result is a set of school rules for student behavior for which both teachers and parents have ownership.

Step 8

The building staff adopts the schoolwide rules for students' behavior, and Ethan begins to encounter uniform expectations for his performance in all classes. After initial protests, he begins to comply with the rules. His classroom teacher is pleased with this change in his behavior and reports positively to the special educator and to Ethan's mother.

Step 9

The special educator, classroom teacher, and Ethan's mother meet. They discuss both his progress and their efforts in identifying adapted computer equipment that might be used with Ethan in developing his typing skills. The classroom teacher, who is able to see a positive change in Ethan's overall behavior, is now willing to modify her standards for his handwriting performance, and she agrees that the development of keyboard skills for use on the computer would be an acceptable substitute for his learning of cursive writing. Ethan's mother has obtained support from the Chamber of Commerce to include adaptive computer equipment in its plan for the whole-school computer lab. The special educator, with assistance from the adaptive technology specialist, has identified the necessary software.

Step 10

The Chamber of Commerce committee approaches the superintendent with a plan to provide the volunteer services of several computer specialists in implementing the lab. When the photographer from the local paper comes to cover the story, Ethan is shown using the new equipment, with assistance from his classroom teacher. The principal is quoted as saying this represents a schoolwide effort to improve the quality of instruction for all students. The superintendent's comment reveals this small step as part of his master plan to make Ethan's school a magnet. Ethan's mother makes a positive statement about the need for professional parents to continue their support of the district's excellent public school program.

The special educator, the team leader (or quality adviser), is present in the background and smiling. This effective leader has empowered others to implement a program that benefits a specific student with special needs, while simultaneously contributing to schoolwide improvement.

◊ ◊

APPLICATION OF THE MODEL IN THE FUTURE

Futurists examine current trends as a knowledge base from which to predict the future. In making their predictions, futurists tend to be optimistic. The authors of this book are optimistic in their prediction that a collaborative model such as interactive teaming will be the major pattern for future service delivery to students with special needs. This optimistic prediction persists, despite acknowledgment of the history of failed past predictions, the barriers to teaming, and the need for continued research, simply because the need for this model is so compelling.

Previous Predictions and Realities

In 1979, forecasting methods employed in the social sciences were used to predict the future of special education for 1993. The 1979 trends in special education were used as a knowledge base to make these predictions along five dimensions: values, social institutions, the economy, technology, and medicine (Safer, Burnette, & Hobbs, 1979). These authors picked variables from these five fields they could use to predict the future. They saw, in 1979, that the traditional values from the Industrial Revolution were beginning to change. From the value system of that era, as reflected in the culmination of the civil rights movement, they suggested that equality and full participation for people with disabilities in education and society might be predicted.

Simultaneously, the 1979 economy was characterized by growth and high inflation, a trend that could open future opportunities for people with disabilities. At that time the nation's social institutions promoted equality and normalization; the family unit was changing from the nuclear model to multiple models with shifting roles and a declining birth rate. Technology was growing rapidly: Compressed speech was possible; and radar, biofeedback, the pacemaker, robotics, and computers seemed to offer limitless opportunities for persons with disabilities. In medicine, new diagnostic procedures—the CAT and amniocentesis, which offered early diagnosis and genetic screening—improved neonatal care, and attempts were being made to remove environmental hazards to children. These advances laid the groundwork for the early identification and treatment of disabilities. In 1979, these futurists predicted a greater emphasis on the quality of life and self-actualization for people with disabilities, although they acknowledged that an economic slowdown could trigger a return to the older values based on workers' productivity.

A few of these predictions came true. The national priority for equality in education did not materialize; it was replaced by the emphasis in the 1980s and 1990s on excellence. The information-service economy reduced unemployment. Social institutions included a greater diversity of family types, although husband and wife roles remained relatively constant; the projected decline in the birth rate did not materialize, and a new teacher and classroom shortage was created when increased national debt reduced public spending for education. Technology has continued to expand at a rapid rate; however, research is underfunded, and the benefits of technology are not generally available to the entire population. Progress in medicine has been related to a lower incidence of some disabling conditions, particularly cerebral palsy and some genetic problems; however, this information is not being disseminated widely. At the same time, new medical crises such as those threatened by drugs, the AIDS epidemic, and antibiotic-resistant bacteria have arisen. Overall, the current conditions from which to predict future trends for children with special needs are similar to those that existed in 1979.

Current Trends That Affect Programs for Students with Special Needs

There is, however, a major difference between the conditions in 1979 and those of the present: Although support for education programs has declined, the number of students at risk for school failure has risen dramatically, and public awareness of the need to collaborate in the solution of this problem has grown. The following discussion summarizes this trend, first, as it relates to the mega level of society along the dimensions of values, social institutions, the economy, technology, and medicine, and second, as it affects the macro level of school restructuring.

Mega Level: Society. The following paragraphs summarize the need for collaboration at the mega level of society.

1. *Trends in values:* The current value system has shifted from an emphasis on human rights to a focus on excellence, as a way of ensuring this nation's economic supremacy. Excellence was initially defined in terms of more rigorous standards and a greater concern with college-bound students. More recently, however, concern has been growing that these standards are, at best, superficial indicators of quality. The educational reforms of the past decade have been focused on the teaching of basic skills, with state control over education and a curriculum driven by standardized achievement tests. There is now a concern that the reforms have overemphasized basic skills while neglecting the teaching of thinking and reasoning.

   Wise (1988) cautioned early in the "excellence" movement that the reforms undertaken have not been based on a common vision and that although the newly implemented regulations have attempted to raise the quality of education, they have instead ultimately decreased the sensitivity of schools to their clients and actually reduced the quality of education.

   The national value system is also characterized by a growth in emphasis on the safety of "old ways." Evidence of this trend is found, for example, in increased censorship and in controversy over bilingual education, both of which emerged in the late 1980s (Gold, 1987; Mirga, 1987). This retreat to the old ways is not entirely negative, however, because it includes a renewed emphasis on the work ethic and on the concept of volunteerism, both of which have positive implications for the future of collaborative programs.

2. *Trends in social institutions:* At least two major trends in social institutions are affecting the climate in which education is delivered. One is the growing mistrust of citizens in their existing bureaucratic institutions. The other is the disintegration of the traditional family structure. These trends, too, may have a

positive side, because they could facilitate a reconceptualization of both school bureaucracies and family systems.

Naisbitt (1982) posited as a major "megatrend" in the informational-service society the increase in individuals' self-reliance as a reaction against dependency. Dolce (1981) summarized the post–Vietnam era mood of the country as one in which individuals had lost faith in their institutions and, as a result, had a sense of helplessness. The emergence of a strong "third-party" mentality was apparent in the national elections beginning in 1992, as new coalitions in both liberal and conservative wings began to grow. Adults had developed the belief that old solutions were no longer valid for current problems. The positive aspect of this trend toward mistrust of institutions was the possibility that it would allow citizens to take the first step in recognizing the need for institutional change.

The statistics on the changes in the family institution have been cited previously. In addition to these data, there were, as early as 1980, other indications of family disintegration. Child abuse increased 55% between 1981 and 1985, with estimates ranging from 150,000 to 1.5 million cases a year (McClellan, 1987). These trends continued into the 1990s: By 1992, there were 2.9 million child abuse cases per year, with an increase of 8% from 1991 to 1992 (Peterson, 1993). Children labeled as "latchkey," who come home after school to an empty house until a parent arrives home from work, were estimated as 41% of the school population (Flax, 1987). These changes in families as a social institution indicated a need for public assistance that is too complicated to be delegated solely to the public schools. Congressional action on family leave was an indication that this need was being recognized.

3. *Trends in the economy:* The amount of money available for special programs continued to decline in the 1980s; this decrease was attributed to the increase in the federal debt (Chiles, 1989). More recently, increasing costs were related to the growing number of persons in the aging population cited in Chapter 1 discussions of demographic changes. Despite this decline, a new positive has emerged: an emphasis on cost effectiveness in education programs.

The initial reaction against increases in the cost of education for special needs students followed the revelation that the average cost of programs for special students is estimated to be between two and four times that of regular education programs (Gough, 1992; Kakalik, Furry, Thomas, & Carney, 1981). Funding for special education programs, authorized at 20% for 1980, with an increase of up to 40%, was cut in half and never regained its previous level (Howe, 1981). As a result of the loss of funds, however, there was a growing backlog of referrals for the placement of students in special programs. These students were not being served effectively in general education programs, which were struggling with fewer teachers and more students, and attempting to respond to individual differences by dividing students into ability tracks (Oakes, 1986). The effect of actions such as these reached the workforce, and in the 1980s business leaders began to recognize that poorly supported education programs increased their costs for training (Iacocca, 1989). In addition, early research summaries showed that money spent on preschool education programs (Hodgkinson, 1988) and transition training for adolescents with disabilities (Viadero, 1989) was particularly well spent in terms of cost effectiveness.

4. *Trends in technology:* The use of computers is a major trend in technology that affects the educational program. Computers are used extensively in school programs, although there is a need for professional development programs that enable teachers to use computers effectively (Garcia, 1998; McGroddy, 1997; Sharp, 1998). Interactive technology is emerging rapidly, as shown by support for e-commerce, wireless communication, multimedia learning, and the paperless office. There is continuing work with computers to develop artificial intelligence; meanwhile, microchips have been used to reactivate neurological responses in people whose limbs have been severed. Though computers promise improvements in education for the future, these innovations are still expensive and not widely available. Recognition of this need has prompted the computer and communications giants to initiate a series of education partnerships that have the potential for school improvement.

5. *Trends in medicine:* A number of diseases—smallpox, TB, measles, polio— seemed to be controlled in the 1980s and 1990s by advances in medicine, better health care, and widespread immunizations. New diseases, however, have become more prevalent as witnessed by transmission of diseases such as ebola and West Nile virus, probably related to worldwide travel patterns. The increased numbers of school-age children with AIDS became, as early as the 1980s, a growing health problem for schools (Reed, 1988). Increased need for funding strained the health care system; new proposals for national insurance may compete with funding of education.

   Mental health problems have increased significantly. It was estimated as early as the 1980s that between 12% and 19% of children today were in need of some sort of mental health treatment, and that 70% to 80% of them were not receiving it (Flax, 1989; Tuma, 1989). The school-related problems of drug abuse have been documented in detail (Newcomb & Bentler, 1989). These conditions exist simultaneously with a dramatic increase in antisocial behavior among youth (Patterson, DeBaryshe, & Ramsey, 1989), and the growth of violence is a major societal concern (American Psychological Association, 1993).

   The encouraging aspect of this trend is that it precipitated a more general recognition of the problems of at-risk students as early as the 1980s (Brown, 1985). Horowitz and O'Brien (1989) provided an analysis of current concerns in their introduction to the 1989 special issue of *American Psychologist*. They pointed out that, in contrast with the last special issue in 1979, the 1989 issue paid more attention to adolescent sexuality, teen pregnancy, culture and identity, and the effects of the environment in its discussion of child development. New topics included substance abuse, accidents, learning disabilities, and computers. However, the most striking difference, they said, is that in the current issue topics are related to questions of social policy.

In his discussion of the need for visionary leadership, Nanus (1992) describes some of the forces that will influence the development of organizations in the 21st century. These include:

1. Explosive technological change caused by simultaneous and mutually reinforcing breakthroughs in materials, genetics, information sciences, space technology, automation, and instrumentation

2. The dominance of postindustrial economies based on information, knowledge, education, and services

3. The globalization of business, politics, culture, and environmental concerns

4. The restructuring of national economies to accommodate intense international competition, and the gradual transition from military to economic dominance in global affairs

5. The erosion of confidence in all institutions, including governments, families, and religion, and the resultant search for self-sufficiency and meaning in work and grass roots activism

6. High economic stress resulting from heavy debt loads, global competition, vulnerable banking systems, and deferred costs of a decaying infrastructure and environmental cleanup

7. Demographic and sociocultural shifts toward far more diversity and fragmentation of values, life-styles and tastes

8. Relative affluence in material goods coupled with "new" scarcities (for example, job security and parental time for children) and increased personal risks from crime and environmental pollution. (p. 174)[1]

The observations of Nanus regarding forces that will influence the future are supportive of those made earlier by others, and suggestive of the need for increasing levels of collaboration between and among individuals and groups.

Macro Level: School Restructuring.   Restructuring of the public education system is one of the major trends with positive implications for the future of interactive teaming. In an extensive report on the status of restructuring in the early 1990s, writers at *Education Week* outlined seven areas in which change must occur if renewal is to succeed:

1. *The balance of power:* This requires a shift in power from administration to groups consisting of the principal, teachers, parents, staff, businesspeople, and students. In this team approach, constituents make decisions about

---

[1] From Nanus, B. (1992). *Visionary leadership.* San Francisco: Jossey-Bass, Reprinted by permission.

issues as diverse as budget, personnel, and curriculum. Although it is difficult for a council that was chosen to represent diverse points of view to develop a shared vision, it is believed that success can be achieved if more team training is provided and results are not expected too soon (Bradley & Olson, 1993).

2. *Time and space:* This involves modification of the regular hours, straight rows, standard way of teaching. Alternatives include the extended day or year, use of learning centers, and incorporation of work outside of school in community projects or real-world applications of learning. Although there are concerns about cost and need for teacher time, there are also some promising innovations, which involve school/university/community partnerships. Again, the need for collaboration is apparent (Sommerfeld, 1993).

3. *The coherent curriculum:* The emphasis on critical thinking requires that teaching and learning become central to reform, using state frameworks for broad concepts, rather than teaching specific lists of competencies. Although there are parental concerns that children will not acquire specific skills, teachers indicate that student interest and risk taking increase with teaching that is interdisciplinary, rather than fragmented into academic specialty areas (Viadero, 1993).

4. *Outcomes for student performance:* This involves a change from a time-based or credit hours enrolled format to an emphasis on what students will know and be able to do as a result of their education program. This movement has been controversial in many states and there are questions about the measurement of outcomes, although several states have progressed in developing ways to deliver these programs effectively (Rothman, 1993).

5. *Professional development:* This requires implementation of learning communities to overcome teacher isolation and link classrooms to outside real-world experiences. Although the need for additional team training is noted, existing models incorporating professional academies and teacher centers have been successful in helping new teachers adapt to special learning needs of the new student population (Bradley, 1993).

6. *Dollars and sense:* This involves attempts to reduce disparities in school spending across rich and poor districts. Initiated by a series of school finance lawsuits against states, it has resulted in development of creative proposals, including the establishment of baseline or supplementary support from state and federal governments (Harp, 1993).

7. *Signing up the public:* This requires development of public awareness of the serious educational problems and their effect on the economy and on global competitiveness. Both the dissemination of information in ways the public can appreciate and the ability of educators to listen to public concerns are suggested. The involvement of business and industry leaders, parents, and volunteers is suggested and examples of success cited (Walsh, 1993).

These trends were still in evidence at the end of the 20th century.

The need for education in interactive teaming skills, including collaboration, communication, and cultural sensitivity, is apparent in these proposed macro-level changes. The relationship of the macro level to the special program changes is seen in the support from the special education community for appropriate inclusion, when possible and appropriate, of special students, as part of the range of services and improvement of the entire educational system (Council of Administrators of Special Education, 1990; Kovaleski, 1992; Turnbull & Cilley, 1999).

MAJOR TRENDS IN PROMISING PRACTICES: THE 1990S

Two major trends in promising practices were seen during the 1990s that relate to and predict success for the interactive teaming model in the future: (1) the growing success of total quality education, that is, the application of TQM in schools; and (2) the rapidly increasing number of efforts to restructure teacher education. Each is summarized briefly below.

Success of Total Quality Education/Learning Communities

Schmoker and Wilson (1993) indicated that the teamwork concepts inherent in total quality management principles have been applied successfully in a variety of schools, including the following:

◆ *Central Park East (Harlem, New York):* In this school district, 95% of the mostly black and Hispanic students go on to college. There was a democratic atmosphere, leadership, a common purpose, and use and analysis of data as a measure of improvement. Teams, consisting of teachers and business and community members, examined student portfolios. Students were required to convince faculty that they were "ready to graduate."

◆ *Comer Schools (New Haven, Connecticut; Prince Georges County, Maryland):* Student achievement scores increased from 35th to 98th percentile. Teams took a scientific approach, involving members of the community and entire staff in decisions. The emphasis was on professional development, no-fault problem solving, and consensus and collaboration, in a process resembling TQM.

◆ *Northview Elementary (Manhattan, Kansas):* Reading and math scores improved from a low of 31% to 70% competency to a high of 97% to 100%. The environment was collegial and purposeful; teams analyzed data to isolate and solve problems.

◆ *Johnson City Schools (New York):* After 6 years, passing scores on the state regent's achievement test rose from 45% to 77%. The district used an outcomes-based model, based on Bloom's concept of mastery learning. The district emphasized continuous improvement, measured by internal and external information.

◆ *Levin's Accelerated Schools (Daniel Webster Elementary, San Francisco, California; Hollibrook, Houston, Texas)*: One school progressed from 69th to 23rd in its district in 3 years. The model was based on a six-step inquiry similar to Deming's, which helps teams focus on problems and their solutions. The focus was on accelerating, rather than remediating, students with poor achievement. The model emphasized work with the school as a whole, building on strengths; using data to isolate problems; and emphasizing continuous improvement.

◆ *Mt. Edgecumbe High School (Sitka, Alaska)*: About 49% of this school's Native American students attend postsecondary schools, and dropouts have been reduced from 40% a year to 1%. The group has eliminated grades, but teachers insist on high-quality work. Faculty members began the school year by helping students see a purpose for learning, then students became their own managers. Teachers supervised a large number of students (100) to free the time for others to work in teams.

Successful implementation of the TQM concepts in educational settings in the early 1990s had positive implications for the need for and predicted success of teaming. This trend was particularly promising when paired with the provision of equal "inputs" (resources) to schools, as well as the expectation of equal outcomes (Miller, 1993).

The changes that continued during the late 1990s in schools are reflected in a new paradigm that includes a view of the effective leader as a facilitator, capable of sharing power with members of a team (Keller, 1998). Within each classroom, the new paradigm has shifted from a focus on teaching to an emphasis on student learning (Lasley, 1998). The new paradigm, derived from the research on school effectiveness, includes a change in the school environment, from a series of separate, individual classrooms to a collaborative learning community, in which participants share a common vision for maximizing the learning of all students (Du Four, 1998; McLaughlin & Schwartz, 1998). Strategies for creation of these new learner-centered environments have attracted the attention of many groups, including the Society for College and University Planning (1998), which has conceptualized the design of new learning "spaces," which are conducive to collaboration among learners and between learners and teachers at the higher education level. These trends are representative of the continuation of development in the new learning paradigm.

Increased Efforts in Restructuring Teacher Education

Public concern about the quality and accessibility of education extended to concern about teacher education. In the 1990s many university programs began to restructure their efforts in teacher education, through initiatives including organized professional networks (American Association of Colleges for Teacher Education, 1990; Goodlad, 1992; Holmes Group, 1990).

These restructuring efforts were further encouraged by a major policy report in 1997, which summarized the importance of quality teacher preparation and support for the kinds of schools that had been identified in the effective schools research. The Report of the National Commission on Teaching and America's Future (Darling-Hammond, 1997) has outlined the conditions for ensuring teachers' professional competence as a "three-legged stool"—preparation program accreditation, (initial) teacher licensing, and (national board) certification.

The first two apply to preservice preparation programs, for which the commission recommends accreditation for the preparing institution. Accredited programs undergo rigorous review by trained colleagues, including an examination of their curriculum and structure, as well as a review of the criteria applied to selection of their faculty and students. Licensing provides the beginner with a permit to teach, after having met specific state and national standards for entrance into the profession. New teachers are expected to demonstrate their competence in knowledge of subject matter, understanding of teaching, learning and development, ability to assess students, plan curriculum, create a positive learning environment, and collaborate with parents and colleagues.

The provision of coordinated programs, such as those found in professional development schools, is highly recommended. These programs enable preservice students to apply what they have learned about teaching within the context of classrooms, under joint supervision of university and K–12 faculty members. Among the most interesting of these restructured teacher preparation programs are those able to create meaningful partnerships with K–12 schools (Kochan & Kunkel, 1998), particularly if they are able to incorporate action research that relates their teaching practices to the learning of their students (Keating, Diaz-Greenberg, Baldwin, & Thousand, 1998).

Additionally, the restructured programs promise to provide preservice teachers with more and better opportunities to understand students from differing cultural backgrounds. This essential feature enables teachers to comprehend the effects of race, ethnicity, social class, and gender on children's formation of knowledge (Banks, 1993; Sleeter & Grant, 1999). Moreover, teachers with a high degree of multicultural expertise will be able to interact effectively in diverse cultural situations (Bell & Morsink, 1986; Liedel-Rice, 1998; Smith, 1992). While about 90% of all teachers are white and female, the number of students from differing backgrounds is increasing rapidly. Kunjufu (1993) emphasizes that the issue is not the race or gender of teachers, but rather the teachers' expectations for students: Too often, teachers believe that children from low-income, single-parent families have no potential. The disproportionate number of students of color who drop out of school or who are placed in low-ability groups or special education programs underscores the importance of preservice education that enables teachers to understand children's individual differences. Increasingly, restructured programs are providing preservice teachers with supervised, directed experiences that prepare them to become culturally responsive (Ford, 1992; Garibaldi, 1992; Klug, Pena, & Whitfield, 1992; Liedel-Rice, 1998; Nel & Sherritt, 1992).

PROMISING SOLUTIONS: THE FUTURE MODEL

These trends support the prediction of a growing awareness of the need for professional collaboration and public support for special needs programs. At the same time that recognition of the need to collaborate has grown, professionals have acquired additional evidence that collaborative efforts result in improved education, both for students at risk and for schools in general. Examples of this evidence include the following:

◆ Heightened awareness of the special needs of children from the diverse subgroups within the African-American, Latino, and American Indian communities, and increased understanding of how collaboration can lessen these children's sense of alienation from school (Altenbaugh, Engel, & Martin, 1995; Kunjufu, 1993; Reeves & McDonald, 1989; Snider, 1990; West, 1990).

◆ Understanding that the current increase in problems such as school dropouts is not simple in origin. These difficulties have multiple causes and manifest medical problems such as teen pregnancy, school problems related to failure, and economic problems such as the need for adolescents to work (Gastright, 1989). Consequently, these problems require intervention by multiple agencies.

◆ Insight into the national commission's (Darling-Hammond, 1997) recommendations for school improvement through empowering school leadership and teacher preparation. Early reforms focused on university–school collaboration, staff development, and teacher empowerment can work in the nation's worst inner city schools, including those in Chicago (Walberg, Bakalis, Bast, & Baer, 1989), Los Angeles (Sickler, 1988), New Haven, Connecticut (Comer, 1989), Miami (Olson, 1989), and Hammond, Indiana (Olson & Rodman, 1988; Schmoker & Wilson, 1993).

◆ Evidence of the effectiveness of collaboration from the synthesis of the knowledge on school-based management (David, 1989), on total quality education (Schmoker & Wilson, 1993), and on professional development involving collaboration through peer coaching, both in general programs (Chrisco, 1989; Glatthorn, 1987; Raney & Robbins, 1989; Showers & Joyce, 1996) and in special education programs (Courtnage & Smith Davis, 1987; Ludlow, Faieta, & Wienke, 1989; Peterson & Hudson, 1989).

◆ A trend for collaboration among community service agencies and a growing body of knowledge to provide assistance to those who establish medical/educational/social services family centers (Burns, 1990; California School Boards Association, 1992; Imel, 1992; National Center for Schools and Communities, 1998; O'Neil, 1997).

◆ Encouraging new studies about the resilience of children who, because of personal and environmental adversities, succeed in spite of predictions that they

will fail; from these studies we can abstract the importance of effective nurturing of teachers, and also regain confidence in the human spirit (Cohen, 1993;
Edelman, 1992; Wang, 1998).

◆ Accumulating data from education reform programs that show the effectiveness of strategies which emphasize the elements important in interactive teaming and in adaptive instruction (Wang, Haertel, & Walberg, 1997). There is also
growing evidence of the value of teaching special educators to collaborate as a
way to increase their effectiveness (O'Shea, Williams & Sattler, 1999; Pugach &
Allen-Meares, 1985; West & Idol, 1987) and their sense of efficacy (McDaniel &
DiBella-McCarthy, 1989).

◆ Research on learning has improved our understanding of how the human
brain functions (Wolfe & Brandt, 1998). New research in the areas of metacogni-
tion and cooperative learning has also sharpened our insight into the teaching–
learning process, showing the similarity between effective programs for special
needs students and for all students (Brandt, 1992; Glenn, 1989; Larrivee, 1985;
Sommerfeld, 1993). New techniques—for using structure and advanced organizers, teaching self-questioning skills, and using mnemonics—can help students learn and retain information (Schumaker & Deshler, 1988). Cooperative
learning (Johnson & Johnson, 1975), the subject of a large amount of research,
shows promise for enhancing the ability of all students to learn and help each
other, and for increasing their social interactions (Villa & Thousand, 1988); it
has been particularly effective in teaching high-order skills.

◆ Realization that the solution to better programs for students at risk lies in the
understanding that these complex problems involve changes in both students
and systems, and that these changes are best implemented by groups of individuals who work together to "make what is into what ought to be" (Cuban,
1989, p. 800) in their individual organizations.

SUMMARY

The failure to collaborate on problem solutions has intensified professionals' difficulties in providing universal, free, appropriate education through our public
schools. Moreover, school failure has been accompanied by economic consequences to industry, and political consequences to the nation. It has, therefore,
attracted the attention of leaders in business and industry who now wish to join
in partnerships with educators and to assist in school improvement. An abundance of evidence shows that (1) collaboration is needed, (2) increased collaboration results in improved schools, and (3) the improvement of programs for students with special needs supports, rather than conflicts with, overall efforts to
improve schools. The interactive teaming model presented in this book has
shown how professionals who work in programs for students with special needs
can collaborate and consult effectively.

Observation Guide to be completed as you watch a real or taped meeting of a professional team in action. As you observe, complete this Observation Guide, "Power/Authority in Teaming (Dykes, 1987)." A sample of this activity, completed by Naomi Miller (1989) follows.

Note: Read this entire description before you begin.

Observe the team for 10 minutes to get an idea of who has the most authority, the nature of the authority (G = group given, S = self-proclaimed, D = declared by 3rd party, R = granted by rules or law). In a second 10-minute observation complete the following table. Identify the team member with the most power or group control at the end of each one minute period. Time each observation separately, take data and record on table. Then, begin next one-minute sample.

P = Power   S = Source

Minute	1	2	3	4	5	6	7	8	9	10
Team Members	P/S	P/S	P/S	P/S	P/S	P/S	P/S	P/S	P/S	P/S
1. Counselor	/S	/S	/S					/S		
2. Psychologist					/D	/D				
3. Sp. Ed. Teacher									/G	/G
4. Parent				/D			/D			
5.										
6.										
7.										

Source: G = Group   **The chart is a record, showing**
               S = Self-proclaimed   **team members who seemed to**
               D = Declared by role   **have the most power at the end of**
               R = Rules/law   **each one-minute sample**
                                            during 10-minute observation.

Reprinted by permission

Responses by Miller, Naomi (1989) to form developed by Dykes, Mary Kay (1987). Observation Guide for Power/Authority in Teaming (assignment for EEX 6786, Fall, 1989). (Unpublished manuscript). Gainesville, FL: University of Florida.

	1	2	3
eg C	/G		/S
D		/R	

Figure 13.1

Observation of an interactive team.

Source: This exercise was designed by Mary K. Dykes of the University of Florida. She uses it to prepare future special education teachers to work effectively as team members and it is reprinted here with her permission.

Upon completion and evaluation of your grid on the previous page, answer the following questions:

      A)   Did one person stay in a more authoritative role than others? Why?

Answer:

> *The counselor in this I.E.P. staffing attempted to exert more control than the other members. She appeared to be trying to prove her role in the team as she is the newest permanent member of the group.*

      B)   Did the power figure change? If so, how did the new person gain power—usurp, demand, request, etc.?

Answer:

> *Power figures changed throughout the meeting. The main leader, the counselor, tended to usurp power that appeared to be resented by the other members of the group. The psychologist, an intern, requested control. She took her cue from the counselor but was received well. The special education teacher demanded control and she spoke from a strong knowledge base. Parent control was requested when the other members indicated a time for involvement.*

      C)   Did individuals use authority (power) to benefit the group or were relations strained within the group? How do you know? (verbal or nonverbal)

Answer:

> *Relations between the counselor and the group appeared strained. The other members were not comfortable with the amount of attempted authority. She exhibited an over exerted trunk-lean, louder voice, and tenser actions. The other members related well together, eye-contact, posture, tone, and gestures all indicated good communication.*

      D)   Were attempts made to get all members to contribute? Were the efforts usually made by the same person(s)? Explain. How were the efforts made (vocal, nonvocal, pause/eye contact, etc.)? Were efforts successful?

Answer:

> *The group functioned collectively. The counselor distributed control between members. First, they went over introductions and then the counselor gave control to the psychologist to go over psychological reports. At certain points throughout the conference, parent participation was invited. Finally, the counselor directed involvement to the I.E.P. formulation, and this is where the special education teacher took over. In the end, the special education representative tried to involve the parent through questions. Control was distributed from the counselor to the psychologist through verbal cues, whereas a gesture was made when the counselor directed the power to the special education teacher. Most other efforts were verbal.*

Figure 13.1, *continued*

E)   What, if any, relation did you observe between power and a team member's use of data? (If the individual brought actual assessment or observation data to conference were they viewed as high or low power? Why?)

Answer:

The psychologist produced data from the psychological report. She gained a high power control base when presenting the data and this was viewed as her knowledge power base. The parent was in agreement with the results of the data.

F)   List observed and personal and/or professional characteristics of those who had (1) the most power and (2) the least power.

Answer:

	Most	Least
Personal:	Empathetic, calm, sincere, and understanding, good eye contact.	Demanding in nonverbal indicators. Overwhelming.
Professional:	Task-oriented, directly involved, invited involvement. Worked from experience.	Pushy on signing of papers. Tried to accept personal responsibility for student improvement.

G)   List procedures a high–power team member used to facilitate the team efforts:

Answer:

Positive: The special education teacher was very confident with her position. She allowed the counselor and psychologist to take their positions also. She displayed verbal and nonverbal cues showing interest. She handled her "duties," explaining the program, I.E.P. formulation and getting signatures with ease. She explained her information in under-standable terms and made the parent feel comfortable.

Negative: There were moments when her involvement could have directed conversation and eased tension rather than the counselor taking control of the situation. She ended the meeting somewhat abruptly by saying that she had to go to another appointment. No opportunities for future interaction were indicated.

H)   Were some team members prepared but spoke only when specifically requested to do so? How could you handle such a situation?

Answer:

Yes, the psychologist took control when it was time to display the psychological reports. The situation will probably be resolved when she becomes more comfortable with the authorita-tive position she holds. It was her first I.E.P. conference and she was just testing her abilities.

Figure 13.1, *continued*

I)   What, if any, role did age, sex, years of experience, professional training, e.g., therapist, physician, educator, psychologist, have in determining who the team members perceived as the authority or power figure? Did you observe a professional or personal "pecking order?" Explain.

Answer:

> As already mentioned, the special education teacher's experience at the position and in this location, enabled her to be very confident in her role. The lack of professional training of the school psychologist stood in the way of her performance. Finally, the counselor's fight for power inhibited her effectiveness. The only person who was involved in a "pecking order" was the counselor, the others ignored the undercurrents.

J)   Identify the most effective team member. Identify the least effective team member.

Answer:

> The most effective team member was the special education teacher. She was involved, prepared, and comfortable, which set the interaction at ease. She did not allow the meeting to stray from the topics, yet still allowed for parent and professional involvement.
>
> The counselor was the least effective in this meeting. She was trying very hard, too hard it appeared. She was the one to greet the parent and pushed too hard to try and appear friendly. Her power–seeking behaviors undermined her effectiveness.

Observe each for three minutes—keep a running log of what each was doing (e.g., eye contact with, posture, attention, etc.). Contrast the two sets of behavior.

Answer:

> Most effective: Attentive, eye contact maintained with person in control. She was in control after the first eight minutes while formulating the I.E.P. She had a relaxed confident posture along with an authoritative voice and tone.
>
> Least effective: Once she was out of her "director" role, she began to slouch and look at her watch. She was writing on some other papers that she was working on. Her attention was minimal.

Figure 13.1, *continued*

◊ ◊

Application

Now that you have completed this book, try to apply your understanding of interactive teaming to the observation of a team meeting, using the observation guide given in Figure 13.1. Watch for examples of effective and ineffective communication, power and empowerment, cultural sensitivity (or lack thereof), and effective or ineffective strategies for running a meeting. Summarize what you see and discuss your observations with others in your class.

◊ ◊

ACTIVITIES

1. Imagine that the year is 2010. You dropped out of teaching during the last decade of the old century. Because you lived in another country and had no further interest in education in the United States, you did not obtain any information about trends and issues. Now in 2010, you return and seek a job as a special education teacher. *You are told that public school special education no longer exists.*

   Debate and discuss this scenario, using evidence gathered from your analysis of current issues and trends. *What might have caused this to happen?*

   ◆ Could it be that the numbers of children with special needs became so large that all education programs were combined into a common, mediocre system?

   ◆ Or are there no more public schools at all? Are some children now educated in private schools, while others receive instruction on home computers or do not receive any education?

   ◆ Did special education programs collapse in failure under the pressure of a new generation of cocaine babies and children damaged by poverty-induced malnutrition and psychological disorders?

   ◆ Could it be that special educators, in whose classrooms students were taught only basic low-level skills, were viewed as incompetent teachers in the new century, and that special education, now outdated, was eliminated from the public schools?

   ◆ Or were special educators so idealistic and so naive about the realities of power and politics that they were unable to work constructively within the system to bring about needed changes?

   ◆ Did teacher's unions, under pressure from child advocates to place all students with severe and multiple disabilities in regular classrooms, lead a parent rebellion that resulted in the repeal of P.L. 94-142 and its antecedents, so that students with disabilities were subsequently expelled from the public school system?

◆ Could it be that the costs of national infrastructure repair, health care spending, and new prison construction, with a simultaneous increase in the number of older Americans, became so great that there were no tax dollars left for special education?

What else might have caused the decline of special education? Choose one of these hypotheses or create your own. Then, outline a series of strategies you could use to implement the reversal of these negative trends.

2. Read the chapter's case study on Ethan carefully. What do you think might have happened behind the scenes to enable things to happen at just the right times? Who could have been responsible for these covert activities? If you were a member of this team, would you engage in such activities? Why or why not?

3. Design a change strategy for the educational organization in which you work or plan to work. Incorporate the facilitating factors discussed in this book. Identify the barriers you will probably encounter. Then provide a step-by-step set of activities to implement this change. Discuss the strengths and weaknesses of your proposal with others in your class and make revisions, based on their suggestions for improvement.

4. Debate this prediction for the future: The majority of programs for special needs students will be delivered by teams, using models such as interactive teaming. Provide evidence, pro or con, to support your point of view.

REFERENCES

Altenbaugh, R., Engel, D., & Martin, D. (1995). *Caring for kids: A critical study of urban school leavers.* London: Falmer Press.

American Association of Colleges for Teacher Education. (1990). Clinical schools update. *AACTE Briefs, 11.* Washington, DC: Author.

American Psychological Association. (1993). *Violence and youth: Psychology's response* (Vol. I). Washington, DC: American Psychological Association Commission on Violence and Youth.

Banks, J. (1993). Multicultural education: Development, dimensions, and challenges. *Phi Delta Kappan, 74,* 22–28.

Bell, M., & Morsink, C. (1986). Quality and equity in the preparation of black teachers. *Journal of Teacher Education, 37*(2), 16–20.

Bradley, A. (1993, March 24). Basic training. *Education Week, 12*(26), 13–18.

Bradley, A., & Olson, L. (1993, February 24). The balance of power. *Education Week, 12*(22), 9–14.

Brandt, R. (1992). On building learning communities: A conversation with Hank Levin. *Educational Leadership, 50*(1), 19–22.

Brown, R. (1985). *Reconnecting youth: The next stage of reform.* Denver, CO: Business Advisory Commission, Education Commission of the States.

Burns, J. (1990). *New start: One stop service center.* Unpublished manuscript. Gainesville, FL: University of Florida Department of Special Education.

California School Boards Association. (1992). *Cutting through the red tape: Meeting the needs of California's children.* West Sacramento, CA: Author.

Chiles, L. (1989, February). *America in debt: The budget deficit.* Symposium conducted at the University of Florida Law Center, Gainesville, FL.

Chrisco, I. (1989). Peer assistance works. *Educational Leadership, 46*(6), 31–34.

Cohen, D. (1993, June 9). Schools beginning to glean lessons from children who "defy the odds." *Education Week, 12*(37), 1, 16–18.

Comer, J. (1989) Children can: An address on school improvement. In R. Webb & F. Parkay (Eds.), *Children can: An address on school improvement by Dr. James Comer with responses from Florida's educational community* (pp. 4–17). Gainesville, FL: University of Florida, College of Education Research & Development Center in collaboration with the Alachua County Mental Health Association.

Council of Administrators of Special Education. (1990, September 29). *Position paper on least restrictive environment.* Las Vegas: CASE Board of Directors.

Courtnage, L., & Smith Davis, J. (1987). Interdisciplinary team training: A national survey of special education teacher training programs. *Exceptional Children, 53,* 451–459.

Cuban, L. (1989). The "at-risk" label and the problem of urban school reform. *Phi Delta Kappan, 70,* 780–784.

Darling-Hammond, L. (1997). *Doing what matters most: Investing in quality teaching.* New York: National Commission on Teaching and America's Future.

David, J. (1989). Synthesis of research on school-based management. *Educational Leadership, 46*(8), 45–53.

Dolce, C. (1981). Conservatism in America: What does it mean for teacher education? *Journal of Teacher Education, 32*(4), 15–22.

Du Four, R. (1998). *The principal series, facilitators guide for tapes 1–3: Creating a collaborative learning community.* Alexandria, VA: Association for Supervision and Curriculum Development.

Dykes, M. K. (1987). *Observation guide for power/authority in teaming.* Unpublished manuscript. Gainesville, FL: University of Florida Department of Education.

Edelman, M. (1992). *The measure of our success: A letter to my children and yours.* Boston: Beacon Press.

Flax, E. (1987, September 9). Teachers cite latchkey situation as cause of learning distress. *Education Week, 7*(1), 17.

Flax, E. (1989). Serious gaps cited in services aiding child mental health. *Education Week, 8*(38), 1, 27.

Ford, B. (1992). Multicultural education training for special educators working with African American youth. *Exceptional Children, 59,* 107–114.

Garcia, R. (1998). Hang-ups of introducing computer technology. *THE Journal, 26*(2), 65–66.

Garibaldi, A. (1992). Preparing teachers for culturally diverse classrooms. In M. Dilworth (Ed.), *Diversity in Teacher Education—New Expectations.* San Francisco: Jossey-Bass.

Gastright, J. (1989, April). Don't base your dropout program on somebody else's problem. *Phi Delta Kappa Research Bulletin,* No. 8, 1–4.

Glatthorn, A. (1987). Cooperative professional development: Peer-centered options for teacher growth. *Educational Leadership, 45,* 31–35.

Glenn, C. (1989). Just schools for minority children. *Phi Delta Kappan, 70,* 777–779.

Gold, D. (1987, November 18). New Jersey relaxes bilingual education rules. *Education Week, 7*(11), 5.

Goodlad, J. (1992). On taking school reform seriously. *Phi Delta Kappan, 74,* 232–238.

Gough, P. (1992). Another bad rap. *Phi Delta Kappan, 74,* 3.

Harp, L. (1993, March 31). Dollars and sense. *Education Week, 12*(27), 9–14.

Hodgkinson, H. (1988). The right schools for the right kids. *Educational Leadership, 45,* 10–15.

Holmes Group. (1990). *Tomorrow's schools: Principles for the design of professional development schools.* East Lansing, MI: Michigan State University.

Horowitz, F., & O'Brien, M. (1989). Introduction to special issue. Children and their development: Knowledge base, research agenda, and social policy application [Special issue]. *American Psychologist, 44*(2), 95.

Howe, C. (1981). *Administration of special education.* Denver, CO: Love Publishing.

Iacocca, L. (1989, March 22). Remarks to the National Association of Manufacturers, Washington, DC.

Imel, S. (1992). *For the common good: A guide to developing local interagency linkage teams.* Columbus, OH: Center on Education and Training for Employment, Ohio State University.

Johnson, D., & Johnson, R. (1975). *Learning together and alone: Cooperation, competition, and individualization.* Upper Saddle River, NJ: Prentice Hall.

Kakalik, J., Furry, W., Thomas, M., & Carney, M. (1981). *The cost of special education* (Report No. N-1792-ED). Santa Monica, CA: Rand Corporation. (Prepared for the U.S. Department of Education, Contract No. 300-79-0733.)

Keating, J., Diaz-Greenberg, R., Baldwin, M., & Thousand, J. (1998). A collaborative action research model for teacher preparation programs. *Journal for Teacher Education, 49*(5), 381–390.

Keller, B. (1998, November 11). Research: Principal matters. *Education Week, XVIII,* 25–27.

Klug, B., Pena, S., & Whitfield, P. (1992). From awareness to application: Creating multicultural reform despite political correctness, a case study. In C. Grant (Ed.), *Multicultural education for the twenty-first century.* Proceedings of the Second Annual Meeting of the National Association for Multicultural Education. New Jersey: Paramount Publications.

Kochan, F., & Kunkel, R. (1998). The learning coalition: Professional development schools in partnership. *Journal of Teacher Education, 49*(5), 325–333.

Kovaleski, J. (1992). *Developing effective instructional support systems in schools: Functions of the IST.* Harrisburgh, PA: Pennsylvania Department of Education.

Kunjufu, J. (1993, February 24). *Developing a positive self-image in black children.* Address to University Community. Slippery Rock, PA: Slippery Rock University.

Larrivee, B. (1985) *Effective teaching for successful mainstreaming.* New York: Longman Publishers.

Lasley, T. (1998). Paradigm shifts in the classroom. *Phi Delta Kappan, 80,* 84–86.

Liedel-Rice, A. (1998). *Program follow-up study of former urban student teachers in their second through sixth year of teaching.* Slippery Rock, PA: Slippery Rock University College of Education.

Ludlow, B., Faieta, J., & Wienke, W. (1989). Training teachers to supervise their peers. *Teacher Education and Special Education, 12,* 27–32.

McClellan, M. (Ed.). (1987). *Child abuse* [Hot Topics Series]. Bloomington, IN: Phi Delta Kappa.

McDaniel, E., & DiBella-McCarthy, H. (1989). Enhancing teacher efficacy in special education. *Teaching Exceptional Children, 21*(4), 34–39.

McGroddy, J. (1997, October). *Transforming the future through technology.* Address to Teacher Education Assembly, annual meeting of PACTE, Grantville, PA.

McLaughlin, M., & Schwartz, R. (1998). *Strategies for fixing failing public schools.* Cambridge, MA: Harvard Graduate School, Pew Forum.

Miller, J. (1993, March 24). Administration readies reform, assessment bill. *Education Week, 12*(26), 1, 44.

Miller, N. (1989). Sample responses to Dykes' *Power/authority in teaming.* Unpublished manuscript. Gainesville, FL: University of Florida Department of Special Education.

Mirga, T. (1987, September 9). Textbooks do not imperil Christians' beliefs, 2 courts rule. *Education Week, 7*(1), 10, 23.

Naisbitt, J. (1982). *Megatrends.* New York: Warner Books.

Nanus, B. (1992). *Visionary leadership.* San Francisco: Jossey-Bass.

National Center for Schools and Communities. (1998). Community schools in the making. In *Conversations: Supporting children and families in the public schools.* New York: Fordham University Center.

Nel, J., & Sherritt, C. (1992). Bridge building and student resistance: Increasing teacher commitment to multicultural education. In C. Grant (Ed.), *Multicultural education for the twenty-first century.* Proceedings of the Second Annual Meeting of the National Association for Multicultural Education. New Jersey: Paramount Publications.

Newcomb, M., & Bentler, P. (1989). Substance use and abuse among children and teenagers. Children and their development: Knowledge base, research agenda, and social policy application [Special issue]. *American Psychologist, 44*(2), 242–248.

Oakes, J. (1986). Keeping track, part 1: The policy and practice of curriculum inequality. *Phi Delta Kappan, 68,* 12–17.

Olson, L. (1989, June 7). Dade County will solicit ideas nationwide for design, structuring of 49 new schools. *Education Week, 8*(37), 1, 21.

Olson, L., & Rodman, B. (1988, June 22). The unfinished agenda, part II. *Education Week, 7,* 17–33.

O'Neil, J. (1997). Building schools as communities: A conversation with James Comer. *Educational Leadership, 54*(8), 6–19.

O'Shea, D., Williams, L., & Sattler, R. (1999). Collaboration preparation across special education and general education: Preservice level teachers' views. *Journal of Teacher Education, 50*(2), 147–158.

Patterson, G., DeBaryshe, B., & Ramsey, E. (1989). A developmental perspective on antisocial behavior. Children and their development: Knowledge base, research agenda, and social policy application [Special issue]. *American Psychologist, 44*(2), 329–335.

Peterson, K. (1993, April 7). Abuse of children is on the rise. *USA Today,* p. D1.

Peterson, S., & Hudson, P. (1989). Coaching: A strategy to enhance preservice teacher behaviors. *Teacher Education and Special Education, 12,* 56–60.

Pugach, M., & Allen-Meares, P. (1985). Collaboration at the preservice level: Instructional and evaluation activities. *Teacher Education and Special Education, 8*(1), 3–11.

Raney, P., & Robbins, P. (1989). Professional growth and support through peer coaching. *Educational Leadership, 46*(8), 35–37.

Reed, S. (1988). Children with AIDS: How schools are handling the crisis [Special report]. *Phi Delta Kappan, 69,* K1–K12.

Reeves, M. S., & McDonald, D. (1989, August 2). Stuck in the horizon: A special report on the education of Native Americans. *Education Week, 8,* 1–16.

Rothman, R. (1993, March 17). Taking account: From risk to renewal. *Education Week, 12*(25), 9–13.

Safer, N., Burnette, J., & Hobbs, B. (1979). Exploration 1993: The effects of future trends on services to the handicapped. *Focus on Exceptional Children, 11*(3), 1–24.

Schmoker, M., & Wilson, R. (1993). Transforming schools through total quality education. *Phi Delta Kappan, 74,* 389–395.

Schumaker, J., & Deshler, D. (1988). Implementing the regular education initiative in secondary schools: A different ball game. *Journal of Learning Disabilities, 21,* 36–42.

Sharp, W. (1998). School administrators need technology too. *THE Journal, 26*(2), 75–76.

Showers, B., & Joyce, B. (1996). The evolution of peer coaching. *Educational Leadership, 53*(7), 12–16.

Sickler, J. (1988). Teachers in charge: Empowering the professionals. *Phi Delta Kappan, 69,* 354–356.

Sleeter, C., & Grant, C. (1999). *Making choices for multicultural education* (3rd ed.). Columbus, OH: Merrill/Prentice Hall.

Smith, G. (1992). Multicultural education: Implications for the culturally responsive teaching of all our children. In C. Grant (Ed.), *Multicultural education for the twenty-first century.* Proceedings of the Second Annual Meeting of the National

Association for Multicultural Education. New Jersey: Paramount Publications.

Snider, W. (1990, March 7). Children's Defense Fund joins call to improve education of Hispanics. *Education Week, 9*(24), 4.

Society for College and University Planning (1998). *Creating tomorrow's learner-centered environments today!* PBS Adult Learning Service Satellite downlink, October 22, 1998.

Sommerfeld, M. (1993, March 3). Time and space: From risk to renewal. *Education Week, 12*(23), 13–19.

Tuma, J. (1989). Mental health services for children. Children and their development: Knowledge base, research agenda, and social policy application [Special issue]. *American Psychologist, 44*(2), 188–199.

Turnbull, R., & Cilley, M. (1999). *Explanations and implications of the 1997 amendments to IDEA.* Upper Saddle River, NJ: Merrill/Prentice Hall.

Viadero, D. (1989, May 3). "7 of 10 handicapped graduates found 'productive.'" *Education Week, 8*(23), 6.

Viadero, D. (1993, March 10). The coherent curriculum. *Education Week, 7*(24), 10–15.

Villa, R., & Thousand, J. (1988). Enhancing success in heterogeneous classrooms and schools: The powers of partnership. *Teacher Education and Special Education, 11,* 144–154.

Walberg, H., Bakalis, M., Bast, J., & Baer, S. (1989). Reconstructing the nation's worst schools. *Phi Delta Kappan, 70,* 802–805.

Walsh, M. (1993, April 7). Signing up the public. *Education Week 12*(28), 9–14.

Wang, M. (1998). Resilience across contexts: Family, work, culture and community. *CEIC Review, 7*(1), 1, 26.

Wang, M., Haertel, G., & Walberg, H. (1997). *What do we know: Widely implemented school improvement programs.* Philadelphia, PA: Mid-Atlantic Regional Educational Lab at Temple University.

West, F., & Idol, L. (1987). School consultation: Part 1. An interdisciplinary perspective on theory, models, and research. *Journal of Learning Disabilities, 20,* 388–408.

West, P. (1990, February 21). Interior Department sets 4 objectives for Indian education. *Education Week, 9*(22), 1, 24.

Wise, A. (1988). The two conflicting trends in school reform: Legislated learning revisited. *Phi Delta Kappan, 69,* 328–332.

Wolfe, P., & Brandt, R. (1998). What do we know from brain research? *Educational Leadership, 56*(3), 8–13.

Name Index

Subject Index